D1064634

Kinship and Capitalism

This uncompromisingly empirical study reconstructs the public and private lives of urban business families during the period of England's emergence as a world economic power. Using a broad cross section of archival, rather than literary, sources, it tests the orthodox view that the family as an institution was transformed by capitalism and individualism. The approach is both quantitative and qualitative. A database of 28,000 families has been constructed to tackle questions such as demographic structure, kinship, and inheritance, which must be answered statistically. Much of the book, however, focuses on issues such as courtship and relations between spouses, parents, and children, which can only be studied through those families that have left intimate records. The overall conclusion is that none of the abstract models invented to explain the historical development of the family withstand empirical scrutiny and that familial capitalism, not possessive individualism, was the motor of economic growth.

Richard Grassby is a member of the Institute for Advanced Study in Princeton, New Jersey. He is the author of numerous books and articles, including *The Business Community of Seventeenth-Century England* (Cambridge University Press, 1995).

WOODROW WILSON CENTER SERIES

Michael J. Lacey, editor, *Religion and Twentieth-Century American Intellectual Life*

Michael J. Lacey, editor, *The Truman Presidency*

Joseph Kruzel and Michael H. Haltzel, editors, *Between the Blocs: Problems and Prospects for Europe's Neutral and Nonaligned States*

William C. Brumfield, editor, *Reshaping Russian Architecture: Western Technology, Utopian Dreams*

Mark N. Katz, editor, *The USSR and Marxist Revolutions in the Third World*

Mary O. Furner and Barry Supple, editors, *The State and Economic Knowledge: The American and British Experiences*

Michael J. Lacey and Knud Haakonssen, editors, *A Culture of Rights: The Bill of Rights in Philosophy, Politics, and Law—1791 and 1991*

Robert J. Donovan and Ray Scherer, *Unsilent Revolution: Television News and American Public Life, 1948–1991*

Nelson Lichtenstein and Howell John Harris, editors, *Industrial Democracy in America: The Ambiguous Promise*

William Craft Brumfield and Blair A. Ruble, editors, *Russian Housing in the Modern Age: Design and Social History*

Michael J. Lacey and Mary O. Furner, editors, *The State and Social Investigation in Britain and the United States*

Hugh Ragsdale, editor and translator, *Imperial Russian Foreign Policy*

Dermot Keogh and Michael H. Haltzel, editors, *Northern Ireland and the Politics of Reconciliation*

Joseph Klaits and Michael H. Haltzel, editors, *The Global Ramifications of the French Revolution*

René Lemarchand, *Burundi: Ethnic Conflict and Genocide*

James R. Millar and Sharon L. Wolchik, editors, *The Social Legacy of Communism*

James M. Morris, editor, *On Mozart*

Theodore Taranovski, editor, *Reform in Modern Russian History: Progress or Cycle?*

Continued on page following index

WOODROW WILSON INTERNATIONAL CENTER FOR SCHOLARS

Lee H. Hamilton, Director

BOARD OF TRUSTEES

Joseph A. Cari, Jr., Chair; Steven Alan Bennett, Vice Chair. *Public Members*: Madeleine K. Albright, Secretary, U.S. Department of State; James H. Billington, Librarian of Congress; John W. Carlin, Archivist of the United States; Penn Kemble, Acting Director, U.S. Information Agency; William R. Ferris, Chair, National Endowment for the Humanities; I. Michael Heyman, Secretary, Smithsonian Institution; Richard W. Riley, Secretary, U.S. Department of Education; Donna E. Shalala, Secretary, U.S. Department of Health and Human Services. *Private-Citizen Members*: Carol Cartwright, Daniel L. Doctoroff, Jean L. Hennessey, Daniel L. Lamaute, Paul Hae Park, Thomas R. Reedy, S. Dillon Ripley, Nancy M. Zirkin. *Designated Appointee of the President from within the Federal Government*: Samuel R. Berger, Assistant to the President for National Security Affairs.

WILSON COUNCIL

Albert Abramson, Cyrus A. Ansary, J. Burchenal Ault, Charles F. Barber, Theodore C. Barreaux, Joseph C. Bell, Jim Blosser, John L. Bryant, Jr., Conrad Cafritz, Nicola L. Caiola, Raoul L. Carroll, Albert V. Casey, Peter B. Clark, William T. Coleman, Jr., Michael D. DiGiacomo, Frank P. Doyle, Donald G. Drapkin, F. Samuel Eberts III, I. Steven Edelson, John H. Foster, Barbara Hackman Franklin, Chris G. Gardiner, Bruce Gelb, Jerry P. Genova, Alma Gildenhorn, Joseph B. Gildenhorn, David F. Girard-diCarlo, Michael B. Goldberg, William E. Grayson, Raymond A. Guenter, Robert R. Harlin, Verna R. Harrah, Eric Hotung, Frances Humphrey Howard, John L. Howard, Darrell E. Issa, Jerry Jasinowski, Brenda LaGrange Johnson, Dennis D. Jorgensen, Shelley Kamins, Anastasia D. Kelly, Christopher Kennan, Steven Kotler, William H. Kremer, Kathleen D. Lacey, Donald S. Lamm, Harold Levy, David Link, David S. Mandel, Edwin S. Marks, Robert McCarthy, C. Peter McColough, James D. McDonald, Philip Merrill, Jeremiah L. Murphy, Martha T. Muse, Gerald L. Parsky, L. Richardson Preyer, Donald Robert Quartel, Jr., Edward V. Regan, J. Steven Rhodes, Edwin Robbins, Philip E. Rollhaus, Jr., George P. Shultz, Raja W. Sidawi, Ron Silver, William A. Slaughter, Timothy E. Stapleford, Linda Bryant Valentine, Christine Warnke, Deborah Wince-Smith, Herbert S. Winokur, Jr.

ABOUT THE CENTER

The Center is the living memorial of the United States of America to the nation's twenty-eighth president, Woodrow Wilson. Congress established the Woodrow Wilson Center in 1968 as an international institute for advanced study, "symbolizing and strengthening the fruitful relationship between the world of learning and the world of public affairs." The Center opened in 1970 under its own board of trustees.

In all its activities the Woodrow Wilson Center is a nonprofit, nonpartisan organization, supported financially by annual appropriations from the Congress and by the contributions of foundations, corporations, and individuals. Conclusions or opinions expressed in Center publications and programs are those of the authors and speakers and do not necessarily reflect the views of the Center staff, fellows, trustees, advisory groups, or any individuals or organizations that provide financial support to the Center.

Kinship and Capitalism

Marriage, Family, and Business in the English-Speaking World, 1580–1740

RICHARD GRASSBY

WOODROW WILSON CENTER PRESS

AND

 CAMBRIDGE
UNIVERSITY PRESS

PUBLISHED BY THE PRESS SYNDICATE OF THE UNIVERSITY OF CAMBRIDGE
The Pitt Building, Trumpington Street, Cambridge, United Kingdom

CAMBRIDGE UNIVERSITY PRESS
The Edinburgh Building, Cambridge CB2 2RU, UK
40 West 20th Street, New York, NY 10011-4211, USA
10 Stamford Road, Oakleigh, VIC 3166, Australia
Ruiz de Alarcón 13, 28014 Madrid, Spain
Dock House, The Waterfront, Cape Town 8001, South Africa

http://www.cambridge.org

© Richard Grassby 2001

This book is in copyright. Subject to statutory exception
and to the provisions of relevant collective licensing agreements,
no reproduction of any part may take place without
the written permission of Cambridge University Press.

First published 2001

Printed in the United States of America

Typeface Sabon 10/13 pt.   *System* QuarkXPress [BTS]

A catalog record for this book is available from the British Library.

Library of Congress Cataloging in Publication Data
Grassby, Richard.
Kinship and capitalism: marriage, family, and business in the English-
speaking world, 1580–1740 / Richard Grassby.
p. cm. – (Woodrow Wilson Center series)
Includes bibliographical references and index.
ISBN 0-521-78203-1 (hb)
1. Family – England – London – History. 2. Marriage – England –
London – History. 3. Businesspeople – England – London – History.
4. Households – England – London – History. 5. Capitalism – England –
London – History. I. Title. II. Series.

HQ616.15.L66 G73 2000   306.8'09421–dc21   00-026197

ISBN   0 521 78203 1   hardback

To all vulgar empiricists.

Contents

Tables   page x
Abbreviations   xiii
Explanatory Notes   xv
Preface   xvii

Introduction: Models and Myths   1

PART I. MARRIAGE

1 Making a Match   37
2 Husbands and Wives   85
3 Widowers and Widows   117

PART II. THE BUSINESS FAMILY

4 Parents and Children   155
5 Adulthood and Old Age   189
6 Kin and Community   217

PART III. THE FAMILY BUSINESS

7 Men in Business   269
8 Women in Business   312
9 Inheritance and Advancement   341
Conclusion: Capitalism and the Life Cycle   387

APPENDICES

Appendix A. Sources for the Database   419
Appendix B. Criteria for Coding Inputs   441

Sources   455
Index   469

Tables

1.1	Status of Spouse (Percentage of Known Cases)	*page* 49
1.2	Marital Status and Survival Rate of Brides (Percentage of Known Cases)	52
1.3	Location of Spouse (Percentage of Known Cases)	55
1.4	Age Distribution of Grooms in First Marriages (Percentage of Known Cases)	59
1.5	Median Age of Marriage (Known Cases)	60
1.6	Age Distribution of Brides in First and Second Marriages (Percentage of Known Cases)	62
1.7	Frequency of Marriage of Businessmen (Percentage of Known Cases)	79
1.8	Businessmen Traveling or Residing Abroad, 1580–1740 (Percentage of Known Cases)	80
2.1	Duration of Marriages (Percentage of Known Cases)	101
3.1	Age at Death (Percentage of Known Cases)	119
3.2	Age at Death (Merchant Adventurers of Newcastle, 1609–1700)	121
3.3	Duration of Widowhood (Percentage of Known Cases)	126
3.4	Executors and Overseers (Percentage of All Wills)	128
4.1	Numbers of Children per Family Who Survived to Maturity (All Marriages Combined [Percentage of Known Cases])	156
4.2	The Children of Richard and Elizabeth Farrington	159
4.3	Distribution of Children by Sex (Percentage of Known Cases)	164
4.4	Number of Orphans per Family (Percentage of Known Cases)	164

6.1   Kin and Friends in Wills (Percentage of Known Cases)   222
6.2   Kin and Friends: Cross-Sectional Analysis, 1580–1740
        (Percentage of Known Cases in Wills)   223
6.3   Primary Beneficiaries (Percentage of Known Cases)   238
6.4   Citizenship and Office (Known Cases Expressed as a
        Percentage of All Subjects in Each Category)   254
6.5   Businessmen outside the Established Church
        (Percentage of All Subjects in the Database)   258
6.6   Charitable Bequests (Percentage of Known Cases)   258
6.7   Charitable Bequests: Cross-Sectional Analysis,
        1580–1740 (Percentage of Known Cases)   261
7.1   Training of Businessmen (Percentage of Known Cases)   272
7.2   Origins of Businessmen (Percentage of Known Cases)   272
7.3   Frequency Distribution of Surnames, 1580–1740
        (Percentage of All Surnames)   274
7.4   Distribution by Trade (Percentage of Known Cases)   276
7.5   Sources of Capital, 1580–1740 (Percentage of Known
        Cases)   287
7.6   Number and Origin of Partners, 1580–1740
        (Percentage of Known Cases)   291
8.1   Women in Business, 1580–1740 (Number of Known
        Businesswomen)   320
9.1   Holdings of Land and Urban Property: Division and
        Rank (Percentage of Known Cases)   347
9.2   Occupations of Sons by Birth Order (Percentage of
        Known Cases)   357
9.3   Generational Continuity in Business   361
9.4   Impact of Father's Occupation on Behavior of
        Businessmen, 1580–1740 (Percentage of Known Cases)   365
9.5   Parental Status of Wives of Sons by Birth Order
        (Percentage of Known Cases)   368
9.6   Status of Husbands of Daughters by Birth Order
        (Percentage of Known Cases)   375
9.7   Dowries of Daughters (Median Value of £ Sterling
        Adjusted for Inflation)   380
10.1 Distribution of Wealth by Cohort, 1580–1740
        (Percentage of Known Cases)   397
10.2 Widows with Children, 1580–1740 (Percentage of
        Known Cases)   400

10.3 Estimated Percentage of Business Assets Held by
     Widows   401
B.1 Number of Known Values in All Fields of the
     Database   442

Abbreviations

Add.	Additional
BL	British Library
Bod	Bodleian Library, Oxford
C	Chancery
CLRO	Corporation of London Record Office
Cal. S.P.	Calendar of State Papers
CUL	Cambridge University Library
E	Exchequer
ESRO	East Sussex Record Office
GLL	Guildhall of London Library
GLRO	Greater London Record Office
HMC	Historical Manuscripts Commission
India Off.	India Office Library, British Library
KAO	Centre for Kentish Studies
LAO	Lincolnshire Archives Office
Occ.	Occasional
PCC	Prerogative Court of Canterbury
PRO	Public Record Office
PROB	Probate records, Public Records Office
RO	Record Office
SP	State Papers
VCH	Victoria County History
WAM	Westminster Abbey Muniments

Explanatory Notes

All statistics cited in the body of the text without a specific reference are derived from a database of London businessmen, the scope and construction of which is fully described in appendices A and B. Data cited from other studies of London without qualification refer to the whole metropolitan population.

A bibliography of manuscript sources has been provided, and the principal quantitative sources for the database have been listed in appendix A. All other works have been fully described on their first citation in each chapter. Place of publication is London for works published in English and Paris for works published in French.

Dates have been given in Old Style except that January 1 has been taken as the first day of the year.

Reference to wills proved in the Prerogative Court of Canterbury have usually been made by the old quire numbers, because the microfilms available to the author had been made before the wills were moved to the Public Record Office and foliated. Those wills read at the Public Record Office have been referenced by the folio numbers in the Probate records 11 class.

The database has been grouped into three subsets by period, wealth, and cohort, full details of which are provided in appendix B. These have been identified in the text as follows: Period I (deceased 1580–1659) and Period II (deceased 1660–1740); Brackets I (£0–500), II (£501–5,000), III (£5,001–50,000), and IV (over £50,000); and Cohorts I (born 1541–80), II (born 1581–1600), III (born 1601–60), and IV (born 1661–1700).

Preface

Although this book is intended to stand on its own feet, it is also a sequel to *The Business Community of Seventeenth-Century England*. When that volume was written the underlying data had not been computerized in a machine-readable format; some general issues were also set aside to be discussed in a separate book, *The Idea of Capitalism before the Industrial Revolution*, which has now appeared. In the present work, most of the relevant data have been presented, albeit in a compressed form, except that some data have been reserved for a planned, but still unfunded, final volume on the material culture of the business community. Although the technicalities of economic history usually provide a cordon sanitaire against the virus of cultural theory, any study of women or the family cannot adopt a neutral stance in the contemporary *methodenstreit* or culture wars. This work will probably be criticized for failing to use theory or to address gender issues. Any such omission is usually taken as a slight and interpreted as a threat to the security and validity of passionately held doctrines. On the other hand, weak scholarship, when dressed up in whatever theory is fashionable, is accepted without demur, providing that it conforms to and confirms orthodox doctrine.

Many of the questions raised in this book occupy that no man's land where empirical history meets theory-based disciplines. A prudent historian would genuflect to the reigning ideologies, drop the right names, and then quietly ignore them. Academics, as their past history of political collaboration suggests, are not noted for their courage or self-denial. Historians who loathe current shibboleths are reluctant to challenge those who control access to funding, preferment, and publication or risk becoming the messenger who is shot. It is safer to massage the egos of the intellectual celebrities and concur that the emperor is fully dressed.

In contrast, the tactic adopted here is full speed ahead with every battery firing and damn the torpedos. So uncompromisingly empirical an approach to the history of the family is likely to alienate all interest groups and provoke retaliation. But it is the duty of the scholar to extirpate error, root, and branch, without regard for the consequences. George Oxenden, when asked why he did not attempt to mollify his critics, replied that he had no time to alight from his horse to cast stones at every cur that barked at him (BL Add. MS 40,700, fo. 36).

Over the past twenty years the history of the family and of women has attracted several distinguished scholars, and this study builds on their work. The literature on the family also includes much pretentious rubbish. It is the practice of the present author to read everything, no matter how absurd, incoherent, derivative, long-winded, or boring, in the hope of finding some germ of an idea or some crucial fact. But many of these works have to be dismissed with the contempt that they deserve; nonsense is still nonsense, no matter how often it is repeated or by whom. Books and articles published after 1996 have only been consulted when available; much depends on random factors, such as the speed and order of cataloging by libraries and the timing of binding of periodicals.

It would have been impossible to complete this work without access to the New York Public Library, the Library of Congress, the Huntington Library, the Bodlean Library, and the library of the Institute of Historical Research in London. Essential funding has also been provided by fellowships from the National Endowment of the Humanities, the Woodrow Wilson International Center for Scholars, and the American Philosophical Society, which provided a grant to microfilm thousands of documents.

Henry Horwitz turned over all his biographical notes on post-Restoration businessmen (which included material originally collected by Robert Walcott), and Sonia Anderson supplied similar information on the Levantine merchants. D. W. Jones responded immediately to an enquiry, enclosing the original copy of his thesis with data from the 1695 port book. The Center for Metropolitan Studies at the University of London provided access to a database on London in the 1690s. Bill Rothfarb helped to install and maintain essential software programs, and Ruth-Ellen Proudfoot provided statistical support. Al Laranjeiro shared the dreary task of inputting data.

The general response rate to letters of enquiry has, on the other hand, been abysmal, and the author has had virtually no opportunity to discuss the ideas of this book with others in the field. Communication between scholars seems to have been easier in the seventeenth than in the late twentieth century. An independent scholar who lacks "accreditation" in effect has pariah status; he is treated with indifference or hostility, charged for access to libraries, excluded from conferences, and shunned by the journals. Specialized cliques seek to monopolize subject areas, exclude outsiders, and resist any competition, particularly if their views are challenged. In such a protectionist academic world there is little room for the free-trading interloper. Indeed, the academy has ceased to be a community of scholars; the writing of history, like soldiering and publishing, is no longer a profession for gentlemen or gentlewomen. Those who study English language and literature are incapable of constructing a meaningful sentence, and those who study the history of culture have no manners.

The battle between the ancients and moderns has been refought by successive generations for at least three centuries. But the destructive capacity of the weaponry has increased, and what began as limited warfare governed by chivalric conventions has become a total war of annihilation. The theoretical revolution also devours its own children. A contemporary obsession with novelty has accelerated the pace of revision and reduced the shelf life of any idea. The intellectual structures of the past have not been adapted to new needs, but bulldozed, leaving a wasteland.

Introduction: Models and Myths

England is often described as the first modern society—a classic manifestation of the modernization model. Whether the great discontinuity is identified with industrialization or with capitalism, it is assumed that England during the seventeenth century made a qualitative transition from an organic, natural order to an artificial, monetary civilization, from gemeinschaft to gesellschaft. An agrarian, immobile, self-sufficient, traditionalist, fully integrated, regional society, based on custom, reciprocity, hierarchy, and status, is alleged to have been replaced by an individualistic, rational, impersonal, mobile, heterogeneous, literate, urbanized, profit-maximizing, national society within a large-scale market economy, based on the division of labor, specific roles, contract, competition, and private property rights.[1]

In the modernization model of the "big ditch," which employs the classic rhetorical device of bipolarization, relationships formulated on historical experience and cultural norms are juxtaposed with those based on the exercise of rational will and anticipation of the future.[2] It is both descriptive and prescriptive; since change is institutionalized as the norm and regarded as irreversible, any regressions are treated as irrational aberrations. By postulating a fundamental and universal break in human

---

[1] The original theory is usually attributed to F. Toennies, *Gemeinschaft and Gesellschaft*, ed. C. P. Loomis (East Lansing, 1957), 165. Both concepts were ideal types: see R. Heberle, "Ferdinand Toennies" in *An Introduction to the History of Sociology*, ed. H. E. Barnes (1965), 151. Emile Durkheim argued that the division of labor made society more complex but rejected the idea of gesellschaft, that a society could exist solely on contract and self-interest: see A. Giddens, *Capitalism and Modern Social Theory* (Cambridge, 1971), 77. The most persistent advocate of the premarket economy is K. Polyani, *The Great Transformation* (Boston, 1985), 53–4, 70.

[2] J. A. Hall and J. C. Jarvie, eds., Introduction to *Transition to Modernity* (Cambridge, 1992), 4.

1

evolution, the model in effect invents the very concept of modernity. It is so simple, convenient, and comprehensive that it has been borrowed, extended, and adapted by theorists with widely different agendas. It was even acknowledged in principle by theorists of social equilibrium; Parsonian models, for example, are both synchronic and diachronic. Historians preoccupied with dividing the past into periods and obsessed with categorizing changes of mentality as well as changes in the economy and society have adopted and merged it with the Whig concept of history as progress.

The original reason why Ferdinand Toennies developed his famous dichotomy was his belief and concern that both the family and the community in which it was embedded had been transmuted into civil society. At the core of the modernization model lies the assumption that the self-sufficiency and intimacy of the traditional family, which was extended and supported by a network of kin, was superseded by the nuclear family, based on the conjugal couple, individualism, and domesticity. At the same time, the traditional community, based on homogeneity, conformity, commensality, and consensus, is assumed to have been destroyed by the division of labor, the market economy, industrialization, and urbanization.

Empirical historians have, of course, queried both the chronology of the great transition and the reality of sudden and irreversible change. It has been argued that individualism and affection emerged in England long before the major economic changes of the early modern period.[3] Family historians have emphasized the continuity of communal forms, that the nuclear family had a long history and coexisted with kinship, and that the household was different from the family.[4] A substantial literature has emerged on the demography and structure of county families and provincial urban elites; a few monographs have even explored kinship networks in business.

---

[3] A. MacFarlane, *The Culture of Capitalism* (Oxford, 1987), 133.

[4] D. B. Smith, "The Study of the Family," *William and Mary Quarterly*, 3rd ser., 39 (1982): 18–19; J. Demos, "Images of the American Family" in *Changing Images of the Family*, ed. V. Tufte and B. Myerhoff (New Haven, 1979), 59; T. K. Haveren, "The History of the Family," *American Historical Review* 96 (1991): 95–124; R. Wheaton, "Observations on Kinship History" in *Family History at the Crossroads*, ed. T. K. Haveren and A. Plakans (Princeton, 1987), 285–301; K. Wrightson, "Household and Kinship," *History Workshop* 12 (1981): 156; J. J. Hurwich, "Lineage and Kin" in *The First Modern Society*, ed. A. L. Beier et al. (Cambridge, 1989), 60; J. D. Faubion, "Kinship is Dead," *Comparative Studies in Social History* 38 (1996): 67–91. The contributions of many other historians of the family will become evident in the course of this book.

A wide gulf still persists, however, between the generality of current theory and the particularism of the research into family and kinship at different social and occupational levels. It is not surprising that theorists rarely cite concrete archival documents because they believe that the past has to be imagined and cannot be distilled from vast numbers of facts. But historians have also sinned by displaying an eagerness to generalize casually about hundreds of thousands of people on the basis of a handful of indiscriminately selected examples.[5] This is tantamount to writing fiction, a task that novelists are far better equipped to perform. Other historians openly admit the inadequacy of their sources as scholarly insurance but then proceed to ignore their own caveats.[6]

The hypothetical relationship between the family and capitalism has never been systematically tested in the urban business community, where it should be most visible. There has been much speculation about the "bourgeois" family as the harbinger and pacemaker of change but no satisfactory or comprehensive research into the business family. The primary purpose of this book is to remedy that omission by studying in depth business families and their kinship networks throughout the English-speaking world, during a period when England emerged as a global economic power. It will both describe and analyze the history of the business family over four generations: what happened to it, how it functioned and responded to events, when and where it changed or failed to change, and why and in what directions it developed. At the very least, this study will provide empirical data either to validate or disprove prior theories of how the modern family developed. At most, it will make the evolution of modern society more intelligible.

MAX WEBER AND KARL MARX

Most theories of the family follow the modernization thesis but emphasize different catalysts. Max Weber, for example, rejected the

---

[5] M. R. Hunt, *The Middling Sort* (Berkeley, 1996), 47, claims somewhat recklessly that there are no records of "non elite" family life before 1650. Those who do not seek do not find. Although it is not clear what proportion of the population would have been adult members of the "middling sort" between 1680–1780, a guesstimate would be at least 750,000. Largely ignoring statistics compiled by other historians, the author generalizes instead from a minute number of random examples drawn from completely different occupations and often a generation apart.

[6] L. Stone, *Family Sex and Marriage* (1977) and "Family History," *Journal of Interdisciplinary History* 12 (1981): 76. The Stone model is still widely used by literary critics, even though it has been totally discredited by historians: see D. Cressy, "Foucault, Stone," *English Literary Renaissance* 21 (1991): 130.

evolutionary approach and did not believe that the logical antecedents of any event constituted a causal explanation.[7] Instead of searching for historical laws, like Karl Marx, he followed Heinrich Rickert and preferred to construct ideal types that were essentially historical models designed to illustrate secular change by analysis of particular events and actions.[8] Weber thought that explaining the origins of any change in terms of that change was tautological; in his view a change of norms had to precede changes in behavior and any change of ethos required an external agent.[9] For Weber, a culture could only be displaced by prior intellectual shifts. The market needed a concept of capitalism before it could become capitalist; therefore, its emergence could not be explained in terms of postcapitalist values.[10]

Weber nonetheless incorporated much of the modernist thesis. He thought that the family had evolved from clans and that it acquired its bourgeois character from Puritanism.[11] The concept of the "calling" depersonalized the family and the neighborhood and created emotional detachment, though in England the feudal and the patrimonial were combined.[12] In the seventeenth century the notion of private property emerged and was guaranteed by the state; the isolation of the household satisfied an essential prerequisite of capitalism.[13] Romantic love, which he considered both irrational and uncontrolled (just like capital accumulation), emerged as a necessary antidote to individual alienation. On the other hand, Weber believed that the extended family stifled economic

[7] R. Bendix and G. Roth, eds., *Scholarship and Partisanship* (Berkeley, 1971), 38.

[8] G. Roth, "History and Sociology," *British Journal of Sociology* 27 (1976): 316; T. Burger, *Max Weber's Theory of Concept Formation* (Durham, N.C., 1987), 210, 227; F. Ringer, *Max Weber's Methodology* (Cambridge, Mass., 1998), chap. 2. T. Parsons, *The Early Essays*, ed. C. Camic (1991), 22, 208, found two kinds of ideal type in Weber and treated Werner Sombart's categories as ideal types. Few sociologists have in fact adopted Weber's methodology because it formulated no laws and required empirical research. The category of "real types" as described by A. Spiethoff, "Pure Theory and Economic Gestalt Theory" in *Enterprise and Social Change*, ed. F. C. Lande and J. C. Riemersma (Homewood, Ill., 1953), 453, has been totally ignored.

[9] G. Marshall, *In Search of the Spirit of Capitalism* (New York, 1982), 133.

[10] D. I. Kertzer, "Anthropology and Family History," *Journal of Family History* 9 (1984): 209.

[11] M. Weber, *General Economic History*, trans. F. H. Knight (New York, 1961), 50. Schumpeter, on the other hand, thought that the bourgeois family was ultimately destroyed by capitalism: see J. A. Schumpeter, *Capitalism, Socialism, and Democracy* (1976), 157.

[12] R. Bendix, *Max Weber* (1960), 70, 375; L. D. Blustone, *Max Weber's Theory of the Family* (Port Washington, 1987), 162.

[13] R. Collins, *Weberian Sociological Theory* (Cambridge, 1987), 291.

development because it put the group before the individual.[14] He considered nepotism, for example, to be a crime, because it impeded the emergence of a universalistic, meritocratic bureaucracy, whereas to kin selection theorists nepotism is a necessary genetic trait.[15]

Karl Marx and his followers identified the great divide with the triumph of the capitalist mode of production that separated work from the household; the family evolved in stages parallel to the stages of capitalism.[16] In the seventeenth century ownership was divorced from use, and labor rather than patrimony became the basis of familial life. The antifeudal family became a unit of consumption, education, and procreation instead of production; external institutions operating in an impersonal market took over its economic functions.[17] Any exceptions in the historical record were treated as abnormalities. The inability of the neofeudal English theater to realize the contradictions within the forces of production has been attributed, for example, to bourgeois "historical immaturity" and the "ideological resistance of feudalism" dismissed as "anachronistic."[18]

To Marxists, rational profit-seeking and individual thrift were emphasized above collective responsibility in a capitalist society. To Crawford MacPherson, the introduction of private property and a free market for land and labor destroyed blood ties and enhanced individual autonomy. Free, equal, and randomly associated individuals now exchanged their labor and competed in an open marketplace. England became a society of possessive individuals who maximized their utility and were bound by contract rather than defined by status.[19] John Locke, and to a lesser extent Thomas Hobbes, are credited with having provided an

[14] Weber argued that the corporate kin group (the sib) throttled capitalism: see Collins, *Weberian Sociological Theory*, 267–9.

[15] R. Fox, *Kinship and Marriage* (1983), 6.

[16] B. Fine and E. Leopold, *Women's Employment and the Capitalist Family* (1992), 8; M. McKeon, "Historicizing Patriarchy," *Eighteenth Century Studies* 28 (1995): 295–322.

[17] E. Zaretsky, *Capitalism, the Family and Personal Life* (1976), xi, 16–7; A. Giddens, *A Contemporary Critique of Historical Materialism*, 2d ed. (Stanford, 1995), 166; J. de Vries, "The Industrial Revolution and the Industrious Revolution," *Journal of Economic History* 44 (1994): 265. Since Marxist histories follow the same script and cite the same secondary sources, one or two examples serves for all.

[18] W. Cohen, *Drama of a Nation* (Ithaca, 1985), 3; S. Bercovitch, "New England's Errand Reappraised" in *New Directions in American Intellectual History*, ed. J. Higham and P. Conkin (Baltimore, 1979), 93.

[19] C. B. MacPherson, *Political Theory of Possessive Individualism* (Oxford, 1964), 53–4, 64.

intellectual justification for this demise of the cooperative, moral
economy by privileging private property rights over communal ownership in civil society.[20] The "critical theory" of Jürgen Habermas postu-
lates that capitalism separated the private from the public sphere and the
family from the economy.[21]

Some contemporary Marxists have reacted to the worldwide rejection
of their doctrines by roping themselves to the mast: "by grace of bourgeois culture in decline, Marxism has emerged as the last bastion of
historical thinking."[22] Others in a desperate attempt to cling to their
faith have downplayed structuralism and the modernization model and
clutched at any new and seemingly popular radical theory that might
reverse their decline, producing some strange hybrids.[23] Elite groups have
been credited with the ability to create an ideology, which served their
interests, and then by fixing the terms of the discussion and through their
control of access to knowledge, persuade their inferiors to accept it as
valid. The concept of mentalities, though treated as an inert force, has
been gingerly accepted as a dialectic between the objective conditions
of human life and the way that people narrate it. Ideologies are
still considered the product of social forces, but it is now conceded
that the egotistic ideology of the bourgeoisie was gender specific, that
women in the household might have contributed to primitive accumulation, that reproduction of the species was a mode of production, and
that the term *culture* could be employed as a shorthand for the activities of a class.[24]

---

[20] N. Bobbio, *Thomas Hobbes and the Natural Law Tradition*, trans. D. Gobetti (Chicago,
1993), 14; R. Holton and B. Turner, *Max Weber on Economy and Society* (1984), 166.
[21] J. Habermas, *The Structural Transformation of the Public Sphere* (Cambridge, Mass.,
1989), 19, 24; D. Held, *Introduction to Critical Theory* (Cambridge, 1980), 41. The
idea that value is objectified by exchange is most brilliantly argued by G. Simmel, *The
Philosophy of Money*, trans. T. Bottomore and D. Frisby, 2d ed. (1990).
[22] E. Fox Genovese, "Literary Criticism" in *The New Historicism*, ed. A. Veeser (1989),
213.
[23] R. Hamilton, *The Liberation of Women* (1978), 98.
[24] G. Therborn, *The Ideology of Power* (1980), 6, 57, 158; C. Middleton, "Patriarchal
Exploitation" in *Gender Class and Work*, ed. E. Gamarnikow et al. (1983), 19; W.
Seccombe, *A Millennium of Family Change* (New York, 1992), 4; M. Pereleman, *Classical Political Economy* (Totowa, 1984), 26–7; C. Meillassoux, *Maidens, Meal, and
Money* (Cambridge, 1981), xiii. Marxism has, like all religions, spawned many heresies;
the Frankfurt School jettisoned both economic and class determination, while continuing to denounce patriarchialism and the bourgeois family. Marxists argue heatedly
among themselves about internal inconsistencies in their theory: see, for example, C.
Mooers, *The Making of Bourgeois Europe* (1994). But this is equivalent to debating the
color and shape of a unicorn's horn without questioning whether unicorns exist.

GENDER THEORY

The central preoccupation of gender theorists has been the exclusion of women from power, often neglecting the family and economic dimensions.[25] The family nonetheless is at least an uninvited guest because it constituted the core of patriarchy. Marxism was linked to feminism through Friedrich Engels, who advanced the proposition that the victory of private over communal property had created patriarchy and the monogamous marriage—the exclusion of the wife from social production and the "subjugation of the one sex by the other."[26] Passion could only occur in bourgeois social relations after the transition from feudalism to capitalism. The capitalist mode of production then divided women into either idle bourgeois, economically and emotionally dependent on their husbands, or into proletarians. By reducing wage earners to a proletariat, the bourgeoisie indirectly created subjectivity and therefore romantic love as well as boosting illegitimacy. Bourgeois civilization made the bourgeois woman.[27]

These views, which were in fact based on the discredited theories of American anthropologist Lewis Morgan, had considerable influence on early gender models of the family.[28] Capitalism was blamed for regulating women's reproduction and their access to economic power.[29] The market economy was credited with responsibility for converting property from a means of exchange between families into capital.[30] Capitalism is also alleged to have marginalized wives by divorcing them from the means of production and forcing them to lead pointless, idle lives in order to fortify the status of their husbands who paid the bills. The bourgeois individual is categorized not as economic man but as domestic woman.[31] The bourgeois public sphere developed the conjugal family as

---

[25] P. Thompson, "Life Histories" in *Biography and Society*, ed. D. Bertaux (1982), 300.

[26] F. Engels, *The Origins of the Family*, trans. A. West and D. Torr (1940), 69; M. George, *Women in the First Capitalist Society* (Urbana, 1988), 4–5.

[27] K. Sacks, "Engels Revisited" in *Women, Culture, and Society*, ed. M. Z. Rosaldo and L. Lamphere (Stanford, 1974), 222. Elements of this model have also been adopted by A. Macfarlane, *Marriage and Love in England* (Oxford, 1986) and by E. Shorter, *Making of the Modern Family* (1976). It also features in general surveys such as M. Mascuch, "Social Mobility and Middling Self-Identity," *Social History* 20 (1995): 55, and in an awkward and somewhat outdated form in D. C. Quinlan and J. A. Shackleford, "Economy and English Families," *Journal of Interdisciplinary History* 24 (1994): 431–63.

[28] Hamilton, *Liberation of Women*, 92–3.

[29] G. Lerner, *Creation of Patriarchy* (Oxford, 1986), 171.

[30] C. Jordan, *Renaissance Feminism* (Ithaca, 1990), 16.

[31] N. Armstrong, *Desire and Domestic Fiction* (Oxford, 1987), 66.

the site of a new form of subjectivity distinct from society.[32] Women now had value in use and men value in exchange.

Gender theorists have also drawn, however, on the modernization model. One popular thesis has been that of Alice Clark who advanced the argument that capitalism marginalized women, but she also argued that they had enjoyed a productive role in an earlier "Golden Age" before the seventeenth century.[33] Followers of this school of thought were prepared to concede that the position of women had evolved, though not necessarily in one or the right direction.[34] Historians have argued, based on the evidence of literary sources and legal texts, that the vocational choices and property rights of women were deliberately narrowed by men in the early modern period.[35] The ideology of family love emerged to endorse male authority and female sacrifice—to control women and conceal their economic contribution.[36] Sexuality and companionate marriage were invoked to legitimate the class and gender hierarchy; the Renaissance woman with her spirit of rational equality became the subordinate wife of later centuries.[37] Traditional paternal patriarchy was converted into modern fraternal patriarchy.[38]

Other theorists have chosen to regard patriarchal repression as omnipresent and changeless over time. Complex debates have occurred over whether or not patriarchy preceded capitalism and over the significance of contract.[39] The idealization of the family as a sanctuary of

---

[32] T. Lovell, "Subjective Powers" in *The Consumption of Culture*, ed. J. Brewer and A. Bermingham (1995), 30.

[33] B. A. Hanawalt, ed., *Women and Work in Pre-industrial Europe* (Bloomington, 1986), xv, and "The Widow's Mite" in *Upon My Husband's Death*, ed. L. Mirrer (Ann Arbor, 1992), 40; M. K. McIntosh, *A Community Transformed* (New York, 1991), 289–90; S. O. Rose, "Proto Industry," *Journal of Family History* 13 (1988): 192.

[34] A. J. Vickers, "Golden Age to Separate Spheres," *Historical Journal* 36 (1993): 383–414.

[35] A. L. Erickson, *Women and Property* (1993), 227; R. E. Archer, "Women as Landholders" in *Woman Is a Worthy Wight*, ed. P. J. P. Goldberg (1992), 162; S. Staves, *Married Women's Separate Property* (Cambridge, 1990), 35, chap. 4; E. Spring, *Law, Land, and Family* (Chapel Hill, 1993), passim; M. Berg, "Women's Property," *Journal of Interdisciplinary History* 24 (1993): 243.

[36] L. S. Robinson, *Sex, Class, and Culture* (1978), 174.

[37] V. Wayne, introduction to A. Tilney, *A Brief Discourse* (Ithaca, 1992), 4.

[38] C. Pateman, *The Disorder of Women* (Stanford, 1989), 35.

[39] C. Pateman, *The Sexual Contract* (Stanford, 1988), 25–7, 37–8; S. Walby, *Theorizing Patriarchy* (Oxford, 1991), passim; H. Hartman, "Capitalism, Patriarchy, and Job Segregation," *Signs* 1 (1976): 137–69; R. Coward, *Patriarchal Precedents* (1983), 88; H. Hartmann, "The Unhappy Marriage" in *Women and Revolution*, ed. L. Sargent (1981), 1–41; J. S. Jaquette, "Contract and Coercion" in *Women Writers and the Early Modern British Political Tradition*, ed. H. L. Smith (1998), 216. R. MacKonough and R. Harrison, "Patriarchy and Relations of Production" in *Feminism and Materialism*, ed. A. Kuhn and A. M. Wolpe (1978), 40, advocate a dual notion of patriarchy.

sentiment is interpreted as a reinforcement of patriarchy. Men have been accused of criticizing women for participating in a system that was designed to entrap them by making marriage and consumption the only outlets for their energies.[40] Historians who argue that women enjoyed power in the household have been dismissed as "duped by the hierarchizing rhetoric of a gendered division of economic labor."[41]

Other gender theorists have mixed economic with cultural determinism. To them, men conquer by internalizing norms and expectations rather than by enforcing obedience. They construct ideals to "uphold the developing apparatus of male bourgeois power"; the character of motherhood therefore has to be reconstructed by imagination, not from "actual material behavior."[42] Male authors have been accused of deliberately defining women's power in terms of sex and their status in terms of desexualized idleness.[43] The importance of the family and kinship is rejected on the grounds that culture and not biology differentiate men from women.[44]

FAMILY MODELS

The family can be regarded as a psychological, biological, social, economic, or political construct. It can be extended upward, downward, and laterally through intermarriage or by incorporating household servants. It can be restricted to male descendants who share the same surname (a house) or expanded to include offspring through daughters. It can consist of solitary bachelors, spinsters, widowers and widows, childless couples, single parents with young children, and coresident siblings. It has never been a rigid institution, and its structure has changed continuously with the life cycle, as its members move in and out, marry, age, and die. Any individual belongs to two families—the family of orientation into which he was born and the family of procreation created by marriage. The family is therefore a moving target and is best defined in terms of what it is not, as occupying all the space not filled by other social institutions.

Historians of the family have devised an elaborate classification

---

[40] L. T. Fitz, "What Says the Married Woman," *Mosaic* 13 (1980): 10.
[41] L. Hutson, *The Usurer's Daughter* (1994), 23.
[42] T. Bowers, *Politics of Motherhood* (Cambridge, 1996), 20.
[43] J. Wiltenburg, *Disorderly Women and Female Power* (Charlottesville, 1992), 257.
[44] J. F. Collier and S. J. Yanagisako, eds., *Gender and Kinship* (Stanford, 1983), 49.

system to distinguish different forms and combinations of forms.[45] For analytical purposes these have been reduced here to three categories: the nuclear family, the extended family, and the household. The nuclear consists of parents, stepparents, or substitute parents, children, and stepchildren. The extended embraces all relations by blood (consanguinial) or marriage (affinal). There was no sharp line of differentiation in the early modern period between agnatic and affinal; the family was an entirety of persons connected by marriage or along filiation lines rather than a dynasty or succession of individuals.

The household was, however, separate from the family. The household was a unit of coresidence that might not include some family members but did include nonfamily members such as servants, apprentices, and lodgers. Grown sons and daughters might live temporarily or permanently in the parental household before and after marriage or move back to assist or replace a parent. From the point of view of the tax-collecting state, the family was a cluster of dependents living under the authority of a household.[46]

Some family models are variations of modernization models. The Parsonian model is ahistorical and predicates a shift from universal to particular, from ascription to achievement, from diffuse to specific roles; the kinship system has to be destroyed and this is effected by industrialization.[47] The Stone model of change is historical but is still based on the proposition that the extended family was superseded by the nuclear family. It also incorporates an assumed psychological revolution in attitudes and sentiments, an idea originally propounded by Philippe Aries. A similar argument has been advanced by Shorter who surmised that the new capitalist society promoted egotism in the emotional sphere as well as in the market.[48] The emergence of sentimentalism in the family has also been interpreted as a mirror image of rationalism and the work ethic—dreaminess is associated with mothers and rational capitalism

---

[45] P. Laslett, "Family and Household" in *Social and Economic Aspects of the Family*, ed. R. Wall and S. Osamu (Cambridge, 1993), table 17.1.

[46] K. Wrightson, "The Policy of the Parish" in *The Experience of Authority*, ed. P. Griffiths, A. Fox, and S. Hindle (1996), 13.

[47] T. Parsons, *Family Socialization and Interactive Process* (Glencoe, 1955), 16, 20. Parsons had no "nostalgic conceptualization of gemeinschaft": see R. J. Holton and B. S. Turner, *Talcott Parsons on Economy and Society* (1986), 23, 218.

[48] Shorter, *Making of the Modern Family*, 259. The views of most academics are determined not by current events but by the political and personal traumas of their youth: see D. Chinot, "Changing Fashion" in *The State of Sociology*, ed. J. F. Short (Beverley Hills, 1981), 260.

with fathers.[49] Yet another approach is to regard the family not as a separate entity but as one component of a whole way of life.

The concept of the development cycle is an influential analytical device introduced as a dynamic alternative to static, demographic, and household models of the family. The family is seen in continuous transition following the life course of its individual members, whose roles and mutual interaction vary with each stage. Three principal stages are envisaged: first the conjugal couple, then dispersion of the children by marriage, and then replacement of parents by their children.[50] The development cycle is studied longitudinally through a succession of cohorts; a distinction is made between individual time, family time, and social time, the latter equated either with age or with the calendar.[51] Families do not necessarily pass through all stages; changes in the configuration of kin over the life course also differ from the family cycle because the stages of parenthood are fixed. The life course approach allows for greater fluidity in family structure and it can be combined with family reconstitution, though it does not explain behavior.[52] It represents more of a strategy than a theory or methodology, and it has been criticized as purely descriptive because the criteria for phases differ.[53]

The family can also be structured as an economic model. Although some economists are willing to concede that the market is not the only determinant, most usually ignore social factors and assume that all humans are motivated by utility; subject to adequate information, families allocate their time and money to maximize satisfaction.[54] A rational choice economic model has been constructed to explain the behavior of families in terms of exchange theory and multiple calculations,

---

[49] C. Campbell, *The Romantic Ethic* (Oxford, 1989), 226.

[50] M. Fortis, introduction to J. Goody, ed., *The Developmental Cycle in Domestic Groups* (Cambridge, 1958), 4–5.

[51] T. K. Haveren, "The Family Cycle" in *The Family Life Cycle in European Societies*, ed. J. Cuisenier (Mouton, 1977), 347; G. H. Elder, "Families and Lives" in *Family History at the Crossroads*, ed. T. K. Haveren and A. Plakans (Princeton, 1987), 182, 196.

[52] T. K. Haveren, "Cycles, Courses, and Cohorts," *Journal of Social History* 12 (1978): 107; M. P. Guttmann, "Family Reconstitutions as Event-History Analysis" in *Old and New Methods in Historical Demography*, ed. D. S. Reher and R. S. Schofield (Oxford, 1993), 159–77.

[53] T. K. Haveren, "Family History at the Crossroads," *Journal of Family History* 12 (1987): xiv.

[54] P. S. Cohen, "Economic Analysis and Economic Man" in *Themes in Economic Anthropology*, ed. R. Firth (1967), 94; H. Coase, *The Firm, the Market, and the Law* (Chicago, 1988), 3.

ignoring the free-rider problem.[55] In such a model the family does not function according to prescription or routine but proceeds by a series of bargains.

Kinship models are standard devices in social anthropology. To Claude Levi-Strauss it was kinship systems that originally created culture.[56] Martine Segalen has argued that kinship should be studied rather than the family.[57] There are, however, important differences between the perceptual categories and definitions of kinship in early societies and the analytical categories of social scientists.[58] Stuart England had no formal system of kinship with sanctions of the kind described by anthropologists. Kinship, like language, had its own grammar and was governed by a largely unknown but still applicable body of rules.[59] Network theory, based on functional mapping and the measurement of clusters, also has some applications to the study of kinship and its influence on individual behavior.[60] A useful distinction can be made between egocentric and sociocentric networks and between the individual actor and all actors in a social system.[61]

Finally, as an extension of family networks, there are models of the community—the gemeinschaft. The holistic concept of the tightly integrated community, which is greater than the sum of its parts, is really a myth; although an organizing concept in sociology, it is an invention that became a method.[62] There are numerous variations of the model; sometimes the community is simply defined as experience, sometimes as an end in itself, sometimes as the opposite of self-interest, sometimes as a totality of common values.[63] There is little consensus as to whether it

---

[55] M. Anderson, *Family Structure in Nineteenth-Century Lancashire* (Cambridge, 1971), 197. The defects of rational choice theory are outlined in J. Elster, *Rational Choice* (New York, 1986), 23–5. In classical theory, moreover, women are regarded as selfless and the family as moral and altruistic: see N. Folbre and H. Hartmann, "The Rhetoric of Self Interest" in *The Consequences of Economic Rhetoric*, ed. A. Klamer et al. (Cambridge, 1988), 185.

[56] M. Csikszentmihalyi and E. Halton, *The Meaning of Things* (New York, 1981), 40.

[57] M. Segalen, *Historical Anthropology of the Family* (Cambridge, 1986), 40.

[58] T. K. Haveren, "Recent Research in the History of the Family" in *Time Family and Community*, ed. M. Drake (Oxford, 1994), 25.

[59] Wheaton, "Observations on Kinship History," 329.

[60] J. C. Mitchell, "Social Networks" in *Annual Review of Antropology*, ed. B. J. Siegel, vol. 3 (Palo Alto, 1974), 297.

[61] A. S. Klovdahl, "Urban Social Networks" in *The Small World*, ed. M. Kochen (Norwood, N. J., 1989), 177. See also S. Nenudic, "Identifying Social Networks" in *History and Computing*, ed. E. Mawdsley, vol. 3 (Manchester, 1990), 189.

[62] A. MacFarlane, "Historical Anthropology," *Social History* 5 (1977): 632.

[63] T. Bender, *Community and Social Change in America* (Baltimore, 1982), 5–8.

should be defined by blood, occupation, neighborliness, social interaction, geographic area, or residential propinquity or whether it exists only as a state of mind, as a reified ideal.[64] Gemeinschaft is really an ideological concept designed to contrast the alleged, face-to-face life of the countryside with urban anonymity. The most practical definition is that it is a bounded social system and not necessarily homogeneous.[65]

THE POVERTY OF THEORY

Models of the family abstract, simplify, and map reality in accordance with specific rules in order to emphasize recurrent and typical forms, display clusters of attributes, predict behavior, reveal trends and connections, and avoid ad hoc interpretations. Historians have been criticized for reducing the value of their analysis by ignoring theory and by studying the domestic family instead of the familial system.[66] Their practice of treating sources as direct descriptions has been challenged on the grounds that "all history is cultural history."[67] Theorists often display great animosity toward empiricism and any appeal to facts, historical or otherwise.[68] A bourgeois mind-set has been identified with an "overmastering obsession with the logic of the real."[69]

Whereas historical sociologists categorize the evidence and then compare and analyze it, social historians usually prefer thick description without an organized system of propositions.[70] Some take great pains to establish the facts and then offer weak explanations, which reflects an inability to analyze rather than the absence of theory.[71] Many family histories make the mistake of comparing past and present instead of

---

[64] A. MacFarlane, S. Harrison, and C. Jardine, *Reconstructing Historical Communities* (Cambridge, 1977), 2.

[65] D. Sachs, "Celebrating Authority in Bristol" in *Urban Life in the Renaissance*, ed. S. Zimmerman and R. F. E. Weissman (Newark, 1989), 188.

[66] S. D. Amussen, "Early Modern Social History," *Journal of British Studies* 29 (1990): 83; R. Winch, et al. *Familial Organization* (New York, 1978), 96–7.

[67] L. Jordanova, "The Representation of the Family" in *Interpretation and Cultural History*, ed. A. Wear and J. H. Pittock (Basingstoke, 1991), 11, 118 (the argument is watered down on page 131).

[68] B. Hindess and P. Q. Hirst, *Pre-Capitalist Modes of Production* (1975), 311.

[69] A. Easthope, "Romancing the Stone," *Social History* 18 (1993): 248; H. Belknap, *Beyond the Great Story* (Cambridge, Mass., 1995), 230; V. H. White, *The Content of Form* (Baltimore, 1987), 3, 36.

[70] V. E. Bonnell, "The Uses of Theory," *Comparative Studies in Society and History* 22 (1980): 170–1; P. Abrams, *Historical Sociology* (Ithaca, 1982), 332; M. Anderson, *Approaches to the History of the Family* (1980), 38.

[71] W. O. Aydelotte, *Quantification in History* (Reading, 1971), passim.

measuring change over successive generations.[72] Observing behavior does not necessarily reveal the reasons for that behavior.[73] Belief can be cautiously inferred from behavior, but a group mentality cannot be inferred from individual beliefs.

The frequent injunction to adopt theoretical rigor, however, betrays narrowness of vision and knowledge.[74] Many theories depend on factual ignorance, on slighting or ignoring the evidence.[75] Labels, like bourgeois, are applied indiscriminately to the family; although they imply class determination, the process of inference is never specified.[76] As Locke observed, "I see it is easier and more natural for Men to build Castles in the Air of their own than to survey well those that are to be found standing."[77] Models used to describe actual families must be tested for empirical validity, because events are governed by fortuitous as well as by systematic factors.[78]

The principal weakness of most theories of society is their denial of individual agency. The apparatus of roles is designed to obviate any need to scrutinize the thoughts or character of individuals. Structures cannot exist without humans; they have to be reproduced across time and space. Every idea has to be conceived by a person.[79] Meaning cannot be a subject of investigation independent of individuals. Economic models of the family are limited in their application, because they predicate a rational economic person who is never ambivalent or conflicted and they treat people like commodities.

Human agency has acquired a new importance, and it is no longer assumed as a matter of course that social systems have their own logic, which humans can neither understand nor influence.[80] Social determinism has been rejected on the grounds that it requires the construction of

---

[72] D. S. Smith, "Parental Power and Marriage Patterns," *Journal of Marriage and the Family* 35 (1973): 419.

[73] S. Wolfan, *In Laws and Outlaws* (1987), 199; R. T. LaPierre, "Attitudes versus Actions," *Social Forces* 13 (1934): 230–7.

[74] A. Marwick, "A Fetishism of Documents" in *Developments in Modern Historiography*, ed. H. Kozicki (New York, 1993), 110–11, 131.

[75] F. Mount, *The Subversive Family* (1982), 63, 187–8.

[76] P. Laslett, "The Character of Familial History" in Haveren and Plakans, *Family History*, 273.

[77] J. Locke, *Correspondence*, ed. E. S. DeBeer (Oxford, 1976–89), Locke to Molyneux 20 January 1693.

[78] H. J. Habbakuk, "Economic History and Economic Theory," *Daedalus* 100 (1971): 311.

[79] M. C. Lemon, *The Discipline of History* (New York, 1995), 176.

[80] S. K. Sanderson, *Social Evolution* (1992), intro.; P. Joyce, "The End of Social History," *Social History* 20 (1995): 84–5.

all the mental states of agents as causes of their actions.[81] There is in fact no objective social reality; societies are what people do.[82]

Most historians are more interested in the typical than in the universal or the structural, and they have developed sophisticated techniques to assess and interpret the evidence without the baggage of theory.[83] Historians' propositions are always existential, because they are ultimately founded on individual behavior, whatever the level of generality.[84] Charles Darwin, it will be recalled, conquered the typology of fixed species by concentrating on the variability of individual organisms within the population. Theory is only applicable at the level of subjectivity of those whose lives are to be explained.[85] It is the evidence and not an agenda that historians of the family must follow; without verification there can be no knowledge.[86]

A grand theory of discontinuity appeals to those who seek simple, monistic explanations for the development of the family. The analytical mode prefers parsimony in explanation and eschews variant causes.[87] Causation can, however, rarely be precisely determined; it is often cumulative, circular, and indirect.[88] A factor can be indispensable without leading inevitably to a particular conclusion.[89] An event can be explained by invoking a particular action or by describing the conditions for that action.[90] Qualitative changes, by definition, cannot be predicted on the basis of past experience.

A different problem is presented by present centeredness, or as Frederick William Maitland defined it, "retrospective modernism." Historians have been accused of reducing the history of the family to a sentimental discourse as an antidote to current values.[91] It is doubtful whether any culture can be analyzed in terms of anachronistic concepts

---

[81] Q. D. R. Skinner, "Social Meaning" in *Philosophy, Politics, and Society*, vol. 4, ed. P. Laslett, W. G. Runciman, and Q. D. R. Skinner (Oxford, 1974), 156.

[82] E. A. Gellner, "Explanations in History" in *Modes of Individualism*, ed. J. O'Neil (New York, 1973), 263.

[83] R. T. Atkins, *Knowledge and Explanation in History* (Ithaca, 1978), 37.

[84] G. Leff, *History and Social Theory* (1969), 77.

[85] P. Abrams, "Historical Sociology," *Past and Present* 87 (1980): 12.

[86] F. W. Fogel and G. R. Elton, *Which Road to the Past?* (New Haven, 1983), 100.

[87] D. S. A. Smith, "A Perspective on Demographic Methods," *William and Mary Quarterly* 39 (1982): 445.

[88] D. S. Landes, "What Room for Accident?" *Economic History Review* 47 (1994): 655.

[89] P. D. MacClelland, *Causal Explanation and Model Building in History* (Ithaca, 1975), 74.

[90] S. Pollard in *Culture in History*, ed. J. Melling and J. Barry (Exeter, 1992), 10; R. Martin, "Causes Conditions," *History and Theory* 21 (1982): 58.

[91] N. Armstrong and L. Tennenhouse, *The Imaginary Puritan* (Berkeley, 1992), 83.

that its members would not have understood.[92] The early modern period had its own obsessions and criteria of what was important; the obsession with image and representation is, however, a preoccupation of the late twentieth century. Historical writing has always been a powerful tool of both radical and conservative propaganda, since it can validate current dislikes and reinforce or destroy myths. Those who abhor market capitalism, because they think that it dissolves fraternity and family ties, prefer to blame blind historical forces rather than accept that it is a product of human choice and voluntary action.[93]

The unifying principles of general theory always have the advantage over conflicted histories. Readers demand simple answers and immutable laws that will invest human history with meaning. They yearn for a moral vision and an intellectually imposed order; a theoretical civilization seeks regularities or what Francis Bacon termed the "idols of the tribe."[94] What begins as theory ends as ideology.[95] Ideologies are both prophetic and exclusive; they consist of assumptions that no longer appear to be assumptions and that are never subjected to critical examination by their disciples.[96]

Because there is no basis to disprove them, ideologies turn into myths.[97] Myths offer comfort, whereas the truth promotes anxiety.[98] Because beliefs endure longer than opinions and usually meet some inner need, they can seldom be refuted; only when the world has lost interest in an issue can the historian treat it objectively.[99] Empirical research on

[92] A. MacIntyre, "Causality in the Social Sciences" in *Rationality*, ed. B. R. Wilson (Evanston, 1970), chap. 6. Sadamer, however, considered prejudice to be a condition of knowledge. See W. Outhwaite, "Hans George Sadamer," in *The Return of Grand Theory*, ed. Q. Skinner (Cambridge, 1985), 26.

[93] R. Grassby, *The Idea of Capitalism before the Industrial Revolution* (Lanham, Md., 1999), chap. 5.

[94] F. Bacon, *Works*, ed. J. Spedding et al. (1857–90), iv. 55–6; E. A. Shils, *The Constitution of Society* (Chicago, 1982), 210; C. Taylor, "Use and Abuse of Theory" in *Ideology, Philosophy, and Politics*, ed. A. Parel (1983), 50–1.

[95] A useful list of the main types of ideology is provided by J. B. Thompson, *Ideology and Modern Culture* (Stanford, 1990), 61–6. To I. Wallerstein, *Historical Capitalism* (1983), 81, truth as a cultural ideal is simply an opiate for the masses; in *The Capitalist World Economy* (Cambridge, 1979), 35, he could confidently predict the *imminent* appearance of socialist world government.

[96] On Marxists as Scholastics see A. MacLachlan, *The Rise and Fall of Revolutionary England* (1996), 122.

[97] R. Boudon, *The Analysis of Ideology* (Oxford, 1989), 204; B. Halpern, "Myth and Ideology," *History and Theory* 1 (1961): 135; K. Walsh, "The Post-Modern Threat to the Past," in *Archaeology after Structuralism*, ed. I. Bapty and T. Yates (1990), 281.

[98] D. C. Coleman, *Myth, History, and the Industrial Revolution* (1992), 40.

[99] K. V. Thomas, *The Perception of the Past* (Creighton Trust Lecture, 1983), 24.

the family cannot hope to compete with the self-fulfilling prophecies of ideologies, which usually claim moral significance and acquire allegorical or symbolic forms as timeless archetypes.[100] Ideologies have much in common with astrology; they are systems of thought that are self-confirming and immune to external argument.[101] Fashions in indignation and methodology do, however, change in the long run. The Oedipal passion invested in the debates over the new economic history has long since metamorphosed into indifference.[102] The econometricians won a Pyrrhic victory because they ignored the first rule of business, which is to protect market share.

It is the business of historians to look for patterns of behavior, to identify trends, and measure change. But it is extremely difficult to generalize from the particular.[103] Studies of human attitude and behavior cannot be entirely objective, because they require empathy and sensitivity to nuance.[104] But they must be impartial and free from cultural assumptions.[105] Where humans are involved, it is only possible to estimate probabilities. Historians have to study the sources systematically and then settle for fragments of the truth.[106] They perform best when they reconstruct the specific sequence of events and refrain from asking unanswerable questions and from having the answers before they even ask the questions. Their principal obligation is to strive to get it right, to explain how rather than why events have occurred.

QUANTIFICATION

Statistical data are limited in their applications because psychic behavior—motives and intentions—is not susceptible to precise measurement. It is impossible, for example, to quantify religious conviction.[107] Figures

---

[100] E. E. Evans-Pritchard, *Anthropology and History* (Manchester, 1961), 8; A. Wilson and T. G. Ashplant, "Whig History," *Historical Journal* 31 (1988): 261. Genuine debate can only occur when all parties are prepared to be proved wrong. The most effective weapon against the invincible ignorance of the true believer is not reason, but ridicule.

[101] K. V. Thomas, *Religion and the Decline of Magic* (1971), 767.

[102] A. Field, ed., introduction to *The Future of Economic History* (Boston, 1987), 1, 35.

[103] G. Levi, "On Microhistory" in *New Perspectives on Historical Writing*, ed. P. Burke (University Park, 1992), 106.

[104] T. Zeldin, "Social History and Total History," *Journal of Social History* 10 (1976): 243.

[105] S. Wilson, "The Myth of Motherhood a Myth," *Social History* 9 (1984): 198.

[106] F. W. Maitland, *Selected Essays*, ed. H. D. Hazeltine et al. (Cambridge, 1936), 241.

[107] M. Spufford, "Can We Count the Godly?" *Journal of Ecclesiastical History* 36 (1985): 437.

do not prove inferences, which have to be logically inferred. It is also difficult to reconstruct process from statistics. Even broadly based official records do not necessarily produce the relational data for anthropological field research.[108]

This is well illustrated by studies of the household. The focus on mean household size conceals variations in structure and differences between localities, occupations, and status groups; a high level of aggregation renders kin networks invisible.[109] By treating the household as an end in itself and by relying exclusively on official records, historians have overlooked the importance of nonresident kin and of economic factors. It is vital to observe individuals, because the average or typical family or household is an abstraction with no counterpart in reality. A family can exist without any children or without one or even both parents.

Historians sometimes use statistical data and introduce graphs and tables as evidence without acknowledging the problems of statistical inference. They rely on a rough correspondence between two variables without asking whether the variables are typical or comparable or whether the association is random or distorted by a third factor or by some change in the independent variable. Statistical correlation can only suggest the strength of linear association, never causation, which can only be established by other evidence.[110] The coefficient of determination can indicate what percentage of the variation in one factor is associated with variation in another. But correlations that technically are statistically significant still have low predictability; the number of alternative factors is usually so high that the effectiveness of the correlation as an explanation is diminished.

Path analysis has been described as a "form of statistical fantasy." A path diagram between two variables can never disconfirm a false causal assumption, even if the variables correlate.[111] Correlation, unlike causation, works in both directions and not necessarily in chronological order, so that it is unclear which variable is active and which passive. Significant coefficients can only be obtained if all complicating factors and all other variables can be controlled. Many statistical procedures work no better than old-fashioned insight or common sense, because they cannot prove any substantial hypothesis.[112]

---

[108] A. Plakans, *Kinship in the Past* (New York, 1984), 249.
[109] Wheaton, "Observations on Development of Kinship," 294.
[110] M. W. Oakes, *Statistical Inference* (New York, 1990), 65.
[111] R. Ling, "Correlation and Causation," *Journal of American Statistical Association* 77 (1982): 490.
[112] N. Fitch, "Statistical Fantasies," *Historical Methods* 17 (1984): 251.

Generational and cohort analysis present special problems for the social historian. Generations have a wider age spread than cohorts, and it is difficult to establish chronological boundaries to compare their behavior. Since a society reproduces itself continuously, where does one generation begin and another end?[113] Unless the sample chosen is random, which often cannot be ensured with historical evidence, it is impossible to generalize from it on the whole population. Changes in the life course of any individual are different from changes in the population of which he is a member.

The hunger for statistics can lead to indigestion and obesity. Figures tend to mesmerize historians, who take them at face value, whereas they sift and critically examine other primary sources.[114] Unless distinctly odd or unless some passionate issue is at stake, statistics are never reworked, because the labor does not seem to justify the effort. The fact is quietly ignored that any data set is probably based on thousands of quick, subjective decisions and distorted by errors of transcription, calculation, bias, and the omission of unknown values.[115]

Collating and interpreting the evidence raises formidable methodological problems.[116] A database can only be constructed by taking complex evidence out of context and reducing it to simple categories. Data has to be coded so that it can be input and then manipulated, and, once aggregated, it cannot be checked without direct access to the program. The labels and categories employed often have an ideological component; cases that do not fit the allocated box are dropped or squeezed to fit; the code determines which questions can be asked, and it cannot be changed once the project is under way.[117]

Adequate statistics are, however, indispensable for establishing the structure of the family. They not only provide a framework for analysis, but they indicate what needs to be explained. The cliometricians did not so much test existing facts as establish new facts that could not be known

---

[113] N. B. Ryder, "The Cohort as a Concept," *American Sociological Review* 30 (1965): 843, 853; A. B. Spitzer, "The Historical Problem of Generations," *American Historical Review* 78 (1973): 1358.

[114] D. Landes, "The Fable of the Dead Horse" in *The British Industrial Revolution*, ed. J. Mokyn (Boulder, 1993), 168.

[115] One insoluble problem of privately held databases is that the reader is unable to check sources, as in conventional historical writing. Although most subjects have been individually documented here in a memo field, it is not feasible to list over 85,000 references in the text and the database will be destroyed once the final volume on material culture is published.

[116] For methods and problems of coding see appendix B.

[117] L. Stone, *The Past and the Present* (1987), 60.

until the evidence was subjected to their kind of questioning.[118] Behavior can be measured and relative changes between different variables compared. The greatest single virtue of statistics is their ability to disprove and thereby eliminate false explanations. They can confirm or reject the null hypothesis that chance will produce the same result. Statistics create a solid basis for probability statements.[119] What emerges are patterns of frequency rather than causal relationships.[120] If the data demonstrate that a high proportion of individuals consistently marry their neighbors over a long time period, it is highly probable that propinquity is a major factor in marriage without knowing the deciding factor or why any particular individual has married. The business family can only be studied through collective macrobiography, through the precise aggregation of individual life histories and genealogies.[121]

DESIGN OF THE PROJECT

Previous historians have usually worked with either a sample occupational group, such as aldermen, or with a block of demographic data, like the records of the Quakers. J. R. Woodhead, for example, included all aldermen and common councilors (1660–89) and Henry Horwitz drew a sample of 379 aldermen and company directors.[122] Sample sizes and time periods have varied. Theodore Rabb identified 3,933 merchants as investors in joint stocks and members of regulated companies.[123] Steve Rappaport analyzed the careers of 1,000 London freemen, 530 in detail.[124] Studies of particular port books have usually involved some 3,000 exporters and importers.[125] Peter Earle analyzed a sample of 375 citizens from the orphans records as well as the interrogatories of 1,994 men and 2,121 women (1660–1725) and 1,794 men and 1,436 women

[118] L. J. Goldstein, "The Sociological Historiography of Charles Tilly" in *Developments in Modern Historiography*, ed. H. Kozicki (New York, 1993), 92.
[119] C. Hay, "Historical Theories," *History and Theory* 19 (1980): 50.
[120] M. Douglas, *Risk and Blame* (1992), 50.
[121] R. M. Taylor and R. J. Crandall, eds., *Generation and Change* (Macon, 1986), 21; W. M. Mason and S. E. Fienberg, *Cohort Analysis in Social Research* (New York, 1985), 35.
[122] J. R. Woodhead, *The Rulers of London, 1660–89* (London and Middlesex Archaeological Society, 1965); H. Horwitz, "Testamentary Practice," *Law and History Review* 2 (1984): 225.
[123] T. K. Rabb, *Enterprise and Empire* (Cambridge, Mass., 1967), 53.
[124] S. Rappaport, *Worlds within Worlds* (Cambridge, 1989).
[125] N. Zahedieh, "London and Colonial Consumer," *Economic History Review* 47 (1994): 243; D. W. Jones, *War and the Economy* (Oxford, 1988).

(1695–1725).[126] Richard Archer compiled a database with 70 fields of 22,164 migrants to America born before 1650.[127] James Alexander has identified 5,498 dealers, 3,871 manufacturers, and 10,379 individuals taxed on stocks in 1693.[128] Lorna Weatherill has sampled 496 and David Cressy 3,261 inventories, though relatively few were of businessmen.[129] Percival Boyd indexed all those citizens whose names appeared in printed registers before 1700, though only 2,744 have known dates of birth.[130] Vivien Brodsky has compiled marriage data on 2,140 men and 2,033 women.[131]

The original plan for this book was to compile lists of businessmen at different points of time, but it soon became apparent that it was more cost effective to input data accumulated over many years rather than to search the records for particular individuals. The project therefore became extensive rather than intensive.[132]

All the evidence has been aggregated in a relational database of 28,000 London businessmen between 1580–1740, or slightly more than half the total business population.[133] Although the subjects are roughly equal in number before and after 1660, the number of cases varies between decades, and many dates of death have been estimated.[134] Although the whole database is large enough to represent a population, the data are

---

[126] P. Earle, *City Full of People* (1994). According to S. R. Jayne, *Library Catalogues of the English Renaissance* (Berkeley, 1956; reprinted Godalming, 1983), 400 inventories of London residents were transcribed by P. A. Kennedy in the 1950s.

[127] R. Archer, "New England Mosaic," *William and Mary Quarterly*, 3d ser., 47 (1990): 478. It is surprising that more dictionaries of occupations and professions, where the basic data is already collected in alphabetical order, have not been computerized.

[128] J. Alexander, "The Economic Structure of London," *Urban History Yearbook* (1989): 50–1, and in *Surveying the People*, ed. K. Schurer and T. Arkell (Oxford, 1992), table 1.

[129] L. G. Weatherill, *Consumer Behavior* (1988), table 8.1; D. Cressy, *Literacy and the Social Order* (Cambridge, 1980), 138.

[130] Boyd compiled one card index of citizens (estimates of the number of entries range from 38,000 to 60,000) and an index of marriages, which is available on microfilm.

[131] V. Brodsky, "Widows in Late Elizabethan London" in *The World We Have Gained*, ed. L. Bonfield, R. M. Smith, and K. Wrightson (Oxford, 1986), 32.

[132] The parameters of research have been governed by the marginal cost of acquiring each datum. At a rate of $100 per day, to devote a whole day to confirm whether a family had an additional child that died in infancy has not, for example, been considered a wise use of limited time and money. Each cell in the database has been allocated 16 cents and 1.2 minutes for research and inputting, assuming a working day of 12 hours and a working year of 360 days.

[133] In 1638 2,238 (21 percent) London households were regarded as substantial: see R. Finlay, *Population and Metropolis* (Cambridge, 1981), 79. For an estimate of the numbers of businessmen see R. Grassby, *The Business Community of Seventeenth-Century England* (Cambridge, 1995), 54–60.

[134] The absolute number of values in each field is given in table 11.1.

unevenly spread and consequently many tables in effect constitute a sample of the whole database.

The data on individual cases have been captured and linked from a broad range of interrelated sources and record sets.[135] Each record in the database consists of one person identified by last and first name. Information on each subject has been stored in both alphanumeric and numeric form in 99 fields; nominal, ordinal, and interval measures have all been employed. The whole database has been manipulated to map relationships between variables and answer broad questions.

For comparative purposes and for cross-sectional analysis, however, the data have also been disaggregated and rearranged in three subsets, which have been utilized as independent variables: one based on period and date of death; one based on financial categories adjusted for price inflation; and one based on successive birth cohorts.[136] This triangular method has allowed the same questions to be approached from three different angles. The main division into two periods has been useful in establishing long-term trends; the four financial brackets have allowed quick and easy assessment of the impact of wealth on any issue; and the cohort divisions make possible a longitudinal analysis of the lifetime experience of groups. When running data and constructing tables, forty years has usually been chosen as the temporal unit rather than a decade.

So much depends on the chance survival of evidence that this cannot be considered a random sample in which every businessman would have an equal probability of being selected. Thanks to errors in the sources and the large number of missing values, there is a high probability of contamination by random error and distortion; some connections may be mere coincidence. The level of risk was not, however, considered sufficient to require testing for confidence and significance, given the limited use of statistical inference and the size of the sample in relation to the total business population and to the number of fields.

The guiding principle of analysis has been simplicity. A method had been adopted that matches the range and type of data. More elaborate techniques would have reduced clarity without remedying defects in the evidence or producing more accurate answers. The data have been analyzed inductively by relating and comparing descriptive

---

[135] The sources for the database are listed in appendix A. On methods of record linkage see E. A. Wrigley, *Identifying People in the Past* (1973), 5.

[136] A precise account of the structure of these subsets is given in appendix B.

observations.[137] In a few cases it has been possible to establish meaningful correlation coefficients.[138] Medians have been uniformly employed to neutralize the impact of extreme values and of wide dispersion around the mean and to establish central tendencies; the difference between the median and the mean has served as an approximate measure of distribution.[139] Quartiles have also been calculated to shape the data and correct for skewed distribution.[140] The results have been presented in contingency tables constructed outside the database. Percentile proportions of frequency distributions have been employed to establish relational and cumulative frequencies, the distribution of variables, and relative changes over time.

THE LIMITATIONS OF PUBLIC SOURCES

Data have been gathered from a broad cross section of records generated by the state, the church, and the city of London.[141] The information available on many subjects is, however, minimal, and the data are uneven and incomplete (see table 11.1). Sometimes the marital history of an individual can be ascertained, but not his business activity, and vice versa. Some bias is inevitable given the nature and distribution of the sources; the best recorded are those who lived longest and those most celebrated. Whereas most overseas merchants have been included, domestic and small-scale businessmen are disproportionally represented among the unknowns.[142]

No source is completely objective or comprehensive. Official records of taxpayers and lenders are often mere lists of names and are incomplete because of evasion or the use of intermediaries. The port books, for example, often list agents or just one member of a firm or distort

---

[137] J. Branner "Combining Qualitative and Qualitative" and M. Hammersley, "Deconstructing the Qualitative" in *Mixing Methods*, ed. J. Brannen (Averbury, 1992), 6, 41.

[138] The data matrix was exported to and run through an SPSS program that performed standard statistical tests and calculated the Pearsons Product Moment Correlation Coefficient between all the interval variables. Several thousand combinations of variables were also run through the database, but the great majority yielded little of significance or answered questions that were not relevant to this book.

[139] L. Auwers, "History from the Mean," *Historical Methods* 12 (1979): 44.

[140] No modes, standard deviations, moving averages, or coefficients of variation have been calculated and the data has been presented exclusively in tables and not in the form of graphs, bar or pie charts, histograms, or scattergrams.

[141] A list of the principal sources for the database is provided in appendix A.

[142] This point was made by J. J. MacCusker in his review of T. K. Rabb, *Enterprise and Empire* in *Historical Methods Newsletter* 2 (1969): 14–18.

names, as is evident when they are compared with private business records.[143] Fiscal records frequently do not indicate the occupation or the real wealth of an individual. The ages declared in marriage allegations (as in legal depositions) cannot be taken at face value; although those recorded for single men and women are probably close to the truth, the ages of widows seem to have been rounded off.[144] Marriage data based on allegations and bonds excludes those married by banns or during the interregnum. Marriages by license constituted only 50 percent of all marriages in the diocese of Canterbury and one-sixth in the diocese of London (1598–1619), rising to 80 percent (1677–1725).[145]

Wills do not survive for all propertied individuals, usually when there was a sole heir or because the family property had been distributed inter vivos. Nuncupative wills are usually brief and other wills were drawn up by third parties or followed printed formulas.[146] Theoretically, the wills of sodomites, suicides, and "a manifest usurer" were voided, though there is no indication of strict enforcement.[147] Nor do they always mention all the wives, heirs, or children of a testator.

Inventories cannot be easily converted into fiscal data because of unspecified debts, distribution inter vivos, the difficulty of equalizing values, and other technical problems.[148] They also reflect the situation of a testator at death, not during his life. The common serjeant's books frequently fail to mention children who were adult, married, or financially advanced during the testator's life and their summaries of estates are bunched by value and not entered in strict chronological order. After 1695 the number of estates passing through the Court of Orphans fell drastically, and a high proportion of them were intestate. Few probate

---

[143] H. Roseveare, "Wiggins Key," *Journal Transport History*, 3d ser., 16 (1995): 14. On possible methods of computerizing port book data see G. J. Milne and M. Paul, "Establishing a Flexible Model for Port Book Studies," *History and Computing* 6 (1994): 106–15.

[144] The accuracy of ages was subjected to several tests by V. Brodsky, "Mobility and Marriage in Pre-Industrial England" (Ph.D. thesis, Cambridge University, 1978), 291, 325, and Brodsky, "Widows," 129. See also R. B. Outhwaite, "Age at Marriage," *Transactions Royal Historical Society*, 5th ser., 23 (1973): 68.

[145] P. Razzell, "The Growth of Population," *Journal of Economic History* 53 (1993): 751; V. Brodsky, "Single Women" in *Marriage and Society*, ed. R. B. Outhwaite (1981), 89.

[146] B. Capp, "Will Formularies," *Local Population Studies* 14 (1975): 49; R. C. Richardson, "Wills and Willmakers," *Local Population Studies* 9 (1972): passim.

[147] H. Swinburne, *A Brief Treatise of Testaments* (1591), 56, 59; G. Meriton, *The Touchstone of Wills*, 2d ed. (1671), 50, 61, 70.

[148] On the technical aspects see A. Schuurman and G. Pastoor, "From Probate Inventories to a Data Set," and C. Litzenberger, "Computer-Based Analysis of Early Modern Wills," *History and Computing* 7 (1995): 126–34, 143–51.

accounts survive for London or before 1660, and the majority of the deceased were married men; the accounts of administrators are more common than those of executors.[149]

Judicial records raise many problems of representation. They highlight the exceptional rather than the normal. Matrimonial cases, for example, only entered the courts when relations between couples broke down; suits over property were brought by the minority of families who failed to agree. Legal proceedings were scripted performances that often represent a victim's viewpoint, and there is no way of determining whether either plaintiff or defendant is truthful. Depositions were tainted by exclusion, collusion, and innuendo and were often false, misinformed, or incomplete; the culture of litigation reduced complex situations to formulas, structured arguments in antitheses, and manipulated language to construct stories; the level of rhetoric increased with the degree of conflict.[150]

Literary sources have the most flaws as evidence, though they are also the most widely used. In addition to their gender bias, authors freely invented facts, wallowed in their prejudices, generalized from their limited personal experience, and pursued their own agendas. It is often impossible to distinguish fact from fiction or advice from reportage; some representations were too far-fetched to be credible.[151] Those authors who eschewed prescription could still only describe what they had personally observed and experienced. Even a man of incomparable intellectual gifts, like Locke, was necessarily limited in his knowledge of the world; Locke probably knew less about his own society than the statistician Gregory King. Puritan writers are hardly the best source for information about the ungodly. The child-rearing manuals represent the values not of children but of their authors.[152]

The same was true of the theater. Plays drew on the real world for

[149] A. L. Erickson, "Introduction to Probate Accounts" in *The Records of the Nation*, ed. G. H. Martin and P. Spufford (1990), 273–86; U. Priestley and P. J. Corfield, "Rooms and Room Use in Norwich," *Post-Medieval Archaeology* 16 (1982): 96; C. Gittings, "Probate Accounts," *Local Historian* 31 (1991): 51–9.

[150] L. Nader, "The Recurrent Dialectic," *University Pennsylvania Law Review* 132 (1984): 645; T. Stretton, "Women and Litigation in the Elizabethan Court of Requests" (Ph.D. diss., University of Cambridge, 1993), 236; L. Gowing, *Domestic Dangers* (Oxford, 1996), passim; L. L. Giese, ed., *London Consistory Count Depositions, 1586–1611*, vol. 32 (London Record Society, 1995), vii–ix; K. Wrightson, "The Family" in *Hanoverian Britain and Europe*, ed. S. Taylor et al. (New York, 1998), 14.

[151] F. E. Dolan, *Dangerous Familiars* (Ithaca, 1994), 32.

[152] J. Mechling, "Advice to Historians," *Journal of Social History* 9 (1975): 47, 53.

inspiration, and they can be read as imaginative constructions of an over-arching mentality.[153] But unless they can be supported by evidence of actual behavior, their message is little more than personal speculation.[154] The dramatists exaggerated the coherence of urban society, parodied the citizenry in hackneyed stereotyped images, personified vices, and employed a defensive rhetoric.[155] Dramatists wrote about businessmen but not necessarily for them; they were particularly keen to juxtapose money, sex, and family and to both mock and defend contemporary values.[156] Comedy depicted the merchant as a predator driven by gain and fear of death, lecherous, intolerably proud, and vulnerable.

THE LIMITATIONS OF PRIVATE SOURCES

Personal records have their own problems. In the first place they have survived randomly in limited numbers. Ralph Josselin is a major source for the history of the family, but, as the editor of his diary has conceded, he was just one clergyman.[157] Of the thousands of letters of Thomas Hall, only one survives that was written to his wife.[158] Some correspondents borrowed their phrases and ideas from books; many letters were modeled on a guide by Nicholas Bretton.[159] To analyze the content of letters, which had a public as well as a private function, it is necessary to know the background and unspoken agenda of both writer and recipient. Affectionate terms may, for example, have been a formality or a device to elicit a particular response.

Diaries and journals, which were a byproduct of a literary culture, vary enormously in subject matter and tone from bald summaries of events to obsessively detailed self-analysis. The great majority were idiosyncratic and written only by those who had self-discipline and an urge to express themselves. The most introspective are usually the least objective. Diaries were kept for many different reasons—as a record of devotion, as an aid to memory, and for self-regulation; frequently they

---

[153] A. Fletcher, "Men's Dilemma," *Transactions of Royal Historical Society*, 6th ser., 4 (1994): 62–3; J. R. Mulryne, *Theater and Government under the Early Stuarts* (Cambridge, 1993), 2.
[154] V. Comensoli, *Household Business* (Toronto, 1996), in her study of domestic tragedies has nothing to say about actual families.
[155] T. B. Leinwald, *The City Staged* (Madison, 1986), 3–4, 80.
[156] A. Leggatt, *Citizen Comedy in the Age of Shakespeare* (Toronto, 1973), 4, 15.
[157] A. Macfarlane, *The Family Life of Ralph Josselin* (Cambridge, 1970), intro.
[158] C. Gill, *Merchants and Mariners* (1961), 133.
[159] J. Robertson, *The Art of Letter Writing* (1942), passim.

were combined with family records and household accounts.[160] A few diarists felt impelled to record everything objectively, including the most mundane events, but frequently information was excluded or edited out at a later stage, and often a diary bumps from one crisis to another.

Memoirs and autobiographies, which were often extensions of journals and commonplace books, differ from diaries in that they were self-conscious and written at one particular point in time. Autobiography is by definition a self-centered narrative, and it has to be constructed; sometimes the text was revised more than once. It was natural that an autobiographer should fashion himself as how he wished others to see him, and accounts could easily degenerate into fantasy. Many life histories in the business community were written as conversion narratives.[161]

It is extraordinarily difficult to reconstruct either the attitudes, motives, or intentions behind behavior. What people do is different from what they think they are doing and what they think they should be doing.[162] What is said or thought to have happened often differs from what actually occurred. Every person has both an actual and a perceived past. Most humans are ambivalent (a crucial fact almost entirely ignored by historians) and procrastinate over decisions of real importance. They often cannot explain their actions to themselves. When it is possible to spend a lifetime with another person without every really understanding him or her, how can historians blithely assume that they can read the minds and make judgments about millions of strangers in a different culture?

The one assumption on which there is universal agreement is that human nature has not changed within recorded history. Whereas modern sensibilities create a barrier to understanding historical cultures, the instinctual life of the past can theoretically be shared and experienced. Emotions such as love, friendship, anger, loneliness, and fear play a central role in the lives of individuals, but they are more ephemeral and less well recorded than interests.[163] Since they cannot be precisely and objectively categorized, they cannot be readily quantified. It is always

---

[160] On various techniques for dealing quantitatively with wills see P. T. Hoffman, "Wills and Statistics," *Journal of Interdisciplinary History* 14 (1984): 813–34; S. K. Cohn, *Death and Property in Siena* (Baltimore, 1988), appendix.

[161] S. Jeake, *Diary*, ed. M. Hunter and A. Gregory (Oxford, 1988), 26.

[162] R. T. Vann, "The Rhetoric of Social History," *Journal of Social History* 10 (1976): 230.

[163] T. Zeldin, "Personal History," *Journal of Social History* 15 (1982): 343.

difficult to distinguish the profession of sentiment from true emotion.[164] Absolute changes in the importance of a particular sentiment have to be carefully distinguished from the same sentiment expressed differently or perceived with a different emphasis.[165] Contradictory feelings coexisted, often in the same person, and changes in behavior may have occurred before they became visible in the sources. On the other hand, what appears to be a change of attitude may merely reflect greater literacy and more surviving evidence. The volume of intimate sources—diaries and correspondence—increases in the early modern period, and written sources are much more persuasive than oral tradition.[166]

QUANTITATIVE AND QUALITATIVE EVIDENCE

The database can nonetheless be regarded as reasonably representative. No one source has been preferred. Inventories, for example, have not been used in isolation, but combined with other sources that reveal age, household size, surviving partners, and occupation.[167] The records of the city and business have been linked with those of litigants and taxpayers to achieve critical mass rather than genealogical precision. The deficiencies in particular sources cancel each other out when aggregated and integrated. The sheer size of the database provides a counterweight to inherent bias. Enough material has survived to observe a sufficiently large number of individual businessmen, to measure the strength and direction of change, and to indicate the influence of one variable on another. The quality of the available data is more than adequate to reconstitute the structure and process of the business family and to describe and analyze its attitudes, functions, and behavior.[168]

The probate evidence, which includes multiple grants of probate, administration records, and cause papers, is of incalculable value. Wills reveal details of marriages, children, and links between families. Through

---

[164] In the seventeenth century the adjective sentimental referred to a judgment of mind, not uncontrolled feelings: see J. H. Hagstrum, *Sex and Sensibility* (Chicago, 1980), 7. The suggestions of P. N. Stearns and Z. Carol, "Emotionology," *American Historical Review* 90 (1985): 813–36, are not particularly helpful.

[165] L. A. Tilly and M. Cohen, "Does the Family Have a History?" *Social Sciences History* 6 (1982): 145; R. Harré, ed., *The Social Construction of Emotions* (Oxford, 1986), 5.

[166] J. Goody, *The Interface between the Written and the Oral* (Cambridge, 1987), 209.

[167] J. Van Vries, "Between Purchasing Power" in *Consumption and the World of Goods*, ed. J. Brewer and R. Porter (1993), 165.

[168] On the inability of high technology to compensate for deficiencies of evidence (garbage in, garbage out) see P. Wiles, "The Necessity and Impossibility of Political Economy," *History and Theory* (1972): 4.

wills the historian can make intimate contact with very large numbers of people; whereas approximately ninety diaries and memoirs of businessmen survive and approximately two hundred sets of correspondence, wills are numbered in the tens of thousands.[169] There is no aspect of the human condition that is not eventually encountered in a will. The format was infinitely varied. John Nicholl chose to make a detailed analysis of his business.[170] One registered will simply consisted of the last letter written by the testator to his wife.[171] Wills were usually made close to death, and testators took the opportunity to review and reflect on their life, issue complex instructions, and record their relationships. They reveal the close attachment of businessmen to both their worldly goods and to the people in their lives. Inventories are usually both detailed and accurate; John Burgis, for example, specified in his will that his wares be appraised at cost (as in his books) and that any disputes over valuation should be referred by his executor.

Because the law both influenced and reflected family attitudes, judicial proceedings and arguments yield valuable insights into the relationship between the family and society. Litigation not only generated abundant information about sources of marital and family conflict, but prompted the deposit of a great number of personal and family papers that were never retrieved and have therefore survived.

The utility of literary works, if carefully interpreted, lies less in the truth of their subject matter than in what they reveal about their intended audience.[172] To use literary sources requires familiarity with the culture, age, background, and prejudices of the author, and with literary conventions of diction, imagery, and syntax. Daniel Defoe's family instructor, for example, describes potential situations with realistic dialogue and believable characters; he was interested in clarifying the issues and analyzing relationships. But he still invented his examples and dramatized his views.[173] The dramatists exposed the discrepancies between how citizens perceived themselves and how they actually behaved.

---

[169] M. Takahashi, "The Number of Wills" in *The Records of the Nation*, ed. G. H. Martin and P. Spufford (1990), 187–213. Of the London businessmen in the database, 153 left major collections of business papers and 56 personal papers. Many others survive for provincial merchants. An excellent survey of wills as sources is R. Houlbrooke, *Death, Religion, and the Family* (Oxford, 1998), chapters 4 and 5.

[170] Prerogative Court of Canterbury (hereafter PCC), Evelyn 72, 1641.

[171] PCC, Berkeley 352, will of Thomas Trenchfield, 1656.

[172] K. McLushie, " 'Tis but a Woman," *Literature and History* 9 (1983): 228.

[173] L. A. Curtis, "A Case Study," *Studies in Eighteenth-Century Culture* 10 (1981): 410.

Private records provide much statistical material. Many journals have notes on births, marriages, and deaths at the front like the account book of Thomas Yardley, glover of Worcester.[174] Business papers name hundreds of clients.[175] But the principal value of personal sources, appropriately filtered, is that they allow direct observation of businessmen; they provide both a window to view daily family life and a passage to the inner soul. Most businessmen wrote their own letters from which their inner feelings can often be reconstucted, shared, and understood. A diary conveys a sense of immediacy, an autobiography, the dreams and longings of the author. Much can be learned from phrasing and even personal handwriting.

Every type of evidence has its limitations and can mislead unless utilized with care. But when the quantitative evidence is combined with qualitative evidence, it is possible to reconstruct on a large scale both the reality and the intimacy of family life. Personal and literary sources reveal the existence of particular attitudes and motives; the distribution and relative importance of those attitudes can then be inferred from the quantitative evidence of behavior. It is human experience that connects structure and process.[176]

THE FRAMEWORK OF PRESENTATION

The approach adopted in this study is therefore both quantitative and qualitative, but not theoretical except in the sense that absence of dogma is itself a dogma.[177] It imitates the bee and the ant but not the spider. It seeks, like Norbert Elias, to clarify the nature and origins of problems without pretending to have all the answers.[178] Every aspect of the family is looked at from a new perspective with greater statistical precision and greater breadth and depth of coverage than earlier studies have attempted. This provides a much sounder basis for generalization and comparison over time. The truth always lies in the details. Ideologies and methodologies come and go, but the facts are eternal.

Since families are created by marriage, the first part of this book considers how marriages in the business community were initiated and

---

[174] Worcester, RO, BA/8541.
[175] A. V. Judges, "History and Business Records," *Genealogical Magazine* 8 (1939): 367.
[176] Thompson, *Poverty of Theory*, 30.
[177] On having a view about having a view see R. Rorty, *Philosophy and the Mirror of Nature* (Princeton, 1979), 371.
[178] N. Elias, *The Civilising Process*, trans. E. Jephcott (Oxford, 1989), xv–xvi.

made. Because freedom of choice to many historians defines the difference between the traditional and modern family, the process of making a marriage is described in some detail to determine how far business marriages were arranged and what was expected. Conventional attitudes to marriage and gender are reconstructed from the legal and didactic literature, and these are then compared with both the quantitative evidence of when and whom businessmen married and with actual cases of individual courtship from family archives.

The next question to be addressed is the quality of married life, whether, as has been suggested by some historians, the roles of husbands and wives have changed over time and whether their private relationship became increasingly intimate. Here again the prescriptions of the advice books are compared with data on the durability of marriages at different levels of wealth and in different periods and with concrete examples of how particular couples dealt with such potential sources of friction as infidelity, personality differences, and household management.

No discussion of marriage would be complete without reviewing the fate of the survivors, both widowers and widows. The database provides precise information on the relative life expectancy of husbands and wives, on the ratio of widowers to widows, on the length of widowhood, the frequency of remarriage, and the appointment of widows as executrix. Contemporary views on remarriage and widowhood are compared with the testamentary evidence and with specific case studies to determine the intentions of husbands and the choices and behavior of widows.

The second part of the book deals with the wider family, focusing first on relations between parents and children. The database clarifies such important matters as the size of business families compared to other occupations and in relation to wealth, the ratio of sons to daughters, and the frequency of orphans and three-generation families. But the principal evidence for parenting is qualitative and anecdotal. Family and legal records have been extensively explored to establish how fathers and mothers handled birth, infancy, childhood, and adolescence, how they interpreted their rights and duties, and how far their attitudes and behavior mirrored the injunctions of contemporary ecclesiastical and secular writings, which have fueled the debate among historians as to when childhood appeared and how children were treated.

A separate chapter examines relationships between parents and those children who had set up independent households as adults. Some statistical tests are conducted to determine whether sons were treated differently from daughters and whether fathers behaved differently from mothers. But the attitude of children to their fathers and mothers in later life and the relationship between siblings in childhood and maturity are mainly reconstructed from family correspondence and probate evidence, which illustrate how conflicts arose and how they were resolved.

Once the character of the nuclear family has been established, it is possible to decide whether the extended family was declining, as some historians have argued, as well as the role of the family in urban society. Quantitative data is assembled on the frequency, breadth, and intensity of relationships with kin. Family records are utilized at this point to determine whether paternal kin were privileged over maternal kin or blood over marriage and to identify who was recognized as family, for what reasons, and with what consequences. Finally, loyalty to family is compared with loyalty to the local community and to urban institutions.

The third part of this book is devoted to the nuclear and extended family as a business institution. Quantitative evidence is presented on the significance of the family as a source of manpower, training, partners, and capital. The records of firms are explored to assess the economic importance of family influence, intermarriage, and kinship networks. The role of women in business is separately considered from men. An estimate is provided of the number and wealth of single women, wives, and widows in business and their preferred trades. Legal, financial, and cultural obstacles are documented to explain why women preferred passive investment to active participation in business.

A final chapter is devoted to the transfer of property between generations and the advancement of business families through their children. The database clarifies who was preferred in wills, the relative importance of partible inheritance and primogeniture, and the careers and marriages selected by parents for their sons and daughters. The probate evidence and marriage settlements are used to determine the motives of testators and the effect on family businesses of efforts to provide adequately for widows and children.

Once the structure and process of the business family have been empirically established, it is possible to judge whether it fits any of the numerous models of the family or validates the modernization thesis. What emerges from this study is that the business family was driven by both external and internal forces, that, contrary to orthodox analysis, the links between the family and the economy did not run in one direction. The patriarchal family and kinship networks coexisted with possessive individualism. The capitalist ethos surfaced in traditional families alongside conventional social ambitions. The business family could not escape the life cycle, but it was still an independent variable of economic growth.

Part I

Marriage

1

Making a Match

In contrast to birth and death, men and women could decide when they wanted to marry. Indeed the exercise of that choice is the central issue in the debate over the origins of the modern family. Family historians have established that arranged marriages were most common among heirs in the upper ranks of landed society and that those with little or no property could marry freely. But the position of the businessman is somewhat obscure. Some clues to general attitudes can be gleaned from the contemporary advice books targeted at urban families, dramas, and legal documents. There is, however, no substitute for systematically studying the behavior of actual business families in the marriage market.

Entry into marriage for all social groups was governed by both legal rules and social conventions that varied in strength from what was normally expected to moral prescription. It was widely assumed that sexual desire had to be controlled and institutionalized in order to maintain the stability of the social and gender hierarchy and the integrity of the culture. But how far did businessmen in practice follow precept and injunction? Why did they marry and whom? When and where did they marry? How did they court and win their brides, who did not necessarily share the same objectives? What were their expectations and options?

LOVE

The power of romantic love was widely acknowledged and represented as a natural emotion in literature.[1] Its physical and mental effects were

---

[1] J. A. Boone, *Tradition, Counter Tradition* (Chicago, 1987), 8.

noted—the ectasy, the self-inflicted pain, the deceit, the despair, and the exhilaration. "For Ovid need not in strikt rules have showne," wrote Wye Saltonstall, "the Art of love which Maids can leave alone."[2] James Harrington, who believed in divorce by consent and observed that the lower orders were privileged in that they were free to follow their affections, paid homage "unto pure and spotless love."[3] *The Power and Pleasure of Love* in 1675 credited the merchant with passion: "When his Love he doth meet and prostrates himself and his wealth at her feet."[4] "Love, this a pretty little soft thing that plays about the heart," warbled the *Ladies Directory* in 1694.[5] William de Britaine argued that "of all Follies in man, there is none more excusable than that of love."[6] Bernard Mandeville regarded love as a sentiment "distinct from all other affections" and innate to both men and women after puberty, though he added "in the making of matches the call of Nature be the very last Consideration."[7]

Although the contemporary romances, with their extravagant escapism and usually chaste ideals, were often attacked, they were widely read and sometimes drew on actual events.[8] Popular ballads and chapbooks spread tales of sexual adventure and romantic love in which an apprentice taken with a serving maid could boldly assert that he would disregard his parents.[9] In the world of fantasy, an apprentice could win the heart of his master's daughter, marry her without parental knowledge, and still receive a portion.[10] Although love can be regarded as a natural instinct that easily becomes infatuation in the young, it was no doubt objectified and reinforced by the romantic literature.[11]

---

[2] W. Saltonstall, *Picturae Loquentis* (1631), C 2–4.
[3] J. Harrington, *Political Works*, ed. J. G. A. Pococke (Cambridge, 1977), 246.
[4] *The Roxburghe Ballads*, ed. J. W. Ebsworth (Hertford, 1884), 459.
[5] *The Ladies Directory* (1694), 259.
[6] W. de Britaine, *Humane Prudence*, 9th ed. (1702), 54.
[7] B. Mandeville, *The Fable of the Bees*, ed. F. B. Kaye (Oxford, 1924), 142–3.
[8] S. M. Mendelson, "The Weightiest Business," *Past and Present* 85 (1979): 129–30; *The Gentlewoman's Companion* (1673), 9, which is no longer ascribed to Hannah Woolley. See E. Hobbs, "Hannah Woolley" in *Culture and Society in the Stuart Restoration*, ed. G. MacLean (Cambridge, 1996), 179–200.
[9] M. Spufford, *Small Books and Pleasant Histories* (1981), 157–8, 164–5; B. Capp, "Popular Literature" in *Popular Culture in Seventeenth-Century England*, ed. B. Reay (1985), 212–13; J. A. Sharpe, "Plebian Marriage in Stuart England," *Transactions of the Royal Historical Society*, 5th ser., 36 (1980): 73.
[10] *The Euing Collection of English Broadside Ballads*, ed. J. Holloway (Glasgow, 1971), no. 1919b.
[11] Adam Smith thought that love in marriage was directly related to the prohibition of divorce: see his *Lectures on Jurisprudence*, ed. R. L. Meek et al. (1978), 150.

Love was feared, however, because it ignored reason and caused instability. Although a distinction was made between love and being "in love," both states were regarded as compelling, dangerous, and likely to conflict with parental, family, and social obligations.[12] Thomas Gainsford, who attacked youthful marriages, argued that "love breeds awful subjection . . . love and the cough and a woman with child can hardly be concealed"; "a citizen is more troubled with his wife than his wares."[13] The chapbooks also mocked passion, and the language of passion became more rhetorical in the course of the century.[14]

Dutiful affection toward authority figures was preferred to self-centered, free outpouring of emotion.[15] Love was valued as an ideal by the preachers, though they preferred it to follow rather than precede marriage. To John Dod and Robert Cleaver "love growing of beauty, riches, lust, or any other like slight, uncertain and frail grounds, is soon lost and vanished."[16] Couples, advised Thomas Gataker, "must take heed not only of ceasing simply to love but of leaving their first love, of suffering their Love to grow lukewarm."[17] Mutual affection and true love, which was allowed a physical dimension, was differentiated from romantic love, blind lust, or unstable affection, which were dismissed as idolatry.[18] Wise love was differentiated from wild love—"the one ever deliberates before it loves and the other loves before it deliberates."[19] The ambivalence toward love is caught in contemporary proverbs: on the one hand "marriage first and love will come after," on the other hand "love has no respect of persons."[20]

Suitors were advised by the chapbooks and courtship manuals to scrutinize the appearance of their intended, because beauty begat beauty, and beautiful daughters found it easier to attract husbands. Businessmen certainly judged women by their physical appearance. John Verney, when

---

[12] L. Gowing, "Women, Sex, and Honour" (Ph.D. diss., University of London, 1993), 127–9.

[13] T. Gainsford, *The Rich Cabinet* (1616), 27–8, 82–5, 102.

[14] G. L. Dillon, "The Seventeenth-Century Shift in the Theory and Language of Passion," *Language and Style* 4 (1971): 143.

[15] L. Jardine, "Companionate Marriage versus Male Friendship" in *Political Culture and Cultural Politics*, ed. S. D. Amussen and M. A. Kishlansky (Manchester, 1995), 235.

[16] J. Dod and R. Clever, *A Godly Form of Household Government* (1630).

[17] T. Gataker, *Marriage Duties Briefly Couched Together* (1620), 37.

[18] R. M. Frye, "The Teachings of Classical Puritanism on Conjugal Love," *Studies in Renaissance* 2 (1955): 159.

[19] *Gentlewoman's Companion* (1673), 95–6.

[20] M. P. Tilley, *A Dictionary of the Proverbs in England* (Ann Arbor, 1950), L 504 and L 5534.

he surreptitiously viewed a prospective match, declared that he would not be dazzled by the eyes of a prospective swain; "her beauty is not like to prefer her to the title of Duchesse, yet she is a very passable woman and well shapt."[21] The Chevalier d'Arvieux was impressed by the youth and beauty of Jonathan Edward's wife.[22] Samuel Pepys, who could rarely keep either his eyes or his hands to himself, noted in his diary that the wife of John Lethieullier was beautiful and fat.[23] John Lethieullier himself recommended a woman as having a "pleasant agreeable temper, witt, face, shape, and fortune."[24] Francis Rogers, who flirted on his ship with a young lady passenger traveling with her uncle, declared that he would take "none over fat" even with a large portion.[25] Thomas Gent described Alice Guy as having "very good natural parts . . . quick understanding, fine complexion, and very amiable in her features."[26]

Women had their own standards of beauty in which size, weight, shape, color of hair, height, and skin all mattered.[27] They were not above improving on nature with the help of cosmetics and the barber surgeons, who treated hair and skin. The *Ladies Directory* gave advice on how to display physical charms including the breasts.[28] Such stratagems provoked a continuous stream of satire and denunciation of the vanity of women. Women were also coy about their age. Streynsham Master, while in India, was informed by his sister that "modesty would not suffer me to give a young man my age" and "my mother is not willing our ages should travel so far."[29]

A few businessmen's marriages are known to have actually been love matches. To some fortunate suitors, passion and interest coincided. Joseph Paice married at twenty-five the woman he loved, as did the worldly John Verney and Phineas Pett.[30] Jonathan Priestley was so infatuated that he married his first wife against the advice of his kin and

[21] M. M. Verney, *Memoirs of the Verney Family*, vol. 4 (1892; reprint 1970), 159–62.
[22] W. H. Lewis, *Levantine Adventurer* (New York, 1962), 35. There were at least seven members of the Edwards family in the Levant, but the "Edouard" mentioned by d'Arvieux was probably Jonathan, who married Abigail Bendysh.
[23] S. Pepys, *Diary*, vol. 7, ed. R. Latham and W. Matthew (1970–1), 41.
[24] Letter, dated 23 Feb. 1724/5, BL, Add. MS 33,085, fo. 110.
[25] *Three Sea Journals of Stuart Times*, ed. B. S. Ingram (1936), xxvii, 216.
[26] T. Gent, *Life* (1832; reprint. 1974), 35.
[27] G. S. Master, *Some Notices of the Family of Master* (privately printed, 1874), 61–2.
[28] *Ladies Directory*, 308.
[29] W. Hedges, *Diary*, vol. 3, ed. H. Yule (Hakluyt Society, 78, 1887), cxxiv.
[30] A. K. Manning, ed., *Family Picture* (1866); P. Pett, *Autobiography*, ed. W. G. Perrin (Navy Records Society, 1918), 9–10.

friends, despite her lack of a portion and reputation for profanity.[31] Robert Pitt fell in love with Harriett Villiers, daughter of Viscount Grandison, and married her without consulting any of his family or kin; his father was furious when he was told seven months later, but his father eventually reconciled to the marriage and became charmed by his daughter-in-law.[32] The Turkey merchant, Thomas Throwbridge, whom Lady Lethieullier had in mind for her son-in-law, married Delitia Bridges; he apologized for marrying "without first consulting these friends," but added that though his bride might have married richer in England "she has one that will make her a kind and tender husband. . . . I'll just hint to you for the present that twas pure love induced me . . . without any thought of her fortune . . . if my wife survive me, I shall leave her every-thing . . . if your good self, Lady, and Friends approve this match pray advise me first that I may know how to deport myself, for at present I am in a maze."[33]

Simon Forman recorded his early amorous adventures, and Marmaduke Rawdon related how at twelve, "before he knew what love was, he fell in love"; in later life Rawdon visited Alice Randall, a former servant in his uncle's household and "one of the great beawties of England and much admired by the King."[34] Even after living in Italy for several years, Philip Williams still pined for his first love who had married in his absence.[35] Richard Mowse left his mistress, Susanne, the wife of Henry Spurstow (presumably his master) £100 to "lay out in a jewell . . . to weare for my sake."[36] Roger Lowe, who was criticized for implying that women were inferior to men, flirted with several women, usually with more passion than success: "at those times my effection ran out violently after her."[37] An apprentice, who was smitten by one of the housemaids, recorded this in his diary when she gave her notice: "I was much thinking of her going away the 19th of September 1704 in the counting house about five of the clock in the afternoon which was of a

---

[31] J. Priestley, *Memoirs*, ed. C. Jackson (Surtees Society, 77, 1883), 12.

[32] *Historical Manuscripts Commission* (hereafter HMC), 13th report, appendix, pt. 3; T. Lever, *The House of Pitt* (1947), 28; Hedges, *Diary*, vol. 3, xciii–xciv.

[33] Letters dated 2 Apr. and 19 July, 1726, BL, Add. MS 33,055, fos 202, 251.

[34] M. Rawdon, *Life*, ed. R. Davies (Camden Society, 75, 1863), xvi, 2, 29.

[35] R. Grassby, "Love, Property, and Kinship," *English Historical Review* 113 (1998): 344. Williams married the daughter of Sir Thomas Bendysh in 1647, not Bowyer as incor-rectly stated in this article. Bowyer was her second husband whom she married shortly after Philip's death: see Essex, RO, Acc 5336/11.

[36] PCC, Hyde 130, 1665.

[37] R. Lowe, *Diary*, ed. W. L. Sachs (1938), 24, 37.

Tuesday and what I should say how she leaves that day twelve month after."[38]

The lovelorn merchant was often the object of much, usually critical comment. Francis Pool warned his brother that passion blinded judgment: "let me shew you the great inconveniency that always attends a young man marrying purely for love"; blemishes become beauties and the woman is "lookt upon as a goddess" whereas after marriage love turns to hate.[39] His warnings had little impact because "the very naming of her . . . used to transport you and to make your eyes and countenance swim with a melting joy."[40] John Lethieullier commented that "men when they are in love form to themselves such extravagant notions of the woman's perfection which no woman ever had."[41] Many of physician Richard Napier's emotionally stressed patients were victims of unrequited passion accentuated by duplicity.[42] Lucy Pelham describes a male acquaintance who had "fallen passionately in love . . . he has a most sad time of it for we all larft at him about it the whole day long"; she also describes a woman "who I think is the most altered that I ever see anybody without a fit of illness."[43]

SEX

The clerics in England and New England rejected Pauline hostility to sex and adopted a functional approach that counseled moderate, but regular sex in marriage, emphasizing utility rather than pleasure. It was assumed, though not explicitly stated, that sex would continue after menopause. William Gouge believed that sexual relations had a value beyond procreation; although the rich were advised to marry the rich, he cited the Song of Solomon to illustrate the importance of physical attraction.[44] The Puritan ministers, although not excessively prudish, were neither enthusiastic nor explicit about sex. They emphasized rational rather than romantic love, control of feelings, and constancy.[45] The Quakers

---

[38] Bodleian Library, Oxford (hereafter Bod), MS Eng misc. F 78.
[39] Letter dated 26 Oct. 1724, BL, Add. MS 33,085, fo. 102.
[40] Letter dated 10 Apr. 1725, BL, Add. MS 33,085, fo. 113.
[41] Letter, BL, Add. MS 33,085, fo. 106.
[42] M. McDonald, *Mystical Bedlam* (Cambridge, 1981), 89, table 3.5. Only one merchant, however, occurs among the patients in table 2.4.
[43] Letter dated 30 Aug. 1718, BL, Add. MS 33,085.
[44] W. Gouge, *Of Domesticall Duties* (1622), 190, 224–5.
[45] E. Leites, *The Puritan Conscience and Modern Sexuality* (New Haven, 1986), 12, 103; E. S. Morgan, *The Puritan Family* (New York, 1966), 52, 63.

denounced temporal passion as idolatry, emphasized spirituality, and regarded the dowry as essential. Premarital sex was condemned, and marriage was mandatory once it had occurred.[46] Richard Baxter, who asserted that wifely obedience was enjoined by divine law, thought that ungodly children claimed sexual desire as an excuse to marry without consent.[47]

Some Restoration writers equated gentility with male libertinism and businessmen with lack of passion; according to *The Spectator*, "the love of business and money is the greatest mortification of inordinate desires."[48] But Elizabeth Grimeston warned that "the darts of lust are in the eyes."[49] Most secular writers feared the power of sex, which provided the amoral energy that drove Jacobean and Restoration comedy. Young men were advised to eschew masturbation, which enfeebled the mind, and to distance themselves from women, who offered sinful temptations and diminished authority and honor, and focus instead on acquiring wisdom. Whoring was equated with venereal diseases, and with some justification, since syphilis spread largely unchecked in London.[50] It has been argued that, in London, sexuality was treated and controlled as a commodity and discussed in the language of debt and obligation.[51] Cuckoldry was employed as an economic metaphor derived from the gendering of labor; money was associated with fertility, prostitution with wholesaling.[52]

Marriage was seen as a sexual release and thought necessary to make an apprentice an honest man.[53] Alexander Niccholes asserted that the true end of marriage was procreation—that a merchant needed "a wife of some phlegmetick humor"; he distinguished between love, where

---

[46] J. W. Frost, *The Quaker Family in Colonial America* (New York, 1973), 156, 180.

[47] R. Baxter, *A Holy Commonwealth*, ed. W. Lamont (Cambridge, 1994), 205–6; R. B. Schlatter, *The Social Ideas of the Religious Leaders, 1660–1688* (Oxford; reprint, 1971), 11.

[48] *The Spectator*, vol. 4, ed. D. F. Bond (Oxford, 1965), 85.

[49] E. Grimeston, *Miscellanea, Meditation, Memoratives* (1604), H3v.

[50] M. Pelling, "Appearance and Reality" in *Making of the Metropolis*, ed. A. L. Beir and R. Finlay (1986), 98–9.

[51] E. Mignon, *Crabbed Age and Youth* (Durham, N.C., 1947), 101, 178; H. Dubrow, *A Happier Eden* (Ithaca, 1990), 25; S. Wells, "Jacobean City Comedy," *English Literary History* 48 (1981): 58; J.-C. Agnew, *Worlds Apart* (Cambridge, 1986), passim. Most literary studies of this genre rely on a limited selection of often unreliable secondary sources for their historical background and frequently betray ignorance of how either urban society or the market actually worked.

[52] D. Bruster, "Cuckoldry and Capital," *Studies in English Literature* 30 (1990): 207–10.

[53] E. Sowernam, *Ester hath Hangd Haman* (1617), 23.

"there is no envy, not jealousy, not discontent, no weariness," and lust, which was "more specious, hath no meane, no bound."[54] Defoe denounced premarital sex, coitus interruptus, nudity, sex during pregnancy, marrying someone and loving another, quick marriages of widows, marriage of infants, and sodomy; a husband should not make a whore of his wife, nor should a wife publicize the sexual inadequacies of her husband.[55]

Women were often blamed for arousing carnal appetites, though Dorothy Leigh argued, in 1616, that the Virgin Mary had taken reproach away from women.[56] Male writers, drawing on a classical tradition, frequently assumed that women had a stronger sex drive than men.[57] The author of *God's Judgement against Whoring* twisted the biblical account of Christ and the woman taken in adultery to argue that lubricious women deserved condemnation.[58] The honor of women of high rank did not depend on chastity, and women were frequently associated with exorbitant appetites and luxury.[59] It was sometimes alleged that businesmen married older women because they were less sexually demanding.[60]

Nonetheless women were expected to be virgins when they married and were taught to expect the worst from men who were not kinsmen, family friends, or clergy. Accusations of unchastity limited their choice of husbands and were grounds for a slander suit. By the eighteenth century literary convention had made men out to be sexual predators, and greater confidence in human rationality had reduced fears of sensuality.[61] Writers' interests shifted from husbands to daughters.[62] Erotic fiction now focused on seduction, while pious and didactic love fiction focused on defending chastity.[63]

[54] A. Niccholes, *A Discourse of Marriage and Wiving* (1620), 16, 32.
[55] D. Defoe, *Conjugal Lewdness* (1727) in *Works*, ed. W. Hazlitt (1843), 12, 23, 46, 61, 67, 76–8, 83, 93. Defoe's *Family Instructors* may have been written for his own children, particularly his son whose seventeen children had made him destitute: see P. R. Backsheider, *Daniel Defoe* (Lexington, 1986), 500.
[56] D. Leigh, *The Mothers Blessing* (1616), 43.
[57] M. Smith, "Gynecology and Ideology" in *Liberating Womens' History*, ed. B. A. Carroll (Urbana, 1976), 114.
[58] *God's Judgement against Whoring* (1697), 111.
[59] F. Dabhoiwala, "The Construction of Honour," *Transactions of the Royal Historical Society*, 6th ser., 6 (1996): 206–8; E. J. Hundert, *The Enlightenment's Fable* (Cambridge, 1994), 209.
[60] R. H. Michel, "English Attitudes towards Women 1640–1700," *Canadian Journal of History* 13 (1978): 44.
[61] Dabhoiwala, "Construction of Honour," 213.
[62] R. Yeazell, *Fictions of Modesty* (Chicago, 1991), passim.
[63] R. Ballaster, *Seductive Forms* (Oxford, 1993), 32–3.

The long interval between sexual maturity and marriage required of those entering business must have tested self-denial to destruction, as is evident in the diaries of apprentices.[64] John Sanderson relates that a whore, disguised as a man, was invited to a meal with the merchants in Turkey, but was sent away because one of the "damned crew" was a cuckold.[65] Thomas D'Aeth advised his son when he went to Italy to "avoid ye great vice of ye country, ye inticement of women."[66] There is abundant evidence in court proceedings and correspondence that apprentices seduced maidservants with the promise of marriage once free and then reneged.[67] John Bailey left a pregnant lover stranded when he left for Constantinople.[68] It is also possible that apprentices vented their sexual frustration by rioting against brothels, though they represented more than 39 percent of the clients of London brothels.[69] A haberdasher, who was about to marry with a portion of £600, belonged to a group of "Whipping Toms" who preyed on female servants.[70] The Merchant Adventurers of Newcastle publicly named apprentices who had fornicated, some of whom married and left their masters while still indentured and all of whom were expelled. Bastards of apprentices appear in the guild records of all towns.[71] George Trosse, before he reformed, flirted and behaved wantonly with the beautiful (and religious) daughter of an Iberian merchant who was betrothed to a man beyond the seas.[72] In a few cases, like that of John Whitson, when both the date of marriage and the birth date of the first child are known, it can be inferred that conception predated a marriage. George Boddington noted, when his prodigal son married, "she being with child."[73] It is also highly probable that pregnancy was the reason why some married while still indentured, though in general the illegitimacy rate in London was low.[74]

---

[64] G. Disney, *Remarkable Passages* (1692), 33–4.
[65] J. Sanderson, *Travels*, ed. Sir William Foster, 2d ser., vol. 67 (Hakluyt Society, 1930), 197.
[66] A. E. J. Hollaender, "A London Merchant's Letter Book, 1698–1704," *Archives* 3 (1957): 34–5.
[67] P. Griffith, *Youth and Authority* (Oxford, 1996), 213–21.
[68] F. G. Emmison, *Elizabethan Life* (Chelmsford, 1973), 5.
[69] P. Griffith, "The Structure of Prostitution," *Continuity and Change* 8 (1993): 55.
[70] S. D. Amussen, "The Part of a Christian Man" in *Politics, Culture, and Cultural Politics*, ed. S. D. Amussen and M. A. Kishlansky (Manchester, 1995), 219.
[71] *Newcastle. Extracts from the Records of the Merchant Adventurers*, ed. J. R. Boyle and D. W. Dendy, vol. 101 (Surtees Society, 1899), 186, 199, 274, 276; P. MacGrath, *Merchants and Merchandise*, vol. 19 (Bristol Record Society, 1955), 130.
[72] G. Trosse, *Life*, ed. A. W. Brink (1974), 59.
[73] Guildhall of London Library (hereafter GLL), MS 10,823.
[74] R. Adair, *Courtship, Illegitimacy, and Marriage* (Manchester, 1996), 203.

WEALTH AND RANK

Several contemporary authors condemned marrying for money or status; they strongly advocated mutual consent and attacked parents who dragooned their children into marriages of convenience. "Fie on this Market-matches," wrote Nicholas Breton, "where marriages are made without affection and obedience is performed by a grieved patience."[75] Oliver Heywood denounced tradesman James Stead, who "used strange ways to get money, married a rich widow."[76] The ability of the market-place to control the pursuit and exchange of love was deplored in comedy.[77] The dramatists pilloried and ridiculed the greed, hypocrisy, and social ambition of businessmen in the characters of Philip Massinger's Sir Giles Overeach or the elderly, stupid, and lecherous alder-men of George Farquahar and William Wycherley. On the stage, fathers who manipulated dowries and deprived their daughters of their lovers were outwitted by their children.[78] Patrick Hannay argued that a woman should no more marry for money than a man, because "love languishes yet till ones death shes forced to live with him."[79] William Fleetwood argued that parents should have no say in the second marriages of their children.[80]

On the other hand, Nicholas Breton had to admit that arranged mar-riages provided a safeguard against lust and folly, and that property and suitability could not be ignored. Frances Rogers argued that parents had a right to consent, because they had brought up the children.[81] Dod and Cleaver asserted that "children are their fathers' goods and riches and therefore they must not bestow themselves in marriage."[82] Many writers sought to have their cake and eat it. Take Francis Masterton, for example, who wrote "by advice of your friends marry in an honest reli-gious family be her portion that it will," and "a good lass is not ye worse of money but never let money be your principal concern."[83] In the view of Joseph Swetnam, beauty without wealth attracted lovers, not hus-

---

[75] N. Breton, *An Olde Man's Lesson* (1605), B3v, and *Choice, Chance, and Change* (1606), H.2.
[76] O. Heywood, *Autobiography*, vol. 3, ed. J. H. Turner (Brighouse, 1881–5), 207.
[77] Wells, "Jacobean City Comedy," 38, 51.
[78] J. Loftis, *Comedy and Society* (Stanford, 1959), 45–6.
[79] P. Hannay, *A Happy Husband*, 2d ed. (1622), 161.
[80] W. Fleetwood, *The Relative Duties of Parents and Children* (1905; reprint, 1985), 41.
[81] D. Rogers, *Matrimonial Honour* (1642), 72.
[82] Dod and Cleaver, *A Godly Forme of Household Government*, Y8v.
[83] Cited by G. Marshall, *Presbyteries and Profits* (Edinburgh, 1980), 230.

bands.[84] Ballads cynically advised women to marry old rich men and have lovers.[85]

In general authors concluded that love, status, and money were not antagonistic ends and that reason and interest as well as emotion should govern choice of partners. The *Complete Tradesman* recommended that younger daughters of gentlemen with small portions should marry younger sons of gentlemen turned tradesmen.[86] The opposition to social advancement through marriage in dramatists, like Thomas Dekker, reflected conflicts within landed society rather than hostility to the citizenry.[87]

Few businessmen could marry an heiress, like Sir Marmaduke Rawdon, Jonathan Priestley, or Arthur Barnardiston, because equality of fortune was a standard requirement. Most expected a portion that would at least defray and preferably cover or exceed the additional cost of maintaining a wife.[88] Marriage was an important source of additional capital and connections; it was the primary mode of assimilation for migrants and of entry by successful businessmen into the municipal elite. Access to a trade could be acquired by marrying the widow of a freeman, though some towns like Abingdon and Bristol and some London companies restricted this method of entry.[89]

Six merchants who were members of the Elizabethan House of Commons married fortunes; families, like the Ibbetsons of Leeds, systematically extended their wealth and position through marriage.[90] Between 1660 and 1740 twelve business families married into the Kentish gentry, five of them having acquired estates in Kent. Ten married into the Northamptonshire gentry. The value of any portion depended, however, on life expectancy. Although a husband had the use of his wife's portion for life, most wives survived their husbands and thereby recaptured their portion.[91] Nor was the search for financial advantage limited

---

[84] J. Swetnam, *The Arraignment of Lewde Women* (1615), 52.

[85] *Roxburghe Ballads*, vol. 3, 369–71; *Broadside Ballads of the Restoration*, ed. F. B. Fawcett (1930), no. 10.

[86] N. H., *The Complete Tradesman* (1684), 36.

[87] P. Seaver, "Thomas Dekker" in *The Theatrical City*, ed. D. L. Smith et al. (Cambridge, 1996), 98.

[88] S. Anderson, *An English Consul in Turkey* (Oxford, 1989), 88.

[89] M. Prior, "Women in the Urban Economy" in *Women in English Society, 1500–1800* ed. M. Prior (1985), 89; *Bristol Ordinances, 1506–1598*, ed. M. Stanford, vol. 41 (Bristol Record Society, 1990), 31–2.

[90] *House of Commons, 1558–1603*, vol. 1, ed. P. W. Hasler (1982), 8; R. G. Wilson, "Merchants and Land," *Northern History* 24 (1988): 81.

[91] On settlements see page 70.

to men. John Whitson may not have been the only husband who suspected that his wife had married him for his money.

To what extent did merchants marry for social advantage? Between
periods I and II the proportion of first wives who were daughters of
businessmen increased from 58.5 percent to 64 percent, daughters
of gentlemen decreased from 31 percent to 29 percent, and daughters of
professionals increased from 4.8 percent to 6 percent with a decrease in
the number of daughters of artisans, aliens, and yeomen.[92] Wives from
business families constituted 75 percent in bracket IV compared with
61.6 percent in bracket I, 68.6 percent in bracket II, and 68.9 percent
in bracket III. The ratio of daughters of businessmen to gentlewomen
increased in each financial bracket from 2.6/2.8 : 1 in brackets II and III
to 4.7 : 1 in bracket IV, which had the lowest proportion of gentlewomen
(16.2 percent) and the highest proportion of professionals (5.9 percent).
The proportion of wives from business families was highest in cohorts I
(66.0 percent) and IV (64.6 percent) but was still 58.5 percent and 61.2
percent in the other two cohorts. Genteel spouses peaked at 37.3 percent
in cohort II and fell to 26.4 percent in cohort IV. Daughters of professionals doubled from 3.4 percent in cohort II to an average of 7.8 percent
in cohorts III and IV. The maiden names of 3,627 brides are known (some
of them recurring); of these, 2,220 (61.2 percent) match the surnames of
businessmen in the database.[93]

Although the relative proportions fluctuated over time, it is clear that
a significant number of businessmen always intermarried with gentry
and professional families. Nonetheless, a majority consistently married
within the business community, and this preference actually increased
with financial success. This pattern was also characteristic of provincial
towns, such as Leeds, York, Newcastle, Norwich, and Bristol.[94] Of all

---

[92] The data is almost certainly biased toward upwardly mobile marriages, since wives of
lower status are harder to identify and many unknowns were probably daughters of
artisans and husbandmen.
[93] The total number of surnames recorded in 778 English parishes in 1601 was 19,650:
see F. K and S. Hitching, *References to English Surnames* (1910).
[94] J. W. Kirby, "Rulers of Leeds," *Thoresby Society* 44 (1985): 33; *Idem.*, "Restoration
Leeds," *Northern History* 22 (1986): 156; D. H. Sacks, *Trade Society and Politics*
(1985), 686; *V.C.H. City of York*, 180–1; J. F. Pound, *Tudor and Stuart Norwich* (Chich-
ester, 1988), 81–2; MacGrath, *Merchants and Merchandise*, 3, 109; *Idem.*, "Wills of
Bristol Merchants," *Transactions of the Bristol and Gloucester Archaeological Society*
68 (1949): 92; R. Welford, "Cuthbert Gray," *Archaelogia Aeliana* 11 (1885–6): 66;
P. Gauci, *Politics and Society in Great Yarmouth* (Oxford, 1996), 77; J. T. Evans,
Seventeenth-Century Norwich (Oxford, 1979), 23–5 (see also chapter 5).

Table 1.1. *Status of Spouse (Percentage of Known Cases)*

	Period I	Period II	Bracket I	Bracket II	Bracket III	Bracket IV	Cohort I	Cohort II	Cohort III	Cohort IV
First Marriage										
Business	58.5	64.0	61.6	68.6	68.9	75.0	66.0	58.5	61.2	64.6
Gentry	31.1	29.1	34.3	26.8	25.1	16.2	28.3	37.3	30.5	26.4
Professional	4.8	6.0	2.7	2.6	5.1	5.9	1.9	3.4	7.2	8.3
Other	5.6	0.9	1.4	2.1	0.9	2.9	3.8	0.8	1.1	0.7
Total Cases	1,257	1,548	73	194	665	68	159	378	732	144
Daughter or Widow of Master	19	44								
Second Marriage										
Business	64.9	64.3	70.0	68.6	68.9	57.1	66.7	67.1	64.4	47.8
Gentry	27.9	28.6	30.0	25.7	27.4	28.6	25.5	28.2	28.2	39.1
Professional	2.0	6.7	–	5.7	3.1	7.1	–	2.4	7.4	13.0
Other	5.2	0.4	–	–	0.6	7.1	7.8	2.4	–	–
Total Cases	154	269	10	35	164	14	51	85	135	23

merchants who were members of the Elizabethan House of Commons, 186 married into business families in their first, 49 in their second, and 7 in their third marriages.[95] Of the active merchants who were members of the House of Commons (1660–90), 47 percent in their first marriages married daughters of merchants, 26 percent gentlewomen, and 1 percent daughters of peers; the proportion of gentlewomen declined in second marriages and increased in third marriages.[96] Of the first 84 directors of the Bank of England (1694–1720), 31 percent married gentlewomen and 38 percent daughters of businessmen.[97]

Edward Osborn was credited by legend with marrying his master's daughter after saving her from drowning. Other celebrated merchants, such as Lionel Cranfield and William Cloberry, followed the same path. Alliances of this kind often happened in particular trades, like gold-smithing.[98] John Harrison married the eldest daughter of his master; his fellow apprentice, Roger Millington, married the younger daughter.[99] Poel Blomefield married the daughter of his master's second wife, and Edward Bramston married the daughter of his master's brother.[100] Joshua Browne married the sister-in-law of his master and George Sawbridge the sister of his master.[101] John Davenant's daughter married her father's apprentice, and they jointly ran his inn in Oxford.[102] The daughter of Thomas Papillon's master married Thomas's cousin, Richard Godfrey.[103] Sometimes a master encouraged such a match: Edward Harvey, who inherited a landed estate while still an apprentice, was given per-mission by his master both to wear his hat in the company of his elders and to chaperone his daughter, though the lad ultimately married a gentlewoman.[104]

[95] *House of Commons, 1558–1603*, vol. 1, 8.
[96] *House of Commons, 1660–1690*, ed. B. D. Henning (1983), 23.
[97] W. M. Acres, "Directors of the Bank of England," *Notes & Queries*, 179 (1940): 38.
[98] T. F. Reddaway, "Elizabethan London," *Guildhall Miscellany* 2 (1963): 187–8; F. G. H. Price, *Marigold Street* (1873), 23.
[99] H. M. Luft, *History of Merchant Taylors School, Crosby, 1620–1980* (Liverpool, 1970), 6.
[100] V. Brodsky "Single Women in the London Marriage Market" in *Marriage and Society*, ed. R. B. Outhwaite (191), 98–9; J. Bramston, *Autobiography*, ed. L. Braybrook (Camden Society, 32, 1845), 21.
[101] A. P. Wadsworth and J. De L. Mann, *The Cotton Trade and Industrial Lancashire, 1600–1780* (Manchester, 1931), 74.
[102] Prior, "Women in the Urban Economy," 97. She was beautiful and witty according to J. Aubrey, *Brief Lives*, ed. O. L. Dick (1949), 85.
[103] T. Papillon, *Memoirs*, ed. A. F. W. Papillon (Reading, 1887), 34.
[104] P. Seaver, "Declining Status" in *Court, Country, and Culture*, ed. B. Y. Kunze and D. D. Drautigan (Rochester, 1992), 145.

Masters also married into the families of their apprentices. For example, the two daughters of George Nodes married the masters of their two brothers, Arthur Upton's sister married his master, and William Holgate married a sister of his apprentice. A few marriages with masters' widows also occurred, like that of John Whitson.[105] James Chetham's second wife was the widow of his master's brother.[106] Such marriages were, however, exceptional. Only nineteen cases of marriage with either the daughter or widow of masters have been identified in period I and only forty-four in period II. The same pattern seems to have been true of other towns like Bristol.[107]

The majority of first marriages were between previously unmarried individuals. In all first marriages by men, the percentage of spouses who were widows dropped from 12.1 percent in period I to 7.9 percent in period II. The percentage of spinsters increased from 88.4 percent in cohort I to 92.2 percent in cohort IV. In contrast, the marriage allegations for London (1598–1619) reveal that 21.8 percent of men aged 25–29 and one-third of men aged between 30 and 34 married widows.[108] At St. James, Duke's Place, bachelors of all occupations marrying widows increased from 21.6 percent (1598–1616) to 22.7 percent (1698–1700) and then fell to 18.7 percent (1680–83).[109] In the whole population, only 75 percent of marriages were between previously unmarried couples.[110]

Many merchants married into families in the same line of business. George Treadway, for example, at the age of forty married the daughter, Ann Lannoy, aged twenty-eight, of his partner. Often they married into the same livery companies, which seem to have functioned as marriage markets.[111] Indeed guild ordinances in London discouraged

[105] P. MacGrath, *John Whitson* (Bristol Historical Association, 1970), 8–9. The couple were probably of the same age.
[106] H. Chetham, *Life*, ed. F. R. Raines and C. W. Sutton, vol. 50 (Chetham Society, 1903), 12.
[107] MacGrath, *Merchants and Merchandise*, 25.
[108] Brodsky, "Single Women," and "Widows in Late-Elizabethan London" in *The World We have Gained*, ed. L. Bonfield et al. (Oxford, 1986), 83, 130; 58 percent of the marriage licenses analyzed by Brodsky were of high status tradesmen, a group that can be equated with the businessmen in this study.
[109] J. Boulton, "London Widowhood Revisited," *Continuity and Change* 5 (1990): table 5; B. J. Todd, "Demographic Determinism and Female Agency," *Continuity and Change* 9 (1994): 450.
[110] E. A. Wrigley and R. Schofield, *English Population History from Family Reconstitution* (New York, 1997), 164.
[111] S. Rappaport, *Worlds within Worlds* (Cambridge, 1989), 229; H. R. Plomer, *Abstracts*

Table 1.2. *Marital Status and Survival Rate of Brides (Percentage of Known Cases)*

	Period I	Period II	Bracket I	Bracket II	Bracket III	Bracket IV	Cohort I	Cohort II	Cohort III	Cohort IV
First Marriage										
Single	87.9	92.1	89.4	90.7	92.4	95.1	88.4	92.7	91.5	92.2
Widow	12.1	7.9	10.6	9.3	7.6	4.9	11.6	7.3	8.5	7.8
Total	2,180	2,936	142	407	981	81	225	549	1,501	309
Second Marriage										
Single	65.9	66.7	61.5	70.5	62.4	66.7	61.3	59.9	68.4	79.4
Widow	34.1	33.3	38.5	29.5	37.6	33.3	38.7	40.1	31.6	20.6
Total	261	610	26	88	263	18	75	147	358	34
Wife predeceased	13.6	23.3	15.8	15.1	23.0	32.9	20.2	28.6	27.0	38.7
Wife survived	86.4	76.7	84.2	84.9	77.0	67.1	79.8	71.4	73.0	61.3
Total Marriages %	3,062	2,428	360	1,692	953	73	188	304	555	124
Widows remarried	8.5	11.6	7.6	8.8	18.7	20.4	21.3	12.0	11.4	18.4

marriage outside the corporation: when Cicely Moore married a "foreign," the Pewterers Company prohibited her husband from taking an apprentice, and a merchant tailor, Wilkes, had to translate to the Vintners company in 1591 in order to marry the widow of Giles Hodgson.[112] The father of Thomas Rawlins gave the Skinners Company a large folio bible to translate him to the Grocers company "by reason of his marriage that he is likely to obtain."[113] With some exceptions and challenges, a bachelor could however acquire the right to the freedom by marrying a widow, a right which in practice represented a capital asset or effective dowry.[114]

A few London businessmen, like John Farnaby, even married their servants or housekeepers, who were often kinsmen from the country; Edward Taylor married the orphan servant of Robert Pain, a salter.[115] Robert Atkinson of Newcastle married his household servant who subsequently took apprentices and on his death married the Bishop of Durham.[116] It is not surprising that shy or busy merchants should choose a woman with whom they had daily and intimate contact, who knew their household, and who, in the case of widowers, may have helped to bring up their children. In some cases marriage may have been cheaper than paying wages; in other cases the servants were pregnant at the time they married.[117]

LOCATION

The marriage horizon of businessmen was circumscribed. They usually lived in close proximity to their eventual spouses, whose families were

from the Wills of English Printers and Stationers, 1492–1630 (1903), iv. Since only occupations have been input into the database, the rate of intermarriage within livery companies cannot be specified precisely. But it is clear from lists of members and from wills that London businessmen frequently married the daughters of fellow liverymen.

[112] C. Welch, *History of the Company of Pewterers* (1902), 153; C. M. Clode, *Memorials of the Merchant Taylors*, vol. 2 (1875), 652–3.

[113] *Skinners Company Records*, ed. J. J. Lambert (1934), 260.

[114] Letter, BL, Harlean MS 2104, fo. 366; Rappaport, *Worlds within Worlds*, 40–1; D. M. Palliser, "Trade Gilds of Tudor York" in *Crisis and Order in English Towns*, ed. P. Clark and P. Slack (Toronto, 1972), 100; *Bristol Ordinances, 1506–98*, ed. M. Stamford, vol. 41 (Bristol Record Society, 1990), 31–2; L. Rostenberg, *Publishers, Printers, and Booksellers*, vol. 2 (New York, 1965), 423.

[115] These and other examples are listed in *London Marriage Licenses, 1521–1869*, ed. J. Foster (1887), 471, 1102, 1152. V. Brodsky, *Single Women in the London Marriage Market, 1598–1619* (Newberry Library Papers, 1980), 11.

[116] *Newcastle Records Merchant Adventurers*, 222.

[117] Brodsky, "Single Women," 89.

often friends and neighbors. Location was usually linked to status with the majority of gentlewomen coming from the country and the majority of daughters of businessmen coming from the metropolitan area. It can also be presumed that many brides whose place of birth is unknown had migrated from the country to London.

Between periods I and II there was a decrease in the proportion of brides from provincial towns from 4.7 percent to 3.5 percent, a reduction from 33.3 percent to 24.8 percent in the number of country wives, and an increase from 58.3 percent to 69.2 percent in the number of London brides. Brackets II (70.8 percent) and IV (73.0 percent) had the highest percentage from London, and bracket I had the lowest (61.4 percent); country wives dropped to 16.2 percent in bracket IV. The proportion of London brides increased from 59.9 percent in cohort I, 62.3 percent in cohort II, 73.1 percent in cohort III, to 73.4 percent in cohort IV. The ratio of London to country brides changed from approximately 2:1 to 3:1. In Southwark, most brides came from nearby parishes or from London.[118] The same pattern seems to have been true of the provincial towns; in Leeds, for example, only five out of forty wives of aldermen came from the country.[119]

A small percentage of wives were of foreign origin—3.7 percent in period I and 2.6 percent in period II. Merchants and factors living in Spain and Germany married natives, despite the threat of expulsion by the Merchant Adventurers.[120] John Burrell, Robert Hilson, and Roger Fludd all married Gdansk women.[121] English merchants in Amsterdam and New York City married Dutch women.[122] Usually, however, neither the husbands nor the wives returned to live in England.

Even after the East India Company allowed employees to take their wives to India, some of them continued to marry Portuguese, Dutch, Jewish, and native women.[123] In Madras eight were married to English

---

[118] J. Boulton, *Neighbourhood and Society* (Cambridge, 1987), table 9.1.

[119] Kirby, "Restoration Leeds," 157.

[120] L. M. E. Shaw, *Trade Inquisition and the English Nation* (Manchester, 1989), 107; W. R. Baumann, *The Merchant Adventurers and the Continental Cloth Trade* (Berlin, 1990), 149.

[121] H. Zins, *England and the Baltic* (Manchester, 1972), 103; N. R. Deardorff, "English Trade to the Baltic" in *Studies in the History of English Commerce* (Philadelphia, 1912), 299.

[122] A. C. Carter, *The English Reformed Church in Amsterdam* (Amsterdam, 1964), 28–9; J. D. Goodfriend, *Before the Melting Pot* (Princeton, 1992), 97.

[123] L. M. Anstey, "William Jearsen," *Indian Antiquary* 34 (1905); B. G. Gokhale, *Surat in the Seventeenth Century* (1970), 157.

Table 1.3. *Location of Spouse (Percentage of Known Cases)*

	Period I	Period II	Bracket I	Bracket II	Bracket III	Bracket IV	Cohort I	Cohort II	Cohort III	Cohort IV
First Marriage										
London	58.3	69.2	61.4	70.8	65.8	73.0	59.9	62.3	73.1	73.4
Other urban	4.7	3.5	4.4	3.1	3.7	4.1	4.4	4.4	3.4	2.6
Country	33.3	24.8	31.6	23.5	28.1	16.2	28.6	31.5	21.9	20.6
Abroad	3.7	2.6	2.6	2.7	2.4	6.8	7.1	1.9	1.6	3.4
Total	1,639	2,496	114	294	833	74	182	477	1,326	267
Second Marriage										
London	61.5	72.1	75.0	77.1	69.6	73.3	63.8	70.7	73.9	55.2
Other urban	3.1	3.3	5.0	3.3	3.3	–	3.5	4.9	2.4	–
Country	32.8	23.8	20.0	18.0	26.6	26.7	29.3	23.6	23.0	44.8
Abroad	2.6	0.8	–	1.6	0.5	–	3.5	0.8	0.7	–
Total	192	484	20	61	214	15	58	123	291	29

women, one to a Dutch woman, five to Casties (Portuguese-born Indians), and one to a Portuguese.[124] Thomas Pitt married the Scottish niece of an East Indian agent.[125] Choice was somewhat limited. Joseph Collett, who declined to keep his female slave in his house and feared venereal disease, mentions five white women—one married but a bawd, one married "free of tongue," one mad, one ugly, and one a propertied widow "too terrible to bear a description," yet "as well shaped as a Madagascan cow."[126]

RELIGION AND KIN

The surge of Protestant writings on marriage in the 1620s and 1630s reflected a desire to create spiritual households to sustain the true faith and counter the errors of the church. The main objective of these writers was to encourage godly matches and direct couples toward God. William Whateley, for example, emphasized that holiness of spirit in a spouse was more important than either beauty or riches—"passion is a short madness."[127] Devout businessmen sought devout wives, and the great majority of marriages occurred within the same denomination.

All the nonconforming congregations exercised tight control over marriage of their members, because the integrity of their communities and the continuity of their faith required that outsiders be excluded. The Quaker Meeting both gave permission to marry and expelled members who married outside the faith. Jews did not marry gentiles and appear to have arranged marriages.[128] Immigrants and religious refugees also married within their communities, although most were eventually assimilated. Two-thirds of the members of the Dutch church in Austin Friars intermarried, though this gradually changed.[129] The Flemish and Dutch communities in Colchester and the Huguenots in both England and the colonies were endogamous in the first generation.[130]

---

[124] H. D. Love, *Vestiges of Old Madras*, vol. 1 (1913), 489.
[125] C. Dalton, *Thomas Pitt* (Cambridge, 1915), 127.
[126] J. Collett, *Private Letterbook*, ed. H. H. Dodwell (1933), letters dated 23 Sept., 16 and 23 Oct., 1712.
[127] W. Whateley, *A Care Cloth* (1624), 73, and *A Bride Bush* (1617), 7, 25.
[128] J. Katz, "Family Kinship and Marriage among Askenazim," *Jewish Journal of Sociology* 1 (1959): 11, which does not provide much evidence of time or place. For Quaker practices see F. B. Tolles, *Meeting House and Counting House* (Chapel Hill, 1948), 119–20.
[129] O. P. Grell, *Dutch Calvinists in Early Stuart London* (New York, 1989), 47–50.
[130] R. D. Gwynn, *Huguenot Heritage* (1985), 163; J. Butler, *The Huguenots in America*

Numerous marriages were contracted within the kinship group within the limits prescribed by the church's *Table of Kindred and Affinity*. Those interdicted included nieces, nephews, aunts, and the brother or sister of a deceased wife; the same rules were applied to a wife's kin as to blood relations and they could be extended to godparents.[131] William Mallett, a glover of Norwich, was prosecuted for marrying his late wife's sister.[132] The Quakers prohibited marriage with first cousins or close relatives of a widow's first husband.[133] George Boddington disapproved of his nephew James Vaughan marrying the daughter of his mother's cousin.[134] But marriage with first cousins was permitted by ecclesiastical law. The Renews, Papillons, and Nathaniel Cholmeley all married cousins, and Thomas Bowrey married his cousin, Mary Gardiner.[135] A son might marry the daughter of his father's second wife by her first marriage and sometimes the stepmother doubled as a mother-in-law.

A few examples will illustrate the process of intermarriage within the extended family. William Boutflower married the niece of the wife of his great uncle.[136] The wives of John and Roger Drake were sisters; two daughters of Nathaniel Tench each married a son of Francis Asty.[137] Nathaniel Cholmley married the daughter of his cousin, and one factor in Naples married his employer's first wife's aunt.[138] Mathilda, widow of Anthony Balam, married as her second husband, Sir Henry Furnese, and her daughter married Robert Furnese, her stepbrother. The brother of Thomas Middleton married the widowed sister of Thomas's first wife; Hugh Middleton married as his second wife his brother's stepdaughter.[139]

(Cambridge, Mass., 1983), 158–9; L. F. Roker, "The Flemish and Dutch Community in Colchester," *Proceedings of Huguenot Society of London* 21 (1965–70): 24–8; C. Littleton, "Social Interactions of Aliens," in *The Strangers Progress*, ed. R. Vigne and G. C. Gibbs, vol. 26 (Proceedings of Huguenot Society of London, 1995), 153; A. A. Houblon, *The Houblon Family* (1907), 97.

[131] J. Week, *Sex, Politics, and Society* (1981), 30, argues unconvincingly that the prohibition of marriage with a wife's sister safeguarded aristocratic interests.

[132] D. Cressy, *Birth, Marriage, and Death* (Oxford, 1997), 314.

[133] *Bristol. Minute Book of the Society of Friends*, ed. R. Mortimer, vol. 26 (Bristol Record Society, 1970), 113; Frost, *Quaker Family*, 160–1.

[134] Diary of George Boddingdon, GLL, MS 10,823/1.

[135] T. Bowrey, *Papers*, ed. Sir Richard Carnac Temple n.s., vol. 58 (Hakluyt Society, 1927), xxvi; Center for Kentish Studies (hereafter KAO), U 1015/C8/3.

[136] D. S. Boutflower, *The Boutflower Book* (Newcastle, 1930), 65.

[137] *Visitation of London Anno Domini 1633, 1634, and 1635*, vol. 1, ed. J. J. Howard and J. L. Chester, vol. 15 (Harlean Society, 1880), 238.

[138] Hugh Cholmeley, *Memoirs* (1788; reprint, Malton, 1870), 57, 80; George Courthop *Memoirs*, 2d ser., vol. 18 (Camden Society, 1907), 114.

[139] J. W. Gough, *Sir Hugh Middleton* (Oxford, 1964), 8.

William Cheslin married the daughter of his father's first wife. Edward Gibbon married Catherine, daughter of Richard Acton who had married his mother, thus making his stepfather his father-in-law. David Otgar Jr. married his stepsister by his mother's second marriage to Thomas Carleton. Elizabeth, daughter of Peter Bradshaw by his first wife, married as her second husband the son of Peter's widow by her second marriage.

TIMING

A standard view of the best age for marrying was "for the young not yet, for the old not at all."[140] "It is better," wrote Andrew Kingsmill, "to look long than to leap lightly."[141] Although the law permitted marriage at a young age, late marriage commanded almost unanimous support, because an older husband was more likely to be financially, emotionally, and morally stable and less likely to err through rashness and inexperience. People in societies that value property above honor usually have a high age of marriage.[142] Defoe spoke for many when he criticized young tradesmen for marrying before they had acquired sufficient capital, though he married at twenty-four with a dowry of £3,700.[143] There was less concern about women marrying young, though William Stout refused to help a niece who married at nineteen, which he considered too young.[144]

Disparities of age aroused greater hostility. The disgust of the dramatists for rich old men who married young girls was presumably shared by their audiences. It was widely assumed that discrepancies in age would lead to loveless marriages. Thomas Gouge thought that husbands should not be more than ten years older than their wives, Joseph Swetnam that a man should marry at 25 a single woman of 17.[145] Gregory King,

---

[140] R. Allestree, *The Ladies Calling* (Oxford, 1623), 227; F. Bacon, *Works*, vol. 6, ed. J. Spedding, R. L. Ellis, and D. D. Heath (1878), 392.

[141] A. Kingsmill, *A View of Man's Estate*, vol. 1 (1574), iii.

[142] J. Goody, *The Development of the Family and Marriage in Europe* (Cambridge, 1986), passim. Late marriage is theoretically characteristic of dynamic, mobile, and diversified societies: see G. S. Becker, *The Economic Approach to Human Behavior* (Chicago, 1976), 243.

[143] D. Defoe, *Complete English Tradesman*, vol. 2 (1727; reprint, New York, 1970), 92; J. Sutherland, *Daniel Defoe*, 2d ed. (1950), 30.

[144] W. Stout, *Autobiography*, ed. J. D. Marshall, 3d ser., vol. 14 (Chetham Society, 1967), 179.

[145] Swetnam, *Arraignment of Women*, 46.

Table 1.4. *Age Distribution of Grooms in First Marriages (Percentage of Known Cases)*

	Period I	Period II	Bracket I	Bracket II	Bracket III	Bracket IV	Cohort I	Cohort II	Cohort III	Cohort IV
Under 18	0.8	–	–	0.6	0.3	–	1.5	0.3	–	–
18–19	0.4	0.2	–	0.6	0.5	–	–	0.9	0.1	0.4
20–21	3.9	2.5	5.2	2.2	3.2	1.8	1.5	2.7	1.7	6.7
22–23	10.5	10.0	14.3	8.8	5.6	5.4	6.2	8.1	9.0	20.4
24–25	17.4	18.7	20.8	19.3	11.8	14.3	7.7	13.0	19.6	20.4
26–27	20.2	18.8	15.6	18.8	14.2	23.2	12.3	18.4	19.3	18.9
28–29	11.6	13.6	14.3	12.2	15.0	7.1	13.9	13.3	13.6	12.6
30+	35.3	36.2	29.9	37.6	49.3	48.2	56.9	43.4	36.9	20.7
Median	27.1	27.0	25.9	27.0	28.9	29.0	29.6	28.7	27.5	25.7
Mean	28.2	28.7	27.4	28.8	30.6	29.7	30.6	30.0	28.6	26.4
1st Quartile	24.8	24.9	23.7	24.9	26.0	25.8	25.9	25.0	24.5	22.8
3d Quartile	30.3	31.0	29.9	30.5	33.9	32.0	32.9	32.9	30.0	28.9
Total Cases	258	1,820	77	181	373	56	65	332	1,335	270

Table 1.5. *Median Age of Marriage (Known Cases)*

	Period I Median	Period I Cases	Period II Median	Period II Cases
Bachelors to Spinsters	28.15	227	27.31	1,586
Bachelors to Widows	29.00	20	30.00	150
Spinsters to Bachelors	20.00	177	20.30	1,264
Spinsters to Widowers	22.50	15	22.00	210
Widows to Bachelors	35.00	16	28.05	101
Widows to Widowers	34.00	10	36.38	86

concerned that disparities in age reduced the number of children, proposed that no person under 16 should marry a partner above 25 and that no person above 60 should marry a partner under 45.[146]

The median age of all businessmen at first marriage was in fact high and remained at 27 between periods I and II with one-fourth marrying under 25 and one-fourth over 30. Bachelors marrying spinsters had a median age of 28.15 in period I and 27.31 in period II. Bachelors marrying widows were older at 29 in period I and 30 in period II. The median age of marriage was 26 in bracket I, 27 in bracket II, and 29 in brackets III and IV. But it declined from 29.6 in cohort I to 28.7 in cohort II, 27.5 in cohort III and 25.7 in cohort IV.

The median age of all brides at first marriage decreased by almost three years from 23 in period I to 20 in period II; there was a slight increase in the first quartile from 18 to 18.5 and a drop of almost one year from 23.9 to 23.1 in the third quartile. Spinsters marrying bachelors had a median age of 20 in period I and 20.3 in period II. The age of brides did not vary much with the wealth of their husbands. The mean age of women was similar in all brackets at 21, but the median age was 20.3 in bracket I compared with 18.9 in brackets II and 19.6 in brackets III and IV. The median age of women did, however, fall from 22 in cohort I to around 20 in cohorts II, III, and IV. The aggregated figures conceal the fact that some bachelors who married spinsters were younger than their wives, usually by one or two years. In period I the median age of widows marrying bachelors was six years higher (N = 16), but in period II the situation reversed and widows were two years younger (N = 201).

---

[146] G. King, "The Burns Journal" in *Graunt and Gregory King*, ed. P. Laslett (Farnborough, 1973), 102.

These statistics are consistent, but not identical, with other data for London and other towns. The marriage allegations for London (1598–1619) reveal that most men married between 24 and 28; the mean/median age of all bachelors marrying was 28.4/28.1, but high-status bachelors had a mean/median age of 26.5/26.3—one year higher than low-status grooms; bachelors marrying spinsters had a mean/median age of 27.6/27.2. The mean age of all London-born spinsters was 20 and of immigrant women 24; there was a 7 year difference between grooms and London-born brides, and the difference was most marked among high-status tradesmen, such as mercers, drapers, and merchants.[147] Some 80 percent of men who married widows were 4.5 years younger than their wives; this difference shrank, however, to 2.2 years for men of high status.[148] In four parishes the mean age of women at first marriage was 19.7 to 23.[149]

In London after 1660 80 percent of brides in first marriages were under 25 and 40 percent under 21, with a mean difference in age of 5 years. The median age of 275 grooms was 27 and that of 216 women was 22, but those grooms with worth above £5,000 married at 30 a bride of 20; those grooms with worth between £2,000–5,000 married at 28 a bride of 22.[150] The median age at marriage of London female deponents in the church courts was 21 for natives and 25 for immigrants.[151] Orphaned daughters of freemen also seem to have married under 21.[152] The marriage allegations between 1660–1714 suggest a mean age for brides in first marriages of 21.9 in London and 23.6 in a sample of five counties.[153] On the other hand, the mean age of all spinsters marrying bachelors at St. James, Duke Place between 1698–1700 was 23.9, and for bachelors and widowers marrying spinsters the mean age was 24.7.[154]

---

[147] V. Brodksy, "Mobility and Marriage in Pre-Industrial England" (Ph.D. diss., University of Cambridge, 1978), 273; Brodsky, "Single Women," 86, tables i–iii. R. Finlay, *Population and Metropolis* (Cambridge, 1981), table 3.7, has similar data from a sample of seventy marriages.

[148] V. Brodsky, "Widows," 127, and "Mobility and Marriage," 254–81, 325.

[149] R. A. P. Finlay, "Population and Fertility," *Journal of Family History* 4 (1979): 31–2.

[150] P. Earle, *Making of the Middle Class* (1989), 181, tables 7.1–2.

[151] P. Earle, *A City Full of People* (1994), table 5.1.

[152] C. Carlton, *The Court of Orphans* (Leicester, 1974), 72.

[153] P. Razzell, "The Growth of Population in Eighteenth-Century England," *Journal of Economic History* 53 (1993): table 3, 752; *Idem.*, *Essays in English Population History* (1994), 184. The data are based on the first one hundred examples in each decade in the printed allegations. P. Earle, "Age and Accumulation" in *Business Life and Public Policy*, ed. N. MacKendrick and R. B. Outhwaite (Cambridge, 1986), 48.

[154] Boulton, "London Widowhood Revisited," table 5.

Table 1.6. *Age Distribution of Brides in First and Second Marriages (Percentage of Known Cases)*

	Period I	Period II	Bracket I	Bracket II	Bracket III	Bracket IV	Cohort I	Cohort II	Cohort III	Cohort IV
First Marriage										
Under 18	13.9	10.7	9.3	6.8	16.5	14.3	9.1	15.8	9.9	13.4
18–19	23.7	25.0	31.5	25.8	25.6	31.4	13.6	26.3	24.5	27.2
20–21	22.2	24.6	20.4	29.6	23.8	14.3	22.7	21.1	25.7	23.0
22–23	12.9	14.7	13.0	13.6	11.6	14.3	13.6	10.5	14.9	15.7
24–25	11.3	10.5	7.4	10.6	9.2	17.1	22.7	10.5	10.2	11.1
26–27	6.2	5.3	7.4	4.6	3.1	2.9	4.6	5.3	5.4	4.6
28–29	3.1	3.0	3.7	0.8	3.7	–	4.6	3.5	3.1	2.3
30+	6.7	6.2	7.4	8.3	6.7	5.7	9.1	7.0	6.4	2.8
Median	23.0	20.6	20.3	18.9	19.6	19.6	22.0	19.7	20.6	19.9
Mean	21.7	21.6	21.9	21.9	21.2	20.7	22.8	21.5	21.7	20.9
1st Quartile	18.0	18.5	17.8	18.8	17.6	17.5	19.0	17.6	18.6	17.9
3d Quartile	23.9	23.0	23.7	22.8	23.6	22.9	23.8	23.7	23.0	22.7
Total Cases	194	1,390	54	132	164	35	22	171	1,071	217
Second Marriage										
Under 18	3.5	3.3	25.0	–	7.0	–	7.1	2.4	3.4	9.1
18–19	10.4	11.0	–	10.8	14.0	–	7.1	9.8	10.1	27.3
20–21	6.9	16.1	–	16.2	12.3	33.3	–	7.3	15.6	45.5
22–23	6.9	11.4	12.5	16.2	8.8	16.7	7.1	7.3	12.2	–
24–25	3.5	11.0	–	8.1	17.5	33.3	7.1	4.9	11.8	9.1
26–27	17.2	7.4	25.0	10.8	5.3	–	14.3	4.9	8.0	–
28–29	6.9	3.7	12.5	5.4	1.8	–	7.1	4.9	3.8	–
30+	44.8	36.1	25.0	32.4	33.3	16.7	50.0	58.5	35.3	9.1
Median	27.0	27.4	–	24.5	23.8	22.0	28.0	28.9	24.8	19.8
Mean	29.1	24.7	–	27.2	26.6	23.5	31.1	31.6	27.2	20.9
1st Quartile	21.5	20.6	–	20.9	19.9	–	23.5	22.8	20.8	17.9
3d Quartile	31.0	31.6	–	29.9	32.9	–	33.0	37.9	31.0	20.9
Total Cases	29	299	8	37	57	6	14	41	238	11

The aldermen of Restoration Leeds also had a mean age at first marriage of 25.[155]

The relative age of marriage partners varied between regions, occupations, and denominations.[156] In the whole population the difference in median age between bachelors and spinsters between 1600–1729 was 1.6 and between bachelors and widows 7.5.[157] The difference in mean age between bachelors and spinsters narrowed from 2.5 (28.1 to 25.6) between 1600–49 to 1.9 years (28.1 to 26.2) between 1650–99.[158] In the diocese of Canterbury marriage licenses suggest a difference of 3 years between a mean/median age of 26.65/25.5 for men and 23.58/22.75 for women.[159] Among Kentish tradesmen, the difference was also 3 years, though the median age of marriage was lower at 24 for men and 22 for women throughout the seventeenth century.[160] In Stratford the difference was 2 years with a mean age of 26 for men and 24 for women.[161] In Shrewsbury the mean age of marriage was 26 for men and 25.5 for women.[162] In Suffolk between 1684 and 1723 there was a difference in mean age of 2 years with men marrying at 26.3 and women at 24.5.[163] In rural Earls Colne the difference was 2 years with a mean age for men of 26 and for women of 24.5; in Lincolnshire it was 1.6 years (28.5 to 26.9).[164] The peers, before 1680, on the other hand, were on average 3 years older than their brides and 6 years thereafter.[165] In Jamaica grooms were 2 years older than their brides (21 to 19), though the difference increased to 7 years after 1705.[166] In New England, before

---

[155] Kirby, "Restoration Leeds," 156.
[156] R. Wall, "Leaving Home," *Continuity and Change* 2 (1987): 88.
[157] Wrigley and Schofield, *English Population from Reconstitution*, table 5.8.
[158] E. A. Wrigley, "Marriage Fertility" in Outhwaite, *Marriage and Society*, table iii; *idem.*, "Age at Marriage," *Family History*, n.s., 12 (1982): table 1; E. A. Wrigley and R. Schofield, *Population History of England* (1981), table 7.26, 162–4; E. A. Wrigley, *People, Cities, and Wealth* (Oxford, 1987), 247.
[159] P. Laslett, *The World We Have Lost*, 3d ed. (1983), table 5.
[160] C. W. Chalklin, *Seventeenth-Century Kent* (1965), 37.
[161] J. Jones, *Family Life in Shakespeare's England* (Stroud, 1996), 90.
[162] J. C. Hindson, "Family Structure, Inheritance, and Kinship" (Ph.D. diss., University of Wales, Aberystwyth, 1991), 120.
[163] R. B. Outhwaite, "Age at Marriage in England," *Transactions of the Royal Historical Society*, 5th ser., 23 (1973): 61.
[164] A. MacFarlane, *Marriage and Love in England* (1985), 216; J. A. Johnston, "Family, Kin, and Community," *Rural History* 6 (1995): 185.
[165] T. H. Hollingsworth, "A Demographic Study" in *Population in History*, ed. D. V. Glass and D. E. C. Eversley (1965), 371, tables 18 and 20; *idem., The Demography of the British Peerage* (1965), table 2.
[166] T. Burnard, "A Failed Society," *Journal of Social History* 28 (1994): 74.

1660, the age difference between grooms and brides was generally 5.9 years and 4.3 thereafter, though in colonial Bristol and Dedham it was 3 years and even less in New York.[167]

In Quaker families the median age of grooms in one urban cohort between 1650–99 was 25 and that of brides 24.8; but the median age at first marriage for all urban males was 28.3. The overall difference in age was 3 to 4 years, though with considerable variations; 20.9 percent of husbands were 5 to 9 years older than their wives and 17.9 percent 10 years older; on the other hand, 4.5 percent of brides were 5 to 9 years older than their husbands, and another 4.5 percent were 10 years older. Wholesalers marrying daughters of wholesalers were only one year apart.[168]

Discrepancies of 30 years in age of the kind portrayed by dramatists did occur with businessmen in their 50s marrying women under 20. Christopher Taylor, in 1602, married at 64 a woman of 30.[169] The difference in median age at first marriage between London businessmen and their brides was, however, 7 years and an age difference of 5 to 10 years seems to have been generally accepted. Widowers were usually richer than bachelors, and an older husband could offer more security because his future was more certain. Provided that couples fell within this range, difference of age does not seem to have been a vital factor in marriage decisions.

The median age of marriage was within one to three years of the age a businessman acquired his freedom.[170] Bachelorhood was mandatory during an apprenticeship, which consequently served as a prudential check. Apprentices who married during their term lost their freedom, though there were exceptions, like the Norwich apothecaries who were sometimes married with children when they took their freedom.[171] A responsible businessman had to postpone marriage until he had estab-

---

[167] R. Archer, "New England Mosaic," *William and Mary Quarterly*, 3d ser., 47 (1990): 492. J. Demos, "Families in Colonial Bristol," *William and Mary Quarterly*, 3d ser., 25 (1968): table ix; K. A. Lockridge, *A New England Town* (New York, 1970), table 1; Goodfriend, *Before Melting Pot*, 186, table 2.2; S. N. Ipswich, "Population Growth in Colonial America," *Population Studies* 25 (1971): 446.

[168] R. T. Vann and D. E. C. Eversley, *Friends in Life and Death* (Cambridge, 1992), tables 3.1, 3.2, 3.3, 3.8, 3.16; R. Wells, "Quaker Marriage Patterns," *William and Mary Quarterly* 39 (1972): 426–8.

[169] *London Marriages*, ed. Foster, 1239.

[170] Clode, *Merchant Taylors*, appendix 26.

[171] M. Pelling, "Apothecaries in Norwich Circa 1600," *Pharmaceutical Historian* 13 (1983): 6.

lished his business and could support an independent household.[172] John Walker of Stratford received insufficient provision from his father so, instead of marrying, he rode to London, sold his horse, and apprenticed himself to a grocer for £10.[173] Overseas factors had to wait until they could afford to take up residence in England.

Just as a woman could not marry until her parents were able and willing to provide an adequate portion, so a young businessman needed whatever funding his father could and would provide in order to negotiate a match. Although he might inherit his share early, if orphaned, the timing of his provision and therefore his ability to marry usually depended on his age and career path, not on the order of his birth or whether his father was alive or dead.[174]

COURTSHIP

A late age of marriage gave a man more time to negotiate with parents and reduced the pressure on a woman to take the first offer. It also enhanced the role of personality in courtship and allowed for light-hearted dalliance with no commitment. A young merchant could learn how to flirt before he entered the matrimonial lists. Thomas Gent was "not very forward in love or desire for matrimony till I knew the world better" and could provide maintenance, "but yet my heart could not absolutely slight a lovely young creature as to pretend I had no esteem for her charms."[175]

The mutual consent of a couple was all that was necessary to create a marriage. The Canons of 1604 and marriage license required parental consent for minors.[176] But an unconditional promise, if accompanied by gifts and especially if sexual consummation had occurred, was a binding contract in canon law, even without witnesses. Men and women over twenty-one were legally "at their own disposal." Self-enactment through spousals and clandestine marriages were, however, rare in the business community.[177]

---

[172] G. Ohlin, "Mortality, Marriage, and Growth in Preindustrial Populations," *Population Studies* 14 (1960): 190.

[173] E. Walker, *The Holy Life*, ed. A. Walker (1690), 11.

[174] This seems to have been true of the whole population: see Wrigley and Schofield, *English Population from Reconstitution*, 171.

[175] Gent, *Life*, 35

[176] M. Ingram, *Church, Courts, Sex, and Marriage in England* (Cambridge, 1987), 136.

[177] R. B. Outhwaite, *Clandestine Marriage in England, 1500–1800* (1995), 41.

Secular law was less liberal. Chancery would not countenance prohibitions on marriage in wills (except for widows) or enforce provisions that required marriage to a particular person in order to receive a portion.[178] But chancery was still willing to enforce restrictions on the legacies of daughters who married before the age of twenty-one without the consent of their parents or guardians. The secular courts recognized the right of parents and guardians to advise and restrict their underage children and, particularly, their daughters. The common law, which encroached on ecclesiastical jurisdiction, did not recognize spousals and ultimately determined the legitimacy of children and the succession of real property. In London male orphans under twenty-one and females under eighteen required permission to marry from the Court of Aldermen.[179] Nonconforming congregations such as the Quakers and the French Church also insisted on parental consent.[180] Parents often acted as though they had a right of veto, even if they could not invalidate a contracted marriage.

Marriages within the business community usually depended on the multilateral consent of all interested parties. Parents could not stand aside, because marriage affected the succession of property and the whole extended family. In established families the fathers and mothers or the guardians of young couples (if both parents were dead) played a crucial role in first marriages and usually negotiated any settlement. Parents usually made allowance for mutual attraction and were prepared to compromise. But parity of status, fortune, family politics, reputation, and religion all had to be taken into account.

Siblings, kin, and friends also had both a direct and indirect influence as advisers and mediators. Male emigrants to London and orphans relied on their kin rather than on their parents in the marriage market. The correspondence of merchants with their kin and friends is full of news of prospective spouses.[181] A Turkey merchant, for example, was told by his brother that his friend was courting Sir Henry Winchcomb's daughter.[182] Richard Blundell was advised, when he was considering marriage

---

[178] S. Staves, "Resentment or Resignation" in *Early Modern Conceptions of Property*, ed. J. Brewer and S. Staves (1995), 205.

[179] *Orders Taken and Enacted for Orphans* (1580); A. Pulling, *Practical Treatise on the Laws and Custom of London*, 2d ed. (1844), 185.

[180] R. T. Vann, "Nurture and Conversion," *Journal of Marriage and the Family* 21 (1969): 643.

[181] Letter dated 7 Oct. 1698, Folger Library, MS UB 18.

[182] Letter dated 29 Jan. 1699/1700, Folger Library, MS UB 18, fo. 179.

with a widow, "be sure of something considerable."[183] David Papillon acted as spokesman for George Papillon; he approached the Nicholson family, listed George's virtues, and set out his finances.[184] Thomas Pitt, while in India where wives were rapidly widowed and voraciously pursued, tried unsuccessfully to assist the courtship by his bookkeeper of a young rich widow in Madras.[185] Thomas Barrow had to negotiate with the whole Oxinden clan.[186] George Warner's uncle, fortified by some of Warner's best wine, negotiated on his behalf with Elizabeth Chester's father, whom he considered "very apt to like your match and as it may be for both our goods I shall do my best indeavour."[187]

Sometimes the advice of kin was counterproductive. Matthew Ashton wrote to his brother-in-law, Edward Franklin: "I take notice of your desire to know the woman I have settled my affections upon but especially her portion, which you write will have a great influence upon my concern. I have formerly wrote you I never could expect one with any great fortune and your constantly pressing of me to marry hath occasioned me to take one that I could fancy."[188] Mature businessmen sometime chose to ignore their kin; James Norris wrote to his cousin, Charles Payne, "I hear . . . that you are arrived to the comfortable state of matrimony . . . altho for sound reasons best known to your self you were pleased in concealing from the world."[189]

Courtship could be initiated directly with the opposite party, since the sexes were not segregated and couples could meet in public, in the street, at church, or at family gatherings. In a few cases, it appears that a couple were mutually attracted without any prior intention to marry, and, although hard to document, it can be presumed that the first step was sometimes taken by the woman. Usually however, businessmen began their search after deciding that they were ready to marry. It was advisable to approach the parents at an early stage, when property was involved. The traditional procedure was for the suitor or his representative to make a formal request to the parents or guardians of his intended for permission to pay court. Fathers differed in their willing-

---

[183] N. Blundell, *Diary and Letter Book 1702–28* (Liverpool, 1952), 45.

[184] KAO, MS U 1015/C5.

[185] *HMC*, 13 report, appendix, pt. 3, 4; Dalton, *Pitt*, 127–8.

[186] *The Oxinden Letters 1607–42*, ed. D. Gardiner (1933), 111–12.

[187] Letter, Public Record Office (hereafter PRO), SP 46/83.

[188] Letter, Bodleian Library, Oxford (hereafter Bod), MS Eng misc. C. 602, July (circa 1680).

[189] Letter dated 11 May 1695, Guildhall of London Library (hereafter GLL), MS 5301A.

ness to allow free access of suitors to their daughters. A sensible father promoted and facilitated a match without seeming to impose. Sometimes the couple courted while their friends and family negotiated. Phineas Pett accompanied his son, Peter, on a courting visit to Suffolk and was entertained by and negotiated with the family of the prospective bride.[190]

Prospective partners were often introduced by the parents. Nicholas Pescod, who wanted his daughter, Mary, to marry a thrifty merchant rather than a spendthrift gentleman, offered a portion of £3,000 to Marmaduke Rawdon and hinted that she would inherit all his considerable estate should his son not survive; Marmaduke was invited to supper and sat up alone until midnight with Mary, but he declined marriage on the grounds that he was obligated to resolve problems in his uncle's business in the Canary Islands. Mary subsequently married a French aristocrat.[191] When Gervaise Disney went to Rebecca Spateman's house, her father told her that Disney was recommended "for a sweetheart"; the parents agreed on the terms, and the couple married in 1671.[192] It was usually essential that the father of the prospective bride be won over, either by the suitor or by the daughter. Approval could be withheld for trivial or irrelevant reasons: Richard Sheppard seems to have been reluctant to have Lionel Cranfield as a son-in-law, because he resented the talents of his apprentice.[193]

A few merchants, like Elihu Yale, used professional brokers, though chancery's refusal to enforce marriage bonds limited their role.[194] "Many hucksters or wife brokers have an admirable talent for matching conditions, families, trades, and estates," wrote Tom Brown, "in short everything except humours and inclinations about which they never trouble themselves." Scriveners and financial brokers also acted as marriage brokers.[195] One merchant sued a broker who produced a relative as a bride, but the court decreed that the merchant had no case because he had received a dowry of £1,200, whereas the wife owed the broker nothing because her husband was penniless.[196]

Serious courtship usually began with correspondence. Model letters

[190] P. Pett, *Autobiography*, ed. W. G. Perrin, vol. 51 (Navy Records Society, 1917), 150–4.
[191] Rawdon, *Life*, 28. He seems to have reveled in the role of eligible bachelor and recorded all portions offered to him.
[192] G. Disney, *Some Remarkable Passages* (1692), 53.
[193] M. Prestwich, *Lionel Cranfield* (Oxford, 1966), 26.
[194] H. Bingham, *Elihu Yale* (Worcester, Mass., 1938), 13.
[195] F. T. Melton, *Sir Robert Clayton* (Cambridge, 1986), 8.
[196] *Chancery Reports of Cases* (1716), 31.

were offered in letter-writing manuals, though they have to be interpreted with care because they were often intended as satire.[197] Apprentices were advised to avoid maidservants looking for a match and not to confuse taking a wife with buying a horse. John Dunton in a love letter focuses on the hair, eyes, mouth, neck, and body.[198] The suitor would introduce himself and clarify his intentions. John Bunyan's Mr. Badman married twice for money and tricked an inexperienced woman by pretending to be devout.[199] The back pages of one of Nathan Simson's copy books contain what appear to be drafts of practice speeches, possibly lifted from some contemporary work by his son: "Talk not of ladies. . . . Above all honour birth and fame. . . . Oh I adore thy name, take this ring as a token of love"; "in costly rich array thou shalt appear and I my self will be ready to wait on thee to admire my beauty my dear."[200] The scraps of actual correspondence that survive range from stiff, formal epistles, long on compliment and short on sentiment, to inventive, spontaneous, and playful addresses. George Oxenden confessed that "when I have a lady to discourse with . . . I find my self . . . as a new married bridegroom that knows not how to begin" though he added, "it is the goodness of your sex to except our weak endeavours and take the will for the deed."[201]

Personal contact would usually follow the exchange of letters. A few couples were married after only one meeting, but usually the suitor made a series of spaced visits during which they would walk, talk, and keep company. Nathaniel Harley told his sister that his master was courting in the country, having shown little interest in the woman Nathaniel liked.[202] When George Warner courted Elizabeth Chester, his uncle contacted her father, who suggested that they meet first at his house and that George should then visit Elizabeth, who was staying with Richard Stone—a journey of "two easy dayes . . . if you think good to take a journey for much out of your way." George met and liked the young lady and was led to believe that he would win the father's consent: "now

---

[197] Many manuals were based on Nicholas Breton's *Poste with a Packet* (1602): see J. Robertson, *The Art of Letter Writing* (1942), 26; G. M(arkham), *Hobson's Horse Load* (1613). Men expressed themselves in verse and women in prose: see G. Duval, "Standardization versus Genre" in *The Crisis of Courtesy 1600–1900*, ed. J. Carré (Leiden, 1994), 44.

[198] J. Dunton, *Life and Errors* (1705), 81–3.

[199] J. Bunyan, *Life and Death of Mr. Badman*, ed. R. Sharrock (Oxford, 1988), 79.

[200] PRO, C 104/13–14. There were several contemporary handbooks on style of address in courtship such as E. Phillips, *The Mysteries of Love and Eloquence* (1658).

[201] Letter dated 24 Jan. 1665, BL, Add. MS 40,700, fos. 32–7.

[202] Letter dated 4 June 1683, BL, Add. MS 70,145.

you have a good ground to walk upon, lay all your traps and strategems you can honorably chuse to win the gentlewoman's affections."[203] Although the courtship of mature businessmen, like George Warner, was ritualized with little physical play, it appears from the sparse evidence that younger couples had some opportunity to explore each other's personality and interests and to contract themselves through secret vows. A witness describes how Rebecca Pereira "with a seeming joy came running into the chamber" having arranged to meet clandestinely with Isaac Coronell.[204]

Flattery, teasing, and subterfuge were all employed in courtship. Thomas Bodley was said to have secured the rich widow of a pilchard merchant by trickery.[205] Baptist Hicks, when he unsuccessfully courted a woman ten years his senior and richer, emphasized his status as a merchant, that he would "love you for yourself and not for that which you have."[206] Soft words were reinforced by gifts and tokens, because "he that courts a Lady without gifts calls an hawk without a lure."[207] John Haynes of Exeter not only traveled thirty-five miles to court Susan Henley but inundated her with gifts.[208] Thomas Gent praised his niece as "a perfect beauty" who could tell him every passage in "a celebrated romance that I had bought for her in London."[209] Extravagant or unsuitable gifts showered by an older or unwanted suitor could also be embarrassing and counterproductive. Elizabeth Torriano had this to say about a box of flowers sent by a suitor: "if his fancy is as dull in the choice of a wife as it is in that of flowers, his adored angel is but a poor dull thing."[210]

SETTLEMENTS

Many brides brought in a simple dowry of linens, household furnishings, and cash; the wife of Nathaniel Tanner, for example, came with two

---

[203] Letter, PRO, SP 46/83.
[204] Earle, City Full of People, 246.
[205] I. G. Philip, The Bodleian Library (Oxford, 1983), 7.
[206] S. E. Hicks-Beach, A Cotswold Family (1909), 88–90.
[207] C. Trenchfield, A Cap of Gray Hairs for a Green Head (1710), 77, 95, 145, 154, 159; O'Hara, "The Language of Tokens," Rural History 3 (1992), 1–46.
[208] R. Haynes, Financial Diary, ed. R. T. N. Brushfield, vol. 33 (Transactions of the Devonshire Association, 1901).
[209] Gent, Life, 35, 49. He did ultimately marry an old flame when her husband died.
[210] Letter dated 15 Oct. 1736, PRO, C 112/24.

featherbeds and bolsters, six feather pillows, two pairs of sheets, a bed-stead, and other goods and plate.[211] Since the interests of the widow and children in London were protected by customary law, many businessmen eschewed any formal settlement. William Webster settled land on his wife at marriage to provide a jointure of £60 p.a., but she formally agreed at his request before his death to relinquish her jointure and take the one-third to which she was legally entitled instead.[212] Although Thomas Mitchell had a settlement in his marriage, when Hester Mitchell in 1719 married William Mingay, a merchant of London, the latter insisted on relying on city custom.[213]

A trend toward making prenuptial agreements can, however, be dis-cerned during this century; the number of known cases rose from 50 in period I to 158 in period II.[214] When a wife survived her husband, but is not named as a specific legatee, it is fairly certain that her inheritance had been separately agreed; 3 percent of wills fall into this category in period I, rising to 9 percent in period II. Often the husband would merely promise, secured by a simple bond, to provide at death cash or property equivalent to the portion received with his wife; in wealthier families, the settlements were more detailed and formal. Wills increasingly cited a prior agreement as a reason for waiving the widow's rights under the custom of London. Henry Lee, for example, settled £150 p.a. on his wife in lieu of her one-third, John Parker settled £2,000 and Robert Bristow £4,000.[215] William Bowyer, tallowchandler, settled extensive real estate in London in lieu of custom and in his will also left his widow his house for one year and a day.[216] James Goff, leatherseller, settled a farm in Hampshire on his wife and agreed to provide £500 in cash at his death, in lieu of custom.[217] In 1673 John Upton agreed to leave his widow either £3,000 or one-third of his personalty and in his will delegated the choice to her.[218] Walter Radcliffe, a merchant, left £2,000 to his widow by prior

---

[211] PCC, Alchin 474, 1654.
[212] PCC, Juxon 26, 1663. On inheritance law, see chapter 9.
[213] Lincolnshire Archives Office (hereafter LAO), Ancaster, MSS 9/A/13, 9/D/11.
[214] While they reveal a trend, there were many more cases that have not been picked up in the database. Nor is it always possible to distinguish agreements made before mar-riage from postnuptial settlements, which were made, even though legally invalid under coverture. In the post-1660 sample of Earle, *Making of the Middle Class*, 196, 372, 15 percent had settlements and 10 percent had jointures.
[215] PCC, Harvey 106; Corporation of London Record Office (hereafter CLRO), CSB IV.
[216] PCC, Rivers 17, 1644.   [217] PCC, Ruthen 631, 1657.
[218] PCC, Dyke 13, 1690.

agreement with a proviso that should his net assets be insufficient, the widow would receive her one-third.[219]

Merchant Richard Newton settled land in Shropshire on his wife for her jointure. John Guyot, also a merchant, agreed to provide his wife £500 at his death.[220] The childless Nicholas Betts, haberdasher, left his house and £1,600 to his widow and the residue to his brother in lieu of custom and "any other agreement I am to leave her at my death."[221] Edmund Harrison made a postnuptial agreement with his father-in-law to provide his wife with an annuity of £600 plus a tenement and her jewels.[222] Sir Richard Hoare, in his will of 1719, confirmed his wife's jointure in land and gave her his house with a proviso that his son would have an apartment in the house for which he would pay rent. This change of practice extended beyond London. Wealthy Liverpool merchants, like William Clayton and John Molyneux, were drawing up settlements by the end of the seventeenth century.[223]

The examples that are referred to in a summary fashion in wills and probate accounts, or which are preserved among business papers and cited in lawsuits, probably represent only a fraction of all settlements, and they may not be representative, because they were tailored to the specific needs, wealth, and circumstances of particular families. But they still have certain features in common. Sometimes it was provided that a specified amount of money, whether in the form of cash, stocks, or loans out at interest, would be transferred outright to the widow. William Dickinson, for example, confirmed in his will of 1619 that he had settled £100 on his wife.[224] This could be equivalent to any property that she had brought in or supplemented from the husband's estate. Some businessmen were reluctant to tie up capital in land because of the low yield; Francis March agreed to settle £6,000 in land on his wife, but in fact put it out at interest. Joshua Morgan sold his wife's jointure lands, though he provided in his will that they be replaced.[225]

Other merchants were content to settle land or urban real estate on their widows, the known rental income of which would constitute a join-

[219] PCC, Bruce 72, 1664.   [220] PCC, Hyde 6 and 114, 1665.
[221] PCC, Nabbs 176, 1660.
[222] P. Wardle, "The King's Embroiderer," *Textile History* 25 (1994): 38.
[223] *Liverpool in the Reign of Queen Anne*, ed. H. Peet, vol. 59 (Transactions of the Historical Society Lancashire and Cheshire, 59, 1907), 144, 151.
[224] *Stockport Probate Records 1578–1619*, ed. C. B. Phillips and J. H. Smith (Record Society Lancashire and Cheshire, 124, 1985), 130.
[225] Earle, *Making of the Middle Class*, 195; PCC, Bunce 48.

ture or annuity. Michael Mitford agreed to put his wife's portion of £1,200 into land; Arthur Lee, girdler, settled £500 on his wife and added £100 p.a. in land.[226] Eliab Harvey settled an annuity of £600 from his Essex lands on his widow in lieu of both custom and her dower rights, together with the right to remain in his great house without paying rent or the servants.[227] The annuities bequeathed in wills, sometimes funded by capital already lent at interest, strongly suggest some form of prenuptial agreement, even when none is specifically mentioned; John Crowther, for example, left his widow £200 p.a. for ten years.[228]

One purpose of a settlement was to protect not only the wife's interest but the interests of her family. The husband might formally agree that his wife should hold separate property in trust (often with the right to dispose of it by will) or that her real estate would revert to her kin on her death.[229] In 1671, when Robert Phillips married Elizabeth Scott, he gave bond to repay £200 of her portion, if his wife died without heirs within one year of the marriage.[230] The advantage of such a settlement was that the widow had priority over other debtors and knew exactly what she could expect, whereas her reasonable part by custom was net of any current debts and could not be ascertained in advance.

Children's portions were often specified as well. When Robert Moore married Sarah Walcott, £2,000 was reserved as a portion should one daughter survive to marry, and £3,000 was reserved to be divided equally if two or more daughters survived; trustees were appointed to raise the children, if orphaned, and any daughters would inherit, should there be no male heirs.[231] In 1660 Edmund Sherman married Jane Wall of Bromley, Essex, who brought in lands plus £500 in money and goods; it was agreed that she would sell the lands and that he would bind himself to provide her with £3,000; should Jane die leaving children, one-third of Edmund's personal estate would be reserved for those children, a protective provision in case he remarried.[232] Derrick Host in his settlement

---

[226] PRO, C 10/381/47: PCC, Coventry 101, 1640. Another example is John Pell in PCC, Pell 16, 1659.
[227] PCC, May 91, 1661. His settlements were probably drawn up during the marriage and the bulk of his wealth passed to his children.
[228] PCC, Pell 439, 1659.
[229] On separate property see chapter 2.
[230] Shropshire, RO, MS 49/615, 26 Dec. 1671.
[231] Marriage settlement of Robert Moore dated 3 Dec. 1701. Shropshire, RO, MS 4572, 4/11.
[232] GLL, MS 3547.

agreed to provide £1,200 for his second son.[233] Richard Lane agreed to settle £11,000 in lands on his wife for life with the remainder to any sons and daughters.[234]

In propertied families, the reconciliation of all interests could require lengthy and elaborate negotiation; blocking tactics were employed, and concessions were extracted by hard bargaining before consensus was reached. One reason that infatuation was condemned by parents was that it undermined bargaining power. George Warner considered that Elizabeth Chester's portion, which had been provided by a grandfather, was too small. His intermediary tried to persuade the father to add to the portion. The father's ploy, as reported to Warner, was "he thankt me your uncle and self . . . but his daughter had noe mind to marry. You may believe and expound it as you please."[235] Warner was advised that room remained for further negotiations but that the family would require a jointure "answerable to the portion."[236] Thomas Papillon had difficulties because the Broadnax family had doubts about a city match and because Thomas did not wish to endanger the finances of his parents by offering too much.[237] Ralph Thoresby, who knew more about antiquities than business, encountered resistance when he sought to marry Mary Cholmeley, because his finances seemed precarious.[238]

Information about the size of portions is spotty, and there is insufficient data to determine any changes in the portion-jointure ratio.[239] James Godschall agreed to provide his widow with £1,000 at death plus his house for life in return for a portion of £500.[240] When William Brand married Frances, the orphaned daughter of Abraham Ash in 1644, her portion was £2,300 and her jointure £60 p.a.[241] John Austen settled £16 per year in return for a portion of £85 after some hard bargaining.[242] The 1728 will of Sir Richard Gough mentions a portion of £4,000 in return for a jointure of £600, secured on land that would revert to male heirs. John Cogge noted that his master was said to have received £1,000

---

[233] PCC, Juxon 36, 1663.   [234] PRO, Prob 11/653/210–11.
[235] PRO, SP 46/83.   [236] Ibid.
[237] KAO, MS U 1015.C10/1; Papillon, *Memoirs*, 35–7.
[238] R. Thoresby, *Diary*, vol. 1, ed. J. Hunter (1830), ix.
[239] For the portions of daughters of merchants, on which there is more data, see chapter 9.
[240] PCC, Lee 351, 1638.
[241] Ipswich and Bast Suffolk Record Office, MS S1/1/77. The amount of the portion is unclear because the document is damaged.
[242] Earle, *Making of the Middle Class*, 38.

with his wife, the same amount received by John Fryer.[243] When Humphrey Morice, a merchant of London, married Mary Trollopp of Stamford in 1669, the portion was set at £1,200.[244] John Priestley received £800 with his partner's daughter.[245] Thomas Fowle received £900 when he married a stationer's daughter.[246] Bristol merchants received portions in the £700 range in the early seventeenth century.[247] John Fryer received £500 in return for giving bond to leave his widow £1,500, but his father-in-law, impressed with his business acumen, later added an additional £500.[248] Samuel Jeake Jr. insisted on £1,200 portion with his intended who was only thirteen; the girl's widowed mother offered £500 plus a house, then raised the offer to £700 plus £100 in goods and the house.[249] Sir Henry Johnson had to provide a jointure of £12,000 for his second wife, the daughter of Lord Lovelace.[250] Frequently portions were paid in installments and payments could be delayed or never made, prompting lawsuits.

Once a "treaty of marriage" had been agreed and parental consent obtained, rings could be exchanged and the couple betrothed. Usually about six months passed between a couple's first meeting and marriage; in the case of Richard Farrington it took five months.[251] Many businessmen chose to marry by license rather than by published banns, because it was cheaper, faster, and more discrete, when there were substantial differences of age or status. The cost of nuptials is obscure; though a tycoon like Sir John Banks could spend £565 on his son, a prominent family might expect to spend around £50.[252] Had weddings been extravagant, they would no doubt have attracted the criticism directed against lavish funerals, which are much better recorded.

A church wedding and the feasting, drinking, and dancing that followed was a public celebration of the exchange of vows, the transfer of

---

[243] Diary of John Cogge, Bod, MS Eng misc. F 78; GLL, MS 12,017.
[244] LAO, Trollopp Bellew MS.
[245] J. Priestley, *Memoirs*, vol. 87 (Surtees Society, 1883), 20.
[246] D. M. Mitchell, "Mr. Fowle," *Business and Economic History* 23 (1994): 28.
[247] MacGrath, *Merchants and Merchandise*, 43, 105.
[248] GLL, MS 12,017, fo. 22.
[249] S. Jeake, *Astrological Diary*, ed. M. Hunter and A. Gregory (Oxford, 1988), 150.
[250] BL, Add. MS 22,187, fo. 175.   [251] GLL, MS 2708.
[252] D. C. Coleman, *Sir John Banks* (Oxford, 1963), 126; L. Weatherill, *Consumer Behaviour* (1988), 64. Expenditure on weddings is rarely recorded in the accounts of businessmen. One example is Haynes, *Financial Diary*, 205. On wedding feasts see D. Cressy, *Birth, Marriage, and Death* (Oxford, 1997), 314; D. M. Palliser, "Civil Mentality" in *The Tudor and Stuart Town*, ed. J. Barry (1990), 237.

property rights, and the transformation of the couple into householders and full members of adult society. The ritual ceremonies—the display of rings, the distribution of gloves, ribbons, and garters, and the bride carried over the threshold—all proclaimed the setting up of a new household. The centerpiece of the ceremony was a sermon on the privileges and duties of marriage, probably lifted from one of the clerical handbooks. Even in India the formalities were observed: when Elihu Yale married the widowed Catherine Hinmer at Fort St. George, Streynsham Master gave away the bride, Henry Oxenden and John Willcox served as bridesmen, and Catherine Barker and Tryphena Ord as bridesmaids.[253] There are, however, no contemporary descriptions of the weddings of merchants, which suggests that the actual ceremony was considered less important than the marriage agreement. Few epithalamia have survived; one example is the marriage contract of Peter DuCane and Jeanne Maurois, which had a celebratory poem by the nephew of the bride.[254] The final act was sexual consummation. As Ned Ward put it, "the City wife . . . never thinks she has a true Right to be called my Lady till his Worship has confirmed her in the Title by his carnal weapon."[255]

REJECTION

According to Caleb Trenchfield, women liked to reject suitors and had to be stalked like partridges; another writer remarked that "citizens wives are like partridges, the hens are better than the cocks."[256] Usually all parties would seek to disengage with goodwill and without embarrassment. *The Gentlewoman's Companion* provided a specimen rejection letter: "if it hath pleased Heaven you should love me, you cannot blame me though you suffer by it."[257] Christopher Jeaffreson was rejected by Francis Russell.[258] Courtship could drag on endlessly without resolution, wasting time and money: a correspondent of William Lawrence describes a long and dismal courtship with a woman, from a wealthy but mad family, who was banished by her father to a dark

[253] *The Genealogist*, n.s., 19 (1903): 182.
[254] Essex, RO, MS D/DDCF3, 9 June 1636.
[255] E. Ward, *The Modern World Disrobd* (1708), 123.
[256] Trenchfield, *Cap Gray Hairs*, 159; W. Notestein, "The English Woman" in *Studies in Social History*, ed. J. H. Plumb (1955), 94.
[257] *Gentlewoman's Companion*, 246.
[258] *A Young Squire of the Seventeenth Century*, vol. 1, ed. J. J. Cordy (1878), 119.

room.[259] Samuel Jeake Sr. was refused because his swain wanted a better jointure and more independence.[260]

Businessmen reacted differently to setbacks. Some tried again. William Phillips wrote to his brother (whom he envied as "happy in the embraces of a pretty wife"): "I can compare my fate to nothing less than a ship who at her first sally out of port is beat back by contrary winds; I am now a second time putting out to sea which hope will prove successful."[261] Samuel Jeake disguised his rejections in shorthand and continued searching.[262] Some just never married, like William Stout who fell in love without reciprocation at age forty. Caleb Heathcote, according to family lore, emigrated to America in 1691, because he had fallen in love with the same woman as his brother, Samuel.[263] John Sanderson fell in love with and wrote poems to Margaret Calthorp, waiting woman and niece of Lady Calthorp; he made no progress and died a bachelor reduced to denouncing his fellow merchants as whoremongers.[264]

Preliminary promises did not always lead to marriage. Daniel Harvey's daughter consented to engagement with her cousin and father's apprentice, but she returned the ring, and the Court decreed that there had been no marriage since no church ceremony had been performed.[265] In 1730 Philip and Jacob Decosta brought an espousal suit against a first cousin, Catherine, the young widow of the wealthy Joseph Decosta; passionate love letters were read in court revealing that Catherine was desolate when her parents refused to allow the marriage.[266] Marriage-contract litigation between business families was rare, and the volume of all cases declined after 1660.[267]

BACHELORDOM

A substantial minority of merchants never married, including famous philantrophists such as Humphrey Chetham, Edward Colston, and

---

[259] BL, India Office, MS Eur 387/C, fo. 28. One of her suitors was Sir Josiah Child.
[260] A. Fletcher, *A County Community* (1975), 31.
[261] Letter to brother Ambrose, Constantinople, dated March 1695/6, Folger Library, MS UB 18.
[262] Jeake, *Astrological Diary*, 36.
[263] E. D. Heathcote, *Account of Some Families Bearing the Name of Heathcote* (Winchester, 1899), 75.
[264] Sanderson, *Travels*, 18, 24.
[265] Edward Dering, *Parliamentary Diary*, ed. B. D. Henning (New Haven, 1940), xiv.
[266] B. R. Masters, "Some Genealogical Sources," *Genealogical Magazine* 20 (1982): 227.
[267] L. Gowing, *Domestic Dangers* (Oxford, 1996), 267; L. Stone, *Road to Divorce*

William Jones. The number of businessmen whose marital status is known and who never married rose from 8.8 percent in period I to 13.4 percent in period II.[268] The proportion increased with wealth from 7 percent in bracket I, 7.7 percent in bracket II, 9.5 percent in bracket III, to 14.3 percent in bracket IV. An increase is also evident in successive cohorts, from 3.5 percent in cohort I to 11 percent in cohort IV.

The number of businessmen who never married seems to have been lower than in the general population, where the proportion rose from 15 to 17 percent in the 1620s to 27 percent in the 1690s; in three successive cohorts (born 1641, 1691, and 1716) the percentage decreased from 19.4 to 8.4 and then rose to 12.1.[269] In landed society 20 to 26 percent of younger sons did not marry.[270] Of active merchants who were members of the House of Commons (1660–90), only 3 percent were unmarried, though the proportion from merchant families was 7 percent.[271] The household surveys for London and Bristol in 1695–6 show a high proportion of bachelors, but many of these would subsequently have married.[272]

Businessmen had many reasons to eschew matrimony. Some must have had homosexual preferences. Some were deterred by rejection or by the prospect of rejection. Others feared or loathed the opposite sex. The bonding of men against women was a commonplace in the war between the sexes as played out in the theater.[273] Some businessmen were misogynists, like Stephen Frewen or Ralph Mayer, who ordered that no women attend their funerals.[274] Sir William Turner recorded in his ledger that "after a full draught of any sensual pleasure we presently loathe it"; the zeal with which he supervised the whipping of whores at Bridewell became the subject of satirical eulogies.[275]

(Oxford, 1990), 86. Matrimonial suits were less profitable for lawyers than other causes, and judges may have been hostile to spousal suits.

[268] The number of bachelors is almost certainly understated in the database, because the sources identify married men more consistently than bachelors.

[269] Wrigley and Schofield, *Population History England*, 260–3; R. Schofield, "English Marriage Patterns Revisited," *Journal of Family History* 10 (1985): 14.

[270] L. Stone, *The Family, Sex, and Marriage* (1977), 44.

[271] *The House of Commons 1660–1690*, ed. B. D. Henning (1983), 20, 23.

[272] J. R. Holman, "Orphans in Pre-Industrial Towns," *Local Population Studies* 15 (1975): 41.

[273] K. E. Westhauser, "Friendship and Family," *Journal of Social History* 27 (1994): 517.

[274] J. Wadmore, *Company of Skinners* (1902), 135; PCC, Fines 211. Misogyny in literature has to be interpreted with care because it became a conceit.

[275] GLL, MS 5109; *Good Sir William Knock* (1693).

Table 1.7. *Frequency of Marriage of Businessmen (Percentage of Known Cases)*

	Period I	Period II	Bracket I	Bracket II	Bracket III	Bracket IV	Cohort I	Cohort II	Cohort III	Cohort IV
Unmarried	8.8	13.4	7.0	7.7	9.5	14.3	3.5	6.7	5.3	11.0
1 Marriage	85.0	75.6	86.9	86.7	72.1	67.6	65.4	72.1	74.8	79.6
2 Marriages	5.5	10.0	5.4	5.1	15.7	15.2	26.3	18.3	18.6	9.0
3+ Marriages	0.8	1.0	0.8	0.5	2.6	2.9	4.8	3.0	1.4	0.5
Total Cases	5,666	6,684	518	2,184	1,687	105	315	842	1,978	402
Settlements	50	158	4	46	96	19	9	14	65	14

Table 1.8. *Businessmen Traveling or*
Residing Abroad, 1580–1740
(Percentage of Known Cases)

	Period I	Period II
Deceased abroad	21.1	25.7
Unmarried	21.7	38.1
Total Cases	1,267	1,613

Others were reluctant to forgo the freedom of bachelorhood in order to find companionship. Marmaduke Rawdon "naturally loved the company of women, yett he was allwayes naturally averse to marriage and some times dreamed he was married, hath wept in his sleep very much"; he never married and, after spending sixteen years in the Canary Islands, lived with his cousin.[276] To Isaac Lawrence, women were "wasps and will sting"; his brother, William, had a friend who "having made it the diversion of thirty years to rage fiercely against matrimony, he will hardly be perswaded to sell his liberty for seven per cent or enter into that politic noose where he must spend some weeks in wooing and all the rest of his life in cooing like the conjugal doves in a cage."[277]

Others, like Ambrose Barnes who rejected the love of a gentlewoman, gave priority to their religious devotion or to their business. Just as many younger sons of peers never married because the needs of the eldest son and the estate took priority, so many merchants concentrated on accumulating capital and building their business. Many died young or lived abroad. Like Montague North, many postponed marriage until it was too late; the proportion of known bachelors among those who lived abroad was 22 percent in period I and 38 percent in period II.[278] Others ultimately had the financial resources to marry, but they were too old and set in their ways to change their lifestyle.

Bachelors could and did live with relatives or with the families of their business partners. John Morris commingled his assets with Sir Robert Clayton and lived with first Robert Abbot and then Clayton. William

---

[276] Rawdon, *Life*, 78.
[277] Letters dated 27 June 1659, 15 Jan. 1692, BL, India Office, MS Eur 387/C.
[278] R. Grassby, *The English Gentleman in Trade* (Oxford, 1994), 209.

Stout's unmarried sister, Elin, acted as his housekeeper, and Edward Colston similarly depended on first his sister and then his niece.[279] But the majority seem to have lived in separate households with paid, professional housekeepers, like Sir William Turner and Sir Andrew King. Some kept mistresses or just lived in sin.[280] Tom Brown alleged that Sir Charles Duncomb had two mistresses.[281] William Cotesworth clearly lived with his housekeeper, and they had a child.[282] Elihu Yale took the widow of a Jewish merchant, Jacques de Paiva, into his house and allegedly had an illegitimate son.[283]

Bequests in wills to housekeepers and female friends often hinted at intimate relationships. Bachelor William Delawood mentioned his housekeeper first in his will, and Hugh Vaughan, a goldsmith, left £100 to his "good friend Elizabeth Silvester" plus all his linens.[284] John Temple left £2,000 to the son of Dr. Pickering and a house to Mrs. Pickering.[285] John Hewitt left the residue of his estate to spinster Elizabeth Cann, a "very loving and dear friend."[286] Sir Robert Peak left £1,000 to my "good friend and valentine Mary St. Loe widow."[287] Bachelor Daniel Elder left his housekeeper "who now lives with me" all his furniture, jewels, and stock and arranged for her to live in his house rent free for life.[288] Walter Kent, who died at seventy-four in 1746 with no surviving children, left his whole estate of over £44,000 to his servant, Jane Morris.

SUMMARY

The debate over choice in marriage is usually framed as a conflict between affection and interest, or between personal inclination and the constraints imposed by family and society. The factors of choice were, however, much more complex. The range of possible motives was too broad to be baldly summarized, and choice is not a simple concept. Indi-

---

[279] Stout, *Autobiography*, 24; Melton, *Clayton*, 68; H. J. Wilkins, *Edward Colston* (Bristol, 1920), 38.
[280] J. Miller, *New York Considered and Improved* (1695), ed. V. H. Paltsits (Cleveland, 1903), 60.
[281] T. Browne, *Amusements Serious and Comical*, ed. A. L. Hayward (1927), 429.
[282] J. M. Ellis, *William Cotesworth* (1981), 201.
[283] Love, *Vestiges Old Madras*, vol. 1, 486.
[284] PCC, Essex 57, 1648.
[285] S. Anderson, *An English Consul in Turkey* (Oxford, 1989), 107.
[286] PCC, Goare 59, 1639.
[287] H. F. Waters, *Genealogical Gleanings in England* (Salem, Mass., 1892), 11.
[288] PCC, Pell 205, 1659.

viduals choose not just on the basis of current needs but for the person they expect to be once they have chosen.[289] Much of the conflict occurred within individual businessmen who had contradictory objectives or were not sure what they wanted.

What role did cultural pressure play in a businessman's decision to marry? The prescriptive literature may have created a disposition to act in accordance with the value system. Some grooms and brides may have generated emotions that fit the roles they were expected to play. But the cacophony of discordant voices, each emphasizing different priorities, did not constitute a universally accepted, binding code of appropriate behavior. The defenders of love, passion, and free choice challenged, but did not displace, traditional arguments that interest, reason, religion, and social compatibility should govern choice. Matrimonial strategy might be embedded in the social order and governed by unconscious habits and unwritten rules, but the tactics of matchmaking were spontaneous and diverse. No body of mechanical rules could have been devised to reconcile all interests and address all situations.[290] Individuals and families just manipulated ideology and culture to meet their own needs; they appropriated from conventional norms what best suited their temperament and interests.

Choice was clearly based on material circumstances. The financial negotiations were as important as the courtship. Women with property were subject to greater control by their families in first marriages; those with little property were often obliged to sacrifice personal preferences for economic security. As William Lawrence put it, "daughters must marry when they can but sonnes may marry when they please."[291] It is tempting to ask whether marriages became more mercenary during the period, but this is not a question that can answered in a meaningful way. Some men and women certainly used marriage as a means of economic advancement, and few businessmen would marry without an adequate portion. The financial objectives of marrying couples can be inferred from their settlements, but not their other intentions. A mutually satisfactory agreement over property was a necessary, but not a sufficient, condition of all marriages. Even if the wealth that changed hands could

---

[289] P. Gardenfors and N. Salin, *Decision, Probability, and Utility* (Cambridge, 1988), 338; D. M. MacCloskey, "The Economics of Choice" in *Economics and the Historian*, ed. T. G. Rawski et al. (1996), 123–4.
[290] P. Bourdieu, "Les strategies matrimoniales," *Annales* 27 (1972): 1123.
[291] BL, India Office, MS Eur 387/C, fo. 79.

be measured precisely over time, it would not provide a reliable index of changing attitudes.

The range of choice was also determined by social and religious factors. Because propertied society was relatively open and mobile, one-third of businessmen were able to marry outside their community. But the majority still took spouses of equivalent status and religious denomination. The successful married into the dominant urban cliques, and, in a society stratified by birth and faith and geographically concentrated, marriages tended to be endogamous and locally centered. Occupation determined both the timing of marriage and the method of courtship. Businessmen married late, were usually older than their brides, and were more likely to marry by arrangement.

As the failure of many suitors illustrates, personality could be a decisive factor. The qualities sought in a spouse were both numerous and different for each individual. A businessman might just look for a woman to bear and raise his children and run his household, or he might consider only those with education and social skills. He might be drawn to someone whose beauty captivated him, who shared his interests, or who would be his friend, nurse, and companion. Humor, understanding, and compatibility of temperament are just a few of the personality traits that made a difference. Women likewise judged the character of their suitors from their own standpoint.

Marriage was a speculative enterprise with unpredictable consequences. The decision to marry carried huge risks for both men and women, because it was a lifetime commitment. It was not just impulsive matches that proved to be mistakes. It is not surprising, therefore, that many consulted astrologers to establish whether a sweetheart was a true love, what was the critical moment to marry, or the best hour to procreate.[292] One merchant reflected that when stocks were down, "we must take all as they do in Matrimony, for better for worse."[293]

Both brides and grooms wanted their spouse to have everything—beauty, wealth, and status. An ideal marriage, however, could only be made in heaven. On earth each partner usually had to compromise, forgo their first choices, prioritize their needs, weigh their chances, and make the best bargain. Women usually had fewer options than men, because they came under greater pressure to marry. The basic objectives of busi-

---

[292] E. Ward, *A Legacy for the Ladies* (1705), 113.
[293] Folger Library, MS UB 818.

nessmen when marrying did not change over time and were shared with the rest of propertied society. But they could be combined in numerous permutations and their relative importance was subjectively determined. The threshold of expectations and wants also probably rose with the growth of individual self-consciousness during the seventeenth century. In the end, however, marriage depended on access to a large pool of prospective partners who met the minimum criteria, and this depended on the balance between supply and demand in the marriage market. The crucial factor was always the window of opportunity.

2

Husbands and Wives

Once a couple joined, how did they relate to each other and how successfully did they cope with the everyday problems of married life? To what extent did business families follow the advice dispensed in marriage literature, much of which was written for the urban bourgeoisie? How far did the seventeenth-century family become a unit of reproduction and consumption instead of production? Did objectives and priorities change and, if so, for what reasons?

THE LAW

The legal maxim that both spouses were united in one person limited the rights of the wife and broadened those of the husband. All personalty passed to him on marriage, and his wife could not make a contract or a will in her first two marriages without his permission unless it concerned a debt or legacy due to her.[1] When the wife of Peter Richardson of Hull wanted to leave £20 in a will, she had to secure a bond from her husband.[2] John Blackburn bequeathed nothing to his married daughter, but instead gave his son-in-law £400 for their joint use.[3] A married woman was described in documents by her husband's name, not by her

---

[1] *Baron and Feme* (1700); J. Godolphin, *The Orphans Legacy* (1674), 17; C. S. Kenny, *History of the Law of England as to the Effects of Marriage on Property* (1879), 14; A. L. Erickson, "Common Law versus Common Practice," *Economic History Review*, 2d ser., 43 (1990): 37; M. Salmon, *Women and the Law of Property* (Chapel Hill, 1986), 88; M. Okin, "Patriarchy and Married Women's Property," *Eighteenth Century Studies* 17 (1983): 125; L. G. Carr and L. S. Walsh, "The Planter's Wife," *William and Mary Quarterly* 34 (1977): 556.
[2] C. Cross, "Northern Women," *Yorkshire Archaeological Journal* 59 (1987): 86.
[3] PCC, Aylett 264, 1655.

occupation. If she could not control her own property, she was economically dependent on her husband.

Nonetheless, "the power of a husband in this Kingdom extends itself farther then it is commonly exercized."[4] A wife still had a separate, autonomous legal existence; "as Adam's punishment was severall from Eves, so in criminal and other special causes our Law argues them severall persons."[5] Men might seek absolute property in women and privilege male descent, but wives enjoyed specific property rights, and, in practice, couverture was as limited as primogeniture.[6] A wife had a legal right to benefit from the joint estate, and her husband was legally responsible for her maintenance and her debts. A prenuptial settlement could give a wife the authority to administer her own property and protect her against a profligate husband. She also had a substantial claim on her husband's personalty under customary law, which was stoutly defended until the late seventeenth century.[7] Women frequently sued for defamation in the Consistory Court of London. Wives of businessmen were also included among those who sued in the equity Courts of Chancery and Requests, though the increase there in the number of female plaintiffs may simply mark a shift in litigation from other courts. In 1627 23 widows and 38 wives were plaintiffs.[8]

A wife could keep her real property, if not her name. She could benefit from property in trust (the title being transferred to feoffees for uses), like the wives of Robert Lant and Peter Briggins.[9] When Margaret Ashe married William Brand, her settlement listed all the goods she brought in and a project for manufacturing soap in Russia.[10] In 1654 Thomasine

---

[4] *Gentlewoman's Companion* (1676), 104. Thomas Smith, in *De Republica Anglorum*, took the same view.

[5] E. T., *The Lawes Resolutions of Women's Rights* (1632), 4; M. L. Cioni, *Women and Law in Elizabethan England* (New York, 1985), 280–6.

[6] Erickson, *Women and Property*, passim; this argument was anticipated by Kenny, *Law as to Effects Marriage*, 14–15, 98–115, 120–1. The legal doctrine of couverture was also attacked by men.

[7] On the entitlement of widows see chapter 9.

[8] H. Horowitz, *Chancery Equity Records* (1995), 37; L. Gowing, "Language, Power, and the Law" and T. Stretton, "Women, Custom, and Equity" in *Women Crime and the Courts*, ed. J. Kermode and G. Walker (1994): 28, 189; T. Stretton, "Women and Litigation in the Elizabethan Court of Requests" (Ph.D. diss., University of Cambridge, 1993), tables 3.3 and 4.1; Erickson, *Women and Property*, table 7.1. Wives usually sued in conjunction with a man, either a father or brother.

[9] PCC, Duke 335, 1670; *Eliot Papers*, ed. H. Eliot (Gloucester, 1893), 54. See also Earle, *City Full of People*, 154. In Connecticut, in comparison, women could have a jointure, but not a separate estate: see C. H. Dayton, *Women before the Bar* (Chapel Hill, 1995), 44.

[10] J. H. Appleby, "Dr. Arthur Dee," *Slavonic and East European Review* 57 (1979): 39.

Skinner arranged to keep £200 of her £700 portion as a separate estate so long as there were no children of the marriage.[11] Henry Wallis, a dyer, left his wife £1,500, his house and its contents, and "the mare my father Blackwell gave her . . . as a token of my love wishing it were more for her"; he also included "those monies she hath of her own."[12] The wife of merchant Henry Boldero inherited a separate estate from her brother, and her husband left her all his lands at his death on condition that all the property would pass ultimately to the children.[13] The Huguenot Judith Duboc managed a substantial portfolio while her husband was still alive.[14]

It was even more common for separate estates to be created by inheritance. Bequests to married daughters and sisters, like those of James Smith in 1617, Richard Mowse in 1665, Joseph Hern in 1699, Sir Edward Clark in 1702, and Sir Richard Levitt in 1711, often provided that the husband should not meddle or were conditional on the husband's behavior. Roger Pettiwood, a salter, left his daughter both money and a ship, her "husband not to intermeddle."[15] Thomas Mun instructed his overseers to purchase land for his married daughters, whose husbands should not meddle.[16] Sir George Merttins left £300 in the hands of a friend for the separate use of his married daughter. Thomas Cook left his sister £100, "provided her husband do give his free consent that she as is intended may have and receive it into her own hands to dispose of the same according to her discretion."[17] Randall Taylor insisted that his daughter's husband not interfere with her inheritance under the custom of London, and in 1696 John Coldham gave his married daughter cash for her own use in addition to her portion.[18] John Bennett, a stationer, bequeathed urban property worth £150 to his married daughter and her heirs, while simply forgiving her husband's debts.[19] Francis Thomson bequeathed more to his daughter than to his son-in-law—"noe part of it to come to the hands of her husband."[20] Sir

[11] Erickson, *Women and Property*, 12. C. Shammas, "Anglo-American Household Government," *William and Mary Quarterly*, 3d ser., 5 (1995): 127, revises Erickson's estimate of separate estates to 1 to 2 percent (with a further 2 to 3 percent created by settlements) by excluding cases where wives gave bond to pay their children's portion in the event of remarriage.

[12] PCC, Ruthen 269, 1657.   [13] PCC, May 55, 1661.   [14] PRO, C 114/182.

[15] PCC, Harvey 75, 1639.   [16] PCC, Evelyn 92, 1641.

[17] PCC, Brent 297, 1653. Another example is the will of George Phinneas dated 1675, PCC, Dycer 115.

[18] W. H. Phelps, "The Will of Randall Taylor," *Bibliographical Society of America Papers* 72 (1978): 337.

[19] PCC, Ruthen 58, 1657.   [20] PCC, Aylett 265, 1655.

Samuel Barnardiston made similar provision for his married niece and Sir Robert Peak for his cousin, Sarah Wildboar.[21] In 1702 Dorothy Wigfall put £2,739 in trust for her son and married daughter and instructed that her son-in-law was not to meddle.[22]

A particularly interesting case is that of Mary Atwood, whose husband's financial difficulties seem to have forced him into hiding from his creditors. She took their young daughter and moved in with her relatives, and her two older boys were put in a boarding school. Her brother then drew up a settlement for her and the children, which she asked her husband to accept in deferential but still firm language:

> it is in the power to do it without father or mother (if not I hope they will not be against it). If so I confess I think I have reason to take it very unkindly if you oppose it considering how readyly I parted with what was settled on me for your convenience. I hope you will not think that I have any designe in desire of it farther then that I may have a comfortable subsistance for my self and children, for do but consider what a miserable condition I should be in if it pleas God to make me a widow (which God forbid) to be left my self and two poor children and but thirty pounds a year to live on. I am sure we must either work hard or beg or starve either of which I believe would trouble you as much as me to think that the poor children should come to want. Therfore let me beg you, if not for my sake for theirs, that this estate may be settled upon me for my life for I think since it please God that it is as it is with us that it is but reason that I and the younger children should have a share of what is left . . . therfore pray consider of it and if you have any kindness for me show it in granting this my request in which you will do me a great kindness and no injury to your self. Pray do not take any thing ill but be as reall in the thing as I am, which is merely for the good of our poor children, and believe me to be the same in affliction as I was in prosperity.[23]

CONVENTION

Both the clerical and secular treatises on marriage drew on classical authorities to construct an ideal and universal model of the family that could be integrated with the dominant culture.[24] Concepts like shame and honor were manipulated, and personal identities were constructed to impose hypothetical order on a chaotic reality. The conduct books,

---

[21] H. F. Waters, *Genealogical Gleanings in England*, vol. 1 (Salem, Mass., 1892), 11.
[22] CLRO, CSB IV.
[23] Letters from Mary to William Atwood dated 31 July and Oct. 1684, PRO, C 109/23/1.
[24] K. M. Davies, "The Sacred Condition of Equality," *Social History* 5 (1977): 563–4; M. Todd, "Humanists, Puritans, and the Spiritual Household," *Church History* 49 (1980):

which tended to supersede the courtesy literature, were often written by bachelors and provide more information about the attitudes of men than women; they offer a definition of the role of wives in business households and suggest how marriage was perceived and represented and how wives could transform their role in the household.[25] Careful analysis can identify some core principles.

What emerges, however, is a contradictory mix of continuously changing cultural imperatives, not a coherent, internally consistent ideology of marriage.[26] Clerical writers felt obliged to cite authorities, like St. Paul, and then faced the problem of explaining away inconvenient maxims that did not meet their needs.[27] The prescriptive works gradually became more descriptive, charting lifestyles and offering practical, if prejudiced, advice.[28] Plays, newspapers, jigs, and ballads viewed marriage in a very different light from the letter-writing manuals and family instructors. There was no consensus among those who expressed their views in print, not even an agreement to disagree.

William Ramesey thought that women "differ nothing from us but in the odd instrument of generation," that they were wittier, quicker of spirit, and, if educated, likely to exceed men.[29] Others recognized that a wife would of necessity sometimes have to assume male functions. Usually, however, men and women were credited with different temperaments that matched their appointed roles. Men were egotistic, driven, and decisive, women adaptable, selfless, and patient; men acted and women responded. Edmund Tilney asserted that men had "a great courage in accomplishment," Thomas Wright that women were merciful and pious.[30] Gender differences were, however, complicated by social stratification. Women of high rank expected deference from males of lower station, even though their authority ultimately derived from their

23; *Idem., Christian Humanism and the Puritan Social Order* (Cambridge, 1987), 116.

[25] N. Armstrong, "Rise of the Domestic Woman" in *The Ideology of Conduct*, ed. N. Armstrong and L. Tennenhouse (New York, 1987), 135.

[26] M. L. Williamson, *The Patriarchy of Shakespeare's Comedies* (Detroit, 1986), 40.

[27] M. Sommerville, *Sex and Subjection* (1995), 255.

[28] K. M. Davies, "Continuity and Change" in *Marriage and Society*, ed. R. B. Outhwaite (New York, 1981), 76–7; S. Baskerville, "The Family in Puritan Political Theology," *Journal of Family History* 18 (1993): 158, argues unconvincingly that Puritan writers asked new questions without making any assumptions.

[29] W. Ramesey, *The Gentleman Companion* (1672), 9–10.

[30] E. Tilney, *A Brief and Pleasant Discours of Duties in Marriage* (1571), E.1; T. Wright, *The Passion of the Minde in Generall* (1601), 74.

husbands or fathers. Men often railed against females while treating their mothers, wives, and daughters with love and respect. Women often adopted male attitudes in their behavior toward other women.

Most writers emphasized the importance of mutual affection in marriage. Clerics Dod and Clever argued "the husband that is not beloved of his wife holdeth his goods in danger, his house in suspicion, his credit in balance and also sometimes his life in peril"; the widow of a merchant tailor was burned at the stake for killing her husband.[31] Love, however, tended to be identified with duty or with a mode of behavior rather than with emotion. The use of nicknames was criticized because it implied equality. The governing ideal was quietness. Thomas Gouge, for example, recommended that a wife be mild, modest, and obedient, that she esteem her husband and have "contentment with her husband's present estate."[32]

A few writers came close to regarding wives as equals of their husbands. Wives should rule in the household, wrote Caleb Trenchfield, "those husbands are fools who think to have the subjection of their wives not by the exercise of affection but the asserting their own authority."[33] Thomas Gwin, when he advised his daughters on how they should behave toward their husbands, stressed prudence rather than obedience.[34] Ned Ward had a fictional wife argue that "man has no title to the upper hand; either may ask, but neither should command."[35]

Nonetheless, the clerical writers, like William Whateley, stressed mutuality and partnership rather than equality.[36] The preachers never made a strenuous effort to reconcile their emphasis on spiritual equality with their acceptance of rule by the husband. Daniel Rogers emphasized submissiveness in gesture and speech and, in common with many, equated chastity with staying at home: the chaste wife "does not prostitute herself to any, not only lusts, but even liberties."[37] A few writers condoned the right of husbands to use physical correction, and, when

---

[31] J. Dod and R. Clever, *A Godly Form of Government* (1630 ed.), Fo L.3; R. Smyth, *Obituary*, ed. Sir Henry Ellis, vol. 44 (Camden Society, 1849), 8.

[32] W. Gouge, *Of Domesticall Duties*, vol. 3 (1622), 10.

[33] C. Trenchfield, *Cap of Gray Hairs* (1671), 163.

[34] T. Gwin, *Journal* (Falmouth, 1837), 45.

[35] E. Ward, *Nuptial Dialogues and Debates* (1710), 71.

[36] M. J. M. Ezell, *The Patriarch's Wife* (1987), 36–61. One feminist interpretation is that the preachers' emphasis on partnership was a rhetorical trick to validate submission: see V. Lucas, "Puritan Preaching" in *The Renaissance Englishwoman in Print*, ed. A. M. Haselkorn and B. S. Travitsky (Amherst, 1990): 229–30.

[37] Rogers, *Matrimonial Honour*, 324.

beating was condemned, it was on the grounds that husband and wife were one flesh and that violence presupposed loss of self-control.[38] There was universal condemnation of husbands who could not control a commanding wife, often vilified as a shrew. A regular prediction of the almanacs was that wives would challenge patriarchy.[39]

The division of labor within a marriage was drawn along gender lines. A few, like Daniel Rogers, might argue that a wife should be consulted about sudden changes of trade, large investments, or family settlements.[40] Gouge allowed that a wife should help her husband in his trade and entertain jointly with him.[41] But modesty and thrift were the virtues usually equated with wifehood. As Henry Smith put it, the wife "sitteth upon the nest to keep all at home."[42] To Leonard Wright, "the keys (were) at her girdle, the purse at his own."[43] "Men get wealth and women keep it," asserted Trenchfield.[44] Gainsford spoke for many when he insisted that wives should not babble, prate, scold, gossip, or slander. Instead, they should be economical, modest, and quiet, working with the needle and distaff, cooking and rearing the children.[45]

The importance accorded to the well-ordered family and the privileges, and obligations associated with the household gave wives, who complemented their husbands, influence if not power within the family; they had an asymmetrical, dual role of subordination and competence.[46] The theorists envisaged marriage as an unequal partnership in which husband and wife had mutual duties, but not reciprocal rights; it was contractual, not consensual. Locke might attack patriarchialism as a basis for government, but he envisaged no public or political role for women; he defended the supremacy of the husband on the grounds that

---

[38] W. Heal, *An Apologie for Women* (Oxford, 1609), 6; S. Rowlands, *Works, 1598–1628* vol. 2 (Glasgow, 1880), 8–10; A. C. Carter, "Marriage Counselling" in *Ten Studies in Anglo Dutch Relations*, ed. J. Van Dorsten (1974), 114; E. Foyster, "Male Honor," *Transactions of the Royal Historical Society* 6 (1996): 223; R. Gwynn, "Marital Problems," *Proceedings of the Huguenot Society of Great Britain* 26 (1995), 217. City regulations prohibited wife beating in London after 9 P.M. as it disturbed the peace: see M. Falkus, "Lighting in the Dark Ages," in *Trade, Government, and Society*, ed. D. C. Coleman and A. H. John (1976), 250.
[39] B. S. Capp, *Astrology and the Popular Press* (1979), 112.
[40] Rogers, *Matrimonial Honour*, 264–5.
[41] Gouge, *Of Domestical Duties*, 18–19, 231–4.
[42] H. Smith, *A Preparative to Marriage* (1591), 55.
[43] L. Wright, *Display of Dutie* (1589), 25.
[44] Trenchfield, *Cap of Gray Hairs*, 152.
[45] T. Gainsford, *Rich Cabinet* (1616), 102–4.
[46] L. T. Ulrich, *Good Wives* (New York, 1982), 8.

the conjugal couple could not decide by majority vote.[47] A private companionship ethic was preached along with the theoretical authority of the male and the public subordination of the female.

MARRIED LIFE

Relationships within actual families were, however, different from those prescribed between men and women. Theorists limited their advice to the nuclear household and, though they included servants in the domestic hierarchy, completely ignored the fact that families had in-laws and other dependents and sojourners in their households. Some division of labor in the household was both necessary and efficient. Wealthy husbands were sometimes inclined to display their economic standing by keeping their wives idle; wives with social aspirations often willingly accepted this role, since deliberate abstention from productive activity was one mark of gentility. But most wives of businessmen were not marginalized, divorced from production, nor converted into idle breeders. Husbands and wives fundamentally worked as a team with flexible strategies.

In many families there was no clear line between household and place of business, thereby creating little need or opportunity to develop a separate domesticity.[48] Both the wife and children participated at several levels.[49] Sir Robert Clayton's wife ran the household, which served as the headquarters of his banking business.[50] Merchants who traveled frequently left their wives in charge of the household, the shop, and local business matters. An attractive wife could entice customers into a shop and ease negotiations; the wife of Thomas Hill allowed Samuel Pepys to kiss her when her husband was lobbying for a naval contract.

In the Chesapeake domestic patriarchy was untenable in the face of

---

[47] D. Gobetti, *Private and Public* (1992), 48, 92; E. Balibar, "What is Man?" in *The Individual in Political Theory*, ed. J. Coleman (Oxford, 1996), 238; J. Locke, *Two Treatises*, ed. P. Laslett (Cambridge, 1964), 364.

[48] A telling example of the complete integration of household and business is provided by the inventory of Giles Crouch in GLL, MS 5677.

[49] Erickson, *Women and Property*, 150; E. C. Sanderson, *Women and Work in Eighteenth-Century Edinburgh* (1996), 168; T. Powell, *Tom of All Trades*, ed. F. J. Furnivall, New Shakespeare Society Series, no. 7 (1876), 143.

[50] F. T. Melton, *Sir Robert Clayton* (Cambridge, 1986), 69. See also A. H. Dodd, "Mr. Myddleton" in *Elizabethan Government and Society*, ed. S. T. Bindoff et al. (1961), 265.

economic and demographic realities.[51] Alexander Barnaby went overseas leaving a pregnant wife and died while abroad.[52] When Thomas Papillon was in exile, his wife had to run his estate as well as the household with detailed instructions from him.[53] Wives often acted as brokers and supplicants for their husbands, raising credit, renegotiating debts, or tapping the goodwill and financial resources of their kin. A weaver sent his wife to pay his fine and persuade the court that the charge was not proven.[54] When James Cole fled his creditors in 1634, he asked his wife to take over the household.[55] John Sanderson told his brother disapprovingly that his sister had "taken over her husband."[56] In ports, like Bristol and Southampton, there were numerous households headed by women whose menfolk were probably at sea.[57]

When, as often happened, there were no men in the household, wives performed all roles—male and female.[58] Husbands had the authority conferred by greater age, but they often depended on their wives to act independently, especially when the age difference was likely to put an elderly and sick husband in the care of his wife. At the deathbed a wife could intervene to influence her husband's testamentary provisions. Roger Green, a cutler, said on his deathbed that "all the estate that he had in the world" should pass to his wife; "his wife replyed unto him in these or the like words, sweetheart you have often said you would give your sister twenty pounds and some thing to her children and likewise something to the girle that he had brought up and kept and did likewise put him in mind of his kinsman, Henry" to which he agreed.[59]

Not only were many family decisions made collectively, but wives developed their own strategies and initiated policy; the spouse of Stephen Fox made her own plans to rebuild Chiswick House.[60] Social and legal

---

[51] A. Kulikoff, *Tobacco and Slaves* (Chapel Hill, 1986), 166.

[52] PCC, Coventry, 24, 1640.

[53] KAO, MS U 1015/C11/9–12; Papillon, *Memoirs*, 262.

[54] A. Plummer, *The London Weavers Company* (1972), 62. See also N. J. Williams, *Contraband Cargoes* (Hamden, Conn., 1961), 79.

[55] P. Seaver, *Wallington's World* (1985), 1–13.

[56] J. Sanderson, *Travels*, ed. Sir William Foster, 2d ser., vol. 67 (Hakluyt Society, 1931), 215, letter dated 7 May 1601.

[57] K. Schürer, "Variations in Household Structure" in *Surveying the People*, ed. K. Schürer and T. Arkell (Cambridge, 1992), 269.

[58] Tilney, *Brief Discourse on Duties in Marriage*, Ciiib.

[59] PCC, Pembroke 198, 1650. It was quite common for widows in their wills to redress what they considered omissions in their husbands' wills.

[60] C. Clay, *Public Finance and Private Wealth* (Oxford, 1978), 263.

subordination did not diminish the importance of self-reliance. The notion that wives should confine themselves to the household was absurd when they had to shop alone in the markets for domestic necessities. They were frequently business partners of their husbands and helped to negotiate loans.[61] The necessary inversion of roles, because of sickness or the absence of a husband, might have reinforced the system, but it also widened the options.[62]

Except for childbirth, which was overseen completely by women and which allowed wives to delegate all their other responsibilities, there was no absolute differentiation of function in the household; tasks were assigned by need and inclination in a bustle of shared activity. Fathers did participate in child rearing, though the main burden fell on the wife (see chapter 4). Although the husband had the final say, the wife usually had primary responsibility for the provision and maintenance of the household. The husband would usually determine the overall budget, which, as was the case with Richard Haynes of Exeter or Stephen Fox, might be a monthly allowance.[63]

It is clear from household accounts that it was the mistress of the household, with the labor of servants, who purchased the food, fuel, and clothing, paid the rent, cleaned and maintained the house, cooked, laundered and mended clothing, tilled the garden, and organized hospitality and entertainment.[64] During the century, some household tasks, like laundry, baking, and brewing, were increasingly farmed out in wealthier families, to specialized providers, as the division of labor was extended in the London economy, reducing the burden on wives. Although retailers' invoices often do not specify whether wives ordered or just collected goods, they usually did make the decisions.[65] Thomas Sutton received a shopping list from his wife, and Robert Abbot paid for goods, like candles and clothes, which had already been purchased

---

[61] B. Lemire, "Petty Pawns" in *From Family Firm to Corporate Capitalism*, ed. P. K. O'Brien (1998), 124; W. S. Prideaux, *Memorials of the Goldsmiths Company*, vol. 1 (privately printed, 1896), 99.

[62] N. Davis, "Women on Top" in *The Reversible World*, ed. B. Babcock (Ithaca, 1978), 154; J. A. R. Abbott, "Robert Abbott," *Guildhall Miscellany* 7 (1956): 31.

[63] T. N. Brushfield, "The Financial Diary of a Citizen of Exeter," *Transactions of the Devonshire Association* 33 (1901): 209; Clay, *Public Finance*, 258.

[64] G. Whetstone, *An Heptameron of Civill Discourses* (1582). The manifold tasks of the housewife were detailed in contemporary handbooks and are well illustrated by household accounts like those in BL, Cott Vesp., F xvii.

[65] C. Shammas, *The Pre-Industrial Consumer in England and America* (Oxford, 1990), 246.

by his wife; the wife of a Seville merchant bought all the household goods, though her husband checked her accounts.[66] Women certainly bought their clothes, in which they had an emotional investment, and often appear in wills and inventories to have more household goods than men.[67]

The universal employment of servants put wives in a position of authority. There is much literary and some judicial evidence that wives could be very authoritarian and even abusive toward both the servants and apprentices.[68] Henry Smith, who regarded husband and wife "like two oars in a boat," suggested that the husband should beat the male, and the wife the female servants.[69] The conduct of one wife is well illustrated in a defense that her husband offered to the mother of his apprentice:

I acknowledge my wife wilbe mistress over her maids, yet she have had mayds that have lived with her longer than an apprentice and that quietly too, else surely would I think have stayed so long . . . but I confesse that when she have mett with a crosse provoking maid it had perplexed and discomposed her. Yet your son do not well to make that a plea or excuse for his misdoeing for though my wife would not bear with saucy provoking Maid servants, to whom she gave wages, yet I gave her not power to meddle with my Apprentice nor doe I think that she ever did with your son unless in a mild and friendly way to give him good Counsaile. I shall say no more but shall refer you unto your son Isaac who have bin I think some time in my house to see and might observe my wife's temper demeanour and carriadge amongst and toward her servants, and let him declare unto you the truth and spare not.[70]

The correspondence of wives reveals both practical shrewdness and a wide range of interests beyond their household, husband, and children. They followed the marriages and careers of their kin, visited friends and the sick, fraternized with their female gossips, attended church, read silently and aloud, chatted, told stories, played cards and games, worked with the needle, strolled around the streets and parks, and exercised

---

[66] Household expenses, WAM, MS 54, 114, 1676–9; P. Bearcroft, *An Historical Account of Thomas Sutton* (1737), 28.
[67] G. Walker, "Women, Theft, and the World of Stolen Goods" in *Women Crime and the Courts*, ed. J. Kermode and G. Walker (1994), 89.
[68] F. Kirkman, *The Unlucky Citizen* (1673), preface.
[69] H. Smith, *Preparative to Marriage* (1591), 52, 75.
[70] Letter from Nathaniel Cock to Mrs. Elizabeth Terry dated 10 May 1667, KAO, MS U 22/E7. The boy had clearly overspent on clothing in excess of the £17 provided by Cock and in addition was short the large sum of £83.5.2 received of customers in the shop.

influence and patronage in matchmaking.[71] The wife of an Elizabethan merchant not only attended civic functions with her husband, but had an independent social life, dining out with her friends in London and the country, while her husband dined with his friends, and attending funerals on her own.[72] It was not just husbands who caroused with their cronies in the taverns and alehouses. The wife of a pewterer was among those killed when a bear-baiting ring collapsed in 1583.[73] Jane Papillon "consulted about my nephew Broadnax his maryage but found noe certaine account of the person to satisfaction."[74] The wife of John Temple, a goldsmith, had a wife who played the harpischord after dinner "till she tired everybody."[75]

Some wives found relief from boredom or mundane tasks in religion, where they could assert their independence. They commandeered their own space and manipulated the gendered conventions of seating and dress to create their own identities. They sustained their self-esteem within a system that curtailed female personal autonomy in theory, but could not stifle strong personalities. Gouge was attacked by city wives for harping on obedience and recommending a diminution of their property rights.[76] Housework was hard work, which Hannah Woolley sought to professionalize, and housewives, like Rachel Pengelly, were proud of their efficiency and skills.[77] Wives felt entitled to their one-third; they valued their labor and expected to receive as widows not only what they had brought into the marriage but a bonus for what they had contributed as wives.[78]

Although housewives did in effect free their husbands for public roles and sometimes took over more than the household when their husbands held public office, the division between public and private was permeable. Wives of businessmen had a social function and accompanied their husbands to city affairs and livery functions.[79] Indeed some often had

---

[71] B. Capp, "Separate Domains" in *The Experience of Authority*, ed. P. Griffiths and S. Hindle (1996), 139.
[72] BL, Cotton Vespasian MS F xvi, fos 39–40.
[73] M. Butler, *Theatre and Crisis, 1632–1642* (Cambridge, 1984), 300.
[74] Letter, KAO, MS U1015/F2, 12 Dec.
[75] Pepys, *Diary*, vol. 8, 82.
[76] A. Fletcher, "The Protestant Idea of Marriage" in *Religion, Culture, and Society in Early Modern Britain*, ed. A. Fletcher and P. Roberts (New York, 1994), 167.
[77] BL, Add. MS 32,456; E. Hoby, *Virtue of Necessity* (Ann Arbor, 1989), 171.
[78] V. Brodsky, "Widows in Late Elizabethan London," 146.
[79] G. Hadley, *Citizens and Founders* (1978), 77; seating list for a dinner given by Sir John Moore as Lord Mayor, GLL, MS 507, 17 Oct. 1681. Sometimes the sexes were segre-

greater social ambitions than their husbands. Jacobean and Restoration comedy consistently lampooned the vanity and affected airs of city wives. In Philip Massinger's *City Madam* of 1632, Lady Frugal entertains grandiose dreams before she is forced to accept the life of a merchant's wife.[80] Thomas Gainsford was one of many who thought that merchants' wives had too much freedom, that their husbands denied them nothing: the wife "goes at her pleasure and will not be restrained from any sights or delights or merry meetings where they may shew their beauties or riches."[81] Such characters had their counterparts in real life who pressed their husbands to acquire a mansion in smart areas of London and a knighthood, who kept fashionable company and aped the gentry.

FIDELITY

Fidelity in marriage is harder to ascertain. The dramatists queried the sexuality of citizens and depicted voracious wives seducing their apprentices.[82] Jacobean and Restoration comedy retold stories of old businessmen routinely cuckolded by young wives; women were depicted as sexual predators, though dependent on men.[83] Thomas Shadwell put a haberdasher's wife of ill repute into the pit at the playhouse, where she indulged in repartee with the gallants.[84] Sir Richard Blackmore attacked the genre, because "the wives of citizens are highly encouraged to despise their husbands."[85] Strangely, however, plays like *The London Cuckold* (1681) were popular with the citizens whom they mocked.[86] The bawdy literature and ballads like *The Quaker's Wife* and *London Libertine* milked the same themes: the sexual inadequacy of husbands, the transmission of venereal disease, and businessmen and their families brought

gated at functions, such as the Corpus Christi plays in York: see D. M. Palliser, "Civic Mentality" in *The Tudor and Stuart Town*, ed. J. Barry (1990), 237.
[80] J. Loftis, *Comedy and Society* (Stanford, 1959), 21.
[81] Gainsford, *Rich Cabinet*, 28.
[82] *A Curtain Lecture* (1638), 198–205; S. Shepherd, *Amazons and Warrior Women* (Brighton, 1981), 47.
[83] R. Thompson, *Unfit for Modest Ears* (1979), 107–10, 114; T. B. Leinwald, "This Gulph of Marriage," *Womens Studies* 10 (1984): 246. It has been argued that men married for sex but wanted harmony, whereas women married for advantage and then wanted sex: see *The Batchelars Banquet*, ed. F. Gildenhuys, vol. 109 (Barnaby Riche Society, 1993), 40.
[84] T. Shadwell, *Works*, ed. M. Summers (1927), 200.
[85] Loftis, *Comedy and Society*, 29.
[86] A. H. Scouten and R. D. Hume, "Restoration Comedy and Its Audience," *Yearbook English Studies* 10 (1960): 48.

to ruin by whoring.[87] Nonetheless, insofar as there was any consensus, citizen comedy seems to have been predicated on the assumption that marriage was a partnership, that sexual desire was natural, and that both husbands and wives should be chaste.[88]

It is difficult to know whether sexual relations continued throughout a marriage, because few diaries survive, like that of Samuel Jeake, Jr., who intermittently recorded his sexual activity in shorthand.[89] Inventories suggest, however, that husbands and wives, at least late in life, had separate chambers when they lived in spacious houses.[90] Thomas Nash, who was not slow to castigate sensuality, noted (with a surfeit of negatives) that Londoners had no "leisure not onely not to watch against sinne but not so much as once to thinke of sinne . . . in bedde wives must question their husbands about housekeeping and providing for the children and familie."[91] Many examples of adultery, impotence, and frigidity are recorded in suits by husbands and wives for restitution of conjugal rights, nullity, and separation, and many more such cases would never have reached the courts because of the expense and public exposure.

A good husband, counseled Francis Lenton, "is satisfied with the breasts of his own bedfellow."[92] But husbands were inevitably unfaithful, sometimes with whores but most commonly within the household, where they seduced their maidservants, sometimes while their wife was delivering a child or in the country.[93] There are scattered but frequent indications in private diaries that the lecherous groping that Pepys recorded in such detail was widely practiced. Nehemiah Wallington fought against filthy thoughts and the fearful sin of adultery: he "had an exceedingly burning desire" for another woman, but "I did consider that God did see me though no other did see me."[94]

---

[87] *Broadside Ballads of the Restoration*, ed. F. B. Fawcett (1930), no. 10; *The London Bawd* (1705); E. Foyster, "A Laughing Matter," *Rural History* 4 (1993): 8.

[88] A. Leggatt, *Citizen Comedy in the Age of Shakespeare* (Toronto, 1973), 128.

[89] Jeake, *Diary*, 25. Although many diaries must have been lost or destroyed, it is doubtful whether many merchants were obsessive enough about sex to keep daily notes.

[90] Inventory of Richard Hill, BL, Add. MS 5488, fo. 115, 1659.

[91] T. Nash, *Christ's Tears over Jerusalem* (1593; reprint, 1970), 74.

[92] F. Lenton, *Characterismi* (1631), 37.

[93] I. W. Archer, *Pursuit of Stability* (1991), 214, 232; P. Griffiths, *Youth and Authority* (Oxford, 1996), 276; A. C. Carter, *The English Reformed Church in Amsterdam* (Amsterdam, 1964), 172; C. Littleton, "Social Interactions of Aliens" in *The Strangers Progress*, ed. R. Vigne and G. C. Gibbs, vol. 26 (Proceedings of the Huguenot Society of London, 1995), 225. One might speculate that many business contacts and deals were made at brothels.

[94] GLL, MS 204, fo. 17.

Wives also seem to have strayed, though they had to face the double standard and more severe penalties than men. Their "honesty" or reputation largely rested on their sexual behavior, though in business circles accusations of idleness were considered equally slanderous. A Newcastle apprentice who called Judith Hall "an idle woman and a base slut" was sent to prison until he recanted, submitted in public, and apologized in person at her house with a witness.[95] Some husbands do appear to have simply ignored their wife's infidelity, and Ned Ward advised husbands to forgive their wives' adultery.[96] But partible inheritance made it important to ensure that all children were legitimate.

Journalists reported many stories that cannot be verified. Ned Ward claimed that "citizens post to their country houses and leave their Prentice to comfort their wives" who were insatiable, younger, and seeking gaiety and attention; they tempted their husbands' apprentices "to open the book of Generation in his master's absence and to point out the third letter in the Alphabet."[97] Although wives were often escorted in public by their maids or the apprentice, the latter could be conspirators rather than watchdogs. Henry Peacham relates the story of a tradesman's wife who went to the theater with the apprentice and had her purse stolen from under her petticoat: she felt a hand there "but I did not thinke he had come for that."[98] Tom Brown claimed that some wives of merchants worked for the infamous Madam Cresswell.[99]

Some examples have been documented. John Mitchell of Wakefield, who had three sons and one daughter, bequeathed his wife, Beatrice, only £8 and her apparel because she "hath plaid the whore with divers and wente awaie from me."[100] Richard Frewin left his estate to his brother and only £10 to his wife "for reasons best known to myself."[101] Wives are known to have slept with the apprentice, once in the presence of a maid, though the incidence of such cases should not be exaggerated.[102] In 1609 Edmund Foster found out that his master's wife was commit-

---

[95] *Newcastle Records Merchant Adventurers*, ed. F. W. Dendy and J. R. Boyle, vol. 93 (Surtees Society, 1895), 169.
[96] E. Ward, *The Forgiving Husband and Adulteress Wife* (1708), 9.
[97] E. Ward, *The Modern World Disrobd* (1708), 155; idem., *The Reformer* (1700); idem., *A Legacy for Ladies*, 117.
[98] H. Peacham, *The Art of Living in London* (1642), 5.
[99] T. Brown, *Amusements Serious and Comical*, ed. A. L. Hayward (1927), 429, 443.
[100] *North Country Wills, 1558–1604*, vol. 121 (Surtees Society, 1912), No. clxiii, 1591.
[101] PCC, Clarke 129.
[102] Griffith, *Youth and Authority*, 270, 278–80. An affair between a journeyman and his mistress is cited in Earle, *City Full of People*, 234.

ting adultery with another merchant.[103] Thomas Pitt considered that his wife had committed some indiscretion at Bath. On at least one occasion, in the household of Samuel Self, bookseller of Norwich, husband and wife cooperated in a ménage à trois, publicly fornicated with third parties, and indulged in flagellation.[104]

DURATION OF MARRIAGES

Death did cut short some unions. Henry Riddell who died at Elbing in 1597 left £50 to Elizabeth Liddell "whom I did meane to make my wife."[105] The daughter of brewer Thomas Courn died of smallpox on her wedding day.[106] Mary Cullum married John Sherbrook and died at age eighteen.[107] But the majority of businessmen could expect to spend many years married, which must for the poorly matched have seemed an eternity. Pepys could not remember in 1666, on his wedding anniversary, how many years he had been married.[108] The record among businessmen seems to belong to Edward Ames, married for 60 years with 23 children, but other long-lived marriages include those of John Ireland (50 years and 12 children), Abraham Elton (50), Francis Covel (42), Henry and Elizabeth Maddison (40 and 16 children), James Yonge (38), and John Beare (34).[109]

The median duration of marriages decreased slightly from 24 to 23.5 years between periods I and II; those lasting more than 30 years stayed constant at 36 percent of the total. Length of marriage was related to wealth. The median length in bracket I was only 12 years, compared with 24.8 in bracket II, 22.7 in bracket III, and 32.8 in bracket IV. A clear downward trend is also visible over time. The mean/median duration in cohort I was 34 years, in cohort II 29, in cohort III 24/25, and in cohort IV 18/19 years.

In comparison, only half of all marriages in Elizabethan London lasted

[103] L. Gowing, *Domestic Dangers* (Oxford, 1996), 191.
[104] L. Stone, "Libertine Sexuality in Post-Restoration England," *Journal of History Sexuality* 10 (1991–2): 512–17.
[105] *Durham Wills and Inventories, 1543–1602*, vol. 112 (Surtees Society, 1906), 167.
[106] J. Stow, *Survey of London*, vol. 4, ed. J. Strype (1720), 109.
[107] *Miscellanea Genealogica et Heraldica*, vol. 2, 160.
[108] Pepys, *Diary*, vol. 7, 318.
[109] E. Hatton, *A New View of London*, vol. 2 (1708), 435, 446, 548; J. Yonge, *Plymouth Memoirs*, ed. J. J. Bickerlegg (1951), 41; Stow, *Survey*, vol. 2, 35; H. Bourne, *The History of Newcastle upon Tyne* (Newcastle, 1736), 66; M. Elton, *Annals of the Eltons* (Stroud, 1994), 44.

Table 2.1. *Duration of Marriages (Percentage of Known Cases)*

Years	Period I	Period II	Bracket I	Bracket II	Bracket III	Bracket IV	Cohort I	Cohort II	Cohort III	Cohort IV
1–5	11.1	10.3	20.0	5.4	10.6	7.4	10.5	8.3	8.5	17.4
6–10	11.1	10.3	20.0	10.8	12.8	3.7	–	10.4	11.6	8.7
11–15	11.1	7.9	10.0	–	9.9	3.7	–	4.2	9.3	17.4
16–20	6.7	11.2	20.0	8.1	8.5	7.4		6.3	8.5	17.4
21–25	11.1	14.1	10.0	27.0	14.9	3.7	10.5	10.4	14.0	13.0
26–30	13.3	10.3	10.0	21.6	7.1	14.8	21.1	12.5	10.0	8.7
Over 30	35.6	36.0	10.0	27.0	36.2	59.3	57.9	47.9	37.2	17.4
Median	24.0	23.5	12.0	24.8	22.7	32.8	34.0	29.0	24.2	17.5
Mean	24.6	24.8	18.0	26.2	24.3	30.0	33.7	28.4	25.4	18.7
Total	45	242	10	37	141	27	19	48	129	23

more than 10 years and one-third 15 years; second marriages had a
median length of 2.1 years.[110] After 1660 the median age of widowhood
was 35, and the average length of marriage was 13 years.[111] In one-third
of first marriages of the peerage (1558–1740) one spouse, usually the
wife, died within 15 years, and the median duration of marriages among
landowners was 22 years in the first and 19 in the second half of the
seventeenth century.[112] In Abingdon it increased from 10 to 12 years
in the sixteenth century to 18 years (1600–59), falling to 15 years
(1660–1720).[113] In Colyton 20 years was a normal span, though one-
fourth of marriages lasted 35 years.[114] In rural Lincolnshire the mean
duration of marriages was 17.9 years and among the Leeds aldermen 36
years.[115] The mean for urban English Quakers (1650–99) was 17.5 years,
though American Quaker marriages lasted 31 years.[116] In sharp contrast,
in Jamaica the mean length of marriage fell from 9 years 6 months
(1666–78) to 6 years 4 months (1679–91) to 4 years 9 months (1692–
1704).[117]

CONFLICT

William Vaughan, a bachelor fellow of Jesus College, Oxford, who
seemed quite knowledgable about brothels, distinguished four kinds
of matrimony: "of honor, of love, of toyle and of grief."[118] Among the
innumerable sources of marital discord, some of which were cataloged
in matrimonial literature, were emotional intensity and deprivation,
food, housing, money, differences of age and interests, religion, and
incompatible personalities. Both husbands and wives could be cruel,
cold, hateful, morose, brutish, obsessive, jealous, venomous, angry,

---

[110] Brodsky, "Widows in Late Elizabethan London," 136.
[111] Earle, *City Full of People*, 162.
[112] L. Stone, *The Crisis of the Aristocracy* (Oxford, 1964), fig. 16, app. xxvi; *idem., The Family, Sex, and Marriage* (1977), 57.
[113] B. J. Todd, "The Remarrying Widow," in *Women in English Society*, ed. M. Prior (1985), table 2.3, 61, 65.
[114] P. Laslett, *Family Life and Illicit Love* (Cambridge, 1977), table 5.1.
[115] J. W. Kirby, "Restoration Leeds," *Northern History* 22 (1986): 170; J. A. Johnston, "Family, Kin, and Community," *Rural History* 6 (1995): 185.
[116] R. T. Vann and D. E. C. Eversley, *Friends in Life and Death* (Cambridge, 1992), table 3.10; R. V. Wells, "Quaker Marriage Patterns," *William and Mary Quarterly*, 39 (1972): 427.
[117] T. Burnard, "A Failed Society," *Journal of Social History* 28 (1994): 67.
[118] For conflict over relations with children and kin see chapters 4 to 6. W. Vaughan, *The Golden Grove*, bk. 2 (1600), chap. 2.

distant, and indifferent. Henry Newcombe could not understand why a substantial tradesman, Mr. Wrigley, was unable to relate to his wife, despite the fact that both led Christian lives, and noted that they lived and died alone.[119] Since urban houses offered less privacy than country homes, it must have been hard for an afflicted spouse to hide or escape. In the absence of resident kin, couples had to fend for themselves.

Even wives who accepted that they had a duty to obey their husbands had difficulty, on occasion, in repressing their personalities or their tongues. As portrayed in the theater, they conspired with their maidservants and outmaneuvered their husbands, exploiting the latter's primary interest in domestic harmony and a smoothly run household. Silence was considered golden in a wife, not just because it enhanced the husband's authority, but because it gave him peace and quiet. Richard Smythe commented on the deceased mistress Franklin in 1663 that she was "a woman very free of her tongue, her husband poor."[120] Catherine Barnaby was such a scold and so litigious that her husband fled abroad to avoid her.[121] John Scattergood took his uncle, Roger, to India but had to send him home because he was too lazy; his uncle, however, "says he would rather live in an oven than with my Aunt Scattergood."[122] Thomas Pitt's invective against his wife was returned in kind (alternating with flattery), and her son, Robert, endorsed one of her letters "my mother's letter about her power to embroil my father's affairs."[123] A common complaint of merchants was that their wives gossiped. Thomas Papillon was enraged when alderman Milner's wife spread rumors about him.[124]

A much more important source of dissension, then as now, was money. Drew Mompesson, who married an older, wealthy widow, wrangled with his wife constantly over property.[125] Husbands sometimes tried to appropriate the separate property of their wives. The most frequent disputes occurred, however, over spending. Some merchants, like Lionel Cranfield, were miserly and made their wives account strictly for all

[119] H. Newcombe, *Autobiography*, ed. R. Parkinson, o.s., vol. 26 (Chetham Society, 1852), 96.
[120] Smyth, *Obituary*, 57.
[121] *Cal. S. P. Dom Chas I*, cccxxxii.
[122] B. P. Scattergood, "John Scattergood," *Contemporary Review* 134 (1928): 219.
[123] H. M. C. *Fortescue*, vol. 1, 35–6; letter from Jane Pitt, dated 19 Dec. 1699, PRO, C 110/87.
[124] KAO, MS U 1015/C25.
[125] *John Isham Merchant Adventurer*, ed. G. D. Ramsay, vol. 21 (Northamptonshire Record Society, 1962), xcvi.

household expenditures. Some wives, once no longer restrained by the sumptuary laws, spent heavily on clothes and jewelry.[126] Defoe blamed such behavior on husbands who exaggerated their wealth.[127] Even the pious Jane Papillon pinned inside her religious journal a list of her diamond and pearl necklaces, numbering each stone and pearl.[128] Matthew Ashton's German wife bought expensive furniture.[129] Thomas Pitt fumed over his wife's extravagance and refused to pay her bills: "if she can't live upon the income of ye land, let her starve and all her children with her."[130]

Often it was the husband whose financial difficulties destabilized the family. When the husband of Sarah Robinson hid behind her to evade payment on a note, she told the lender: "would have you give him no quarter for hee is a digraceful roog."[131] Mary Atwood alternated between sympathy with and resentment at her husband's financial predicament.[132] She moved away and gave excuses for not visiting him or writing. "You complain of me for not writing and I think I have the most cause for I have writ so many letters that I resolved to write no more till I had heard from you. . . . I thank you for your wine you sent me, I would not have had you send me so much. Pray let me hear from you which is all the comfort I have." On the one hand, she wanted him to "have your liberty without which all the world to me is nothing"; on the other hand, "pray let me beg you to do all you can to get some imployment tho it be but small; it will be better than to spend your time as you do now without either profit or content. . . . I wish to God I could be any ways a comfort or assistant to you or servicable to my father or mother in your troubles. I would do it with all my soul. . . . I will write to my father, but I doubt it is too soon to write to him yet for money, so if you pleas to send me 3 or 4 pound or what you can conveniently spare."

Mary needed money for the children's clothes, health, and education, to pay her bills, and repay her loans from kin. "I hope when you have

---

[126] Bill for fabrics for Madam Taylor, ULL, MS 473, 29 June 1677.
[127] D. Defoe, *Complete Tradesman* (1727), 120.
[128] KAO, MS U 1015/F12.
[129] Receipts of Matthew Ashton, Bod, MS German C 21.
[130] W. Hedges, *Diary*, ed. H. Yule, vol. 78 (Hakluyt Society, 1888), xciiii; PRO, C 110/81.
[131] Letter to Nathan Simpson dated 12 May 1723, PRO, C 104/13–14.
[132] Letters from Mary to William Atwood dated 10 April, 12 June, 19 and 31 July, 21 Oct., 19 Dec 1685, PRO, C 109/23/1. From the context it appears that the "father" in her correspondence is her father-in-law, William Atwood, Sr., though some ambiguity remains. Usually she signs herself "your ever loving wife," but when angry or upset, she signs "your disconsolate wife."

money to spare you will remember me for your poor children will quickly want clothes and my father's allowance will not maintain us here." Atwood had promised "that you would send me some money and I think I may expect it long enouf for I see you think no more of it but I must be contented for it is but as I did expect that when I was out of sight I should be out of mind." At the same time she sent him a hamper with puddings for Christmas, chatted about their daughter, wished him a better New Year, and expressed concern about his bout of ill health. "I have now some hopes that in time you may live to see an end of your troubles," but in the meantime she asked him if he would object if she moved farther away to Norfolk.

Wills sometimes suggest that relations between husband and wife had been strained or that the wife rated a low priority. In some cases provision was stingy or a wife just received back what she had originally contributed to the marriage. Husbands might will their goods to other beneficiaries in order to prevent their personalty from passing to their widows.[133] Sometimes a wily husband left his wife more than her mandatory one-third part, but conditional on her assuming unwanted responsibilities or accepting other provisions that she disliked. John Lemming even used his wife's personal effects as an enforcement mechanism: "if she be content with what I give her and not otherwise I give her a gould chaine with all her rings jewels and apparell."[134]

Sometimes the widow only received houseroom together with the contents of her widow's chamber, plus an annual allowance.[135] Henry Shershaw, for example, left his widow £100 and the feather bed, household implements, and other goods, "which she had when I married her," her chamber rent free, and £5 p.a. rent from the house for maintenance.[136] William Sanderson just gave his wife her chamber in the house and its contents, the goods she had brought into the marriage, plus £60.[137] William Fellows, a cooper, gave his widow £2,000 plus his house, but

---

[133] Inheritance by widows is discussed fully in chapter 9 and distribution between widows and children in chapter 5.

[134] PCC, Cambell 95, 1642.

[135] Although beneficiaries and creditors sometimes challenged what a widow regarded as her paraphenalia, the "widow's chamber" was broadly defined in London. Thomas Greenley (PCC, Ruthen 166, 1657) thought it necessary to specify that some childbed sheets, linens, and a holland apron in his wife's chamber should pass to his daughter. Rooms in the former conjugal residence constituted a scaled-down version of the dower house. See also *Wills from the Archdeaconry of Suffolk*, ed. M. E. Allen (Woodbridge, 1989), xi.

[136] PCC, Berkeley 19, 1656.   [137] PCC, Berkeley 19, 1656.

she was required to provide a chamber for the apprentice, a cousin who was named executor and beneficiary.[138] Richard Sheriff, a barber surgeon, left his widow his house with a provision that his brother could also use it.[139] The childless Thomas Arnold, a clothworker, named a nephew joint heir with his wife and instructed that all his household goods "be divided when my wife gives up housekeeping or a year after my decease."[140]

Businessmen did not always make the widow their residual legatee, and sometimes they preferred kin, servants, or friends. John Mills, a clothworker, gave his wife only £5 for a ring, plus her chamber and diet, in addition to her one-third.[141] Grocer Arthur Young left his wife only £5 and the residue of his estate to his two brothers and cousins.[142] In 1605 Francis Saire deducted from his wife's one-third the amount he was owed by his father-in-law.[143] Joseph Chaffer, a pewterer, left his widow an annuity of £90, but it was to be paid out of a loan of £1,370 he had made to his brother-in-law.[144] John Vassall made his brother his residual legatee and just gave his widow back the "dowry or portion which was promised me by her father and mother or that should have been given me with her for and respect and in lieu of her jointure settled upon her."[145]

Marital violence also occurred. Usually it was the husband who was the aggressor, often after heavy drinking with his cronies at the tavern. Abuse could be triggered by imagined disobedience, laziness, or incompetence, by personal frustration, by resentment at one's wife's friends and relations, or by efforts to appropriate the wife's separate estate.[146] George Churchouse, a failed goldsmith, treated his wife cruelly. Mary Pepys, if even half of her deposition is true, was brutally treated by her husband, Charles.[147] The Begynhof church in Amsterdam examined several resident English merchants for beating their wives.[148] Sarah Boddington's

---

[138] PCC, Nabbs 183, 1660.   [139] PCC, Skynner 66, 1627.   [140] PCC, Laud 94, 1662.
[141] PCC, Ruthen 298, 1657.   [142] PCC, Pile 341, 1636.
[143] *Durham Wills, 1604–49*, vol. 142 (Surtees Society, 1929), 10.
[144] PCC, Pell 126, 1659.   [145] PCC, Hyde 29, 1665.
[146] M. H. Hunt, "Wife Beating," *Gender and History* 4 (1992): 16–17; the number of cases cited is very small.
[147] M. Ingram, *Church Courts, Sex, and Marriage* (Cambridge, 1987), 184; J. Cox, *Hatred Pursued beyond the Grave* (1993), 25–7; T. Hearne, *Reliquiae Herniana*, ed. J. Bliss and J. B. Brown (1966), 339. A particularly brutal case of both verbal and physical abuse is that of Thomas Bifield, cited in Earle, *City Full of People*, 236; the Quaker Skinner, Thomas Bifield, must have been a different person.
[148] Carter, *English Reformed Church*, 61–2.

husband, Robert Wakeman, pulled her out of bed by her hair, tore off her clothes, abused her verbally, threatened her life, and took her separate maintenance; she decided to stay in the house, when he absconded because of losses in business, "that nothing might be embezzled," but eventually she was turned out. Her father had to support her children, and she had to live with her father and brother until she "grew very fat" and died.[149]

Sometimes, however, the wife was the aggressor, asserting her rights forcibly, screaming insults, or acting belligerently toward servants, lodgers, and customers. A young Quaker wife traveling with her husband, a ship captain, was proud and not Quaker-like, according to a passenger.[150] George Trosse describes his drunken master and "sensual and irreligious" wife fighting constantly with words and blows, in and out of bed.[151] More ominously, the wife of Gilbert Wright consulted a cunning man to find out if she would outlive her husband.[152] Ambrose Asty asked in his will for an autopsy, should he die within twenty-five miles of his wife. Elizabeth Tichborn was bequeathed two shillings and sixpence, "it being so much as she would have given for Rattsbarn . . . to poison me."[153] A few cases of mental disorder and suicide can be traced to marital difficulties.[154] Madness sometimes afflicted one spouse and occasionally ran in the family; in Bristol one merchant "went by the name of mad Pitman," and his wife was said to have been a "crazy woman."[155] The beautiful second wife of Abraham Brown, a vintner, drowned herself in the Thames after the fire of 1666.[156]

Some marriages ended in failure, though they could only formally end with death. Under ecclesiastical law, a contract of marriage could be annulled, or husband and wife could be separated by bed and board. Annulments, the grounds for which were rather unsavoury (bigamy, impotence, incest, or murder), were rare in the business community.

---

[149] GLL, MS 10,823/1, fo. 60. Several examples are given by Gowing, *Domestic Dangers*, but the occupations of offenders are not specified.

[150] J. Danhers and P. Sluyter, *Journal of a Voyage to Newport 1679–80*, ed. H. C. Murphy, vol. 1 (Memoirs Long Island Historical Society, 1867), 103.

[151] G. Trosse, *Life*, ed. A. W. Brink (Montreal, 1974), 58.

[152] W. Lilly, *History of His Life* (1715), 28–9.

[153] *Barbados Records, Wills, and Administrations, 1639–80*, ed. J. M. Sanders (1979), 359.

[154] M. MacDonald and T. R. Murphy, *Sleepless Souls* (Oxford, 1990), 262; MacDonald, *Mystical Bedlam* (Cambridge, 1981), 47.

[155] *Barbados Records, Wills, and Administrations, 1700–1725*, ed. J. M. Sanders (Baltimore 1982), 82; BL, Add. 5540, fos. 29–32.

[156] K. Rogers, *Old London* (1935), 92.

Separation, usually on grounds of extreme cruelty, adultery, or absence for more than five years, was more common. Private separations by deed, usually arranged by family members, occur from the 1650s onward. Thomas Frederick was separated by deed from his estranged wife, who left him with three daughters.[157] The wife of Sir Samuel Starling secured a separation and ultimately married Viscount Villiers. Divorce with the right of remarriage, although possible by private act after 1670, was not a practical option for businessmen. Paul Bayning refused to provide maintenance for his second wife, after they had separated, and tried to divorce her through the archbishop of Canterbury, the lord treasurer, and a bill in Parliament.[158] Stephen Jermyn claimed that he was entrapped by Sarah Bell at the age of eighteen while apprentice to a wine merchant; the church courts found that his wife had committed gross adultery, but his bill for divorce was rejected in the House of Lords.[159]

HARMONY

In literature, as in real life, differences between spouses and reproach were frequently followed by concessions and compromise, if not connubial bliss.[160] As Ned Ward wisely observed, "marrying is but putting two lovers into a Ring, to fight for the britches," but after fighting they usually relapsed into fondness.[161] Although it is impossible to quantify and compare successful and failed marriages, there are numerous individual cases where conflict was resolved. Many couples worked hard to sustain their marriages. Mutual solidarity, shared friendship, and a host of other factors often proved sufficient to neutralize clashes of personality or overcome economic difficulties.

Matrimonial cases represent a tiny fraction of all marriages; in 1697 and between 1705 and 1707 the Consistory Court of London only heard sixty-one matrimonial cases and between 1700 and 1710 only 140.[162]

---

[157] E. H. Fellowes, *The Family of Frederick* (Windsor, 1988), 31.
[158] H. G. Gillespie, "The Rediscovery of an Elizabethan Merchant Adventurer," *Genealogical Magazine* 9 (1944): 432.
[159] HMC., House of Lords MSS (1706–8), 40–1.
[160] For some hypothetical marital quarrels see R. Snawsel, *A Looking Glasse for Married Folkes* (1610).
[161] E. Ward, *Marriage Dialogue* (1709), preface.
[162] T. Meldrun, "A Womens Court in London 1700–45," *London Journal* 19 (1994): table 1; P. Earle, "The Female Labour Market in London," *Economic History Review* 42 (1989): 329. Of 10,412 suits in the Court of Arches (1660–1913) brought by all social

Between 1660 and 1700, only forty-four separation suits were brought to the Court of Arches by wives on grounds of cruelty.[163] Although suits regarding marriage settlements increased in the late seventeenth century, the number was still small; only 2 percent of bills in chancery relate to settlements and only four merchants and one draper appear in a sample (1603–1712).[164]

Wives could be staunchly loyal, though loyalty came from the mind rather than the heart. William Sharpe's wife, pregnant and eager to return to England from Barbados, wrote to her sister that she could not leave her husband because that "is a treason I dare not trust my thoughts with."[165] Frequently mutual love for their children drew couples together, though some childless couples appear to have been particularly close, perhaps because they had no children to distract them and create friction. There is no doubt that some couples sustained a high level of affection over many years of marriage. In their letters, when separated, they were tender, solicitious, anxious about news, sad about being alone, and keen to anticipate the return of their partner.[166]

As early as the 1550s John Johnson wrote affectionately to his wife.[167] Edward Allen wrote charming letters to his wife stating "as welcome to me shall you be with your rags as yf you were in cloath of gold or velvet. Trye and see."[168] John Verney expressed his feelings openly to his first wife.[169] Jane Papillon was completely obsessed with spiritual matters in her journal, but in her frequent letters to her husband, Thomas, while he was in exile, she tells him about the house, the health and habits of the children, family gatherings, births and deaths, local events, and the

---

and occupational groups, only some 10 to 14 percent were matrimonial cases: see B. R. Masters, "Some Genealogical Sources," *Genealogical Magazine* 20 (1982): 226; L. Stone, *Road to Divorce* (Oxford, 1990), 32–4. Some cases were clearly initiated to make trouble, not to reach a settlement, and others were collusive. On slander cases, which were much more common in the ecclesiastical courts of first instance see Gowing, *Domestic Dangers*.

[163] E. Foyster, "Male Honour," *Transactions of the Royal Historical Society*, 6th ser., 6 (1996): 216.

[164] Erickson, "Common Law," 28, and *Women and Property*, 127, table 7.3; S. Amussen, *An Ordered Society* (Oxford, 1988), 109.

[165] Letter to Mary Brook dated 12 Oct. 1665, Shropshire, RO, MS Acc 567.

[166] KAO, MS U 1015/C 27. Few poems were, however, penned about conjugal love, as distinct from love outside marriage: see M. Prior, "Conjugal Love" in *Women as Mothers in Pre-Industrial England*, ed. V. Fildes (1990), 180.

[167] B. Winchester, *Tudor Family Portrait* (1955), 69.

[168] Letter dated 21 Oct. 1603, *Henslow Papers*, vol. 2, ed. R. A. Foakes (1961), 18.

[169] *Verney Memoirs*, vol. 2, ed. F. P. Verney (1930), 364.

debauchery of the lower orders.[170] Merchants traveling abroad welcomed letters from their wives: Vallentine Franci, writing to Hoare and Company from Denmark, concluded "pray give my love to my wife and children and let her write to me per the 1st post."[171] Peter Ducane signed his letters "your affectionate husband."[172] John Dubois told his wife, "I love thee as my own soule."[173]

A perfect example of a warm relationship can be seen in the letters exchanged between the great ship captain and projector, Thomas Bowrey, and his wife, Mary, who spelled entirely by ear. Here is Mary writing to Thomas at his ship:

My dear tomee. Pray my dear let me hear from you as soon as you can that I may not whorry to write to you. . . . I take leave with my affectionate love to you and remain your ever loving wife till death . . . pray send word hou Vincy [presumably a dog] and pus doth . . . [he must write to her] for that's the only cumfort I have now.[174]

Here is Thomas writing to Mary at Bath, where she was taking the waters (with a gift of a small lacquered punch bowl):

My dear Molly . . . if you want anything else write me word and it shall be sent you for. I would not have you destitute of anything which may contribute to your health and satisfaction. . . . [Her dog Delle is] as rude as ever. . . . [The dog ate raw fish guts and became ill but he recovered] . . . and can play at Romps very well. Mistress if you please to come and play a little and then you may go back again to the Bath . . . I would not have you bathe beyond your strength. . . . I mightily want your company but will rather be without that enjoyment so long as it is for your good. . . . I cannot possibly be so long absent from the ship as a journey to the Bath does require else would very gladly be with you. . . . I am dear ducold, your every loving husband.[175]

RECOGNITION

The affection of businessmen for their wives was expressed in many ways. Richard Farrington in his diary thanked God for his marriage.[176]

[170] KAO, MS U 1015/C11/1, 15/4, F12.
[171] Letter dated 4 July 1696, PRO, C 104/11–12.
[172] Attachment to will of 11 May 1711, Essex, RO, MS D/DDCF3.
[173] D. Ormrod, "Puritanism and Patriarchy" in *Studies in Modern Kentish History*, ed. A. Detsicas and N. Yates (Maidstone, 1983), 134.
[174] Undated letter from Mary Bowrey to Thomas Bowrey, commander of the St. George galley at Spit Head, Portsmouth, GLL, MS 3041/1.
[175] Letters from Thomas Bowrey to Mary Bowrey dated 23, 26, 30 May and 8 June 1704, GLL, MS 3041/1.
[176] GLL, MS 2708, 30 Oct. 1705.

John Dunton wrote a eulogy to his wife.[177] Gervaise Disney was more patronizing, listing among his wife's virtues frugality, subjection, and sympathy: "she is a truly good woman, yet but a woman and therefore subject to humane Frailties."[178] Robert Perry on his deathbed "spake Dear Harte [speaking to his wife] I have a fair estate which I leave to thee."[179] John Harvey described his wife as "loving and kind to me but especially a good nurse to all my children."[180]

Both husbands and wives commemorated each other with plaques, gravestones, and monuments.[181] It is true that some monuments, like that of Customer Smythe, his wife, and twelve children, formally glorified the husband; the wives of Sir Hugh Hammersley and Sir Thomas Green were depicted on their knees praying.[182] But others were more egalitarian and intimate. Richard Farington recorded in his diary that his wife had died "to my unspeakable losse and griefe as also of many others and . . . she was interred in the middle aisle against the pulpit in Iver church . . . by my twelve children"; six months later "I erected a monument of marble in Iver church to the dear memory of my most loving and beloved wife and also of my 12 children."[183] Inscriptions recited the personal virtues of the deceased spouse and their arms were displayed to emphasize their dignity and status. In 1611 the widow of Barne Roberts erected a monument to her husband, one year after his death, with the inscription "if human worth could have preserved him still, he had been much too strong for Death to kill."[184]

Businessmen also expressed their feelings for their wives through gifts. Robert Gray, while traveling on business, frequently sent his wife tokens "from the trewe love of my hart."[185] Sir Henry Johnson spoiled his wife with gifts of expensive jewelry.[186] Husbands frequently made extravagant

---

[177] J. Dunton, *Life and Errors* (1705), 354–5.
[178] G. Disney, *Some Remarkable Passages* (1692), 54.
[179] Nuncupative will, PCC, Goare 78, 1637.   [180] PCC, Swann 58, 1623.
[181] There are innumerable monuments in churches and churchyards, dutifully recorded in county, urban, and parish histories. J. Stow, *Survey of London*, ed. Strype (1720) is a useful overall guide to London, but many monuments to London business families were placed in suburban churches, as businessmen moved their residences to the country: see, for example, *Northamptonshire Families*, ed. O. Barron (1906), 63.
[182] J. F. Wadmore, "Thomas Smythe," *Archaeologia Cantiana* 17 (1887): 203; E. Hatton, *A New View of London* (1708); B. Mackerell, *History and Antiquities of Kings Lynn* (1736), 128.
[183] GLL, MS 2708, 11 Aug. 1727, and 8 Feb 1727/8.
[184] T. Delaune, *The Present State of London* (1681), 58.
[185] T. S. Willan, *The Inland Trade* (Manchester, 1976), 123.
[186] BL, Add. MS 22,186, fo. 108.

or sentimental bequests to their widows, like the coach and horses presented by Sir Richard Dean, Nicholas Crisp, John Harvey, John Currer, and Sir Hugh Hammersley.[187] In 1709 Sir Godfrey Copley left his widow his collection of paintings, including five William Van de Veldes and his own portrait by Sir Godfrey Kneller.[188] In 1638 James Carcas left his widow "one long pillow of tentwork wherein is the history of 88 and the Powther plott of the fifth of November."[189]

Wills offer an index of the devotion of husbands to their wives, though they can be misleading because the widow's inheritance may have been specified in a prenuptial settlement. Nicholas Machell, for example, bequeathed his whole estate to his father because his widow had a jointure.[190] Widows were usually bequeathed the residue of an estate, particularly if the children were minors or there were no surviving children. Eliab Harvey settled his land on his sons, but they were instructed to let their mother live in his grand house for life with a full complement of servants at no charge.[191] Although a bequest of a couple of chambers of the marital residence may seem paltry, there was often only one house to share between widow and children. Having even two rooms gave a widow her own enclave where her authority was not challenged.

Merchant John Battie was one of several who left their wives one-third of their land as well as their personalty.[192] Thomas Wardle, a merchant tailor, gave his son his urban property but instructed him to give his widow the rental income in addition to her one-third.[193] Robert Bowyer, a grocer, gave his widow more than her one-third because she had been "loyal and kind."[194] Oliver Denner, a cutler, "in respect of the love and affection which I bear" gave his wife her full one-third plus the £400 that had been stipulated in their marriage settlement in lieu of her one-third.[195] Ralph Boyer, a haberdasher, gave his wife £100 in addition to her one-third in "testimony of my intire love and affection towards her."[196] Humphrey Bury, a clothworker, left his wife his entire estate "in consideration of intire love which I have."[197] Richard Lane was so impressed with how his wife had nursed him in his old age that he gave her more than £11,000 in land as well as some tenements in London.[198] Henry Meese left his Virginia estate to his four orphans, and his entire

[187] PCC, Sadler 82, 1635; PCC, Pile 103, 1636; PCC, Alchin 43; CLRO, CSB, iv.
[188] ULL, MS 186/3.   [189] PCC, Coventry 5.   [190] PCC, Seager 87, 1634.
[191] PCC, May 91, 1661.   [192] PCC, Pell 515, 1659.   [193] PCC, Nabbs 92, 1660.
[194] PCC, Hele 53, 1626.   [195] PCC, Ruthen 374, 1657.   [196] PCC, Pell 530, 1659.
[197] PCC, Nabbs 260, 1660.   [198] PRO, Prob 11/653/210–11.

English estate to his wife, even though her marriage settlement had only specified £200.[199] Mark Ewen left his widow more than her one-third to provide better subsistence for her and their children.[200] Richard Dyer, who devoted his entire will to spiritual reflections and recited the formula that "God would be his widow's husband, yea a father, a patron and defender" still left her all his worldly goods because "she is my flesh."[201]

LOSS

It is clear that spouses worried about each other's health. Husbands were tormented when their wives were sick or giving birth. "My wife is in a very afflicted condition soe that I know not what to do with her," wrote Sir Benjamin Bathurst.[202] Matthew Ashton apologized for complaining about delays in response to his requests, when he discovered that his correspondent had suffered from ill health and the loss of his dearest.[203] Thomas Firmin dreamed that his first wife died, and he did in fact lose her and all his children.[204]

Husbands often took extraordinary care in their wills to provide for every contingency. Sir Thomas Low provided that a woman who knew his wife's medical condition should stay with her, urged his children to allow their mother to live peacefully in the house without molestation, and suggested that the most dutiful second son should live with her.[205] A particular servant was often asked to stay with the widow.[206] Christopher Kaley bequeathed his wife £200 above her customary part "in token of my lovey towards her" and instructed his apprentice to help her, as did Thomas Lane and Thomas Walker.[207] George Simpson instructed his apprentices to help his widow and "all that I have I give to my wife [not giving one groat from her] and I think all too little for her."[208] Sometimes testators tried to control their widows from the grave: Edmund

---

[199] *American Wills Proved in London, 1661–1775*, ed. P. W. Coldham (1992), 33.
[200] PCC, Alchin 160, 1654.
[201] PCC, Twisse 621; the same wording was used by Jonas Wellin in PCC, Fines 63.
[202] Letter to William Fortrey dated 24 Sept. 1698, BL, Loan MS 57/102.
[203] Letter to Edward Franklin dated 18 Feb. (circa) 1680, Bod, MS Eng misc. C. 602, fol 4v°.
[204] J. Cornish, *The Life of Mr. Thomas Firmin* (1780), 20.
[205] PCC, Swann 31, 1623.
[206] Will of William Rodway, PCC, Hele 48, 1626.
[207] PCC, Audley 77, 1632; PCC, Alchin 471, 1654; PCC, Aylett 265, 1655.
[208] PCC, Parker 88, 1619.

Hale gave his wife their house and garden but specified that the "long
table with the forms and benches" should remain in the hall and the
drawing table with two leaves in the parlour"; his widow was, however,
permitted to "lop the trees for firewood."[209]

Loss of either spouse was a traumatic experience. Richard Smythe
commented cynically on the death of Lady Vyner: "a great loss to Sir
Robert Vynor she having during her life 2000 li per ann."[210] But
bereavement was a heavy burden to carry, and although death concentrated the mind of the survivor, ritual mourning was often necessary to
Christianize the grief, alleviate the shock, and accept permanent separation. The surviving spouse had to overcome melancholy and adapt to a
new life.[211] Yonge described the year 1709, when he lost his wife, his
grandson, and some friends, as "my grand climatoric."[212] Sarah Savage
noted in the back of her husband's pocketbook "my dear husband died
the first of September."[213] A few cases occur of one spouse dying very
soon after the other. The widows of Sir Cuthbert Buckle and Jacob
Delilliers were buried three weeks after their husbands, and the widow
of Benjamin Steele only survived for four days.[214]

Businessmen frequently stipulated that they should be buried near
their wives or their first wives, if they had remarried.[215] William Weston
instructed that he be buried against the pulpit in the middle aisle of St.
Gregory's near his wife's pew door; Jasper Chapman made the same provision.[216] John Quince left money and detailed instructions on the upkeep
of the vault that was to house first him and eventually his wife.[217] Robert
Stiles, a clothworker, gave £5 to the poor of Whitechapel to ensure that

---

[209] PCC, Berkeley 352, 1656.   [210] Smythe, *Obituary*, 104.
[211] Some of Richard Napier's patients were unable to cope with a spouse's death: see
MacDonald, *Mystical Bedlam*, table 3.3.
[212] Yonge, *Plymouth Memoirs*, 41.   [213] PRO, C 107/172.
[214] *London Visitation Pedigrees, 1664*, ed. J. B. Whitmore and A. W. H. Clarke, vol. 92
(Harlean Society, 1940), 52; GLL, MS 10,823.
[215] *Durham Wills and Inventories, 1543–1602*, 172, *1604–49*, 10, James Grey (1599) and
Francis Saire (1605); will of James Marshall, PCC, Audley 67, 1632; PCC, Russell 107,
1633; PCC, Pile 6, 1636; will of Humphrey Hawkins, PCC, Rivers 129, 1645; will of
John Barker, PCC, Fines 80, 1647; will of William Essington, PCC, Fairfax 181, 1649;
wills of William Bow and Edward Burton, PCC, Grey 169 and 180, 1651; will of
Francis Taylor, PCC, Aylett 197, 1655; will of Richard Bradshaw, PCC, Ruthen 272,
1657; will of George Tench, PCC, Ruthen 273; will of Benjamin Ward, PCC, Pell 9,
1659; will of Richard Davis, PCC, Nabbs 170, 1660; will of William Bowes, PCC, May
67, 1661; will of John Tufnall, PCC, Swann 72, 1699; 1694 will of Gilbert Upton in
W. Upton, *Upton Family Records* (1893).
[216] PCC, Bowyer 123, 1652; PCC, Alchin 367, 1654.
[217] PCC, Berkeley 435, 1656.

"he and his wife might have a burial place together next to his children in the churchyard" with a tombstone.[218] Nicholas Johnson instructed, on his deathbed, that his body be embalmed and carried to London to be buried beside his first wife.[219] Thomas Liddell of Newcastle instructed that he be buried next to his two wives.[220] The same was true of widows. Elizabeth Castelyn, when she remarried Roger Martin, had the body of her first husband, Thomas Knowles, moved to London so that she could be buried alongside both her husbands.[221] By this means the married couple was united in death.

SUMMARY

The married lives of seventeenth-century businessmen were infinitely diverse. No model can encapsulate the actual experience of marriage or adequately express the variations in human personality and behavior. It is impossible to generalize about changes in the character of marriage on the basis of opinions voiced in literary sources, as so many historians have misguidedly attempted. Where specific cases can be documented, the objectives and priorities of married couples in the business community do not appear to have changed fundamentally over time or in any linear direction. Nor were their marriages cut short by premature death as might be expected from other studies of the whole urban population.

There is certainly evidence of friction, infidelity, mistreatment, and disillusionment, of martyred wives and henpecked husbands, but there is just as much evidence that marriages were loving, chaste, and happy, that they gave couples the means and the will to withstand the trials of life. The majority, no doubt, fell somewhere between these two extremes. No index of uxorious bliss can be constructed and quantified, because contentment cannot be defined by objective criteria. In marriage, as in life, one man's or woman's meat is another's poison. Obvious cases of abuse and dysfunction can be identified, but there is no way of judging their proportional importance, because the overwhelming majority of families have left no record of their domestic life. It is clear, however, that marriage was not a static condition with fixed norms; it was a relationship that continuously evolved throughout life.

[218] PCC, Pell 248, 1659.   [219] Nuncupative will, PCC, Aylett 301, 1655.
[220] *Durham Wills, 1604–49*, 101; Palliser, "Civic Mentality," 110.
[221] M. B. Donald, *Elizabethan Monopolies* (Edinburgh, 1961), 57.

At a theoretical level, patriarchal attitudes were not seriously undermined by intellectual challenges, because they served to validate the gender hierarchy, to reassure men, and reinforce their dominance in the business community. In order to preserve the principle of female subordination, both law and convention chose to depict any compromise between equals as acquiescence to a superior. The wives of businessmen clearly benefited from municipal custom, and, if their customary rights were reduced at the end of the seventeenth century, they received greater recognition in the equity courts. But no comprehensive or exclusive ideology of marriage emerged, because objectives diverged too widely.

In reality, the advice literature and all the talk about marriage was largely irrelevant to the needs of actual families. Marriages were working partnerships based on reconciliation of differences, not a device to marginalize women or force them to sacrifice their independence and property to men in return for emotional security. For most spouses inequality and relative power were just not issues. They were preoccupied with handling the daily stress of cohabitation, with the realities of sickness and death, with both giving and receiving succor, not with esoteric theories of gender. Demographic factors, economic needs, and force of personality gave wives much more power and independence than they were supposed to have. Wives defined their own standards of acceptable behavior and reconstructed themselves with their husband's identity. Marriage in the business community did not just transfer power over women from father to husband. Companionate marriage required concessions from both partners and met needs overlooked or downplayed by theorists and historians of the family.

3

Widowers and Widows

All marriages ended with the death of one partner, leaving the survivor with new needs and responsibilities. Widowhood was not a fixed state or uniform experience but, like marriage, had its own life cycle, which was different for each individual and varied with wealth, the number of offspring, and length of bereavement. The relationship of widowers and widows to their children and kin necessarily changed as they and their siblings aged and their children matured and married.

What was the relative life expectancy of husbands and wives, the ratio of widowers to widows, and the length of widowhood? How often was the widow appointed executrix, and what did this entail? How frequently did survivors remarry, and when and who did they marry? What determined whether a widower or widow would remarry? What were the benefits and disadvantages of widowhood?

LIFE EXPECTANCY

John Aubrey intended to ask Sir William Petty "what is the medium of all lives whether fifty or sixty years" and settled for sixty-four, though he added "real time or age is but 32 years" allowing for childhood, sleep, devotion, and sickness.[1] Sir Thomas Browne identified "the great climactericall year, that is sixty three."[2] In the 1690s Edmund Halley put the life expectancy of men and women at 33.93 years at age twenty and 27.64 years at age thirty.[3] Death was not closely identified with old age,

---

[1] J. Aubrey, *Idea of Education*, ed. J. E. Stephens (1972), 104, 144.
[2] T. Browne, *Pseudoxia Epidemica*, vol. 1, ed. R. Robbins (Oxford, 1981), 334; multiples of seven were always credited with significance.
[3] Laslett, *The World We Have Lost*, 93.

because of high infant mortality, and contemporaries lacked a clear concept of when old age began, though the age of gravity conventionally began at fifty and old age at seventy.[4]

Longevity always caught the attention of antiquarians; Daniel Lysons listed many cases in London, and Ralph Thoresby, whose widowed aunt still retained her memory at ninety, in Leeds.[5] Although reports of centerians were probably exaggerated, a few businessmen, including some Jewish immigrants, reached and passed ninety.[6] A high level of infant mortality did not preclude a high life expectancy for those who reached twenty-five; indeed those tough enough to survive infancy were predisposed to have a long life span.[7] In the Wallington family John Sr. lived to eighty-six, John Jr. to sixty-four, and Nehemiah to sixty, but most of their children died young.[8]

The mean/median age at death of London businessmen fell from 62/64 in period I to 60/57 in period II; in the first quartile the median declined from 53 to 50 and in the third quartile it stayed constant at 72/71. The mean/median rose with wealth from 56/54 in bracket I, to 57/58 in bracket II, 66/66 in bracket III, and 69/70 in bracket IV; it fell sharply during the seventeenth century from 68/68 in cohort I to 58/59 in cohort II and 49/48 in cohort IV. This is consistent with other data for London. In Elizabethan London, the average life expectancy of 93 freemen at 26 was 28 years, and one-third lived to 60; freemen in the great companies lived longer, but there was no obvious difference between native Londoners and migrants.[9] In 1600–3 51 out of 488 residents (10.5 percent) of one London parish were over 65 and 8 were over 85.[10] The mean age of assistants in the Haberdashers Company in 1641 was 63.[11] The life expectancy of the children of Elizabethan aldermen at age 5 was 50 and

---

[4] R. Steele, *A Discourse Concerning Old Age* (1688), 9.

[5] D. Lysons, *London and Its Environs*, vol. 4, (1792–6), 227, 273; R. Thoresby, *Ducatus Leodiensis* (Leeds, 1816), 622–4; *idem., Diary*, vol. 2, ed. J. Hunter (1830), 427.

[6] A. S. Diamond, "The Community of the Resettlement," *Transactions of the Jewish Historical Society of England* 24 (1974): 143.

[7] Life span is different from average length of life; for methods of calculating life expectancy, which is not employed here in its strict technical sense, see L. I. Dublin, A. J. Lotka, and M. Spiegelman, *Length of Life* (New York, 1949), 21. On differential mortality see R. Woods, "On the Historical Relationship between Infant and Adult Mortality," *Population Studies*, 47 (1993): 195–219. On life expectancy in medieval England see J. T. Rosenthal, *Old Age in Medieval England* (Philadelphia, 1996), 124.

[8] P. S. Seaver, *Wallington's World* (Stanford, 1985), 70–1.

[9] Rappaport, *Worlds within Worlds*, 69.

[10] M. F. and T. H. Hollingsworth, "Plague Mortality Rates," *Population Studies*, 25 (1971): table 2; T. R. Forbes, *Chronicle from Aldgate* (New Haven, 1971), table 4. It is not clear how far these percentages are distorted by migration.

[11] I. W. Archer, *History of Haberdashers Company* (Chicester, 1991), 47.

Table 3.1. *Age at Death (Percentage of Known Cases)*

Age	Period I	Period II	Bracket I	Bracket II	Bracket III	Bracket IV	Cohort I	Cohort II	Cohort III	Cohort IV
Under 30	2.77	2.36	2.27	1.53	0.27	1.19	–	1.16	2.50	8.76
30–39	6.81	9.27	9.09	11.88	2.65	–	1.92	3.19	10.88	23.11
40–49	8.09	12.89	19.32	17.24	7.69	4.76	2.24	5.95	16.15	21.51
50–59	19.57	20.01	30.68	24.14	18.04	14.29	17.31	18.29	21.86	19.12
60–69	29.79	25.88	20.45	24.90	31.30	26.19	33.97	30.77	24.26	17.53
70–79	23.19	20.38	13.64	14.18	26.66	34.52	29.49	27.87	17.04	8.37
80+	9.79	9.22	4.55	6.13	13.40	19.05	15.06	12.77	7.32	1.59
Mean	62.21	60.20	55.88	57.35	65.67	68.50	68.04	65.39	58.19	49.02
Median	63.61	57.06	54.10	57.75	66.00	69.86	67.92	66.82	58.59	47.63
1st Quartile	53.44	50.06	46.17	46.81	57.65	60.88	60.93	57.93	47.02	37.36
3d Quartile	71.69	71.41	65.00	67.90	74.53	76.58	75.67	73.70	69.15	60.75
Total	470	1,909	88	261	754	84	312	689	1,121	251

the median age of the Jacobean aldermen was 71.3.[12] In every trade and town there were active merchants in their 60s and 70s.[13] John Whitson had 76 and Nicholas Farrar had 75 old men at their funerals, gowned as mourners to celebrate their longevity; Samuel Vassall sailed for Virginia with his children at the age of 80.[14]

Between 1590 and 1729 the life expectancy at age 25 of all London freemen improved steadily except for a relapse during 1630 and 1649: those dying under age sixty rose from 58 percent (1610–29) to 68 percent (1630–49), but then fell to 60 percent (1670–89) and 43 percent (1710–29), 9.9 percent lived beyond 60.[15] Freemen who left orphans (1660–1730) had a median age at death of 44.5, though the merchants in this sample reached 52 compared with 43 for haberdashers and 40 for apothecaries; clothworkers and mercers had a higher life expectancy than freemen of artisan companies; 10.4 percent of a sample of deponents in the Consistory Court were aged 55 or more.[16] Death rates were always higher in London than the country, because the numerous immigrants can be presumed to have lacked immunity to urban diseases, and they peaked in the 1670s and 1680s when the median age at death of London citizens fell to forty-four. There is an apparent contradiction between the high age at death and the high number of legal orphans. But it was late marriage and late fatherhood rather than early mortality that produced orphans.[17] The mean/median age of Jacobean aldermen who left orphans was 62.5/61; fourteen of them had a mean/median age of 71/72.[18] A father would also have been considered to have left an orphan if just one unmarried son or daughter under twenty-one remained in the family at his death.

[12] R. G. Lang, "The Greater Merchants of London" (D. Phil. diss., University of Oxford, 1963), 280.

[13] T. Gent, *History of Hull* (1735; reprint, Hull, 1869), 34, 36, 41.

[14] *Prerogative Court of Canterbury, Register of Soame*, ed. J. H. Lee (Boston, 1904), 120; J. Horn, *Adapting to a New World* (Chapel Hill, 1994), 263.

[15] P. Earle, "Age and Accumulation" in *Business Life and Public Policy*, ed. M. MacKendrick et al. (Cambridge, 1986): tables 3.1, 3.2. J. Boulton, "London Widowhood Revisited," *Continuity and Change* 5 (1990): 352, queries these figures because they clash with the burial evidence and suggests that they may only apply to the wealthy and may reflect some other bias in Boyd's list of citizens.

[16] Earle, *Making of the English Middle Class*, figure 11.3, table 4.7, 310, 390; life expectancy improved steadily after 1690. P. Earle, "The Female Labour Market in London," table 1.

[17] Late parenthood also reduces the value of marriage allegations as a means of calculating the life expectancy of the parents of those marrying.

[18] Lang, "Greater Merchants," 280.

Table 3.2. *Age at Death (Merchant
Adventurers of Newcastle, 1609–1700)*

Age	1609–59 % of Known Cases	1660–1700 % of Known Cases
Under 30	0.94	15.04
30–39	12.74	29.02
40–49	20.75	16.36
50–59	15.09	20.32
60–69	21.70	13.46
70–79	22.64	5.28
Over 80	6.13	0.53
Mean	58.12	44.92
Median	59.70	42.58
1st Quartile	36.07	33.10
3d Quartile	71.00	55.82
Total Cases	212	379

*Source: Newcastle Extracts from the Records of the
Merchant Adventurers*, ed. J. R. Boyle and D. W. Dendy
(Surtees Society, vol. 93, 1895, and vol. 101, 1899).

The life expectancy of provincial businessmen varied between region,
trade, and period. The mean/median age at death of those free of the
Merchant Adventurers Company of Newcastle was 58/60 (1609–60),
falling to 45/43 (1660–1700).[19] In Stratford (1570–1630) 31.5 percent
of men and 20.5 percent of women lived beyond 60, with a median age
at death of around 50 for men and under 40 for women.[20] The mean
age of those leaving the bench at Gloucester (1580–1800) was 66, and
the mean age of magistrates was 67 in Tudor York and 48–52 in Restoration Leeds.[21] The mean/median age at death of the magistrates of King's
Lynn was 62/63.[22] The apothecaries of Barnstable and the aldermen of
Norwich had a mean age at death of 63.[23] In Glasgow the mean age at

[19] It has been assumed that all subjects were aged 18 at binding. Where actual dates of
birth are known, the age of indenture ranges from 17 to 20. The age of apprenticeship
in London was 17.7 to 18.5: see Rappaport, *Worlds within Worlds*, 297, and Earle,
Making of the English Middle Class, 359.
[20] Jones, *Family Life in Shakespeare's England*, table 5.
[21] P. Clark, "Civic Leaders of Gloucester" in *The Transformation of English Provincial
Towns, 1600–1800*, ed. P. Clark (1984), 318; J. W. Kirby, "Restoration Leeds,"
Northern History 22 (1986): 146; D. M. Palliser, *Tudor York* (Oxford, 1979), 120.
[22] G. A. Metters, "The Rulers and Merchants of King's Lynn" (Ph.D. diss., University of
East Anglia, 1982), 36.
[23] G. E. Trease, "Devon Apothecaries," *Devon and Cornwall Notes and Queres* 32 (1972):
46; J. T. Evans, *Seventeenth-Century Norwich* (Oxford, 1979), 55.

death of charitable donors was 63.4.[24] The life expectation of Quakers
at ages 25–9 (1650–99) was 29.8 years for men and 25.7 for women;
for urban Quakers, based on actual ages at death, life expectation at age
40–45 was 22.8 to 24.4 years.[25]

In comparison, the peers at 25 could expect to live 26 years before
1675, 28 years until 1700, and then 29 years; females could expect to
live 2 to 3 years longer and their life expectancy improved faster than
males after 65.[26] Of 243 peers (1540–1640) 103 lived into their 50s and
60s, 33 into their 70s, and 15 into their 80s.[27] Scholars of Caius College,
Cambridge, at 23 had a life expectancy of 37 years, members of Parliament at 25 of 25.7 years, barristers and benchers at age 30 of 28 to 31
years, and subscribers to the 1693 tontine (30 percent of whom were
businessmen) 28 years.[28] The advocates of Scotland could expect to live
28.6 years at age 30 (1532–1649) and 31.1 years (1650–99).[29] In New
England one-half of the men and women who survived beyond 20 could
expect to live into their 60s; in the Chesapeake, however, the normal life
span was 48 years, and businessmen in Connecticut died, on average, at
47—younger than farmers or professionals.[30]

In the whole population, expectation of life at birth declined from 42
years in 1581 to 36 years in 1661; 40 percent never reached maturity.
Life expectancy at age 25 for males, however, was 26–32 before 1650,
28–31 between 1650 and 1699, and 31–34 after 1700.[31] A man of 25
had a 1-in-16 chance of reaching 80; the probability of his reaching 70

[24] T. C. Smout, "The Glasgow Merchant Community," *Scottish Historical Review* 47 (1968): 61.
[25] R. T. Vann and D. E. C. Eversley, *Friends in Life and Death* (Cambridge, 1992), tables 5.11 and 5.12. They also provide alternative calculations.
[26] T. H. Hollingworth, "A Demographic Study" in *Population in History*, ed. D. V. Glass and D. E. C. Eversley (1965), 36, tables 4, 6, and 9, and *Demography of the Peerage* (1965), 53, 65.
[27] Stone, *Crisis of the Aristocracy*, 168.
[28] P. Razzell, *Essays in English Population History* (1994), 201, table 10; M. Curtis, "The Alienated Intellectuals," *Past and Present* 23 (1962): 31; R. A. Houston and W. A. Prest, "To Die in the Term," *Journal of Interdisciplinary History* 26 (1995): 243–9.
[29] R. A. Houston, "Mortality in Early Modern Scotland," *Continuity and Change* 7 (1992): table 1.
[30] R. Archer, "New England Mosaic," *William and Mary Quarterly*, 3d ser., 47 (1990): 497; J. T. Main, *Society and Economy in Colonial Connecticut* (Princeton, 1985), 298; D. B. and A. H. Rutman, *Small Worlds, Large Questions* (Charlottesville, 1994), 205; J. Demos, *Past, Present, and Personal* (New York, 1986), 151; D. H. Fischer, *Growing Old in America* (Oxford, 1978), 56.
[31] P. Razzell, "The Growth of Population," *Journal of Economic History* 53 (1992): table 10.

was 0.348 (1591–5) and 0.310 (1691–5).[32] Less than two-thirds of those who reached 25 lived to 55; but at 55, they had a 1-in-3 chance of surviving to 75.[33] In a sample of twelve parishes, the life expectancy of men at age 30 fell from 29.2 (1550–99) to 28.4 (1650–99), rising to 30.4 (1700–50), that of women was slightly lower (1600–49) and slightly higher (1650–99).[34] Extrapolating from marriage data, a married man at 25 could expect to live 26.9 years (1600–50) and 28.6 years (1650–99).[35] The proportion of the population over 60 may have increased from 8 percent in 1581 to 9 percent in 1661 and 9 to 11 percent in 1696.[36]

RATIOS

Which spouse was more likely to survive? Four-fifths of the wives of Tudor aldermen outlived their husbands; wives of London businessmen had a clear advantage, though the gap closed during the seventeenth century. The ratio of widowers to widows changed from 1:6.4 (398: 2,558) in period I to 1:3.3 (548:1,798) in period II (see table 1.2). The percentage of wives surviving their husbands declined with wealth from 85 percent in brackets I and II to 76 percent in bracket III and 68 percent in bracket IV. A similar decline is evident between successive cohorts, from 82 percent in cohort I to 70 percent in cohort II, 72 percent in cohort III, and 59 percent in cohort IV.

It is clear that widows far outnumbered widowers, though the number of widows heading households declined after 1650.[37] In London 12.5 percent of all households and 10 percent of estates that passed through

[32] P. Laslett, *A Fresh Map of Life* (1991), table 6.3; L. A. Clarkson, *Death, Disease, and Famine* (New York, 1975), chap. 3.
[33] J. E. Smith, "Widowhood and Agency," *Ageing and Society* 4 (1984): 430.
[34] E. A. Wrigley and R. Schofield, *The Population History of England, 1541–1871* (Cambridge, Mass., 1981), table 7.21; J. Landers, *Death and the Metropolis* (Cambridge, 1993), table 4.10; D. V. Glass, "Two Papers on Gregory King" in *Population in History*, ed. D. V. Glass and D. E. C. Eversley (1968), 206. Adult-mortality estimates relate only to those who married. V. M. Cowgill, "The People of York," *Scientific American* 222 (1970): 106, suggests that women had lower life expectancy, but many may have moved out of observation.
[35] Razzell, *Essays English Population*, table 10.
[36] P. Laslett, "Necessary Knowledge" in *Aging in the Past*, ed. D. Kertzer and P. Laslett (Berkeley and Los Angeles, 1995), table 1.3, and *Family Life and Illicit Love* (Cambridge, 1977), chap. 5; Wrigley and Schofield, *English Population History*, 250; Glass, "Two Papers," 215; R. Wall, "The Household" in *Social and Economic Aspects of the Family Life Cycle*, ed. R. Wall and S. Osamu (Cambridge, 1993), 504.
[37] Wall, "The Household," 504.

the Court of Orphans were headed by widows; of 684 female deponents, 370 were widows.[38] Among all residents of forty London parishes in 1695, there were 3.4 widows to every widower.[39] In the whole population one-third of all brides were widowed and lived to age 55; 10 percent of adult females were widowed, and two-thirds of widows were under 65; 12.9 percent of households were headed by widows compared with 5 percent by widowers.[40] In Cambridge 20.93 percent of households were headed by widows, and in Lichfield 32.6 percent of women in 1695 lived alone.[41]

It is not surprising that more wives than husbands survived their partners. Males had a higher life expectancy up to 45, but women had the advantage from 45 to 65, and more females reached 60.[42] In a 1681 birth cohort 82 percent of males but only 79 percent of the females were dead by 65.[43] Women ran the additional risk of death in childbirth, not necessarily with the first child. Mary Burnell, for example, died at 20 in childbirth, and the wife of Abraham Ash at 33 after bearing 10 children.[44] Propertied wives may have been more vulnerable because midwives may have wanted to show their skills.[45] Despite a high rate of maternal mortality in London of 21 per 1,000 (1657–1700) and 15 per 1,000 baptisms (1666–1758) compared with 10.34 per 1,000 live births for the aristocracy, the risk was still small compared with death from other causes.[46]

Although sex ratios have been the subject of debate, by the 1690s the London marriage market seems to have moved against women, who now

---

[38] Brodsky, "Single Women," 86, tables 2 and 3; Earle, *City Full of People*, table 5.2.

[39] D. V. Glass, "Notes on Demography of London," *Daedalus* 97 (1968): 581–92.

[40] J. E. Smith, "Widowhood and Agency," 431–4; R. Wall, "Regional Variations in Household Structure" in *Regional Demographic Development*, ed. J. Hobcraft and P. Rees (1977), tables 4.5, 4.8.

[41] J. W. Kirby, "Restoration Leeds," 156; Vann and Eversley, *Friends in Life*, table 3.12; R. Wall, "Women Alone," *Annales de demographie historique* (1981): 312; P. Laslett, "Mean Household Size" in *Household and Family in Past Time*, ed. P. Laslett (Cambridge, 1972), 147; R. Houlbrook, "The Making of Marriage," *Journal of Family History* 10 (1985): 342; N. Goose, "Household Size and Structure," *Social History* 5 (1980): table 13.

[42] D. V. Glass, "Two Papers on Gregory King," 207; E. A. Wrigley and R. Schofield, *Population History from Family Reconstitution* (New York, 1997), 348; R. Wall, "Elderly Persons" in *Aging in the Past*, ed. D. Kertzer and P. Laslett (Berkeley, 1995), 90; A. Laurence, *Women in England and America* (New York, 1994), 28.

[43] Introduction to M. Pelling and R. M. Smith, eds., *Life, Death, and the Elderly* (1991), 10.

[44] E. Hatton, *A New View of London* (1708), 99, 102.

[45] A. Eccles, *Obstetrics and Gynaecology in Tudor and Stuart England* (1982), 121.

[46] B. M. Willmott-Dobbie, "An Attempt to Estimate the True Rate of Maternal Mortality," *Medical History* 26 (1982): 80; A. Eccles, "Obstetrics in the Seventeenth and

outnumbered men.[47] Since brides were on average seven years younger than their grooms in first marriage and since they lived longer than men, the high ratio of widows to widowers is understandable.[48] Another reason is the differential rate of remarriage. Widowers were more likely to remarry than widows, whose eligibility declined with age. And if they remarried young women, they were more likely to leave widows. It is harder to explain why more husbands should have outlived their wives after 1660, but the relevant factors are probably an increase in the age at marriage of women and a decline in the frequency of remarriage by men.

For many bereaved wives, widowhood was permanent or of long duration. The median length increased from 9.9 to 12.5 years between periods I and II; those widowed for more than 25 years increased from 15.4 percent to 16.6 percent. In brackets I and II the median was 11/12 years and in brackets III and IV 12 years, with many remarrying in their 20s and 30s and an overall mean of close to 15 years. The mean/median duration increased from 11/12 years in cohort I to 15/14 in cohort II to 16 in cohort III before declining to 15 years in cohort IV. Wives whose husbands died young and whose marriages were short could expect a long widowhood.[49] A weak statistical correlation can be detected between the duration of widowhood and the number of children who survived.[50] In comparison, aristocratic widows in Northamptonshire survived 12 years and in Kent 16 years.[51]

WIDOWS AS EXECUTRIX

A majority of London businessmen named their wives executrix, but there was a gradual shift from sole to joint appointments; an increasing

Eighteenth Centuries," *Bulletin of Social History Medicine* 20 (1977): 49; J. Lewis, "Maternal Mortality in the British Aristocracy," *Journal of British Studies* 37 (1998): table 3; P. Crawford, "The Experience of Maternity" in *Women as Mothers*, ed. V. Filders (1990), 47; R. Schofield, "Did the Mothers Really Die," in *The World We Have Gained*, ed. L. Bonfield et al. (Oxford, 1986), 260.

47 R. W. Herlan, "Aspects of Population History," *Guildhall Studies in London History* 4 (1980): 137.
48 Boulton, "London Widowhood Revisited," 341–2.
49 The Pearson R coefficient of correlation between age at death of husband and number of years married is +0.399 and between age at death of husband and number of years widowed is –0.292. The Pearson R between number of years married and number of years widowed is –0.304. The Pearson R between length of widowhood and the number of surviving orphans is +0.441.
50 The Pearson R is +0.139.
51 L. Bonfield, "Affective Families," *Economic History Review*, 2d ser., 39 (1986): 344, and *Marriage Settlements, 1660–1740* (Cambridge, 1982), 117–18.

Table 3.3. *Duration of Widowhood (Percentage of Known Cases)*

Years	Period I	Period II	Bracket I	Bracket II	Bracket III	Bracket IV	Cohort I	Cohort II	Cohort III	Cohort IV
1–5	34.3	24.0	27.3	27.3	22.5	21.9	30.9	25.3	21.1	22.6
6–10	20.7	17.1	9.1	20.0	18.1	21.9	18.2	19.5	10.6	16.1
11–15	17.8	18.6	36.4	23.6	17.2	21.9	23.6	17.2	16.2	22.6
16–20	5.3	12.3	–	10.9	11.9	12.5	9.1	10.3	13.4	12.9
21–25	6.5	11.4	9.1	3.6	13.2	6.3	5.5	11.5	14.8	12.9
26–30	6.5	6.0	–	5.5	7.1	9.4	5.5	3.5	9.9	3.2
Over 30	8.9	10.6	18.2	9.1	10.1	6.3	7.3	12.6	14.1	9.7
Median	9.85	12.7	11.8	10.8	12.5	12.0	10.6	15.5	16.0	14.6
Mean	12.5	14.7	14.6	12.5	15.1	14.4	12.4	14.4	16.5	15.1
Total	169	350	11	55	227	32	55	87	142	31

number of husbands, particularly in the higher financial brackets, also made alternative arrangements toward the end of the seventeenth century. Between periods I and II the percentage of surviving widows appointed sole executrix decreased from 77 percent to 69 percent; those named joint executors with their children or kin increased from 8 percent to 9 percent.[52] Wealthier husbands were much more likely to bypass their widows or make them joint executors. The percentage of widows who were named sole executrix was 81 percent in bracket I, 78 percent in bracket II, 50 percent in III, and only 31 percent in bracket IV. Meanwhile joint appointments increased from 4 percent in bracket I to 6 percent in II, 19 percent in III, and 31 percent in bracket IV. The number of sole executrixes remained within a range of 43 to 53 percent in successive cohorts, but the percentage named jointly fluctuated from 21 percent in cohort I to 14 to 15 percent in cohorts II and III, to 27 percent in cohort IV.

The appointment of wife as executrix was an ancient practice and common within and outside London, though there were both regional and chronological variations.[53] If her husband died intestate, the widow was entitled to act as administratrix.[54] In north England joint executorship was common without any overseers, whereas in the south, overseers were usually designated to supervise a single executor.[55] In London after 1660, of 164 wills of testators who died before their wives, 21 percent named the widow sole and 57 percent joint executrix; joint appointments increased after 1690.[56] In Great Yarmouth overseers were named to help 58 percent of those widows who were appointed executrix.[57] Whereas in Abingdon the proportion of executrixes was 81.5

---

[52] Brodsky, "Widows in Late Elizabethan London," 145, also finds that 80 percent of Elizabethan Londoners appointed their wives sole executrix.

[53] Erickson, *Women and Property in Early Modern England*, table 9.1; J. Boulton, *Neighbourhood and Society* (Cambridge, 1987), 241; *Elizabethan Life*, ed. F. G. Emmison (Chelmsford, 1980), passim; B. J. Todd, "Freebench and Free Enterprise" in *English Rural Society*, ed. J. Chartres and D. Hey (Cambridge, 1990), 198; *Life and Death in Kings Langley*, ed. L. M. Munby (1981), xx–xxi; J. Murray, "Kinship and Friendship," *Albion* 20 (1988): 376; D. M. Palliser, "Civic Mentality" in *The Tudor and Stuart Town*, ed. J. Barry (1990), 239; *Derbyshire Wills and Inventories, 1600–1625*, ed. J. A. Atkinson et al., vol. 201 (Surtees Society, 1993), 8; M. Spufford, *Contrasting Communities* (Cambridge, 1974), 114–15. It is not always clear in some secondary sources whether their percentages are based solely on the wills of testators who died before their wives.

[54] Statute 21 Hen VIII. C.5.

[55] Erickson, *Women and Property in Early Modern England*, 71.

[56] Earle, *Making of the Middle Class*, 369, table 11.2.

[57] P. Gauci, *Politics and Society in Great Yarmouth* (Oxford, 1996), table 2.3.

Table 3.4. *Executors and Overseers (Percentage of All Wills)*

	Period I	Period II	Bracket I	Bracket II	Bracket III	Bracket IV	Cohort I	Cohort II	Cohort III	Cohort IV
Unmarried Testators										
Parents and Siblings	46.58	41.67	25.00	38.27	34.69	–	22.22	38.46	39.29	58.33
Kin	23.29	27.98	50.00	28.40	30.61	66.67	44.44	23.08	32.14	25.00
Kin and Other	2.28	5.95	–	6.17	6.12	–	11.11	–	7.14	–
Other	27.85	24.41	25.00	27.16	28.57	33.33	22.22	38.46	21.43	16.67
Total	438	168	12	81	49	6	6	13	28	12
Childless Testators										
Widows	75.39	44.12	85.71	43.14	35.19	–	10.00	42.11	29.03	25.00
Widows and Other	4.67	5.88	–	15.69	5.56	12.50	10.00	5.26	9.68	–
Parents and Siblings	3.74	6.86	–	11.76	5.56	12.50	–	5.26	–	12.50
Kin	11.21	29.41	14.29	19.61	35.19	62.50	60.00	42.11	41.94	50.00
Kin and Other	0.94	–	–	–	1.85	12.50	20.00	–	–	–
Other	4.05	13.73	–	9.80	16.67	–	–	5.26	19.35	12.50
Total	321	102	7	51	54	8	10	19	31	8
Overseers										
Widow	1.08	1.64	4.35	2.24	1.00	–	2.17	2.41	2.90	–
Children	1.08	3.28	–	3.14	3.00	–	6.52	4.82	4.35	–
Parents and Siblings	6.49	3.28	–	7.17	4.50	–	8.70	3.61	5.80	–
Kin	29.81	42.62	26.09	34.08	43.00	50.00	43.48	43.37	50.72	50.00
Kin and Other	6.25	1.64	8.70	6.73	5.00	7.14	6.52	2.41	–	–
Other	55.29	47.54	60.87	46.64	43.50	42.86	32.61	43.37	36.23	50.00
Total	832	244	23	223	200	14	46	83	69	12

When Widow Survives

Widow	77.38	68.60	80.93	78.00	49.74	29.73	45.24	53.55	55.10	46.00
Widows and Eldest	3.97	3.39	1.56	2.28	9.63	18.92	11.90	5.81	5.78	6.00
Widows and Other	4.19	6.02	1.95	4.11	10.16	13.51	8.33	8.39	7.82	20.00
Eldest son	3.07	5.05	2.72	2.89	8.58	10.81	10.71	10.97	9.18	2.00
Daughter	0.48	0.69	0.78	0.15	1.23	–	2.38	1.29	1.02	2.00
Children	2.42	1.04	0.39	0.53	3.33	2.70	4.76	2.58	3.40	2.00
Parents and Siblings	1.43	1.31	0.78	1.22	1.40	–	1.19	1.29	1.36	4.00
Kin	2.42	5.12	1.95	3.35	7.88	8.11	8.33	8.39	7.82	10.00
Kin and Other	2.98	0.97	0.39	0.76	1.58	5.41	4.76	1.29	2.38	–
Other	0.43	7.81	8.56	6.70	6.48	10.81	2.38	6.45	6.12	8.00
Total	2,316	1,446	257	1,314	571	37	84	155	294	50

When Widow Predeceases Husband

Eldest son	32.29	23.64	6.25	24.17	29.30	30.00	27.78	30.61	34.09	35.48
Daughter	9.40	10.86	3.13	5.69	8.28	5.00	5.56	14.29	9.09	3.23
Children	1.88	8.63	6.25	3.32	12.74	10.00	11.11	12.25	14.77	12.90
Parents and Siblings	4.39	3.19	3.13	4.74	0.64	–	–	4.08	1.14	6.45
Kin	21.63	17.89	9.38	16.11	22.93	25.00	38.89	20.41	15.91	19.35
Kin and Other	5.96	4.15	–	2.84	7.64	15.00	5.56	2.04	4.55	6.45
Other	24.45	31.63	71.88	43.13	18.47	15.00	11.11	16.33	20.46	16.13
Total	319	313	32	211	157	20	18	49	88	31

percent (1600–59) and 87.5 percent (1660–1720), and in Shrewsbury it was 29.7 percent.[58] In business communities outside of England, in Belfast and New York, the situation was similar to London; in New York 75 percent of husbands (1664–95) named their widows sole executrix.[59]

Many husbands clearly credited their wives with sound judgment, loyalty, and fiscal responsibility and considered them able to administer their estates. Nicholas Warner placed his trust in his widow, though he felt it necessary to add that "she will answer the contrary before Almighty God at his dreadful day of Judgement."[60] Thomas Brockett more typically put "my trust in her of which I make no doubt."[61] Frequently the widows were given custody of the children's legacies until they came of age or married. In some cases testators, like John Crowther and Thomas Gaseley, made their widows responsible for allocating portions between the children; John Jennens, an ironmonger, asked his wife to distribute his testator's one-third.[62] George Breton asked his widow "by that love she ever bore me not to cast off my weak sonne nor his poor children."[63] Robert Johnson, a goldsmith, asked his widow to raise their son "and bestow what portion soever she pleases upon him."[64] Men, like Simon Whitcombe, whose estate was largely abroad, asked their wives to determine their charitable distributions.[65] Samuel Cook was one of many who left all disposition to his widow.[66] In 1638 Christopher Beeston counted on his wife to deal with his debts, "which no one but my wife understands."[67]

In the late seventeenth century, however, the disposal of property by will, especially in wealthier families, became more complex. Although widows were not specifically excluded from participation, they were not explicitly included. They were named interim executrix until the heir came of age or they had to share control with brothers or male kin from

---

[58] B. Todd, "Widowhood in a Market Town" (D. Phil. diss., University of Oxford, 1983), table 4, 175, and "Remarrying Widow" in *Women in English Society, 1500–1800*, ed. M. Prior (1985), 68; J. C. Hindson, "Family Structure, Inheritance, and Kinship" (Ph.D. diss., University of Wales, Aberystwyth, 1991), 191.

[59] J. Agnew, *Belfast Merchants* (Dublin, 1997), 34; D. E. Narrett, *Inheritance and Family Life* (1993), tables 3.5 and 3.10.

[60] PCC, Saville 61, 1622.   [61] PCC, Brent 291, 1653.

[62] PCC, Pell 436, 437, 439, 1659.   [63] PCC, Coventry 38, 1639.

[64] PCC, Berkeley 126, 1656.   [65] PCC, Lee 19, 1637.

[66] PCC, Rivers 128, 1645.

[67] *Playhouse Wills, 558–1642*, ed. E. A. J. Honigman and S. Brock (Manchester, 1993), 21.

either side of the family or with friends. It is noticeable that women rarely served as witnesses of wills (though witnesses could not be beneficiaries, which usually excluded family and kin), as appraisers, or as guardians of children (unless they were the mother). Although widows were usually made guardians of young children, a significant minority of fathers named kin or friends as sole or joint guardians, sometimes distributing their children between different guardians. Often sons were separated from daughters, and the children were allocated a guardian of the same gender. In 1622 Francis Burnell of Newcastle, for example, entrusted his two daughters to his widow but his son to his brother-in-law.[68] Martin Archdale made his brother guardian of his sons and left his daughters to the widow.[69]

No doubt gender prejudice played a role in determining whether or not a widow was named executrix, but the decision also depended on the number of reliable candidates, the availability of adult children and kin, and the age and competence of the widow.[70] A major concern of businessmen, especially if they had young children, was continuity and efficiency of administration, which depended on the longevity and capacities of their executors. If both husband and wife lived longer, there was a greater likelihood that the surviving widow would be elderly and infirm, thus less able to function as executrix.

Some businessmen certainly had doubts about their wives' ability to act. In 1613 Richard Collins asked his son to help his mother because "a woman shall not so easily of herself make thorough and dispatch."[71] Peter Ducane wrote in his will "I joyn you both together . . . that you live in mutual love and my son's duty is that he be tender of a loving mother and helpful to her in managing her accounts . . . and shewing her my last ballance whereby with a little instruction she may understand the state of all my affairs."[72] But many more, like Sir Dudley North, just wanted to spare their relicts the work and worry of managing complex

[68] *Durham Wills, 1604–49*, vol. 142 (Surtees Society, 1929), 153. A typical will making the widow executrix and guardian of all the children is that of brewer William Kildale in PCC, Clarke 138, 1625. Although the number of widows named guardian has not been systematically recorded, it approximates closely to the number named executrix.
[69] H. F. Waters, *Genealogical Gleanings in England*, vol. 1 (Salem, Mass., 1892), 316.
[70] For gender as a factor in eighteenth-century Halifax see J. Smail, *The Origins of Middle-Class Culture* (1995), 169–70, tables 6, 7. For a similar trend in colonial America; see D. S. Smith, "The Demography of Widowhood" in Kertzer and Laslett, *Aging in the Past*, 269.
[71] Donald, *Elizabethan Monopolies*, 59.
[72] Will, Essex, RO, MS D/DDC/F3, 11 May 1711.

business estates and leave them instead a secure property that produced an easily managed income.[73] Sir Francis Child revoked his appointment of his widow as executrix "to save her trouble." In 1644 Thomas Wetherall, a merchant tailor, recognized that "in regard of the sadd tymes it (may) prove a hard difficult and tedious tyme and business for my wife being my Executrix to gett in my debts with the help of some of her friends."[74] John Dunster, a clothworker, made his friends executors because "a great part of my estate is abroad whereby some trouble and suits in law may arise too troublesome and hard a burthen for a woman."[75] William Cloberry left his widow his house but asked his brother to take care of her and his sons.[76]

THE BURDEN OF EXECUTORSHIP

As executrix or administratrix, a businessman's widow acquired formidable responsibilities. She had to arrange and pay for the funeral and find appraisers for the inventory and sureties and witnesses for bonds; then she had to liquidate his stock and goods and collect debts owing to the estate, which often required extensive personal travel and lawsuits; then she had to pay all fees, charges, and taxes, provide maintenance for children, satisfy all creditors of the estate in order of priority, and pay all the individual legacies designated in the will; finally she had to file an account within a year, showing the net value of the estate after deducting all legal disbursements, and defend it in court.[77] A surge in mortality among her kin might require that she handle more than one estate at the same time. The widow of John Howes was simultaneously executrix for both her late husband and father; the widow of Adam Chapman was named executrix not only of her husband but his mother.[78] Disgruntled legatees could drag widows into court, like the widow of Francis Brerewood.[79]

---

[73] R. Grassby, *The English Gentleman in Trade* (Oxford, 1994), 214.
[74] PCC, Rivers 20, 1644.   [75] PCC, Clarke 147, 1625.
[76] PCC, Coventry 4, 1640.
[77] A lucid account of probate administration is provided by A. L. Erickson, "An Introduction to Probate Accounts" in *The Records of the Nation*, ed. G. Martin and P. Spufford (1990), 167–86. A typical example of what was involved are the 1625 accounts of Elizabeth, widow of Cantrell Legg, in *Abstracts from the Wills of Printers of Cambridge, 1504–1699*, ed. G. J. Gray (Bibliographical Society, 1915), 83–5. The accounts of administrators, male and female, occur frequently among business papers: one example is in Ashe papers, PRO, C 107/17.
[78] PCC, Pell 443 and 530, 1659.
[79] PRO, C 7/292/54. It is often difficult to tell in contested suits who is at fault or whether the action was collusive.

Business estates could be extremely complex. Margaret Courteen, widow of Martin Boudaen, was ensnared by the intricate confusion of Sir William Courteen's estate.[80] The widow of Sir Horatio Palavicino remarried to escape the burden of handling his estate.[81] Litigation could be expensive, time consuming, and a source of anxiety. The widow of John Sell, for example, was sued by a relentless Josiah Child regarding some houses that had been destroyed by fire.[82]

Liquidating a working business in seventeenth-century England demanded skill and knowledge. The widow of John Herlan, for example, had to unload his entire inventory.[83] Merchant Francis Summers listed over £2,300 of debts owing to him that he had not posted to his books and, aware of the problems facing his executors, appointed his father and three friends jointly with his wife.[84] The ghost of a citizen is said to have returned during the interregnum to advise his married daughter on the intricacies of his estate.[85] The executrix of John Leigh, a stationer, had to visit the Fleet prison to investigate the status of her late husband's debts.[86] In 1705 the administratrix of the intestate estate of Thomas Jones, a draper, had to sell his wares and shop goods "by way of auction."[87] The widow of Thomas Tyrell, an apothecary, had to dispose of his shop, drugs, and equipment.[88] Matthew Clarke of King's Lynn left his widow a ship.[89] When the business was overseas, it could require a chancery suit to secure a proper account.[90] Mary, the widow of Richard May, had to sue two Jewish merchants to recover investments in the Iberian trade.[91] Sarah Gibbs took three years to wind up her husband's commercial investments.[92]

Robert Williams left his wife "all my debts which are fair and written in a little book covered with parchment," but she had to collect them.[93] The widow usually needed the help of friends, partners, kin, or the

[80] BL, Sloane MS 3515.
[81] L. Stone, *Sir Horatio Palavicino* (Oxford, 1956), 294.
[82] PRO, C 110/140, 1671.   [83] PCC, Clarke 126, 1625.
[84] PCC, Hyde 8, 1665.
[85] K. V. Thomas, *Religion and the Decline of Magic* (1971), 716.
[86] M. Pitt, *The Cry of the Oppressed* (1691), 130, 135.   [87] CLRO, CSB IV.
[88] M. Pelling, "Apothecaries in Norwich," *Pharmaceutical Journal* 13 (1983): 7.
[89] Metters, "Rulers of King's Lynn," 356–7.
[90] A useful example of the problems of liquidating an estate overseas is the daybook of the executor of John Freeman in BL, Lansdowne MS 1,156. See also Farrington v. Flavell, PRO, C 9/489/20, 1685; PRO. C 2/Jas I/55/15; PRO C 104/13–14; J. H. Appleby, "Dr. Arthur Dee," *Slavonic and East European Review* 57 (1979): 50.
[91] C. J. Sisson, "A Colony of Jews in Shakespearian London," *Essays and Studies* 23 (1938): 41.
[92] R. Davis, *Aleppo and Devonshire Square* (1967), 7.   [93] PCC, Brent 205, 1653.

apprentice. Husbands, like John Wildgoose, left their apprentices legacies on condition that they serve out their time with the widow.[94] Hugh Stanford, a cutler, bequeathed his apprentice all his tools in return for helping the widow liquidate his business, and William Hill gave his apprentice £150 to do the same.[95] Adam Chapman, a draper, asked his partner to help his widow, and William Chadwell asked his son-in-law to assist in recovering foreign debts.[96] The widow of John Wightwick tried to secure an early grant of freedom for the apprentice so that he could help her administer the estate.[97] In 1689 widow Oliver employed Edward Millington to come to Norwich to auction her stock.[98] Sir Benjamin Bathurst's widow turned to Gregory King for help.[99]

Indebtedness constituted a major problem. Dorothy, widow of John Harvey, found that her husband's estate shrank from £4,000 to £2,222 after the debts were paid.[100] When liabilities exceeded assets, all a widow could do was divide what remained pro rata among her late husband's creditors.[101] A widow could be sued if she selectively paid off creditors.[102] Anne Brudenell went bankrupt thanks to her late husband's debts.[103] Sometimes creditors went after the widow's separate estate or even her personal effects, and it was not always easy for her to prove independent ownership. Widows often needed to raise cash to pay debts and support children, but they could not realize capital assets as easily as guardians, because the income from those assets was their subsistence.

Some widows just declined to act as executrix. When they took out letters of renunciation, it was usually because of old age and infirmity, because the estate was too dispersed, or because they suspected that it was bankrupt. The widow of Nicholas Gore renounced the executorship to a creditor of the estate.[104] On the other hand, a widow might still serve as administratrix, because that would allow her to track the course of

---

[94] PCC, Eure 68.
[95] PCC, Ridley 61, 1629; PCC, Lee 24, 1638; will of John Foy, PCC, Clarke 144, 1625.
[96] PCC, Pell 530, 1659; PCC, Cottle 206.
[97] B. M. Berger, *The Most Necessary Luxuries* (University Park, 1993), 226.
[98] D. Stoker, "Prosperity and Success," *Publishing History* 30 (1991): 35.
[99] Business letter book of Gregory King, BL, Loan MS 57/73, 1704–7.
[100] CLRO, CSB IV, 1706.
[101] *Upperside. Minute Book of Friends 1669–90*, ed. B. S. Snell, vol. 1 (Buckingham Architectural and Archaeological Society, 1937), 35; PRO, Req/2/397/60.
[102] W. J. Jones, *The Foundations of English Bankruptcy* (Transactions of the American Philosophical Society, 69, 1979), 30.
[103] KAO, MS U 1015/C1/8.
[104] *Miscellanea Genealogica et Heraldica*, vol. 2, 348.

probate and protect her own property without incurring liability for debts.[105]

FREQUENCY OF REMARRIAGE

Some widowers seem to have preferred close relations with a woman without remarrying. William Weston, whose wife predeceased him, left "my Valentine Mrs Judith Hewitt if she shall be living at my decease twenty shillings to buy her a ring."[106] The widower and grandfather, Tobell Aylmer, made his "good friend Edith Perrin widow" his executrix and beneficiary.[107] Other widowers ran through several wives. John Whitson married four times, though he left no surviving children.[108] James Silverlock married four times, and his third wife had had two previous husbands.[109] Sir John Fryer married three times, and Sir Owen Buckingham married six times.

A few remarried while their first partner was still alive. Although concubinage was more common than bigamy, bigamous marriages did occur, principally among merchants who resided abroad, and many others must have passed unnoticed.[110] Sir Nicholas Wyett, president of Surat, married his niece when he already had a wife.[111] Often bigamy was unintentional since it was difficult for some wives, when their husbands had traveled abroad, to determine whether they were still alive. The act of 1603 that prohibited bigamy exempted an offender whose spouse had been absent without news for at least seven years.

The marriage habits of the whole population of Elizabethan London have been described as serial monogamy; 45 percent of marriages by license were remarriages, and 35 percent of all brides were widows.[112] But only one-third of 208 widows of Tudor aldermen remarried, and the rate of remarriage in London fell during the century.[113] Multiple

---

[105] Although the number of widows renouncing has not been systematically counted, it is clear that they represented a small percentage.
[106] PCC, Bowyer 123, 1652.
[107] PCC, Juxon 113, 1663.
[108] J. Aubrey, *Brief Lives*, ed. A. Clark (Oxford, 1898), 367.
[109] *London Visitation Pedigrees 1664*, ed. J. B. Whitmore and A. H. H. Clark, vol. 92 (Harlean Society, 1940), 125.
[110] A. C. Carter, *The English Reformed Church* (Amsterdam, 1964), 164.
[111] Hedges, *Diary*, ed. H. Yule, vol. 75 (Hakluyt Society, 1887), cccxix.
[112] Brodsky, "Widows in Late Elizabethan London," figure 5.1.
[113] Rappaport, *Worlds within Worlds*, 46, citing an unpublished thesis by N. Adamson; Boulton, "London Widowhood Revisited," table 1; C. Carlton, "The Widow's Tale," *Albion* 10 (1978): 119–27.

marriages were in fact uncommon among businessmen. Of those who married at least once, 6.9 percent remarried in period I and 12.7 percent in period II (see table 1.7). Taking all cases where the marital status is known, including those never married, 5.5 percent married twice in period I and 10 percent in period II; the respective percentages for third and subsequent marriages were only 0.8 percent and 1 percent. In period I, of widows who survived their husbands, 8.5 percent remarried and in period II, 11.6 percent (see table 1.6).

Remarriage certainly increased with wealth. A total of 4.5 percent of widowed businessmen remarried in bracket I, 5 percent in bracket II, 17 percent in bracket III, and 15 percent in bracket IV. In comparison 7 percent of widows remarried in bracket I, 10 percent in bracket II, 15 percent in bracket III, and 14 percent in bracket IV. Of all businessmen whose marital status is known, 28 percent remarried in cohort I, 20 percent in cohort II, 18 percent in cohort III, and 12 percent in cohort IV; the respective percentages for widows remarrying at least once were 23 percent, 15 percent, 13 percent, and 21 percent. Few businessmen during the whole period married more than twice—5 percent in cohort I, 0.03 percent in cohort II, 2 percent in cohort III, and 0.94 in cohort IV. Although the data are very slim, about 50 percent of third wives were widows.

In comparison, the proportion of marriages in the whole population that were remarriages has been put as high as 30 percent, though levels as low as 10 percent have been detected in the countryside.[114] In the diocese of Canterbury the percentage of widows/widowers remarrying was 31.8 (1619–46), 28.3/31.6 (1661–76), and 26.1/32.6 (1677–1700).[115] Of 262 married businessmen in the Elizabethan House of Commons, 64 married twice and 17 married three times; of all active merchants in the House of Commons (1660–90), 23 percent married twice and 5 percent three or more times.[116] In Gloucester 25 percent of the councilors and 33 percent of the bench married more than once.[117]

---

[114] R. Schofield and E. A. Wrigley, "Remarriage Intervals" in *Marriage and Remarriage in Populations of the Past*, ed. J. Dupaquier et al. (New York, 1981), 212–14; Wrigley and Schofield, *Population History England*, 258–9; B. A. Holderness, "Widows in Pre-Industrial Society" in *Land Kinship and Life Cycle*, ed. R. M. Smith (Cambridge, 1984), 430.

[115] Razzell, *Essays English Population*, table 6.

[116] *The House of Commons, 1558–1603*, vol. 1, ed. P. W. Haslter (1982), 8; *The House of Commons, 1660–1690*, ed. B. D. Henning (1983), 23; the percentage for all merchant families was 20 percent and 8 percent, respectively.

[117] Clark, "Civic Leaders of Gloucester," 316.

In Tudor York 27 aldermen married once and 19 twice.[118] In Aldenham, Hertfordshire, remarriages were more common before 1700.[119] In Abingdon they declined from 37.5 percent of all marriages (1600–50) to 23.5 percent (1660–1700).[120] About one-fourth of heads of gentry families and 28 percent of the peers (1558–1641) married more than once.[121] Almost twice as many widowers as widows remarried among urban Quakers (1650–99); of all Quaker marriages, 20.4 percent were remarriages by men and 11.3 percent remarriages by women.[122] In Belfast remarriage by merchants' widows was quite common.[123]

TIMING

A few businessmen were not deterred from remarrying by advanced age or by the ridicule directed at lust among the elderly. Sir Stephen Fox remarried at age 77 and had four children. Widower William Cary of Bristol married his servant at the age of 74 and had one son.[124] Sometimes they robbed the cradle. Sir Hugh Middleton's second wife was twenty years younger, whereas his first wife had been eighteen years older.[125] John Jeffereys's second wife was also young, and Alexander Norman, a cooper, remarried at 56 a girl of 19.[126]

The median age of spouses of widowers hovered around 27 in periods I and II. The median age of spinsters who married widowers was particularly low: 22.5 (N = 15) in period I and 22 (N = 210) in period II. The median age of widows marrying widowers rose from 34 (N = 10) in period I to 36 (N = 86) in period II; the median age of widows marrying bachelors, however, dropped from 35 (N = 16) in period I to 28 (N = 101) in period II. The median age of brides marrying widowers was 28 in cohort I, 29 in cohort II, 25 in cohort III, and 20 in cohort IV. The age of second wives declined with wealth from a median of 24.5 in bracket II to 22 in bracket IV (see tables 1.5 and 1.6).

---

[118] Palliser, *Tudor York*, 129.
[119] J. D. Griffith, "Economy, Family, and Remarriage," *Journal of Family Issues* 1 (1980): 486.
[120] Todd, "Remarrying Widow," table 2.1.
[121] L. Stone, *Family, Sex, and Marriage*, 56; *idem., Crisis of the Aristocracy*, 168.
[122] Vann and Eversley, *Friends in Life*, table 3.11.
[123] Agnew, *Belfast Merchant Families*, 29.
[124] F. Harrison, *The Devon Carys* (New York, 1920), 522.
[125] J. W. Gough, *Sir Hugh Middleton* (Oxford, 1964), 8.
[126] J. Youings, *Tuckers' Hall* (Exeter, 1968), 97; *London Allegations for Marriage Licenses*, ed. J. L. Chester and G. Armytage, vol. 26 (Harlean Society, 1887), 275.

The situation among all residents of London was somewhat different.[127] Widows of Elizabethan tradesmen often took younger men as second husbands, sometimes as much as 15 years younger, and 60 percent married bachelors.[128] Many widowers, 64 percent under 50, married younger single women; 21.8 percent of daughters of high-status tradesmen married widowers, and the London-born brides of widowers had a mean age of 22.5, compared with 28.5 for migrant brides. In St. James, Duke's Place, while the number of widowers fell, the percentage of widowers marrying spinsters increased from 38 percent (1598–1619) to 48 percent (1680–83) and 52 percent (1698–1700); in Stepney widows did marry younger men, but most widows of businessmen remarried older men.[129]

A wife who lost her husband when she was still in her twenties was the most likely to marry again, and many of these remarriages took place relatively early in life. In the whole population widows marrying bachelors were younger than widows who married widowers; both bachelors marrying widows and widowers marrying spinsters had a similar age difference (7.5 and 7.9), but widowers marrying widows were only six years apart.[130]

Age discouraged some widowers from remarriage. The widower Joseph Collett continued to dance and chat with the ladies, but he told his brother, "I had always an aversion to an old fellows marrying a young girl . . . so I think he ought to expect the horns"; he considered himself too old to provide for children and intended either to marry an old nurse or content himself with a housekeeper "as might take care of me without scandal."[131] Samuel Bufford visualized an old man married to a young

---

[127] W. K. Jordan, *Charities of London, 1480–1660* (New York, 1960), 281; Glass "Notes Demography London," 581–92; Brodsky, "Widows," 127; Earle, *City Full of People*, table 5.1, 162; Rappaport, *Worlds within Worlds*, 40; Todd, "Remarrying Widow," 65.

[128] V. Brodksy, "Mobility and Marriages in Pre-Industrial England" (Ph.D. diss., University of Cambridge, 1978), 330; Brodsky, "Widows in Late Elizabethan England," 86, table V. The database records the age of bachelors who married widows and the age of widows on their second marriage, but not the age of widowers on their second marriage. It is clear nonetheless from the ages of men at first marriage that the majority of remarrying widows chose men of the same age or older, whereas it was less common for widowers to marry older women.

[129] Boulton, "London Widowhood Revisited," 336; Carlton, "Widow's Tale," 127; Earle, *City Full of People*, 162.

[130] Wrigley and Schofield, *English Population from Reconstitution*, tables 5.7, 5.8; McIntosh, *A Community Transformed*, 295; D. J. Loschky and D. F. Krier, "Income and Family Size," *Journal of Economic History* 29 (1969): 445.

[131] J. Collett, *Private Letter Book*, ed. H. H. Dodwell (1933), 144 (letter dated 14 Dec. 1716).

wife with children "got for him by some good Neighbour hanging about him and calling Daddy, Daddy."[132]

On the other hand, John Des Carrière, after spending more than two years as a widower, married a 20 year old with a portion of £150, "a young woman very much to my liking"; he told his daughter that he felt like a 40 year old, that his new wife could read and write well, and that she would take care of him.[133] Sir John Moore in his dotage received the following advice from Lady Frances Gressley, when he was thinking of marrying her young daughter, Anne: "As to that of age you desired me to consider of I have taken notes of some of our neighbours," and one had married at 80, another at 68 with six children, and another at 69 and still breeding. Her daughter would suit him well if he did not expect a large portion, "I do believe my daughter can like you as well as a young man and do believe she be very affectionate unto you."[134]

The interval between remarriages was shorter for widowers than for widows, though comprehensive information on this point is lacking for the business community. Some widowers, particularly when they had young children or lacked heirs, were more inclined to marry soon after bereavement and were probably less fussy about a portion. Widows usually took longer, and a year of mourning was recommended by convention. The much-cited case of the genteel widow who married the journeyman draper on the second day of her bereavement, when he called on her to sell her mourning clothes, is a somewhat unlikely story.[135] But Elinor Harvey did remarry within one month of her bereavement and Ambrose Barnes's widow within four months.[136] Merchants in India often remarried quickly the widows of factory members. In Elizabethan London the median interval between marriages was nine months, and it rose at St. James, Duke's Place, during the century.[137]

SELECTION

As with first marriages, the new spouse was often connected by business, kinship, and residence nearby. John Blunt remarried the widow of

[132] S. Bufford, *An Essay against Unequal Marriage* (1696), 30.
[133] G. Sherwood, *The Pedigree Register*, vol. 3. (1913–16), 118 (letter 27 Dec. 1695).
[134] GLL, MS 507, 20 and 28 Feb. 1692. Similar arguments were advanced when Thomas Sutton was widowed: see Stone, *Crisis of Aristocracy*, 295.
[135] H. M. C., Gawdy, vol. 10, 172.
[136] *London Allegations Marriage Licenses*; A. Barnes, *Memoirs of the Life*, vol. 50 (Surtees Society, 1866), 37.
[137] Brodsky, "Widows of Late Elizabethan England," 133.

Benjamin Tudman, former partner of his associate, Stephen Child.[138] Well-to-do widows could rise socially in their second marriages; the widows of William Lane and Geoffrey Elwes, for example, remarried baronets.[139]

The proportion of brides of widowers who were widows declined slightly from 34 percent in period I to 33 percent in period II (see table 1.2). It fell, however, from 39 and 40 percent in cohorts I and II to 32 percent in cohort III and 21 percent in cohort IV. The only change in the status of wives between periods I and II was a slight increase from 28 to 29 percent in the number of gentlewomen and a significant increase from 2 to 7 percent in daughters from professional families; 64 to 65 percent came from business families (see table 1.1). The percentage of gentlewomen was 30 percent in bracket I, 26 percent in bracket II, 27 percent in bracket III, and 29 percent in bracket IV. But the percentage of wives from business families dropped from 70 percent in bracket I to 57 percent in bracket IV; daughters of professionals rose to 7 percent in bracket IV. The proportion of daughters of businessmen and gentlewomen remained within the same range in cohorts I to III at 64 to 67 percent and 25 to 28 percent respectively; in cohort IV (N = 20), the proportions were 48 percent and 39 percent.

Between periods I and II wives from the country fell from 32 percent to 24 percent and those from London rose from 62 to 72 percent with no change in those coming from other towns (see table 1.3). In all brackets, 70 to 77 percent were from London. In cohorts I to III 64 to 73 percent of wives came from London and 23 to 29 percent from the country; in cohort IV, however, Londoners declined to 55 percent and country brides rose to 45 percent. What little data there are for third marriages suggests no major change in either status or location.

OPPOSITION TO REMARRIAGE

A few writers emphasized the need to counsel widows and train them as executrixes.[140] The letter-writing manuals advised widows about how to

---

[138] P. G. M. Dickson, *The Financial Revolution in England* (1967), 115. See also chapter 7.

[139] Although the second husbands of widows of businessmen have not been systematically tracked in the database, the impression from cumulative individual examples is that widows who had property and chose to marry, usually married well.

[140] Rogers, *Matrimonial Honour*, 79.

approach remarriage and how to deal with their late husband's debts. But many male authors were imaginatively vituperative; their invective was so vehement than one can only suppose that they ran foul of some particularly imperious widow. Playwrights depicted rich widows as over-sexed figures of fun; social commentators treated them as menacing harpies who seduced and married younger men, using their wealth to compete unfairly with poor maids.[141] Alexander Niccholes, for example, treated the sexuality of widows as scandalous and condemned their power to reject suitors without consulting fathers or male kin.[142] Even widows who did not remarry were not spared. "No more pity," exclaimed Ned Ward, "to see a widow weep than to see a goose goe barefoot."[143] To Wye Saltonstall, "a widdow is like a cold pye thrust downe to the lower end of the table that has had too many fingers in't."[144] Joseph Swetnam argued that widows were already "framed to the condition of another man" and inveighed against rich, proud, and demanding widows.[145]

Many husbands did not relish the thought of their wives remarrying and tried to discourage them by restrictive bequests. Some wills, like those of Customer Smythe, Sir John Robinson, Sir Abraham Reynard-son, Nicholas Crisp, Edmond Underwood, Thomas Petchell, Christopher Langley, Edmund Andrews, and Robert Herrick, provided that a widow would forfeit all but her mandatory inheritance, if she remarried.[146] Samuel Wood left his widow a house on London bridge for life or until she remarried.[147] Nicholas Penning left his widow the bulk of his estate because she had promised not to remarry. Even though John Barker had no children, he instructed his widow to surrender the executorship to his brother if she remarried.[148] Some testators no doubt feared that their wives would forget them or mock them in someone else's arms. Others may just have felt that the person who their widow married should contribute to her upkeep.

---

[141] Carlton, "Widow's Tale," 119.
[142] A. Niccholes, *Discourse of Marriage* (1615); T. B. Leinwald, *The City Staged* (Madison, 1986), 147.
[143] E. Ward, *A Legacy for the Ladies* (1705), 168.
[144] J. Saltonstall, *Picturae Loquentis* (1631), 4.
[145] J. Swetnam, *Arraignment of Lewd Women* (1615), 46, 54.
[146] CLRO, CSB IV, 1706; PCC, Harvey 126, 1639; PCC, Lee 133, 1648; PCC, May 163; *Elizabethan Life*, ed. F. G. Emmison (Chelmsford, 1978), 294; J. F. Wadmore, "Thomas Smythe," *Archaelogia Cantiana* 17 (1887): 202; PCC, St. John 78, 1631. The same was true in New York: see *New York Abstract of Wills*, vol. 1 (1892), 389, 416.
[147] PCC, Grey 178, 1651.   [148] PCC, Russell 105, 1633.

The incidence of restrictive bequests varied over time and between regions.[149] The lesser tradesmen, both in London and in Abingdon, do not seem to have even raised the subject of remarriage.[150] The great majority of London businessmen neither encouraged nor discouraged remarriage in their wills, though silence does not necessarily imply indifference.[151] William Barton, a draper, merely provided that his apprentice be placed with another master by his widow if she did not continue his business or remarried someone with a different trade who could not take over the apprentice.[152] John Jones, a girdler, gave his wife his house and one-third of his land, but required her to transfer his "household stuff" to their son if she remarried.[153] Richard Pearson, a rich merchant tailor, whose mourning rings were inscribed "remember thy end," was concerned about the occupation of his widow's future husband. He stipulated that she could keep the lease of his house if she remarried a merchant or tradesman, "but if my said wife doth marry a lawyer or gentleman" the lease passed to his sons.[154]

A primary objective of testators was to avoid couverture.[155] Although some testators bequeathed real property outright to their wives, they usually preferred to give them a life interest, the property reverting to their children or kin. If they had no male heirs, businessmen were usually content that their estate should pass to daughters and their sons-in-law. But they did not want it to pass into the hands of a new husband through couverture; they wanted to preserve the family name and line. Edmund Bull, for example, wanted his house in London to pass to his sons if

---

[149] Erickson, *Women and Property in Early Modern England*, table 9.4; Earle, *Making of the Middle Class*, 369; R. T. Vann, "Wills and the Family," *Journal of Family History* 4 (1979): 366; *Inheritance in America*, ed. C. Shammas et al. (New Brunswick, 1987), 59; N. Evans, "Inheritance, Women, Religion" in *Probate Records*, ed. P. Riden (1985), 66; J. A. Johnston, "Family, Kin, and Community," *Rural History* 6 (1995): 183. Only 3 percent of wills in the Hustings Court of London vetoed remarriage in the fifteenth century: see B. A. Hanawalt, "Remarriage as an Option" in *Wife and Widow in Medieval England*, ed. S. S. Walker (Ann Arbor, 1993), 148.

[150] Brodsky, "Widows in Late Elizabethan London," 145; Todd, "Remarrying Widow," 73. Brodsky's conclusions are based largely on Consistory Court wills, which were written primarily by tradesmen with little property to bequeath.

[151] Although no specific count has been made, approximately 10 percent of all PCC wills of London businessmen raise the question of remarriage. In the sample of wills in Earle, *Making of the Middle Class*, 393 n. 38, only 5 testators voided bequests on remarriage, though many more made alternative arrangements for the children.

[152] PCC, Parker 74, 1619.

[153] PCC, Nabbs 268, 1660.   [154] PCC, Hele 90, 1626.

[155] Erickson, *Women and Property in Early Modern England*, 168.

his widow remarried, and then by elaborate male descent.[156] Richard Rogers, a goldsmith, required any subsequent husband of his widow to give bond that half his estate would pass to his kin.[157] Robert Mann provided that any subsequent husband of his widow would not have authority to sell or mortgage his urban leaseholds, the income from which was designated for his kin.[158] Samuel Rivers provided that his London tenements would pass to the children of his kinsmen if his widow remarried.[159] New husbands were often loose cannons; they could and did challenge the provisions of a will, suing the executors to regain control of the estate or increase the widow's share. Sir William Humphries, who had married the widow of Robert Lancashire, sued his daughter-in-law who was acting as administratrix.[160]

The other principal concern of most testators was their children's future. They had reason to worry. When a widow was appointed guardian, she was usually given free use of the children's portions until they matured, when she was supposed to hand them over; the testator's one-third was also bequeathed initially to the widow for eventual transfer.[161] John Christian, a merchant tailor, bequeathed his son one-third of his estate to be managed by his widow, who received two-thirds out of which she was expected to raise, educate, and apprentice the boy.[162] Without safeguards, the portions of children would be at the mercy of a second husband, should a widow die. Even during her lifetime, a second husband might act as administrator of his predecessor's will, and could, like Thomas Grey, cheat the children.[163] Sir Josiah Child was accused of appropriating £20,000 from his wife's jointure intended for educating her children.[164] The Court of Orphans required executrixes to give recognizances with sureties for orphans' portions and to prove their inventory before they remarried.[165]

Edward Proctor, who had no children but whose wife was pregnant

---

[156] PCC, Aylett 313, 1655.   [157] PCC, Berkeley 340, 1656.
[158] PCC, Berkeley 211, 1656.   [159] PCC, Aylett 265, 1655.
[160] PRO, C 6/269/113, 1688.
[161] PCC, Ruthen 56, 1657; PCC, Berkeley 318, 1656.
[162] PCC, Ruthen 295, 1657.
[163] CLRO, CSB I. The guardianship of children did not pass to a second husband: see T. Barrett-Lennard, *The Position in Law of Women* (1883; reprinted Littleton, 1983), 47.
[164] C. Brydges, *Continuation of the History of the Willoughby Family*, ed. A. C. Wood (1958), 124, 136; T. Woodcock, *Extracts from the Papers*, ed. G. C. M. Smith, 3d ser., vol. 13 (Camden Miscellany, 1907), 75.
[165] *Orders Taken and Enacted for Orphans* (1580); C. Carlton, *The Court of Orphans* (Leicester, 1974), 43.

when he made his will, urged the widow not only to nurse, feed, clothe, and educate the child properly, but to remain unmarried until the child was either twenty-one or married; if she did marry, she should settle half her inheritance on the child.[166] Bartholomew Hemming left his whole estate to his widow, but specified the amount that she must give to their youngest daughter, should she remarry.[167] Henry Plaisterer, a weaver, made his widow custodian of their son's half share, but required her to transfer it to him "within one week after the marriage day," should she remarry.[168] Robert Joyce instructed that his four children should each receive £100 on the death or the remarriage of his widow.[169] Thomas Bishop instructed his widow, should she remarry, to transfer one-third of his estate to their daughter along with a complete account.[170] Bartholomew Selwood, a salter, and Joseph Wells, a tallowchandler, required their widows to give security for the children's portions if they remarried.[171] Samuel Wheatley, a woollen draper, whose wife was pregnant when he made his will, left the unborn child £100 at twenty-one and required his widow to give sureties if she remarried.[172] Henry Reeve, a merchant, delegated the distribution of his estate between his children to his widow but added that all his estate would pass to his children if she remarried, with an extra £100 to the eldest son.[173] Edward Berry asked his widow to give her portion to the children, should she remarry.[174] John Horner, a weaver, left his widow his whole estate for thirteen years (after which the sons would presumably inherit) so long as she remained a widow.[175]

Sometimes a widow was only made guardian of the children and trustee of their property so long as she remained a widow.[176] Thomas Walker provided, "if it shall please God" that his wife should remarry, that his overseers would protect the interests of his children.[177] Many, like Joseph Haskins Stiles, Joshua Marshall, and Francis Moore, provided alternative executors or guardians, either a sibling, kinsman, or

---

[166] PCC, Fairfax 153, 1649.   [167] PCC, Alchin 473, 1654.
[168] PCC, Ruthen 371, 1657; see also will of John Woodward, PCC, Pell 1, 1659.
[169] PCC, Grey 160, 1651.   [170] PCC, Alchin 80, 1654.
[171] PCC, Ruthen 62, 1657; PCC, Pell 434, 1659.
[172] *Banbury Wills and Inventories*, ed. E. R. C. Brinkworth and J. S. W. Gilson, vol. 14 (Banbury Historical Society, 1976), 49.
[173] PCC, Russell 102, 1633.   [174] PCC, Clarke 143, 1625.
[175] PCC, Nabbs 185, 1660.
[176] Will of Peter Le Noble, PCC, Juxon 121, 1663; *Durham Wills 1604–49*, 13.
[177] PCC, Alchin 295, 1654.

friend, in case the widow remarried. Silvester Poulton provided that his overseers would become guardian of his daughter; Thomas Wynn made his friend, Richard Sherman, guardian of his children, and Rimbold Jacobson, a brewer, put his son by his first marriage in the hands of a friend rather than his second wife.[178] Nicholas Harris, a grocer, George Bowcock, a clothier, and Richard Buckeridge, a cooper, required that their widows give sureties for payment of their children's portions to the overseers if they remarried.[179] In 1701 Hugh Grange left his wife her one-third, but provided that should she marry without the consent of his overseers, the latter would take over the children's portions.[180] In 1711 Henry Kellett provided that responsibility for his six children would pass to trustees if his widow remarried.[181]

A widow intending to remarry could also run into opposition from the kin of her late husband, from single women who disliked competition, and from the children of her first marriage. The husband's kin feared that property would pass out of the family, the kin of the widow that her jointure might be endangered.[182] Leonora Marescoe quarreled bitterly with her daughter over her remarriage to Jacob David, the young, former prentice of her late husband.[183] Sarah Pitt's legacy to her widowed sister was conditional on her not remarrying in India and returning to England with her son.[184] Azariah Pinney wrote to his sister about their father: "I hope he is not inclinable to marry now in his old age."[185]

THE DECISION TO REMARRY

Widowers shared some objectives in common with widows—such as the desire for companionship—but their priorities and needs often differed. Widowers might want to provide a mother for young children or, if childless, to start a family. Thomas Boddington, when his first wife died in childbirth, immediately married his niece, and his father promoted the

---

[178] PCC, Berkeley 211, 1656; PCC, Rivers 27 and 44, 1645.
[179] PCC, Ruthen 272, 1657; PCC, Pell 436 and 547, 1659.
[180] CLRO, CSB IV. [181] CLRO, CSB IV.
[182] MacFarlane, *Marriage and Love in England*, 231–5; Jordan, *Charities London*, 281; Carlton, "Widow's Tale," 119, 127; Boulton, "London Widowhood," 341; Todd "Remarrying Widow," 65, 83.
[183] *Marescoe-David Letters*, ed. H. Roseveare (British Academy, 1987), 5.
[184] Will of Sarah Pitt, BL, Egerton MS 1,971, 1700.
[185] J. Pinney, *The Letters, 1677–93*, ed. G. F. Nuttall (Oxford, 1939), letter dated 14 Oct. 1697.

marriage as "best for the children," on whom he settled his first wife's portion of £2,000.[186] Some widowers were mainly interested in finding a wife to run their household or to take care of them as they aged.

Often widowers preferred virgins and wanted young and active spouses without young children from a prior marriage; stepchildren constituted negative capital and absorbed time and money, though the prospect of borrowing an orphan's portion cheaply could be an incentive in London. A widower might anticipate conflict between his own children and any children that his second wife might bring to the marriage or bear for him. Benjamin Ward, a scrivener, put his two youngest children by his first marriage in the care of his eldest daughter and insisted that his second wife should only have what she had brought in plus the specific goods that he had given her and £10 if she did not dispute the will.[187] William Hill, however, married a widow with children and told his nephew "I live very comfortable."[188]

The prospect of a second portion could be a powerful incentive for widowers. Philip Henslow benefited from his marriage to a wealthy widow; Peregrine Pelham, the regicide merchant of Hull, married as his second wife the widow of Sir Peter van Lore.[189] Sir William Courteen married as his second wife Catherine Crommelin, who was deaf and dumb but had a dowry of £60,000.[190] George Boddington received £3,000 with his second wife, having received £2,000 with his first.[191] Josiah Child, before his rise to fame, married as his second wife the twenty-year-old daughter of William Atwood and widow of Thomas Stone, receiving a portion of £3,000 plus £250 and household goods.[192] Streynsham Master acquired a portion of £15,000 with his second wife.[193]

Rich widows had always presented a tempting target for predatory suitors. Impecunious Elizabethan peers pursued aldermanic widows with zest. "Widows of wealth," wrote John Sanderson, "do dayly faule and ar taken up before they come to ground."[194] A typical refrain of Restoration ballads was "tis good to strike while the iron 's hot"; a *Catalogue*

---

[186] GLL, MS 10,823, fo. 52.   [187] PCC, Pell 9, 1659.
[188] Letter to Abraham Hill dated 20 July 1670, BL, Add. MS 5488, fo. 171.
[189] *Henslowe Papers*, ed. R. A. Foakes (1961), xviii.
[190] *Miscellanea Genealogica et Heraldica*, vol. 2, 160.
[191] GLL, MS 10,823.
[192] Marriage articles, PRO, C 109/19, 1663.   [193] Stone, *Family*, 58.
[194] J. Sanderson, *The Travels*, ed. Sir William Foster, 2d ser. (Hakluyt Society, 67, 1930), 255.

of Ladies for disposal by auction listed a vintner's widow with £4,000 and a grocer's widow with £3,250.[195] In one extreme case, the widow of a businessman was kidnapped and forced into a remarriage.[196] The widow of Alderman Bennett attracted the attention of both Heneage Finch and Sir Edward Dering, the latter unsuccessfully making his play through the children.[197] Women could be equally predatory. The widowed Frances Dowcett married the rich, but senile, timber merchant, Robert Weedon, nine months before his death and was accused of altering his will.[198] A widow who managed to outlive several rich husbands could accumulate a fortune.

Widows with independent property and no parents or guardians to veto their wishes, could exercise greater choice in their second marriages. They could and sometimes did disregard all social restraints and marry for love or sex. When George Bamforth IV died at twenty-eight from a fall, his widow married the butler.[199] The widow of Thomas Clark in India married a Venetian.[200] Widow Wright, who married four months after her bereavement, said that she was tired of old men and wanted a man who would love her.[201] A Manchester wig maker who had lost two wives and five infants commented in his diary on a woman's reaction to his advances in 1712: "she does not like on't, but I believe she does."[202]

Nonetheless, impulsive matches were rare, and widows had to consider hard realities. Often they had young children to rear who might benefit from a substitute father. In 1659 Mary Fenn, the widow of a grocer, remarried Richard Awdesley on the condition that he maintain her two orphans.[203] Widows also had to consider their long-term economic needs. Wealthy widows could afford to stay widowed, but poorer widows often had to remarry to secure sufficient financial support.[204]

---

[195] N. Wurzbach, *The Rise of the English Street Ballad, 1550–1650* (Cambridge, 1990), 72–3; C. J. S. Thompson, *Love, Marriage, and Romance in Old London* (1936), 48.
[196] L. Stone, *Uncertain Unions* (Oxford, 1992), 96–104.
[197] *Conway Letters*, ed. M. H. Nicolson (1930), 3.
[198] Cox, *Hatred Pursued*, 91.
[199] D. Hey, *Fiery Blades* (Leicester, 1991), 181.
[200] H. D. Love, *Vestiges of Old Madras, 1640–1800*, vol. 1 (1913), 466.
[201] M. Abbott, *Life Cycles in England, 1560–1720* (New York, 1996), 105.
[202] *Collectanea Relating to Manchester*, ed. J. Harland, vol. 68 (Chetham Society 1866), 197.
[203] CLRO, CSB II.
[204] R. O'Day, *The Family* (New York, 1994), 114; I. K. Ben-Amos, "Women Apprentices," *Continuity and Change* 6 (1991): 240.

Widows who had a business that required male assistance were more likely to remarry.

Remarriage technically put a widow back under couverture. Whereas a widower kept his own and his new wife's property, she could lose both the capital and income from her first marriage and control over the portions of her children. The reason that widows appear to have tolerated testamentary restrictions without much fuss is that they would have been anxious to protect their offspring. The widow of Richard Whitelocke, who succeeded in raising four sons and providing them with £600, had to cope with an abusive second husband whose creditors pursued her.[205]

A sensible widow could, however, protect herself against such hazards. The widow of Roger Hatton sold her estate to her new husband and put the proceeds into a trust for her sons from her first marriage.[206] When the widower David Le Noble remarried a widow with children, their settlement protected the £1,500 that she brought in and allowed £1,000 for her prior children; he agreed to add £300 but reserved £200 for a child by his first wife.[207] Giles Ellbridge of Bristol, who had at least five children from his first marriage, settled £3,000 on his second wife with whom he had four more children.[208] Although Ralph Akehurst sold the annuity of £20 p.a. that his wife had inherited from her prior marriage, by agreement he not only left her land and a share of his house and furniture, but he also provided that his sons make good the annuity out of the land they inherited.[209]

The decision whether or not to remarry was made with difficulty and for many different reasons depending on individual circumstances. As with first marriages, recourse was had to astrologers.[210] Remarriage did not imply lack of feeling for a deceased spouse, and indeed fond memories and sexual jealousy often proved a deterrent. Widows remarried both for sound business reasons and to satisfy their physical and emotional needs. They often chose not to remarry so that they could be better

[205] J. Whitelock, *Liber Familicus*, ed. J. Bruce, 1st ser., vol. 70 (Camden Society 1858), ii; J. R. MacConica, "Social Relations of Tudor Oxford," *Transactions of the Royal Historical Society*, 5th ser., 27 (1977): 125.
[206] PRO, PROB 11/444/77; M. Prior, "Women and Wills" in *English Rural Society*, ed. J. Chartres and D. Hey (1990), 206.
[207] PCC, Hyde 132, 1665.
[208] F. W. Todd, *Humphrey Hooke of Bristol* (Boston, Mass., 1938), 60.
[209] PCC, Aylett 289, 1655.
[210] Thomas, *Religion and Magic*, 374.

mothers or pursue religious and other interests.[211] Many were unwilling to surrender their property to another man or risk forfeiting their status by marrying outside their late husband's livery company.[212]

One example of why a widow might choose not to marry is Katherine Austen, widowed at twenty-nine with three young children. Her mother remarried Alderman Highlord, but Katherine decided to honor the memory of her husband, who had made it clear in his will that he opposed her remarriage. Here is her caustic response to one suitor and her advice to her daughter:

A gentleman tried to say he would like her if she was poor . . . then he took me by the hand, he said what a hand was there to be adored. I answered him looking upon a tuft of grass which had growing in it a yellow flower, that that spire of grass was fitter to be adored then my hand. [She did not believe] that men had rather be in the society of women and women love better that of men. Noe I doe discover by a comparison not to give credit to words. The King courts the City and loves it because its rich. And then it will be safe to the King. As a rich wise woman is loved. And if she does not love again, it is noe matter if she is not wise and rich. [She warned her daughter against] fond affection and deluded judgement, [that] too great love occasioned much unhappiness [that singular virtues could be found in a rich as well as a poor man.] For my part I doe not injury to none by not loveing. As for my body it can be enjoyed but by one. And I hope its the worst part of me and that which every servant maid and country wench may excel mine and can give the same satisfaction as mine. . . . If any thing in me is to be loved, I hope tis my mind.[213]

DRAWBACKS AND BENEFITS

Widowhood did not necessarily bring economic security. A widow could only be as rich as her late husband, and her income would fall unless she inherited the whole estate. Widows of small tradesmen were usually poor because the income from one-third of a modest personal estate was simply insufficient. Families whose male head had not earned adequate reserves, were impoverished should he die prematurely with young children. A widow who chose not to remarry might be forced to continue the business. She could also be at the mercy of her children, if they were grown and responsible for paying her an annuity.

[211] B. J. Todd, "Demographic Determinism and Female Agency," *Continuity and Change* 9 (1994): 422, 426.
[212] T. Young, *Annals of the Barber Surgeons* (1890), 272.
[213] BL, Sloane MS 4454, fos. 9, 94–96 (1665).

Widows could also suffer from lack of knowledge. If inexperienced, they could mismanage their inheritance; if timid or sickly, they could be cheated by aggressive relatives or unscrupulous executors. Defoe and others pointed out that many widows, though not helpless, were uninformed about their husband's business and dependent on the help of others or forced to marry the apprentice.[214] Katherine Austen complained bitterly that her ignorance of business was exploited by those with whom she had to deal. In fact Max Weber would have been proud of her; she meticulously recorded her loans, rents, taxes, and losses from pickpockets and claimed proudly that she doubled the value of the estate she had inherited.[215] On the other hand, the widow of Christopher Tomlinson was alleged to have squandered £25,000 of the £35,000 she handled as administratrix; Leonora Marescoe went shopping for jewelry with her late husband's capital.[216]

Living as a solitary could be lonely, if the children were married and resident elsewhere. Alternatively, a widow might have to share her home with an adult child or become dependent on and tied to children with whom relations were strained. Anthony Gomes Serra in his will of 1706 left money to his sister as long as she did not live with his widow. In 1652 Arthur Juxon, a salter, gave his widow the choice of £1,200 or £50 p.a. if she lived with one of their sons.[217]

Nonetheless, widowhood combined with age gave a woman power, a legal identity, and independence.[218] Many became matriarchs surrounded by dependents. Some, like Rachel Pengelly and Mary Ferrar, were heads of households that could include unmarried children, elderly parents, sisters, kin, and lodgers.[219] Widows usually did not take over their husband's business, but instead they managed portfolios of passive investments and collected their rents and interest (see chapter 9). They were less likely than landed widows to be manipulated by kinsmen or bound by restrictive settlements.

As executrices, widows of businessmen gained in status, business knowledge, and authority. They asserted themselves against other beneficiaries of their husbands' wills. Sir Thomas Gresham's widow created endless problems for the Mercers Company, since she had a son from a

[214] D. Defoe, *Complete English Tradesman* (1727; reprint, New York, 1970), 215.
[215] BL, Sloane MS 4454.   [216] *Marescoe-David letters*, 151, 206.
[217] PCC, Bowyer 59.
[218] E. T., *The Lawes Resolutions of Women's Rights*, 242.
[219] BL, Add. MS 32,456; O'Day, *The Family*, 270.

previous marriage and was given a life interest.[220] Sir Thomas White's widow created similar headaches for St. John's College, Oxford.[221] The widow of Michael Mitford stood by her marriage settlement and refused to pay some annuities under her late husband's will.[222] The enterprising widow of John Hind was accused of concealing assets from her late husband's creditors.[223]

Even when widows were not appointed executrix they could still sue the executors and dispute the authenticity of the inventory, as did Rachel Turner.[224] The widow of Thomas Cope, a London dyer, sued in chancery to recover her entitlement in the 1680s, and Anne Kersteman sued to enforce the terms of her marriage settlement in 1712.[225] James Tandin left his wife £1,000 and her jewels and personal effects, as agreed, but his widow believed that his estate was worth £6,000–10,000 and sued for her one-third.[226] In 1705 the widow of Sir Jeremy Sambrook, acting for her infant children, contested her husband's will on the grounds that the testator had not been compos mentis.[227] Francis Glover claimed that she had been cheated of her share of her husband's estate, and chancery eventually gave her the administration.[228] Widows sometimes proved adept at claiming inexperience in the law to further their claims in court.

SUMMARY

Thanks to differential age and life expectancy, wives of businessmen were likely to survive their husbands. Widows were usually appointed as executrix, but increasingly husbands, particularly when they had major assets, made their wives joint executors or chose their children or kin. Widows were excused the responsibility, not because their husbands distrusted their efficiency, but because executors had a hard, thankless, and risky task.

Widows were less likely to remarry than widowers and waited longer. In part this reflected the hostility of contemporaries to remarriage and the opposition of husbands, children, and kin; in part it was a function

---

[220] I. G. Doolittle, *History of the Mercers Company, 1579–1629* (1994), 33.
[221] W. H. Stevenson, *Early History of St. Johns College, Oxford* (Oxford, 1939), 155, 387.
[222] PRO, C 10/381/47.
[223] B. H. Johnson, *Berkeley Square to Bond Street* (1952), 120.
[224] CLRO, MC 6/10.
[225] Horwitz, *Chancery Equity Records*, 78; PRO, C 107/12.
[226] Earle, *Making of the Middle Class*, 196.   [227] PRO, C 10/304/59.
[228] Appleby, "Dr. Dee," 51.

of age and the availability of partners. But in many cases it was the personal choice of the widow. Consequently there were more widows than widowers, and the wife of a businessman could expect to spend around one-fifth of her life as a widow. Although widowhood could be financially insecure and often involved loss of a beloved partner, it still gave a woman independence, often for the first time in her life, and the benefits probably outweighed the disadvantages. The crucial factor was always the wealth at her disposal.

Part II

The Business Family

4

Parents and Children

Henry Cuffe divided the life course into the following stages: infancy (0–4), boyhood (5–10), "budding and blossoming age" (11–18), youth (19–25), "flourishing and middle age" or prime and manhood (25–40/50), old age (over 50), and "decrepid old age."[1] The three crucial stages in multiples of 7 for boys and 6 for girls, were 7/6 for the end of innocence, 14/12 for discretion, and 21/18 for majority.[2] Each stage of the life cycle raised different problems for parents and provoked different responses.

What was the size of business families in comparison with other occupations and in relation to wealth? What was the ratio of sons to daughters and the frequency of three-generation families? How many children were orphaned and raised by substitute parents? In what ways did parents handle birth and infancy, childhood and adolescence, and how far did they follow prescriptive advice? How did they interpret their rights and duties, and did their attitudes and behavior change over time?

SIZE OF THE FAMILY

In period I, of 3,578 families whose progeny is known, 10.3 percent had no children; in period II, of 3,763 families, 12.8 percent were childless.

---

[1] H. Cuffe, *The Differences of the Age of Man's Life* (1607), 118–20. On the cultural construction of ideas about childhood see J. Cunningham, "Histories of Childhood," *American Historical Review* 103 (1998): 1195–208.
[2] K. V. Thomas, *Age and Authority in Early Modern England* (Raleigh Lecture, 1976), 20. Rights were acquired at different ages and the rules varied over time and with status; a boy could choose his curator at fourteen, but an indentured apprentice had to wait several years beyond twenty-one until he came of age with his freedom; the age of majority under Roman law was twenty-five. The law recognized only three stages—childhood, service, and adulthood: see L. Bonfield, "Was There a Third Age?" in *An Aging World*, ed. J. M. Eekelar and D. Pearl (Oxford, 1989), 40.

Table 4.1. *Numbers of Children per Family Who Survived to Maturity*
(All Marriages Combined [Percentage of Known Cases])

	Period I	Period II	Bracket I	Bracket II	Bracket III	Bracket IV	Cohort I	Cohort II	Cohort III	Cohort IV
0	10.3	12.8	10.1	7.4	11.9	14.1	8.1	6.5	12.4	15.5
1	27.1	24.0	27.5	16.4	17.9	5.9	14.3	19.8	20.0	24.9
2	18.5	20.0	22.5	21.9	14.6	9.4	9.7	18.4	18.2	15.5
3	13.3	13.4	16.3	18.7	11.5	11.8	10.8	12.3	12.9	12.7
4	10.3	10.3	10.1	13.8	12.8	12.9	13.5	12.7	11.6	11.1
5	7.3	7.5	6.2	10.2	9.2	11.8	8.9	10.9	9.0	3.3
6+	13.2	11.9	7.4	11.7	22.2	34.1	34.8	19.4	16.0	17.1
Total Families	3,578	3,763	258	1,896	1,389	85	259	479	809	181
Median Children	1.8	1.7	1.8	2.7	3.0	4.2	3.7	2.6	2.0	1.9
Mean Children	2.8	2.7	2.5	3.1	3.5	4.4	4.6	3.5	3.1	2.7

This was a consequence of high infant and child mortality rather than of infertility or late marriage.[3] Six to seven births were required just to replace the two parents. If there was only a 1-in-2 chance of reaching adulthood, there was a 1-in-8 chance that no sons would survive. In the whole population out of every five families, only three were likely to produce a male heir, one would have a female heir, and one no heir.[4]

A few business families were over endowed with children. Humphrey Brown, a girdler, had ten surviving children, · to each of whom he gave £500.[5] Ralph Woodcock had twenty-four children, Richard Wich eighteen, Anthony Lambert and Thomas Barlow thirteen, John Rogers seventeen, Sir John Langham sixteen, Thomas Cony nineteen, Thomas Robinson sixteen, and John Davenant fourteen. Customer Smythe had six sons and six daughters, and John Offley, who lived to seventy-four, had seventeen children of whom thirteen survived. The wife of a Minehead merchant had eighteen children, and George Badger, draper of Stratford, lived to eighty-three and had sixteen children.[6] In Hull Henry Maister had nine sons and two daughters, all of whom survived; John Rogers had seven children and Mark Kirby ten, five of whom survived.[7]

When children from more than one union were combined, families could be huge. Dereham Baldwin, a mercer, had several children by his first wife, three daughters and nine stepchildren with his second wife, and two daughters by his third.[8] William Hough, a clothworker, had one son and four daughters of his own and several stepchildren from his wife's former marriage.[9] Edmund Sheaffe, a clothier, had four stepchildren from his wife's first marriage plus three daughters and seven sons of his own.[10]

---

[3] In the eighteenth century the rate of involuntary infertility has been put at 8 percent: see C. D. Rogers, *Local Family History* (Manchester, 1991), 103.

[4] E. A. Wrigley review of Habakkuk, *Economic History Review*, 2d ser., 26 (1973): 727, and "Fertility Strategy for the Individual and the Group" in *Historical Studies of Changing Fertility*, ed. C. Tilly (Princeton, 1978), tables 3.1–3; J. Goody, *Production and Reproduction* (Cambridge, 1976), appendix 2; R. Schofield and E. A. Wrigley, "Remarriage Intervals" in *Marriage and Remarriage in Populations of the Past*, ed. J. Dupaquier et al. (New York, 1981), 239.

[5] PCC, St. John 112, 1631.

[6] D. McLaren, "Marital Fertility and Lactation," in *Women in English Society, 1500–1800*, ed. M. Prior (1985), 38; Jones, *Family Life in Shakespeare's England*, 91.

[7] T. Gent, *History of Hull* (1735; reprint, Hull, 1869), 34–41.

[8] M. Edmond, "Limners and Picture Makers," *Walpole Society* 47 (1978–80): 120.

[9] PCC, Grey 67, 1651.

[10] A. B. Langdale, *Phineas Fletcher* (New York, 1937), 9.

High fertility was, however, usually offset by high infant and child mortality. Jacob Turner had eight children, two of whom survived; Ambrose Crowley III had eleven children, five died young and only one son survived.[11] Ralph Thoresby had ten children, but only two sons and one daughter survived.[12] Children also died in their adolescence and early adulthood before their parents, as in the Gresham and Cotesworth families. This accounts for the large number of residual legatees named in wills.

The roller coaster of births and deaths is well illustrated by the memorandum book of Richard Farrington. Ten months after his marriage, he recorded "on Saturday the 31 Aug 1706 about 8 minutes past 8 a clock at night, my most dear wife was safely delivered of a daughter," but seven days later the child was dead, and this was just the first of a desolate progression of deaths of thirteen babies and children, leaving him with just one male heir.[13]

The median number of children per business family who survived was 1.8 for period I and 1.7 for period II; but 30 percent of families in both periods had more than four children and 13/12 percent (mean/median) had more than six (see table 4.1).[14] The mean/median number of surviving children per family rose with wealth from 2.5/1.8 in bracket I to 3.1/2.7 in bracket II, 3.5/3 in bracket III, and 4.4/4.2 in bracket IV. There is a slight statistical correlation between the number of surviving children and both wealth and age at death; the wealthier the family and the older the father at death, the more children survived.[15] The mean/median number of children per family declined, however, during the seventeenth century from 4.6/3.7 in cohort I to 3.5/2.6 in cohort II, 3.1/2 in cohort III, and 2.7/1.9 in cohort IV. The average number of surviving children per wife was 2.8 in cohort I, 1.7 in cohort II, 1.5 in cohort III, and 2 in cohort IV.

The number of children born was determined by fertility, age at marriage, the life span of the husband, and the number of years his wife or

[11] M. W. Flinn, *Men of Iron* (Edinburgh, 1962), 42.
[12] Thoresby, *Diary*, ix.
[13] GLL, MS 2708.
[14] Although the number of children who survived can be picked up from a number of sources, those who were born and died young can only be recovered systematically from parish birth and burial registers. All known births have been recorded in the database, but the data has not been used because it understates the true numbers to an unacceptable degree.
[15] The Pearson R correlation between number of surviving children and wealth of father at death = +0.073; the correlation with age of father at death = +0.110.

Table 4.2. *The Children of Richard and Elizabeth Farrington*

Date	Name	Age and cause of death
1706	Elizabeth	7 days
1708	Elizabeth I	33 yrs, 4 mons, 2 days (dropsy)
1709	Hester	2 yrs, 3 mons, 10 days (small pox)
1711	Richard	Survives father
1713	Margaret	4 yrs, 22 days
1714	Sara	7 wks, 1 day
1715	Anne	8 wks, 1 day
1716	Sara I	11 mons, 10 days
1718	Mary	7 yrs, 2 mons, 8 days
1719	Robert	2 yrs, 7 mons, 2 days
1721	Joseph	9 mons, 25 days
1722	Martha	5 mons, 2 days
1723	Thomas	7 wks, 6 days
1725	Anna Christina	19 days
1726	Ann Maria	5 yrs, 8 mons, 6 days (smallpox)
1727	Wife dies	
1706–26	11 daughters, 4 sons	1 son survives the father

Source: Memorandum book of Richard Farrington, distiller of London, GLL, MS 2708. The couple were married in 1705.

wives could bear children. Whereas a marriage of under five years was likely to produce only 1.26 children, a marriage of eleven to fifteen years would produce 2.94, and a marriage of sixteen to twenty years 3.22 children.[16] The number who survived to maturity depended in part on factors such as wealth and upbringing, but mainly on luck and genes. Wet nursing may have increased the number of both births and infantile deaths. Though the number of children per family rose with remarriage (except when the first wife died very young), the majority of children appear to have been conceived during the first marriage.[17]

COMPARISONS

In London (1580–1650) the wealthier parishes had higher fertility and lower mortality rates; 60 percent of children survived to age fifteen

---

[16] Earle, *A City Full of People*, table 5.3.
[17] When businessmen remarried, it is only possible to allocate children between their wives in that minority of cases where detailed records or pedigrees survive. Wills list the children surviving at the time of composition, but usually do not indicate the mother—therefore precise data on the distribution of children between successive marriages are not available.

compared with 50 percent in poorer parishes.[18] London was particularly unhealthy. Respiratory infections may have been responsible for high neonatal mortality, though smallpox and measles increasingly killed children in the first year of life.[19] In St. Botolph within Aldgate (1550–1625) 70 percent of children survived to age one, 48 percent to age five, and 27–30 percent to age fifteen.[20] A sample of 494 Consistory Court wills (1580–97) reveals an average of two children per family with 42 percent testators having no surviving children and 24 percent only one son or daughter.[21] In the parish of St. Leonards, Eastcheap, the mean number of baptisms per family was only 4.4.[22] Infant mortality may have been lower among tradesmen, but in aldermanic families, of 4.75 children born, only 2.5 survived infancy and 1.9 to maturity.[23] In the early eighteenth century 45 percent of the aldermen had no male issue.[24]

Gregory King thought that there were 2.6 children per couple in London. However, in a sample of forty London parishes in 1695 the mean number of persons per house was 6.0 and the mean number per household was 5.2 within and 3.8 outside the walls; the mean number of children per house was 1.4 (ranging from 0.8 to 1.6) with 1.5 in the richer parishes.[25] By 1700 infant mortality was 300 per 1,000, and there were only 1.2 offspring per family, though the houseful (including lodgers and servants) was 6.1, and the household (including stepchildren and kin) was 8.3.[26] In 1708 Edmund Hattor recorded five to a family in London.[27] The mean size of households in Southwark was 3.8–4.3 with apprentices and lodgers raising business households to six or more;

[18] R. Finlay, *Population and Metropolis*, 16; J. Landers, *Death and the Metropolis* (Cambridge, 1993), 192.

[19] W. F. Bynum and R. Porter, *Living and Dying in London* (Medical History Supplement, 11, 1991), 11.

[20] T. R. Forbes, *Chronicle from Aldgate* (New Haven, 1971), table 4.

[21] Brodsky, "Widows in late Elizabethan London," 136, table 5.3.

[22] P. S. Seaver, *Wallington's World* (Stanford, 1985), 70–1.

[23] D. McLaren, "Fertility and Infant Mortality", *The Seventeenth Century* 22 (1978): 381.

[24] N. Rogers, "Money, Land, and Lineage", *Social History* 4 (1979): 450.

[25] D. V. Glass, "Social economic status" in *Studies in London History*, ed. A. E. J. Hollaender and W. Kellaway (1969), table 1, and "Notes on Demography of London," tables 1–3; *London Inhabitants within the Walls, 1695*, ed. D. V. Glass, vol. 2 (London Record Society, 1966), table 4, xxx–xxxii; J. Alexander, "The City Revealed" in *Surveying the People*, ed. K. Schurer and T. Arkell (Cambridge, 1992), 186.

[26] Landers, *Death and Metropolis*, 190; R. Wall, "Regional and Temporal Variation" in *Regional Demographic Development*, ed. J. Hobcraft and P. Rees (1977), table 4.6–7.

[27] E. Hatton, *A New View of London* (1708), v.

victualers in Romford had a household mean of four.[28] The mean size of alien households was 4.8 with 1.9 children.[29]

In other towns much the same was true. One-third of Bristol citizens had one child, 27.3 percent two children, and 19.3 percent three or more.[30] In Worcester the mean household size of tradesmen was 4.8 with 2 children, in Coventry 7.4, in King's Lynn 4–4.5, in Southampton 4.3, and in Poole 5.1.[31] In Chester the mean household size of merchants was 5.9 with 3.6 adults.[32] In Norwich 131 mayors at death had 168 living sons.[33] In Cambridge the mean household size was 3.8, but it was 4.8 for merchants and retailers with 2.6 children, and 15.25 percent of couples were childless.[34] In Stratford (1600–30) 32 percent of children died before the age of sixteen; on average 5.1 children were born, of whom 2.3 survived.[35] In Chilvers Cotton, Warwickshire, the mean household size of tradesmen and craftsmen was 4.55 with three offspring.[36] In Shrewsbury 33.6 percent of the population had no children and 13.2 percent had four or more; mean household size was 4.3 with 1.6 children; tradesmen and craftsmen had a mean of 4.8.[37] In Tudor York the mean household size was 4.7 with 2.7 children, though among the aldermen four children were common after 1550.[38] In Leeds twelve of forty-one aldermen (1660–1700) had no male heir and ten only had one son.[39]

[28] A. L. Beir and R. A. P. Finlay, eds., *London, 1500–1700* (1986), 46; Boulton, *Neighbourhood and Society*, 122–4; M. McIntosh, "Servants and the Household," *Journal of Family History* 9 (1984): tables 2, 4.

[29] C. Littleton, "Social Interactions of Aliens" in *The Strangers Progress*, ed. R. Vigne and G. C. Gibbs (Proceedings of the Huguenot Society of London 26, 1995), 152.

[30] J. R. Holman, "Orphans in Pre-Industrial Towns," *Local Population Studies* 15 (1975): 41.

[31] I. Roy and S. Porter, "Social and Economic Structure," *Bulletin of the Institute Historical Research* 53 (1980): 211, table 6; R. Tittler, "The Economy of Poole," *Southern History* 7 (1985): 96.

[32] N. J. Alldridge, "House and Household in Restoration Chester," *Urban History Yearbook* (1983): 44, table 4.

[33] J. T. Evans, "Decline of Oligarchy," *Journal of British Studies* 14 (1974): 58.

[34] N. Goose, "Household Size and Structure" in *The Tudor and Stuart Town*, ed. J. Barry (1990), 100, 104, tables 7–9.

[35] Jones, *Family Life in Shakespeare's England*, figure 1.

[36] G. Shochet, "Patriarchialism in Stuart England," *Historical Journal* 19 (1969): 419.

[37] J. C. Hindson, "Family Structure, Inheritance, and Kinship" (Ph.D. diss., University of Wales, 1991), 93, 214, and tables 1.17, 2.3, and 2.10.

[38] Palliser, *Tudor York*, 118; V. M. Cowgill, "Marriage and Progeny in York, 1538–1751," *Kroeber Anthropological Society Papers* 42 (1970): 61. V. M. Cowgill, "The People of York 1538–1812," *Scientific American* 222 (1970): 112, suggests 3.56 with an excess of females, but has only used the printed registers for the wealthier parishes.

[39] J. W. Kirby, "Restoration Leeds and the Aldermen," *Northern History* 22 (1986): 167.

In Elizabethan Exeter, on the other hand, 40 percent of merchant families had five to six children and 15 percent seven or more.[40] In Edinburgh, in 1694, the mean sibling group was 1.2 with one to four children in upper-status households.[41]

In the general population, out of every 1,000 born, 799 survived to age 1, 668 to age 5, and 624 to age 10.[42] The probability of anyone at 44 having one brother or sister was 0.30 and the probability of anyone having a descendant aged 77 was 0.84.[43] The size of households always varied between occupational groups.[44] The mean household size was 4.75 with two children (2.9 for tradesmen and craftsmen).[45] Most families probably lived in households of six or more, and 14 percent of couples were probably childless.[46]

The peers lost one-third of their children before they reached fifteen; the number of children per married peer fell from around five (before 1660) to three to four (1660–1730); 18.6 percent of all peers ever married were childless and 29 percent of marriages had no issue; the extinction rate was 40 percent (1558–1641).[47] Of the 1,226 baronetcies created (1611–1800) 55 percent were extinct by 1800, and only 295 existed by 1928; only fourteen of ninety-three families achieved succession in single direct male line, often through grandsons.[48] The proportion of gentry families with no male heir rose from 25 percent to 40 percent.[49] The Quakers lost 22.5 percent of their infants and had a mean

[40] W. G. Hoskins, "The Elizabethan Merchants of Exeter" in *Elizabethan Government and Society*, ed. S. T. Bindoff et al. (1961), 177.

[41] H. M. Dingwall, *Late Seventeenth-Century Edinburgh* (Aldersley, 1994), 42–4.

[42] R. Schofield and E. A. Wrigley, "Infant and Child Mortality" in *Health, Medicine, and Mortality*, ed. C. Webster (Cambridge, 1979), 95; E. A. Wrigley and R. Schofield, *Population History of England from Reconstitution* (1997), 218, 249, 306; A. Burgière, *History of the Family*, vol. 2 (Cambridge, 1996), 14.

[43] P. Laslett, "La parenté en chiffres," *Annales* 43 (1988): table 2.

[44] J. Flandrin, *Families in Former Times: Kinship, Household, and Sexuality* (Cambridge, 1979), 57.

[45] Laslett, "Mean Household Size," 125, 148, and tables 1.6, 13, 4.15, 16.

[46] J. Patten, "The Hearth Taxes, 1662–1689," *Local Population Studies* 7 (1971): 23; R. Schofield and E. A. Wrigley, "Remarriage Intervals," 220.

[47] T. H. Hollingsworth, *Demography of the Peerage*, vol. 18 (Population Studies Supplement, 1965), 29–32, 36, 45; *idem.*, "Demography of Ducal Families" in *Population in History*, ed. D. V. Glass and D. E. C. Eversley (1965), table 29; Stone, *Crisis of the Aristocracy*, 168–9.

[48] P. Roebuck, *Yorkshire Baronets 1640–1760* (Oxford, 1980), 276; A. R. Wagner, *English Genealogy*, 3d ed. (Oxford, 1983), 241; K. M. Wachter and P. Laslett. "Measuring Patrilinear Extinction" in *Statistical Studies of Historical Structure*, ed. K. M. Wachter (New York, 1978), 134–5. Extinction of title is not identical with failure of male heirs.

[49] Stone, *The Family, Sex, and Marriage*, graph 9; G. H. Jones, *The Foundations of Modern Wales* (Oxford, 1987), 94.

family size (1650–99) of 6.6.[50] Jewish families lost 48 percent of their children before the age of ten, and their mean household size in 1684 and 1695 was 4.5–5 with 2.5 children.[51]

Infant mortality was much lower in New England, though some 40 percent of sons in New York did not survive to adulthood. In Philadelphia seven out of thirty-two elite business families had no children, and seventy-eight had no male heirs.[52] The mean number of children per family was three in colonial Bristol, 7.8 in Plymouth, 7.2 in Andover, and 4.6 in Dedham and Hingham.[53] The mean number of children of emigrants to New England was 3.1.[54] In Jamaica, in contrast, over one-half of 302 testators (1665–1734) had no surviving children.[55]

SEX RATIOS AND GRANDCHILDREN

Thomas Lodge took wagers with his factor on the sex of his unborn children, and chance determined the birth order and sex ratio of surviving children in any particular family.[56] In the whole population males had a slight advantage: John Graunt calculated from the bills of mortality (1628–62) that the ratio of males to females at birth was 110:100 and at death 106.8:100.[57] The actual ratio of surviving sons to daughters in the database was 118:100 (5,463:4,632) in period I and 103.6:100 (5,078:4,902) in period II.[58] It changed from 112:100 in cohort I to

---

[50] R. T. Vann and D. Eversley, *Friends in Life and Death* (Cambridge, 1992), table 2.4, 241.

[51] A. S. Diamond, "The Community of the Resettlement," *Transactions of the Jewish Historical Society of England* 24 (1974): 143–4.

[52] G. E. Byers, *The Nation of Nantucket* (Boston, 1987), 92; J. D. Goodfriend, *Before the Melting Pot* (Princeton, 1992), 31; B. Nash, "The Early Merchants of Philadelphia" in *The World of William Penn*, ed. R. S. and M. M. Dunn (Philadelphia, 1986), 343.

[53] R. S. Seward, "The Colonial Family in America," *Journal of Marriage and the Family* 35 (1973): 61.

[54] V. D. Anderson, *New England's Generation* (Cambridge, 1991), 23.

[55] T. Burnard, "Family Continuity and Female Independence in Jamaica," *Continuity and Change* 7 (1992): 186.

[56] C. J. Sisson, "Thomas Lodge" in *Thomas Lodge and Other Elizabethans*, ed. C. J. Sisson (Cambridge, 1933), 15, 353.

[57] J. Graunt, *Natural and Political Observations*, ed. W. F. Willcox (Baltimore, 1939), 70.

[58] The ratio in period I seems somewhat unbalanced and the data may reflect a bias toward the recording of sons in the sources, since it is unlikely that mortality among daughters would have been disproportionately high. The ratio of males to females born in modern populations is 105:100: see R. A. P. Finlay, "Differential Child Mortality," *Annales de démographie historique* (1981): 76. On the other hand Hollingsworth found a 122:100 ratio for first births: see T. H. Hollingsworth, "Studies in Quantitative History," *History and Theory* 9 (1969): 74.

Table 4.3. *Distribution of Children by Sex (Percentage of Known Cases)*

	Period I	Period II	Bracket I	Bracket II	Bracket III	Bracket IV	Cohort I	Cohort II	Cohort III	Cohort IV
No children	10.3	12.8	10.1	7.4	11.9	14.1	7.0	6.5	12.4	15.5
Only sons	12.6	11.5	15.9	14.8	7.3	4.7	8.5	8.8	11.4	12.2
Only daughters	11.5	12.1	14.0	13.9	10.9	9.4	11.2	10.4	10.0	13.3
Sons and daughters	65.6	63.7	60.1	63.9	69.9	71.8	73.4	74.3	66.3	59.1
Total families	3,578	3,763	258	1,896	1,389	85	259	479	809	181
Total sons	5,463	5,078	338	2,977	2,399	175	635	861	1,233	257
Total daughters	4,632	4,902	309	2,816	2,444	200	566	788	1,246	244
Grandchildren	207	122	3	75	91	7	23	24	37	8

Table 4.4. *Number of Orphans per Family (Percentage of Known Cases)*

	Period I	Period II	Bracket I	Bracket II	Bracket III	Bracket IV	Cohort I	Cohort II	Cohort III	Cohort IV
1 Orphan	25.5	25.3	30.6	24.0	19.4	–	16.1	32.0	19.8	37.9
2 Orphans	21.8	28.6	25.0	27.1	22.3	42.9	22.6	26.0	27.8	24.1
3 Orphans	20.1	19.2	18.1	19.3	19.1	28.6	25.8	12.0	21.4	13.8
4 Orphans or more	32.5	26.9	26.3	29.6	39.2	28.6	35.5	30.0	31.0	24.1
Median	2.6	1.9	1.8	2.0	2.9	2.5	2.1	1.7	1.9	1.8
Mean	3.00	2.7	2.5	2.8	3.1	1.5	2.9	1.9	2.8	2.3
Total Families with Orphans	864	1,059	232	1,304	309	8	31	50	126	29

109:100 in cohort II, 99:100 in cohort III, and 105:100 in cohort IV. Among all residents of London, more boys seem to have been born, though more girls survived; the ratio in 1695 was 98:100.[59] The ratio for children born to peers (1558–1641) was 102.6:100 (879:857).[60]

In period I 401 first marriages and 23 second marriages produced only daughters; 437 first and 9 second marriages produced only sons. Of all marriages whose progeny are known (3,578), 24.1 percent had either only sons or daughters, and 21.8 percent had no sons. In period II the situation was much the same: 440 first and 15 second marriages produced only daughters; 414 first and 13 second marriages produced only sons. Of all marriages whose progeny is known (3,763), 23.6 percent had either only sons or daughters and 24.9 percent had no sons.

A late age of marriage led to wider spacing between generations. A businessman who married at twenty-eight, for example, could still expect a child at thirty and a grandchild at sixty.[61] George Boddington lost many infants but still had grandchildren.[62] In period I 62.8 percent of businessmen lived beyond sixty and in period II 55.5 percent (see table 3.1). A significant number of business families, therefore, had three generations. Grandchildren are mentioned by 204 testators in period I and 122 in period II.[63]

Several families had numerous grandchildren. Thomas Lyon, a merchant tailor, had eight granddaughters from two daughters.[64] William Tirrey, a goldsmith, had four grandchildren by his daughter's first marriage and two by her second marriage.[65] Gerard Gore, who died in 1607, had seven sons and twenty-nine grandchildren.[66] William Atwood had ten grandsons and seven granddaughters when he died.[67] Thomas Hollis, who died in 1718 at eighty-four, had ten grandchildren.[68] James Denew, when he died at seventy-eight in 1705, had thirteen grandchildren. John Babington, a salter, had at least seven grandchildren, whom he made his heirs since his sons were already advanced.[69] John Godschall had eleven

---

[59] R. Thompson, "Seventeenth-Century English and Colonial Sex Ratios," *Population Studies* 28 (1974): 163; *London Inhabitants in 1695*, table 5.

[60] Stone, *Crisis of Aristocracy*, appendix XIII.

[61] In comparison, a Connecticut husband had a fifty-fifty chance of becoming a grandfather: see J. T. Main, *Society and Economy in Colonial Connecticut* (Princeton, 1985), 12.

[62] GLL, MS 10,823.

[63] Of the wills sampled by Earle, *Making of the Middle Class*, table 11.3, 4.4 percent mention grandchildren.

[64] PCC, Fines 255, 1647.   [65] PCC, Ridley 84, 1629.

[66] *Miscellenea genealogica et heraldica.*   [67] PRO, PROB 11/398.

[68] PCC, Tenison 178, 1718.   [69] PCC, Bowyer 199, 1652.

grandchildren and Richard Welby, a leatherseller, five grandchildren.[70] The usual number was, however, two to three, as were the cases of Rowland Wilson, Jereman Mayor, Samuel Bridges, and William Essington.[71] Some even outlived their grandchildren since wills, like that of Thomas Lait, occasionally mentioned grandparents.[72]

A few businessmen, like Nehemiah Bourn, Humphrey Hooke of Bristol who lived to seventy-seven, Simon Smith who lived to eighty-two, and Gideon Delaun who died at eighty-nine, even had great-grandchildren.[73] When Mary Herrick died at ninety-seven, she had 142 children, grandchildren, and great-grandchildren, many in business; James Houblon had sixty-seven direct descendants when he died.[74] Richard Farrington noted "in the year 1710 I had 4 generations living in my family, all Elizabeth," that is his daughter, mother, grandmother, and greatgrandmother.

In comparison, some 27 percent of all London families had a grandparent alive; 2.3 percent of all children were grandchildren.[75] In Salisbury and Essex 20 percent of a sample of wills mention grandchildren, with an average of 1.2 grandsons and 1.3 granddaughters.[76] In the whole population, however, few parents lived to be grandparents.[77]

ORPHANS AND BASTARDS

Despite the fact that most businessmen lived into their fifties, many children were orphaned because of late fatherhood and remarriage by widowers.[78] A child born when his father was forty had a fifty-fifty chance of being orphaned by the age of twenty-one. Since it was the death of a father that created a legal orphan, most orphans had in fact a living mother and would today be categorized as children of one-parent families.

[70] PCC, Seager 80, 1634.
[71] PCC, May 160, 1661; PCC, Aylett 161, 1655; H. F. Waters, *Genealogical Gleanings in England*, vol. 1 (Salem, Mass., 1892), 835; PCC, Fairfax 181, 1649.
[72] PCC, Clarke 128, 1625.
[73] PCC, Vere 201; PCC, Pell 380; PCC, Mico 14; F. W. Todd, *Humphrey Hooke of Bristol* (Boston, Mass., 1938), 38–40.
[74] S. Nichols, *History of Leicester*, vol. 2 (1795), 616; J. Houblon, *Pious Memoirs* (1863), 44.
[75] *London Inhabitants*, xxxiv; Brodsky, "Widows in Late Elizabethan London," 152.
[76] D. Cressy "Kin and Kin Interaction," *Past and Present* 113 (1986): 54.
[77] Laslett, "Mean Household Size," table 4.10.
[78] F. F. Mendel, "Notes on the Age of Maternity," *Journal of Family History* 3 (1978): 245.

In families where the father died leaving at least one child under age, the median number of orphans was 2.6 in period I and 1.9 in period II.[79] The mean/median number of orphans was 2.5/1.8 in bracket I, 2.8/2 in bracket II, 3/2.9 in bracket III, and 1.5/2.5 in bracket IV. The median number was close to 2 in all four cohorts. As might be expected, the number of orphans was statistically related to the age at death of the father and to the number of children who survived.[80] Fathers who died young left more orphans; fathers who had long lives left more children.

Several wills reveal that a wife was pregnant when a will was made.[81] Children were born after their father's death, like those of Samuel Thornburn, a cooper, and, in 1710, William Langford.[82] Provision for the unborn could be elaborate. John Hodges, a merchant, left his widow £2,000 and his unborn child £1,000.[83] John Wilding, a London gold-smith, and John Hope, a Bristol vintner, provided for twins, just in case.[84] Jarvis Cartwright in 1674 left money to the unborn children of his two daughters.

Orphans were common in all towns, and 25 to 34 percent of appren-tices were orphaned at time of binding; in the London Weavers Company 57 percent of apprentices bound were orphans.[85] Only 53 percent of daughters in Elizabethan London had fathers alive at age twenty; half of the orphans apprenticed had London fathers.[86] Many of the children at

---

[79] These are minimum numbers based on probate through the Court of Orphans of London or on wills that specify (usually when guardians were named) that particular children were still minors. The percentage of legal orphans omitted could be as high as 10 percent. The post-1660 sample in Earle, *Making of the Middle Class*, table 8.5, puts the mean number per case at 3.1.

[80] The Pearson R correlation between number of orphans and age of father at death = −0.172; the correlation with numbers of children who survived = +0.758.

[81] *Sudbury Archdeaconry Wills, 1636–38*, ed. N. Evans (Suffolk Record Society, 35, 1994), 321; PCC, will of John Maycott, Audley 78, 1632; PCC, will of William Moore, Pile 7, 1636; PCC, will of Thomas Agard, Lee 5, 1638; PCC, will of Thomas Wilson, Harvey 90, 1639; PCC, will of Henry Hopkins, Seager 77; PCC, will of Lancelot Topper, Twisse 150, 1646; PCC, will of John Pauncfort, Lee 19, 1648; PCC, Essex 56, 1648; PCC, will of Henry Arnold, Fairfax 175, 1649; PCC, Pembroke 108, 1650; PCC, will of William Pratt, Alchin 127, 1654; PCC, Berkeley 127, 1656. Sometimes the testator just anticipates the possibility, as when Robert Chapin writes "if shee bee with child" (PCC, Bowyer 24, 1652). But when a wife is described as "big with child," the meaning is clear. The date wills were signed is usually close enough in time to the date of probate for the testator to be aware of his wife's pregnancy but unaware of her delivery.

[82] CLRO, CSB 1693–1713.   [83] PCC, Harvey 96, 1639.

[84] PCC, Essex 77, 1648; *Tudor Wills Proved in Bristol, 1546–1603*, ed. S. Lang and M. MacGregor (Bristol Record Society, 44, 1992), 45.

[85] A. Plummer, *The London Weavers Company* (1972), 85.

[86] Brodsky, "Mobility and Marriages in Pre-Industrial England," 193.

Christ's Hospital were orphans of freemen from major London companies.[87] Of 150 apprenticeship disputes brought before the Lord Mayor's
Court, one-third had living fathers, 19 percent widowed mothers, and
22 percent guardians or stepfathers.[88] In Bristol 33 to 40 percent of
apprentices were orphans.[89] Most fathers in Rye did not live to see their
children reach twenty-one, and in Manchester (1654–60) 59.5 percent
of fathers were dead when their daughters married.[90]

In the whole population 20.7 percent of children were orphans.[91] It
is probable that 17 percent had lost a mother by eleven, 35 percent by
twenty-two, and 46 percent at time of marriage; the respective percentages for loss of father are 20 percent, 40 percent, and 51 percent.[92] One-
third of the peers had lost one parent by age fourteen.[93] In East Kent
18.6 percent of brides marrying at twenty and 43.7 percent of brides
marrying at twenty-five had no father alive; among artisans and tradesmen 17.9 percent (1619–46) and 19.9 percent (1661–1700) of fathers
were dead when their daughters married.[94]

Bastards were less common. The bachelor Ralph Cole, a merchant
adventurer of Newcastle, left "my base begotten son" £40 in 1584.[95]
John Smith had an illegitimate daughter in London to whom he left 40
marks in his will.[96] William Culpepper, unmarried and a resident in
Elbing, left a daughter of fourteen.[97] John Sadler left a pregnant lover
behind in Stratford when he moved to London, where he became a prosperous grocer.[98] Tycoon Thomas Sutton, who married late at fifty and
had no legal issue, had a bastard whom he ignored in his will and left

---

[87] *Christs Hospital Admissions, 1554–1599*, vol. 1 (1937). In late medieval London
   60 percent of the sons of aldermen were orphaned by the age of twenty-one: see
   S. V. Thrupp, *Merchant Class of Medieval London* (1962), table 14.
[88] M. Pelling, "Apprentices Health and Social Cohesion," *History Workshop Journal* 37
   (1994): table 2.
[89] I. K. Ben Amos, *Adolescence and Youth in Early Modern England* (New Haven, 1994),
   48; F. Grubb, "Fatherless and Friendless," *Journal of Economic History* 52 (1992): 105.
[90] G. Mayhew, "Life Cycle Service," *Continuity and Change* 6 (1991): 205.
[91] P. Laslett, "Parental Deprivation in the Past," *Local Population Studies* 13 (1974): 12;
   Family Life and Illicit Love (Cambridge, 1977), 162–3; and Laslett, "Mean Household
   Size," table 4.10.
[92] D. Cressy, "Private Lives" in *Attending to Women*, ed. B. Travitsky and A. F. Seef
   (Cranbury, 1994), 194.
[93] Stone, *Family, Sex, and Marriage*, 58.
[94] P. Razzell, *Essays in English Population History* (1994), 192–7.
[95] *Durham Wills and Inventories, 1543–1602* (Surtees Society, 112, 1906), 110.
[96] *Smythe Family of Ashton Court. Calendar of the Correspondence, 1548–1642* (Bristol
   Record Society, 35, 1982), xi.
[97] *Prerogative Court of Canterbury, Register of Scroope*, ed. J. H. Morrison (1934), 129.
[98] Jones, *Family Life in Shakespeare's England*, 98.

in poverty.[99] Sir William Dansell left an annuity of £12 to his bastard daughter.[100] James Gordon, a merchant, left £10 to apprentice Jane Gordon, a child boarding in Hertfordshire to "some honest calling"; since she was not identified as kin, she may have been his bastard.[101] In 1713 bachelor Thomas Coulson left £4,000 to his "reputed" daughter by widow Jane Radcliffe and left the widow £500 plus two houses and his household goods; this may not have been his only bastard. Bastards were relatively common in India; Elihu Yale had an illegitimate son who died at twenty-one.[102]

BIRTH

The first child appeared soon after marriage. The limited data on the interval from first marriage to baptism in business families suggest that it was usually twelve months, as in the general population, but the mean delay in fertility and the mean interval between successive births remains a matter of conjecture.[103] George Boddington had children at yearly intervals between 1675–81 and 1685–92, and two-year intervals were regarded as the norm.[104] The wife of a businessman, who had her first child at twenty-two and then every two years to forty, would theoretically have ten children, but the mean number of births seems to have been six to seven, as in the general population.[105] There was clearly greater variation in the age of paternity than in the age of maternity; remarriage of widowers created delays of paternity.[106]

Whether or not parents deliberately spaced having children has not been determined. Although medical knowledge was too primitive for

[99] N. R. Shipley, "The Foundation of Charterhouse," *Guildhall Studies in London History* 1 (1975): 243.

[100] T. S. Willan, *The Muscovy Merchants of 1555* (Manchester, 1953), 90.

[101] PCC, Berkeley 24, 1656.

[102] H. Bingham, *Elihu Yale* (Worcester, Mass., 1938), 302; T. Fitzhugh, "East India Company Families," *Family History* 12 (1982): 282. In the Indian records bastards are described as "natural son" whereas in England usually as "baseborn son."

[103] R. Schofield, "English Marriage Patterns Revisited," *Journal of Family History* 10 (1985): 18; A. MacLaren, *Reproductive Rituals* (1984), 86. Although some diaries, commonplace books, and family genealogies provide exact dates of birth, the intergenesic intervals can only be reconstructed by systematic analysis of parish registers.

[104] GLL, MS 10,823. The minimum interval between births is usually put at eighteen months with wet nursing and twenty-seven months with breast feeding: see R. G. Potter, "Birth Intervals," *Population Studies* 17 (1963): 155. The shorter the intergenesic interval, the greater the chance of death in childbirth.

[105] Burguière, *History of the Family*, vol. 2, 13.

[106] F. F. Mendels, "Note on the Age of Maternity," *Journal of Family History* 3 (1978): 237, 244.

effective artificial contraception, it was always possible for families to control births by abstinence, coitus interruptus, and breast feeding.[107] It is noticeable that widows, even the younger ones who remarried bachelors, had relatively few children.[108]

The wife obviously bore the burden of pregnancy and the risk of delivery, which was at its highest level at first births and then with advanced age. Advice on prenatal care was usually given by female kin and midwives, though some commonsense and many dubious recommendations appear in the printed manuals: Thomas Tryon, for example, discouraged strong drink and sex during pregnancy.[109] Wives received special treatment and support from their female kin and gossips while carrying to term.[110] Although husbands were largely excluded from the birth rituals, they recorded successful births with evident relief, noting the day and the hour of delivery and celebrating the event with pride.

Wives were always anxious during pregnancy and delivery, which could be difficult or end in a miscarriage. Richard Farrington's wife, for example, was in labor for two days. They also feared that their child might be born deformed or mentally deficient. When that happened, the child was not rejected but accorded special attention. One of George Boddington's sons had no thumb and two of his fingers were joined.[111] In 1720 Peter Paggen left a trust for his incompetent daughter, Sarah, as did Robert Atwood, in 1738, for his "afflicted" son.

Before an infant could be baptized, a first name had to be chosen. In this task, parents usually adopted a familial rather than an individual approach, though Puritan zealotry, political loyalties, and individual eccentricity produced some deviations from the norm.[112] Most first names were necronyms and usually commemorated lineal ancestors rather than aunts or uncles.[113] Hannah, the eldest daughter of Walter Tucker, a mercer of Barnstable, who revered her father, died in childbirth

---

[107] D. MacLaren, "Wet Nursing and Prolonged Lactation," *Medical History* 23 (1979): 441; R. V. Schnucker, "Elizabethan Birth Control," *Journal of Interdisciplinary History* 5 (1975): 666.

[108] Brodsky, "Widows in Late Elizabethan London," 135.

[109] T. Tryon, *A New Method of Educating Children* (1695), 19–28.

[110] For some cautionary reservations about female bonding see L. A. Pollock, "Childbearing and Female Bonding," *Social History* 22 (1997): 286–303.

[111] GLL, MS 10,823, fo. 60.

[112] S. Smith-Bannister, *Names and Naming Patterns in England, 1538–1706* (Oxford 1997), 2, 8, 184.

[113] R. M. Taylor and R. J. Crandale, eds., *Generation and Change* (Macon, 1986), 47. The 28,216 subjects in the database shared 1,412 first names, the most common in order of popularity being John, Thomas, William, Richard, and Robert.

but produced another Hannah "phoenix like to succeed her."[114] The Huguenots usually named their eldest child after the grandfather.[115] When a child died in infancy, the name was frequently transferred to the next birth of the same sex. Indeed one of the most persistent problems in differentiating subjects in the database is the frequency that parents gave their eldest son their own first name. But children were also named after both paternal and maternal kin, their godparents, and even their father's partners and friends. In Shrewsbury about half the children were named after the father and half after close kin.[116] Double first names were extremely rare, except among aliens.

INFANCY

Infancy evoked curiosity and was recognized as a special period of development.[117] Henry Cuffe asked himself why infants slept more and why children had short memories.[118] Tryon believed that an infant's mind was a tabula rasa, that the capacity and desire to learn was greatest in the first five years, that children learned the virtues of temperance and order by imitation, and that vices could not be eradicated after the age of ten.[119] The almanacs offered advice on how to inculcate traits desired by the parents.[120] The majority of parents, however, relied on advice from their parents, kin, and friends—not books. Motherhood was seen primarily as a physical activity.[121] In a patrilinear descent group, mothers were able to develop emotional links with their children and a relationship that, though necessarily unequal and asymmetrical, was one of unconditional trust.[122]

The first need of the infant was food. Breast feeding was strongly advocated as healthy and natural, particularly by Puritan preachers, like

---

[114] P. Le Neve, *Monumenta Anglicana*, vol. 4 (1715–19), 14.
[115] Houblon, *The Houblon Family*, vol. 1, 97.
[116] Hindson, "Family Structure," 212.
[117] The concept of childhood has a long history and was clearly recognized in late medieval Florence: see L. Haas, *The Renaissance Man* (1998), 180; for different attitudes see M. J. M. Ezell, "John Locke: Images of Childhood" in *John Locke: Critical Assessments*, ed. R. Ashcraft, vol. 2 (1991), 231–9.
[118] Cuffe, *Difference of Ages*, 122, 125.
[119] Tryon, *New Method of Educating Children*, 19–28, 34.
[120] B. S. Capp, *Astrology and the Popular Press* (1979), 290.
[121] M. Salmon, "The Cultural Significance of Breast Feeding," *Journal of Social History* 27 (1994): 263.
[122] S. D. M. Schneider and K. Gough, eds., *Matrilinear Kinship* (Berkeley, 1961), 22; S. N. Eisenstadt and L. Roniger, *Patrons, Clients, and Friends* (Cambridge, 1984), 31.

Gouge.[123] Henry Smith thought that wet nursing could alter the character of children and compared it to hatching a hen's egg under a hawk.[124] Some mothers did breast-feed their children, but wet nurses and surrogate mothers were widely employed.[125] Indeed the high rate of infant mortality in business families may in part be related to that practice. Richard Farrington, who lost most of his children in infancy, sent at least two out to nurse at 4 shillings per week, though both of these died after weaning.[126] The use of wet nurses should not be interpreted as indifference or neglect; some nurses were resident in the home, and parents visited infants who had been sent out. Nurses were sometimes remembered in wills: the widower Benjamin Baron, a grocer, left "the woman nurses of my said sons £3 a piece" and £5 to nurse Dunn and goodwife Wilson; John Brook left his nursemaid £30.[127]

In addition to feeding, infants had to be kept clean, minded, and toilet trained. These tasks were undertaken by mothers, elder daughters, female kin, nursemaids, and servants. Some infants were swaddled for a month or two, though this does not seem to have been common; one of Henry Offley's infants died "in his swaddling clothes."[128] If it is true that early weaning creates aggressive personalities, aggression would not have been a problem. The age of weaning varied from one to two years, but was most commonly sixteen months.[129] It is clear from paintings and woodcuts and from the customs' records of imports that a great variety of toys, such as whistles, rattles, and dolls, were acquired to divert and train infants.[130]

Fathers were not aloof about child rearing. Thomas Papillon, Sir Dudley North, and Samuel Jeake systematically recorded when their infants were weaned, when they cut their first teeth, and when their sons

---

[123] Gouge, *Of Domesticall Duties*, 81, 512.
[124] H. Smith, *A Preparative to Marriage* (1591), 100.
[125] V. Fildes, ed., *Women as Mothers* (1990), 128; G. Clark, "London Nurses," *Genealogical Magazine*, 23 (1989), passim; V. Fildes, "The English Wet Nurses," *Medical History* 32 (1988): 149–50. D. Harley, "From Providence to Nature," *Bulletin of History Medicine* 69 (1995): 200, suggests, without presenting any evidence, that the wives of shopkeepers adopted wet nursing as the elite rejected it.
[126] GLL, MS 2708.
[127] PCC, Hele 84, 1626; Earle, *Making of the Middle Class*, 321.
[128] L. De Mause, ed., *History of Childhood* (New York, 1974), 331; G. C. Bowen and H. W. Harwood, "Pedigree of Offley," *Genealogist*, n.s., 19 (1903): 219.
[129] L. A. Pollock, *Forgotten Children* (Cambridge, 1983), table 10; P. Crawford, "The Sucking Child," *Continuity and Change* 1 (1986): 35–9; V. Fildes, *Breasts, Bottles, and Babies* (Edinburgh, 1986), 90, 163.
[130] Peter Blayney kindly provided details of imports from his study of the London port books in the 1580s. Metalworkers who made toys were called "triflers" according to C. Welsh, *History of the Pewterers' Company*, vol. 2 (1902), vi.

were put into breeches.[131] Fathers showed considerable interest in the antics of their children and how their personalities developed—their first words and their first upright steps on leading strings. Portraits of children were commissioned at different stages of their children's life. John Blunt had in his house a "picture of Mr Blunt, one of Mrs Blunt, one of Mrs Blunt's mother, one of Mrs Blunt and child, one of two children and seven small pictures, mainly of children."[132]

Fathers readily acknowledged that the mother played a crucial role. William Ashwell, a cutler, made his widow guardian "nothing doubting of her goodness and motherly affection towards her children as it hath been ever."[133] A succession of births and premature deaths and the burden of dealing simultaneously with an infant and growing children must have taken its toll on mothers, who may not have welcomed every new baby with open arms. But in those business families for which evidence survives, the quality of mothering seems to have been high. Mothers displayed tenderness and affection and may sometimes have been overprotective. In the Houblon family the children were "sweet ones," and Mary Houblon died at forty nursing a child with the plague.[134] If it is true that personality develops primarily in infancy (a view challenged by those who emphasize continuing development throughout life and the importance of culture), then the characters of businessmen would have been determined by their mothers.[135]

Parenthood required both fatalism and resilience. Most parents had to face absolute separation from their children by early mortality, which, though an expected event, was still all too frequent and traumatic. Even when they survived infancy, children could still die from drowning, burns, falls, and traffic accidents as well as from disease; John Hull was scalded and nearly trampled by horses at the age of two.[136]

Preachers considered it idolatry to mourn too long and offered the comfort of Christian ritual and salvation: "the untimely death of a hopeful child is indeed a very sore affliction to the Parent, but tis a blessing to the child himself who dies in the Lord."[137] Infants who were

[131] KAO, MS U 1015/C1/6; Jeake, *An Astrological Diary*, 85.
[132] Inventory of John Blunt, PRO, C 114/164, 22 May 1697.
[133] PCC, Twisse 168, 1646.   [134] Houblon, *Houblon Family*, vol. 1, 122, 160.
[135] A. and C. Clarke, *Early Experience: Myth and Evidence* (1976), 290. This may be an area where women exercised real power, although historians have neglected this issue, perhaps because they are reluctant to put women back into the nursery.
[136] H. F. Clarke, *John Hull* (Portland, 1940), 5.
[137] O. Blackall, *Of Children Bearing the Iniquities of the Father* (1708), 15. Some parents did adopt this attitude: see the diary of Elias Pledger in Dr. Williams Library, MS 28.4c.

stillborn or who died shortly after birth generated less grief, because they had no time to develop personalities. Parents had every reason to be pessimistic about the chances of their child's survival, and their only practical remedy was continuous procreation. Babies were never, however, regarded as expendable, and parents carefully recorded their deaths, worried about infant damnation, and suffered bereavement with every child.[138]

CHILDHOOD

Although conceptualized in different ways, childhood had long been recognized as a distinct stage of life.[139] Some writers emphasized the innocence and purity of children, others that they had been born in sin and should never be allowed to forget their sinful nature; most agreed that every child was different.[140] More perceptive authors recognized both the promise and the vulnerability of childhood. To Earle, a child "is natures fresh picture newly drawne in oyle," but he added "his father hath writ him as his owne little story."[141]

When children reached the age of seven, they were treated with greater firmness, because they were thought to be capable of distinguishing right from wrong. Sons were now treated differently from daughters; they were no longer instructed by women, and they exchanged their petticoats for breeches and acquired a masculine identity. Gender now became a factor in their relationship with their parents—fathers were drawn to daughters and mothers to sons.

There is no hard evidence showing that children were ever treated as pets or regarded as family property in business households. On the contrary, they were valued for themselves and given nicknames and a peaceful refuge from the world outside. Parents seem to have enjoyed talking, playing, and walking with their children and watching them develop.

---

[138] P. Crawford, "The Experience of Maternity" in *Women as Mothers*, ed. V. Filders, (1990), 23; R. Houlbrook, ed., *Death, Ritual, and Bereavement* (1989), 245.
[139] S. Shahar, *Childhood in the Middle Ages* (1990), 103–5.
[140] Despite arguments to the contrary, it was possible for contemporaries to conceive of an irreducible self: see R. Wunderli and G. Broce, "The Final Moment before Death," *Sixteenth Century Journal*, 20 (1989): 275. In Puritan theology, as in literary theory, attempts to glorify God by self-effacement actually make the self the locus of reality: see D. S. Bercovitch, *The Puritan Origins of the American Self* (New Haven, 1975), 18–19.
[141] J. Earle, *Microcosmography* (1628), A1, B2.

Ned Ward describes how "tradesmens wives treat the child at the far-thing pye-houses."[142] Ralph Thoresby took his children to visit London, though whether they were interested in comparing his transcriptions with the tombs is debatable.[143] Adoring parents often spoiled their children or bribed them into compliance with rewards.

Monitoring their progress, fathers had more interest in grown children than in infants. In their correspondence, they often discussed the character and behavior of their children. John DesCarrier, for example, describes one of his sons learning to read, another learning to write, and the cleverness of a third.[144] William Atwood was told that his youngest daughter, who lived with her mother, was a "witty one" and "learns her book very prettily" and "makes everybody fond of her. . . . She talks every day of pappe . . . she says he gone to London to fetch her some chestnuts and a hobbey horse which is her great delight."[145]

Children in business families were well supplied with books and toys—hobbyhorses, cardboard windmills on sticks, drums, hoops, and balls; Nicholas Oram, an Oxford fishmonger, gave his children a doll house.[146] In the household accounts of a London alderman's wife, some child had scrawled "Dorothie" and great "P"s across the page.[147] Children spent much of their time with other children; Thomas Papillon relates how his son found a playmate.[148]

It can be hypothesized that some busy or harassed parents might have starved their children of care, affection, and attention and that some children would in consequence have been lonely, withdrawn, and unable to sustain emotional relationships in later life. But it is extremely difficult to reconstruct the mental world of children or determine whether or not they were happy or felt neglected. Children had their own model of reality and perceptions.[149] Childhood is a state of being rather than becoming. Although dependent on their parents, children still enjoyed sufficient freedom to test their physical limits, to play and dream, and to

---

[142] E. Ward, *A Legacy for the Ladies*, 128. Sir Stephen Fox also indulged his children in these pies: see C. Clay, *Public Finance and Private Wealth* (Oxford, 1978), 329.
[143] Thoresby, *Diary*, vol. 2, 77.
[144] G. Sherwood, *The Pedigree Register*, vol. 3 (1913–16), 116.
[145] Letters to William Atwood from his wife dated 10 April and 21 Oct. 1685, PRO, C 109/23/1.
[146] D. G. Vaisey, "Probate Inventories" in *Probate Records and the Historian*, ed. P. Riden, 104.
[147] BL, Cotton MS Vespasian F xvii, fo. 24v°.   [148] Papillon, *Memoirs*, 405.
[149] K. V. Thomas, "Children in Early Modern England" in *Children and Their Books*, ed. G. Avery and J. Briggs (Oxford, 1996), 45–77.

develop their own rhymes, vocabulary, rules of conduct, and games, which often mirrored adult concerns.

The only surviving evidence, usually autobiographical memories rec-ollected in maturity, projects an adult view of how children thought and acted. The incidents remembered in later life tend to be dramatic, shame-ful, or life threatening. Marmaduke Rawdon decribes how he declined to play with a boy in another house until he was invited, how he indulged in archery, bowling, riding, and swimming, how he broke his arm, and how he burned and temporarily blinded himself while playing with gunpowder.[150] Samuel Jeake, who learned to write at nine, illustrates a common tendency of children to record all monetary gifts.[151]

Parents were aware that each child was different and were always con-scious of their responsibilities. Sometimes they pushed when they should have led, and sometimes they acted from duty rather than from inclina-tion. No doubt they often repeated the mistakes of their parents. In some households, strict formalities of speech and behavior were observed; the father wore his hat while his children knelt before him. But the limited evidence suggests close and frequent contact between parents and their children, and a rich communal life in business households. In the Papillon family, for example, the children were boisterous and affectionate, leaping up and kissing their father and passing judgment on their new house.[152]

SUBSTITUTE PARENTS

In some business families children were deprived of continuous access to their fathers, their work frequently taking them away from home. William Ball left his wife and children in London when he went to Virginia.[153] William Bolton left his youngest children in Chelsea when he went to Madeira.[154] Jacob Turner went to live in Smirna and left a wife and three children in England.[155] James Maxwell apologized to David Papillon for calling him to London: "I know your affairs are many and this my demand unreasonable to call you away from your house and family (but necessity has no law)."[156] Serle Daniel had to abandon

---

[150] Rawdon, *Life*, 3.   [151] Jeake, *Diary*, 87.
[152] Letter from Jane to Thomas Papillon dated 23 April 1668, KAO, MS U 1015/C11.
[153] N. T. Mann, "William Ball Merchant," *Northern Neck Virginia Historical Magazine* 23 (1973): 2523–9.
[154] *The Bolton Letters, 1695–1714*, ed. A. L. Simon (1928), introduction.
[155] Palmer to Lane and Wood dated 22 March 1688/9, PRO, C 114/55–56.
[156] Letter dated 24 July 1630, KAO, MS U 1015/01.

his family to avoid his creditors during the Civil War and travel abroad.[157]

When either father or mother was unavailable, the other parent filled the gap. In the Papillon family the children clearly adored their father and missed him while he was in exile; when his letters were read to them, Philip wept and Sarah thanked God for such a father.[158] But Thomas Papillon was told by his daughter that "mother is as a father and mother both to us."[159] Joseph Collett maintained regular contact with his daughters when he was in India, which he thought no place for his family: "tell your sisters that when they can write to me, they may expect a particular answer."[160] Samuel Jeake, who lost his mother, brother, and sister when he was an infant, had a compensatory, close relationship with his father.[161]

Sometimes children were brought up by their grandparents. Nicholas Farrar, who lived into his seventies, tended to his granddaughter from the cradle.[162] If a son died young with children, his father might care for the widow and children, as did William Dobbins.[163] Sir Stephen Fox lost most of his children and virtually adopted his daughter Elizabeth's son after her death.[164]

Grandparents loved to play with and teach their grandchildren; they were often more relaxed, confident, and affectionate than the parents. William Williams wrote to his married daughter expressing his love for her but principally asked to see the children.[165] Jane Papillon complained that her three-year-old daughter was spoiled by her grandmother and threatened to give her up.[166] One grandfather describes how his grandson caused trouble by flying into a passion and how he had to take him up and walk him and "by means of singing, the little knave would be appeased sometimes for half an hour."[167] Humphrey Hooke of Bristol described his grandson as a "most stubborn and unruly" boy.[168]

[157] C. Durston, *The Family in the English Revolution* (Oxford, 1989), 104.
[158] Papillon, *Memoirs*, 394, 396, 405.   [159] Ibid., 390.
[160] J. Collett, *Private Letter Book*, ed. H. H. Dodwell (1933), letter to his daughter, 22 Sept. 1712.
[161] Jeake, *Diary*, 4.
[162] *Prerogative Court of Canterbury, Abstracts of Register of Soame, 1620*, ed. J. H. Lea (Boston, Mass., 1904), 120.
[163] Letter from William Dobyns to Thomas Pitt dated 25 Jan. 1702/3, BL, Add. MS 22,852.
[164] Clay, *Public Finances*, 266, 278.
[165] Letter dated 3 June 1698, LAO, Pearson Gregory MS 2P.G./12/5/1.
[166] KAO, MS U1015 C/11/14; I. Scouloudi, "Thomas Papillon," *Proceedings of the Huguenot Society of London* 18 (1947): 71.
[167] Sherwood, *Pedigree Register*, vol. 3, 117.   [168] Todd, *Humphrey Hooke*, 38.

Some testators made their grandchildren their principal legatees (see chapter 9). Ralph Yardley, an apothecary, and William Abell, a merchant, made detailed provisions for the education and upbringing of their grandchildren.[169] Margery Shaker petitioned the Company of Barber Surgeons on behalf of her grandson, who had been turned out by his master.[170] In some cases, testators preferred their grandchildren because their own children had predeceased them; examples include Robert Bristow, John Woodward, Robert Tichborn, and Richard Alley.[171]

Nonetheless, premature death did break up families and reduce the influence of the biological parents. Many children never knew their parents as adults and grew up in other households, like John Verney who lost his natural mother in infancy. Death could be traumatic for a child and interpreted as rejection. Henry Newcombe noted the cries of the children at the burial of a dyer in 1659.[172] George Boddington records how he "fetched my grandson George Wakeman from Newington boarding school not letting him know his mother was dead. In the coach he expresst sorrow [his schoolmaster had told him], which he received with an affectionate sorrow more like a man of great grace then a child. After walked with me in my garden to my great comfort expressing himself."[173]

The loss of one parent during adolescence was less devastating than the loss of both parents during childhood. Some children seem to have compensated by seeking paternal or maternal figures among their kin and friends or in their marriages. Widowed fathers sustained the link between their children and their natural mother by passing on mementos. For example, Humphrey Hawkins, a merchant tailor, gave his daughter her dead mother's bible, and James Piton gave his daughter his wife's "best diamond ring sett with two turtle doves."[174]

Through remarriage many children also acquired stepfathers or, more frequently, stepmothers, who assumed the function of child rearing without childbearing.[175] It was not always easy for children to transfer their affection to stepparents, making their relationships tense, resentful,

---

[169] PCC, Berkeley 18, 1656; PCC, Swann 30, 1623.
[170] T. Young, *Annals of the Barber Surgeons of London* (1890), 267.
[171] PCC, Rivers 24, 1645; PCC, Audley 87, 1632.
[172] H. Newcombe, *Autobiography*, ed. F. Parkinson (Chetham Society, o.s., 26, 1852), 101.
[173] GLL, MS 10,823.   [174] PCC, Rivers 129, 1645; PCC, Pell 8, 1659.
[175] Children from first marriages of widows who remarried subjects in the database have not been recorded, though some appear under their father's name if he was a London businessman. Although sometimes mentioned in wills, stepchildren are quite difficult to track.

hostile, bitter, or angry, as in the Marescoe family. Robert Robinson was caught in the middle of a conflict between his father and stepmother.[176] Children did not, however, necessarily live in the same household as a stepparent, since they were often adolescents by the time their surviving parent remarried.

Kin, principally uncles or aunts from both sides of the family, and friends also served as guardians of orphans—in effect substitute parents. William Stout brought up two orphaned children of a neighbor, and John Dunton adopted a child.[177] The daughter of the widowed John Jackson, an innholder, was brought up by Widow Hide.[178] Sir Thomas Browne was orphaned at eight and brought up by the impecunious Sir Thomas Dutton.[179] In some households dry nurses (nannies) or servants brought up the children and fulfilled the role of parents. Jane Papillon relates how she "came home I found all ye family absent and my children in the hands of strangers and I thought one of them very much dispirited and my house open."[180]

PARENTAL RIGHTS AND DUTIES

No contract governed the relationship between parents and children. Children were, like wives and servants, subordinated to the father in a hierarchical structure. The head of any household, whether husband or widow, was responsible for maintaining morality, religion, and order, and a mother had independent authority, if no legal rights, over the children.[181] Independence only came with adulthood; until then parents enjoyed the right to determine what their children ate, wore, and said. Apprentices were supervised by both their father and their master. It was a relationship of total dependence in which brute force could prevail. Parental authority was not necessarily biological, and it was not patriarchal; Hobbes thought that it derived initially from the mother, but later he believed it came from the father.[182]

Contemporary handbooks, however, emphasized the duties of parents

[176] Letter from Robert Robinson dated May 1725, PRO, C 104/13–14.
[177] *American Wills Proved in London, 1611–1775*, ed. P. W. Coldham (1992), 148.
[178] PCC, Pile 97, 1636.   [179] J. Bennett, *Sir Thomas Browne* (Cambridge, 1962), 2.
[180] KAO, MS U 1015/F12, fo. 338.
[181] M. Sommerville, *Sex and Submission* (1995), 67; Barrett-Lennard, *The Position in Law of Women*, 46.
[182] G. J. Schochet, "Thomas Hobbes on the Family," *Political Science Quarterly* 82 (1967): 433.

and the mutual interests of parents and children.[183] Parenthood was viewed as a conditional trust with an obligation to help children develop as individuals and as members of society. All the manuals asserted that parental love was natural and axiomatic, that parents had a responsibility to feed, clothe, and shelter their children and prepare them for adulthood. Increasingly the authority of parents and the obedience of children was justified by the love and care that the former gave and the latter received.[184] Richard Allestree advised parents to secure obedience through love and not servility, to give their children some freedom, and teach by example.[185] The ideal parent exercised control without coercion. Children also enjoyed important rights, such as the rights to hold property and enjoy the fruits of their labor.[186]

The authority of parents ultimately rested on their control of property and was underpinned by their considerable and irrecoverable investment of money as well as time. The maintenance of a child in a business family, including medical costs and laundry and excluding schooling, setting up and daughter's portions, was at least £5 a year and usually more.[187] A few examples will illustrate the magnitude of the financial commitment. Raymond King, a merchant of Harwich, allocated the profits from several voyages just to pay for his son's schooling.[188] William Atwood paid Mr. Glascock £33.18.5 for eight months of schooling, food, and books.[189] One East India Company factor allocated half of the salary paid to him in England for his nine-year-old child.[190] In 1733 Nathaniel Torriano had to find a premium of £300 to apprentice his son Nathaniel Jr. and £16 for binding plus £349 for shoes, flute lessons, tailor's bills, apothecary fees, French lessons, stockings, buttons, and a wig; his son Peter, who was at Cambridge, cost him £133.6.0 for one year; and he also had to subsidize his married son, George.[191] Robert Pitt reminded his son that "your mother and I . . . have lived in straits for our childrens' sake."[192]

[183] Shochet, "Patriarchal Politics," 416; M. J. M. Ezell, *The Patriarch's Wife* (Chapel Hill, 1987), 161.
[184] W. Fleetwood, *Relative Duties of Parents and Children* (1716), 68–70.
[185] R. Allestree, *The Ladies Calling* (Oxford, 1673), 197.
[186] Macfarlane, *Marriage and Love in England*, 80; J. Waldron, *The Right to Private Property* (Oxford, 1988), 245–6.
[187] Erickson, *Women and Property*, 47–50.
[188] *Elizabethan Life. Wills of Essex Gentry and Merchants*, ed. F. G. Emmison (Chelmsford, 1978), 293.
[189] PRO, C 109/21/1.   [190] BL, Add. MS 22,186, fo 127v°.
[191] PRO, C 112/24/2.   [192] *H. M. C. Fortescue*, vol. 1, 84 (letter 25 Nov. 1726).

The clerical writers on marriage unsurprisingly emphasized the spiritual duties of parents—that they instill godliness and piety into their children. The secular advice books were more concerned that parents socialize their children and develop their obedience and manners. It was unusual, as writer Samuel Bufford did, to question whether parents should mold their children in their own image or whether they alone knew what was best for their children.[193] Usually, it was taken for granted that the behavior of children must be modified by education and moral instruction to conform to expected norms. Children were judged by their outward behavior, not by their inner feelings.

Devout parents tried to instill godliness into their children and condition them to the brevity of life.[194] In this regard it was often the mother who served as a role model. John Fryer claimed that his mother had taught him godly habits.[195] Devout families worshipped together and strictly controlled the contacts of their children to ensure their spiritual conformity.[196] The Puritan Ambrose Barnes allowed no smutty conversation and no visits to plays or taverns.[197] In Quaker narratives, which were highly artificial and formulaic, the children emerge as miniature adults, serious, pious, and dutiful.[198]

Most parents in the business community, however, wanted to instill morality rather than piety and teach their children skills rather than civility. Their primary objective was to impart the virtues of self-control—whether control of their spending habits or of their bodies and appetites. They recognized the value of good manners, learning, bearing, obedience, and respect; their children were dressed to impress and display their social station.[199] But they were mainly interested in preparing their children for survival as adults.[200] Fathers also wanted their sons to construct an identity suitable for entering a male-dominated world.

---

[193] S. Bufford, *An Essay against Unequal Marriage* (1696), 93.
[194] It is difficult to reconstruct the attitude of children about death because the evidence consists of spiritual works whose authorship is uncertain.
[195] GLL, MS 12,107, fos 13–14.
[196] D. Ormrod, "Puritanism and Patriarchy" in *Studies in Modern Kentish History*, ed. A. Detsicas and N. Yates (Maidstone, 1983), 135.
[197] A. Barnes, *Memoirs*, vol. 50 (Surtees Society, 1866), 37.
[198] J. W. Frost, *The Quaker Family in Colonial America* (1973), 80–1.
[199] E. Ewing, *History of Children's Costume* (1977), 32, 35.
[200] There was an inherent conflict between independence and socialization: see A. Bryson, "The Rhetoric of Status" in *Renaissance Bodies*, ed. L. Genty and N. Llewellyn (1990), 152.

DISCIPLINE

Some child rearing books advocated an intrusive method of harsh discipline for children to repress frivolous instincts and destroy their sense of fun. An extreme example of this approach is Caleb Trenchfield who believed that children brought their parents to financial ruin and advocated breaking a child to silent obedience: "The less the child is hold in arms the better."[201] William Whateley advised that the wife not interfere when her husband corrected the children.[202]

But even supporters of using the rod usually agreed that parents should act from love when they instilled obedience. Most writers, increasingly aware that brutality was coarsening, settled for wielding both carrot and stick; discipline should be carefully modulated and accompanied by parental support.[203] Locke is notorious for recommending the suppression of crying, but he also saw the value of play and curiosity and only approved of physical discipline when a child was too young to be rational; thereafter shame, verbal reproof, and social sanctions would suffice.[204]

Since children, unlike apprentices, could not bring suits against abusive parents, there is no way of ascertaining how many parents or stepparents imposed stern discipline. Only extreme cases of neglect and abuse surface in the courts. Fishmonger John Rowse, for example, is known to have murdered his two children in 1621, and cutler Robert Robinson was hanged for ravishing his stepdaughter.[205] But most parents would probably have agreed with Sir William Turner, who noted in his ledger "the rod and reproof give wisdom but a child left to himself bringeth his mother to shame."[206]

Responsible parents seem to have combined permissiveness with repression. They tried to internalize social values through moral indoctrination and preferred mental pressure to physical punishment. William Stout complained that his master's wife overindulged her children. An increase in complaints about "cockering," or spoiling, suggests that

[201] C. Trenchfield, *Cap for Gray Hairs* (1710), 184–6, 197–9.
[202] W. Whateley, *A Bride Bush* (1617), 18.
[203] The major works are summarized in C. J. Sommerville, *The Discovery of Childhood in Puritan England* (Athens, 1992).
[204] J. Locke, *Some Thoughts Concerning Education*, ed. J. W. and J. S. Yolton (Oxford, 1989), passim; *Correspondence*, vol. 4, ed. E. S. De Beer (Oxford, 1976–89), 713.
[205] J. A. Sharpe, "Domestic Homicide," *Historical Journal* 24 (1981): 42; R. Smythe, *The Obituary*, ed. H. Ellis (Camden Society, 44, 1849), 8.
[206] GLL, MS 5109.

parents were becoming more lenient during the century.[207] If all else failed, parents could always resort to emotional blackmail; some made dramatic pleas for their children's reformation on their deathbed.

Once sons passed ten they were usually sent away from home, though they remained in someone's household until they married. Primary education took place in the family, but most boys were sent to carefully chosen schools and often, like James Fretwell, boarded with a schoolmaster. In contrast to other occupations, few children of businessmen were "tabled," or fostered, with kin.[208] Those destined for trade were, however, apprenticed to masters with whom they lived.[209] Only children of artisans and those who could not afford an apprenticeship stayed at home to learn their trade.[210]

Parents did not send their children away because of indifference or neglect of their responsibilities. They thought that schoolmasters could provide more professional instruction; schools supplemented, but did not replace, parental guidance and emotional support. Ironically, children may have ended up in the hands of merciless schoolmasters because their parents were too soft-hearted to administer discipline. Sending children away removed adolescent crises from the family and reduced the danger of friction or incest. The authority of strangers was thought to be more effective because it was easier to control the children of others.

Living outside the cosy, intimate atmosphere of the family gave children a degree of autonomy and fostered individualism and self-sufficiency. Caleb Trenchfield argued that "children when put out to board are taught betimes . . . to oversee their own concerns."[211] Sending children away also widened the range of contacts of both the child and his family. Sarah Savage sent her son a hat, recommended daily spiritual exercises, and explained that "you will learn more experience by going further from us" and "as you now draw near 16 yr old" she and his father "had some careful discourse" and decided that a grammar school would be "of no great advantage" whereas he could learn accounts at

---

[207] R. V. Schnucker, "Puritan Attitudes" in *Women as Mothers*, ed. V. A. Fildes (1990), 115.
[208] R. Wall, "Age of Leaving Home," *Journal of Family History* 3 (1978): 191; P. Laslett, "The Gentry of Kent," *Cambridge Historical Journal* 9 (1948): 150.
[209] Ben Amos, *Adolescence and Youth in Early Modern England*, 60–1. See also chapter 7.
[210] G. Mayhew, "Life Cycle Service," *Continutiy and Change* 6 (1991): 25.
[211] Trenchfield, *Cap for Gray Hairs*, 197–9.

Chester."[212] Parents living abroad, as in India, had to send their children back to England for their education.[213]

Once indentured, apprentices ceased to be children because they owed obedience to another, although the handbooks disagreed on whether apprenticeship was a paternal or contractual relationship.[214] Parents usually kept an eye on the master of their children and, when disputes arose, as with Nathaniel Harley, were prepared to believe their sons.[215] Richard Steele and Francis Kirkman, who was beaten by his master when he complained to his father about his treatment, argued that masters should treat apprentices like their children.[216] Edward Stephens argued that "tacit trust and confidence of kindness to and care of the apprentice [was] reposed in the master by the parent or relations."[217] Through service, apprentices were introduced to the rigors of life outside the family and learned how to accept the conventions of the social hierarchy.[218] Marmaduke Rawdon, when apprenticed to his uncle, was made to wait on tables and dine with the servants "to breed him with more humility."[219]

ADOLESCENCE

What Henry Cuffe called "budding and blossoming age" the modern world would call adolescence. This is a stage of life when, in the Erik Erikson model, a child reaches sexual maturity and struggles for autonomy, self-control, and identity.[220] These are years of inner turmoil and withdrawal in which a youth examines himself, asserts his independence, mocks his elders, displays both energy and laziness, and is dependent on peer approval.

Although puberty was little discussed by handbook authors in the

---

[212] Letters dated 5 Aug. 1712, 15 Jan., 25 May 1713, Dr. Williams Library, MS Henry 4.
[213] C. Gill, *Merchants and Mariners* (1961), 125.
[214] S. R. Smith, "The Ideal and the Reality," *History of Education Quarterly* 21 (1981): 450.
[215] Letter from Nathaniel French dated 15 July 1686, BL, Add. MS 70,223.
[216] F. Kirkman, *The Unlucky Citizen* (1673), 43, 147; R. Steele, *The Tradesman's Calling*, 2d ed. (1698), 118.
[217] E. Stephens, *Relief of Apprentices* (1687), 5.
[218] Burgière, *History of the Family*, 40.
[219] Rawdon, *Life*, 53.
[220] E. H. Erikson, *Identity and Life Cycle* (New York, 1959), 68. Some historians regard adolescence as a late modern concept: see J. Demos, *Past, Present, and Personal* (New York, 1986), 98; I. K. Ben Amos, "Adolescence as a Cultural Invention," *History of Human Sciences* 8 (1995): 69–89.

seventeenth century, the behavior of "youth" provoked much comment. *The Gentlewoman's Companion*, for example, recognized that children had different "humours, inclination and dispositions" and even used the expression "teens."[221] Others remarked on the pride in display, the different body language, gestures, and terms of speech; Dr. Daniel Williams noted, for example, that youth were subject to violent passions and inordinate mirth.[222] Preachers were aware that young apprentices were ripe for spiritual conversion.

Some insight into the problems of adolescence can be gained from apprentice's diaries and correspondence with their parents. Although such evidence is sparse, it seems clear that children had minds of their own and that at least some parents understood their children and were prepared to compromise between exercising control and letting their child develop.

The mentality of an apprentice is well illustrated by the letters of John Scott to his father and the diary of John Cogge.[223] Scott describes in detail all his trials—his bouts of sickness, his accidents, his shortage of money, and his relationship with his master. Cogge's diary describes his routines and preoccupations—his fascination with time and knowledge, the new people he constantly met, his relations, his clothes, shoes, and accessories, such as a clasp knife with a tortoiseshell handle. He records every gift of cash as well as a visit from his mother who brought him a hat, wig, gloves, and shoes and a visit by his master to his father and mother.

Even more revealing are the letters to William Atwood from his wife, his son, William, and his son's schoolmaster.[224] Atwood's wife had moved away with her young daughter, leaving her husband "to be mother and father to the boys," William and Richard, who were both at boarding school. Although she perceptively remarked "I doubt poor Willie is troubled that I am come so far from him," she worried about the boys, suggesting ways of refurbishing their winter clothes for summer use and sending a tape measure to their schoolmaster and money to the boys.

---

[221] *The Gentlewoman's Companion* (1673), 14–15. Several writers like J. Aubrey, *Idea of Education*, ed. J. E. Stephens (1971), 29, regarded the years between seventeen and twenty as having peculiar difficulties.
[222] D. Williams, *The Vanity of Childhood and Youth* (1691), 36, 46.
[223] KAO, MS U 1015 C163/1–15; Bod, MS Eng misc. F 78.
[224] Letters dated 9 Sept., 17, 25, and 26 Oct., 3 Dec. 1685, 2, 12, 24, and 25 Jan. 1685/6, 18 Feb. 1685/6, PRO, C 109/23/1.

William Jr. pressed his father for the usual playthings—a penknife, bird lime and hooks, flies, packthread, a tin box, and worms—so that he could catch a pike for his mother. "I hope you will be so kind as not to deny me that but if you have any love for me let me have it next Thursday or Saturday at your fathers." To the alarm of his parents, he used a present from his mother of 5 shillings to purchase a half share in a gun. Here is a perfect example of the obligatory letter from a boy at school to his father:

Ever honoured Father, my master told me that you have not been very well which I am very sorry to hear, but I hope you are now well again. I received your letter. . . . I am sorry to hear so many complaints but I will do my best endeavour to amend them and I do not mind my play but when I am at it and you must consider that I must have something to play with. . . . My Brother and I remember our duty to you and grandfather and Mother and our service to all our friends and remain begging your prayers your ever obedient son to serve you whilst I live. I had wrote a letter to my Honoured Mother but it was late before I thought to write to you. I will write to her next time I write to you.

William also had his own views on the right education for him, requesting

that you would not let me come to school any more for I am very well satisfied that I cannot learn if you put me to school any more. You will spend your money in vain and I am never the better. My Master is so very harsh and sets me so much to get and then if I do not say it, he makes me get my book when they play so that it doth make me so dull that I hate to goe to my book so that I cannot learn. . . . I believe it is time for me to goe to learn to cast accounts for almost all the boys in our form do, as I believe it tis high time for me. Pray . . . send me a summing book from London for I believe my master has none.

His schoolmaster, Benjamin Stebbing, took a different line:

"Books and birdlime agree not well together. However the former may prove a good diversion if it will make him stick to his book." [Stebbing made William compose an essay on the consequences of idleness, a copy of which he enclosed to the father.[225]] But his actions correspond not his words. . . . I do desire you to write to him [if not to command him] to persuade him to his business against this folly he seems to finds in that Latin . . . will do him no good for an Apprentice. I know not your resolutions for his disposal in the world. I am sure that learning will facilitate any Employ.

[225] "Idleness is the mother of all mischief and those that are given to Idleness never come to good though they be never so rich for in that short time they become beggars and are forced to turn to thievery and kill men for their estate for which they are hanged."

William's mother took her son's side:

I am infinitely troubled for poor Wille but I confesse it is but what I feared would proceed from the harsh and churlish carriage of his master and I am very sure that that is not the best way to deal with such tempers. As I have heard you say yourself you would do more for a good word then with all the beating and so I am sure would he. He is not of such a nature as his master takes him to be . . . my cousen Sheering and those gentillmen that taught him when his master was sick which are as competent judges as Mr Stebbing and thay all say that he larnt as well as any boy in the school.

SUMMARY

Contrary to what might be expected, business families had few children and their households, even though swollen by servants, apprenticer, and lodgers, were still small. Inventories suggest that wealthier businessmen had separate rooms and furniture for their children. Space was more confined in urban houses, which facilitated greater intimacy and mutual discussion and encouraged emotional bonding, affection, and attention, though possibly at the cost of reduced privacy and freedom for the children.

Although many married couples had no surviving children or only sons or daughters, a significant proportion were nonetheless three-generation families. Many children lost their fathers at a young age and were brought up either by their mothers or by substitute parents. Despite the care exercised by parents in child rearing, the rate of infant and child mortality remained high.

Not only was childhood recognized as a discrete stage of the life cycle, but maturity was delayed by the educational process and by inheritance customs. Parents were vested with complete authority over their children and usually took their duties seriously, but many chose to give their children some slack and to accommodate their personalities within the traditional structure. Their priority, it should be noted, was to nurture and steer their children through the trials of adolescence and prepare them for adulthood. It was the family rather than the state, the church, or the educational system that integrated children with adult culture.

The arbitrary factor of death constantly undermined the stability of family formation, which was a serial process. The composition of house-holds changed as parents died and were replaced by substitutes, as survivors remarried, and as children accumulated from different marriages. But the cohesion of the family survived even in locations of exceptional mortality, like Barbados.[226] The business family was not, as is sometimes assumed, a static institution. It was a dynamic hybrid and a set of relationships that varied with mortality, remarriage, and the life cycle.

[226] G. A. Puckrein, *Little England* (New York, 1984), 186.

5

Adulthood and Old Age

Children eventually moved away from their parents and set up independent households as adults. In the seventeenth century adulthood was a social construct based on economic independence rather than than on biology or age, and it was delayed well beyond puberty by apprenticeship or other forms of training. At this stage were sons treated differently from daughters? Did the behavior of fathers differ from that of mothers? How did parents relate to their children when grown, and how did children regard and treat their parents in later life? Were siblings united by mutual affection or divided by rivalry? By what means were conflicting objectives, expectations, and interests resolved within the nuclear family?

SONS

Occasionally sons, like those of John Cary, were still resident in their parents' household in their late teens, usually apprenticed to their fathers. Even after marriage a son might stay (temporarily) with his parents, often at his own expense. John Burkin, in his will of 1731, released his son, James, from debt for boarding his family. A few parents continued to treat their offspring as children even when they were grown, working, living outside the family, or even married. But few business families were stem families in which sons remained in the household until married. Although daughters usually lived with their parents or surviving parent until married, the majority of sons were sent away in their teens and never returned to live in the parental household, even if their fathers were still alive after they had completed their training.

Parents continued to help and supervise their children after they had

189

left the family hearth. Some apprentices ran home to their mothers.[1] Richard Hoare counseled his son, Jim, to watch his step, to improve his writing and spelling, and to safeguard his health.[2] A young factor in Turkey was sent detailed fatherly advice along with his mother's love, some beer, clothes, and other delicacies. He was instructed to learn Italian bookkeeping, to correct his spelling, to improve his handwriting, and to use courteous expressions and capitals for place names: "I would not have you forget that you are an apprentice and a younger brother and that you are sent out to make your fortune and not sett up for the fine gentleman and only take your pleasure." Meanwhile, the young man's principals were asked both to "excuse all his youthful slips" and to "not indulge my son too much but keep him strict to business."[3]

James Phipps, before he left for Africa, was bombarded with lengthy epistles from his pious mother, urging him to remember his baptismal vows and seek the glory of an omnipresent God.[4] His father was more down-to-earth:

I understand that mother hath writ to you. You know she is a pious woman and doth not cease to pray for you. . . . I was not ignorant that I sent you into a heathen country that you would miss of all those helpes and advantages to instruct you in the way to heaven as you might have had in Europe, but I considered you had been religiously educated and that you were not so young but you understood good and evil . . . you have your bible and many good books which I recommend to you to read often. . . . Your business in Africa is to raise your fortune . . . that you may return again and live in your own country with more honour.[5]

Elizabeth Torriano had a dutiful son, Nathaniel, whom she smothered and a prodigal son, Peter, who treated her with contempt. When Nathaniel visited Berwick on family business, he had to reassure his mother that he would not delay or drink in taverns. She inundated him with letters that well illustrate how personality determined the relationship between mother and son:

My dearest Nat, I bless almighty God with all my heart for his infinite mercy to me in preserving you this far on your journey. The morning you went I [went] to church to recommend you to his almighty protection . . . he will still keep you

[1] Plummer, *The London Weavers Company*, 88.
[2] K. Woodbridge, "Accounts Rendered," *History Today* 19 (1969): 784–5.
[3] Letters to son dated 9 Feb., 28 April, and 1, 16 Sep. 1728, Folger Library, MS UB 18.
[4] Letter from Brigett Phipps dated 21 June 1703 to her brother, James, containing letters from his mother dated 23 and 30 June 1704, PRO, C 113/280.
[5] Letter to James Phipps dated 28 Oct. 1703, PRO, C 113/280.

under the shadow of his wings and let no real evil happen unto you . . . if it be his blessed will to us his unworthy servants . . . let me intreat you my dear life to be very cautious both in your words and actions for people are prodiguously sharp in the north and upon an unwary word all your endeavours may be frustrated. . . . I must now acquaint you . . . that Peter sent me a very impertinent letter telling me . . . I should be in town about ten a clock tonight telling me I should get a bed aired for him and if I was desirous he should study, a room to himself and a fire that . . . he hoped he might see his friends whenever he please. . . . I order Mr Bruton to keep the counting house locked and have emptied some of the desk drawers to lock the things in . . . for there wont be a crick nor corner he can get at he wont look into . . . Postscript. Pray dont travel late and be very careful of your bed and drying the things and pray either wrap a . . . stocken round you that as the country people do.[6]

Peter lived up to expectations:

I am at present pestered with fetching things and carrying them to him tho he is very well, but had rather wear out the easy chair then his legs in helping himself to what he wants. He sends for his tea in the morning. If I ask him to come down to dinner, unless somebody is here he wont come down and at supper the same, so tho he pays nothing he wastes me as many coles and gives me as much uneasiness and my servants as much trouble as if he paid the most plentiful board. . . . He asked me in his dogmatical way when the desk in the parlour was to be standed up for him. . . . I told him when it was time. He told me it was time. . . . The other morning he was resolved to go out and had no money in his pocket, so as I was eating my breakfast he came in and said he wanted money. I asked him for what. I thought he could not want it till he went to College and then I would give him some . . . all he wants is a bed and . . . he wondered I would allow you to trade . . . and deal of such pragmaticall stuff. I told him you did nobody any harm by what you did and that indentures only bound you to serve your master faithfully . . . he told me he pittied you very much and was very sorry a fine gentleman should be spoiled by my confining him to my way that prevented you from seeing company which must be of use to you when you set up in business. . . . I bless God you dont think all happiness of life consists in eating drinking and indolence and wish he did not neither. He does indeed read something but what it is I can't tell. . . . I believe but he hasn't read a quarter of those few [books] he brought and therefore I am very glad I nailed up your door or else they would have been continually hauled about whether read or not. I have now done with this nonsense and wish I could as readily rid my thoughts of it as I can stop my pen.[7]

Even when overseas, adult sons maintained contact with their parents. William Sharpe, in Barbados, and Heigham Bright and Richard Lake, in

---

[6] PRO, C 112/24.
[7] Letters from "your truly affectionate mother and sincere friend," Elizabeth Torriano dated 2 Sept., and 23 Oct. 1736, PRO, C 112/24/2.

Aleppo, corresponded regularly with both their parents, who anxiously waited for news about their safe arrival, their health, and prospects.[8] John Hall, a goldsmith, wrote regularly to his mother in America, sending tokens and gifts, retailing gossip and news, discussing politics, religion, and the plague, and describing his daughter and her early attempts at speech.[9] John Sanderson relates how his mother, when on her deathbed, said that she wanted "joy at my death as I had at your birth."[10]

DAUGHTERS

Although fathers often hoped for a male heir to continue their name and inherit their land, there are few explicit indications that they were unhappy if they had daughters rather than sons. Daughters were raised differently and would have spent much of their time in the company of other females. On occasion, a father may have distrusted the influence of the mother. Valentine Bowles, a vintner, instructed that his two daughters be "put forth to some good Christian woman to be educated and taught in Religion and manners, but not to abide with their mother but to come now and then to see her and doe their duties as good children ought to do."[11] But there is little specific evidence that daughters learned by imitating their mothers how either to accept or circumvent their subordinate status.

In business households fathers seem to have been close to their daughters, though they could be separated by absence on business or by death. When Benjamin Boucher died in India, his widow remarried Samuel Blunt, and Boucher's daughters were sent to England.[12] Peter Briggins exhorted his teenage daughters to devotion when they were at school, but he also sent them chestnuts and expressed love and tenderness.[13] Elizabeth Papillon feared that God would shut her out of her father's affections, because she had sinned by breaking the Sabbath.[14] Betty Scattergood told her father "I desire no greater pleasure than that of

[8] Letters, Shropshire RO, Forester MS 1224, 1660–4; PRO, SP 110/16; J. B. Bright, *The Brights of Suffolk* (Boston, 1858), 175, 180; PRO, SP 110/111.
[9] D. Cressy, *Coming Over* (Cambridge, 1987), 230.
[10] J. Sanderson, *Travels*, ed. Sir W. Foster, 2d ser., vol. 67 (Hakluyt Society, 1931), 22.
[11] PCC, Goare 101, 1637.
[12] LAO, Ancaster MS 9/A/5.
[13] *Eliot Papers*, ed. E. Howard (1895), 73–4.
[14] Papillon, *Memoirs*, 408. Thomas wrote addresses to his children, including his reflections on the Sabbath.

pleasing you."[15] Sir Stephen Fox was devoted to his daughter, Jane, and in his old age was upset when she forgot to thank him for her birthday present.[16] In 1680 alderman Hart of Bristol thought that he saw his daughter's ghost in London on the day that she died at home.[17] Joseph Collett sent a stream of presents to his daughters, including a diamond ring, and had their portraits painted; William Haselden had his daughter's portrait hanging in his house.[18]

In business households most daughters were literate, many receiving schooling outside the family and through their teens. Sons, however, took priority, and education was gendered.[19] William Fleetwood advised parents to tailor the level of education to the size of their portions.[20] A few even received a learned education, like Mary Astell, the daughter of a Newcastle merchant.[21] Joseph Collett was "pleased to hear of my daughter Betty's proficiency and thank you for your care to improve her mind as well as direct her hands."[22]

The majority of daughters were expected to marry and were consequently trained in "housewifery," or housekeeping skills.[23] In the household of Ambrose Barnes the daughters were put to sewing.[24] In one of Ned Ward's imaginary dialogues, a tallow chandler wanted his daughter to learn housework and not dancing.[25] David Taylor insisted in his will that his daughters should not attend boarding school.[26] Joseph Collett sent his daughters home to England to be educated "as may best qualify them for the charge of a family which I take to be a woman's main business."[27] Many daughters were taught elementary arithmetic at school. Based on the format of the household accounts, like those of

[15] BL, Add. MS 42,122; B. P. Scattergood, "John Scattergood," *Contemporary Review* 134 (1927): 218.
[16] Clay, *Public Finances and Private Wealth*, 314.
[17] Thomas, *Religion and the Decline of Magic*, 717.
[18] J. Collett, *Private Letter Book*, ed. H. H. Dodwell (1933), 76, 89; PCC, Pile 6, 1635.
[19] On the high rate of literacy among London women, see Cressy, *Literacy and the Social Order*, 115, 129, table 7.2; L. Pollock, "The Making of Women," *Continuity and Change* 4 (1989): 236–9; Earle, *City Full of People*, table 2.1.
[20] W. Fleetwood, *The Relative Duties of Parents and Children* (1705; reprint, 1985), 55.
[21] F. M. Smith, *Mary Astell* (New York, 1916), 173–7.
[22] Collett, *Private Letter Book*, 19 (letter to his sister dated 19 Sept. 1712).
[23] For marriages of daughters see chapter 9. In most cases it has not been possible to track the lives of unmarried daughters, though many seem to have lived with their siblings or kin.
[24] A. Barnes, *Memoirs*, vol. 50 (Surtees Society, 1866), 69.
[25] E. Ward, *Nuptial Dialogues* (1710), 260.
[26] E. S. More, "Congregationalism and the Social Order," *Journal of Ecclesiastical History* 38 (1987): 225.
[27] Collett, *Private Letter Book*, letter to his brother dated 18 Sept. 1713.

Anne Crowche, some women must have received more advanced instruction in bookkeeping.[28]

Weathier businessmen, however, tended to educate their daughters for gentility at the finishing schools that specialized in teaching dancing, French, and needlework and sometimes they employed private tutors.[29] An alderman's wife paid 30 shillings for "teaching Judith to play the lute for ½ year."[30] Edward Oakley's daughter was placed with a wine cooper's wife for £20 to be taught needle work and playing the virginals.[31] The dressmaker's bill of £5.10.0., which Elizabeth Abberley ran up in three months in 1658, suggests that daughters learned fast how to spend money.[32] Sir Stephen Fox took his children to the theater, employed French governesses, and provided lessons in singing and dancing.[33] Sir Josiah Child hired a Huguenot refugee woman as a tutor for his daughter.[34] Nehemiah Grew approved of women studying but noted with disapproval that "every ordinary Tradesman's wife will have her daughter learn to dance that she may be a gentlewoman."[35]

Marriage did not necessarily mark the conclusion of parental responsibility. Sometimes daughters had to be retrieved from failing marriages. Richard Banks, a draper, supported his married daughter for four years before his death, because her husband had spent her portion and disappeared to Ireland.[36] Thomas Barefoot, a merchant tailor, left his married daughter "one shilling and noe more in regard she hath had more then her share of my small estate already and been a great charge unto me from time to time."[37] Margaret Vanderput had to confront Robert Vansittart about his cruelty to her daughter.[38]

Some parents took a great interest in their daughters' marriages. Sir Henry Johnson watched over his daughter's pregnancy, having married her at great expense to Lord Stafford: "I am writing this in your bedchamber by my dear daughter . . . I hope will bring an Aire to your lordships estate."[39] Sir John Kempthorne was informed by his daughter's father-in-law when she had a son, though the christening was too sudden for him to attend: "I was last night with Nancy who I bless God is as

[28] BL, Add. MS 30,494; Earle, *City Full of People* 25, 35.
[29] A. F. Kendrick, *English Needlework*, 2d ed. (1967), 119, 159.
[30] BL, Cotton MS Vespasian F xvii.   [31] WAM, MS 9977, nos. 10, 139.
[32] C. Carlton, *Court of Orphans* (Leicester, 1974), 54.   [33] Clay, *Public Finances*, 258.
[34] B. W. Manning, *History and Antiquities of Surrey* (1808–14; reprint, 1974), iii.
[35] Huntington Library, MS 1264, fo. 148.   [36] PCC, Rivers 28, 1645.
[37] PCC, Pembroke 195, 1649.
[38] M. Hunt, "Wife Beating," *Gender and History* 4 (1992): 22.
[39] W. Hedges, *Diary*, ed. H. Yule, vol. 75 (Hakluyt Society Publications, 1887), cci–ccii.

well as we could expect . . . give me leave to joyn with you in joy for our grand son John Kempthorne, whom God bless he was christen'd this evening, and the ceremony past with few people, it being by the mother resolved on soe sudden, which indeed I cannot think was improper, your self and son being absent."[40]

Daughters fulfilled other roles in the family. Elder daughters often acted as mothers to their younger siblings. Sometimes they were appointed executrices by their fathers. Abraham Ashe in his will computed all his assets for his daughter, Margaret.[41] Edward Field, a merchant tailor, made his daughter executrix when she came of age and his widow merely overseer; he bequeathed all the goods he had before his marriage to his daughter and named a friend to give consent when she married.[42] Richard Thacker, a salter, ignored his sons and named a daughter "my said poor executrix."[43] Mothers also frequently chose daughters as their executrices.[44]

TRIALS OF PARENTHOOD

Despite their care and exhortation, many parents were often disappointed by the character and unpredicted behavior of children who did not follow the prescribed path or live up to expectations. Extravagant habits could be adopted in reaction to a strict upbringing or from spoiling during childhood. Several parents were bewildered and angered when their sons became insolvent and feared that they would become liable for their son's debts. Edward Chard was reluctant to leave anything to his son because it would be seized by his son's creditors.[45] Lawrence Ashton, a clothworker, forgave his eldest son's debts but only bequeathed him 10 shillings.[46] The hands of William Atwood shook when he wrote to his father to explain why he had cancelled his visit to "pay my humble duties": "by the way was informed that a Creditor or two of mine had some designe upon me so to avoid trouble either to your honored selfe or me I thought it better to return back."[47]

Other parents were dismayed by their sons' character and behavior. Richard Bell, a merchant tailor, gave his son, Joseph, more than his cus-

[40] Letters to Sir John Kempthorn dated 29 Apr. and 4 May 1676, GLL, MS 18,760/1.
[41] East Suffolk RO, Ipswich branch, MS S1/1/77.
[42] PCC, Alchin 84, 1654. [43] PCC, Brent 298, 1653.
[44] S. D. Amussen, *An Ordered Society* (Oxford, 1988), 92.
[45] PRO, B 11/307. [46] PCC, Sadler 77, 1635.
[47] Letters dated 16 March and 15 Nov. 1685, PRO, C 109/23/1.

tomary one-third, "which he hath ill deserved."[48] Several testators, like apothecary Henry Dickinson, provided that their sons would not inherit if they pursued "dissolute, disordered and wicked courses."[49] Richard Yearwood, a grocer, made his son his heir only if he "reformed and become a frugal man."[50] Richard Sheppard regarded his son's drunkenness as "a punishment that God hath laid upon me in my prosperity."[51] Richard Hoare's son, Thomas, defrauded his father and succumbed to lust and drink.[52] Sir Joseph Hodges ran through an inheritance of £7,000 to £8,000 per year and died unmarried and bankrupt.

The death of grown children was particularly difficult to accept. Joseph Collett told his brother that the "loss of an only son just entering into the World with personal merit and great advantage must affect me deeply . . . his death destroyed the little ambition I had of raising a Family."[53] George Boddington, who had a separate section for each of his children in his diary, had this comment on his son, John, who died at nineteen: "to my great grief being a diligent comfortable child very understanding in business . . . full of holy expressions . . . too good to live."[54] Abraham Gonsales, when his daughter died, wrote how it had "pleased God to take her from this miserable world . . . it has caused us a great deal of grief and sorrow . . . give us strength to withgo so much sorrow for it has touched our hearts."[55]

Businessmen expected to derive some benefit from their children, many infrequently employing their sons though they did not need their labor.[56] Parents who were preoccupied with economic and social advancement could be adversarial and manipulative and exploit youth and inexperience. An authoritarian parent, like James Bankes who was both self-made and proud of the family name, might attempt to control his sons from the grave.[57] But many more parents gave priority to their offspring over all other members of the household. They were proud of the appearance and accomplishments of their children, worried constantly about their welfare, and suffered when they moved away. Wills were drafted with painstaking care to secure their surviving children's

---

[48] PCC, Twisse 70, 1646.   [49] PCC, Ruthen 372, 1657.   [50] PCC, Audley 98, 1632.
[51] *HMC Sackville*, vol. 1, 228 (letter dated 2 Feb. 1598/9); P. Le Neve, *Pedigrees of the Knights*, ed. G. W. Marshall, vol. 8 (Harlean Society, 1873), 202.
[52] Woodbridge, "Accounts Rendered," 787–8.
[53] Collett, *Letters*, letter dated 14 Dec. 1716.   [54] GLL, MS 10,823.
[55] Letter to Nathan Simpson in Port Royal dated 25 April 1724, PRO, C 104/13–14.
[56] Fleetwood, *The Relative Duties of Parents and Children*, 4. See also chapter 7.
[57] *Bankes Family Early Records*, ed. J. Bankes and E. Kerridge, vol. 21 (Chetham Society, 1973), 1.

future, particularly if they were underage. A typical example is the widower, John Ferrers, who asked his kin, friends, and neighbors to ensure that his orphaned son was "well educated and brought up in learning and virtue."[58]

Parents regularly asked to be buried near their children, sometimes, like Humphrey Levins, in the same grave.[59] Robert Buckland, a glover, erected a monument to his only son, John, who died in the plague of 1625; in 1622 Samuel Simmons commemorated his son with an epitaph listing his charities.[60] Richard Lane arranged to have a marble monument to his daughter, Elizabeth, erected inside his parish church with an epitaph.[61]

OPPOSITION TO PARENTS

Children were expected to show obedience, affection, and respect to their parents and to address them, both in speech and writing, with formality and deference. William Gouge and William Fleetwood argued, for example, that both parents had an equal right to love and respect and that "restraint and awe is best" in children, who would recognize the value of a strict upbringing in later life; children were denied the right to disobey even an unjust command.[62]

In fact filial response was conditioned by conflicts of personality, emotions, and interests. Children could be hostile when thwarted, suspicious of parental initiatives, committed to self-improvement, and eager for personal advancement. They asserted their independence against parental authority causing confusion, tension, and dissension. The three most combustible issues in relations between parents and children were choice of career, marriage, and inheritance (see chapter 9). Many children contested their fathers' wills in the courts, suing the executors and overseers.[63]

Youngsters sometimes rebelled by running away, like William Morrice who left his father, to whom he was apprenticed, and probably fled to

---

[58] PCC, Saville 86, 1622.
[59] Will of John Jennings, PCC, St. John 73, 1631; will of George Chalfont, PCC, Aylett 313, 1655; E. Hatton, *New View London* (1708), 105; wills of Nicholas Smith and Christopher Gaylor, PCC, Ridley 5 and 12, 1629.
[60] Boulton, *Neighbourhood and Society*, 149. [61] PRO, Prob 11/653/210–11, 1732.
[62] Fleetwood, *The Relative Duties of Parents and Children*, 8–15, 25; Gouge, *Of Domesticall Duties* 484.
[63] PRO, Req 2/307/Rep 15, 1622; C 10/5/4/90, 1677; C 8/356/30; C 7/363/34 and C 7/373/40, 1705.

Ireland.[64] John Dore left home at eighteen after his father beat him for
dancing, though he returned home two years later and was welcomed.[65]
A few children committed suicide to retaliate against their parents and
masters.[66]

The conflict between age and youth was a common theme of contemporary dramatists. The attitude of children toward their parents did
change between different stages of the life cycle. When grown, they developed their own interests and reacted against their upbringing and their
parents' values. Once away from home, they resented parental interven-
tion in their affairs. Lionel Cranfield's mother, who was both tough and
active on his behalf, complained to him that he ignored her once apprenticed.[67] John Dunton was happy to escape from his mother, who seems
to have been a shrew. Maurice Wynn sought to assert himself against his
domineering father. Some were estranged from their parents by religion.
Moses Marcus, the eldest son of a Jewish East India merchant, turned
Anglican and was supported by the courts against his father.[68] In 1701
Jacob Mendez de Breta's daughter turned Christian at the age of eighteen.[69] There is little evidence, however, that children identified more
with their peer group than their parents. Youth was a period of transition, not a culture; particular birth cohorts do not seem to have shared
attitudes and experiences that set them apart from other generations.

Separate residence, which was normal even for unmarried sons, isolated children from their parents and weakened parental control. Marriage accentuated this process, because the first loyalty of a husband and
father was usually to his wife and children, not to his parents. When
fathers lived to an old age, greedy children became restless about their
inheritance, waiting impatiently for their fathers to die.[70] Entrepreneurial children were frustrated by their inability to take over or revamp the
family business. Younger sons were likely to be jealous if preference was
given to the eldest.

---

[64] H. Prideaux, *Letters*, ed. E. M. Thompson, vol. 15 (Camden Society, n.s., 1875), 140.
[65] Demos, *Past, Present, and Personal*, 8.
[66] T. R. Murphy, "Woeful Childe of Parents Rage," *Sixteenth Century Journal* 17 (1986):
259ff; M. McDonald, "Secularization of Suicide," *Past and Present* 111 (1986): 72.
[67] M. Prestwich, *Cranfield* (Oxford, 1966), 50.
[68] C. Roth, *Anglo Jewish Letters, 1158–1917* (1938), 97–8; S. Staves, "Resentment or
Resignation" in *Early Modern Conceptions of Property*, ed. J. Brewer and S. Staves
(1995), 207.
[69] D. S. Katz, *The Jews in the History of England 1485–1850* (New York, 1994), 192–3.
[70] Letter dated 16 May 1715, Hertfordshire RO, Radcliffe MSS; Thomas, *Religion and
the Decline of Magic*, 369.

Disputes between the parents sometimes alienated the children. In the Pitt family, the daughters took the mother's side against the father, and the son, Robert, on the other hand, turned his mother and sisters out of his house, though he raised no monument to his father. Thomas Pitt constantly threatened to disinherit all his children and was involved in endless rows and switches of affection. "It will ruin the children to put them in Expectation of any thing from me more then what I have allowed above" he argued, but in the end he tried to be fair to all his children and grandchildren.[71]

Children's disobedience is reflected in wills. Thomas Frederick, who in fact neglected his children while running the East India Company, diverted £9,000 to charity because of the disaffection of his children.[72] In 1667 Richard Darnell excluded his son, Daniel, from his testator's one-third, because he had been disobedient, exorbitant, and lewd. In 1693 Francis Dorrington left his son only £30 a year because of his disobedience. William Eyon, an ironmonger, appealed to the Almighty to reform his son, John, "whom I beleave God by the prayers and tears of a dying father to bless and turn his heart and make him a dutiful childe to his careful mother."[73] John Bathurst left his disobedient son, Henry, his books "hoping he will make a good use of them."

The misbehavior of some children seemed so outrageous to their parents that they were disinherited. Even eldest sons were cut off by Sir Martin Bowes, Thomas Chamberlain, William Kendale, Francis Dorrington, Robert Dornell, Alexander Jacob, and Thomas Priestley.[74] William Yeats, a mercer of Chipping Camden, excluded three sons from his will, and alderman John Bathurst of London disinherited his son.[75] John Chapman, an apothecary, instructed that his lands be sold and his estate equally divided between his children, but he cut out one son entirely.[76] Malachy Thurston of Bristol was disinherited when he refused his father's command to return from Virginia.[77] Thomas Banks disowned

[71] BL, Add. MS 22,852, fo. 135; T. Lever, *House of Pitt* (1947), 22–6.
[72] *Marescoe-David Letters*, ed. H. Roseveare (British Academy, 1987), 9.
[73] PCC, Evelyn 51, 1641.
[74] *John Isham Merchant Adventurer*, ed. G. D. Ramsay, vol. 21 (Northamptonshire Record Society, 1962), xliii; T. S. Willan, *Muscovy Merchants* (Manchester, 1953), 50; J. Priestley, *Memoirs*, vol. 77 (Surtees Society, 1883), 26.
[75] I. E. Gray, "Some Token Issues," *Transactions of the Bristol and Gloucester Archaeological Society* 74 (1965): 108; *V. C. H. Middlesex*, vol. 5 (1970), 161.
[76] PCC, Nabbs 179, 1660.
[77] M. H. Quitt, "Immigrant Origins of the Virginia Gentry," *William and Mary Quarterly* 45 (1988): 633, 641.

his son because he had "unnaturally and undutifully forsaken his native country and natural parents," causing grief to his mother.[78] Lawrence Lee left his land in Virginia to his eldest son and then to his brother rather than his younger son.[79]

Some daughters also suffered from disapprobation. John Bott, a haberdasher, cut off one daughter with five shillings, because "she hath been very unjust and undutiful unto me," and gave his obedient daughter his estate.[80] Joseph DeBritto refused even to support his daughter when she converted from Judaism. Henry Fletcher, a stationer, gave his daughter, Prudence, all his lands, but his married daughter, Lucy Laughton, received only twelve pence.[81]

WIDOWS AND CHILDREN

Sometimes the widow took second place to the children. In 1621 the merchant Jonas Raynold preferred his son and minimized his wife's inheritance.[82] Nicholas Cox, a haberdasher, bequeathed his house to his son, but instructed him to pay his mother an annuity of £28 p.a. and allow her the use of one chamber plus its contents.[83] Nathan Potts, for example, only gave his wife £100 and left his house to his two sons, who were named executors and instructed to pay her £20 p.a.[84] John Buttermore, a tobacconist, favored his grandchildren and bequeathed his widow just the goods she had brought in plus an annuity of £12 p.a. to be paid by his overseers from £200 he had set aside.[85] Richard Wright, a skinner, was generous to his sons but just gave his widow the furniture.[86] George Cutler, a goldsmith, gave his whole testator's one-third to his son and grandchildren, though he added "I wish my condition was such that it were better for her sake."[87] Richard Warner provided that his widow would have the use of the parlor and one chamber in his house with their furnishings "with free liberty of ingress, egress and regress into the same with the necessary use of the yard pump and washhouse," but in return for a two room apartment and access to the laundry room she was expected to surrender her dower rights over all land to her son, a somewhat unequal exchange.[88]

---

[78] PCC, Lewyn 48, 1598.   [79] PCC, Clarke 37, 1625.
[80] PCC, Lee 17, 1638.   [81] PCC, Aylett 200, 1655.
[82] *Suffolk Archdeaconry Wills, 1620–1624*, ed. M. E. Allen (Woodbridge, 1989), 82.
[83] PCC, Ruthen 269, 1657.   [84] PCC, Aylett 378, 1655.   [85] PCC, Pell 331, 1659.
[86] PCC, Pell 414, 1659.   [87] PCC, Pell 248, 1659.
[88] PCC, Alchin 386, 1654. The widow was named joint overseer with her brother of the will and guardian of the children, but not executrix.

Usually, however, husbands privileged their widows, thereby creating grounds for conflict. One son, who believed that his father would die within a year, made the point well: "my father often desired we would live in peace and love among each other and not fall out amongst ourselves which he seemed to fear and be civil to my mother when he is gone, I suppose he have put her in such a good case as she need care for none of us and . . . I suspect to have done so well by her at his death as he thinks twill disgust us. This is only my fancy so pray burn this when read, I pray."[89]

Many men, like Henry Holmes, William Palmer, Thomas White, and Nathan Potts, urged their children to comfort and support their widows and "love and live together in all fitting respect and obedience."[90] Philip Henslowe urged his well-beloved son, "I praye you forget not your mother."[91] William Clark, a haberdasher, like John Foote, a grocer, urged his son to be dutiful to his mother "to whom he is dear."[92] But as William Quarles anticipated, "discontent and unkindness can ensue" between the widow and the children.[93]

The widow was often named guardian, particularly of daughters, and had the right to administer and even change the children's portions (see chapter 3). William Hunt, a stationer, made his widow guardian of their orphan son "hoping my son will bee obedient unto her and be ruled by her."[94] Hugh Hulse, a haberdasher, in his nuncupative will, said "I doe give her all that I have and doe leave my children to her disposing, they being hers as well as myne."[95] Hugh Capell left land to his daughters but gave the widow the right to change their portions if they disobeyed.[96] John Worrall, a salter, left his son in the sole care of his widow "in her motherly respect of his good welfare."[97] Sir William Ashurst instructed his widow to give the most to the children who were dutiful after his death. William Derrack, a grocer, bequeathed £100 to his daughter but only £5 to his sons, because he wanted his widow to determine their residual inheritance "as they shall apply themselves unto virtuous courses and behave themselves well."[98] Widows exercised this power. Thomas

[89] Letters to Thomas Palmer Mercer from M. Meynell, dated Jan. 1702, GLL, MS 3723.
[90] PCC, Pembroke 79, 1650; PCC, Clarke 125, 1625; PCC, Skynner 7, 1627; PCC, Aylett 378, 1655.
[91] *Henslowe Papers*, ed. R. A. Foakes, vol. 2 (1961), 18.
[92] PCC, Cope 127, 1616; PCC, Saville 47, 1622.
[93] PCC, Meade 117, 1618.   [94] PCC, Nabbs 186, 1660.   [95] Ibid.
[96] R. M. Berger, *Most Necessary Luxuries* (University Park, 1993), 243.
[97] PCC, Clarke 50.   [98] PCC, Nabbs 263, 1666.

Plampin's son was disobedient to his widowed mother, so she favored her daughters in her will of 1724.

Husbands usually defined the widow's territory in their wills. The widow was often given control or a veto over disposition of the estate and usually the principal house or part of it (see chapter 3). Samuel Hodgson, a draper, left his widow everything, the son inheriting at her death: "I injoyne my said wife that she doe assist my said sonne in her life time with such of my goods and household stuffe as she shall think fit," hoping that both would "live in unitie and peace."[99] Edmund Lewis left his son a tenement, but he was required to give "in a submissive manner" on bended knee to his mother the sum of 20 guineas each year.[100] William Waller, a merchant tailor, provided that his widow could deduct her legal fees from the children's portions, should they sue her.[101]

One alternative adopted by Patrick Banford, a merchant tailor, was to name the son executor and hope that he and the widow would achieve a "heartie correspondence."[102] Richard Archdale acted as his father's executor and gave him a handsome funeral.[103] The percentage of sole executors who were sons, usually eldest sons (often when there was no surviving widow), rose from 3.1 percent in period I to 5.1 percent in period II (see table 3.4). The percentage also increased with wealth from 2.7 in bracket I to 2.9 percent in bracket II, 8.6 percent in bracket III, and 10.8 percent in bracket IV. It fell from 11 percent in both cohorts I and II to 9 percent in cohort III and 2 percent in cohort IV. An insignificant number of daughters was, however, appointed executrix by their fathers and few children were appointed overseers.

Another compromise was to make the widow and one or more of the children joint executors. Arthur Abdy made his two elder sons coexecutors with his widow "requiring them that in the fear of God and with a good conscience they carry themselves dutifully and loving to their mother."[104] Sometimes overseers were charged with the role of arbitrator. Robert Trelawney of Plymouth, who had remarried a widow with children, left his stepchildren only 5 shillings each but his own daughter £400; he asked his overseers to arbitrate, should there be a dispute.[105]

[99] PCC, Pell 203, 1659.   [100] PCC, North 366.
[101] PCC, Berkeley 340, 1656.   [102] PCC, Juxon 46, 1663.
[103] The accounts for the funeral are in GLL MS 23,955.   [104] PCC, Coventry 120, 1640.
[105] Trelawney Papers, 1631–1770, ed. J. P. Baxter, 2d ser., vol. 3 (Maine Historical Society, 1884), 441.

Many testators made their bequests conditional on acceptance of the will as written. Peter Vanlore asked his son not to litigate against his widow.[106] But inevitably some families still ended up in court. Discontented children exploited ambiguities in their fathers' wills, contesting both the terms and the executors. They sometimes challenged the bequest of more than one-third to their mother, though the widow was entitled to deduct the cost of bringing up a child from their portion. In 1696 Elizabeth, daughter of Sir Richard Chiverton and wife of Sir James Tilly, sued for £2,000 held in trust under her father's will.[107] The estate of Frederick Hern, who had made more than one will, split the family and generated a complex chancery case.[108] When Benjamin Coles died intestate in 1708, his orphans sued the administrix in chancery claiming that the personal estate had been used to buy real estate to fulfill a marriage settlement.[109] Children could even be sued by the widow, as when the widow and creditors of Robert Daton, Sr., sued Robert, Jr., for debt.[110] One widow and her eldest son were alleged to have concealed a will that named other beneficiaries.[111] In 1709 the grandchildren of Robert Bristow sued their mother and elder brother over payment of legacies.[112]

Children were even more likely to challenge a widowed stepmother or stepfather. In 1712 a plaintiff claimed that their stepmother had ignored customary distribution.[113] Roger Faucus, a shipmaster, died leaving his daughter in the hands of his second wife who had three children of her own and was allegedly harsh to her stepdaughter who, once married, sued her stepmother and accused her of falsifying the inventory.[114] Elihu Yale was sued by his stepchildren.[115] In 1706 William and Robert Hedges filed a bill in chancery claiming that their two stepbrothers from their father's second marriage, John and Charles, should receive either the £3,000 that their mother had brought in or their share of the personalty, but not both; although initially successful, a petition from the widow and executrix based on her marriage settlement ultimately prevailed.[116]

---

[106] PCC, Skynner 88, 1627. [107] PRO, C 7/334/9.
[108] PRO, C 5/35/13, 1702; GLL, MS 6372. [109] CLRO, CSB, 1693–1713.
[110] D. S. Lawless, "Robert Daborne Senior," *Notes and Queries* 222 (1977): 515.
[111] Shropshire, RO, Scott MS 49/605–13.
[112] PRO, C 8/484/6. [113] PRO, C 7/356, 1712.
[114] J. Cox, *Hatred Pursued beyond the Grave* (1993), 81–3.
[115] Bingham, *Elihu Yale*, 302.
[116] *HMC*, House Lords, MSS, 1708–10, 277.

SUPPORT FOR PARENTS

Children may often have deferred to their parents because the latter had the property and the connections. The elderly relied on their wealth and status rather than on ritual deference to counterbalance their declining physical powers.[117] Businessmen tended to cling to their property to preserve their authority, which could decline with old age. Adults were always hierarchically superior to minors, but the elderly were not necessarily superior to their middle-aged sons.[118] Several appear to have postponed drawing up their wills through fear of losing control and becoming dependent on children whose trustworthiness was uncertain.

Parents were frequently advised not to transfer their estates to their children in their lifetime. Ned Ward expressed the King Lear syndrome well: "he that gives his children all and on their curtesy relies, will fare but ill and surely shall Repent his Folly ere he dies."[119] William Whateley warned that children could ill treat their parents when given property.[120] Some fathers did, however, transfer their property to their children before death, usually in return for a regular income. John Upton, for example, transferred his estate to his eldest son on the condition that he would receive an annuity of £60.[121]

Children had no legal obligation to support their parents, and some sons expressed reluctance to help their parents when old. But many provided financial help either directly or through their other legatees.[122] When one or both parents were still alive, their children usually bequeathed them at least a token, and sometimes substantial, legacies. For example, Henry Hopkins, a vintner, left his mother an annuity of £8, and Jacob Moyer, a merchant, left his mother £200.[123] William Blencoe, a grocer, left his father an annuity; Richard Bayman, a goldsmith, left his father and mother jointly £20 per year for life.[124] Robert Overton, a merchant, left his grandmother an annuity of £5.[125] Bache-

---

[117] M. Fortes, "Age Generation and Social Structure" in *Age and Anthropological Theory*, ed. D. I. Kertzer and J. Keith (Ithaca, 1984), 107.

[118] C. D. Hemphill, "Age Relation and the Social Order," *Journal of Social History* 27 (1994): 271–2.

[119] E. Ward, *Nuptial Dialogues*, vol. 1 (1710), xxxii.

[120] W. Whateley, *A Care Cloth* (1624), 52.

[121] W. Upton, *Upton Family Records* (1893), 76.

[122] P. Thane, "Old People" in *Charity Self Interest and Welfare in the English Past*, ed. M. Daunton (1996), 134.

[123] PCC, Seager 77, 1634; PCC, May 76, 1661.

[124] PCC, Hele 101 and 102, 1626.   [125] PCC, Laud 88, 1662.

lor Thomas Deane, a haberdasher, gave his "dear and well beloved" widowed mother £70 plus the goods in his shop "as a free acknowledgment of the dutye and the due respect I owe and bear unto her and for . . . her better livelihood and subsistence in her declining years."[126] Richard White, a distiller of Chipping Sodbury, divided his house between his mother and his wife.[127] John Hayward, an armorer, left his aged mother 20 shillings a year for life; Thomas Woodrow left the residue of his estate to his mother.[128] Robert Smith, a grocer, left his lands in Yorkshire to his eldest son, but the income was to be first enjoyed by his mother for the rest of her life and then by his widow.[129] Bachelor Thomas Melling left the residue of his estate in trust for his father and mother to provide income for them.[130]

Occasionally, a widow or an elderly widowed father would move in with one of their married children. Richard Farrington at seventy-one left London to live with his son and daughter-in-law in Iver.[131] Thomas Papillon's mother lived with him in Acrise in 1667. John West, a merchant tailor, had his mother move into his house and provided in his will that she would have an "upper chamber or room in my now dwelling house with her diet and other necessaries as she hath had heretofore during her natural life."[132] The mother of William Stout was shunted around by her children and eventually lived with her bachelor son. In 1615 Sir Thomas Pullis was given a pension, which was paid in advance for three years, by the Drapers Company provided that he gave up housekeeping and lived with his daughter.[133] Catherine Coytmore, who had seven children by her first husband, emigrated to Charleston in 1637 with her grandchildren.[134]

The household was not designed for large families. Many children were not keen on coresiding with their parents at any age, and their parents were most likely to move in when widowed, old, sick, and poor. It was hard to reconcile joint residence with individual property rights and authority, because a household could only have one head. A widow living with her married son might have to subordinate herself not only to her son, but also to his wife. A son, whether married or not,

---

[126] PCC, Ruthen 269, 1657. She was also named executrix.

[127] J. Addy, *Death, Money, and the Vultures* (1992), 145.

[128] PCC, Swann 31, 1623; PCC, Evelyn 50, 1641.   [129] PCC, St. John 109, 1631.

[130] PCC, Swann 59, 1623.   [131] GLL, MS 2708.   [132] PCC, St. John 87, 1631.

[133] A. H. R. Johnson, *The History of the Company of Drapers of London*, vol. 3 (Oxford, 1914–20), 110.

[134] R. Thompson, *Mobility and Migration* (Amherst, 1994), 197.

might feel that his authority as head of the family was usurped by his mother.

Separate residence was therefore the norm, though this did not mean less contact. Parents visited frequently to see their grandchildren or tend the sick. Some widowed parents must, however, have suffered from isolation and loneliness in old age.[135] The mobility of children also scattered the family. "When you come," wrote Edmund Stead, "you'll finde a great alteration in conversation and manners, my family is much dispersed which you know is the consequence of matrimony, my self and wife at home."[136]

Unmarried daughters were more likely to tend to their elderly parents and were often compensated in wills. Thomas Green, a Lancaster grocer, at age seventy-four sent for his two daughters from London to look after him and his wife.[137] Looking after her father, Judith Crowley delayed marriage until forty-three.[138] Azariah Pinney complained that her father did not write; his father complained that his daughter was throwing herself away on a poor man with children, when she should be attending to him.[139]

Even allowing for lip service and stylized forms of address in correspondence, it is clear that many children loved and respected their parents and thought of them after they had passed away. They independently sought parental blessing on their marriage and at the deathbed. Sons paid tribute to their mothers and fathers in their correspondence.[140] John Burnell honored his mother in his will "and her love again was no less towards me."[141] Joseph Collett wrote to his mother from India, "I hope to see you once again in the world."[142] One of the first actions of merchants, like Marmaduke Rawdon and Sir Dudley North, when they returned from living abroad was to visit their parents.[143] John Hudson commiserated with his brothers about their sick mother: "our dear

---

[135] R. Wall, "The Household" in *Family Forms in Historical Europe*, ed. R. Wall et al. (Cambridge, 1983), 493.
[136] Letter to Edward Stedd dated, 9 Oct. 1680, GLL, MS 18760/1.
[137] W. Stout, *Autobiography*, ed. J. D. Marshall, 3d ser., vol. 14 (Chetham Society, 1967), 140–2.
[138] Flinn, *Men of Iron*, 21.
[139] J. Pinney, *Letters, 1677–93*, ed. G. F. Nuttall (Oxford, 1939), letters dated 14 Dec. 1700, 28 April 1701.
[140] KAO, MS U 1015/C1; letter dated 5 Jan. 1666/7, BL, Add. MS 40,713.
[141] PCC, Swann 7, 1622.
[142] Collett, *Private Letter Book*, 64 (letter dated 16 Oct. 1713).
[143] Rawdon, *Life*, 27.

mother was very bad for fower or five weeks but is now pretty well recovered but yet is feeble in body then she was before she began."[144]

William Phillips assured his father that "I never have to my knowledge kept any matter of my concerns since you were pleased to set me out in the world secret from you . . . were I thereby to gain all the imaginable good this world can afford I would not act any thing in such nature to disoblige you."[145] William Cotton recalled in his will how he feared his mother's rebuke when he joined a mob that plundered Sir Henry Audley's house during the civil wars.[146] Sir William Turner recorded in his ledger the deaths of "my dear father" and "my dear mother."[147] Ralph Thoresby observed an annual meditation for his father, Roger Lowe visited his parents' grave, and the Moore family had epitaphs inscribed over the family vault.[148] Daughters were even more dutiful. Sarah and Elizabeth Papillon corresponded regularly with their father, and Sarah visited him in Holland.[149] Sir Henry Johnson's daughter visited him daily when he had gout.[150] The daughter of Simon Burton erected a monument to her parents.[151]

Children often asked to be buried with their parents.[152] Matthew Bateson, a skinner, wanted to be buried in the family vault near his father and left £150 to erect a tomb to commemorate both of them; he also left his house to his mother, Lady Ayloff, for life.[153] Nathaniel Mann, a merchant, instructed that he be buried next to his father and that a squadron of lifeguards place his corpse in the ground.[154] Marmaduke Rawdon asked to be buried in the same grave as his father and mother or, if that were impractical, near his cousin, Bowyer.[155] James Stanier, a merchant, specified burial near his father and his two deceased sons; Thomas Ballard, a vintner, wanted to be laid to rest near his mother and

---

[144] Letter to James Hudson from his brother, John, dated 25 Feb. 1733, PRO, C 105/15.
[145] Letter dated 1 Jan. 1697/8, Folger Library, MS UB. 18.
[146] PCC, Aylett 382, 1655.   [147] GLL, MS 5105.
[148] R. Thoresby, *Diary*, ed. M. Hunter (1830), 71–2; Ledger of Robert Moore, Shropshire RO MS 4572.
[149] Letter dated Aug. 1668, KAO, MS U 1015 C.14/23.
[150] W. Hedges, *Diary*, ed. H. Yule, vol. 75 (Hakluyt Society Publications, 1887), cci–ccii.
[151] E. Hatton, *New View London* (1708).
[152] W. Coster, "Kinship and Inheritance," *Borthwick Papers* 83 (1993): 7; P. MacGrath, "Wills of Bristol Merchants," *Transactions of the Bristol and Gloucester Archaeological Society* 68 (1949): 101; will of Luke Lucy, PCC, Juxon 121, 1663.
[153] PCC, Hyde 2, 1665.
[154] PCC, Bruce 81, 1664. Other examples include Matthew Chapman and Thomas Stower: PCC, Audley 73, 1632; *Durham Wills, 1604–49*, vol. 142 (Surtees Society, 1929), 7.
[155] Rawdon, *Life*, xxxi.

children.[156] Daniel Elder, a merchant, wanted to be buried near his mother and father, and Arthur Bickerstaff, a skinner, wanted a short inscription on his tombstone and to be placed near his mother's grave.[157]

SIBLING RIVALRY

Many families had so few children that rivalry between them did not constitute a problem, but in the few large families antipathy could develop between elder and younger children and between sons and daughters. Although parents tried their best to foster amicable relations between their children and deflect their egos, friction was still created by parental favoritism and by conflicts of personality and interest. Parenting handbooks advised treating all children the same, but one child (sometimes the youngest rather than the eldest) could be preferred by one or both parents. Siblings often had little in common with each other and much to dispute; as the proverb says, no one hates like a brother. Although birth order provided one possible source of authority, children's relationships could not be governed by patriarchal principles.

Locke argued that "children who live together often strive for mastery."[158] William Atwood's wife clearly understood this:

As to his unkindness to his brother I look on that only to proceed from his masters telling him how much better schollar his brother is then he and how much apter to learn and alas they are both but children and I know the young one is ready to insult over the other and he has not discretion to govern his nature and so I guess do many times fall out and be at difference but I hope no great hurt to either and tho Dicke be of much quicker parts which I know, is most pleasing to the master it being less trouble and pains to him to teach him and more credit in the end yet let us thank God Wille is no fool and I am still confident that were he with a master that would a little comply and sute himself to the childs disposition that he will make scholar good enouf for what you designe him. Now my great desire is [may it be with your approbation of you and the rest of our friends] that he may be removed to Mr Glascocks school which I verily believe would be better for them both, for it cannot but be a great disheartening to Wille to see his brother before and I believe the other would learne better if he were gone, for then they would strive which should do best.[159]

[156] PCC, Juxon 147, 1663; PCC, Pell 436.
[157] PCC, Aylett 312, 1655. Other examples include Adam Chapman and Humphrey Hardwick in PCC, Pell 205 and 530, 1659.
[158] Locke, *Some Thoughts Concerning Education*, 169.
[159] Letter from Mrs. Atwood dated 18 Feb. 1685/6, PRO, C 109/23/1.

The main source of tension between siblings was distribution of property. Sons and daughters fought over portions, legacies, settlements, and executorships. John Stow quarreled with his brother over his mother's will; his brother told his mother that John needed no part of her goods and had neglected her.[160] John Earle's shopkeeper "sayes he would use you as his brother, for he would abuse his brother."[161] In 1678, in the Elwes family, the younger son was given the furniture, goods, and chattels as well as a rent charge; the father, exhorting brotherly love, expected him to sell the furniture to the eldest, but strife and financial difficulties ensued.[162] In the Radcliffe family the grandfather's legacy was disputed, and the younger sons banded together against their two elder brothers.[163]

In a few families disputes between siblings led to litigation.[164] Elizabeth, daughter of Sir Charles Rich, had married Peter Civill without her father's consent; after his death she and her husband exhibited a bill in chancery, arguing that Sir Charles's other daughter had received real estate that had not been counted against her customary inheritance.[165] George Boone's unmarried daughter sued her married sister in 1709.[166] John Christian, a merchant tailor, clashed with his married sister over a piece of property, and William Cloberry sued his brother to recover a debt.[167] In the Daniel family difficulties arose over gardens that had been left jointly to several brothers.[168] One son and the daughters of Thomas Chamberlain brought pressure on another son to release land to satisfy legacies, though this may have been a collusive action.[169]

Siblings also competed for love and attention. Daughters were sometimes rivals for their husbands' or fathers' affection. Sanderson debated with himself whether his elder brother loved him; in 1606 he wrote on the back of a bill, "love me and not money, you are my brother and I am yours."[170] The son of Sir James Harvey, once executor of his

[160] Stow, *A Survey of London*, liv. [161] Earle, *Microcosmographie*, 54.
[162] *Lincolnshire Archivists Report* (1968–9), 112–13. The earlier settlements of the family worked smoothly.
[163] R. Davis, *Aleppo and Devonshire Square* (1967), 12–14.
[164] Although the number of cases has not been quantified, it is clear that the great majority of siblings did not resort to litigation.
[165] GLL, MS 507. [166] PRO, C 8/672/12.
[167] PCC, Ruthen 295, 1657; PCC, Fairfax 17, 1649.
[168] Letter from John Daniel dated 18 April 1693, KAO, MS U 119/C2.
[169] PRO, C 5/460/31, 1674.
[170] BL Lansdowne, MS 241, fo. 365; J. Sanderson, *Travels*, ed. Sir William Foster, 2d ser., vol. 67 (Hakluyt Society Publications, 1931), 33.

father's estate, left the city and put his sisters on the street.[171] Preferential treatment of any kind for the eldest, of which the most common but not the only form was primogeniture, could arouse jealousy. Younger sons often had mixed feelings about gaining from the death of their elder brother. When this happened to Richard Lane it was noted "by which he will gain [at death of his wife also] minimum 1,000 li p annum."[172]

Sometimes siblings just disliked each other. For example, Mary Gresham, a spinster and trader who died in 1726, ignored her brother, John, and made her sister her heir and then her nephews.[173] Friction could also be generated by accusations of improper behavior: "I have wrote my sister my mind concerning her, together with a few lines either to bring her to repentance or misery . . . she being now unworthy of anyone's pity."[174] Usually, however, animosity was provoked by unsatisfactory performance. Thomas Trenchfield wrote to his wife from Leghorn after his brother left in high dudgeon: "I wish he were here with me. I might prevaile with him to lead a new course of life and I should once more be a loving brother unto him."[175] "What I doe or have done or shall do for you," wrote Thomas Povey, rebuking his brother, William, for his business conduct, "is not without continual expence of my tyme, of my Interest and something also of my Purse, which three they are my subsistence."[176]

SIBLING HARMONY

The surviving evidence suggests, however, that most siblings enjoyed warm, intimate relationships. In their correspondence they expressed strong emotions. Richard Hill ended a letter, "kinde brother, my love being remembered not forgotten."[177] John Scattergood asked forgiveness of his brother "for the many juvenall abuses I have offered you."[178] As an apprentice, Nathaniel Harley wrote to his sister, Abigail, in a childish hand, concluding "I am your brother and truly loves you."[179]

---

[171] H. M. Pinchbeck, *Children in English Society*, vol. I (1973), 88.
[172] Letter to Woolley dated 15 Feb. 1698/9, Folger Library, MS UB 18, fo. 165.
[173] G. Leveson-Gower, *Genealogy of the Family of Gresham* (1883), 123.
[174] Undated letter to brother Cobb from his sister, Shropshire RO, MS 4572, 2/11.
[175] PCC, Berkeley 352, 1656. His relations with his other brothers were amicable.
[176] Letter to brother William dated 18 Jan. 1678, BL, Egerton MS 2395, fo. 32.
[177] Letter dated 13 Apr. 1631, BL, Add. MS 5488 fo. 88.
[178] Letter dated 12 March 1702/3, BL, Add. MS 43,730, fo. 19.
[179] Letters dated 25 Feb. 1681/2, 6 Dec. 1682, 4 June 1683, 15 Jan., 16 Feb., and 29 March 1684, BL, Add. MS 70,145.

Heigham Bright thanked his brother for "reall love and friendship."[180] Nicholas Blundell assured his brother that he would "find in me a father as well as a brother."[181] Janet Warner worried about her brother and kept in constant touch by correspondence.[182] The sister of Charles Payne hoped "that you and yours may have joy and comfort in this world which is the prayer of your sister."[183] Lucy Pelham told her brother that she "sincerely loves him" and asked for his portrait.[184] The letters between Richard Oxenden in India and his sister, Elizabeth Dalison, were delightfully affectionate: "dearest brother, it is impossible to express the great want I find in thy absence." His sister, Anne, also longed for his company and insisted that he could not live in India forever, though "all things in this world are bitter sweet."[185]

The death of a sibling was a hard blow. Sanderson wrote an emotional letter to his mother on the death of his sister.[186] William Lawrence confessed that "my brother's death shooke me so rudely that my Soule seem'd depriv'd of all its organs."[187] Anne Masters feared for her brother's survival in India after she learned that "it hath pleased the Lord to put an end to my son Robert's days in that remote place."[188] William Phillips was "much concerned at the ill news of my dear brother's death and although by Providence I am placed his successor, I must own my self a chief partaker in the loss of him."[189] Richard Oxenden was devastated by the premature death of his sister.[190] Sir William Turner bought black marble to raise a monument to his brother, Richard.[191]

The relationship between brothers Isaac and William Lawrence serves as a somewhat melodramatic example.[192] In 1674, after a spell as a slave in Algiers and a tourist in Rome, Isaac decided to become an interloper in India "to make some great and sudden increase in his fortunes and then to live at home in full peace and plenty." To his brother, William, the "absence of my best friend fixeth my soul" and "robbs me of your society and steals away that blessing to which I have a natural as well

---

[180] Bright, *The Brights of Suffolk*, 177.
[181] N. Blundell, *Diary and Letter Book, 1702–28* (Liverpool, 1952), 44.
[182] PRO, SP 46/83.   [183] Letter dated 20 May 1696, GLL, MS 5301a.
[184] Letters dated 30 Aug. 1718 and 25 Apr. 1719, BL, Add. 33,085.
[185] Letter dated 10 March 1665/6, BL, Add. MS 40,700, fos 50, 53. On the Oxenden/ Dallison connection, see S. Robinson, "Dalison Documents," *Archaeologia Cantiana* 15 (1883): 391.
[186] BL, Lansdowne MS 241, fo. 341.
[187] W. Lawrence, *The Diary*, ed. G. E. Aylmer (Beaminster, 1961), 60–1.
[188] Letter dated 20 April 1667, BL, Add. MS 40,713.
[189] Letter to his uncle, Marseille, dated 24 June 1697, Folger Library, MS UB 18.
[190] BL, Add. MS 40,700, fos 69, 223.   [191] GLL, MS 5105.
[192] Letters to and from William Lawrence, BL, India Off Eur MS 387/C, fos 212–15, 239.

as a civil right." In 1676 Isaac was admitted to the private trade in India and was in Bengal when the plague arrived. He wrote to his "dearest brother" in England that he was dying and wanted to bid farewell:

The weakness of my sight permits me not to add more than to tell you you have lost the most loving of brothers and the best of friends. Shed not needless tears for me, though Nature may require and can hardly resist 'em. My little prophet-ick Merlin read my doom at my departure when she told me she should never see me more . . . receive with these lines the latest breath and the very soul of your affectionate brother Isaac Lawrence, adieu, adieu my dearest friend.[193]

Many times siblings exchanged gifts with their correspondence. Baptist Hicks sent his brother and sister silks.[194] John Hudson received shaving materials from one brother and books from another.[195] George Warner had a long list of requests from both his sister, Janet, and his married sister, Elizabeth: eels from Holland, linens, underclothing, a mantua, a neck scarf, a cap for her child, 24 pounds of currants, prunes, and raisins, powdered sugar, pepper, spices, lemons, starch, and vinegar; in return Warner was sent cheese, brawn, and 43 pounds of bacon.[196] Nathaniel Harley sent his sister chocolate, perfume, wine, coffee, and tobacco. Sanderson, like several brothers, augmented his sister's marriage portion.[197] Thomas and Hugh Middleton provided £250 "marriage goods" for their sister, Barbara.[198] Matthew Skinner, a merchant, left £1,000 for dowries for his four unmarried sisters, provided that they married with the consent of their brother or brothers-in-law.[199]

Bequests to siblings were a stock feature of wills, particularly if the testator died young, unmarried, or abroad, like Reginald Kitch who died at Archangel or Christopher Ware of Ipswich.[200] William Bowyer of New York gave his real estate to his brothers and sisters.[201] Some even remembered their step-siblings: Robert Kaley, a merchant in Oporto, left money to the children of his mother's new husband; John Deleat left everything to his stepmother and three stepbrothers; Edward Bewick left land to his

---

[193] He in fact recovered from this particular bout of illness, but died shortly afterward.
[194] S. E. Hicks Beach, A Cotswold Family (1909), 193.
[195] Letter to James Hudson from his brother, John, dated 25 Feb. 1733, PRO, C 105/15.
[196] Letters dated 26 Feb., 20 March, 25 April, and 10 May 1642, and some undated, PRO, SP 46/83. A continuous correspondence was also maintained with his other brothers, Nathaniel and William.
[197] Sanderson, Travels, 17, 33.
[198] J. W. Gough, Sir Hugh Myddleton (Oxford, 1964), 7.   [199] PCC, Rivers 12, 1644.
[200] North Country Wills, 1558–1604, vol. 121 (Surtees Society, 1912), no. clxiv; Suffolk Archdeaconry Wills, 1620–1624, ed. M. E. Allen (Woodbridge, 1989), 77–8.
[201] New York Abstract of Wills, vol. 25 (1892), 416.

half brother.[202] When a testator had children, however, his legacies to siblings were usually tokens—a ring, personal mementos, or clothing. Humphrey Smallwood, a tallowchandler, for example, left his brother "my night gown with money to make it into a suit."[203]

Regular communication was maintained, even with married siblings. Francis Forbes, while in India, obtained the family news from his brother, William.[204] Nathaniel Harley told his sister when he cut his hair, reported gossip about London and his master, and described how he had met his young cousins who "are not in the least afraid of me."[205] Joseph Collett wrote to all his brothers and sisters, telling them about the earthquakes and the native religions of India.[206] A gap in correspondence usually created anxiety. Nathan Simpson wrote to his brother "I have not heard from you in such a long time which I am mighty troubled about therefore I pray you to let me hear from you otherwise I shall have no rest at all."[207]

Siblings participated fully in each other's lives and provided many kinds of assistance. Eldest sons accepted responsibility for orphans, unmarried sisters, and younger brothers. When Charles Blunt's son heard about his sister's marriage he commented "pray God they may doe well. I wish them all happiness."[208] Phineas Pitt, in contrast to his elder brother, helped his siblings. Nathaniel Torriano confessed to his mother that "I had nearly forgot my brother's birthday."[209] The widow of Thomas Juxon left her house in London to her son on the condition that he let his sisters dry their clothes in the garden without charge.[210] Brothers watched out for their sisters. Nicholas Buckeridge had to give assurance to his wife's brother that he had provided for his wife and children when he went to India.[211] Sisters took care of their sibling's children.[212] When Anthony Lowther died while still indentured, his brother approached his master, Michael Mitford, to recover some of the premium. Mitford insisted "that neither law nor custome can oblige me

[202] PCC, Berkeley 427, 1656; PCC, Hyde 112, 1665; *Durham Wills, 1543–1602*, vol. 112 (Surtees Society, 1906), 125.
[203] PCC, Goare 106, 1637.   [204] BL, Add. MS 43,730, 12 March 1702/3.
[205] Letters dated 25 Feb. 1681/2, 6 Dec. 1682, 4 June 1683, 15 Jan., 16 Feb., and 29 March 1684, BL, Add. MS 70,145.
[206] Collett, *Private Letter Book*, passim.
[207] Letter dated 9 Aug. 1705, PRO, C 104/13–14.
[208] Letter to Charles Blunt dated 18 Jan. 1697, PRO, C 114/164.
[209] Letter from Nathaniel Torriano to his mother dated 10 Oct. 1736, PRO, C 112/24/2.
[210] PCC, Lee 5, 1637.   [211] BL, Add. MS 40,700, fo. 19.
[212] Letter to Messrs Hudson and Co., London, 31 Oct. 1704, GH, MS 11,892A.

to return one penny of what received with your brother" and added that he had spent £125 on the lad's funeral "and soe as he had a good exit, he is well provided for and needs noe more portion."[213]

Siblings also provided direct financial help to each other. In 1715 John Hunter left £50 a year for any sibling who might need it. Humphrey Williams, a goldsmith, left his "poor brother Owen Williams xx li (£20) if that will free him out of prison."[214] Hannah Parsons wrote to her brother recognizing his role in rescuing her husband from his debts: "I am sorry to hear you have not bine well and the more because my unfortunate husband should occasion your remove into those cold parts. Pray let me hear how you doe for I dreamt you was dead which almost over whelmed me with grief but hope the contrary. . . . I have bine hard put to it to preserve my family but hope it will be better if it please God."[215]

In a surprising number of cases, siblings related their nighttime dreams to one another. Richard Prowde told his sister "I have dreamed three nights since I came up that I have been in your company."[216] William Lawrence tells how:

I had this dream. Methought my great desire to see you had landed me at Surat where thinking to have surprised you with a unexpected visit I entered into your lodgings, but to my own greater surprise, I saw you wrapt up in your winding-sheet and lying pale, thin and dead in your coffin. . . . [William called his brother to life again before waking up.] Perhaps it is high friendship can make such a perfect union that one cannot suffer but the other must have some share in it.[217]

A final example could have been lifted from John Bunyan's *Pilgrim's Progress*:

Last night tho my Body was in profound sleep my Mind was awake and fancy was introduced into my soul which imployed all its faculties. I supposed myself near that noble fabrick which you described [a moated castle guarded by beasts] and encountered two charming persons the one nam'd faith and the other hope . . . a gay aiery phantom appeared called vanity. . . . At last she prevailed with me to withdraw with her . . . to a strange ridiculous place where there was several odd figures some in the likeness of Men and some of Women some were kings

---

[213] Letter from Michael Mitford to John Lowther at Dantzig dated 21 Oct. 1703, GLL, MS 11,892A.
[214] PCC, Hele 100, 1626. See also BL, Add. MS 32,456.
[215] Letter dated 18 Nov. 1697, PRO, C 110/158.
[216] Letter dated Aug. 1670, Shropshire RO, MS Acc 567.
[217] Letter dated 20 Sept. 1670, BL, Add. MS 40,713.

and queens and others milkmaids, devils, shepardesses, dogs, cats, monkeys, friers etc a great part dancing others singing . . . a witch beating a king with a broom stick. . . . I . . . wished my self out of this hell . . . immediately by some conjuration out goes the candles. Then I thought it high time to go away but how to do it was the question. However with great difficulty I got away with the loss of my money. . . . Reason comforted me and told me that for the future I must take care to avoid the evil creature as my greatest enemy . . . they call it [said she] a Masquerade. . . . Goodness she took me into a large dining room . . . hung with tapestry in which was wrought scripture stories and the pictures of several of the fathers as Eusebius, Hugo Grotius, St Chrystome, St Jerome, St Austin etc and also some of our late writers as Beveridge, Stillingfleet, Tillotson. . . . I was more pleased to see two men truly religious sitting discoursing upon the tapestry and of a future judgment a thing so little spoke of in these days. . . . I continued to admire his conversation . . . till my body began to awake.[218]

SUMMARY

The attitude and behavior of parents changed as their children matured, gender becoming more important. Sons were treated differently from daughters, and fathers often responded differently than mothers. But the emotional commitment of both parents did not waver. Parents usually put their children first and were always worried about their children's future, particularly how they would fare after their parents were dead. Fathers attempted in their wills to anticipate all contingencies, to provide for stepchildren as well as children, for younger as well as eldest sons, and especially for the unmarried and the underaged.

Although parents were well aware that their children represented a long-term investment with heavy costs for training and placement, they rarely dwelled on the fact that children reduced their opportunity to increase their own material possessions. On the contrary, most wished to perpetuate themselves through their children, and they suffered from grief and disappointment when their children died young or matured into adults whose character, ability, or behavior did not meet expectations.

The response of grown children both to their parents and to their siblings ranged from active dislike and rejection to love and support. Inevitably there was generational conflict as children developed their egos, reacted against authority, and acquired their own identity through

[218] Letter from Elizabeth Moore to her brother, Robert, Shropshire RO, MS 4572, 7/2/1.

self-assertion. Marriage and mobility undermined the unity of the business family; egotism, greed, and conflicts of interest always threatened its integrity. Relations between parents and children and between siblings could be driven by self-promotion and were usually based on personal choice, not on prescription. It is often difficult to determine who was the manipulator and who was manipulated. But the majority of children seem to have bonded permanently with their parents, whom they loved, cherished, accepted, and supported in later life. In most cases that have been recovered here, conflicts were resolved by compromise and harmony restored by reconciliation.

The mutual interaction of parents and children was certainly influenced by external social and economic forces. The business family, like other propertied families of the period, had a patriarchal structure, a gender hierarchy, and predetermined priorities for distribution of resources. But family historians in their attempts to distinguish the premodern family from the modern one, have neglected to acknowledge the importance of individual personality and raw emotion. When relations between parents and children are reconstructed in particular families, the range of behavior is infinitely varied, volatile, and remarkably similar to later periods. Love, grief, and self-sacrifice coexisted with enmity, indifference, and aggressiveness. Both parents and children had aspirations and expectations that could not always be fulfilled, which led to jealousy, resentment, and regret. The desire to belong conflicted with the desire for independence. Individuals simultaneously sought and resisted the emotional embrace of the family; they often could neither live with nor without their kin.

Some of the new ideas that emerged in the outside world to challenge old values must have filtered through to individual families, though there is little hard evidence of direct influence. There are some indications that parents faced increased pressure from their children for personal autonomy—everyday contact slowly became less formal. But the stresses visible in relations between parents and children were inherent in the family structure. Their objectives and interests remained the same. What did change in the early modern period was the frequency with which the respective rights and obligations of family members became the subject of public debate.

6

Kin and Community

Kinship is partly a biological fact and partly a cultural construct; it can be either consanguineous or affinal. A lineage can descend either from a common male ancestor (patrilineal or agnatic) or through females (matrilineal or cognatic). A bilaterally extended kin group, which descends through either father or mother, is more egalitarian and favors living relatives at the expense of future generations.[1] Whereas blood kin are inherited, affinal kin are acquired through the marriage of unrelated couples (including cousins in England). The exchange of women between patriarchal families continuously expands and integrates the kinship group.[2]

The potential kindred of any businessman, even when uterine kin from remarriages are omitted and allowance is made for unmarried and childless collaterals, was vast: it included the spouses and children of his own brothers and sisters, the parents and siblings (and their spouses) of his own wife, the spouses of his own children, the brothers and sisters of his own parents (aunts and uncles) with their children (cousins), and the spouses and children of his cousins.

Whenever a new conjugal family was created by marriage, it could either reject or submit to the prior family of birth of each spouse. Were most wives of businessmen absorbed into their husbands' families, and was priority normally accorded to paternal over maternal kin and to blood over marriage? What range of kinsfolk, both spatially and

[1] J. J. Hurwick, "Lineage and Kin" in *The First Modern Society*, A. L. Beier et al. (Cambridge, 1989), 59. See also J. Goody, review of M. J. Maynes et al., *Gender Kinship Power* (New York, 1996), in *Journal of Early Modern History* 2 (1998): 182.
[2] H. Levi-Straus, *Elementary Structures of Kinship*, trans. J. H. Bell et al. (Boston, 1969), 480–1. This model is rejected by L. Leibowitz, "In the Beginning" in *Womens Work, Mens Property*, ed. S. Coontz and P. Henderson (1986), 75.

genealogically, was recognized, and were they cultivated from duty or
affection or because there was a utilitarian benefit? What was the quality
of contact—how frequent, how broad, and how intense? Were obligations to kin optional or so vague as to be meaningless; how were the
claims of kin defined, justified, and balanced against the interests of the
nuclear family, and how valuable was the interaction? By what means
did the business family reconcile its priorities with those of the urban
community and the rest of society? Did it reject or embrace rival institutions and with what consequences?

RECOGNITION

"God," wrote Gouge, "hath yet further extended this natural affection
[toward wife and children] to brethren, cousins and other kindred."[3] The
ecclesiastical table of kindred and affinity provided a fairly comprehensive guide, and every landowner knew the common law of descent. But
in everyday use the terminology of kinship was imprecise, changeable,
and employed inconsistently and erratically. The qualification "in-law"
was frequently dropped after brother, father, and mother; stepparents
and stepchildren were not distinguished from natural parents and
children. Grandchildren were often described as godchildren or even
sons-in-law; in many documents the term "daughter" turns out to mean
stepdaughter or daughter-in-law. Walter Myers, a skinner, referred to his
grandchildren as the children of his son-in-law.[4]

The terms "brother" and "sister" were widely used outside the family
to designate members of corporate institutions, such as the guilds or
Trinity House. Little distinction was made between first cousins (those
sharing common grandparents) and second cousins (those sharing common great-grandparents); indeed the term "cousin" was used so casually
that it often seems little more than a mode of address. Despite a growing
interest in heraldry and genealogy, little attempt was made to measure
degrees of relationship by generation, which suggests a lack of interest
in distant kin.

Some testators in their bequests and their choice of mourners discriminated against their wife's kindred or privileged their paternal
kin. The allegiance of a wife on marriage traditionally passed to her
husband's family. Daughters-in-law were less likely to receive legacies

---

[3] Gouge, *Of Domesticall Duties*, 81.   [4] PCC, Meade 60, 1618.

than sons-in-law. But the majority of kin were affinal rather than consanguineous, and this explains why parents wished to control the marriages of their children. In practice little distinction was made between
ties of blood and marriage; maternal kin were treated in the same way
as paternal kin.[5] Sons-in-law were regarded as natural sons if a testator
had no male heirs. Children belonged to the family of both their father
and mother. Lineal descent was usually preferred, but if there was no
direct heir, family property was passed to nephews or cousins by lateral
descent.

As the proverb says, "at marriage and burials friends and kinsfolk be
known."[6] Thomas Russell, a vintner, instructed that his property be sold
and distributed to all his kindred "next allied in blood to me."[7] Thomas
Stead, a girdler, wanted "my kindred, household, neighbours and familiars" to accompany his corpse "but mourning cloth for my executor,
household and neere kindred onelie."[8] On the other hand, alderman
William Gore selected as mourners his wife, children, grandchildren,
sons-in-law, servants, and "all the brethren and sisters of the whole bloud
of mee and my wife."[9] Testators both included their wife's kindred
among the mourners, like William Rodway, a merchant tailor, and left
them substantial bequests, like Richard Crowche, a salter; the widower,
girdler George Tench, even included friends of his kindred.[10] John Amy,
a haberdasher, let his wife decide his bequests to her kindred.[11]

Differences of degree were of course taken into account. Some testators took a narrow view: Ellis Crispe asked for no pomp at his funeral
and just "my own family, my son, daughters and grandchilde and myne
owne and my wife's brother and sisters"; Sir Nicholas Butler specified
just his "own family."[12] Others took a broader approach: Samuel
Pennoyer provided for all "collateral cousins not exceeding the 2nd
degree."[13] The order of preference after the family of orientation, was
most commonly the father and mother-in-law (if alive), then the children
of siblings, and then uncles and aunts. Bachelors gave first to their siblings and then to their nephews and nieces. Distant kin received little
property unless they were the closest living relatives. Many testators
made children their ultimate legatees (the adult kin serving as trustees

---

[5] D. Cressy, "Kin and Kin Interaction," 48.
[6] M. P. Tilley, *Dictionary of Proverbs* (Ann Arbor, 1950), 445.
[7] PCC, Parker 85, 1619.   [8] PCC, Campbell 3, 1642.   [9] PCC, Byrde 62, 1624.
[10] PCC, Hele 48, 1626; PROB, 11/98/173, 1601; PCC, Ruthen 273, 1657.
[11] PCC, Bowyer 215, 1652.   [12] PCC, Clarke 120; PROB, 11/457/125.
[13] PCC, Alchin 388, 1654.

until the children came of age or married) and thereby privileged future generations of the family.

Several factors determined who was recognized as kin—the age and marital status of the testator, accessibility, and wealth. Older men and widows had more living kin and a greater incentive to look beyond their immediate family. A distinction was made between remote kin, effective kin (with whom there was some contact), and "loving kin" (with whom there was intimate contact). Kin were divided by wealth and prestige; the rich had more property to distribute and more extended kin.[14] Those considered failures could be dropped from the list.

Kinship was therefore a negotiable process of exclusion, both descent-centered and ego-centered, and a flexible and permissive system with no fixed rules.[15] Selection was based primarily on personal preference, and different families had different priorities. The core of kinship was in fact friendship. When distributing property or when there was no direct heir, testators did not automatically include all their kin or select by degree, but favored those who they liked. Richard Walter, a girdler, left bequests to twenty-five kin but excluded some individuals by name and left a legacy to William Heath, only if his sister "does not marry Mr Prowde," a neighbor.[16] Rowland Powell, a merchant, endowed the children and grandchildren of his siblings but excluded one nephew, as did Thomas Chilton, a clothworker.[17]

NUMBERS

The number of kin may have been reduced by high mortality in the seventeenth century, with fewer uncles and aunts and more cousins; one estimate puts the decline at 50 percent.[18] But the kin universe was still huge and it expanded outward at great speed like the universe after the big

---

[14] K. Schürer, "Variations in Household Structure" in *Counting the People*, ed. K. Schürer (Cambridge, 1994), 275; N. Goose, "Household Size and Structure" in *The Tudor and Stuart Town*, ed. J. Barry (1990), passim.

[15] R. Wheaton, "Family and Kinship in Western Europe," *Journal of Interdisciplinary History* 5 (1974–5): 624.

[16] PCC, Rutland 20, 1587.   [17] PCC, Rivers 2, 1644; PCC, Pile 6, 636.

[18] Cressy, "Kin and Kin Interaction," table 4, suggests that the numbers of close kin for an individual aged forty-four fell from twenty-seven to fifteen and the number of first cousins from eleven to five. A reduction in the mean number of cousins also occurs in the simulated model of J. E. Smith and J. Oeppen, "Estimating Numbers of Kin" in *Old and New Methods in Historical Demography*, ed. D. S. Reher and R. S. Schofield (Oxford, 1993), 298.

bang; genealogies, in other words, are long and broad.[19] Families spread horizontally through kin rather than vertically through generations. New kin were continuously accumulated through marriage, remarriage, and new births. As a postscript, Alexander Stuart wrote "all your friends are well and for news, the number of your relations are increased, your aunt being safely delivered . . . of a son."[20] Bilateral descent through either father or mother created a new range of kin in each generation. Given that any individual after fifteen generations will have 32,000 ancestors, it is somewhat difficult to trace the distant kin of businessmen, and attention has been focused here on first-order links.[21]

Some testators named legions of kin, like Edmund Hale and the bachelor William Haines, a goldsmith, who named 116 kin and 29 children; John Banks, a mercer, who allotted 2,000 marks for his funeral, named 77 kindred and 104 friends; Sir Nicholas Rainton listed 102 kin and 8 friends.[22] Robert Parker, a merchant tailor, knew the exact addresses of his relatives all over the country and the names of their spouses.[23]

But kinship is limited by memory, and many businessmen often lacked precise or current details. Sir John Cutler left £2,000 for any relations he might have forgotten.[24] Standard clauses in wills, like that of Thomas Fox, a clothworker, allowed "unto all other my kindred that shall make it appear that they are truly and lawfully allied unto me twelve pence apiece."[25] Ralph Ingram, an ironmonger, knew the names of three children of his brother, Robert, but "one other name I doe not remember."[26] Daniel Elliott, a merchant tailor, was generous to his wife's relations, including one daughter "who is married to a taylor in Beawley whose name I know not."[27] Jasper Chapman, a grocer, could not recall the names of his sister's two daughters, and Ralph Ingram of one nephew.[28]

---

[19] A. R. Wagner, *Pedigree and Progress* (1975), 129; B. Dyke and T. M. Warren, eds., *Genealogical Demography* (New York, 1980), 91.

[20] Letter dated 22 Jan. 1732, PRO, C 111/95.

[21] E. Shils, *Tradition* (Chicago, 1981), 164.

[22] PCC, Berkeley 352, 1656; PCC, Audley 43, 1632; PCC, Twisse 129, 1646; PCC, Scroope 84, 1630.

[23] PCC, Clarke 76, 1625.   [24] J. B. Heath, *Company of Grocers*, 3d ed. (1869), 288.

[25] PCC, Sadler 59, 1631. Other examples are will of Peter Hearn, PCC, Fines 72, 1647; will of William Hounsell, PCC, Aylett 186, 1655; will of John Shirley, PCC, Fairfax 177, 1649; wills of William Hearn and John Tanner, PCC, Ruthen 162 and 273, 1657; PCC, Pell 326, 1659; will of Startup Jackson, PCC, Alchin 161; will of Thomas Howes, PCC, Twisse 157.

[26] PCC, Rivers 16, 1644. Other examples include Thomas Finch in 1684 and Sir Robert Peak.

[27] PCC, Ridley 71, 1629.   [28] PCC, Alchin 367, 1654; PCC, Rivers 16, 1644.

Table 6.1. Kin and Friends in Wills (Percentage of Known Cases)

	Period I	Period II	Bracket I	Bracket II	Bracket III	Bracket IV	Cohort I	Cohort II	Cohort III	Cohort IV
Number of Kin										
None	22.46	11.96	20.51	13.06	7.59	3.45	6.49	9.71	7.77	12.07
1–2	23.98	25.69	23.08	22.80	19.17	22.41	15.58	23.43	21.55	25.86
3–4	15.61	15.92	12.82	13.78	15.01	17.24	9.09	16.00	17.67	13.79
5–10	22.57	28.76	33.33	28.74	32.73	31.03	33.77	28.00	33.92	31.03
11–20	10.64	13.94	7.69	15.91	17.36	12.07	22.08	14.29	15.55	12.07
Over 20	4.74	3.73	2.56	5.70	8.14	13.79	12.99	8.57	3.53	5.17
Mean	5.55	6.06	5.28	6.87	8.17	10.11	12.06	7.19	6.77	5.88
Median	3.09	3.98	4.00	4.55	5.47	5.00	8.33	4.61	4.89	4.25
Total	1,710	911	39	421	553	58	77	175	283	58
Number of Friends										
None	27.18	23.60	25.64	21.24	17.55	19.61	9.23	22.45	25.00	20.00
1–2	31.48	37.14	35.90	33.33	30.44	27.45	13.85	29.25	33.61	43.64
3–4	15.86	17.27	12.82	18.27	20.30	15.69	24.62	18.37	16.80	20.00
5–10	17.80	16.65	15.39	17.78	22.20	19.61	35.39	21.77	17.21	16.36
11–20	5.75	4.22	10.26	7.41	7.40	11.76	10.77	6.80	5.33	–
Over 20	1.94	1.12	–	1.98	2.11	5.88	6.15	1.36	2.05	–
Mean	3.62	3.14	3.33	3.91	4.44	6.06	8.17	3.90	3.50	2.25
Median	2.01	1.90	1.60	2.28	2.67	2.80	5.00	2.39	1.96	1.67
Total	1,652	805	39	405	473	51	65	147	244	55

Table 6.2. *Kin and Friends: Cross-Sectional Analysis, 1580–1740*
(Percentage of Known Cases in Wills)

	List Kin (%)	Omit Kin (%)	Total Number	List Friends (%)	Omit Friends (%)	Total Number
Never Married	83.67	16.33	594	77.03	22.97	492
Widowed	87.29	12.71	417	83.33	16.66	372
Married with children	81.19	18.81	1,595	73.62	26.38	1,463
Married without children	80.88	19.12	408	75.93	24.07	511
Lived abroad	78.61	21.39	416	74.61	25.39	382
Deceased under 50	92.22	7.78	90	83.33	16.66	84
Deceased over 50	91.31	8.69	495	77.73	22.27	422
London origin	89.08	10.92	348	87.66	12.34	632
Country origin	89.84	10.16	679	82.53	17.47	1,076
Major office	92.88	7.12	379	91.20	8.80	341

Thomas Botheby, a merchant tailor, forgave his brother's executors for failing to repay a debt "the which I took very unkindly," but could not remember the name of the husband of one of his nieces.[29]

Richard Arnold, a goldsmith, was vague about the location of his kin; he thought that one of his father's brothers might be in New England and a child of his father's sister in the Isle of Thanet.[30] Sir John Moore received a letter from a kinsman that began "I presume my letter will be very surprising to you. . . . I humble crave your pardon for this troublesome and perhaps impertinent relation it being occasioned through the earnest and longing desire I had to hear from some of my kindred." Moore's comment was "I do not remember who Sarah Linch alius Webb is."[31]

Between periods I and II the median number of kin mentioned in wills rose from 3 to 4, and testators who ignored their kin fell from 22 percent to 12 percent; in both periods 23 to 28 percent mentioned 5 to 10 kinsman, and 11 to 14 percent mentioned 11 to 20 kin. The median number rose with wealth from 4 in bracket I to 5 in brackets II through IV. The median number declined, however, during the seventeenth century from 8 in cohort I to 5 in cohorts II and III to 4 in cohort IV. The percentage of testators who listed some kin was constant at 79 to 82 percent, whether they were bachelors, widowed, married with

[29] PCC, Clarke 114, 1625. [30] PCC, Rivers 7, 1644. [31] GLL, MS 507.

children, resident abroad, or holders of public office; neither age nor place of birth seems to have made any difference. The number of kin mentioned did, however, fall as the number of surviving children increased.[32]

In comparison, another sample of London wills reveals a mean of 2.3 kin among legatees, and 7.2 percent of testators named 11 to 20 kin and 1.7 percent named over 20.[33] A horizontal network of close-knit kin with an extended cousinhood was visible in Southwark, Norwich, Exeter, St. Ives, Gloucester, King's Lynn, and Belfast.[34] In Gloucester 51 percent of the elite were related, though the clusters of kin became smaller over time.[35] In East Anglia 215 nuclear families made up 55 extended families.[36] Although diluted by mobility, weakened by lack of sanctions, and frequently invisible, the extended family was a social fact. Kinship created social networks.[37]

CORESIDENCE

Unless they were apprentices or servants, kin did not usually reside in the household, which was predominately two-generational and limited to the conjugal couple and their children and stepchildren. In the whole population 10.1 percent of households had resident kin and 12 percent had extended families; in 1695 23.9 percent of all households in one London parish and 8.3 percent in 7 other parishes had resident kin.[38]

---

[32] The Pearson R correlation between number of kin and total number of surviving children = −0.108.

[33] Earle, *Making of the English Middle Class*, 392, n 29, table 11.3.

[34] Boulton, *Neighbourhood and Society*, 251; G. A. Metters, "The Rulers and Merchants of King's Lynn" (Ph.D. diss., University of East Anglia, 1982), 49; M. Carter, "Town or Urban Society" in *Societies, Cultures, and Kinship, 1580–1850*, ed. C. Phythian-Adams (Leicester, 1993), 111; P. Clarke, "The Ramoth Gilead of the Good" in *The Tudor and Stuart Town*, ed. J. Barry (1990), 259; J. Agnew, *Belfast Merchant Families in the Seventeenth Century* (Dublin, 1996), 35.

[35] P. Clark, "The Civic Leaders of Gloucester" in *The Transformation of English Provincial Towns, 1600–1800*, ed. P. Clark (1984), 325.

[36] Thompson, *Mobility and Migration*, 200.

[37] S. Cooper, "Household Forms" in K. Schurer, *Counting the People* (Cambridge, 1994), 220; R. A. Houston, *Social Change in the Enlightenment: Edinburgh, 1660–1760* (Oxford, 1994), 28.

[38] Laslett, "Mean Household Size," table 4.12, and P. Laslett, "Family, Kinship, and Collectivity," *Continuity and Change* 3 (1988), 154. R. Wall, "Family Forms" in *Family Forms in Historical Europe*, ed. R. Wall (Cambridge, 1983), table 1.11, and "Regional and Temporal Variation" in *Regional Aspects of British Population Growth*, ed. J. Hobcroft and P. Rees (1979).

In Southwark 18 percent of households were related to at least one other.[39] Kin were resident in only 7.4 percent of households in Southampton.[40] In Shrewsbury 938 families were organized in 261 kinship groups, but only 0.11 percent of the whole population had resident kin.[41] On the other hand, in Great Yarmouth and Ryton extended households were common.[42]

Joint residence occurred occasionally from choice and frequently because of death, widowhood, orphanage, migration, or spinsterhood. On the day after his marriage Richard Farrington's "mother and grandmother came to lodge and board at my house."[43] Samuel Jeake lived with his wife's mother, sister, and brother. Aunts and uncles fostered their nephews and nieces: John Sanderson and William Joyce both lived with their nieces.[44] Migrants to the towns, particularly women, often had to live with kin. Some of the lodgers who are listed with relative frequency, except in the wealthier business households, were kin.

The godson and kinsman of Francis Griffin, a childless merchant tailor, lived with him.[45] George Frere lived with his cousin, Bridget, and arranged for his nephew to be taught English and Latin and apprenticed to a merchant.[46] Robert Wilson, a draper, and James Williams, a merchant tailor, were both living with kinswomen at their deaths, as was the widower and merchant tailor Augustin Bullock, who made his godson and kin his heirs.[47] Coresidence, moreover, defined the household rather than the family, which extended itself through common activities, such as sharing meals. Rachel Pengelly's household was swamped with kin.[48] The Bowreys seem to have swapped houses with their in-laws in Newcastle, though Thomas Bowrey's sister-in-law paid £48.15.0. for nine months board for herself, her mother, and a maid.[49]

[39] Boulton, *Neighbourhood and Society*, 253.   [40] Goose, "Household Size," 377.
[41] Hindson, "Family Structure, Inheritance, and Kinship in Shrewsbury," 48–57, 63–7, 243. Merchants represented 10 percent of this sample.
[42] M. Chaytor, "Household and Kinship," *History Workshop Journal* 10 (1980), 47; P. Gauci, *Politics and Society in Great Yarmouth* (Oxford, 1996), chapter 2.
[43] GLL, MS 2708.
[44] *Prerogative Court of Canterbury, Abstracts of Register Wootton*, vol. 5, ed. W. Brigg, 84.
[45] PCC, Rivers 146, 1645.
[46] N. Currer-Briggs, *Virginia Settlers* (Baltimore, 1970), 185.
[47] PCC, Coventry 11, 1639; Waters, *Genealogical Gleanings in England*, 328; PCC, Barrington 10, 1628.
[48] BL, Add. MS 32,456.   [49] GLL, MS 3041/1.

FREQUENCY OF CONTACT

Dense networks reflect genetic relationships but not necessarily close ties. The importance of kinship must be gauged not just by numbers, but by the frequency of contact and the services that kin could provide. The center could easily lose touch with the periphery. Stephen Abberley, a grocer, asked for no pomp at his funeral, because "most of my kindred wilbe absent living far off."[50] Continuous mobility led to separation and undermined lineage loyalty. Even though kinship was entrenched in the social order, it could decay by default. In families that lacked the magnetism of wealth and the esteem of high status, kinship ties had to be reinforced through continuous effort.

In business families distance seems sometimes to have even stimulated communication, which was sustained through correspondence. Geography separated but did not sever contact—cousinage bridged the oceans. West Indian merchants, like Christopher Jeaffreson, exchanged letters and gifts with their kinsmen and friends in England.[51] New Englanders and Virginians nurtured their kin in England, though the second generation relied more on local kin.[52] In Barbados and New York many merchants left property to relations and friends in England; Charles Lambert sent money to his mother and sister in Exeter.[53] Jacob Jesson, a merchant, left his brother-in-law, John Walley of Boston, £5.[54] Joseph Cruttenden inquired after a kinsman whom he eventually located.[55] William Sharpe corresponded with his mother-in-law, sending her sugar, a parrot, and a monkey.[56] Richard Oxenden had a chatty correspondence with all his relatives; his mother reminded him that it was a "noble principle to love family and kin."[57]

Michael Mitford was succinct and businesslike with his sister-in-law

[50] PCC, Rivers 46, 1645.
[51] *A Young Squire*, vol. 1, ed. J. C. Jeaffreson (1878), 311.
[52] Morgan, *The Puritan Family*, 150; Anderson, *New England's Generation*, 211; J. Horn, *Adapting to a New World* (Chapel Hill, 1994), 15; *American Wills Proved in London, 1611–1775*, ed. P. W. Coldham (1992), 6, 20, 29; J. Horn, "To Parts Beyond" in *To Make America*, ed. J. Horn and I. Altman (Berkeley, 1991), 9, 112–14; Waters, *Genealogical Gleanings*, 152.
[53] *New York Abstract of Wills in Surrogates Office*, 25 (1892), 198, 395, 442; ibid., 26 (1893), 38–9, 189; *Barbados Records. Wills and Administrations, 1639–80*, ed. J. M. Sanders (Houston, 1979), passim.
[54] PCC, Lloyd 108, 1686.
[55] J. Cruttenden, *Letters, 1710–17*, ed. I. K. Steele (Toronto, 1977), 93.
[56] Shropshire RO, Forester MS Acc 224.
[57] Letter dated 7 May 1666, BL, Add. MS 40,700.

in Newfoundland: "My wife recd your letter and find little to answer therein. I send you inclosed a bill on Mr Procter for 10 li for the Xmas quarter. Your daughter is very well. I am sorry for the death of cosen Grey. Pray give mine and my wife' duty to my mother and when you see cos Milbourn give my service to her and tell her I recd the 5 guineas I disbursed for her."[58]

Within England mobility was offset by clustering in towns, and immigrants maintained links with their country kin. Bachelors were especially dutiful: Henry Parvis explained to his mother that "having no children (as yet I have none) amongst my blood must be divided the fruit of my labours for which I desire the rather to hear how they are married and increased with children."[59] Robert Booth, a London merchant, corresponded with his country cousins, and Peter Mitton with his kin in Shropshire.[60] Daniel Wigfall informed his uncle, Sir John Gell, when his cousin, Philip, was captured by Tripolitans.[61] Charles Payne corresponded with his cousins and was congratulated on his marriage and the birth of a daughter by James Norris.[62] Henry Ashton gave his cousin all the family news:

Mrs Worthington is dead, her eldest son married at St Kitts . . . who I recommended to be her sons correspondent. . . . I was not at the funerall of her mamma nor had a ring. Old Halstead is in good head. Your brother Jack is in good recovered . . . my mother dyed about 5 weeks ago. Your brother John was then indisposed and could not attend her funeral. One of your nieces is at Newton so I am afraid he has taken them from school . . . my little girl has had a violent fever having had 3 blisters at a time but is now pretty well recovered.[63]

Edward Blackett received a letter from his brother, which illustrates the fondness that could develop between uncle and niece: "I have one standing by me who desires to be remembered unto you and will not go away till I advise you that you forgot your promise unto her about your Pretty Dog. No news but to say that my Lady upon Saturday last fell over a dogg and broake her Arme."[64] John Daniel received news of his kin from his sister-in-law, who had recently lost her husband and brother and was

---

[58] Letter dated 21 Oct. 1713, GLL, MS 11,892A.
[59] Letter dated 21 July 1613 in S. E. Hicks-Beach, *A Cotswold Family* (1909), 192.
[60] Papers of Robert Booth, Hertfordshire RO, Pashanger MSS, 1670–80; T. C. Mendenhall, *Shrewsbury Drapers* (Oxford, 1953), 232.
[61] Derbyshire RO, MS D 258, box 41/31/c.
[62] Letters dated 11 May 1695 and 20 May 1696, GLL, MS 5301a.
[63] Letters, one undated and one dated 9 Oct. 1730, PRO, C 110/140.
[64] Letter dated 22 Aug. 1676, CUL, MS Add. 91.

left with a seven-year-old son: "A very fine child who often talks of his unckell but god knows when ever he will see you or noe and my daughter Ann which you knew when she was young, she is married and has two fine children a boy about 3 years old and a girl about 4. They live in Kent but are with me now at Greenwich and give their duty to you and my sister."[65]

William Atwood, Sr., received a sad letter from his father-in-law who had left his house and moved away:

I am sorry for my poor friends and kindred as I shall not be able to do for them as I . . . intended, but we have all a good god to rely upon, blessed be his name, we are all heer in health and I am as well accommodated (except a minister) as I can expect anywhere (out of a howse of my owne), but I am not pleased in my mind to live and die so far from you and my sonn Hampton and my other friends, but god[s] will bee done. If we meet in heaven (as we have good hopes through free grace in our dear redeemer) then it is no great matter where we die.[66]

Kin did not just correspond; they attended and participated in birth, marriage, and death ceremonies. The baptisms of Nicholas Wheeler's children were all witnessed by his kin.[67] Indeed weddings and wakes were often large gatherings at which the extended family was reunited; members ate and drank together and, at funerals, perpetuated the memory of the deceased by wearing mourning rings. Testators usually expected their kin to attend their funeral. Robert Clark, a dyer, willed no mourning but "all the kindred may have rings and ribbons" to follow his corpse.[68] Arthur Bickerstaff, a skinner, allowed mourning apparel only for his "own family," but he still expected his neighbors and friends to attend his burial.[69]

Contact of a more personal kind was also maintained. Nehemial Wallington noted the birthdays of his kin and when his cousin, Hester Holland, brought a parrot.[70] Parents often became closely attached to their sons-in-law and daughters-in-law; Richard Hoare was upset by the death of his son's wife.[71] Many businessmen had warm relations with both their mothers-in-law and their brothers-in-law; John Isham's constant companion was his brother-in-law.[72] Indeed kin often served as

[65] Letter dated 6 Jan. 1695/6, KAO, MS U 119/C2.
[66] Letter dated 16 Oct. 1666, PRO, C 109/23/1.
[67] M. Edmond, "Limners and Picture Makers," *Walpole Society* 47 (1978–80), 142.
[68] PCC, Aylett 295, 1655.   [69] PCC, Aylett 312, 1655.   [70] GLL, MS 204, fo. 88.
[71] H. P. R. Hoare, ed., *Hoares Bank: A Record* (1955), 27.
[72] *John Isham Mercer*, vol. 21, ed. G. D. Ramsay (Northamptonshire Record Society, 1962), xxxix.

companions, both within and outside the household. Abraham Nichols commiserated with Nathaniel Harley in Aleppo: "you are now tho (never so rich) distant from all your dear relations and friends the sole enjoyment of your life."[73]

The scattering of kin through mobility was offset by visiting relations on both sides of the family.[74] James Levett visited his relations in Lancashire, and when Marmaduke Rawdon returned from the Canaries, all his relatives came to visit.[75] Kin could appear without warning and overstay their welcome; some hosts were stingy (or practical) when entertaining kin and made them pay.[76] When George and Richard Oxenden left for India, Richard's brother came aboard their ship with his wife and cousin, Dalison, to wish them well.[77] When Thomas Papillon as a young apprentice went to France with his fellow apprentice and kinsman, Michael Godfrey, "we were called by my cozen Papillon with a coach ... there was in company my aunt, her son and daughter, her sister and her daughter and my cosen Gerbrandt."[78]

DISSENSION

Hostility could be generated by inequalities of wealth and power and undermine cooperation between different branches of the family. Kin came under pressure to place or advance relations with neither talent nor interest. Thomas Papillon wrote from experience that relatives could be unkind and envious. He was incensed when William Brodnax first asked him peremptorily for a £500 bond for his son, a factor in the East India Company, and then took umbrage when he demurred: "I must tell thee that it was a litle disobliging ... your uncharitable and unchristian letter dated the 16th instant is before me and although you insert that you expect no answer ... yet you must excuse me if I cannot with silence lye under such a severe censure." His wife, on the other hand, when visited by kin, sensibly took the view that "these are not times ... to have differences between such relations."[79]

[73] Letter dated 11 March 1702/3, BL, Add. MS 43,730.
[74] O. Harris, "Households and Their Boundaries," *History Workshop* 13 (1983): 146.
[75] Wallis, "Diary of a London Citizen," *The Reliquary* 4 (1890): 137; Rawdon, *Life*, 25.
[76] R. Spalding, *Contemporaries of Bulstrode Whitlock* (Oxford, 1990), 486.
[77] BL, Add. MS 54,332, fo. 30, 9 Apr. 1656.   [78] KAO, MS U 1015/F4, 12 Oct. 1647.
[79] Letter from Jane Papillon dated 2 Jan. 1691, KAO, MS U 1015/C18; draft of a letter from Thomas Papillon, KAO, MS U 1015/F/24; letter from William Brodnax dated 26 March 1691, KAO, MS U 1015/F15/5.

Businessmen lived in fear of being dragged down by their kin and were understandably reluctant to help the spendthrifts, misfits, and black sheep in their families. Kin did sometimes prove to be both financially and administratively burdensome: loans, handouts, and sureties had to be provided, and impecunious relations, who could not or would not repay their debts, could become an embarrassing and costly nuisance. Ambrose Barnes was hurt by the failure of a son-in-law for whom he stood surety.[80] Thomas Papillon's nephew, William Brudenell, fell into debt and Thomas had to help.[81] Sir George Sondes acted as executor for his father-in-law, alderman Freeman, and ran into trouble when the assets of the estate would not cover the legacies.[82]

Unscrupulous and greedy relatives sometimes abused their position as masters, arbitrators, feoffees, trustees, executors, administrators, and guardians. John Bland, a grocer, cut out a kinsman who "played the knave with me."[83] Sir Pelatia Barnardiston in his will of 1712 mentioned his suit against his "late barbarous and unjust" uncle, Sir Samuel Barnardison, who had cheated him out of his inheritance.[84] Thomas Tite, who died in 1692, claimed that his kinsman, Thomas Sheppard, had foisted a will on him when senile.[85] Richard Pargiter took a deceased relative's child as an apprentice and sent him abroad as a factor while milking his estate in England.[86] The kin of John Kendrick frustrated his charitable intentions.[87]

Business deals with in-laws, including marriage settlements, could create friction. Cranfield fought with his father-in-law, who ultimately failed in business.[88] When the father-in-law of his daughter tried to evade his financial commitments by casting blame, Thomas Boughey retorted: "Pray Sir, lay not your own mistakes on me, for I never advised you thereto but allways the contrary . . . who have never bin wanting to seek allways to promote friendship with you."[89] Sir Henry Johnson was sued by a kinsman who enclosed some edifying sermons for Johnson to read and complained that he did not pay his debts "whereas several instances

[80] A. Barnes, *Memoirs of the Life*, 29–30.   [81] KAO, MS U 1015/C17/3.
[82] G. Sondes, *His Plaine Narrative to the World* (1655) in *Harlean Miscellany* 10 (1813), 44.
[83] PCC, Audley 44, 1632.   [84] Anderson, *An English Consul in Turkey*, 88.
[85] PRO, C 8/352/248.   [86] Anderson, *An English Consul in Turkey*, 88.
[87] C. Jackson, "The Kendricke Bequests," *Southern History* 16 (1994), 58.
[88] *HMC*, Sackville, vol. 2, 89.
[89] Letters from Thomas Boughey to Anne Kempthorne dated 15 March 1675/6, and to Sir John Kempthorn dated 31 May 1677, GLL, MS 18760/1.

may be given ... of persons of honour and great estates do not treat their tradesmen ... at the rate you have."[90]

William Atwood received little sympathy in his financial predicament from his wife's family, as his wife admitted to him:

I am mighty sorry there cannot be a right understanding between my brother and you. ... [H]e pretends a great deal of kindness but I am sure it is no kindness to himself but a great unkindness to us to let our house run so out of repair that it is like to fall ... but pray lay aside passion and comply as far as you can and I hope so will he but you must give losers leave to talk.[91]

Marriage was another possible bone of contention. Thomas Povey lectured the woman whom his brother had married secretly and whom he probably fancied himself:

not that I think you unworthy to be my sister (whom I could most willingly have chosen to have been my Mistress had my Fortune rendered me capable of making my own election) but that I could noe way approve a marriage between you and my brother ... considering the narrowness and hardship of the condition you were then both in ... some other wife less beautiful and desirable might much better suit his state of affairs and, my sweet sister, prudent persons have many things to consider when they join themselves in marriage and must not, I am sure ought not, to forget that it is the most important act of their life, for which they are to be accountable to more then their own fancies, it being a matter wherein the family they relate to are concerned.[92]

Thomas Papillon, who ran the business of his late partner, Peter Fountain, for his widowed sister, ran into trouble when he opposed a proposed marriage by Mary Fountain.[93] Sir John Frederick broke with his niece when she married without his consent.[94] Sir Samuel Ongle, who died in 1726, worried that his nephew, when overseas, would marry a woman of inferior fortune.

When an estate had no direct heir, there were endless grounds for conflict, given the numbers of kin who would have some claim. Relatives frequently expressed disappointment over their legacies. Thomas Pitt execrated his cousin, John, whom he had set up in business but failed to show his gratitude in his will; Thomas in turn was blackmailed by his own son to increase his provision.[95] In a dispute between kin in the Brooke family over a will, Thomas Mompesson described one

---

[90] Letters dated 3 Oct. 1672 and 10 June 1709, BL, Add. MS 22,186.
[91] Letter to William Atwood, Jr., from his wife dated 30 Nov. 1685, PRO, C 109/23/1.
[92] Letter dated 31 May 1659, BL, Add. MS 11,411, fo. 80.
[93] KAO, MS U 1015/B/1/4.   [94] Fellowes, *The Family of Frederick*, 7.
[95] Lever, *The House of Pitt*, 59.

party as "minding nothing but his gutt."[96] When the son of John Ramsey died, his sister's husband claimed his orphanage share from the executor.[97]

Disputes led of course to litigation. The executors of John Scattergood were sued by the widow, uncle, aunt, and daughter of the deceased.[98] The childless John Whitson cut his nephew, Richard Partridge, out of his will because he considered him a coxcomb, and he reduced his bequest to Sarah Hynde because she had not taken his advice on marriage; his kin unsurprisingly contested his will.[99] Susan Cope sued the estate of her uncle, Sir Thomas Fowle, for a legacy, as did the son-in-law of Joseph Fern.[100] The estates of both Sir Richard Ford and Joseph Finch were much contested by their kin.[101]

Dissension in all these forms generated anger and resentment, such as that expressed by William Boulter who left 5 shillings for a halter to be delivered by the common hangman to his uncle.[102] All it took to create rancor was a conflict of personalities. Some kin just did not like each other or were paralyzed by the enmity of others. The brother of James Phipps wrote that "the unhappy disagreement between my wife's mother and my father makes me uncapable of serving anybody which adds much to my trouble."[103] Hannah Parsons told her brother: "my brother and sister Kiffen are pretty well but have their hearts full. The old gentleman's wife and her brother has bine at law with the suit they say has cost two hundred pound, but . . . he is as hearty as ever."[104]

MUTUAL AID

The conflicts that arose between kin only underline the essential and wide-ranging services they offered. Reciprocal obligations, even toward distant kin, were recognized and honored without any effective sanctions. Kin played an effective role in both major events, like birth and marriage, and in recurrent family crises—such as sickness and death. They provided support and advice during pregnancy, nursed and solaced

---

[96] Letter dated 12 Jan. 1696/7, Shropshire RO, Forester MS Acc 224.
[97] CLRO, Suits, box 4, no. 3, 1680.
[98] *The Scattergoods and the East India Company*, ed. L. M. Anstey, B. P. Scattergood, and R. C. Temple (Harpenden, 1935), 278.
[99] P. MacGrath, *John Whitson* (1970), 19–20.   [100] PRO, C 6/301/18.
[101] PRO, C 5/90/117, 1682; PRO, C 8/522/45, 1689; PRO, C 5/501/110.
[102] GLRO, MS E/TD/30, 1714.   [103] Letter dated 20 Feb. 1710, PRO, C 113/280.
[104] Letter dated 22 July 1694, PRO, C 110/158.

the sick, minded children, consoled the bereaved, assisted the widow and orphans, and supervised probate. Wherever parental mortality was high, networks of kin replaced the nuclear family.[105]

Kin were less likely to be appointed executor when a widow survived, though they were more prominent in brackets III and IV and represented 8 percent of all primary executors in all cohorts (see table 3.4). When there was no surviving widow, kin numbered 22 percent of executors in period I and 18 percent in period II; the proportion increased with successive financial brackets, though it fluctuated between successive cohorts (see table 3.4). Bachelors appointed kinsmen as their executor in 23 to 28 percent of wills, the percentage rising with wealth and fluctuating around 25 percent between cohorts. The same pattern held true for childless testators, whose percentage of kin as executors rose from 11 percent in period I to 29 percent in period II and increased with each financial bracket, while fluctuating between cohorts.

A few examples will suffice. John Lead's brother-in-law collected his debts after his death.[106] Charles Peers administered the estate of his mother-in-law.[107] In 1689 Charles Blunt acted as executor for his cousin, John Blunt, inventorying and selling his effects and taking 12 shillings "for my self, 2 dayes travel and 3 days work hanging the room, covering the table and desk."[108] Richard Farrington was executor for his cousin, mother-in-law, and grandmother.[109] Thomas Bright of Ipswich, a widower with no surviving children, named kinsmen as both his executor and overseers; Richard Lewis made his son-in-law executor.[110] Tristram Clark, a clothworker, made his aunt executrix, and Richard Astell, a merchant tailor, made his mother-in-law executrix, until their children came of age.[111] Benjamin Baron, a grocer, asked his widow to bring up his niece and made his mother-in-law overseer.[112] Philip Papillon was executor for his cousin, Samuel, and his brother-in-law, Charles Henshawe.[113]

Less wealthy testators sometimes chose notable dignitaries as their

[105] R. W. Beales, "The Child in Seventeenth-Century America" in *American Childhood*, ed. J. M. Hawes and N. R. Hines (Westport, Conn., 1985), 41.
[106] Metters, "Rulers King's Lynn," 360.   [107] GLL, MS 10,188/1.
[108] Account for cousin Blunt dated 16 Jan. 1689, PRO, C 114/164.
[109] GLL, MS 2708.
[110] *Fiske Family Papers*, ed. H. Fiske (Norwich, 1902), 102; *Suffolk Archdeaconry Wills, 1625–26*, ed. M. Allen (Woodbridge, 1992), 121–2.
[111] PCC, Ruthen 159, 1657; PCC, Pell 8, 1659.   [112] PCC, Hele 84, 1626.
[113] KAO, MS U 1015 T/45/1.

overseers, to elevate their families.[114] Kin were, however, appointed overseers by 30 percent of testators in period I and 43 percent in period II; the proportion increased with each bracket and ranged from 43 to 51 percent in successive cohorts. Titus Talbot made his son executor, but he was to account to his mother-in-law and a friend.[115] Richard Baynam, a goldsmith, asked his overseers (three kinsman and a friend) to help his son (who was appointed executor when of age) recover property abroad and purchase land.[116] Charles Manwaring, a grocer, made his uncle overseer and asked him to help his widow rear the children.[117] James Kent, a barber surgeon, asked his uncle and godfather to help his eldest son.[118]

Few kin, except for uncles, seem to have been appointed guardians in the diocese of York.[119] But John Ellison, widowed draper of Doncaster, made his father, uncle, and brothers-in-law guardians of individual daughters.[120] Francis Liddell of Newcastle had custody of two infant sons of kinsmen.[121] In London wills kin were frequently appointed guardians. Robert Kent, a haberdasher, made his mother-in-law, not his widow, guardian of his child.[122] John Hall, a goldsmith, named a cousin and friend guardian of his only daughter.[123] Thomas Proctor appointed his "loving uncle and friend" guardian of his orphan son.[124] Sons-in-law were sometimes appointed guardians if the widow was young. Thomas Pitt removed his younger children from his son's care and transferred them to a kinsman.

Children frequently spent much time in the homes of their relations. Some kinsfolk became foster parents and in effect (though there was no legal procedure) adopted children. Samuel Jeake helped his mother-in-law with her difficult son.[125] John Staverd, a haberdasher, hoped that his aunt "nay rather a mother" would be grandmother to his children.[126] Thomas Beazley, a haberdasher, left everything to his brother's widow to bring up his only daughter.[127] Child rearing was often left to kin in the

[114] M. Zell, *Industry in the Countryside* (Cambridge, 1994), 198.
[115] PCC, Bowyer 28, 1652.   [116] PCC, Hele 101, 1626.
[117] PCC, Russell 106, 1633.   [118] PCC, Hele 85, 1626.
[119] W. Coster, "Guardianship in York, 1500–1668," *Continuity and Change* 10 (1995): 28.
[120] PCC, Hart 22, 1603.
[121] *Durham Wills and Inventories, 1604–49*, vol. 142 (Surtees Society, 1929), 123 (1617).
[122] PCC, Goare 97, 1637.   [123] PCC, Vere 81.   [124] PCC, Byrde 117, 1624.
[125] Jeake, *An Astrological Diary*, 38.   [126] PCC, Tirwhite 31, 1582.
[127] PCC, Hyde 110, 1665.

Chesapeake, because of high mortality, in contrast to New England where parents survived long enough to accomplish this task.[128]

The unmarried and the childless found substitute children among their nephews and nieces, acting as godfathers, attending christenings, and bestowing presents.[129] Sir William Turner noted the ages of all the children of his brother, Richard, and helped his nephews; he brought Charles Turner to London, provided him with a writing master, paid for four months' tuition, and supplied him with writing books and clothes.[130]

Kin also advised on careers and acted as patrons. Joseph Collett had to explain that he had not preferred a kinsman for one post because it paid so poorly.[131] Some supplicants pulled out all the stops: Sir George Oxenden received a letter in India from a cousin who wanted him to find a place for her son; it was addressed to "Noble Sir George" from "your affectionate, loving and obliged kinswoman and servant Susan Mercer . . . with my most endeared love and respects."[132] Sir Stephen Fox found offices, spouses, benefices, and tutors for his kin. The entire extended family decided jointly whether Nicholas Collett should be apprenticed.[133] In Belfast kinsmen advised on apprenticeship, marriage, and all major decisions.[134] When Grace Kendall wanted advice about whether to let James Kendall travel to Jamaica, she wrote to Jack Kendall asking him to forward her letter to Thomas Papillon: "He spends a way his time and his money vainly here and if he go it may prove dangerous. I beseech god to direct me for the best."[135]

As well as acting as witnesses and sureties, kinsmen also provided direct financial assistance, as in the Isham family (see also chapter 7). Loans to relations, like those provided by John Walbank, were almost universal.[136] Sometimes debts of this kind were subsequently forgiven, as when Michael Mitford cancelled a debt of £100 owed by Sir John Delaval.[137] Robert Keayne, a Boston merchant, paid the debts and the cost of passage to New England for his English brother-in-law.[138]

---

[128] D. B. and A. H Rutman, *Small Worlds, Large Questions*, 207.
[129] WAM, MS 10,367.   [130] GLL, MS 5105.
[131] Letter to his sister dated 24 Sept. 1712. in Collett, *Private Letter Book.*
[132] BL, Add. MS 40,708, fo. 28.   [133] R. O'Day, *The Family* (New York, 1994), 271.
[134] Agnew, *Belfast Merchant Families*, 27–32.
[135] Letter dated 15 Nov. 1667, KAO, MS U 1015/F32.
[136] Account book, BL, Egerton MS 2224, 1674–86.
[137] GLL, MS 11,892, fo. 49.   [138] Cressy, *Coming Over*, 104, 204, 277, figure 13.

Sir William Turner paid his brother's bills in London, and his brother reciprocated in Yorkshire; he also bought Africa Company stock for his niece and gave her silk for a petticoat.[139] Thomas Papillon mortgaged his estate to his son-in-law, Samuel Rawston, when he fled to Holland. Michael Mitford prepared his niece for balancing her books:

> your daughter Mary has removed to school at Stepney for some reason that my wife had that she should not be continued at Kensington. I now pay 20 li a year for her diet besides all other extraordinaries. She is well and keeps her correspondency with her aunt. I have nothing to do but to pay money when desired. ... [She has to] keep an account of every particular thing thats laid out for her, for if that were not done she might forget hereafter ... if she did not keep an account herself of every penny. But she is a very good girl and I hope will answer expectation.[140]

BEQUESTS

Businessmen regularly exchanged gifts with their kin. George Warner provided all his relatives with cloth.[141] Charles Blunt thanked his cousin "for the nightcoat and apron which came very safe. ... All persons that have seen it like your fancy."[142] John Cogge was given money, while an apprentice, by his uncle and aunt and noted when his uncle had his sixty-third birthday.[143] George Boddington gave his niece £100 on her marriage.[144] Sir William Turner gave New Year's gifts to his relatives and housekeeper.[145] George Warner paid 14 shillings toward the funeral of his uncle, Walton.[146]

The bulk of any estate was always left to the immediate family. Sir Stephen Fox, after having children late in life, scaled down his bequests to his nephew (who would have continued his name) and his sons-in-law.[147] Some testators simply ignored their relations. William Caswell, a clothworker, left everything to his widow, "having no kindred that I am bound either in duty or in conscience to bequeath or give any legacy unto."[148] Some kin were overlooked, particularly if they were poor and on the fringe.

But kin usually received at least token legacies or they were forgiven their debts; if there were no surviving children or grandchildren, they

[139] GLL, MS 5107/2.   [140] Letters to sister Webster, 1 Aug. 1704, GLL, MS 11,892A.
[141] Letter dated 9 May 1642, PRO, SP 46/83.
[142] Letter dated 2 Jan. 1705, PRO, C 114/164.   [143] Bod, MS Eng misc. F 78.
[144] GLL, MS 10,823.   [145] GLL, MS 5100.   [146] PRO, SP 46/85.
[147] Clay, *Public Finances and Private Wealth*, 306, 338.   [148] PCC, Pell 205, 1659.

could be made the principal beneficiaries. Robert Sowers, a grocer, provided that, if his only daughter should die, his estate would be distributed among the children of his kin.[149] John Williams, a haberdasher, insisted that "my cozens and kindred to be first paid."[150]

When a widow survived, bequests to kin were negligible. But 37 percent of bachelors made kin their primary beneficiaries in period I and 52 percent in period II; the proportion rose from 30 percent in bracket I to 60 and 61 percent in brackets II and III to 100 percent in bracket IV. Over time an increase is also visible between cohorts, though the number of cases is too few for comfort. In both periods I and II kin represented 9 to 10 percent of primary beneficiaries of widowers; the proportion increased with wealth and reached 12 to 13 percent in cohorts II, III, and IV. When no children survived the percentage was even higher: 11 percent in period I, 34 percent in period II, 10 percent in bracket II, 39 percent in bracket III, and 42 to 47 percent in all cohorts. A similar pattern is visible in provincial towns, like Bristol.[151]

Some bequests had conditions attached. Philip Culmer composed a long, complex will with moral and spiritual injunctions both at the beginning and the end.[152] Robert Mann, a haberdasher, made his legacies contingent on his kin eschewing "a wicked and disorderly life."[153] Joas Denew left money to a kinsman's son only if he reformed his stubbornness and disobedience to his mother.[154] Arthur Robsart left bequests to kinswomen on marriage provided that they married with the consent of his executors.[155]

Testators with married daughters, like John Carpenter, a clothworker and merchant adventurer, might favor their sons-in-law.[156] But the most frequent beneficiaries were nephews and nieces, usually named as residual legatees in case no children of the testator survived; a typical example is Robert Walker, an apothecary.[157] George Janus, a vintner, willed that, should he die without children, his land would pass to his kin.[158] Robert Hayward made the youngest sons of his brother his heir and apprenticed them.[159] Kin who were distant both geographically and genealogically, were not, however, excluded. Henry Higginbottom left

---

[149] PCC, Lee 21, 1638.   [150] PCC, Essex 91, 1648.
[151] MacGrath, *Merchants and Merchandize*, passim.   [152] PCC, Lee 29, 1638.
[153] PCC, Berkeley 211, 1656.   [154] PCC, Barrington 81, 1628.
[155] PCC, Fairfax 175, 1649.   [156] PCC, Pile 25, 1636.
[157] PCC, Sadler 78, 1635.   [158] PCC, Nabbs 187, 1660.
[159] R. Gough, *History of Myddle* (1723; reprint 1979), 118–19.

Table 6.3. *Primary Beneficiaries (Percentage of Known Cases)*

	Period I	Period II	Bracket I	Bracket II	Bracket III	Bracket IV	Cohort I	Cohort II	Cohort III	Cohort IV
Unmarried Testators										
Siblings	38.76	27.21	10.00	16.98	10.20	–	–	16.67	9.38	9.09
Siblings/Other	9.69	6.12	30.00	7.55	8.16	–	16.67	8.33	6.25	–
Father/Mother	4.65	4.08	10.00	3.77	2.04	–	–	–	3.13	–
Kin	36.82	52.38	30.00	60.38	61.25	100.0	66.67	50.00	75.00	72.73
Other	10.08	10.20	20.00	11.32	18.31	–	16.67	25.00	6.25	18.18
Total	258	147	10	53	49	12	6	12	32	11
When No Children Survive										
Parents/Siblings	1.26	3.19	–	–	–	11.11	–	–	–	–
Widow	47.06	24.47	40.00	42.86	17.31	11.11	27.27	17.65	12.90	11.11
Widow/Kin	19.33	28.72	40.00	36.73	36.54	–	18.18	29.41	41.94	33.33
Widow/Other	20.17	5.32	–	10.20	1.92	–	–	–	–	–
Kin	10.92	34.04	20.00	10.20	38.46	66.62	45.46	47.06	41.94	44.44
Other	1.26	4.26	–	–	5.77	11.11	9.09	5.88	3.23	11.11
Total	238	94	5	49	52	9	11	17	31	9

When Wife Predeceases

Eldest/Son	8.09	17.19	6.25	6.98	14.40	45.00	6.67	12.20	20.59	50.00
Sons	3.40	0.78	–	0.58	0.80	–	–	–	4.41	–
Daughters	6.38	6.25	–	4.07	5.60	5.00	–	9.76	4.41	3.33
Children	62.98	59.38	81.25	79.07	60.00	15.00	60.00	48.78	54.41	30.00
Grandchildren	2.98	3.13	–	1.74	6.40	–	6.67	9.76	4.41	–
Children/Grandchildren	5.11	0.78	–	2.33	0.80	–	–	2.44	–	–
Kin	9.79	8.59	12.50	4.07	8.80	25.00	20.00	12.20	13.24	13.33
Other	1.28	3.91	–	1.16	3.20	10.00	6.67	4.88	2.94	3.33
Total	235	256	16	172	125	20	15	41	68	30

When Widow Survives

Widow	10.19	4.05	–	1.59	3.24	–	4.41	4.07	5.02	2.78
Widow/Children	11.46	6.60	2.90	4.98	7.34	8.82	1.47	10.57	8.22	8.33
Widow/Kin	3.65	3.51	2.90	2.29	4.97	2.94	2.94	4.88	5.48	11.11
Widow/Other	1.79	0.32	–	0.20	0.43	–	–	–	0.46	2.78
Eldest/Son	0.97	4.58	4.35	0.90	5.83	32.35	4.41	8.94	10.05	13.89
Children/Grandchildren	1.04	2.02	–	1.00	2.59	8.82	–	3.25	4.57	–
Equal	69.57	76.68	89.85	88.76	72.35	44.12	80.88	65.85	61.64	61.11
Kin	0.97	2.02	–	0.30	3.02	2.94	5.88	2.44	4.11	–
Other	0.37	0.21	–	–	0.22	–	–	–	0.46	–
Total	1,344	939	69	1,005	463	34	68	123	219	36

money to his cousins in Cheshire.[160] Edward Colston left land in trust for his grandniece.[161]

Many bequests had a specific reason and purpose. Innocentius Harris, a woodmonger, left his niece his household effects because she had taken "care of me and my domestic affairs in the time of my sickness."[162] Samuel Towlin left £100 to redeem his brother-in-law from corsairs.[163] Sir James Campbell who named two cousins coexecutor with his widow, was quite generous to his kin, bestowing dowries and leaving £100 to a nephew toward his costs at Cambridge University.[164] John Harvey, a grocer, provided for the education of his nephew at the university.[165]

Bachelors unsurprisingly made kinsmen their legatees. John Billings, a mercer, left money to his fellow apprentice, siblings, friends, master, and also to his "poor kindred."[166] Henry Currer, a grocer, left £1,000 to his nephew, and John De Deuxville left his entire estate to his sister and her children.[167] Thomas Wriothesley, a haberdasher, John Sanderson, a clothworker, and William Browley, a leatherseller, bequeathed everything to the children of their siblings.[168] Neville Tennant, a merchant, left £300 for distribution among his poor kindred.[169]

Some testators privileged their kin in their charitable bequests. Robert Tichborn, a skinner, and Edward Mallory, a vintner, left loan funds to their respective companies with preference for their kin.[170] Henry Hebblethwaite, a draper, Thomas Hallwood, an ironmonger, and Richard Platt, a brewer, gave their kin priority in their charities.[171] Charity was usually more direct. John Gatley, a haberdasher, left "to every of my kindred something as I conceived where was most necessary" and sought "peace love and amity" among his kindred and friends.[172] Thomas Pitt told his son, Robert, that he wanted him to help his uncle and aunt, that his fortune was not just for his children but for "necessitous relations and friends."[173]

[160] PCC, Pile 102, 1636.
[161] H. J. Wilkins, *Edward Colston, 1636–1721* (Bristol, 1920), 128.
[162] PCC, Nabbs 85, 1660.   [163] PCC, Bath 100.   [164] PCC, Campbell 1, 1642.
[165] PCC, Swann 58, 1623.   [166] PCC, St. John 85, 1631.
[167] PCC, Aylett 378, 1655; PCC, Alchin 42. Another example is the will of John Thompson, PCC, Hele 95, 1626.
[168] PCC, Barrington 68, 1628; PCC, Ridley 65, 1629; PCC, Alchin 362, 1654.
[169] PCC, Ruthen 373, 1657.   [170] PCC, Rivers 24, 1645; PCC, Rudd 8.
[171] G. D. Squibb, *Founders Kin* (Oxford, 1972), 30; PCC, Clarke 40.
[172] PCC, Bowyer 133, 1652.
[173] Letter dated 21 Jan. 1707/8 in *H. M. C. Fortescue I*, 35.

In 1715 John Jefferyes left £2,000 for his brother to distribute among his poor relations; aldermen Henry Smith left £1,000 as well as a fellowship at Cambridge.[174] Edward Bowater, a Hamburg merchant, left the residue of his estate to his brother to distribute among "the poorest and neediest of my kindred."[175] Philip Rogers, a grocer, left money to be distributed equally among "the poorest of my kindred."[176] Robert Bowyer, a grocer, left an annuity of 20 shillings to a poor cousin, and Wolfran Smith, a grocer, £50 "for poor kindred."[177] Richard Coish, a skinner, who wanted to convert all bishops' lands "unto the uses of religion and learning," left his third part to poor kindred and the poor in general.[178] Caleb Cockcroft, a skinner, left money to the "poorest of my mother's kindred in Lancashire."[179] In 1719 Samuel Levy of New York gave his brother and son in London £200 to be distributed to poor relations in Germany.[180]

FRIENDS

Some merchants developed their own friendships and "affinity" outside the family; in some respects friends can be regarded as "fictive kin."[181] The basic difference was that friends were voluntarily and spontaneously chosen, whereas kin just accumulated. Friends often played a larger role than distant kin and became a surrogate family to single and widowed businessmen.

Unfortunately, if the term "kin" is opaque, the term "friend" is transparent. It was used to describe practically every kind of relationship from mere acquaintances to colleagues, business associates, ministers, and influential patrons; to compound the problem, it was also a synonym for both kinsman and neighbor. William Lawrence wrote "it makes me almost think there is no society in nature beyond that of acquaintance and that the appellation of friend is but an idle title that hath a name but no being."[182] It is hard to judge when a customer became a friend. One broker who specialized in collecting rents spent much of his time drinking with customers.[183] The term has meaning only in relation to its

---

[174] D. Lysons, *Environs of London*, vol. I (1792–6), 512.   [175] PCC, Skynner 83, 1627.
[176] PCC, Capell 89, 1613.   [177] PCC, Ridley 17, 1629; PCC, Hele 53, 1626.
[178] PCC, Bowyer 3, 1652.   [179] PCC, Rivers 55, 1645.
[180] *New York Abstracts of Wills, 1708–28*, vol. 26 (New York Historical Society, 1893), 189.
[181] D. O'Hara, "Ruled by My Friends," *Continuity and Change* 6 (1991): 40.
[182] Letter dated 27 June 1659, BL, India Office, Eur MS 387/C.
[183] Bod, Rawlinson MS D 1114.

opposite, that is enemies or complete strangers. Here it has been employed to describe all those, including godchildren, who were not clearly designated as blood or affinal kin.

Some businessmen may have had no friends, and certainly some testators and correspondents never mention them. William Millward, a stationer, when making a nuncupative will, was asked about his bequests to friends and declined to name any.[184] Between periods I and II the median number of friends mentioned in wills declined slightly from 2 to 1.9, but the proportion of testators who did not mention friends also declined from 27 percent to 24 percent; wills that listed 5 to 10 friends fell from 18 percent to 17 percent and those listing 11 to 20 friends from 6 percent to 4 percent (see table 6.1). The median number mentioned increased steadily with wealth from 1.6 in bracket I to 2.7 in bracket IV; it declined however in successive cohorts to 1.7 in cohort IV (see table 6.1).

The median number of friends corresponds closely with the number of overseers, a function they frequently performed. Neither marriage, surviving children, widowhood, age, foreign residence, or place of origin had any significant impact on the number of friends, though they were most numerous in the wills of public officials. One slight statistical correlation suggests an inverse relationship between the number of children who survived and the number of friends mentioned; another correlation suggests that those who remembered many kin, also remembered many friends.[185] In comparison, in Shrewsbury 22.6 percent of wills mention friends, usually in the same wealth bracket.[186] In a sample of wills of London citizens 26.5 percent mentioned friends, and the mean number listed was 2.5.[187]

Who did businessmen select as their friends? Some were acquired in boyhood. Several of Marmaduke Rawdon's friends had been his schoolmates.[188] Apprentices visited their former masters and named their children after them.[189] Robert Knight mentioned his master, mistress, and three other servants in his will.[190] Most were citizens and often members of the same livery company; many of Sir Thomas Ramsey's twenty-seven

---

[184] PCC, Ruthen 374, 1657.
[185] The Pearson R correlation of kin mentioned with total number of surviving children = −0.115 and the correlation between kin and friends = +0.420.
[186] Hindson, "Family Structure," tables 5.1 and 5.12.
[187] Earle, *Making of the English Middle Class*, table 11.3.   [188] Rawdon, *Life*, 3.
[189] P. Griffiths, "Some Aspects of Youth" (Ph.D. diss., Cambridge University, 1992), 410.
[190] *Prerogative Court Canterbury, Register Scroope*, ed. J. A. Morrison (1934), 13.

friends in his will were grocers.[191] London citizens, according to John Earle, had "a kind of gossiping friendships and those commoner within the circle of his trade."[192] Other friends were acquired in the normal course of business; often they were partners, but several factors in Smirna were close even when they did not transact business together.[193] Michael Mitford, writing to a business correspondent, signed "I am with all kind love your real friend."[194] James Claypoole insisted that a dispute be arbitrated in England, not Hamburg, because "they are friends and intimates and I know no man there."[195] On occasion, the lists in wills, like that of John Banks in 1630, read like a biographical dictionary of the London elite.[196] Lewis Roberts dedicated his *Merchants Map of Commerce* to the seven Harvey brothers and was honored in a prefatory poem by several of his kinsmen and friends.[197] Christopher Langley of Colchester had several London merchants as friends.[198]

Some beneficiaries were lifetime friends. Robert Bell, a skinner, remembered thirty-six friends, including "my old acquaintance and very good friend Mr Edward Gregory scrivener and his wife" and "antient friend Edward Higgens of Deptford."[199] Frequently friendship was gendered—males bonding with males and females with females. Some friends were probably resident in the household; the names of lodgers in Walbrook ward in 1684 and the immigration returns of 1653 reveal many merchants lodging together.[200] Friends were not confined to the business world. The merchant William Langhorn dined regularly with the country gentleman Sir Humphrey Mildmay.[201]

Godchildren were usually children of siblings, but some were unrelated. Businessmen, especially bachelors, often served as godfathers; parents would choose a wealthy or well-connected businessman and even name a child after him to secure future bequests and patronage.[202] The number of godchildren mentioned in wills was usually one to two, though as many as four are recorded for individuals, such as Richard

---

[191] F. W. Fairholt, "Inventory of Sir Thomas Ramsey," *Archaeologia* 40 (1866): 316.
[192] Earle, *Microcosmographie*, 93.
[193] Anderson, *An English Consul in Turkey*, 76.
[194] Letter to Mallaber and Lowther dated 13 April 1705, GLL, MS 11,892A.
[195] J. Claypoole, *Letter Book, 1681–1684*, ed. M. Balderston (San Marino, 1967), 98.
[196] *Register of Scroope, 1630*, 121–2.
[197] L. Roberts, *Merchants Map of Commerce* (1638), preface.
[198] F. G. Emmison, ed., *Elizabethan Life* (Chelmsford, 1978), 294.
[199] PCC, Ruthen 72, 1657.   [200] GLL, MS 507; BL, Add. MS 34,015.
[201] R. P. Lee, *Sir Humphrey Mildmay, 1633–52* (New Brunswick, 1947), 17–18.
[202] Smith-Bannister, *Names and Naming Patterns*, 184–5.

Bowmer.[203] Bachelor Anthony Baron had several godsons, and John Whitson's godson, John Aubrey, stayed with him during the holidays.[204] John Egerton, a bachelor and a merchant tailor, left "my little girl Anne Lyle whom sometime I have kept upon charity" an annuity of £12 plus his furniture.[205] A godfather could intervene to protect his godsons:

I found two of them . . . in such a deplorable condition, that they had not six-pence to buy them a dinner and I may be bold to say if I had not taken care of them they must of necessity have taken ill courses. . . . I shall desire that hee in a speciall manner take care of the education of his grandchild and my godson Michael Mitford. Pray press him to promise it to you for altho the father might have offended him yet the innocent child is noe wayes to blame.[206]

The social life of businessmen often revolved around their friends. Apprentices shared the male camaraderie of unmarried youth and spent their leisure hours in the company of their peers. Thomas Papillon con-fessed his folly as a young man in encouraging his friends to drink.[207] Older, married businessmen had a regular circle of friends with whom they socialized. Dining lists, like those of an alderman's wife, reveal a core of four to five friends as well as guests invited for social or political reasons.[208] Aldermen Newton of Cambridge had his cronies to his home for dinner. Thomas Bowrey told his wife: "We are all going this evening with Mr Gray and wife and Miss Boucher to the Cherry Garden. I wish you with us. I yesterday met father Halfpenny of whom I have some very fat stories to tell you when we meet."[209] Merchants corresponded and exchanged gifts with their friends as well as with their relatives. Leonard Rich sent Thomas Palmer some lampreys for helping his daughter.[210] William Phillipps wrote to his old friends in Constantinople: "Dear rogues, I am no sooner out of your sight but I am forgot by both which verifies the old proverb out of sight out of mind."[211]

William Alchorn sent his reflections on the impending demise of a

---

[203] In the database godchildren not identified as kin have been classified as friends. Although they have not been systematically counted, the practice of naming godpar-ents does not seem to have declined at least until the end of the seventeenth century.
[204] J. Aubrey, *Brief Lives*, ed. A. Clark (Oxford, 1898), xxiii.
[205] PCC, Ruthen 369, 1657.
[206] Letter to Sir John Delaval dated 1 Aug. 1704, GLL, MS 11,892A, fo. 49.
[207] KAO, MS U 1015/F15/5.   [208] BL, Cotton MS Vespasian F xvi.
[209] Letter dated 8 June 1704, GLL, MS 3041/1.
[210] Letter dated 13 Apr. 1712, GLL, MS 3723.
[211] Letter to Goodfellow and Clutterbuck dated 25 Oct. 1699, Folger Library, MS U B 18, fo. 174.

relation together with a couple of capons to his "honoured friend" William Atwood:

We entreat your acceptance of this little taste of my wife's housewifery. . . . I am apt to fear him in danger however God is very gracious to him in giving him so leisurely a warning for another world, though I have good hopes that he was not a stranger to such thoughts in his health. To be sure that is the safest course and god grant we may make this good use of all the providences of God . . . so as seriously and timely to provide for our own eternal condition. My wife hath not yet outgrown her sadness at Mrs Atwood's death. Such impressions are apt to dwell long upon those who are under the bondage of a melancholy temper. Her bodily health is somewhat impaired by it, but I am assured she's otherwise a gainer by it.[212]

The loyalty of friends was expected, but sometimes faltered. Daniel Cooper implored Lionel Cranfield "to stand my friend so much as now in my adversity not to forget me."[213] John Parsons, when he advised Madam Dashwood on business matters, warned her that "you must not expect but that those friends who seem so warm for you now, when they come to be frustrated of their expectations . . . they will then grow cold enough."[214] Jeremiah Elwes was angry that Thomas Antrobus had not paid his bills for him during his sickness.[215] Isaac Lawrence had to apologize for causing offense: "Friend . . . misfortunes have been heapt upon me, otherwise my correspondence with you would have been of another nature then hitherto hath been. I expect not always a clowded fortune but that one day a bright sunshine of this worlds favour may make me acceptable to my friends, however now despised and forgotten."[216] Friends, like kin, served as intermediaries in a wide range of transactions. They advocated, arranged, and sanctioned marriages and acted as sponsors for baptisms.[217] Maurice Wynn asked his father to provide £50 for his friend, Thomas Owen, who was visiting Wales from Germany.[218] Heigham Bright asked his elder brother to find out which of his friends had recommended him.[219] George Warner addressed Bryan Ball, who had sent him two hats and a band, as "loving friend," though

[212] Letter dated 4 Jan. 1673, PRO, C 109/23/1.
[213] Letter dated 19 July 1597, in *H. M. C. Sackville*, vol. 2, 2.
[214] Letter dated 5 July 1711, PRO, C 110/158.
[215] Note dated 17 June 1710, PRO, C 107/161.
[216] Letter to William Bowtell in London from Surat dated 18 Jan. 1670, BL, India Office, European, MS 387/A.
[217] D. S. Boutflower, *The Boutflower Book* (Newcastle, 1930), 67.
[218] National Library, Wales, Wynn MSS F 111.18.
[219] Bright, *The Brights of Suffolk*, 175.

he added that the hats were too small.[220] Michael Mitford provided money and clothes for visiting friends.[221]

Friends were particularly important in probate administration. They acted as witnesses and appraisers and were frequently appointed as trustees.[222] The proportion of wills that named nonkin as executor when a widow survived rose from 0.4 percent in period I to 7.8 percent in period II, with a range of 6 to 8 percent in all brackets and cohorts. When no widow survived, the proportion rose from 24.5 percent in period I to 32 percent in period II with the highest percentage in brackets I and II and a range of 11 to 20 percent in all cohorts. Between one-fourth and one-third of unmarried testators chose nonkinsmen as their executors (see table 3.4).

Here is one example of the pains that friends would take to settle an estate. When Edward Peak died in Oporto, a will was found in a drawer of his secretaire, but it was not signed or witnessed, because he had wanted to keep the contents private. Two of his friends explained to his uncle how hard they had worked, despite suffering from gout, to collect Peak's debts, inventory his estate, and verify what was still owed to others:

You may be assured that we have on our part assisted and with all affection attended him as if he was a near and dear Relation having both on your account and for his own sake ever had a very particular esteem for him, his modest and mild temper and curt behaviour obliging us and every one. . . . I am now picking out the payments made him out of loose papers for he kept no book of recovery and as soon as it is done I shall call at every shopkeeper he had accounts with and examine their books.[223]

Friends, usually business associates rather than neighbors, also served as overseers. Nonkin constituted 55 percent of the overseers in period I and 48 percent in period II; the proportion never dropped below 43 percent in any bracket or below 33 percent in any cohort (see table 3.4). Sometimes the overseer acted as investment manager. Sarah, widow of John Pitt, made her "good friend" Gulston Addison overseer and trustee and gave him discretion to invest her assets in either trade or usury.[224]

[220] Letter dated 20 Sept. 1639, PRO, SP 46/85.
[221] Letter dated 6 March 1707, GLL, MS 11,892A.
[222] M. Pelling, "Apprentices Health and Social Cohesion," *History Workshop Journal* 37 (1994): 46.
[223] Letters to Matthew Kenrick dated 16 March 1709/10 and 12 July 1711, PRO, C 108/44.
[224] BL, Egerton MS 1971, 1706.

Businessmen frequently appointed friends, often their partners and associates, as guardians for their children. Alderman Richard Chamberlain entrusted two sons to Thomas Gore and another to alderman James Harvey. Thomas Coke, a resident of Constantinople, put his children in the hands of the Levant merchant Thomas Palmer. Arthur Calcott instructed his only son to be obedient to his friend, William Nicholls.[225] Richard Richards, a clothworker, asked his cousin to inter him "in some convenient dry place within the cathedral church of St Paul . . . with [after one year] a stone of the most durable and best sort over him" and appointed three friends as guardians of his infant son.[226] William Green, a cooper, asked two of his friends to be guardians of his grandchildren, should his wife die.[227] George Anglesey, a grocer, put out his daughters' portion to a friend, Francis Needham, at 6 percent and made him responsible (with his widow) for his daughters.[228]

Married testators with children rarely named their friends as primary beneficiaries, though there were exceptions. Abraham Orton, a merchant tailor, gave his wife 12 pence and the rest of his estate to his friend, William Coleman, and his wife, in return for their kindness.[229] Those with heirs usually left token legacies—gowns, rings, and cups.[230] Thomas Gilborn, a clothworker, left rings for his friends "with the poesie aske not what my ring did cost, I had it by a friend I lost."[231] On the other hand, testators without children could be generous. Francis Solomon, an apothecary, left his whole estate to a friend; William Steeg, a merchant tailor, gave extensively to the children of friends as well as to his kin.[232]

In periods I and II 10 percent of all unmarried testators (and an even higher percentage in brackets III and IV) left the bulk of their estate to nonkin, most of whom can be presumed to have been friends; married testators without surviving children made a similar disposition in 1.3 percent of cases in period I and 4.3 percent in period II (see table 6.3).

Some bequests were broad in scope. Bachelor John Clurgeon just listed "friends and acquaintances."[233] John Gravener, a merchant tailor, asked his partner and executor, George Warren, to distribute his goods "among my kinsfolke and friends."[234] Luke Cropland, a mercer, empowered his

---

[225] PCC, Clarke 139, 1625.   [226] PCC, Lee 121, 1648.
[227] PCC, Alchin 173, 1654.   [228] PCC, Parker 99, 1619.
[229] PCC, Evelyn 53, 1641.   [230] Willan, *Muscovy Merchants of 1555*, 19.
[231] PCC, Cambell 102, 1642.   [232] PCC, Savill 33, 1622.
[233] PCC, Twisse 172, 1646.   [234] PCC, Byrde 112, 1626.

executor to distribute "amongst such of my kindred and friends as he in his discretion shall see fit."[235] Robert Labon, a saddler, compiled a long list of "loving friends."[236]

Other wills were specific and suggested personal attention. Malachy Marten, a merchant in Bantam, distributed his jewels and all his lavish clothing among his friends.[237] Abraham Mancio, a brewer, left 30 shillings apiece to "my adopted father Mr William Bowyer merchant and to his twelve sons of our ancient society."[238] Thomas Thynn left equal amounts to his partners and friends.[239] Samuel Moyer remembered his fellow prisoners in the Tower of London.[240] Thomas Parker, a skinner, ignored his kin but made many bequests to the poor "and some other special friends."[241] Simon Wood, a merchant tailor, left a diamond ring to a friend.[242] Richard Knipe, a merchant who died at sea, left his goods, which included his share "of sow and pigs," to his servant and the ship's company.[243] John Moore, a mercer, left his friend, Richard Franklin, his "hardwood desk whereon I usually write."[244]

Servants often outnumbered children and kin in the household. Richard Farrington had twenty-three male and thirty-four female servants in his lifetime, plus several nurses.[245] In London 80 percent of households in 1694 had one to two servants.[246] In Boroughside 31 percent of households had adult servants, compared with 58 percent in London.[247] Domestic servants were not always distinguished from business employees or apprentices. Humphrey Brown, a girdler, refers to "menservants which shalbe my apprentices."[248] Servants were sometimes treated as members of the family (or like children); many were in fact poor relations. Michael Steel, a merchant tailor, Thomas Smith, a girdler, Humphrey Chetham, and Thomas Stevens, a tallowchandler, all had kinswomen as servants.[249] Edward Berry asked his widow to keep on his kinswoman as a servant until she reached the age of sixteen.[250]

Domestic service, although an integral part of the patriarchal household, had not yet acquired the low status it was to have in the nineteenth century; many servants, who cannot always be distinguished from

[235] PCC, Nabbs 69, 1660.   [236] PCC, Skynner 88, 1627.   [237] PCC, Goare 69, 1637.
[238] PCC, Pell 217, 1659.   [239] PRO, PROB 11/372/28; PRO, PROB 3/25/468.
[240] PCC, Drax 372.   [241] PCC, Rivers 21, 1644.   [242] PCC, Fines 86, 1647.
[243] PCC, Berkeley 257, 1656.   [244] PCC, Pile 90, 1636.   [245] GLL, MS 2708.
[246] Earle, *Making of the English Middle Class*, table 4.6.
[247] Boulton, *Neighbourhood and Society*, 135.   [248] PCC, St. John, 1631.
[249] PCC, Clarke 56 and 105, 1625; PCC, Parker 73, 1619; F. R. Raines and C. W. Sutton, *Life of Humphrey Chetham*, vol. 49 (Chetham Society, 1903), 26.
[250] PCC, Clarke 143, 1625.

apprentices in documents, were not just hired help. A faithful servant was important to a widower or bachelor householder. A loose-tongued or revengeful servant, however, could inflict enormous damage on a family's reputation.[251] In several unambiguous cases in both wills and correspondence, servants were treated like friends or with an intimacy and sense of caring characteristic of blood relations.

It was normal to bequeath a legacy to present and past servants. Widowers or bachelors often left substantial sums to their staff. Humphrey Burgess, a merchant tailor, left the residue of his estate to a kinswoman who was his servant.[252] The childless Michael Hancorn, a merchant tailor, left his kindred 12 pence a piece and gave everything to his maidservant, who he named executrix.[253] Thomas Carter, an ironmonger, left his kinswoman and servant, Susan Carter, £100 and the same amount to another servant.[254] Thomas Watson, a goldsmith, left £100 to his niece "now living in the house a servant with me" and had another niece whom he asked his widow to educate.[255] The widower Richard Irish, a brewer, left his land to a maidservant who was a kinswoman from Yorkshire.[256]

NEIGHBORS

The borderline between friends and neighbors was as permeable as that between kin and friends. The nuclear family was too small to provide a complete social life. Individual members went out into the streets of their parish, where they could intermingle with their familiars, equals, and betters and take advantage of public amenities and festivities. The street, with its noisy, bustling activity, was the center of retail marketing and gossip. Individuals met, conversed, and entertained at the ale house, the inn, the bowling green, the park, rather than in the home.[257] Communal drinking had an integrative function. Children played together in the streets. Business families lived in a face-to-face society.

Neighbors had many functions. They helped to preserve order in the locality and reconcile differences. Communal sanctions and arbitration by neighbors reduced the need for litigation, which tended to aggravate rather than resolve disputes. Neighbors acted as witnesses, executors,

---

[251] Capp, "Separate Domains," 117. [252] PCC, Alchin 154, 1654.
[253] PCC, Nabbs 126, 1660. [254] PCC, Coventry 101, 1640.
[255] PCC, Bowyer 123, 1652. [256] PCC, Hele 44, 1626.
[257] F. Heal, *Hospitality in Early Modern England* (Oxford, 1990), 318.

overseers, administrators, and appraisers.[258] John Phillips, a tallowchandler, and John Gardiner, a mercer, made their neighbors overseers.[259] Neighbors also came to the rescue in crises and were a source of financial credit.[260] They provided essential character references for those seeking to borrow money or defend themselves in court. Wives and widows developed supportive networks among their neighbors as well as their kin.

Businessmen frequently remembered their neighbors in wills. John Page, a weaver, gave his neighbor and tenant 20 shillings.[261] Samuel Foot, a merchant, allowed forty rings for his relations, friends, and acquaintances.[262] Henry Waller remembered twenty-six friends and neighbors in comparison with forty-three kin.[263] It was standard practice to invite neighbors to attend funerals as mourners. William Weston, a merchant tailor, left ribbons and gloves for his kindred "and some few neighbors to be invited."[264] Warwick Founes, a merchant, wanted no pomp at his funeral but that his kindred, household, neighbors, and familiars accompany his corpse to burial.[265] Sometimes legacies were left to children of friends and neighbors, though these were often godchildren.

A common method of remembering neighbors was to provide a dinner. John Wooleey, having lost his wife and only daughter, left his estate to his grandchildren and charity and provided a dinner for the parishioners of St. Magnus "and such other friends and old acquaintances of mine dwelling elsewhere as he shall think fit . . . by parishioners I do not mean every dweller in the parish without exception but only those my executor with the advice of his friends shall think convenient."[266] Edward Chard bequeathed £40 for a dinner for his neighbors and mourners.[267] John Hertau, a merchant, left a dinner for "loving neighbors and friends" of his parish.[268]

Common values and interests underpinned the neighborhood and created a relatively harmonious, moral community at the parish level, based on residential proximity and exclusion, with its own support system. Reciprocal obligations between effective equals were recognized and business relationships thrived on localism. Neighborliness nurtured the desire to belong. The local community gave an individual a sense of

[258] Boulton, *Neighbourhood and Society*, 240, 247.   [259] PCC, Meade 6 and 60, 1618.
[260] Horn, *Adapting to a New World*, 231.   [261] PCC, Alchin 381, 1654.
[262] PCC, Young 55, 1710.   [263] PCC, Savile 2.   [264] PCC, Bowyer 123, 1652.
[265] PCC, Coventry 103, 1640.   [266] PCC, Welldon 66, 1617.
[267] PRO, PROB 11/307.   [268] PCC, Clarke 126, 1625.

place and status. Women did not have a separate social identity, but they could develop their own gossip networks, which, however, excluded their social inferiors. Although the cohesiveness of towns was always threatened by massive migration and by residential segregation, there was a stable core of permanent residents in neighborhoods that, like households, could simultaneously combine many different roles. Even London, with its large transient population, was basically a federation of neighborhoods, not an impersonal space. It is anachronistic to employ concepts like anonymity.

Indeed it can be argued that urban life was too public and devalued the private sphere. All individual behavior had collective implications.[269] The business of the household was the business of the community.[270] Even private ceremonies had public attendees and witnesses. The deathbed was a stage with a choreographed social performance, and the intimate events of family life were displayed to the local community.

The importance of neighborliness must not, however, be exaggerated. In Edinburgh the rhetoric was not translated into effective action.[271] In Elizabethan London the elite rejected commensalism in favor of hierarchy, citing as justification (or excuse) the problems of the underclass; despite the formal rhetoric of corporatism, the city was in fact a matrix of overlapping communities with different loyalties.[272]

Relations with neighbors could be unstable and episodic. Increased litigation, particularly to recover debts, suggests that many disputes could not be resolved by consensus and arbitration.[273] Order was increasingly maintained by binding over aggressive individuals rather than relying on community pressure. Living in close proximity did not necessarily lead to frequent interaction and often reinforced dependence rather than promoted mutuality. The poor were increasingly isolated from the community by discriminatory legislation and by the eligibility requirements for relief.

[269] D. Cressy, "Private Lives, Public Performance" in *Attending to Women*, ed. B. Travitsky and A. F. Seef (Cranbury, 1994), 187; L. C. Orlin, *Private Matters and Public Culture in Post-Reformation England* (Ithaca, 1994), passim.
[270] D. Cressy, "Death and the Social Order," *Continuity and Change* 5 (1990): 114; *idem.*, *Birth, Marriage, and Death*, 476.
[271] Houston, *Social Change in the Enlightenment*, 30.
[272] I. W. Archer, *Pursuit of Stability* (1991), 258–60.
[273] The volume of litigation did fall at the end of the century for reasons that are not entirely clear. One possible explanation is the decline of communal institutions: see W. A. Champion, "Recourse to the Law" in *Communities and Courts*, ed. C. W. Brooks and M. Lobban (Rio Grande, 1997), 183.

Families did not necessarily wish to submit to communal authority. Neighbors could be intrusive or watch and denounce families. Since the reputation of a family depended on how others thought its members behaved, it was vulnerable to gossip. Families did not relish outside interference in their affairs or invasion of their privacy. One possible boundary between public and private space was the parlor, where the family met outsiders.[274] Increasingly the home was regarded as a separate sphere.

The character of the local community must not be romanticized or viewed out of context. Neighborhoods were densely populated and segregated by status, wealth, and, above all, occupation.[275] In Newcastle the merchant oligarchy dominated one residential area.[276] There was always the potential for conflicts of interest between family and neighborhood and between kinship networks that were geographically diffuse and groups of residents. The local community was a federation of households rather than a federation of families. Heads of households might have to choose between loyalty to their family and obligations to their neighbors.

THE CIVIC COMMUNITY

An even greater rival to the family was the city, which in its ideal form (*civitas*), was a world unto itself. London absorbed hordes of unattached, young migrants and sought to mold a common civic identity though the ritual of passage from apprenticeship to the freedom. It was the city that excluded aliens and outsiders, conferred the right to reside and trade, dispensed privileges, and sustained the social hierarchy. Families were expected to submerge their individual interests and serve the city by participating in municipal government and paying taxes.

The main instrument of civic corporatism and the core of the urban community was the guild, which was a macrocosm of and an alternative to the family. Businessmen were not just heads of families and households, but freemen with fraternal obligations to their livery companies. For most of the seventeenth century, the guilds competed effectively with

---

[274] F. E. Brown, "Continuity and Change in the Urban House," *Comparative Studies in Society and History* 28 (1986): 590.
[275] Boulton, *Neighbourhood and Society*, 183.
[276] J. Langhorn, "Residential Patterns in Pre-Industrial Cities," *Transactions of the Institute of British Geographers* 65 (1975): 1, 14.

the family, imposing their own discipline and holding the loyalty of their members. Despite a hierarchial structure and internal divisions, they integrated their members and gave them a civic identity. As corporations they were, unlike families, exempt from mortality. They promulgated the fraternal spirit through common dining, the wearing of livery, the provision of charity for their less fortunate, and through burying the dead. Their halls and gardens were communal space. Guilds arbitrated disputes within families between husband and wife and between parents and children. In 1634 the company of turners settled a dispute between two members over a woman; the saddlers and the founders intervened in matrimonial cases.[277]

Businessmen participated regularly in the fraternal activities of their guilds. Even residents of Southwark identified with their London companies, rather than with their locality or actual occupation.[278] Testators described themselves by their company and sought the presence of their fellow liverymen at their burial. Wives and widows participated in the social functions and often chose a livery funeral, which in the Haberdashers Company cost a husband 5 marks.[279]

Many testators bequeathed plate as a remembrance to their guild or money and property to endow a dinner or establish a charity. In 1626 John Juxon, a merchant tailor, provided for a dinner for the livery, plus kinsmen and friends.[280] In 1639 George Breton gave the Skinners Company plate as "a token of my respectful love unto them."[281] Richard Fishborn established a loan charity to benefit first shopkeepers and then merchants.[282] When establishing charities and schools, priority was often specified for members of the guild.[283]

The majority of native London businessmen who were not permanently resident overseas, were free of the city. Most also displayed a willingness to contribute to the public good by serving in unpaid, time-consuming offices at the ward and precinct level. Those who qualified financially sat on the bench; aldermen who did not also hold a national office represented 3 percent of the database in both periods I and II; the percentage was expectedly highest in brackets III and IV; there appears

---

[277] A. C. Stanley-Stone, *The Company of Turners* (1925), 79; J. W. Sherwell, *Historical Account of the Saddlers* (1889; reprint 1937), 171; G. Hadley, *Citizens and Founders* (1976), 80; J. P. Ward, *Metropolitan Communities* (Stanford, 1997), 5.

[278] Boulton, *Neighbourhood and Society*, 150–3.

[279] Archer, *History of Haberdashers Company*, 43.

[280] PCC, Hele 112, 1626.   [281] PCC, Coventry 381, 1640.   [282] PCC, Clarke 57, 1625.

[283] I. G. Doolittle, *History of Mercers Company* (1994), 91.

Table 6.4. *Citizenship and Office (Known Cases Expressed as a Percentage of All Subjects in Each Category)*

	Period I	Period II	Bracket I	Bracket II	Bracket III	Bracket IV	Cohort I	Cohort II	Cohort III	Cohort IV
Not Free	0.04	0.61	0.18	0.27	2.26	9.91	–	0.37	1.67	3.74
Free	57.60	47.70	41.90	71.20	60.50	46.90	76.10	71.10	57.50	36.50
Alien	2.03	1.75	0.18	1.01	1.72	1.80	5.62	1.83	0.63	0.44
Aldermen	3.09	3.16	2.03	1.98	37.40	13.50	29.80	14.20	4.66	2.20
National Officer	0.64	2.20	1.00	1.05	14.10	46.90	9.27	7.31	5.38	13.60
All Subjects	14,060	14,156	1,132	2,577	2,035	111	356	1,094	2,210	455

Note: Although holders of lesser civic offices in the parish, ward, and precinct and members of common council have been recorded in the database, they have been excluded here because all subjects have not been systematically matched with all the available lists. Only those known to have taken their freedom have been recorded, so that the number of freemen is almost certainly understated. Businessmen who held office under the Crown or served as members of Parliament have not been included among the aldermen, even though the great majority were also aldermen.

to have been a drop in participation in cohort III, though this may just reflect the greater number of subjects in that cohort.

Richard Farrington provides an illustration of the civic-minded businessman. He "never lay (but one night) out of my dwelling house in Grubb St" for fifty-five years, and he listed all his engagements with the city: commissioner for administering oaths, common councilman, deputy of his ward, commissioner of the land tax, judge in the Court of Conscience, governor of Christs Hospital, St. Bartholomew, Bridewell, and the London workhouse, trustee of charity schools and almshouses, a committee member for London Bridge and Gresham College, organizer of royal processions, petitioner to the House of Lords, master of the Distillers Company, grand and petty juryman, and vestryman.[284]

Nonetheless, civic consciousness often took second place to the family and other institutions. By the end of the century an increasing minority, particularly of wealthier businessmen, chose not to take the freedom, as is evident in bracket IV and cohort IV. Aliens, who represented around 2 percent of all subjects in both periods and in the higher financial brackets, remained outside the citizenry (see table 6.4). Evasion of service in city offices became increasingly common.

The fraternal life and representative nature of the guild also declined during the century. Some of the major companies were too big to sustain the spirit of association; attendance at meetings and dinners grew smaller. The economic and functional divisions between merchants and artisans, the latter usually excluded from the livery, erased craft identities and undermined occupational solidarity.[285] Women disappeared from view, though they had always been marginal.[286] The volume of benefactions declined. The companies retained their political importance in London, thanks to the city's constitution, but they abandoned their former regulatory role and became oligarchic institutions. The same story was repeated in other towns. In Norwich only one-sixth of the wealthier businessmen served in civic office by 1725; in Coventry guild culture had declined a century earlier in the face of a pluralistic society.

---

[284] GLL, MS 2708.
[285] M. Berlin, "Broken All in Pieces" in *The Artisan in the European Town*, ed. G. Grossick (Aldershot, 1997), 76.
[286] M. A. Clawson, "Early Modern Fraternalism and the Patriarchal Family," *Feminist Studies* 6 (1980): 381.

The guilds survived but in a more pragmatic, impersonal, and bureau-cratic form.[287]

The traditional civic community had to adapt to a rapidly changing world, to economic expansion, and social mobility. The loss of civic mindedness was blamed on such novelties as the stock market or on the influx of aliens, Dissenters, and Jews.[288] In Bristol the loss has been credited to the impact of the Atlantic trade.[289] One method of adaptation was to replace the face-to-face group with voluntary associations that could act collectively.[290] Another and probably more effective solution was the fusion of aristocratic and urban values into a new civility.[291] But the ideology of civic humanism was more successful in promoting individual autonomy than communitarianism. If the city had ever shared common cultural assumptions, they could not survive the increasing polarization between elite and populace.[292] The trend, as in Edinburgh, was toward greater informality and less ceremony.[293] In London the presence of the royal court allowed civic ceremonies, which exalted the magistracy, to survive longer than in other towns, but private affluence still coexisted with public squalor.[294]

An interesting comparison is provided by New England where, it has been argued, a disciplined individualism was combined with collective solidarity in a libertarian communalism.[295] The Puritan covenant is alleged to have preserved social cohesion without repressing affection or friendship, to have both deferred gratification and built trust.[296] Individualism was embedded in a homogenous local community, which was held together by reason, emotion, exclusion, and ritualism.[297] In

---

[287] C. Branford, "Powers of Association" (Ph.D. diss., University of East Anglia, 1993), 151; C. Phythian-Adams, Desolation of a City (Cambridge, 1979), 276–8; R. M. Berger, The Most Necessary Luxuries (University Park, 1993), 250.

[288] B. G. Carruthers, City of Capital (Princeton, 1996), 85.

[289] D. H. Sacks, The Widening Gate (Berkeley, 1991), xvii, 10.

[290] J. Barry, "Bourgeois Collectivism" in The Middle Sort, ed. J. Barry and C. Brooke (1994), 84–112.

[291] J. G. Jones, "Concepts of Order and Gentility" in Class, Community, and Culture in Tudor Wales, ed. J. G. Jones (Cardiff, 1989), 124.

[292] R. Tittler, Architecture and Power (Oxford, 1991), 128. The argument is much exaggerated with much speculative nonsense drawn from social anthropology (p. 136).

[293] Houston, Social Change in the Enlightenment, 122.

[294] M. Berlin, "Civic Ceremony in Early Modern London," Urban History Yearbook (1986): 21, 24.

[295] R. P. Gildrie, The Profane and the Civil and the Godly (University Park, 1994), 9.

[296] A. Porterfield, Female Piety in Puritan New England (New York, 1992), 12.

[297] S. Innes, Creating the Economic Culture of Puritan New England (New York, 1995), 29; Bender, Community and Social Change in America, 69; J. F. Marin, Profits in the Wilderness (Chapel Hill, 1991), 304.

Gloucester and Marblehead, Massachusetts, a communitarian culture survived the challenge of economic change and social mobility.[298] On the other hand, in Andover, Massachusetts, the family, revitalized by faith, replaced the community.[299]

In England it was ultimately family ties and intermarriage that gave the urban elites cohesion and a common ethic.[300] Despite its hierarchial structure, the city had a familial base. The extended family functioned as a collective group with a voluntary membership. The main threat to the family now came not from the guilds, but from their descendants— the professional associations of the law, medicine, and the army, which had their own self-perpetuating esprit de corps.

CHURCH AND STATE

The church (together with a variety of unorthodox denominations) assumed responsibility for defining the duties of individuals toward their family, their society, and their God. The church theoretically absorbed and validated the family, monitored social obligations, and controlled large sectors of the educational system. A family head might have immediate responsibility for the spiritual and secular well-being of his household, but ultimate responsibility lay with the church and the state.

The line between domestic and sacred space was thin. Ecclesiastical ceremonies linked families with the community. The parish church, despite its provision of privileged seating for the better sort, was not only a place of communal worship, but a meeting place for the neighborhood. The vestry was a miniature society with meetings and dinners. Religious oaths still authenticated binding contracts. The family rituals of birth and death were also religious rituals, which rearranged the status and rights of individuals, defined relationships, and made activities reverent and thereby acceptable. Children were socialized in church schools by professionals outside the family.

A substantial minority of businessmen worshipped outside the established church. Although known Catholics were few and Jews only became significant late in the century, nonconforming Protestants numbered around 2 percent of all subjects and were prominent in bracket III

[298] C. L. Heyrman, *Commerce and Culture* (New York, 1984), 8–9.
[299] J. Henretta, "The Morphology of New England Society," *Journal of Interdisciplinary History* 1 (1971): 396–8.
[300] R. G. Wilson, "Georgian Leeds" in *A History of Modern Leeds*, ed. D. Fraser (Manchester, 1980), 36.

Table 6.5. *Businessmen outside the Established Church (Percentage of All Subjects in the Database)*

Denomination	Period I	Period II	Bracket I	Bracket II	Bracket III	Bracket IV	Cohort I	Cohort II	Cohort III	Cohort IV
Catholic	0.06	0.10	0.18	–	0.10	–	0.28	0.18	0.23	–
Dissenter	2.14	1.43	2.39	3.65	13.17	22.52	5.90	15.27	6.74	7.91
Quaker	0.01	0.42	0.09	0.97	0.74	–	–	0.09	0.41	0.88
Foreign Protestant	1.92	2.64	0.80	7.07	5.50	10.81	5.06	3.20	3.94	6.37
Jews	0.26	2.11	–	1.24	1.28	–	0.28	0.37	0.18	0.44
All Subjects	14,060	14,156	1,132	2,577	2,035	111	356	1,094	2,210	455

Table 6.6. *Charitable Bequests (Percentage of Known Cases)*

Volume	Period I	Period II	Bracket I	Bracket II	Bracket III	Bracket IV	Cohort I	Cohort II	Cohort III	Cohort IV
Major	32.93	32.66	38.60	37.35	57.47	72.86	78.11	47.75	46.46	46.55
Minor	30.96	38.59	24.56	38.33	29.88	12.86	19.53	36.94	32.92	29.31
None	36.11	28.75	36.84	24.32	12.65	14.29	2.37	15.32	20.62	24.14
Total	2,235	1,047	57	514	743	70	169	222	325	58

(14 percent) and bracket IV (23 percent). French and German Protestants numbered 1.9 percent in period I and 2.6 percent in period II after the massive immigration of Huguenots; they represented 7 percent in bracket II and 11 percent in bracket IV.[301]

The independent churches functioned as familial institutions, providing a base, for example, for migrants to the cities. The Quakers were in many respects an extended family, sharing communal affection and offering conciliation services for married couples.[302] The sects had to control the family and marriages, because they could not rely on new conversions to sustain their numbers and had to fall back on family patrimony to carry the faith from one generation to the next. Personal belief could have adverse effects on a family. Businessmen who rejected orthodoxy in religion cut their children off from the larger society. Nonconformists who married outside the church ran a risk of having their widows and orphans disinherited, despite the effective acceptance of Quaker marriages.[303]

Spiritual devotion must have interfered with attention to spouses and children. Richard Farrington "never was absent [if in London] both forenoon and afternoon on Sunday from my parish church . . . for 33 years excepting 4 times in the afternoon and when one of my family has been dead in the house."[304] Husbands sometimes spent more time preparing their souls in their wills than providing for their wives. Some wives, like Jane Papillon, were obsessed with their salvation. Spiritual loyalty delayed the assimilation of the Huguenots and restricted their contact with other families.[305] Testators, especially nonconformists, frequently left bequests to ministers and for sermons and church furnishings.

Although it is virtually impossible to gauge, there are some signs that businessmen were reluctant to share or surrender authority over their families. There is little reason to suppose that they observed the

---

[301] The relative importance of Jews is almost certainly exaggerated in the database, because they are relatively easy to identify in the sources, whereas the number of Dissenters is underrepresented because they often cannot (particularly before 1640) be clearly distinguished from Anglicans.

[302] J. K. Gardiner, "Regendering Individualism" in *Privileging Gender in Early Modern England*, ed. J. R. Brink (Kirksville, Missouri, 1993), 223; *Bristol, Minute Book Mens Meeting Society Friends, 1667–86*, vol. 26, ed. R. Mortimer (Bristol Record Society, 1970), xxii.

[303] A. Lloyd, *Quaker Social History* (1950), 51; C. W. Horle, *The Quakers and the English Legal System* (Philadelphia, 1988), 234–8.

[304] GLL, MS 2708.

[305] C. Littleton, "Social Interactions of Aliens" in *The Strangers Progress*, vol. 26, ed. R. Vigne and G. C. Gibbs (Proceedings of the Huguenot Society of London, 1995), 156–7.

teaching of their respective churches on matrimonial and family issues any more than they followed the moral advice of the clerics on business behavior. There was a growing trend to regard baptisms and burials more as private, family affairs rather than public, religious rituals.[306] During the century, the decreasing willingness of London businessmen to endow the church rather than their families is evident when John Stow's *Survey* is compared with John Strype's revision.[307]

The religious and social pressures on merchants to make philantrophic bequests created another conflict of obligation. Parents had to choose between helping their children or helping the poor. The percentage of testators who made more than token bequests to charity remained constant at 33 percent in both periods I and II, but the number leaving minor gifts increased by 8 percent and the number making no charitable bequests declined by 7 percent. The rich gave both more frequently and on a larger scale. In bracket III only 13 percent gave nothing to charities and 30 percent made minor bequests; in bracket IV 14 percent left nothing and 73 percent made major bequests. The proportion of major charitable donors remained fairly constant in successive cohorts at 46 to 47 percent, but the percentage of minor bequests declined and those mentioning no charities increased.

Surprisingly, 46 to 48 percent of bachelors and those with no surviving children (some of whom probably died young, poor, and abroad) contributed nothing to charity, compared with 35 percent of those leaving children. Age was certainly a factor: 34 percent of those who died under age fifty made no bequests compared with 14 percent over fifty. Only 19 percent of those outside the established church left nothing to charity compared with around 32 percent for the whole database. The form in which assets were held seems to have had no impact on charitable giving.

In London, after 1660, a sample of wills confirms that one-third of testators left charitable benefactions, though many bequests were quite modest.[308] The same pattern can be discerned in other towns, such as Belfast, Coventry, Shrewsbury, and Manchester.[309] Old-fashioned nonconformists, like Samuel Jeake and Thomas Papillon, still allocated

[306] R. A. Houlbrooke, ed., *Death Ritual and Bereavement* (1989), 7; C. Gittings, *Death, Burial, and the Individual* (1984), 14.
[307] Stow, *Survey of London.*
[308] Earle, *Making of the English Middle Class*, 318, table 11.3.
[309] Agnew, *Belfast Merchants*, 67; Hindson, "Family Structure," 157; T. S. Willan, *Elizabethan Manchester* (Chetham Society, 1980), 104; Berger, *Necessary Luxuries*, 251.

Table 6.7. *Charitable Bequests: Cross Sectional Analysis, 1580–1740*
(Percentage of Known Cases)

	Major	Minor	None	Total
Never married	25.15	28.83	46.01	489
Surviving children	30.30	34.63	35.07	1,825
No surviving children	27.59	24.38	48.03	406
Deceased under age 50	40.57	35.85	23.59	106
Deceased over age 50	56.20	29.86	13.94	653
Landholder	41.22	33.25	25.53	1,128
Urban real estate	39.25	38.67	22.08	1,037
Capital in business	38.71	35.02	26.27	217
Outside Church of England	53.23	28.36	18.41	402

one-tenth of their income to the poor, and it was common to forgive the debts of kin friends, and clients.[310] But the great majority of testators gave only a small percentage of their estate; the rich gave more in absolute terms, but their proportionate contribution was often less than their poorer counterparts. Only a tiny number of businessmen were truly beneficient; legacies were also often contingent on other beneficiaries. Whereas William Jones gave 48 percent of his estate, his fellow haberdashers with £3–£10,000 gave 2.23 percent, and those with £10,000 or more 4.43 percent.[311] Most testators would have paid out much more in poor rates during their lifetime than they gave at their death.

Business families of course bestowed casual alms during their lifetime, and their philanthropy was cumulative. Frequently a widow on her death augmented the gifts of her late husband. London businessmen favored the poor of their parish, trade, and company and then city hospitals and prisons, though they also remembered their birthplace. Many gifts were however token or intended to secure mourners; testators often spent more on gowns and gloves for their friends than on the poor. By the end of the century charitable societies had become the preferred instrument of social amelioration; endowment through guilds and bequests by individual families declined.[312] Indeed, the charitable societies of Bristol, which were managed by retailers and had common dinners, resembled

---

[310] East Sussex, RO 145/11; Papillon, *Memoirs*, 382; C. Muldrew, *The Economy of Obligation* (1998), 304.
[311] Archer, *History of Haberdashers Company*, 74.   [312] Bod Rawlinson, MS D 1312.

guilds.[313] But private philanthropy was increasingly regarded as an act of beneficence and virtue toward carefully chosen causes rather than a community-based obligation.

The family was also embedded in the state. In 1601 Gerard Malynes described the commonwealth as a family, and Sir Robert Filmer wrote that "we may call Adam's family a commonwealth."[314] Because the household was the fundamental unit of governance, the state could not afford to leave the family to its own devices and constituted yet another potential rival. Although the contemporary debate over political obligation was framed in terms of individual rights, those rights could be asserted and exercised more effectively by families than by persons.

The number of businessmen who served as members of Parliament or in offices under the Crown did increase. The proportion rose from 0.6 percent of the whole database in period I to over 2 percent in period II, and from 1 percent in bracket II to 14 percent in bracket III to 47 percent in bracket IV. A similar pattern can be seen in successive cohorts (see table 6.4).

Although most business families were unaffected by national politics, a parent who opposed the government for political or religious reasons could put his family at risk. In a few cases political loyalties and service to the state conflicted with the welfare of children and kin. For some individuals politics took priority over other obligations. Lawrence Green, a merchant who died in Constantinople, left a major bequest to Parliament.[315] Public office of course advanced families in wealth and prestige. But the quest for office could undermine a family business, privilege personal careers, and challenge the primacy of family values and interests. Although controlled in this period by nepotism and family enclaves, public institutions had an inherent interest in detaching the individual from the family; bureaucracy does not welcome any competition and seeks to replace family patronage and kinship networks with an impersonal, universal meritocracy homogenized by a common education.[316]

[313] J. Barry, "Popular Culture" in *Popular Culture in Seventeenth-Century England*, ed. B. Reay (1985), 73.

[314] R. Filmer, *Patriarcha*, ed. J. P. Sommerville (Cambridge, 1991), 16.

[315] PCC, Alchin 159, 1654.

[316] Fox, *Kinship and Marriage*, 7; S. N. Eisenstadt, *From Generation to Generation* (Glencoe, Ill., 1956), 54. Emile Durkheim thought that professional groups filled a vacuum created by the decline of the family: see S. Lukes, *Emile Durkheim* (1973), 185.

SUMMARY

England had no formal system of kinship with sanctions and a coherent structure. Wives and children always took priority over kin, and no family was obliged to give exclusive loyalty to a large tribe of relations. Kinship was voluntary and could be either drawn on or ignored; familial relationships were based on personal bonding, not on prescription. Some individuals saw more of their friends and neighbors than their kin, and some treated outsiders as though they were kin. Business families tended to be more separated by distance than were families of artisans.

Differences of wealth and rank divided kin. Business families regarded self-reliance as a virtue and showed greater interest in wealthier relations than in their poor kindred. Wealthy households dominated large kin networks with poorer satellite branches, which tended to be takers and not givers. Conflict was generated by differences of personality and values. The interests of the extended family often conflicted with those of the nuclear household.

The kinship universe was, however, huge and families managed to maintain contact with a wide range of kin over great distances. The frequency and intensity of communication varied with individual temperament, opportunity, need, distance, and unpredictable events. Some networks were inherited and some constructed; they both converged and diverged according to occupation. Paternal kin were not usually privileged; accessibility and particular circumstances determined who was recognized and which kin were chosen as companions and advisers.

The boundaries between the nuclear and the extended family were infinitely flexible because it was a living organism; they changed continuously along with the attitude and behavior of individuals.[317] Conjugal couples acknowledged the need to belong to a larger group and took pride in their families beyond their own children. Conflicts were inevitable but usually resolved, and most families recognized a collective responsibility. Kin and friends provided crucial advice and assistance at moments of crisis and stress, and their help was recognized and rewarded by testators. The family was too fragile to survive without their support.

---

[317] K. Berkner, "The Use and Misuse of Census Data," *Journal of Interdisciplinary History* 5 (1975): 738.

Contrary to what is often assumed, the business family embraced much more than those members who resided together. Important family relationships were sustained outside the household, which was a more tangible, but separate, institution with members from outside the family. Households expanded and contracted according to age distribution, demographic events, current needs, and the life cycle of different family members. The preindustrial society of England was not just an agglomeration of individuals but a bifurcated network of extended families and local and regional communities each with their own group norms, mutual obligations, and moral discipline.[318] The local community was created not just by genetic transmission but by culture.[319]

The business family, however, increasingly bypassed the community. Although there was no lineal decline in neighborliness, the center of gravity shifted.[320] The old ties of solidarity were challenged by self-consciousness. The household was increasingly closed to routine neighborly regulation, and privacy became valued above communality. Although it is not clear what were regarded as private matters, the family home with its interior, domestic life could offer a refuge from the outside world.[321] Continuous bonding within the family could serve as a substitute for communitarian values. This may have reinforced patriarchal authority; men were liberated by market individualism, but women were deprived of community support, while not substantially increasing their choices for action.[322]

Once the moral economy of the community lost its authority, the concept of civil society, based on private interests and values, emerged to bridge the gap between the household and the market.[323] Elite families began to distance themselves from the populace and fence off and redefine their culture. Public interference in family affairs declined, but new rival institutions emerged at both the local and national level. The family ideal was appropriated by both church and state, and the expan-

---

[318] Bender, *Community and Social Change*, 122.
[319] E. Gellner, *Anthropology and Politics* (1995), 45.
[320] M. Anderson, "New Insights into the History of the Family" in *New Directions in Economic and Social History*, ed. A. Digby, C. Feinstein, and D. Jenkins, vol. 2 (1992): 127.
[321] L. Pollock, "Living on the Stage" in *Rethinking Social History*, ed. A. Wilson (New York, 1993), 78–90.
[322] A. Lawrence, *Women in England, 1500–1760* (New York, 1994), 274.
[323] The use of the term "civil society" is discussed by G. Schochet, "Vices, Benefits" in *The Intersection of the Public and Private Sphere*, ed. P. R. Backscheider and T. Dystal (1996), 257.

sion of government encroached on family responsibilities. But the family remained the root institution of society because there was no viable alternative.

The core of the family consisted therefore of the conjugal couple with their children, orbited first by a circle of kin and then by a circle of friends. Each family had both diachronic vertical links with their ancestors and synchronous bonds with their horizontal kin; individual members grouped and regrouped with different functions.[324] It is rarely noted that businessmen had multiple and conflicting obligations toward their wives, children, kin, friends, and neighbors, their guild and parish, their church, the city, and the Crown. Heads of families had to wear many hats simultaneously, and they lacked the time to give equal weight to all responsibilities. They had to constantly resolve conflicts of loyalty and transfer in and out of different roles.[325] But these conflicts, far from destabilizing the family, only confirmed its importance and strengthened the status quo.

[324] T. K. Haveren, "Cycles, Courses, and Cohorts," *Journal of Social History* 12 (1978): 100.
[325] T. K. Haveren, "Recent Research" in *Time, Family, and Community*, ed. M. Drake (Oxford, 1994), 25; K. Wrightson, "Sorts of People" in *The Middle Sort*, ed. J. Barry and C. Brooks (1994), 38.

Part III

The Family Business

7

Men in Business

The basic unit of business was the household, not the biological family spread over numerous occupations. A household could be organized as a nuclear family, but it could just as well consist of a bachelor with apprentices or a widower (or widow) with or without children. The family firm extended, however, beyond the household to include nonresident kin, and it was an informal and not a bureaucratic institution. The organization chart of a major business resembles a family tree.

Most businesses were conducted in partnership, usually in a succession of short-term arrangements between two or three persons, though longer partnerships with one individual, like that of Thomas Church, did occur.[1] The Elizabethan trade to Barbary and the Atlantic tobacco trade well illustrate a persistent trend from isolated, individual trading to continuous short-term partnerships.[2] In Hull the partnership developed into an extra-familial organization.[3]

A typical long-term arrangement was that between Robert Fowle and Thomas Wotton, goldsmiths. Each put up £1,000 for ten years; Fowle would live above the shop with the bookkeeper giving Wotton right of way, and each partner could draw a maximum of £33 per month.[4] Partnerships were hostage to mortality and were inherently impermanent. Even in a large firm, death created a crisis: in one case when a senior partner died, the survivors had to face the questions of replacing

---

[1] Inventory of Thomas Church, ULL, MS 71.
[2] T. S. Willan, *Studies in Elizabethan Foreign Trade* (Manchester, 1959), 159; J. M. Price, *Tobacco in the Atlantic Trade* (Aldershot, 1995), 6.
[3] G. Jackson, *Hull in the Eighteenth Century* (1972), 111.
[4] Indenture of partnership, PRO, C 104/108, March 1692.

him, whether or not to change the company's name, and whether or not to implement decisions made by the deceased.[5]

The line between the partnership and other business institutions was blurred.[6] Regulated chartered companies, like the Levant Company, were in effect an aggregate of individual partnerships with monopolistic privileges. The company provided a framework of regulation but expected its members to conduct their own business. Colliery partnerships had all the characteristics of joint stocks.[7] A holding company could also be created without incorporation by combining several partnerships. Although the great ironmaster, Ambrose Crowley, retained sole control of his business, Quakers managed the iron industry through interlocking family partnerships.

An interesting example of a complex extended-family firm is the Foley iron business.[8] In the 1660s, Thomas Foley divided his ironworks, each worth some £60,000, among his three sons, so that each sector would be managed independently. Since Paul Foley received the furnaces and Philip Foley the forges, they had to work together. However, in 1692 the sons recombined through unified partnerships, creating in effect a company with a board of directors. Additional associates, like Henry Glover and Samuel Wallis, were integrated into the business by marriage.

Scotland had a different partnership law. There, a partnership was a separate legal entity that generated rentier income for passive investors and had a managing partner paid both a salary and in shares. Levels of borrowing and suits by creditors were restricted, and the yield on shares was limited to 5 percent until the partnership was dissolved.[9] The Glasgow merchants were bound by articles for four to seven years and often interlocked with other partnerships; the legal obstacles to dissolution were such that firms lasted for more than one generation.

All joint-stock organizations, whether incorporated or not, were dis-

[5] Letters from Nathaniel Galpin dated 20 May 1699, PRO, C 104/11–12. Surviving partners might have to sue to recover their investment: see, for example, H. Horwitz and C. Moreton, *Samples of Chancery Pleadings and Suits*, vol. 257 (List and Index Society, 1995), no. 248.
[6] M. M. Postan, *Medieval Trade and Finance* (1975), 89–91.
[7] J. U. Nef, *Rise of the Coal Industry*, vol. 1 (1932), 49–56.
[8] R. G. Schafer, "Genesis and Structure of the Foley Ironworks," *Business History* 13 (1972): 19–30; *Philip Foley Stour Valley Ironworks, 1668–1674*, ed. R. G. Schafer, vol. 9 (Worcester Historical Society, 1978), xii; B. L. C. Johnson, "The Foley Partnerships," *Economic History Review*, 2d ser., 4 (1951–2): 325–31; M. B. Rowlands, *Masters and Men* (1975), 74.
[9] T. M. Devine, *Tobacco Lords* (Edinburgh, 1975), 76.

tinguished by a division between ownership and management. But there was no clear line between a syndicate and a partnership, because one partner usually dominated and because the division of labor between partners and their respective capital contributions were not necessarily equal. Nonetheless, businesses financed as alienable joint stocks raised from silent partners or passive investors and run by elected or appointed managers were different from partnerships, whether they were temporary, unincorporated syndicates, or self-perpetuating, bureaucratic, joint-stock corporations. Even corporations, however, succumbed to nepotism and kinship. Certain families dominated the great companies through interlocking directorships, and in every company sons succeeded their fathers in office.

How important was the family as an instrument for recruiting and training manpower? Was a family business self-financed or dependent on outsiders? Were partners and employees drawn from the immediate family, from kin, or from the general population? To what extent did business firms depend for their successful operation on family influence, intermarriage, and networks of kin? Were kin preferred to strangers, and if so, for what reasons?

RECRUITMENT

Sons born to freemen of London could enter business by right of patrimony, though many who chose this route also voluntarily served an apprenticeship. Sons of provincial businessmen and aliens were denied this option, though they could purchase the freedom by redemption. The proportion of businessmen known to have taken their freedom as sons of citizens declined from 44 percent in period I to 13 percent in period II, but this overall trend conceals major fluctuations. The proportion varied between 11 and 17 percent in brackets I to III and fell to only 6 percent in bracket IV; it also fell from 17 percent in cohort I to 6 percent in cohort III, only to rise again to 16 percent in cohort IV.[10] The number entering by patrimony also varied inversely with the number entering by redemption.

In comparison, among all citizens of Elizabethan London, one-third

---

[10] The figures for patrimony may be distorted in period I because they include data from the 1640s, which does not indicate whether those taking their freedom had also been apprenticed. Entry by patrimony may have been more common in artisanal trades, which are excluded from the database.

Table 7.1. *Training of Businessmen (Percentage of Known Cases)*

	Period I	Period II	Bracket I	Bracket II	Bracket III	Bracket IV	Cohort I	Cohort II	Cohort III	Cohort IV
Immediate Family	1.09	4.57	2.30	3.87	3.56	7.84	1.01	1.91	7.87	12.04
Apprenticeship with Kin	2.35	6.07	11.49	5.31	7.46	13.73	5.05	6.46	5.78	11.11
Apprenticeship with Other	46.90	58.57	47.13	58.45	63.22	54.90	66.67	77.75	70.63	48.15
Patrimony	43.62	12.58	11.49	17.39	12.71	5.88	17.17	9.33	6.42	15.74
Redemption	2.85	14.52	8.05	5.31	3.39	9.80	7.07	2.39	2.25	5.56
Professional Other	3.19	3.70	19.54	9.66	9.66	7.84	3.03	2.15	7.06	7.41
Total	1,192	1,598	87	207	590	51	99	418	623	108

Table 7.2. *Origins of Businessmen (Percentage of Known Cases)*

	Period I	Period II	Bracket I	Bracket II	Bracket III	Bracket IV	Cohort I	Cohort II	Cohort III	Cohort IV
Occupation of Father										
Businessman	52.57	51.68	51.09	51.84	49.02	55.81	47.34	46.15	53.63	76.29
Gentleman	32.56	30.03	31.52	28.09	32.10	22.09	33.51	32.17	28.77	15.46
Professional/Public official	1.48	5.59	4.35	3.01	4.56	6.98	2.13	2.80	7.02	4.64
Artisan/Tradesman	0.81	2.44	2.17	2.34	2.50	5.81	1.06	3.32	3.11	1.03
Farmer	1.86	5.55	8.70	4.35	7.27	4.65	6.38	11.89	5.52	1.03
Alien	10.73	4.71	2.17	10.37	4.56	4.65	9.58	3.67	1.96	1.55
Total	2,098	2,378	92	299	922	86	188	572	869	194
Place of Birth										
Abroad	11.30	8.02	3.57	8.79	4.58	6.74	8.86	3.74	3.50	2.94
Distant region	37.87	37.61	39.29	46.32	44.82	31.46	44.73	44.15	39.34	22.55
Local region	10.34	10.98	10.71	11.16	15.22	14.61	13.08	16.69	10.71	5.89
London	40.50	43.38	46.43	33.73	35.39	47.19	33.33	35.41	46.45	68.63
Total	2,699	2,667	112	421	1,071	89	237	641	943	204

of sons chose a different trade than their fathers, and 89.5 percent were freed by service.[11] In the seventeenth century few entered by redemption, and, after 1681, about 12 percent of London freemen entered by patrimony.[12] In the Drapers Company (1660–88) only five entered by apprenticeship compared with eight by patrimony and one by redemption; the same surnames recur, as in most companies, but some families also disappeared.[13] In the Turner's Company only 5.5 percent entered by patrimony.[14] Practice varied considerably in different towns. In York over one-third entered by patrimony (1600–99).[15] In Norwich admissions by patrimony rose from 22.7 percent (1590–1640) to 36.1 percent (1640–90).[16]

Approximately half of known apprentices were sons of businessmen: 52 to 53 percent in both periods and 49 to 56 percent in all brackets; the proportion rose from 46 and 47 percent in cohorts I and II, to 54 percent in cohort III to 76 percent in cohort IV. Sons of artisans and small tradesmen (who cannot always be distinguished from businessmen in the sources) fluctuated between 1 and 2 percent with an increase to 6 percent in bracket IV and 3 percent in cohorts II and III. Half of the sons of the London elite (1660–1725) followed their father's occupation.[17]

There was little change in the relative distribution of parental occupations of apprentices over time or between financial brackets: 30 to 33 percent were sons of gentlemen, declining to 22 percent in bracket IV and 15 percent in cohort IV. Sons of professionals and public officials rose from 1.5 percent in period I to 6 percent in period II; an increase is also visible in brackets III and IV and cohorts III and IV. Sons of husbandmen and yeomen rose from 2 percent in period I to 6 percent in period II, with a concentration in brackets I and III and cohort II. Sons of aliens rose from 1 percent in period I to 5 percent in period II, with a concentration in bracket II and cohort I. A surprisingly large number of businessmen were neither preceded nor followed by blood kin: 60 percent of all surnames in the database only occur once, and 15 percent only twice.

---

[11] Rappaport, *Worlds within Worlds*, 291–2, 308–10, 341–3.
[12] M. T. Medlycott, "The City of London Freedom Registers," *Genealogical Magazine* 19 (1977): 45.
[13] A. H. Johnson, *History of the Company of Drapers* (Oxford, 1914–22), vol. 2, appendix 31 and vol. 3, 321.
[14] P. S. Seaver, *Wallington's World* (Stanford, 1985), 113.
[15] *V. C. H. City of York*, ed. P. M. Tillott (1961), 166.
[16] J. T. Evans, *Seventeenth-Century Norwich* (Norwich, 1980), 10.
[17] H. Horwitz, "Testamentary Practice," *Law and History Review* 2 (1984): table 7.

274 The Family Business

Table 7.3. Frequency Distribution of Surnames, 1580–1740
(Percentage of all Surnames)

Frequency	1	2	3–4	5–8	9–16	17–32	33–64	65+
Percent	56.95	14.80	12.09	8.13	4.91	2.20	0.76	0.16
Total names	8,556							

In another sample of all entrants to fifteen companies (1570–1640), sons of merchants (47) were outnumbered by sons of gentry (762), clergy (236), yeomen (1,977), and husbandmen (1,452).[18] Sons of gentlemen represented 11 to 38 percent before 1646 and 14 to 29 percent between 1674 and 1690. An increasing number of sons followed their fathers in King's Lynn during the seventeenth century.[19] The same was true of Bristol: one-fifth (1600–30) and one-fourth (1670–90) of the merchants were sons of practicing merchants; 5.8 percent of the fathers of apprentices were gentlemen, 40.9 percent businessmen, and 3.2 percent professionals.[20] In Norwich 11.5 percent (1601–23) and 19.6 percent (1625–50) were sons of gentlemen.[21] In Coventry (1558–1660) 50 percent of the mercers had sons in business, but only three families had more than one son in business, and some migrated to London; 60 percent of new recruits had no relatives in the company, and only 40 percent of apprentices became freemen.[22] In the Scottish towns sons did follow their fathers, and kin were favored by masters and charged lower entry fees, but most came from outside.[23] In Glasgow 71 of 163 merchants were sons of merchants.[24]

The geographical origins of London businessmen were constant over time and between brackets: 37 to 38 percent came from distant regions

[18] Brodsky, "Mobility and Marriage in Pre-Industrial England," tables 7, 10; these statistics include all apprentices, including artisans who would never qualify as businessmen.
[19] S. M. Cooper, "Intergenerational Social Mobility," Continuity and Change 7 (1992): 287.
[20] MacGrath, Merchants and Merchandize, appendix B; I. K. Ben Amos, "Service and Coming of Age," Continuity and Change 3 (1988): 62; D. H. Sacks, The Widening Gate (Berkeley, 1991), 113–16.
[21] J. Pound, Tudor and Stuart Norwich, tables 5.1 and 5.2, 50.
[22] R. M. Berger, Most Necessary Luxuries (University Park, 1993), 272–3, table 9.5.
[23] T. M. Devine, "The Merchant Class" in Scottish Urban History, ed. G. Gordon and B. Dicks (Aberdeen, 1983), 99, 104.
[24] Devine, Tobacco Lords, 11.

with an increase in brackets II and III and a decrease in successive cohorts from 45 percent to 23 percent; 10 to 11 percent came from counties adjacent to London and Middlesex, with an increase in bracket III and cohort II; 41 to 43 percent came from London, with an increase in bracket IV and cohorts III and IV. Those born abroad fell from 11 percent in period I to 8 percent in period II, with a concentration in bracket I and cohort I. Migrants from the country did include some sons of provincial businessmen in search of greater opportunities, often in an allied trade; provincial clothiers, for example, apprenticed their sons to merchant adventurers. Some London companies were closely associated with particular regions: the Levant Company, for example, drew heavily on Suffolk and the West country.[25] But the data on place of birth of apprentices confirms the data on parental occupation and demonstrates that about half of businessmen were recruited from within the local business community.

In comparison, 24.1 percent of merchants listed by the heralds in the 1633–5 London Visitation were sons of London citizens.[26] A sample of birthplaces of apprentices shows 38.5 percent from London and Middlesex and 20.8 percent from the Southeast (22.3 percent from the gentry and 14.2 percent from the yeomanry); a sample of deponents in church courts (1665–1725) suggests that total migration to London from distant regions increased after 1660, with migrants from the hinterland declining from 38 to 28 percent.[27] Between one-fourth and one-third of those entering the freedom (1690–1750) were sons of Londoners.[28]

The data available on the distribution of businessmen between different sectors of the economy has to be interpreted with caution. Foreign trade is clearly overrepresented at 53 to 67 percent of known cases, and the concentration of overseas merchants in bracket III and cohorts I and IV reflects their greater visibility in the sources. Half of the Jacobean aldermen were engaged in the domestic trade, distributing imported and manufactured goods to the provinces and supplying London with raw materials and foodstuffs.[29] It had been estimated that 40 percent of

[25] Anderson, *An English Consul*, 75.
[26] J. Grant, "The Gentry of London," *University Birmingham Historical Journal* 8 (1962): 198.
[27] Earle, "Age and Accumulation," tables 3.2, 3.4; Earle, *A City Full of People*, tables 2.4, 2.5 (divided into four regions).
[28] W. F. Kahl, "Apprenticeship and the Freedom," *Guildhall Miscellany* 7 (1956): 18–19.
[29] R. G. Lang, "The Greater Merchants of London," (D. Phil. thesis, University of Oxford, 1963), passim.

Table 7.4. *Distribution by Trade (Percentage of Known Cases)*

Trade	Period I	Period II	Bracket I	Bracket II	Bracket III	Bracket IV	Cohort I	Cohort II	Cohort III	Cohort IV
Foreign	67.25	53.39	33.84	46.43	63.24	50.93	61.15	52.45	55.16	69.78
Domestic	12.24	16.03	29.10	16.68	14.42	3.70	11.49	20.61	20.84	7.43
Retail	6.43	9.37	11.28	13.93	3.84	–	8.45	9.38	7.35	3.84
Manufacturing	12.69	12.28	12.59	19.08	6.93	5.56	8.45	10.80	8.51	6.72
Financial	0.82	6.85	8.66	1.94	5.01	13.89	4.05	3.05	4.28	7.19
Combined	0.57	2.07	4.53	1.94	6.56	25.93	6.42	3.71	3.86	5.04
Total	9,835	11,120	993	1,751	1,616	108	296	917	1,891	417

London citizens participated in manufacturing and 36 percent in retailing (1665–1720), and it is almost certain that most of those whose trades cannot be identified in the database would have been in the domestic trade or manufacturing.[30]

The data, however, yield some useful information. An increase in those with multiple interests in different economic sectors is evident between periods I and II as well as a modest increase in the number of retailers who qualified as businessmen. No subject in bracket IV was in the retail trade, but 4 percent were in the internal trade, 6 percent in manufacturing, 15 percent in financial services, and 26 percent had multiple economic interests. Businessmen were closely identified with distribution (both overseas and internal) and with finance (of production as well as consumption).

TRAINING

A minority of businessmen had no formal instruction: 3 to 4 percent in both periods I and II, 20 percent in bracket I, 8 to 10 percent in brackets II to IV, and 7 percent in cohorts III and IV. The majority, however, served an apprenticeship. A few wills note the contribution by young children to the family business. The sons of James Denew worked in his business in return for their board. Apprenticeship was often treated as a familial relationship, as in the case of Roger Lowe. But an apprenticeship indenture was still a contract, and children of businessmen did not usually labor for their parents.

Only 1 percent of known apprentices were bound to their father in period I, rising to 4.6 percent in period II; the proportion rose to 8 percent in bracket IV and 12 percent in cohort IV. In comparison, the proportion apprenticed was 1.9 percent in Bristol between 1542 and 1565, 9 percent in Southampton in the 1610s (rising to 27 percent in the 1670s), and 12.6 percent in Oxford; examples can also be found in Norwich and King's Lynn.[31] In the West India trade sons continued to

---

[30] Earle, *Making of the English Middle Class*, 19; A. L. Beier, "Engine of Manufactures" in *London 1500–1700*, ed. A. L. Beier and R. Finlay (1986), 150–3.

[31] A. Yarborough, "Apprentices as Adolescents," *Journal of Social History* 13 (1979): 68; *Southampton Calender of Apprentices*, ed. A. J. Willis and A. L. Merson, vol. 12 (Southampton Record Society, 1968), xxxiv; *Oxford City Apprentices, 1697–1800*, vol. 31 (Oxford Historical Society, 1987), xiv; *Norwich Apprentices*, vol. 29 (Norfolk Record Society, 1959); G. A. Metters, "The Rulers and Merchants of King's Lynn" (Ph.D diss., University of East Anglia, 1982), 345.

be apprenticed to their fathers in the eighteenth century.[32] Sir Thomas
Davies was apprenticed both to his father and to a stationer.[33] George
Boddington trained some of his children and took his son, Benjamin,
into his counting house.[34] A fellow apprentice of Francis Kirkman was
the son of his master.[35] Thomas Purcell was master of two of his sons as
well as of his nephew.

Siblings sometimes acted as master. William Crooke was apprenticed
to his brother, Andrew, and ultimately became his partner.[36] Abraham
Elton was bound to his brother, a cooper, but transferred to another
master who could offer a wider scope; his own sons were apprenticed
within his family and eventually became partners.[37] William Marshall, a
grocer, took two of his brothers apprentice.[38] In Abingdon Anne Turton
bound her son to her second husband.[39] The Fredericks and the Lethieul-
liers were all apprenticed to each other. In New England partnerships
between siblings were relatively common.[40]

The proportion of businessmen apprenticed to kin rose from 2
percent in period I to 6 percent in period II, and fluctuated between 5
and 14 percent between different financial brackets; the proportion
ranged from 5 to 6 percent in cohorts I to III, rising to 11 percent
in cohort IV. In Elizabethan London 15 percent of seven hundred
Londoners had at least one apprentice with the same surname.[41] Kin
feature prominently among the masters of the Elizabethan Muscovy
merchants.[42] In Newcastle fourteen merchant adventurers had masters
with the same surnames (1580–1660), dropping to five (1660–1700) and
three (1700–40).[43]

[32] K. Morgan, "Bristol West India Merchants," *Transactions of the Royal Historical
Society*, 6th ser., 3 (1993): 189, 200.
[33] C. Rivington, "Sir Thomas Davies," *The Library*, 6th ser., 3 (1981): 188.
[34] GLL, MS 10,823, fo. 68.   [35] F. Kirkman, *The Unlucky Citizen* (1673), 34.
[36] T. Hobbes, *Correspondence*, vol. 2, ed. N. Malcolm, 824.
[37] M. Elton, *Annals of the Elton Family, 1654–1728* (Stroud, 1994), 13–19.
[38] PCC, Bruce 81, 1664.
[39] M. Prior, "Women and the Urban Economy," in *Women in English Society*, ed. M. Prior
(Cambridge, 1985), 121.
[40] P. D. Hale, "Family Structure and Economic Organization" in *Family and Kin in Urban
Communities*, ed. T. Haveren (New York, 1977), table 1.
[41] S. Rappaport, "Reconsidering Apprenticeship" in *Renaissance Society and Culture*,
ed. S. Rapport, et al. (New York, 1991), 248.
[42] Willan, *The Muscovy Merchants*, 40.
[43] *Newcastle Records Merchant Adventurers*, vol. 101, ed. F. W. Dendy and J. R. Boyle
(Surtees Society, 1899).

Uncles were often the first choice, as for James Fretwell and Marmaduke Rawdon.[44] William Byrd was sent out to Virginia to a childless, maternal uncle, Thomas Stegg, who had in turn been set up by Byrd's father.[45] William Lowther was apprenticed to his father's younger brother for £200.[46] Francis Saire took on his nephew and made him his trustee.[47] John Cogge was bound first to his uncle and then to John Stevens.[48] Brothers-in-law and cousins were also common as apprentices. Elizabeth Hicks, whose son was thought too short for a haberdasher's shop, apprenticed him to her brother-in-law.[49] Gervaise Disney was bound to his cousin, a silkman, and Ralph Thoresby to his cousins, Joseph and Benjamin Milner.[50] Heigham Bright was apprenticed to his cousin, Philip Wheake.[51] Often the master came from even more distant kin, or the exact relationship is not specified. William Boulton, a mercer, had Ambrose Boulton as his servant.[52] Jonathan Dickinson's son, an American Quaker, was apprenticed to a kinsman in London.[53] The nephew of Robert Wilson, a draper, was bound to Rowland Wilson.[54]

The proportion of all those apprenticed to masters outside the family fluctuated around 50 percent: 47 percent in period I and 59 percent in period II; the proportion was 47 to 63 percent in all financial brackets and 67 to 78 percent in cohorts I to III, falling to 48 percent in cohort IV. Few masters of goldsmiths were kinsmen, though former apprentices constituted a trading network.[55] Only 82 apprentices in the Stationers Company were sons of stationers compared with 404 gentlemen, 218 clothworkers, and 126 tailors.[56] Fewer than 4 percent of Norwich apprentices had the same surname as their master; the same was true of

[44] M. Rawdon, *Life*, vol. 95, ed. R. Davies (Camden Society, 1863), 8.
[45] P. Marambaud, "William Byrd I," *Virginia Magazine of History and Biography* 81 (1973): 132.
[46] D. Hainsworth, "The Lowther Younger Sons," *Transactions of Cumberland and Westmoreland Archaeological and Antiquarian Society*, 88 (1988): 151.
[47] *Durham Wills, 1604–49*, vol. 142 (Surtees Society, 1929), 13.
[48] Bod Library, MS Eng misc. F 78.
[49] S. E. Hicks-Beach, *A Cotswold Family* (1909), 191.
[50] G. Disney, *Some Remarkable Passages* (1692), 30.
[51] Bright, *The Brights of Suffolk*, 175.   [52] PCC, Grey 62, 1651.
[53] J. W. Frost, *The Quaker Family in Colonial America* (1973), 139.
[54] PCC, Coventry 11, 1639.
[55] S. Quinn, "Balances and Goldsmith Bankers" in *Goldsmiths and Silversmiths*, ed. D. M. Mitchell (1995), 62.
[56] D. F. MacKenzie, "Apprentices in the Stationers Company, 1555–1640," *The Library*, 5th ser., 13 (1958): 292–9.

the Newcastle merchant adventurers, though many masters appear to have mutually exchanged their children.[57]

Businessmen did, however, help to place their kin and supervise their apprenticeships. Family patronage determined access to the major companies of London and the pace of advancement of young men in the early years.[58] Thomas Gent was assisted by his father and brother-in-law.[59] Sir Benjamin Bathurst assisted the son of a cousin: "I am of your opinion that a little time at the university might doe my cousin . . . noe hurt, but if he is to be bred up to business . . . at the East India house I think any further [delays] . . . are not useful and may make him look higher. . . . I will see what may be done."[60] George Warner instructed his nephew: "You see how careful your uncle is for the managing of this . . . business. However it will be wisdom in you to be punctual in the observance of his instructions and to give him a just account. . . . This day we have received a fresh token of your loving remembrances namely a barrell of oysters."[61]

Masters frequently expected recommendations from third parties before they took on an apprentice. William Raikes, for example, sent the following reference for Christopher Richardson's son to Sir John Moore: "To my knowledge, very frugally educated and very hopeful, not addicted to any vice soe if yourself or any friends have occasion for service no question but you or they will find him tractable."[62] The outcome was sometimes unexpected. A poor relation, placed by the Earl of Clare with a jeweler, robbed his master.[63]

John Sanderson was bound by his uncle to Martin Calthorp, who already had his own son as apprentice; John and Thomas Mun were placed by their stepfather.[64] Kinsmen in London helped find a master for Richard Oxenden; Edward Mellish arranged for his kinsman, Robert, to serve Samuel Harvey in Aleppo.[65] Thomas Calverley exploited his con-

[57] *Norwich. An Index of Indentures of Apprentices, 1510–1749*, ed. P. Millican (Norwich, 1934); *Newcastle Merchant Adventurers Records*; M. Zell, *Industry in the Countryside* (Cambridge, 1994), 193.

[58] F. F. Foster, *The Politics of Stability* (1977), 94.

[59] T. Gent, *Life* (1832; reprint 1974), 51.

[60] Letter dated 29 Nov. 1698, BL, Loan MS 57/70, fo 12.

[61] Letter dated 10 Nov. 1638, PRO, SP 46/83, fo. 10.

[62] Letter dated 12 March 1668, GLL, MS 507A.

[63] G. Holles, *Memorials of the Holles Family, 1493–1656*, ed. A. C. Wood, 3d ser., vol. 45 (Camden Society, 1937), 36.

[64] J. Sanderson, *Travels*, ed. Sir W. Foster, 2d ser., vol. 67 (Hakluyt Society, 1930), 2, 7, 9.

[65] Letters dated 1692–3, University of Nottingham, Mellish of Hodscock MSS.

nections through marriage to place his nephew with a merchant adventurer in Newcastle.[66] Richard Hill secured the apprenticeship of his nephew, Thomas, to banker George Clifford.[67] George Trosse was recommended by his brother-in-law in London to a Portuguese merchant.[68] John Randall and William Bullwart were both helped by their uncles during their apprenticeships.[69]

Some businessmen recruited kin as their apprentices. In 1693 Samuel Heathcote took a son of his cousin apprentice, though the lad eventually became a liability.[70] John Foote, a grocer, Richard Glover, a mercer, and Robert Stubbs, a draper, all had cousins as apprentices, and Edward Westcomb had his nephew.[71] Cary Helyar took on the godson of his father and brought him to Jamaica.[72] Thomas Wallis, a vintner, accepted a son of his brother-in-law.[73] John Kendrick took two kinsmen apprentice and kept his former master, John Quarles, as his bookkeeper.[74] But merchants mainly recruited outside the family. Nathaniel Galpin and his partner relied on the local schools.[75] The number of unrelated apprentices in business families also increased in tandem with the number of surviving children.[76]

Most businessmen were therefore sent away from home to be trained by unrelated masters. Parents often chose friends or close business associates. Thomas Glover, a Dedham clothier, asked his friend Edmund Sherman to take his son apprentice and gave him the use of his son's portion until his son took his freedom.[77] But many masters were complete strangers chosen by recommendation. There are several explanations for this preference for outside training. It was thought to develop motivation and self-sufficency, whereas instruction by loving and lenient

[66] C. M. Fraser and K. Einsley, "Some Early Recorders of Newcastle," *Archaeologia Aeliana*, 4th ser., 49 (1971): 147.
[67] D. Woolley, "Thomas Hill of Tern," *Archives* 21 (1994): 156.
[68] G. Trosse, *Life*, ed. A. W. Brinks (1974), 57.
[69] Earle, *Making of the English Middle Class* (1989), 90, 92.
[70] E. D. Heathcote, *Families of Heathcote* (Winchester, 1899), 104.
[71] PCC, Cope 127, 1616; PCC, Aylett 379, 1655; PCC, Evelyn 86, 1641; PCC, Hele 73, 1626.
[72] J. H. Bennett, "Cary Helyar," *William and Mary Quarterly*, 3d ser., 21 (1964): 113.
[73] PCC, Saville 37, 1622.
[74] Stow, *Survey of London, 1720*, vol. 2, 129; J. Kendricke, *Last Will and Testament* (1625).
[75] Letter dated 10 Feb. 1699, PRO, C 104/11–12.
[76] The Pearson R correlation between numbers of children and unrelated apprentices = +0.123.
[77] *Wills of Essex Gentry and Merchants*, ed. F. G. Emmison (Chelmsford, 1978), 288, 1596.

parents was assumed to breed complacency and dependence (see also chapter 5). Fathers also wanted to broaden the range of their children's contacts, to find a prestigious master, or secure entry into a trade other than their own. Often the death of a father reduced the number of options.

CONSANGUINEOUS CAPITAL

Capital was essential to businessmen. Benjamin Bangs had to become a shoemaker because his mother lacked capital.[78] The amount of capital needed varied with each type and stage of business. Every newcomer had first to invest in his freedom, whether through outright purchase or by payment of an apprenticeship premium, then to find sufficient working capital to set up, and then muster venture capital for further expansion. Heavy industry required fixed capital; small-scale production and distribution required circulating capital, usually sunk into inventory and credit to suppliers and customers. It was also advisable to have financial reserves and assets that could serve as collateral for loans.

Capital could be acquired without cost through direct transfer within the family. A son's provision and the legacies he received from either parents or kin usually constituted a free gift, though testators might impose conditions on their bequests. Usually, however, children received only a small percentage of the family's capital while the father was alive. Capital could also be raised within and outside the family by temporary loans, by extension of credit, or by setting up partnerships with active or passive investors who took a share of the profits.

Starting capital was usually provided by the father, sometimes as an advance against the son's ultimate inheritance. William Atwood advanced his son, William, when he went to Genoa, with £1,500 of the £3,000 he had intended as his full portion.[79] Roger Pettiwood, a salter, advanced his son £2,000 and gave him an additional £1,000 in his will.[80] Nathaniel Harley, Thomas Pye, Nathaniel Hunter, James Cope, Giles Pargiter, Humphrey Chetham, Robert Saville, and Rowland Sherman were all financed by their immediate family.[81] Daniel Tanturier

---

[78] B. Bangs, *Memoirs* (1757), 10.   [79] PRO, C 109/21/1.   [80] PCC, Harvey 75, 1639.
[81] Berkshire RO, EZ5/B1; Shropshire RO, Pye MS 7 (b); PRO, SP 110/116; *Verney Family Memoirs*, ed. F. M. Verney, vol. 3 (1892–99), 374; Bod Library, DD Ashurst; PRO, C 104/11; F. R. Raines and C. W. Sutton, *Life of Chetham*, vols. 49–50 (Chetham Society, 1903); *Yorkshire Abstracts Wills*, ed. J. W. Clay, vol. 9 (Yorkshire Archaeological and Topographical Association, 1890), 14.

was set up by his father, as was Thomas Lethieullier, with £1,200.[82] George Boddington was financed by his father and in turn financed his son-in-law.[83] George Sitwell gave his son £200 to trade in Aleppo, though £1,000 was regarded as the norm.[84] George Seracole, who lived and traded with his brother, Ralph, was set up by his father with £500.[85] John Everenden and his younger brother used their portions to set up as mercers, and their kin provided them with custom.[86] Widowed mothers often funded their sons. William Clarke was financed by his widowed mother from the sale of land and was also helped by his master.[87]

A careful parent also arranged and financed entry into a partnership or firm. Edward Bellamy gave £1,000 to two Hamburg merchants to establish his son, Edward in the trade with a one-sixth share in the business after five years and one-third at expiration of the agreement.[88] William Phillips set up his son, Charles, in Turkey with £1,000 and much advice: "be thrifty and do not lend to great Turks at high rates. . . . You know my small stock at present will not permit of trading, but hereafter I hope I shall have a good opportunity of serving you that way." Phillips made sure all his sons were provided with commodities to trade and placed in partnerships.[89]

A few parents continuously injected capital or shared directly in ventures with their sons. Henry Cleev, a dyer, took his second son apprentice and gave his eldest son £200 in installments, expecting that he would "in the meantime set up his trade by himself or with some partners."[90] Richard Sherman received £2,619 from his father's estate and £80 from his mother, borrowed at 10 percent, and put £1,000 into a partnership with John Scudamore; his father also invested in his business.[91] In the Cokayne and Lowther families all the sons were set up in trades connected with their father; Sir Thomas Cokayne borrowed over £500 to

---

[82] ESRO, MS Barnes, HA 53/4090/vii; letter dated 7 Apr. 1720, BL, Add. MS 33,085.
[83] GLL, MS 10,823/1.
[84] G. Sitwell, *Letter Book 1662–66*, ed. P. Riden, vol. 10 (Derbyshire Record Society, 1985), 64; account of the estate of John Barrington, Bod Library, MS Rawlinson D 1483, fo. 20.
[85] PCC, Lee 126, 1649. [86] A. Fletcher, *A County Community* (1975), 30.
[87] P. R. Harris, "An Aleppo Merchant's Letter Book," *British Museum Quarterly* 22 (1960): 65.
[88] GLL, MS 16,823, 30 Dec. 1724.
[89] Letters dated 16 Dec. 1698, 15 Feb. 1698/9, 22 May 1699, 29 Jan. 1699/1700, 1 Sept. 1726, Folger Library, MS UB 18, fos 179–80, 188, 222.
[90] PCC, Dale 40, 1621. [91] National Maritime Museum, MS AMS/1.

trade in partnership with his father and Nicholas Pearson.[92] Robert Ashe gave his son, James, £500 toward his shop (half his stock) in return for half the profit.[93]

Although parents provided the principal funds, grandparents and siblings also helped. Richard Masters paid a £500 premium for his brother to Randolph Knipe.[94] John Gell received £1,000 from his father plus a legacy of £100 from his grandfather.[95] Edmund Bramston went to Barbados with capital he had appropriated from his younger brother's portion.[96] William Stout benefited from his father's estate, but he also used his sister's dowry of £80. The Middleton brothers, like many Bristol siblings, financed each other with loans.[97] Sir Thomas Cullum, who bought into a partnership with his master, borrowed from his stepfather and was financed by his father, his eldest brother, his sister, and his wife (through her dowry).[98]

The example of the Hudson family well illustrates how parents struggled to find capital for their children and siblings and then supervised its employment. James Hudson, who had borrowed his own seed capital from his sisters' portions, called in loans and drew on an inheritance from his brother:

Thou talks of going to America and committing thy body to the merciless waves of the sea. Is there not bread enough in England and to spare. I am willing to do what I can for thee . . . thou may pay me after or give me a note for the money . . . thou is of such a temper thou cannot deal in a little but must put thy self and others to inconvenience . . . make one half of thy wage serve thee for clothes and do not buy them so costly, one bird in the hand is worth two flying. . . . Mother and I borrowed most part sisters money to stock our selves with. . . . I desire thee not to stretch thy arm further than thy sleeve will reach. If thou sell to good prophit, length of time will increase thy stock and I desire thou give not too much credit especially to people of mean circumstances.[99]

[92] A. E. Cokayne, *Cokayne Memoranda* (privately printed, 1873), 101.
[93] PRO, C 107/20/1. Ashe bought £17,000 of cloth in six months.
[94] J. Newman, "A Very Delicate Experience" in *Industry and Finance in Early Modern History*, ed. I. Blanchard, A. Goodman, and J. Newman (Stuttgart, 1992), 123.
[95] Derbyshire RO, Gell MS D. 258/ box 16.1.
[96] J. Bramston, *Autobiography*, ed. L. Braybrook, vol. 32 (Camden Society, 1845), 22.
[97] J. W. Gough, *Sir Hugh Myddleton* (Oxford, 1964), 6–7; MacGrath, *Merchants and Merchandise*, 23.
[98] A. Simpson, *Wealth of the Gentry* (Chicago, 1961), 116–20.
[99] Letters dated 20 and 29 Oct. 1731, 8 Apr. 1732, and 10 July 1733, PRO, C 105/15.

AFFINAL CAPITAL

Kin were also a source of capital. The principal beneficiaries were nephews. James Godchall made his brother, Samuel, "my servant" trustee of the money he left to his brother's children on which Samuel had to pay 4 percent.[100] Thomas Baldwin, a merchant, left £10 to the son of Robert Garland "to buy 2 pieces of colchester bays ready to send to sea for a stock for his sonne."[101] Bachelors like Sir John How favored their nephews; Sir William Turner set up a nephew with £1,000.[102] William Jennings left £50 for starting capital for his nephew John.

In-laws and cousins were also helped financially. Richard Prowde financed his brother-in-law's voyage to the Levant.[103] Samuel Bradley was originally financed by his brother-in-law.[104] Thomas Muschamp, a grocer, placed the son of his cousin with Henry Shuttleworth of Amsterdam for seven years and gave him £50 stock and £10 p.a. maintenance "to begin the world with wishing that he may improve the same by good husbandry."[105] John Hardwin, a waxchandler, took a kinsman apprentice and bequeathed him £30 plus a share of the mill presses, provided that he help the widow.[106]

Sometimes assistance took the form of loans, often without interest or below the market rate. Debts from relations were often waived in wills as a bequest. Ralph Thrale, a brewer, had the use of his uncle's money, and Drew Mompesson borrowed capital from his relations.[107] John Fryer obtained a loan of £300 from his maternal uncle to start his shop.[108] Alexander Hosea made loans to young relations to set them up.[109] Philip Papillon hoped that his cousin would not be charged as much interest on a loan as a stranger.[110] John Priestley was financed by his aunt at 5 percent.[111] John Kempster lent his cousin, John Wilkins, the money to set up as a glassmaker.[112] Edward Harris, son-in-law of James Ashe, bor-

---

[100] PCC, Berkeley 341, 1656.   [101] PCC, Rivers 115, 1645.   [102] GLL, MS 5105.
[103] Shropshire RO, Acc 567.   [104] *New York Abstracts of Wills*, vol. 25 (1892), 366.
[105] PCC, Ruthen 64, 1657.   [106] PCC, Ruthen 162, 1657.
[107] *John Isham*, ed. G. D. Ramsay, vol. 21 (Northamptonshire Record Society, 1962), xcvi; B. A. Holderness, *Pre-Industrial England* (1976), 155.
[108] GLL, MS 12,017.   [109] Plummer, *The London Weavers Company*, 261.
[110] Letter to William Brudenell dated 2 Feb. 1702/3, KAO, MS U 1015/C17/2.
[111] J. Priestley, *Memoirs Concerning the Family of Priestley*, vol. 77 (Surtees Society, 1883), 14.
[112] PCC, Foot 79, 1687.

rowed £100 of the portion of Mary Harris.[113] James Hudson borrowed
on favorable terms from his family: "Ann says she will forgive the first
year's interest but she wants the second and I want mine. If I can get the
hats sould that will serve but have sould none of them yet. They are too
dear for this country."[114]

Uncertain trades were best financed within the family, because siblings
and kin were less likely to imprison for debt.[115] Alexander Ethersey, a
draper of Buckingham, lent money to his brother without any paper-
work.[116] The extended family spread risk, provided a cushion against
misfortune, and acted as an insurer of last resort. Kin also provided
valuable sureties for loans from third parties, for factors and writers in
India, and for transfers of stock.[117] George Warner agreed to act as
suretor despite some doubts: "I much wonder that your master should
soe soone change his resolution for certainly he was not so resolved when
he was with me. If he had he would in all likelihood have spoken to
me about it. . . . I am willing you should cast about where you may
to borrow this sum of 2,000 li and I am well content to stand your
security."[118]

Dowries were a crucial source of additional capital for businessmen
like Jonathan Priestley, John Verney, Nicholas Spencer, Maurice Gethen,
Edward Allen, Samuel Moyer, and Richard Bagnall. Peter Mitton benefited from his marriage to the daughter of Rowland Lee, and Thomas
Norris benefited from marrying the daughter of Sir Henry Garway;
Thomas Jeffereys of Exeter received both a dowry of £1,600 and an
additional £4,000 from his father-in-law.[119]

Two other sources of funding for young merchants existed that were
familial in spirit. The first was the master of an apprentice, particularly
if he left a widow or children who needed assistance. Ralph Yardley, an
apothecary, left his apprentice all the implements in his shop for three

---

[113] Cashbook, PRO, C 107/17.
[114] Letter to James Hudson from his brother, John, dated 25 Feb. 1733, PRO, C 105/15.
[115] P. Mathias, "Business History and Management Education," *Business History* 27 (1975): 10–11.
[116] *Buckinghamshire Probate Inventories, 1661–1714*, ed. M. Reed, vol. 24 (Buckingham Record Society, 1988), 299.
[117] *East India Company Calendar of Court Minutes, 1640–43*, ed. E. B. Sainsbury (1907–38), 148; ibid., *1668–70*, 376, 384–5; ibid., *1674–76*, 396–407.
[118] Letter dated 1 Nov. 1641, PRO, SP 46/83, fo. 34.
[119] T. C. Mendenhall, *Shrewsbury Drapers* (Oxford, 1953), 23; *The Norris Papers*, ed. T. Heywood, o.s., vol. 9 (Chetham Society, 1846), 10–12; Exeter City, MS 61/6/1. See also chapter 1.

Table 7.5. *Sources of Capital, 1580–1740*
(Percentage of Known Cases)

	Immediate family	Kin	Wife	Master
Percentage	41.20	10.11	41.95	6.74
Total	267			

years.[120] Paul Bayning left his apprentice, Jefferey Kirby, £100 "on condition he help my son and executor in setting straight and perfect my books and accounts."[121] Henry Canham was left £150 by his master plus £20 if he took care of the estate for nine months and collected debts.[122] William Cotesworth finished his apprenticeship with his master's widow and then borrowed her capital.[123] In 1683 William Ladds left his servant, Jacob Webster, £1,000 at 4 percent for twenty years to carry on his draper's business. Many more, such as Richard Nelthorp and Elihu Yale, received financial help from their masters. Capital was also available in small quantities from one of the numerous charitable loan funds at low or negative rates of interest. Some of these had preferences for kin: James Howell suggested that his two younger brothers "when they are out of them time may join stock together" and discovered that the Drapers Company had a loan fund for descendants of Thomas Howell.[124]

The data suggest that in London 41 percent of internally generated capital in the early years of a business came from the immediate family, 42 percent from marriage portions, 10 percent from kin, and 7 percent from masters. There are no comparable figures for other towns, though it appears that Coventry and Glasgow drew on both consanguineous and affinal capital.[125] The clothiers of Kent borrowed from relatives and the portions of orphans.[126] Despite the lack of precise data on capital flows, it is nonetheless clear that external finance was indispensable. A young merchant was normally obliged to borrow at the start, and only the richest

[120] PCC, Berkeley 18, 1656. [121] PCC, Cope 99, 1616.
[122] N. Evans, *The East Anglian Linen Industry* (Aldershot, 1985), 88.
[123] J. M. Ellis, *William Cotesworth* (1981), 5.
[124] Letter dated 30 Sept. 1629, in J. Howell, *Familiar Letters.*
[125] Berger, *Most Necessary Luxuries*, 236; Devine, *Tobacco Lords*, 97.
[126] M. Zell, "Credit in the Pre-Industrial English Woollen Industry," *Economic History Review* 49 (1996): 673–4.

extended families were self-financing. Major enterprises, like the Foley ironworks, needed outside capital either from passive lenders or passive investors. The shipping industry relied on unincorporated, joint-stocks.[127]

Money could be borrowed on the open market in several ways. Merchants could negotiate short-term credit from suppliers or delay payment up to the limit (if they were sensible) of their equity or of the credit they had advanced their customers. Alternatively they could borrow short and long term, depending on their collateral, through a variety of more formal debt instruments. Venture capital was usually raised by floating syndicates and attracting investors as silent partners; by this means, projectors had the use of other people's money without the burden of carrying any debt or the penalties for default.

Facing a cash-flow problem and in need of £1,000 to finance a ship, a partner of alderman Richard Hoare forwarded the names of sureties and supporting letters to a friend in London who was rumored to have £5,000 to invest; he had considered taking up £400 from Mr. Collier "but he is so nippy that he will not lett us owe him a penny."[128] William Clarke responded to the accounting shenanigans of the firm of Robert Main, in which he had invested, with veiled sarcasm:

> As I took an interest in your house from the motive of friendship, a full confidence in your integrity and honour and desire of promoting our mutual interest I flatter myself that you engaged and will always continue to act upon the same principles which leave noe room to doubt my receiving a full statement when it shall suit your convenience to send one. . . . I must say it is a little hard that I should be quite in the dark as to what is past and of consequence unable to determine what is proper for me to propose for the future. . . . I am at a loss to find out what is meant by the House ruling on R M stock, whether R M signifies ready money or Robert Main, but I think whatever stock was in the House must from the course of your business be there still with the addition of a handsome profit if you have not entered into engagements which I am a stranger to.[129]

PRINCIPALS

When children were apprenticed within the family, they often went into business with their fathers.[130] Sir Abraham Reynardson, John Kendall,

---

[127] R. Davis, *Rise of the English Shipping Industry* (1972), chapter 5.
[128] Letter dated 2 April 1698, PRO, C 104/11–12.
[129] Letter dated 11 Sept. 1740, ULL, MS 628, letter book of William Chalmers, fo. 4.
[130] The Pearson R correlation between the number of partners and the number of apprentices from the immediate family = +0.704.

and James Phipps formed partnerships with their sons.[131] Nicholas Mosley was in a partnership with his son, Rowland, who acted as the London agent.[132] Lionel Cranfield initially traded for his mother, father, master, and uncle, William, and was helped by his maternal grandfather, Vincent Randall.[133] William Bolton took his son into partnership in the wine trade "only for the sake of my business running on currently."[134] Several sons joined their fathers among the Shrewsbury drapers and the Chester merchants.[135] Even when they were not formally associated with their fathers, young men often entered the same trade, as was the case of Sir James Campbell, the Cokaynes, the Gores, and the Rowes.

Siblings also became partners in the Delabarr and Wright families.[136] Thomas Trenchfield, a Leghorn merchant, traded with his brother, John, as William did with John Pynchon.[137] Alexander Bisby, a salter, shared a house and warehouse with his brother.[138] John Stratford and his brother, Ralph, were partners, as was John Jennens with his brother, Ambrose, in the Birmingham iron trade.[139] Even when in separate businesses, brothers entered closely linked trades. There were five Barnardistons, seven Harveys, five Chamberlains, three Lees, and eight Howlands in the same area of trade at the same time. Brothers could share a business without living together. George Ravenscroft, a glassmaker, had two brothers in Venice as well as an uncle in Brussels.[140] Samuel Meux was a resident agent in Narva and Archangel while his brother, Thomas, stayed in London; a similar division of labor occurred in the Iberian trade.[141] Nicholas Blundell bought goods for his younger brother, Richard, in Virginia and invited him to form a joint partnership with him in Liverpool.[142]

[131] KAO, MS U 1015/F32; PRO, C 113/280.
[132] Willan, *Elizabethan Manchester*, 56–7.   [133] *H. M. C. Sackville*, vol. 1, 3.
[134] *The Bolton Letters*, ed. A. L. Simon (1928), 21.
[135] Mendenhall, *Shrewsbury Drapers*, 102; D. M. Woodward, *The Trade of Elizabethan Chester* (Hull, 1970), 110.
[136] K. R. Andrews, *Ships, Money, and Politics* (Cambridge, 1991), 52.
[137] PCC, Berkeley 352, 1656; *The Pynchon Papers*, ed. C. Bridenbaugh and J. Tomlinson, vol. 2 (Colonial Society of Massachusetts, 1985), 41.
[138] PCC, Ridley 79, 1629.
[139] J. Thirsk, *The Rural Economy of England* (1984), 265; V. C. H. *Warwick: The City of Birmingham*, ed. W. B. Stephens (1964), 83.
[140] R. Rendel, "The True Identity of George Ravenscroft," *Recusant History* 13 (1975): 102.
[141] J. Newman, "A Very Delicate Experience" in *Industry and Finance in Early Modern History*, ed. I. Blanchard, A. Goodman, and J. Newman (Stuttgart, 1992), 123; L. M. E. Shaw, *Trade Inquisition and the English Nation* (1989), 107.
[142] N. Blundell, *Diary and Letter Book, 1702–28* (Liverpool, 1952), 42, 46.

It was common for overseas merchants, like John Manifold, to trade with their kin.[143] William Sanderson had a business association with Sir Walter Raleigh who was related by marriage.[144] Thomas Wick was a partner of his brother-in-law, Clement Harby, in the Russia trade. Louis Boucher of Boston was a partner of his kinsman, Paul Boucher of London, in the shipping industry.[145] Sir John Banks was in business with his brothers-in-law, the Dethicks; Charles Dethick's dealings with his kinsmen were used as examples by John Collins in his accounting textbook.[146] In the Russian tobacco trade, William Dawson was a partner of his brother-in-law, Samuel Heathcote, and John Gould of his two brothers-in-law; William Brown was the London correspondent of his cousin, Adam Montgomery, a merchant in Stockholm.[147] John Burnell and Peter Ent traded with their brothers-in-law.[148] When William Freeman returned from the West Indies, he formed a partnership with his brother-in-law.[149] Walter Atwood had a one-third share in a joint stock with his brother-in-law, Walter Hampton, and handled business for his cousin, Thomas Atwood, a Russia merchant.[150] Twenty families had multiple members in the Morea joint stock; partnerships between kin recur frequently in the port books.[151]

Trading among kin was also quite common in the domestic trades.[152] Philip Henslowe's partner in the entertainment business was his son-in-law, Edward Alleyn.[153] Richard Bagnall's long-term partner in the salter's trade was his brother-in-law, Lemuel Leppington.[154] In King's Lynn Thomas Grave was in business with his son-in-law, and William Atkin

---

[143] Letter dated 14 April 1666, BL, India Office Home Misc., MS H/40/54, fo. 58.
[144] R. A. MacIntyre, "William Sanderson," *William and Mary Quarterly*, 3d ser., 12 (1956): 190.
[145] B. and L. Bailyn, *Massachusetts Shipping, 1697–1714* (Cambridge, Mass., 1959), 73.
[146] D. C. Coleman, *Sir John Banks* (Oxford, 1963), 80; O. Kojima, "Accounting Textbooks," *Accounting Historian's Journal* 4 (1977): 73.
[147] J. M. Price, *The English Tobacco Adventure to Russia* (Transactions of the American Philosophical Society, 1961), 16, 106.
[148] S. E. Astrom, *From Cloth to Iron* (Helsingfors, 1963), 122, 137; H. Zins, *England and the Baltic* (Manchester, 1972), 104; PCC, Rivers 118, 1645.
[149] C. and R. Bridenbaugh, *No Peace beyond the Line* (New York, 1972), 322.
[150] PRO, C 109/21/1.
[151] G. L. Ambrose, "The Levant Company" (B. Litt. thesis, University of Oxford, 1933), 102; N. J. Williams, *The Maritime Trade of the East Anglian Ports, 1550–1590* (Oxford, 1988), 187–9, 202.
[152] Willan, *The Inland Trade*, 108.
[153] J. H. Forse, *Art Imitates Business* (Bowling Green, Ohio, 1993), 47.
[154] D. Dawes, *Skillbecks Drysalters, 1650–1950* (1950), 18.

Table 7.6. *Number and Origin of Partners, 1580–1740*
(Percentage of Known Cases)

	1 partner	2 partners	3 + partners	Total Partners
Immediate Family	44.96	32.14	23.42	41.46
Kin	9.81	11.79	3.80	9.61
Unrelated	45.22	56.07	72.79	48.92
Total	1,559	280	158	1,997

with his brother-in-law and his father-in-law.[155] Edmund Hopegood was in a partnership with both his son and son-in-law.[156] George Hanger had £200 invested in the Irish Adventurers in association with his son-in-law.[157] Humphrey Chetham was closely involved with his brother-in-law as well as his brothers.[158] Francis Griffin, a merchant tailor, formed a partnership with his nephew.[159] Daniel Tiberkin, a silkman and dyer, lived with two sons-in-law, one of whom was also a dyer.[160] Thomas Walter was in a sugar partnership with his mother-in-law and brother-in-law.[161] Abraham Dashwood traded with his brother-in-law, John Parsons.[162]

Almost half of partners were, however, outsiders. Although the documentation on partnerships is limited, 10 percent of known partners (1580–1740) were kin, 42 percent were immediate family members, and 49 percent were outsiders; individuals in multiple partnerships were usually unrelated. Numerous businessmen established themselves without dealing with their kin. Richard Fishborne, a mercer, for example, was apprenticed to Baptist Hicks and then traded with John Browne, a merchant tailor.

Some businessmen relied on their masters to begin business ventures.

---

[155] G. A. Metters, "The Rulers and Merchants of King's Lynn," (Ph.D. diss., University of East Anglia, 1982), 284–8.

[156] PCC, Ent 177, 1689.

[157] PCC, Fairfax 77, 1649.

[158] F. R. Raines and C. Sutton, vol. 49, *Life of Humphrey Chetham* (Chetham Society, 1903), 15; A. P. Wadsworth and J. De L. Mann, *The Cotton Trade and Industrial Lancashire, 1600–1780* (Manchester, 1931), 29.

[159] PCC, Rivers 146, 1645. [160] Boulton, *Neighbourhood and Society*, 79.

[161] PCC, Wootton 5, 1657.

[162] Account general of Parsons and Dashwood, PRO, C 110/158.

Richard Farrington served eight years with Thurstan Withnall and "then entered into copartnership with him which continued together until . . . it pleased God to take out of this world my loving master."[163] Thomas Papillon, who had been apprenticed to a distant relation, was first agent of and then partner with his master.[164] But many others found a suitable long-term partner among their friends in the business world or fell back on multiple short-term associations, as was common in the Levant. James Smythe, a salter, was in business with his son, but he also formed a partnership with four other merchants for three years to trade in logwood.[165]

AGENTS

Fathers employed their eldest and, more commonly, their younger sons as their overseas factors.[166] George Sitwell had two sons serving overseas, whom he treated with patient care, as well as several cousins acting for him within the country.[167] Sir Thomas Earle had one son in Bilbao, William Colston one in Marseille and one in Lisbon, George Lane one son and a kinsman in Portugal.[168] The Lowther family had Richard in Holland, Christopher in Seville, two sons in Ireland and Germany, and uncle Robert in London.[169] Gilbert Heathcote remained in London with his sons, William and Gilbert Jr. but Samuel went to Danzig, George died at sea, John and Josiah resided in the West Indies, and Caleb was in New York. Two of the four sons of Sir Henry Lee were in the wine trade, like their father. Of Richard Hoare's sons, John was in Genoa, James in Amsterdam, and Richard in Hamburg.[170] William Colston the elder of Bristol had five sons working in Spain.[171] Sons also served as agents in London for provincial merchants, like Thomas Marsden of Bolton.[172]

[163] GLL, MS 2708.
[164] Papillon, Memoirs, passim.   [165] Tripartite indenture, PRO, C 112/4, 24 Sept. 1647.
[166] C. M. Wilson, Anglo-Dutch Commerce and Finance (Cambridge, 1941; reprint 1977), 28.
[167] G. Sitwell, Letter Book, 1662–66, ed. P. Riden, vol. 10 (Derbyshire Record Society, 1985), xxviii, xxxiii.
[168] MacGrath, Merchants and Merchandise, xvi–xvii.
[169] Hainsworth, "Lowther Younger Sons," 152, 156; C. Lowther, Commercial Papers, 1611–44, ed. D. R. Hainsworth, vol. 189 (Surtees Society, 1977), 43.
[170] K. Woodbridge, "Accounts Rendered," History Today 19 (1969): 784.
[171] J. Latimer, Annals of Bristol in the Seventeenth Century (Bristol, 1900), 409; T. Garrard, Edward Colston (Bristol, 1852), 5.
[172] Wadsworth and Mann, Cotton Trade, 8, 94.

Siblings also acted as agents for each other. Three Lambtons worked together in the private trade to India in 1667, and the Hardwicke family had representatives in Brazil, Italy, and India.[173] Thomas Parker, a skinner, had a brother in Rotterdam, a brother in New England, and several kinsmen as apprentices.[174] Richard Povey was in Jamaica and his brother William in Barbados, both acting for Thomas and Martin Noell; there were three Heyshams and two Goulds in the Barbados trade.[175] Charles Barcroft, a London merchant, joined his brother in Virginia in 1636 and then became a factor.[176] Paul Bayning took his brother, Andrew, apprentice and made him his agent in Spain.[177] In the Priestley family several brothers worked together in the textile trade, and John was sent to London as a Blackwell Hall factor.[178] Hercule, Thomas, and James Coutts were distributed between London, Newcastle, and New York.[179]

Kin acted even more frequently as correspondents. In Northern Europe, Thomas Wingrave was factor in Dantzig for Robert Wingrave; the Maisters of Hull had kinsmen as factors in Stockholm.[180] Samuel Avery's brother and father-in-law acted together in the Hamburg trade, and the Bladwells did the same in the Russia trade. Thomas Hill corresponded with Samuel Hill in Amsterdam.[181] Edinburgh merchants had relatives as factors in Spain and Norway.[182]

In the Mediterranean trades Thomas James went to San Lucar, while his brother stayed in London.[183] George Ball was based in Genoa with his two nephews, Robert and Thomas, at Leghorn.[184] The Levant was

---

[173] R. Maloni, *European Merchant Capital and the Indian Economy* (New Delhi, 1992), 423; A. H. R. Johnson, *History Company Drapers*, vol. 4 (Oxford, 1914–22), appendix 48, 503.

[174] PCC, Rivers 21, 1644.

[175] L. M. Penson, *The Colonial Agents of the British West Indies* (1924), 13; N. Tattersfield, *The Forgotten Trade* (1991), 16, 30; R. B. Sheridan, *Sugar and Slavery*, 2d ed. (Kingston, 1994), 283.

[176] J. Horn, "To Parts Beyond" in *To Make America*, ed. I. Altman and J. Horn (Berkeley, 1991), 87.

[177] R. G. Lang, "Greater Merchants," 84.

[178] Priestley, *Memoirs*, 11, 19.

[179] T. C. Smout, *Scottish Trade on the Eve of Union* (1963), 80.

[180] S. E. Astrom, *From Cloth to Iron* (Helsingfors, 1963), 122, 137; H. Zins, *England and the Baltic* (Manchester, 1972), 104.

[181] Letter dated 12 Sept. 1664, BL, Add. MS 5489.

[182] M. H. B. Sanderson, "The Edinburgh Merchants" in *The Renaissance and Reformation in Scotland*, ed. I. B. Cowan and D. Shaw (Edinburgh, 1983), 191.

[183] A. J. Loomie, "Thomas James," *Recusant History* 11 (1972): 167.

[184] A. E. J. Hollaender, "A London Merchant's Letter Book," *Archives* 3 (1957): 36.

awash with kinsmen: four Bettons, at least six Williams, three Metcalfs, and one Edwards at Aleppo and four at Smirna.[185] Thomas Pengelly traded with his uncle, Thomas Davis, and with two cousins.[186] William Blois's agent in Marseille was John Baker, whose partner was his cousin.[187] William Atwood employed a kinsman, William Halford, as his factor in Venice.[188] Nathaniel Torriano, Sr., worked closely with his brother-in-law, Daniel Renew, with Peter Renew "father-in-law and best of friends," and with his cousin, John Rogerson.[189]

In the Atlantic family networks connected England, New England, and the West Indies. Many migrated to regions where they had relatives; kinship gave coherence to expatriate communities. Many members of the Newfoundland Company were interrelated. The Pepperells of Piscataqua came from Devon via the Newfoundland fisheries.[190] John Dellbridge of Barnstable employed his nephew as a factor in Bermuda, and Richard Dodderidge had a son-in-law in the Guinea trade.[191] Bermuda and Barbados settlers and merchants traded jointly with their kin in England.[192] Richard Hutchinson was in London, and his brothers and nephews were in Boston.[193] John Hull traded with his uncle and cousins in England, and Valentine Hill served as a Boston agent for his brother in London.[194] The Codrington family were distributed between England, Barbados, and New York. Henry Corbin emigrated to Virginia, while his two brothers stayed in London as merchants.[195] William Ball went to Virgina with his two younger sons, and his eldest

---

[185] Grassby, "Love, Property, and Kinship," 340; PRO, SP 10/14.

[186] Letters dated 19 March 1657 and 24 Jan. 1659/60, Bod Library, Add. MS C 267.

[187] Account book of William Blois, ESRO, HA 30/787.

[188] Letter dated 30 Nov. 1682, PRO, C 109/23/2.

[189] Journal and letter dated 7 Dec. 1717, PRO, C 112/24.

[190] B. Fairchild, *Messrs Pepperell* (Ithaca, 1954), 8; G. T. Cell, *English Enterprise in Newfoundland* (Toronto, 1969), 55.

[191] A. Grant, "Breaking the Mould" in *Tudor and Stuart Devon*, ed. T. Gray, M. Rowe, and A. Erskine (Exeter, 1993), 126, 132.

[192] Bermuda Archives, Colonial Records, MS II, 231; G. A. Puckrein, *Little England* (New York, 1984), 210; K. G. Davies, "The Origins of the Commission System," *Transactions of the Royal Historical Society*, 5th ser., 2 (1952): 91.

[193] J. R. Perry, *The Formation of a Society on Virginia's Eastern Shore, 1615–1655* (Chapel Hill, 1990), 144; Horn, "To Parts Beyond," 86, 106–9, 117; B. Bailyn, "Communications and Trade," *Journal of Economic History* 13 (1953): 380, and *idem., The New England Merchants* (1955; reprint New York, 1964), 35, 82, 87, 135–7; R. C. Ritchie, "London Merchants," *New York History* 57 (1976): 18.

[194] E. S. Morgan, *The Puritan Family* (New York, 1966), 155; Cressy, *Coming Over*, 204, 268; H. F. Clarke, *John Hull* (Portland, 1940), 102; R. Thompson, *Mobility and Migration* (Amherst, 1994), 65.

[195] J. Horn, *Adapting to a New World* (Chapel Hill, 1994), 61, 181.

stayed in England as an agent.[196] Nathan Levy was based in New York with Moses Levy and his nephews, Samuel and Isaac, resided in London; he also traded with his brother-in-law, Joseph, his uncle, Oliver, and his father-in-law.[197] Maurice Thompson was at the center of a complex web of kin with worldwide interests.[198] The Atlantic tobacco trade was organized through networks of kin, like the Perrys and the Glasgow merchants.[199]

The same was true of internal trades, like cutlery, ironmongery, book-selling, or brewing.[200] The clothiers of Manchester were linked by marriage with each other and with London.[201] James Pillston of Manchester supplied his cousin, a London haberdasher, with cottons.[202] The Yorkshire cloth dresser and factor, John Lister, and his son sent their wares to a cousin in London.[203] Thomas Hollis was apprenticed to his uncle and acted as his London agent.[204] Shipmasters in the Wirral were all related.[205] Samuel Cust's eldest daughter married John Freeman, Jr., who acted as London agent for his father-in-law.[206] The apothecaries of Norwich cooperated with their relatives in London.[207] John Aylward worked with his brother-in-law, James Carter.[208] Thomas Bowrey let one of his shops to a kinsman furnishing goods as a starting inventory; the tenant paid 11 pence daily but retained the profit on sales, though not the capital supplied by Bowrey.[209] Samuel Jeake sold goods through his

---

[196] N. T. Mann, "William Ball Merchant," *Northern Neck Virginia Historical Magazine* 23 (1973): 2646.

[197] PRO, C 104/13–14. In Albany, in contrast, sons-in-law were accepted in artisan trades more commonly than in business: see S. Bielinski, "A Middle Sort," *New York History* 73 (1992): 273–5.

[198] J. R. Pagan, "Growth of the Tobacco Trade," *Guildhall Studies in London History* 3 (1979): 260; J. E. Farnell, "The Navigation Act of 1651," *Economic History Review* 2d ser., 16 (1964): 454; K. R. Andrews, *Ships, Money, Politics* (Cambridge, 1991), 52.

[199] J. M. Price, *Perry of London* (Cambridge, Mass., 1992), 1, 13; Devine, *Tobacco Lords*, 11.

[200] A. Everitt, *Landscape and Community in England* (1985), 311; D. G. Hey, *Fiery Blades* (Leicester, 1974), 228; P. G. Mathias, *The Transformation of England* (1979), 210; G. Mandelbrote, "From the Warehouse to the Counting House" in *A Genius for Letters*, ed. R. Myers and M. Harris (Winchester, 1995), 51; M. B. Rowlands, *Masters and Men* (Manchester, 1975), 112.

[201] Willan, "Manchester Clothiers," 178–81.

[202] Wadsworth and Mann, *Cotton Trade*, 8, 94; Willan, *Elizabethan Manchester*, 56–7.

[203] J. Smail, *The Origins of Middle-Class Culture* (1995), 55.

[204] Hey, *Fiery Blades*, 158.

[205] D. Woodward, "Shipmasters of the Wirral," *Mariners Mirror* 43 (1977): 243.

[206] E. and L. Cust, *Records of the Cust Family* (1898–1927), 169.

[207] M. Pelling, "Apothecaries of Norwich," *Pharmaceutical Historian* 13 (1983): 7.

[208] Letter from John Fortrey dated 23 Oct. 1702, Bod Library, MS Eng. Lett. C. 192.

[209] Articles of agreement between Bowrey and James and Martha Davis, GLL, MS 3041/1.

relations in London, and Jonathan Scott distributed his wines through his brother-in-law in Shropshire.[210] The London contact of Richard Showell, a Banbury mercer, was his brother-in-law, John Tanner, a grocer.[211]

The majority of associates, agents, and regular customers were not, however, kin.[212] Many of the factors employed by Elizabethan merchants were strangers.[213] Only 6.5 percent of merchants registered in the 1633–5 London heraldic Visitation entered relatives in the same branch of trade.[214] Businessmen were exceedingly clannish, but the sheer size of the market made it inevitable that most of their contacts would be friends and acquaintances, not kin. Merchants were obliged to rely on brokers and other intermediaries, selected by referral, to employ outsiders as agents and employees. The Foleys hired John Wheeler as their managing director and salesman at an annual salary of £100.[215] Joshua Holland explained to Isaac Herd: "if they deale abroad they cannot expect to have persons of the Company to serve them, soe they must make use of Managers."[216] Local, regional, and distant kin networks were essential to absorb immigrants and help beginners. Ambitious entrepreneurs, however, moved beyond their families to seize the opportunities of a wider market.

The indexes to the ledgers of businessmen demonstrate the predominance of outsiders. William Atwood listed ten kin among 193 correspondents. Among the twenty-nine clients in the ledger of an Aleppo factor, twelve were sons of Levant merchants, but none were obviously kin.[217] Of the 457 individuals listed by Henry Phill, only three were relations.[218] Richard Hill listed his brother and seven kin among the seventy-seven names in his books.[219] The major transactions of Robert Ashe were with James Ashe, clothier of Westcombe, John Ashe, clothier of Freshford, Edward and Jonathan Ashe, in Paris, and

[210] Letter dated 17 Jan. 1710, Shropshire RO 49/637.
[211] Banbury Wills and Inventories, ed. E. R. C. Brinkworth and J. S. W. Gibson, vol. 14 (Banbury Historical Society, 1976), 214.
[212] Although the data on employees is too sparse to tabulate, a trend is evident.
[213] Willan, Studies in Elizabethan Foreign Trade, 31.
[214] Grant, "The Gentry of London," 91.
[215] Schafer, "Genesis and Structure," 32.
[216] Letter dated 12 May 1696, PRO, C 104/11–12.
[217] Bod Library, MS Rawl D. 1483, 1682–90.
[218] PRO, C 111/127/1.   [219] BL, Add. MS 5488.

his son, James, in London, but he had 129 substantial clients.[220] Charles Blunt traded with his cousin, John, acted as investment banker for another cousin, and mentioned three other kin; but he treated his relatives exactly like his other 104 clients.[221] Richard Archdale listed 115 names but no obvious kin.[222] An anonymous merchant trading to Germany (1617–18) traded with sixty-seven individuals, none identified as kin.[223] John Hill, whose partner was George Legatt, listed forty-six English clients and correspondents, but no kin.[224] George Warner recorded one uncle, one cousin, one brother, and one brother-in-law among almost one hundred names in his account book.[225] None of the forty-two names in the letter book of Matthew Ashton were obvious kin.[226] Charles Peers records the names of seven relations, including his brother-in-law, Anthony Reynolds in Malaga, but his index contained 350 names.[227]

THE VALUE OF FAMILY

Family members did not always meet expectations. Disputes generated harsh words and recrimination: "I thank God I have a Kinsman's heart to you though you have not had a faithful and friendly Kinsman's tongue toward me."[228] William Phillips wrote to his brother: "I chide you now because I hope twill have the effect of making you a better correspondent . . . put yourself boldly into the business as soon as you can."[229] One disappointed correspondent expostulated: "I could hardly have thought it possible for any man of trade or credit to have failed of his promise for now allmost four months together in sending the coppy of an account. . . . I never found such treatment from either your father or uncle."[230] Isaac Lawrence was peeved by a relative, whose husband had invested (and lost money) and who complained to him: "I have given both to her and my father an ample and large account of his square deal-

[220] PRO, C 107/20/1. [221] PRO, C 114/164–5.
[222] Journal dated 1623–30, GLL, MS 23,953.
[223] KAO, MS U 119/A1. [224] KAO, MS U 1515/02.
[225] Account book dated 1638–43, PRO, SP 46/85.
[226] Bod Library, MS Eng misc. C. 563.
[227] GLL, MS 10,188/1. [228] Morgan, *Puritan Family*, 157.
[229] Letter dated 16 Dec. 1698, Folger Library, MS UB 18.
[230] Letter dated 5 Oct. 1710, PRO, C 104/11–12.

ings with me which I doubt will make her frett, though it be nothing but the simple truth."[231]

There was frequent in-fighting between relations over management.[232] Transferring control of a business from father to son was a delicate process with complex psychological aspects. Henry Morse accused his father of incompetence: "I need not tell you how great a misfortune it is to think of such an estate being ruined by his governing contrary to the advice of all his factors."[233] Samuel Dashwood responded angrily to his brother who sought sole management of their business by challenging Samuel's figures and his expenses.[234] Sir Samuel Moyer, in his will of 1716, refers to his brother's "querulous demands" regarding his books. Samuel Marriott was chastised by his family when he decided to lend to the City Corporation instead of investing in his brother's hosiery and iron-mongery business.[235] Michael Blackett thought his uncle acted too much on his own: "I do take notice how you have carried on the business . . . but you do drive things so to the last that I know not what to say."[236] John Paige quarreled with his partner and father-in-law "like two lovers."[237]

Kin could be financially unreliable and become a burden, requiring loans and handouts; to give sureties was to assume a considerable risk (see also chapter 6). Sir John Moore was approached by Richard Moore for a surety for a bond, and, when he declined to answer, Richard wrote to his cousin asking him to intercede; Richard's cousin replied that he did not want to become involved.[238] Wilfrid Hudleston's business was damaged by his eldest brother's irresponsibility.[239] Thomas Starkey claimed, in a bill of 1592, that he had been defrauded by his son-in-law, who had traded on his stock, withheld his goods, and then slandered him.[240] Thomas D'Aeth had difficulty extracting money he was owed by

[231] Letter to his brother, William, 30 Nov. 1677, BL, India Office, Eur MS 387/C, fo. 23.
[232] PCC, Romney 183; letter from John Heal dated 21 April 1671, PRO, SP 110/113.
[233] Letter to George Radcliffe dated 28 May 1715, GLL, MS 6645.
[234] Letter dated 5 July 1690, Bod Library, MS Dashwood A/1.
[235] A narrative of S. Marriott dated 1728, Bod Library, MS Rawlinson D 114.
[236] CUL, Add. MS 91, fo. 39.
[237] J. Paige, *The Letters, 1648–58*, ed. G. F. Steckley, vol. 21 (London Record Society, 1984), xxii, xxxiv.
[238] Shropshire RO, MS 4572, 2/16.
[239] G. P. Jones, "Wilfrid Hudleston," *Transactions of the Cumberland and Westmoreland Archaeological Society* 67 (1967): 188.
[240] Willan, *Studies in Elizabethan Foreign Trade*, 289–92.

Charles Balle from his brother, Robert Balle, at Livorno.[241] John Gell had to deal with his bankrupt cousin, William Bradley, a Manchester chapman, who went to Virginia; he also warned his father that his cousin, Wrigley, was "not to be trusted with the cash . . . all the while that his master was out of town he followeth cocks and gaming and when his master came home he ran away and lay at a tavern 2 or 3 nights. . . . I suppose he has gamed away some of his master's money."[242]

The most frequent source of trouble was indebtedness. Hillary Hill expressed "my true love to you and to my cosen and to my little cozen" and then made excuses for the late payment of what he owed: "I do promise you that at the spring I will pay part of it."[243] Paul Rycaut found himself £700 in debt because of his nephew and apprentice, James Rycaut.[244] Author Daniel Defoe had to be bailed out by his mother-in-law.[245] Ezekiell Hall claimed that he would settle his own debts out of "£10,000 standing out at the Canaries and when peace comes with Spain," but he reneged on the debts of his brother and partner: "will not pay one farthing of his brother's debts as to Insurance, neither has any body entered any actions against him for his brother died not worth a groat so that it is but good moneys thrown after bad."[246] Deborah Clarke apologized for a loss from a debtor: "we had not cause for suspicion at the time. . . . I am certain he acted for thy interests as for his own in that and all the concernes between you and as thou had noe reason to think otherwise in his life its my hope thy friendship wont cease now he is gone".[247]

Nonetheless the services of kinsmen were indispensable. In long, risky overseas trades, merchants needed correspondents and agents who would honor their obligations and pay their debts. In all trades businessmen were much more comfortable when they could deal with a kinsman no matter how distant: "if thou hath a mind to deal in hats there is a man that married cousin Manuel Clemensons daughter thats a hatter which I would advise thee to deal with."[248] One merchant confessed his poor judgment in selecting a stranger rather than his

---

[241] Letter dated 29 Sept. 1704, GLL, MS 9563.
[242] Letter dated 18 Apr. 1675, Derbyshire RO, Gell MSS D 258/Box 31/34/t, 34/B.
[243] Letter dated 30 Jan. 1666/7, BL, Add. MS 5488.
[244] Anderson, *English Consul*, 100.
[245] P. R. Backscheider, *Daniel Defoe* (Lexington, 1986), 50.
[246] Letters to William Procter dated 10 and 19 Oct. 1704, GLL, MS 11, 892A.
[247] Letter dated 24 Sept. 1733, PRO, C 105/15.
[248] Letter dated 9 Sept. 1731, PRO, C 105/15.

cousin: "Mr Ellis and I are parted. If he and I can agree on reasonable terms I shall go on and design to let you in. . . . I regret I did not take you in instead of Ellis he has every way deceived me."[249] William Byrd was prepared to trust a Barbados merchant whose brother was known to him.[250]

The core of any business relationship was always trust. Thomas Pelham warned of the danger of "ill reputation with the trading part of the world among whom your dealing chiefly lye."[251] Hugh Hassall, who had waited eight years in vain for an order to be filled by a Barbados merchant, said that he "never yet was as good as his word."[252] Dishonesty and fraud were still seen as moral failings, as is evident in this judgment by John Hudson on Robert Jackson: "I think him as wicked a man as lives here about. Our father and my self have lost many pounds by him. Be no more conserned neither for him nor anie belonging to him nor nobody else except some friend that thou may trust. Let this be a warning to thee for the future."[253]

Long-range credit required more than neighborly trust; the legal machinery for enforcing obligations became more effective and was more frequently employed as the market expanded.[254] But unfair bargains were inherently unstable, and morality came into play whenever the market failed.[255] John Lloyd, in a dispute with Clement Nicholson over twenty hogsheads of tobacco consigned by his brother, invoked morality as well as the law: "Let me tell you sir, plain dealing is best. . . . I doe assume in case you doe not very soon render to me a more satisfactory account I shall give you trouble and if soe, I fear disgrace will attend."[256] Many businessmen disliked the cost, the uncertainties, and the time-wasting intricacies of litigation. Although debtors could be sued for loss of property, suits of trespass upon the case only had the status of oral contracts.[257] It is not surprising, therefore, that business-

---

[249] Undated letter to Captain Blackburn, C110/140.
[250] *Correspondence of the Three William Byrds of Westover, Virginia*, ed. M. Tinling (Charlottesville, 1977), 106.
[251] Letter dated 20 Sept. 1718, BL, Add. MS 33,085.
[252] PCC, Hyde 148, 1665.   [253] Letter dated 9 Feb. 1732, PRO, C 105/15.
[254] C. Muldrew, "Interpreting the Market," *Social History* 18 (1993): 183; *idem., The Economy of Obligation* (1998), conclusion.
[255] D. Gauthier, *Morals by Agreement* (Oxford, 1986), 197; J. S. Kraus, *The Limits of Hobbesian Contractarianism* (Cambridge, 1993), 318.
[256] Letter dated 4 Oct. 1698, PRO, C 107/161.
[257] Muldrew, "Interpreting the Market," 180.

men preferred to reconcile differences through the kinship network, which had established procedures for claims without recourse to law.[258] Contracts were often considered less reliable than ties of blood and marriage.

Kinsmen could be counted on for many different favors. Captain Blackburn told Henry Ashton: "I have given your services to Mr Prater and acquainted him of the particular regard you will have for his kinsman."[259] Failing businesses were rescued by kinsmen, as in the Radcliffe and Papillon families.[260] Matthew Ashton begged his brother to keep him afloat while he tried to negotiate a composition of 50 percent with his creditors:

If you refuse to help me I must either beg or take up some imploy which may shorten my days being I cannot longer subsist without assistance. Therefore dear brother do good whilst it is in your power and let not the remembrance of my misfortune hinder your benevolence but do good against evil that good may come thereof and I kept imployed by your charitableness in my profession . . . your poor brother who hath noe other friends to depend on but you.[261]

The obligations of kinship could also be invoked by elderly, widowed, and retired businessmen. The widowed Sir John Moore in old age relied on his nephew and cousin.[262] William Atwood was expected to provide his retired father-in-law with current investment advice:

I should be glad you would write me more largely something of the times. Though you goe but seldome to london yet you are near and hear more than I can, whether all our debts at London be not very doubtful if not desperate and what you think of Sir Robert Vyner, Richard Thorowgood, Jacob Strange Mathew Carleton the East India Company, the Company of merchants . . . [and] the king's debt upon the security we have. Trewly I looke upon my personal estate as very uncertain and my real estate in Chester . . . is my chief prop.[263]

[258] Muldrew, "Culture of Reconciliation," 937; C. Tilly, "Family History," *Journal of Family History* 12 (1987): 327.
[259] Letters dated 21 June 1730 and 20 Jan. 1730/1, C 110/140.
[260] Letter from Henry Morse to George Radcliff dated 28 May 1712, Hertfordshire RO, Radcliffe MSS; KAO, MS U 1015/C6/3.
[261] Letter 1 Aug. 1687, Bod Library, MS Eng misc. C. 602.
[262] GLL, MS 3504.   [263] Letter dated 16 Oct. 1666, PRO, C 109/23/1.

CONNECTION

Some businessmen, like Michael Mitford, liked to think that their success was due entirely to their own enterprise, as he explained to his apprentice who was acting as his factor abroad:

I am sorry you say you have not earnt bread to your mouth. I am sure I paid for your maintenance till you came to be in Company with Mr Mallabar and a man for your selfe and if you cannot earn your bread abroad I question if ever you will doe it at home. However, if you are weary of your station, you may come home to me again. I have both bread for you to eat and work for you to do, so long as you are under covenant with me I will perform the part of an honest master to you but for shame let it never be said that you cant earn your bread. For if so you are a very silly idle fellow. Would you have bread brought to your bed and stopt into your mouth. Noe surely. I hope you doe not yet play so much the sluggard. You are in a plentiful country for bread and a diligent man that will seek it may find it. I thank God I found mine there and never had the tenth part of your estate from my parents to help me to it, neither the advantage of any recommendation to be brought into a comptoir of business to shew me any way or method as you have had and yet could find out a way and means to earn bread to my mouth.[264]

In fact, business was based on connection. Every region had its own networks, based on family, marriage, and religion and usually organized around specific commodities, with a division of labor between family members. In the records of many trades and ports the same names recur over several generations. Those with connections had a decisive advantage. Family cartels controlled trades, passed on clients and properties, circulated advice, controlled information, and maintained secrecy. In the victualling trades, export licenses for food were resold between brothers and sons; international commerce was built on personal contacts initially developed at the local level.[265] Access to markets, principals, agents, and suppliers depended on referral, patronage, and clientage. An alliance of kinsmen could corner a market more effectively than a simple partnership or syndicate of individuals. Cousinage and the group solidarity of family networks linked different sectors of the economy.

The most important task for any new businessman was creating a network of business associates and a client base. William Phillips, when

[264] Letter to John Lowther at Dantzig dated 21 Oct. 1703, GLL, MS 11,892A.
[265] A. Everitt, "The Marketing of Agricultural Produce" in *The Agrarian History of England IV, 1500–1640*, ed. J. Thirsk (Cambridge, 1967), 513, 523, 530–1.

he left the Wood *ragione*, had to find new principals but was confident that "I have friends at home that are able to support and make me a house of a good business"; he was later able to help his brother when he was sent to Turkey.[266] Matthew Ashton approached John Mann of York: "if you have a minde to make a triall of me, I will use my utmost endeavour to give you all the satisfaction our market will afford both in the sale of your dozens or any other sort of goods."[267] Michael Mitford encouraged his cousin, Henry Norris, who was in his first year abroad, to build his own trade beyond his master:

It is the tarr trade that there hath been money got by this year, as for the iron trade, it hath been a certain loss to us and for wire it is a very dull commodity so that I have had no encouragement to give you any commissions last summer and soe long as iron is soe dear with you and cheap with us you find but little commissions . . . however let me desire the favour of you if you can procure any pitch or tar especially the latter. . . . I will not give your Master to find any more fault with you for the buying any pitch and tarr for me as he did for the last parcel you bought for Mr Collet and me though I think it is very unreasonable in him to think you must not have the liberty to serve any but him, for you will and must have occasion to create your selfe as many friends as you can for it is not by him alone you will be able to live. Your letters to Mr Wm Benson I have delivered who you know hath no great respect for your Master but saith when his son comes home, he may give you for my sake some part of his business.[268]

Businesses were built through kinsmen. In 1700 John White (and his partner, Nicholas Geraldine) approached his kinsman, John Aylward, for business, expressing his disgust that his principals had prohibited them from taking commissions on trade or trading on their own account: "Finding us not in a condition to set up for ourselves . . . doe oblige us to what they please. . . . I have thought to settle my self alone tho I begin with a small matter."[269] Family news was often mingled with offers of business:

We should be glad to hear from thee and we desire that thee would write a few lines to brother John Nicholson in York and acquaint him that his mother and

---

[266] Letters dated 25 Feb. 1695/6 and 26 Aug. 1698, Folger Library, MS UB. 18; see also S. Whyman, "Land and Trade Revisited," *London Journal* 22 (1997): 22.

[267] Letter dated 4 July 1682, Bod Library, MS Eng misc. C. 563.

[268] Letter to his cousin, Henry Norris, in Stockholm dated 1 Feb. 1703/4, GLL, MS 11,892A.

[269] Letter dated 3 Feb. 1700, Bod Library, MS Eng lett. C. 192.

sisters and her husband and children is as before. . . . [We are in a] very good way of business with the cooper trade and shopkeeping. We have been marryed above 3 years and have two children a girl about 2 years ould and a boy about two months ould and their names is Rebecka and Isaac and we desire a small favour of thee if you wilt take the trouble to buy some hobnayles and send us the prime cost per Thousand . . . and we would do any service for thee heare if it be in our power for we buyes abundance of goods and we and thee might do service to each other in the way of trade if thee was free to it. So no more at presant but our kind love to thee and to cousen peeter Hudson and his wife and cosin Jane Wilson and to our relations in Cumberland.[270]

Business careers were also advanced by family patronage. John Cutler of Ipswich was linked by kinship with the merchants of Norwich and had a cousin who was secretary of the Eastland Company.[271] Charles Blunt, whose son, Samuel, was in the Irish trade, recommended a cousin for a post in the East India Company, though when pressed later for additional help he replied, "I live in the country and do not trouble my self with business as formerly and therefore can noe way help."[272] William Hill sought a favor from his cousin for his son; John Fleet, Gilbert Heathcote, and Nathaniel Hern wrote on behalf of Daniel Mann as a favor to his father.[273] Baptist Hicks benefited in his trade from the political influence of his brother, Michael.[274] Alderman John Langley saved his son, Richard, from discipline by the Levant Company and obtained the treasurership for him, which he then abused.[275] William Farrington's uncle agreed to consign 20,000 lion dollars to Vernon and Company if they admitted his nephew.[276]

The limitations of family networks must, however, be noted. Some areas and types of business required large-scale, permanent institutions. It was not feasible or cost effective for a family to provide all the services of a company, nor could business be conducted exclusively within the family. The Foleys, for example, made cartel agreements with other ironmasters to establish marketing territories. The success of any businessman was heavily influenced by his master, by his company, and by

[270] Letter from Philadelphia dated 15 Sept. 1731, PRO, C 105/15. There is a hole in the center of the letter.
[271] H. F. Waters, *Genealogical Gleanings in England* (Salem, Mass., 1892), 175.
[272] Letters dated 18 Jan. 1697, 2 Jan. 1705, and 19 June 1708, PRO, C 114/164.
[273] Letter dated 10 July 1663; BL, Add. MS 22,852, fo. 136. BL, Add. MS 5488.
[274] Hicks-Beach, *A Cotswold Family*, 87.
[275] Anderson, *English Consul*, 96.   [276] Ambrose, "The Levant Company," 28.

the friends and acquaintances he made outside his family. The kinship network was only one of many business networks.

MARRIAGE AND RELIGION

Marriage consolidated networks as well as providing an important source of additional capital. Business marriages secured mutual interests, eliminated competition, merged firms, and reinforced other ties.[277] What began as referral or friendship was often cemented by a blood tie. It was principally through marriage that individual fortunes were enlarged and transferred.

The dominant cliques in every town were closely linked by affinity. In Elizabethan and Jacobean London the Bonds were related to the Gores and the Gores to the Campbells and the Lees. Alderman James Campbell had as brothers-in-law Sir Christopher Clitherow, Sir John Gore, and Anthony Abdy; Thomas Campbell was linked through marriage with Edward Bright. In 1580 four London aldermen sat on the court with brothers-in-law, three with a son-in-law, and one with two sons-in-law; George Whitmore was connected with seven aldermen, and the Offley clan had relatives in twelve aldermanic families and marriage ties with nineteen others.[278] A century later Sir Richard Hoare, a goldsmith banker, married into the city oligarchy as did his son and junior partner.[279] A similar pattern of marriage existed in Manchester, Norwich, Bristol, Exeter, Cambridge, King's Lynn, Leeds, Belfast, Edinburgh, and New York.[280]

---

[277] C. Branford, *Powers of Association* (Ph.D. diss., University of East Anglia, 1993), 419, appendix 9.

[278] Foster, *Politics of Stability*, 96–102.

[279] C. G. A. Clay, "Henry Hoare Banker" in *Landowners, Capitalists, and Entrepreneurs*, ed. F. M. L. Thompson (Oxford, 1994), 117.

[280] Willan, *Elizabethan Manchester*, 87; J. Agnew, *Belfast Merchants* (Dublin, 1996), 29, 35; Evans, *Seventeenth-Century Norwich*, 31; MacGrath, *Merchants and Merchandise*, 93, 109; *idem.*, "Wills of Bristol Merchants," *Transactions of the Bristol and Gloucester Archaeological Society* 68 (1949): 92; J. W. Kirby, "Restoration Leeds," *Northern History* 22 (1986): 135; N. Goose, "Household Size" in *The Tudor and Stuart Town*, ed. J. Barry (1990), 237; F. W. Todd, *Humphrey Hooke of Bristol* (Boston, 1938), 38; *Bristol, Africa, and the Slave Trade*, ed. D. Richardson, vol. 38 (Bristol Record Society, 1986), xxii; W. T. MacCaffrey, *Exeter 1540–1640*, 2d ed. (Cambridge, Mass., 1976); M. H. B. Sanderson, "The Edinburgh Merchants" in *The Renaissance and Reformation in Scotland*, ed. I. B. Cowan and D. Shaw (Edinburgh, 1983), 184; Metters, "Rulers King's Lynn," 50–3; C. D. Matson, *Merchants and Empire* (1998), 27.

Partnerships were cemented by marriage; junior partners married the daughters of senior colleagues.[281] John Nelson of Boston married the daughter of his partner, William Tailer (who committed suicide in 1684), and had six children.[282] The firm of Henry Colthurst and Company was created by marriage; John Watts and Sir Thomas Middleton were partners of their fathers-in-law.[283] Masters married the sisters of their apprentices, and partners married into the same family; examples include Sir Anthony Abdy and Sir Christopher Clitherow, Arthur Dawbeney and Gerard Gore, and the Bennetts.[284] Sir John Buckworth's daughter married first Sir William Hussey and then his partner.[285] Samuel Heathcote married the sister of his partner, William Dawson, and his son inherited the Dawson estate.

The Levant trade provides a perfect illustration of the affinal network.[286] Edwin Brown, assistant of the Levant Company, had a sister who married Sir John Buckworth and had a daughter, Elizabeth, who married Sir William Rawstorn and had two sons who became assistants, and a third son, John, who became an Aleppo factor along with his cousin. Sir John Langham, governor of the Levant Company, had a brother, Samuel, whose son became a Smirna factor, a sister, Elizabeth, whose son, Sir William Vincent, became deputy governor, and a brother, Sir Stephen, who became an assistant. Heneage Twisden, a Smirna factor, had a sister, Margaret, whose son, Sir Oliver Stile, became a Smirna factor. Eliab Harvey's son, Sir Eliab, became an assistant, and his brother Daniel's son became ambassador in Constantinople. Sir Thomas Bludworth married, as his second wife, the mother-in-law of Mun Brown, an Aleppo factor. Sir John Buckworth's first wife was Elizabeth Dennis, a relation of an assistant; one of their daughters married Sir Peter Vanderput and had a daughter who married Sir Philip Jackson, a Smirna factor, whose son became an Aleppo factor; another daughter, Elizabeth, married Thomas Hartopp, an assistant. By his second marriage Sir John

[281] Devine, *Tobacco Lords*, 91.
[282] R. R. Johnson, *John Nelson, Merchant Adventurer* (Oxford, 1991), 32.
[283] K. R. Andrews, *Elizabethan Privateering* (Cambridge, 1964), 101, 105, 114; A. H. Dodd, "Mr Myddelton" in *Elizabethan Government and Society*, ed. S. T. Bindoff and others (1961), 253.
[284] E. Gethy-Jones, *George Thorpe and the Berkeley Company* (Gloucester, 1982), 266. See also chapter 1.
[285] P. Le Neve, *Pedigrees of the Knights*, ed. G. W. Marshall, vol. 8 (Harlean Society, 1873), 432.
[286] R. Davis, *Aleppo and Devonshire Square* (1967), 64; R. Brenner, *Merchants and Revolution* (Cambridge, 1994), 72; Anderson, *An English Consul*, 115.

Buckworth had a son who became an Aleppo merchant and assistant; his daughter, Mary, married first Sir William Hussey, an Aleppo factor, and second John Evans, a wealthy Levant merchant and assistant; his stepson, Moses Goodyear, also became an Aleppo factor.

East India servants were all related.[287] Sir Henry Johnson was told that "the chief of the factory . . . is related to Mr John Bull the Turkey merchant whose son is married to Sir John Fleet's daughter and now one of the committy."[288] William Hedges wrote to Sir Henry Johnson, when Johnson's nephew married his niece, "my enemies have the malice to compare it to Cpt Pitt's marrying Mr Vincent's niece . . . but all men are not alike."[289] Business marriages were standard practice among merchants and shipmasters in the Barbados trade.[290] The Haswell, Boldero, and Cutler families were linked by marriage in the Baltic trade.

In the domestic economy marriage linked both trade and region. Migrants from Yorkshire, Warwickshire, and Wiltshire had regular meetings in London to exchange information; Maidstone was connected with London through marriage.[291] Some industries and trades were notably incestuous. In the shipping industry the Aldeburg clan of Bences, for example, intermarried with the Johnsons.[292] The Fell tribe of ironmasters was located around the country with a division of labor.[293] The Lloyds were connected by marriage with the ironmasters of the West Midlands.[294] Bankers married the widows and daughters of other bankers: the families of Child, Wheeler, Blanchard, Abbott, and Morris were all closely related.[295]

Alien businessmen were endogamous and usually lived in close proximity. Jacob Wittwrong married Germain Tileman, a brewer, and his two

---

[287] T. Fitzhugh, "East India Company Families," *Family History* 12 (1982): 281–2; H. V. Bowen, *Elites, Enterprise, and the British Overseas Empire* (New York, 1996), 109.

[288] BL, Add. MS 22, 186, fo. 127.

[289] Letter dated 30 Jan. 1682, BL, Add. MS 22,186.

[290] L. D. Cragg, "Shipmasters in Early Barbados," *Mariners Mirror* 77 (1991): 108.

[291] D. A. Dawe, *Skilbeck's Drysalters* (1950), 25; Coleman, *Banks*, 120; P. Morgan, "Warwickshire Apprentices," *Dugdale Society Occasional Papers* 25 (1978): 10.

[292] Andrews, *Ships, Money, Politics*, 49.

[293] Hey, *Fiery Blades*, 172.

[294] M. W. Flinn, *Men of Iron* (1962), 29; G. M. Jenkins, *The Foundations of Modern Wales* (Oxford, 1987), 121.

[295] "Childs and Company," *Three Banks Review* 98 (1973): 43; J. A. R. Abbott, "Robert Abbott," *Guildhall Miscellany* 7 (1956): 36; *The Mystery of the New-Fashioned Goldsmiths* (1676), reprinted in J. B. Martin, *The Grasshopper in Lombart Street* (1892); R. D. Richards, "Edward Backwell," *Economic Journal Supplement* 3 (1928): 338; F. G. H. Price, *Handbook of London Bankers*, 2d ed. (1890–1).

daughters married sons of Mathias Otton, his partner.[296] Alien merchants sustained connections with their country of origin, as did the Lombe family in Amsterdam and Norwich. Even the second generation of aliens still intermarried. Sebastian Bonfoy married the sister of Henry Audley, and of his three sons, two became merchants.[297] Peter Fountain had one daughter married to Christopher Parker, another married to Peter Paravicini, and a third married to James Carswell.[298] Philip Burlamachi and David Papillon married sisters from the Calandrini family, and Philip Papillon was connected through marriage with the Jolliffes.[299]

Religious and ethnic ties were often indistinguishable from and as important as blood ties. Religious refugees and nonconformists of all stripes were linked by a common faith, morality, and marriage, and they had access to the international networks of their fellow believers.[300] Although native English Catholic merchants were few, some of them had links with Catholic communities abroad; the Catholic-Irish networks were extensive.[301] Business families, like the Ashursts, the Jolliffes, and the Foleys, were linked by dissent as well as by marriage with each other to New England and the West Indies; Sir Gilbert Heathcote was associated with Arthur Shallett, an Independent wine merchant.[302] Presbyterian kinship links were prominent in towns such as Norwich.[303] Worldwide financial and trading networks were created by the Huguenot diaspora, though the Huguenots, unlike the Quakers, outmigrated, married outside the faith, and had fewer children.[304] The Jews in London, Barbados, and the American colonies were closely connected; in the journal of Nathan Levy 33 out of 162 named entries were Jews.[305]

---

[296] J. Wootton, *Baronetage* (1771 ed.), I.   [297] Le Neve, *Pedigrees of the Knights.*
[298] KAO, MS U 1015/F/31.   [299] KAO, MS U 1015/ L1.
[300] B. G. Carruthers, "Homo Economicus and Homo Politicus," *Acta Sociologica* 37 (1994): 180; Frost, *Quaker Family in Colonial America*, 204.
[301] Agnew, *Belfast Merchants*, 180.
[302] G. S. De Krey, *A Fractured Society* (Oxford, 1985), 76.
[303] Branford, "Powers of Association," 385.
[304] L. M. Cullen, "The Huguenots" and D. Dickson, "Huguenots in the Urban Economy" in *The Huguenots and Ireland*, ed. C. E. J. Caldicott, H. Gough, and J. B. Pittion (Dublin, 1987), 131, 330; R. D. Gwynn, *Huguenot Heritage* (1985), 154; B. Butler, *The Huguenots in America* (Cambridge, Mass., 1983), 153; J. F. Bosher, "Huguenot Merchant and the Protestant International," *William and Mary Quarterly*, 3d ser., 52 (1995): 77–8, 98.
[305] W. S. Samuel, *Jewish Colonists in Barbados* (1936), 24–5, 95; R. C. Ritchie, *Captain Kidd* (Cambridge, Mass., 1986), 66–7; E. R. Samuel, "Portuguese Jews in Jacobean London," *Transactions of the Jewish Historical Society in England*, 18 (1958): 180; PRO, C 104/13–14.

Quakers tended to continue in the same business, and were subject to their own strict business codes, though some still did not pay their bills on time.[306] The family connections of Quaker merchants stretched from England to New England, Virginia, and the West Indies; young Quakers traveled abroad with certificates from their meetings, and the family was deliberately treated as an instrument of business.[307] A kinship web bound the Quakers of Pennsylvania, New Jersey, and Barbados to the sugar importers in London. Joseph Pike of Cork was in a partnership with his brother and son-in-law and traded with his cousin.[308] It is sometimes forgotten that the Quakers were exclusive and rejected market principles. Friends were expected to help other Friends and not compete with each other in business.[309]

SUMMARY

Business was not an aggregation of individual entrepreneurs operating in an impersonal market, but a network of family partnerships. Because they were unable to produce sufficient competent male heirs, most family firms could not be based exclusively on the nuclear family. New manpower was continuously recruited from and trained by the whole extended family, which also provided capital resources through direct transfers, loans, passive investment, and financial guarantees. Family firms could build a reputation for good credit, and they were better positioned to borrow long term than individuals because the responsibility for repayment did not depend on the life of one person. Complex business transactions between principals and agents could be initiated and sustained by ties of kinship, which also served to cement contractual obligations. Kin were preferred to strangers because they were considered more trustworthy. Networks of kin, continuously extended by marriage and reinforced by religious ties, dispensed patronage, information, and advice.

Nonetheless, in an increasingly sophisticated economy, no business could be based solely on the family. At least half of businessmen were recruited from and trained outside the family. Many trades could not be

---

[306] J. M. Price, "The Great Quaker Families" in *The World of William Penn*, ed. R. S. and M. M. Dunn (Philadelphia, 1986): 378–82; Sitwell, *Letter Book*, xxvii.
[307] Frost, *Quaker Family*, 134, 204.
[308] Pike, *Life*, 121. [309] A. Lloyd, *Quaker Social History* (1950), 74.

adequately capitalized even by pooling the capital of several branches of a family; loans from and investment by outsiders were essential. The family lacked the borrowing capacity of a joint-stock corporation, which could carry permanent debt. It was Dutch capital that financed the English Atlantic commodity trade.[310] Kin could be a liability because of fraud and disputes. Without friends and associates drawn from the whole society, it would have been impossible to sustain large-scale industries and trades, secure adequate supplies, or maintain and develop the economy. Families, like religious minorities, were too homogeneous, too endogamous, and too few to exploit a world market. As the towns moved from communality toward a market economy, private businesses moved from gemeinschaft to gesellschaft.[311] The old metropolitan networks were challenged by individual enterprise, alternative institutions, new mafias, and waves of ethnic, religious, and provincial immigrants.

The tenacity of family values should not, however, be underestimated. Outsiders who infiltrated family businesses were treated as family members and frequently absorbed by marriage. Just as families continuously expanded their kin through intermarriage, business families grew by taking in apprentices and partners; new recruits were integrated into the family structure. Small-world theory has suggested that a high degree of interconnectedness occurs even in modern societies, and, given the relatively small size of preindustrial England, it is not really surprising that so many businessmen had intimate contact. What mattered, of course, was the quality and reliability of the connections. Clusters of families continued to dominate, if only for finite periods, particular areas, and types of trade by borrowing and cooptation and by piggybacking on kin networks. Covert family enclaves preserved intimacy within the more impersonal business organizations.

Some historians have argued that capitalism was promoted by thrusting individuals in an impersonal market; others have regarded business as a social activity conducted through traditional institutions. To ask whether business was rooted more in the family or in the individual is like asking which parent is responsible for the conception of a child. Business had in fact a hybrid structure. Management was in the hands of individual heads of households, but diffused through the extended

[310] D. Ormrod, "The Atlantic Economy," *Historical Research* 66 (1993): 208.
[311] J. M. Price, *The Atlantic Frontier of the Thirteen American Colonies* (Aldershort, 1996), 429.

family. The basic unit was small, based on personal relations, fluid, and never completely independent. A bilaterally extended, dense, tribalistic web of relatives linked different sectors of the domestic and world economy. In preindustrial England the family was a necessary, if not a sufficient, business institution.

8

Women in Business

Thomas Tryon, an advocate of fuller education for women, reflected that "we do not approve of their being employed in Robust and Masculine offices" such as selling goods.[1] To what extent were women excluded from business by law or convention? How many were in practice engaged in trade and in which sectors? What was the relative importance of single women, wives, and widows? Did women prefer to be passive investors rather than active entrepreneurs? What obstacles did they face and how did they respond?

EXCLUSION BY GENDER

Under the custom of London, spinsters could trade as femes soles and so could wives with their husbands' consent, provided they chose a different trade from their spouse; a feme covert who "useth any craft on her sole account, wherewith the husband meddleth nothing . . . such a woman shall be charged as a feme sole."[2] Widows of freemen of London were always entitled to follow their late husband's trade and were exempted from the provisions of the Statute of Artificers by the city charter.[3] Daughters could be apprenticed, if unmarried, and were entitled to claim the freedom by patrimony at twenty-one, though that right could be lost by marriage to a nonfreeman.[4]

---

[1] T. Tryon, *A New Method of Educating Children* (1695), 17.
[2] A. Pulling, *Laws and Customs of the City of London*, 2d ed. (1844), 179.
[3] G. Jacob, *City Liberties* (1732), 114–15; E. Bohun, *Privilegia Londini* (1702), 124–5; M. Bateson, *Borough Customs*, vol. 21 (Selden Society, 1906), cxiv. Husband and wife still had to be free of the same company, and while the husband forfeited all legal rights to his wife's business assets, he was still responsible for her contracts.
[4] T. Girtin, *The Triple Crowns* (1964), 165; C. Welch, *History of the Pewterers* (1902), ii.

Similar provisions existed in other boroughs and business institutions; the East India Company allowed female shareholders to vote for members of committees.[5] Women also qualified under the law of bankruptcy, which was strictly limited to those who bought and sold goods.[6] In New York and Virginia women were allowed to trade as femes soles; in Salem they could act for their husbands, and in Pennsylvania they were allowed to peddle goods.[7]

Nonetheless, women suffered from serious restrictions. Single women were in practice excluded by London guilds from working as masons, tanners, and smiths. Only widows were allowed to use looms in the Weavers Company under the ordinances of 1596. However, Richard Bunby, a clothworker, bequeathed his wife "six frames or engines to make silk stockings," and Thomas Hawkins, in 1610, left a loom to each of his three daughters.[8] Women were excluded from skilled work like silk throwing, though some were numbered among the weavers employed by the Lustring Company.[9] Coventry and York limited the number of apprentices and journeymen that a widow could take and restricted the transfer of the freedom.[10] A married woman technically needed her husband's signature on an indenture if she took an apprentice.[11] Many towns, like Nottingham, increasingly prosecuted women who traded without taking the freedom.[12]

[5] *East India Company Court Minutes, 1677–79*, ed. W. Sainsbury, vol. 2 (Oxford, 1938), 25.

[6] W. J. Jones, *The Foundations of English Bankruptcy*, vol. 69 (Transactions of the American Philosophical Society, 1979), 24.

[7] R. Morris, *Studies in the History of American Law* (New York, 1930), 171–3; C. D. Hemphill, "Women in Court," *William and Mary Quarterly*, 3d ser., 39 (1982): 168; C. Shammas, "The World Women Knew" in *The World of William Penn*, ed. R. Dunn (Philadelphia, 1986), 103; M. Salmon, *Women and the Law of Property* (Chapel Hill, 1986), 44–53; J. R. Gunderson and G. V. Gampel, "Married Women's Legal Status," *William and Mary Quarterly*, 3d ser., 39 (1982): 133.

[8] F. Consitt, *London Weavers Company* (Oxford, 1933), 320; PCC, Pell 547, 1659; N. Evans, *The East Anglian Linen Industry* (1985), 82.

[9] W. B. Stern, "The Trade of Silk Throwing," *Guildhall Miscellany* 6 (1956): 28; M. Manchée, "Some Huguenot Smugglers," *Proceedings of the Huguenot Society of London* 15 (1936–70): 412.

[10] C. Phythian Adams, "Ceremony and the Citizen" and D. M. Palliser, "The Trade Gilds of York" in *Crisis and Order in English Towns, 1500–1700*, ed. P. Clark and P. Slack (Toronto, 1972), 58, 100.

[11] On the origins of the convention whereby the husband's name was added to a contract or indenture, even though the wife was trading independently, see Bateson, *Borough Customs*, vol. 2, cxiv.

[12] R. O'Day, *The Family* (1994), 143; O. J. Dunlop, *English Apprenticeship and Child Labour* (1912), 145.

Women were rarely full members of guilds or companies with the right to hold office, vote, or exercise political authority; often only wives and daughters of freemen were permitted to follow the trade.[13] In Norwich they were excluded from the freedom of the city.[14] In Maryland wives were even more restricted than in England; in northern New England wives engaging in business needed a letter of attorney from their husband.[15] Most women were described in official documents by their marital status, not by their occupation, though some exceptions occur in wills.[16] Priscilla Good of Southwark was described as citizen and skinner, Jane Larrett as widow and merchant tailor, Grace Hardwin as citizen and waxchandler, and Anne Cooper as widow and grocer.[17]

During recessions, or whenever men competed with women for limited openings and opportunities, particularly in artisanal trades, discrimination against women tended to increase.[18] But English towns had from an early period made extensive, if unequal, provision for women, who had always benefited from any decline in population and labor shortages.[19] There were few areas of business where women were specifically barred. The interests of the family took priority over gender; wives, widows, and daughters could not be excluded without undermining the integrity and economic self-sufficiency of the household.

APPRENTICESHIP

Women migrated to London and were admitted as apprentices in the livery companies.[20] A few entered one of the major companies: Kather-

---

[13] K. E. Lacey, "Women and Work in London" in *Women and Work in Pre-Industrial England*, ed. L. Charles and L. Duffin (1985), 57; S. Shahar, *The Fourth Estate* (1983), 196; A. M. Johnson, "Politics in Chester" in Clark and Slack, *Crisis and Order*, 256.

[14] *Norwich Register of Freemen*, ed. P. Millican (Norwich, 1934), xv.

[15] G. V. Gampel, "Planter's Wife" in *Women and the Structure of Society*, ed. B. J. Harris and J. K. MacNamarro (Durham, N.C., 1984), 28–9; L. T. Ulrich, *Good Wives* (New York, 1982), 40.

[16] G. H. Kenyon, "Petworth Town and Trades," *Sussex Archaeological Collections* 96 (1958): 96.

[17] *Prerogative Court of Canterbury, Index to Wills, 1671–5, 1676–85, 1693–1700*.

[18] I. Archer, *The Pursuit of Stability* (Cambridge, 1991), 196.

[19] *York Mercers and Merchant Adventurers*, ed. M. Sellers, vol. 129 (Surtees Society, 1917), 64; R. Thompson, *Women in Stuart England and America* (1974), 76–7; H. Hewell, *Women in Medieval England* (1996), 92.

[20] Among the London companies whose apprenticeship registers include women are the cutlers, pewterers, drapers, glass sellers, girdlers, basketmakers, scriveners, gunmakers, weavers, clockmakers, goldsmiths, carpenters, and stationers. See also Dunlop, *English Apprenticeship*, 150–1; P. A. Clark and D. Souden, eds., *Migration and Society in Early Modern England* (1987), 35.

ine Wetwood was freed by patrimony in the Pewterers Company in 1634, after the master and wardens of the Merchant tailors and two silk weavers swore that she was a virgin.[21] But most entered minor companies. Andrew King apprenticed his niece to a wine cooper.[22] In the Scriveners Company James Windus and his wife took Elizabeth Billingsley, in 1665, and Lucy Sanderson, in 1666, as apprentices; Sarah, daughter of Thomas Dutton, was admitted by patrimony in 1675.[23] Many women were apprenticed to the needle-working trades: Lady Katherine Petrie bound the daughter of a Clerkenwell surgeon to a London embroideress.[24] Some companies, however, took few or no women. Anne Story was freed by apprenticeship in the Founders Company in 1729, but thereafter women were excluded.[25] In the Carpenters Company only twenty-one women (1654–70) were admitted out of 1,658.[26] Although women were not formally excluded from the Apothecarys Company, none were apprenticed.[27]

Women were also apprenticed in provincial towns such as Bristol and Coventry, though a shift toward lesser trades and a preponderance of orphans became increasingly evident during the seventeenth century.[28] In Bristol one-fifth of the women were apprenticed to distributive trades as drapers, grocers, haberdashers, apothecaries, fishmongers, brewers, vintners, and mercers; 50 percent were daughters of craftsmen and 20 percent daughters of merchants, retailers, or professionals, with 33 percent from agricultural backgrounds. The daughter of a deceased esquire was apprenticed to a haberdasher for £24.[29] The Newcastle merchant adventurers had "sisters" who took apprentices.[30] In Norwich, in the early eighteenth century, 113 women, including the daughter of a deceased alderman, were apprenticed to grocers, mercers, and cord-

[21] C. Welch, *History of the Company of Pewterers* (1902), 92.
[22] WAM, MS 9, 977.
[23] F. W. Steer, *History of the Company of Scriveners* (1973), 27.
[24] A. C. Edwards, "Sir John Petrie," *London Topographical Record* 23 (1972): 80.
[25] G. Hadley, *Citizens and Founders* (1976), 137.
[26] *Carpenters Company Records*, ed. B. Marsh (1913), vol. 1.
[27] E. A. Underwood and C. Wall, *History of the Apothecaries*, ed. H. C. Cameron (Oxford, 1963), 84.
[28] L. Fox, "The Coventry Gilds," *Transactions of the Birmingham Archaeological Society* 78 (1962): 199.
[29] Ben Amos, "Women Apprentices in the Trades and Crafts of Bristol," 229–33, tables 1–2; *idem., Adolescence and Youth* (New Haven, 1994), 140–3.
[30] *Newcastle Merchant Adventurers Records*, ed. F. W. Dendy and J. R. Boyle, vol. 93 (Surtees Society, 1895), 7.

wainers.[31] The number of women apprentices does not appear to have declined at the end of the seventeenth century; women still constituted 5.2 percent of all apprentices in five counties between 1710 and 1731.[32] Only a tiny percentage of all apprentices were ever women. Although 37 percent of migrants to London were female, few of them entered the major companies and trades.[33] In 1690 only twenty-three were admitted to the freedom of London, twelve by apprenticeship.[34] In Tudor York only 44 out of 6,231 admitted to the freedom were women, and few women were apprenticed in Edinburgh.[35] The majority of female apprentices came from poor families and entered the craft or retail trades; in many cases they were bound to a wife to learn "howsewifry" rather than to a husband to learn his trade.[36]

TYPE OF TRADE

Apprenticeship records are not a satisfactory indicator of the number of women in business or of changes over time, because guild enforcement declined. It is clear from indictments that women traded surreptitiously in market towns without a formal apprenticeship.[37] In the bakers and weavers guilds of York few women were indentured, but 5 percent of

[31] P. Corfield, "A Provincial Capital" in Clark and Slack, *Crisis and Order*, 288; *Norwich Index Indentures Apprentices*, ed. W. M. Rising and P. Millican, vol. 29 (Norfolk Record Society, 1959), 86, 112, 148; *Norwich City Records*, ed. W. Hudson and J. C. Tingey, vol. 2 (1910), 308–9.

[32] K. D. M. Snell, *Annals of the Labouring Poor* (Cambridge, 1985), table 6.4, 272–3, 318; M. Kitch, "Capital and Kingdom" in *London, 1500–1700*, ed. A. L. Beier and R. Finlay (1986), 225–6.

[33] S. Rappaport, "Reconsidering Apprenticeship" in S. Rappaport et al., *Renaissance Society and Culture* (New York, 1991), 240, and Rappaport, *Worlds within Worlds*, 37; J. M. Bennett, "Medieval Women" in *Culture and History*, ed. D. Aers (1992), note 53, citing a thesis by N. Adamson who found only seventy-three female apprentices in Tudor London; Brodksy, "Single Women," 91–2, table VI; Brodsky, "Widows," 141.

[34] D. V. Glass, "Socio-Economic Status and Occupations" in *Studies in London History*, ed. A. E. J. Hollaender and W. Kellaway (1969), 386. Only a handful of businessmen in the database took a woman apprentice, and they appear to be servants rather than trainees in the business: one example is John Woodward, a fishmonger, who left "my apprentice," Dorothy Mayo, 20 shillings: see PCC, Pell 1, 1659.

[35] Palliser, *Tudor York*, 150, 156; Houston, *Social Change in the Enlightenment*, 370.

[36] *Southampton Calendar of Apprentice Registers*, ed. A. J. Willis and A. L. Merson, vol. 12 (Southampton Record Society, 1960), li. The majority of such apprentices were paupers: see J. Lane, *Apprenticeship in England, 1600–1914* (1996), 127.

[37] Dunlop, *English Apprenticeship*, 145; W. Thwaites, "Women in the Market Place," *Midland History* 9 (1984): 25; J. A. Twemlow, ed., *Liverpool Town Books* (1935); H. Reed, ed., *Liverpool in the Reign of Queen Anne*, vol. 59 (Transactions of the Historical Society of Lancashire and Cheshire, 1907).

those fined for infractions were women (1560–1700).[38] It has been estimated from Consistory Court depositions (1695–1725) that 60 percent
of married women were maintained by their own work and that half of
the wives in substantial families followed their own trade.[39] In Oxford
10 percent of widows who were heads of households had a business.[40]

A few women were overseas merchants, though importers of goods
for retail distribution were more common than exporters.[41] In Bristol
(1654–6) 30 out of 423 importers of sugar and tobacco were wives or
widows.[42] In the Atlantic tobacco trade (1606–60) 55 out of 1,304
adventurers were female; 17 appear in the port books for 1627–8.[43] In
1706 a woman acted as a shipping agent at Hull.[44] But these are the
exceptions. Few women appear in the port books or other records of the
regulated export companies.[45]

Women were more prominent in the domestic trade and in manufacturing. They were particularly active in the textile trades, mostly at the
lower end as seamstresses and dressmakers working with fine fabrics like
silk and lace; Hester Wansey ran her late husband's clothing business for
thirty-two years.[46] In the 1692 poll tax records for London fourteen out
of thirty-nine women whose occupations are given were seamstresses;
the others included an exchangewoman, goldsmith, ironmonger, and
skinner.[47] Katherine Childey supplied stockings for the army, and
others served as contractors for the navy; women were noticeable in
the knitwear trade of Leicester and in the Yorkshire textile industry.[48]

[38] Willen, "Guildswomen in York," *The Historian* 46 (1984): tables 1–2, 218.
[39] Earle, *City Full of People*, 118, 149, 162, 203.
[40] M. Prior, "Women and the Urban Economy," in *Women in English Society*, ed. M. Prior, (Cambridge, 1985): 106.
[41] *Welsh Port Books, 1550–1603*, ed. E. A. Lewis, vol. 12 (Cymmrodorion Society Record Series, 1927), xli; *London Port and Trade*, ed. B. Dietz, vol. 8 (London Record Society, 1970), 48.
[42] D. H. Sacks, *The Widening Gate* (Berkeley, 1991), 259.
[43] Price, *Tobacco in Atlantic Trade*, 4; N. J. Williams, "The English Tobacco Trade," *Virginia Magazine of History and Biography* 65 (1957): 416; R. Pares, *A West India Fortune* (1950), 9; M. J. Blake, ed., *Blake Family Records, 1600–1700* (1905), 247.
[44] J. Holroyd, *Letter Book*, ed. H. Heaton (Halifax, 1900), 18–25.
[45] T. S. Willan, *The English Coasting Trade* (Manchester, 1938), 49; R. W. K. Hinton, ed., *Boston Port Books, 1601–40*, vol. 50 (Lincolnshire Record Society, 1956), 256.
[46] B. Lemire, *Dress, Culture, and Commerce* (1997), 4, 98; J. de L. Mann, "A Wiltshire Family of Clothiers," *Economic History Review*, 2d ser., 9 (1956–7): 241.
[47] Glass, "Socioeconomic Status," table 8.
[48] C. Cross, "Northern Women," *Yorkshire Archaeological Journal*, 59 (1987): 89; I. Gentles, "London Levellers," *Journal of Ecclesiastical History* 29 (1978): 297–303; E. Kerridge, *Textile Manufacture in Early Modern England* (Manchester, 1985), 199; A. Clark, *Working Life of Women*, new ed. (1992), 31–2.

Women were also a significant force in publishing. Although many were probably binders, as many as 10 percent of English books were published by widows, like Elizabeth Calvert, Ann Brewster, and Susanna Moore.[49] Occasionally they appear in the metal trades as cutlers, silversmiths, ironmongers, and even gunmakers; there were forty working female goldsmiths in 1697.[50] Two women had a lead mine and asked Ambrose Barnes to be their partner.[51] Women also participated as wholesalers in the distributive trades, as mercers and corn and coal dealers.[52]

Throughout England and in the American colonies women were, however, most prominent in the retailing of food and in service industries, like victualing, lodging, and surgery.[53] Of 2,461 tradesmens' tokens current in London and its vicinity (1648–72), 80 were issued by women, 33 of which specifically related to taverns and coffee houses.[54] Inventories of women reveal few merchants, but in one sample there was one brewer, one carrier, two grocers, one ironmonger, and twenty shopkeepers.[55] There were several shopkeepers in the Exchange, like Ursula Hobson, and female retailers were common in Southwark.[56] Almost three-fourths of the brothels were run by women and a few keepers, like

---

[49] P. Morgan, "Warwickshire apprentices to Stationers Company," *Dugdale Society Occasional Papers* 25 (1978): 2; E. Arber, ed., *Stationers Company, Transcripts of Registers, 1554–1640*, vol. 5 (1876), lxxx–cxi; D. P. Ludlow, "Shaking Patriarchy's Foundation" in *Truth over Silence*, ed. R. L. Greaves (Westport, Conn., 1985), 114; H. M. Petter, *The Oxford Almanacs* (Oxford, 1974), 23–4.

[50] H. L. Blackmore, *A Dictionary of London Gunmakers* (Oxford, 1986), 22; C. Welch, *History of the Cutlers*, vol. 2 (1916–23), 59; P. Glanville and J. Goldsborough, *Women Silversmiths, 1685–1845* (1990), 22–6.

[51] A. Barnes, *Memoirs*, vol. 50 (Surtees Society, 1866), 168.

[52] S. Wright, "Churmaids, Huswyfes, and Hucksters" in *Women and Work in Pre-Industrial England*, ed. L. Charles and L. Duffin (1985), 115; M. R. Brailsford, *Quaker Women* (1915), 15; R. Champness, *Company of Turners* (1966), 125; Earle, *City Full of People*, 144–6, 199–201, tables 4.3, 4.9; C. Shammas, *The Pre-Industrial Consumer* (Oxford, 1990), 237.

[53] E. W. Dexter, *Colonial Women of Affairs*, 2d ed. (Boston, 1931), 5; Earle, "Female Labour Market," 338–9, table 10; S. Young, *Annals of the Barber Surgeons* (1890), 267, 270–2; N. Evans, "Inheritance Women, Religion, and Education" in *Probate Records*, ed. P. Riden (1985), 66; T. Powell, "Tom of All Trades" in *New Shakespeare Society*, ed. F. J. Furnivall, 6th ser. (1876), 164.

[54] J. Y. Akerman, *Tradesmens Tokens Current in London 1648 and 1672* (1849; reprint, New York, 1969); J. H. Burn, *A Descriptive Catalogue of the London Traders Tavern and Coffee House Tokens* (1853).

[55] L. G. Weatherill, *Consumer Behaviour and Material Culture in Britain* (1988), table A2.1.

[56] Boulton, *Neighbourhood and Society*, 75, 82; L. Bonfield, "Testamentary Causes" in *Communities and Courts*, ed. C. W. Brooks and M. Lobban (Rio Grande, 1997), 150.

Elizabeth Creswell, were wealthy.[57] In the play *The London Jilt* the daughter of a merchant became a whore when her father died.[58] A few midwives also bought and sold medicines, and one, Hester Shaw, accumulated £3,000.[59] The women who insured with the Sun Fire office were mainly caterers, shopkeepers, and pawnbrokers.[60] Women were also active in the used-clothing business and as receivers of stolen goods.[61] Sir John Fleet declared that he had no objection to sitting for a female artist when he had his portrait painted for the Coopers Company.[62] In Liverpool several female retailers were fined for fore-stalling (1583–1602).[63]

The overwhelming majority were not, however, businesswomen with equity capital of at least £500.[64] Only a minority of all businesses were managed by women, and they were predominately small-scale. In a sample from London only five out of fifty female decedents had businesses, and these were mainly small shops.[65] In a sample drawn from different localities the mean estate of thirty-nine women traders was only £137, and for innkeepers and victualers it was only £224.[66] Only seventy-five businesswomen have been identified in period I and eighty-five in period II.

Although women may be disproportionately represented among those numerous firms whose records have not survived, there is little direct or indirect evidence of widespread participation at the higher levels. Many businesswomen, particularly unmarried daughters, wives, and single women, are undoubtedly invisible in official sources, which are heavily biased toward men. But, given the need to record all business transac-

---

[57] N. Ward, *The Comforts of Matrimony* (1780 ed.), 57; E. J. Burford, *Bawds and Lodging* (1976), 144, 171–2, and *Private Vices, Public Virtues* (1995), chapter 10; P. Griffiths, "The Structure of Prostitution," *Continuity and Change* 8 (1993): 46, 56.

[58] R. Thompson, "The London Jilt," *Harvard Library Bulletin* 23 (1975): 289–94.

[59] H. J. Cook, *The Decline of the Old Medical Regime* (1986), 33; P. Crawford, "Printed Advertisements," *Bulletin of the Society of History and Medicine* 35 (1984): 69; Young, *Annals of the Barber Surgeons*, 260; A. L. Wyman, "The Surgeoness," *Medical History* 28 (1984): 40; J. Donnison, *Midwives and Medical Men*, 2d ed. (1988), 23.

[60] Earle, *Making of the Middle Class*, 168, 172, table 6.2.

[61] G. Walker, "Women, Theft, and Stolen Goods" in *Women, Crime, and the Courts*, ed. J. Kermode and G. Walker (1994), 92.

[62] W. Foster, "Sir John Fleet," *English Historical Review* 51 (1936): 683.

[63] J. A. Twemlow, ed., *Liverpool Town Books* (1935), passim.

[64] C. R. Erlington, "Records of the Cordwainers," *Transactions of the Bristol and Gloucester Archaeological Society* 85 (1966): 168.

[65] Earle, *Making of the Middle Class*, 171–4.

[66] L. Weatherill, "A Possession of One's Own," *Journal of British Studies* 25 (1986): tables 2 and 6.

Table 8.1. *Women in Business, 1580–1740*
(Number of Known Businesswomen)

	Period I	Period II
All active traders	75	85
Widows running a business	25	28
Widows surviving husband	2,644	1,861

Note: Wives and daughters assisting their husbands have been excluded. Most of the widows enumerated had taken over their late husband's business, but some had an independent trade.

tions, any woman running a major business would eventually surface in the correspondence and accounts of other businessmen, and few such examples occur.

FEMES SOLES

Dramatists depicted women as tavern owners, or as competent saleswomen. Daniel Defoe's famous heroine Roxana was a prototype "she merchant."[67] When a wife ran her own business, however, it was usually an informal and relatively simple operation. Wives gravitated toward home-based activities; their outside economic activities were governed by gender conventions, family constraints, and their life cycle.[68]

Spinsters in business certainly occur in London. Anne Porter and Elizabeth Chauncey had shops; Gertrude Rolles, a milliner in the royal exchange (1680–98), paid £50 rent for a stall.[69] In the burial records of St. Giles within Cripplegate (1654–93) two unmarried females are identified as merchants and one as a goldsmith, fishmonger, and grocer respectively, plus fourteen brewers, thirteen button makers, and twenty-four glovers.[70] Mary Gresham and Judith Gresham were described as "of London and trades therein being spinster."[71]

---

[67] J. E. Gagen, *The New Woman* (New York, 1954), 102.
[68] P. Sharpe, "Literally Spinsters," *Economic History Review* 44 (1991): 55, 63.
[69] PRO, C 112/181; Brodsky, "Single Women," 91. On contemporary usage of the term "spinster" see J. H. Baker, "Male and Married Spinsters," *American Journal of Legal History* 21 (1977): 259. Female retailers are illustrated by Hollar: see G. Parry, *Hollar's England* (Salisbury, 1980), figure 51.
[70] T. R. Forbes, "Weavers and Cordwainers," *Guildhall Studies in London History* 4 (1980): table 2.
[71] G. Leveson-Gower, *Genealogy of the Family of Gresham* (1883), 123.

In the provinces Salisbury had a few solitary women merchants and craftswomen in 1612, as did Oxford in the early eighteenth century.[72] In Steyning two women were clearly substantial traders. In 1706 Martha Lucke had a mercer's shop worth £1,406.[73] Sarah West was a tallow-chandler with a shop in King's Lynn.[74] Joyce Jeffereys, a usurer, dealt in bonds, pawns, mortgages, and government stock.[75] Elizabeth Parkin took over the family business because there were no sons.[76]

The same was true outside of England. Elizabeth Howatt traded as feme sole in Port Royal, and businesswomen were common in New York; Andrew Tellen had a female friend who set up a milliner's shop.[77] In seventeenth-century Edinburgh thirty-five women were overseas traders, mainly importers, and eleven traded in the Merchants Company in their own right, while many others were small retailers; in the early eighteenth century women retained their importance in the textile and grocery trades—one hundred were featured in the ledger of John Bell, a linen draper.[78]

Some wives had independent businesses, including midwivery. Abell Druce, a salter, was given £100 to invest in the Indies by the wives of Samuel and Nicholas Crispe.[79] David Briggs, a skinner, gave his widow "the house she brought me called by the name of the Boar's head in Eastcheap. I give her over above her stock which she hath under me in a particular trade what doth not come into my books or any way into my estate."[80] Catherine, wife of John Nicks, traded on her own account in India while her husband was still alive.[81] In the 1680s Madame Cockey was the correspondent of an anonymous merchant, probably in the York-

---

[72] Wright, "Churmaids," 115; Thwaites, "Women in Market Place," 24.

[73] J. Pennington and T. Sleight, "Steyning Town," *Sussex Archaeological Collection* 130 (1992): 168, 176.

[74] S. M. Cooper, "Intergenerational Social Mobility," *Continuity and Change* 7 (1992): 287.

[75] R. G. Griffiths, "Joyce Jeffries," *Transactions of the Worcester Archaeological Association* 11 (1935); R. Tittler, "Moneylending in the West Midlands," *Historical Research* 67 (1994): table 4.

[76] D. Hey, *Fiery Blades* (Leicester, 1991), 198.

[77] M. Pawson and D. Buisseret, *Port Royal Jamaica* (1975), 91; letter to Nathan Simson dated 23 Oct. 1723, PRO, C 104/13–14.

[78] E. C. Sanderson, *Women's Work in Eighteenth-Century Edinburgh* (New York, 1996), appendixes 1–4, 26, 38, 168–70; H. M. Dingwall, *Late Seventeenth-Century Edinburgh* (Aldershot, 1994), 203–5; R. A. Houston, "Women in Scottish Society" in *Scottish Society, 1500–1800*, ed. R. A. Houston and I. D. Whyte (Cambridge, 1989), 122.

[79] PCC, Lee 13, 1638.

[80] PCC, Hele 85, 1626.

[81] J. J. Cotton, *Inscriptions on the Tombs in Madras* (Madras, 1905), 11.

shire cloth trade.[82] The wife of Adam Lawrence, a merchant, was in her sister's thread trade in partnership with Abraham Cullen and Philip van Cassel.[83] Mary Cranfield kept a linen drapery shop in 1617, and the wife of Jean Arnaud a shop in Taunton.[84] Thomas Kent, a mercer, instructed his apprentice to help the widow "soe long as shee shall keep her trade of vintner."[85] Judith Du Boc, a Huguenot, lent her husband money from her separate estate, though she seems to have been a rentier.[86] In both London and the provinces some wives were silversmiths; Anne Willaum began with her father's apprentice whom she subsequently married.[87]

An interesting case is Elizabeth Dallison who, although married to a gentleman, clearly traded for and with her brother in India, buying commodities for him that she kept in the East India Company warehouse and conveying information about other merchants: "I will to a penny be accountable for it would break my brains to reconcile what is past, so prithy Deare President do not require it at my hands and withall I will promise you to be better then I will say, for it is high time we begin to lay up for a wet day."[88]

WOMEN IN THE FAMILY BUSINESS

Unmarried daughters, adult spinsters, and wives assisted their husbands and relatives in the shop in return for subsistence rather than wages.[89] Wives bought raw materials, supervised apprentices, hustled for customers, and sold finished goods.[90] Indeed some wives were extremely aggressive toward their servants, apprentices, and even customers, and

[82] Bod Library, MS Eng misc. C. 260.   [83] PCC, Ruthen 376, 1657.
[84] J. Fontaine, *Memoirs, 1658–1728,* ed. D. W. Ressinger, vol. 2 (Huguenot Society London, 1992), 129; M. Edmond, "Limners and Picture Makers," *Walpole Society* 47 (1978–80): 97.
[85] PCC, Nabbs 269, 1666.   [86] PRO, C 114/182.
[87] Glanville and Goldsborough, *Women Silversmiths,* 22–6.
[88] Letters dated 13 and 24 March 1665, BL, Add. MS 40,700; letters dated 3 and 6 Apr. 1663, BL, Add. MS 40,711.
[89] India Office Library, MS 40/5; M. Roberts, "Women and Work" in *Work in Towns, 850–1850,* ed. P. J. Corfield and D. Keene (Leicester, 1990), 93; O. Hufton, "Women without Men," *Journal of Family History* 9 (1984), 357; W. Stout, *Autobiography,* ed. J. D. Marshall, 3d ser., vol. 14 (Chetham Society, 1967), 90, 105.
[90] E. Ward, *London Spy,* ed. K. Fenwick (1955), 56; S. Shepherd, *Amazons and Warrior Women* (Brighton, 1981), 47; R. A. Foake and R. T. Rickert, eds., *Henslowe's Diary* (Cambridge, 1961), xxii.

they were frequently named as the offending party in cases of abuse involving apprentices.[91] Many wives traded as agents for their husbands, while the latter were traveling or sick, and assumed independent responsibility.[92] Edward Coxere's wife kept his shop and sold Holland cloth while he was at sea; Robert Gray's wife did likewise while he traveled on business.[93] In Chester the wife of a cooper was prosecuted for coloring some train oil in her husband's absence; the wife of William Edwards, an ironmonger, took over the sale of his corn in Chester.[94] When John Davis, a linen draper and Baptist, was imprisoned, his wife kept his shop.[95] Thomas Pitt put his wife in charge of his affairs in England in conjunction with Peter Godfrey and Samuel Ongley and dispatched goods to her. When she neglected his instructions and furnished no accounts, he replaced her, however, with his son: "I find great inconvenience by trusting a woman with busyness which I will avoid for the future."[96]

Wives were also active overseas, and on occasion the spouses of shipmasters sailed with their husbands.[97] In colonial America a labor shortage made the services of wives essential.[98] In New York the wife of Robert Livingstone was an active partner, and in northern New England wives worked alongside the shipmasters, though none of their account

[91] S. R. Smith, "Almost Revolutionaries," *Huntington Library Quarterly* 43 (1978–9): 316; J. Thirsk and J. P. Cooper, eds., *Seventeenth-Century Economic Documents* (Oxford, 1973), 234; S. Forman, *Autobiography*, ed. J. O. Halliwell (1849), 6; P. Rushton, "The Matter of Variance," *Journal of Social History* 25 (1992): 97; T. C. Jeaffreson and W. J. Hardy, eds., *Middlesex County Records* (1886), vol. 4, xi. Although it cannot be adequately documented, it is possible that wives played a major role in training apprentices: H. Swanson, "The Illusion of Economic Structure," *Past and Present* 121 (1988): 36–7, 45, suggests that this may also have been true of the fifteenth century.
[92] Ulrich, *Good Wives*, 42, 46; G. P. Jones, "Wilfrid Hudleston," *Transactions Cumberland and Westmoreland Archaeological Society* 67 (1967): 189; J. Thirsk, ed., vol. 4 *Agrarian History of England, 1500–1640* (1967), 513; Pepys, *Diary*, ed. R. Latham and W. Matthew, vol. 5, 266; W. Notestein, "The English Woman" in *Studies in Social History*, ed. J. H. Plumb (1955), 94.
[93] E. Coxere, *Adventures by Sea*, ed. E. H. W. Meyerstein (Oxford, 1946), 51, 80; T. S. Willan, *The Inland Trade* (Manchester, 1976), 123.
[94] M. J. Groombridge, ed., *Chester City Council Minutes*, vol. 106 (Historical Society Lancashire and Cheshire, Record Series, 1956), 60, 123.
[95] P. Crawford, *Women and Religion in England, 1500–1720* (1993), 190.
[96] C. Dalton, *Thomas Pitt* (Cambridge, 1915), 390.
[97] J. Danhers and P. Sluyter, *Journal of a Voyage to Newport, 1679–80*, ed. H. C. Murphy, vol. 1 (Memoirs Long Island Historical Society, 1867).
[98] Thompson, *Women in Stuart England*, 77; J. C. Spruill, *Women's Life and Work in the Southern Colonies* (Chapel Hill, 1938), 345; E. J. Perkins, "The Entrepreneurial Spirit in Colonial America," *Business History Review* 62 (1989): 184–5. Independent women traders were, however, rare in Maryland: see Gampel, "Planter's Wife," 28, 35.

books have survived from the seventeenth century.[99] Wives were also active in India from an early date.[100] Alien women were prominent in London in all trades, including brewing.[101] Ferdinand Albin of Bordeaux had his wife as his correspondent, as was common among Jewish families.[102]

Businesses that utilized all family members existed in all sectors of the economy. James Claypoole's wife and daughter helped him in his export business.[103] In 1653 Blanche, the wife of William Freeman, made a deposition regarding the lading of a cargo in Bristol.[104] The Mangies, goldsmiths of Hull, were a conjugal team, and the wife, when widowed, took her son into partnership.[105] Wives were particularly involved in the book trade.[106] John Dunton acknowledged the contribution of his wife: "Dear Iris gave an early specimen of her prudence and diligence . . . and . . . bookseller, cash-keeper, managed all my affairs for me."[107]

Joint management was most frequent, however, in the food and drink trades and in retail shops.[108] In 1714 a draper in Amthil enumerated the items that his wife was to prepare for sale to peddlers.[109] Jane Davenant ran her father's tavern with his former apprentice whom she married; she continued the business after her husband's death.[110] Thomas Bowrey's wife, Mary, helped him to let property, ran a brewhouse, acted as his broker, and kept shop.[111] Henry Guston, a haberdasher, left his

[99] L. Biemer, "Business Letters of Alice Livingston," *New York History* 63 (1987): 186; T. J. Archdeacon, *New York City, 1664–1710* (Ithaca, 1976), 63–4; R. B. Morris, ed., *New York, Select Cases Mayor's Court* (Washington, 1935), 25; Ulrich, *Good Wives*, 44–8.

[100] Diary of Richard Mohun, BL, India Office Library, G 19/36, 1676–77, fo. 94; C. Lockyer, *An Account of the Trade to India* (1711); T. G. P. Spear, *The Nabobs* (1932), 13.

[101] I. Scouloudi, "Alien Immigration," *Proceedings of the Huguenot Society of London* 16 (1938): 36.

[102] BL, Add. MS 34,015, fo. 89; M. Woolf, "Foreign Trade of London Jews," *Transactions of the Jewish Historical Society England*, 24 (1974): 56.

[103] J. Claypoole, *Letter Book, 1681–1684*, ed. M. Balderston (San Marino, 1967), 23.

[104] *Bristol Deposition Books II 1650–1654*, ed. H. E. Nott and E. Ralph, vol. 13 (Bristol Record Society, 1947), 148.

[105] A. Bennett, "The Mangies of Hull," *Yorkshire Archaeological Journal* 57 (1985): 157.

[106] G. Mandelbrote, "From the Warehouse" in *A Genius for Letters*, ed. R. Myers and M. Harris (Winchester, 1995), 52.

[107] J. Dunton, *Life and Errors* (1705; reprint, 1818), 79.

[108] N. Evans, "Inheritance, Women, Religion" in *Probate Records and the Local Community*, ed. P. Riden (1985), 66.

[109] Lemire, *Dress, Culture, and Commerce*, 60, 66.

[110] M. Edmond, *Rare Sir William Davenant* (New York, 1987), 14.

[111] GLL, MS 3041/4.

widow his house and shop, and "she gives over the shop and trade at her discretion."[112]

Husband and wife sometimes worked together as full partners inside and outside the household. Both, therefore, could be named in law suits in the royal and municipal courts.[113] John Dunch owned a ship with his wife, and Joshua Brown's wife "was a great occasion of his profiting in the trade by her personal industry as by her understanding of the trade."[114] But partnerships of this kind represented only 12 percent of a sample for London.[115] The private business papers that survive suggest strongly that most wives played a subordinate role in their husbands' businesses.

WIDOWS AND APPRENTICES

One indication that some women were much more than housewives is the fact that widows could and did take over and present their late husbands' apprentices. Some even took new apprentices; a Bristol widow took the son of a Somersetshire gentleman for a premium of £400.[116] In the Stationers Company apprentices were taken by thirty-one widows (1603–40) and by eighty-one widows (1641–1700).[117] Other examples occur in Chester, Coventry, Bristol, York, Oxford, and Newcastle.[118] In Kingston upon Thames thirty widows had apprentices; Mary Dodson, a cooper, had several over a period of years.[119] Some widows assumed responsibility for family members. Susanne Havel took her grandson apprentice, and Timothy Parker was apprenticed to his aunt.[120] Joseph Bromley's son was apprenticed to his mother with some later friction.[121]

---

[112] PCC, Clarke 137, 1625.   [113] PRO, Req 2/389/ A 183.

[114] Wadsworth and Mann, *Cotton Trade*, 75.

[115] Earle, *City Full of People*, 116–23.   [116] ULL, MS 554.

[117] D. F. MacKenzie, ed., *Stationers Company Apprentices, 1605–1640* (Charlottesville, 1961); *idem.*, *Stationers Company Apprentices, 1641–1700* (Oxford, 1974).

[118] *Chester Council Minutes*, 60; Prior, "Women and Urban Economy," table 3.1; R. M. Berger, *The Most Necessary Luxuries* (University Park, 1993), 217; S. Lang and M. MacGregor, eds., *Tudor Wills Proved in Bristol*, vol. 44 (Bristol Record Society, 1993), no. 182; Ben Amos, "Women Apprentices," 239, table 3; *idem.*, *Adolescence and Youth*, 135–41; *Newcastle Merchant Adventurers Records*; Willen, "Guildswomen in York," 216–18.

[119] A. Daly, ed., *Kingston upon Thames Register of Apprentices, 1563–1713*, vol. 28 (Surrey Record Society, 1974), xi, no 164.

[120] W. Brigg, ed., *Prerogative Court of Canterbury. Abstracts of Wills*, vol. 3 (Leeds, 1894), 66; MacGrath, *Merchants and Merchandise*, xii.

[121] Rappaport, *Worlds within Worlds*, 204.

The overall numbers were, however, low. Only 5 percent of 1,000 men were presented for the freedom of London by widows between 1551 and 1553, and only 2 percent of 32,000 apprentices between 1598 and 1619 were bound to women.[122] Only 2 percent of apprentices in the Weavers Company were bound to women in 1681.[123] In Oxford the proportion was less than 1 percent, and in Norwich 1 percent.[124]

Widows were obliged either to take over or translate any apprentices in their household, and they were frequently so instructed by their husbands. Dru Tindale, a Hamburg merchant, asked his widow to place his apprentices.[125] John Bush, a draper, instructed his wife to turn over his apprentice if she "shall not keep my trade."[126] Charles Owen, Charles Harvey, and Sampson Cotton insisted that their apprentices complete their term with the widow.[127] In 1625 William Rutter, a dyer, left his apprentice £15 if he served the widow "in my trade" and £35 if the widow declined.[128]

Some apprentices, like Thomas Atherall, ran the business with their master's widow.[129] John Waythman traded in joint stock with his mistress in Newcastle.[130] Henry Liddell was encouraged by widow Anne Clavering: "let your age be what it will your aptness to business will not I daresay fail you."[131] The Barber Surgeons decreed that when a wife kept shop with an apprentice, that the apprentice must account for all proceeds and remain under the command of his mistress; widow Sanderson made an apprentice who started his own business agree not to set up shop within the same parish.[132] In 1614 Agnes Smith appealed to the Burgess Court of Westminster to prevent her husband's apprentice from leaving, and the court decreed that he must stay until he found a new master.[133]

Many testators advised their widow to take over their business. Edward Cheney, a merchant tailor, left his widow his house and tenements in Jerusalem Alley with his "beer goods" "to the end she may hold

---

[122] Brodsky "Widows," 141–2; Rappaport, *Worlds within Worlds*, 39–41.
[123] Plummer, *London Weavers Company*, 64.
[124] B. Todd, "Widowhood in a Market Town," (D. Phil., University of Oxford, 1983), 186; *Norwich Index Apprentices*.
[125] PCC, Hyde 54, 1665.   [126] PCC, Dale 103, 1621.
[127] PCC, Evelyn 50, 1641; PCC, Sadler 82.
[128] PCC, Clarke 42.
[129] R. M. Berger, "Thomas Atherall," *Warwickshire History* 5 (1981–2): 40.
[130] *Newcastle Merchant Adventurers Records*, vol. 1, 270.
[131] H. Liddell, *Letters, 1673–1717*, ed. J. M. Ellis, vol. 197 (Surtees Society, 1987), 3.
[132] Young, *Annals Barber Surgeons*, 267, 270–2.
[133] M. H. Manchée, *The Westminster City Fathers* (1924), 128.

and keep the said house in trade for her better subsistence."[134] John Juxon wanted his widow to continue his sugar business and so she did with Sampson Cotton, her daughter's husband.[135] Thomas Lane advised his wife to let his business partnership continue until it expired, because dissolution would be financially disadvantageous.[136]

Often a testator recommended that his widow combine with a son or kinsman. Thomas Jupe, a girdler, invited his wife to enter into business with their son, and Edward Brent wanted his wife to take their son in as a partner when he reached twenty-one.[137] Joshua Lee expected his wife to trade with his son and partners.[138] Robert Clark, an apothecary, left his wife the lease of his house and "the benefit and advantage of my trade" for two years with his son, Robert.[139] William Haines, a plumber, wanted his kinsman, Samuel Emms, to "continue partner with my wife and executrix hereafter named in and for the one half of my trade during so long time as my wife shall desire to keep the trade"; if the widow should decline, Emms was to receive the house and pay the widow £60 per year.[140] Simon Selly, a leatherseller, recommended that his widow trade with his eldest son and invest, thereby increasing the portions of the four younger children.[141]

WIDOWS IN BUSINESS

Widows sometimes inherited and managed the family business.[142] A few even engaged in overseas trade; several appear in the 1567 London port book, including the widow of Peter Peterson, with nine entries; two are listed in the 1677 London *Directory*.[143] The widow of Thomas Antrobus carried on his former business in the Atlantic wine trade, and the widows of Whitehaven merchants were active in freighting tobacco.[144] Elizabeth Reynolds, a widow, borrowed from William Hawke on the security of shipping shares.[145] Most were, however, engaged in one of the domestic

---

[134] PCC, Ruthen 373, 1657.   [135] PCC, Lee 5; PCC, Hele 112, 1626.
[136] PCC, Alchin 471, 1654.   [137] PCC, Fines 219, 1647.
[138] J. Smail, *Origins of Middle-Class Culture* (1995), 172.
[139] PCC, Pell 431, 1659.   [140] PCC, Pell 4, 1659.   [141] PCC, Goare 96, 1637.
[142] Berger, "Mercantile Careers," 40; Clark, *Working Life Women*, 25, 305; J. A. Johnston, ed., *Probate Inventories of Lincoln*, vol. 75 (Lincolnshire Records Society, 1991), lxii, nos. 3, 27; J. T. Swain, *Industry Before the Industrial Revolution*, vol. 32 (Chetham Society, 1986), table 8.1; Devon RO, Tucker MSS.
[143] *A Collection of the Merchants Living in and about London* (1677); B. Dietz, ed., *London. Port and Trade*, vol. 8 (London Records Society, 1972).
[144] Letter to Bridge Antrobus dated 8 June 1710, PRO, C 107/161; C. Churches, "Women and Property in Early Modern England," *Social History* 23 (1998): 177.
[145] CLRO, MCD 1/131.

trades, ranging from victualing the parliamentary armies to glassmaking, coal, and saddlery.[146] The widow of Philip Lea was a mapseller; Hannah Allen, widow of an overseas merchant, was a publisher, as was Hannah Sawbridge, widow of a stationer.[147] Sir Andrew King listed several widows among traders granted dispensations in 1696.[148] The Goldsmiths Company renewed the lease of a shop to a widow in 1578; in 1726 there were four active women goldsmiths in London running the business of their late husbands.[149]

Outside of London widows occur in all the distributive trades. In Bristol the widows of the merchants Nicholas Cutts and Youngs continued their business, as did Anne Brent.[150] In Chester one widow imported iron, and Dorcas Stone managed the grocery business that she inherited.[151] The widow of Francis Burgess of Norwich continued to publish his newspaper.[152] The widow of Ralph Shaw, a wool merchant, carried on her late husband's business, and some of the widows who occur in the ledger of Robert Ashe may have been more than customers.[153] The widow of George Chetham stayed in business with her husband's nephews, and Elizabeth Hellinas of Devon left £1,275, including debts owed by a factor at Blackwell Hall.[154] Susanna Lee and Susanna Riles were active in the Yorkshire clothing trades, as were widows in Telford and Norwich.[155]

The same was true in manufacturing. Anne Smallbridge of Lichfield was a substantial dyer, and Judith Delamotte, widow of a Calvinist

---

[146] Stone, *Uncertain Unions*, chapter 9; E. S. Godfrey, *Development of English Glassmaking* (Chapel Hill, 1975), 82.

[147] S. Tyacke, *London Mapsellers, 1660–1720* (Tring, 1978), xv, xx; M. Bell, "Hannah Allen," *Publishing History* 26 (1989): 46. See also L. Rostenberg, *Publishers, Printers, and Booksellers*, vol. 2 (New York, 1965), 423.

[148] WAM, MS 54,982.

[149] W. S. Prideaux, *Memorials of the Goldsmiths Company* (1896–7), 84. For several examples in the records of the Fishmongers and Grocers Companies, see S. Mendelson and P. Crawford, *Women in Early Modern England* (Oxford, 1998), 330.

[150] MacGrath, "The Wills of Bristol Merchants," 99; *idem.*, *Merchants and Merchandize*, vol. 19 (Bristol Record Society, 1955), 117; *idem.*, *John Whitson* (Bristol Historical Association, 1970), 8.

[151] D. M. Woodward, *The Trade of Elizabethan Chester* (Hull, 1970), 60; J. S. W. Gibbon, "Inventories in the Prerogative Court of Canterbury." *Local Historian* 14 (1980): 224.

[152] D. Stoker, "Prosperity and Success," *Publishing History* 30 (1991): 32.

[153] E. R. C. Brinkworth, *Shakespeare and the Bawdy Court* (1972), 102; PRO, C 107/20/1.

[154] F. Raines and C. W. Sutton, *Life of Humphrey Chetham*, vol. 49 (Chetham Society, 1903), 122; M. Cash, ed., *Devon Inventories*, vol. 1 (Devon and Cornwall Record Society, 1966), no. 217.

[155] Smail, *Origins of the Middle Class*, 172; B. Trinder, *Yeomen and Colliers of Telford* (1980), 90; Priestley and Corfield, "Rooms and Room Use," 110.

refugee, took over her husband's dyehouse in Southampton.[156] The widow of Francis Sitwell continued to produce iron, and the widow of Samuel Willetts took over his pinmaking trade.[157] Isobel Tiffin carried on her husband's business for six years, and was worth at least £1,500 when she died.[158] Isabel Lancaster was the commercial caterer for Hull corporation; widow Crane and Mrs. Holbach provided bricks for the almhouses in Warwick; Katherine Power of Hull left an interest in a Humber ferry, and Elizabeth Casson of Leeds left fulling mills.[159] Sarah Fell's interests ranged from the iron and grain trades to banking for her Quaker neighbors.[160] The widows of Abingdon ran mills as well as ale houses.[161]

Even more widows operated in the retail trades. In Petsworth Anne Edsaw was described as a mercer, and three other widows continued their husbands' business, as did those of Cambridge and Sevenoaks.[162] Whereas single women were often discouraged in Kent, Northampton-shire, Norwich, and Leicester, widows ran 10 percent of the ale houses, and they kept inns in Manchester.[163] In York there were seventy-four widows in the bakers guild (1566–1700) and forty-nine other active widows (1581–1660).[164] The widow of Thomas West of Wallingford took over the shop that she had probably kept while her husband was alive.[165] Anne Turton was an active vintner in Oxford.[166] Samuel Lucke, a mercer of Steyning, left his wife, Martha, two thriving businesses valued at £1,406, which she ran for another twenty years;

[156] *Southampton Calendar Apprentices*, xxxiv, lxxv; D. G. Vaisey, ed., *Lichfield Probate Inventories*, vol. 5 (Coll. History Staffordshire, 1969), 12, 29, 36, 189.
[157] G. Sitwell, *Letter Book*, ed. P. Riden, vol. 10 (Derbyshire Record Society, 1985), xxxiii; N. Herbert, ed., *VCH City of Gloucester*, vol. 4 (1988), 108.
[158] Willan, *Elizabethan Manchester*, 60, 79.
[159] A. Laurence, *Women in England, 1500–1760* (New York, 1994), 150–2, 235.
[160] B. Y. Kunze, "Poor and in Necessity," *Albion* 21 (1989): 568; *idem., Margaret Fell* (1994), 78, 123. Her accounts are described as double entry (p. 71) though they sound like charge and discharge.
[161] B. J. Todd, "The Remarrying Widow" in *Women in English Society*, ed. M. Prior (1985), 70.
[162] Kenyon, "Petsworth Town," 96; N. J. Williams, *The Maritime Trade of the East Anglian Ports* (Oxford, 1988), 184: M. C. F. Lansberry, ed., *Sevenoaks Wills and Inventories* (Kent Archaeological Society, 1988), xii.
[163] P. Clark, *The English Alehouse* (1983), 79; H. Swanson, "Artisans in the Urban Economy" in *Work in Towns*, ed. P. J. Corfield and D. Keene (Leicester, 1990), 51; Willan, *Elizabethan Manchester*, 94.
[164] Willen, "Guildswomen in York," 216–18.
[165] T. West, "Accounts of Thomas West," ed. M. Prior, vol. 46 (Oxoniensa, 1981), 75.
[166] Prior, "Women and the Urban Economy," 106–8.

John Blackfan, a brewer, provided that his daughter and wife could use the malthouse, and Elizabeth Taylor followed her husband as a shoemaker.[167]

The same was true outside of England. In Edinburgh widow Boog was in brewing and Agnes Campbell in printing.[168] Widows also took over from their husbands in Belfast.[169] In Connecticut widows became innkeepers; in New York Elizabeth Jourdain, Duffy Simson, and Helen Rombouts were major businesswomen; Margaret Hardebroeck traded both before and after her widowhood and had a father, brother, uncle, and three cousins in business.[170]

Sometimes a widow traded jointly with a second husband or with her sons and daughters.[171] Leonora, the widow of Charles Marescoe, traded aggressively in partnership with other merchants after her husband's death; after waiting five years she married Jacob David, whom her late husband had employed as a clerk.[172] The widow of a fustian maker took over the family business with her sons and daughters.[173] Ellen Dodson, a cooper, continued with an apprentice until her son, James, entered the business in 1633.[174] Widows carried on with their sons in Rye.[175] Thomas Walters was copartners with his mother-in-law and brother-in-law.[176] Sometimes a widow employed a male manager, like the widow of John Crowley.[177] Martha, the widow of Anthony Gay, continued to trade to Virginia and Jamaica in 1678, but her cargoes were selected by Thomas Walden.[178] Thomas Gent helped widow Dod run a printing business.[179]

---

[167] Pennington and Sleight, "Steyning Town," 175–6, 180.
[168] Sanderson, *Womens Work*, appendixes 1–4, 26, 38, 168–70; Dingwall, *Edinburgh*, 203–5; W. Mackey, "Edinburgh" in *The Early Modern Town in Scotland*, ed. M. Lynch (1987), 208.
[169] Agnew, *Belfast Merchant Families*, 28.
[170] J. T. Main, *Society and Economy in Colonial Connecticut* (Princeton, 1985), 285; T. J. Archdeacon, *New York City, 1664–1710* (Ithaca, 1976), 63–4; letter to Mrs. Simson dated, 27 June 1726, PRO, C 104/13–14; J. B. Biemer, *Women and Property in Colonial New York* (1984), chapter 3.
[171] Bennett, "The Mangies," 157; G. Mayhew, "Life Cycle Service," *Continuity and Change* 6 (1991): 216; Hufton, "Women without Men," 359.
[172] H. Roseveare, ed., *Marescoe-David Papers* (British Academy, 1987), 4, 121, 151, 203.
[173] Wadsworth and Mann, *Cotton Trade*, 82.
[174] *Kingston upon Thames Apprentices*.
[175] G. Mayhew, "Life Cycle Service and the Family," *Continuity and Change* 6 (1991): 216.
[176] Brigg, ed., *Prerogative Court Canterbury Abstracts*, vol. 2, 8.
[177] M. W. Flinn, *Men of Iron* (Edinburgh, 1962), 77.
[178] MacGrath, *Merchants and Merchandise*, 60.
[179] T. Gent, *Life* (1832; reprint 1974), 155.

Nonetheless, most widows liquidated the business. Only twenty-five widows are known to have continued their late husband's business in period I and twenty-eight in period II (see table 8.1). In London wives of masters rarely worked, and only 2 out of 295 took over from their husbands, usually in minor trades.[180] Of widows whose inventories were presented to the Court of Orphans (1666–75) only nine out of twenty-four were in business.[181] Widows were much more likely to take in lodgers or live as rentiers than to run a business.[182] The numerous widows who did work in London were not widows of businessmen. The widow of Willam Crooke, a bookseller, continued his business for two years and then sold it.[183] The same was true outside of London. The widow of a Bristol tailor helped the apprentice but did not undertake the trade; Nottingham widows were more inclined to lend money than take over the family business.[184] In Abingdon the percentage of widows following their husbands declined from 41.7 percent (1620–59) to 33.3 percent (1660–1720); it was the poorer widows with a mean estate of £258 who were most likely to continue.[185] The number of widows entering baking, brewing, and ale selling steadily declined.[186]

PASSIVE INVESTMENT

The inventories of widows of businessmen suggest that they predominately invested in real estate, joint stocks, annuities, or loans.[187] If they invested an inheritance in cash, it was usually at a fixed rate in a mixed portfolio. Although it is possible that some liquidated a business shortly before their decease, the more probable conclusion is that the majority sought safe, passive outlets for their capital. They kept the rentier investments—stocks, bonds, and leases—and sold the inventory and the working assets, which required full-time management.

[180] Earle, "Female Labour Market," 338–9; Earle, *City Full of People*, 116–23.
[181] Earle, *Making of the Middle Class*, 171.
[182] Brodsky, "Widows," 141; list of lodgers in Walbrook ward, GLL, MS 507, Feb. 1684.
[183] T. Hobbes, *Correspondence*, ed. N. Malcolm, vol. 2, 825.
[184] Laslett, "Family, Kinship, and Collectivity," 55; S. Dunster, "An Independent Life," *Transactions of the Thoroton Society of Nottingham* 95 (1991): 32–5.
[185] Todd, "Widowhood in Market Town," 175, tables 4.4, 4.6.
[186] M. MacIntosh, *A Community Transformed* (New York, 1991), table 4.5.
[187] Wright, "Churmaids," 112; P. J. Goldberg, ed., *Woman is a Worthy Wight* (1992), 162–3; B. A. Holderness, "Credit in a Rural Community," *Midland History* 3 (1975): 101; *Ipswich Probate Inventories*, 89, 107; Pennington and Sleight, "Steyning Town," 173, 180.

Seventy widows inherited printing shops (1553–1640), but fifty of them disappeared within one year.[188] In Edinburgh widows delegated management of the business to others and lived off the proceeds.[189] Some handled their own money, but widows who lacked the knowledge and connections used the services of others: relatives, scriveners, brokers, bankers, or the attorneys who assumed this role in Gloucester and Liverpool.[190]

Women were minority shareholders in most of the joint-stock companies. Although less than fifty women invested in the colonial and trading companies (1575–1630), relicts did hold shipping shares and were numbered among subscribers to the Eastland, Northwest, and Russia Companies.[191] In the later seventeenth century widows were represented in the African, East Indian, and South Sea Companies.[192] Of eighteen stockholders in the Hudson Bay Company, seven were widows.[193] Women held 18 percent of Bank stock, with an average value of £680; 14.6 percent of the United East India Company's stock in 1712 was held by women, with an average value of £643.[194] In 1685 ten women, mainly widows like Elizabeth Howland, had sufficient shares in the East India Company to be eligible to vote; by 1700 the number was 109.[195] Jane Borough, a widow, was admitted an adventurer in 1679 on paying £5 for redemption, having bought £200 of stock; several women are recorded in transfers of stock (1671–3).[196] Chapwoman Joan Dant had shares in the East India Company and the bank, as well as in ships.[197]

Widows also lent short-term on bond to corporations, like the Hudson Bay Company. Mary Brocas had to petition the House of Lords regard-

[188] P. Hogrefe, *Tudor Women* (Ames, Iowa, 1975), 48.
[189] Houston, *Social Change*, 78.
[190] *V. C. H. City of Gloucester*, 105; B. L. Anderson, "The Attorney in the Early Capital Market" in *Liverpool and Merseyside*, ed. J. R. Harris (1969), 57.
[191] T. K. Rabb, *Enterprise and Empire* (Cambridge, Mass., 1967), 27; H. Zins, *England and the Baltic* (1971), 117; T. S. Willan, *Muscovy Merchants of 1555* (Manchester, 1953), 55; C. Shammas, "Invisible Merchant," *Business History* 17 (1975): note 6; G. V. Scammel, "Shipowning," *Historical Journal* 15 (1972): 397; *idem., Ships, Oceans, and Empires* (1995), 397.
[192] K. G. Davies, "Joint Stock Investment," *Economic History Review*, 2d ser., 4 (1952): 285; *idem., Royal Africa Company* (1957), 66.
[193] A. Carlos and J. Van Stone, "The Hudson Bay Company," *Business History* 38 (1996): table 9.
[194] Carruthers, *City of Capitalism*, tables 6.4, 6.5.
[195] *East India Company. List of Adventurers* (1685, 1700); BL, Add. MS 22,185.
[196] E. B. Sainsbury, ed., *East India Company. Calender of the Court Minutes* (Oxford, 1907–38), vol. 9, 306–14; vol. 11, 247.
[197] M. Spufford, *The Great Reclothing of Rural England* (1984), 46–9.

ing a debt of £1,000, which she had lent to the Muscovy Company in 1617 on bond that had not been repaid.[198] In 1685 20 percent of East India bonds were held by women.[199] They also held a significant percentage of the various financial instruments that collectively constituted a national debt.[200] Women made up 12 percent of subscribers to the tontine of 1693, and Nathaniel Torriano bought annuities for a spinster in 1717.[201] One powerful argument deployed against reducing the legal maximum rate of interest was that it would impoverish numerous widows.[202]

Widows also became silent partners in a variety of trading firms, like Perry and Company or the business of Henry Phill.[203] They deposited funds with goldsmiths and appear in the client lists and correspondence of bankers; 12 percent of Vyners clients were widows or spinsters, as were 14.6 percent of bankers' assignees (1677–83).[204] Thomas Key, a goldsmith, was financed on a voyage by his "loving friend," widow Turner.[205] John Knight raised £600 from Helena Smythe and £500 from Elizabeth Appleton to build his sugar house.[206]

Active traders also borrowed on bond extensively from women.[207] John Isham borrowed £30 from an old maid at $6\frac{2}{3}$ percent.[208] John Hill borrowed small sums from women, and in 1623 Richard Archdale borrowed £200 from Francis Low, a widow, at 7 percent and mentions three widows in his journal whose money he may have invested directly in the wine trade.[209] Charles Peers borrowed £500 from Ann Hanger at 5.5 percent.[210]

---

[198] BL, Harlean MS 243, fo. 71.

[199] BL, Harlean MS 7497; E. E. Rich, *History of the Hudson Bay Company*, vol. 21 (Hudson Bay Company Record Society, 1958), 317.

[200] CLRO, MS 40/35; *Calendar Treasury Books, 1689–92*, vol. 9, Pt. 5, 2,004; P. G. M. Dickson, *The Financial Revolution* (1967), 426, table 38.

[201] PRO, C 112/24.

[202] *HMC 8th Report*, Pt. 1, appendix, 133 ff.

[203] J. M. Price, *Perry and Company* (Cambridge, Mass., 1992), 157; PRO, C 111/127/1.

[204] H. Roseveare, *The Financial Revolution* (1991), 19; J. K. Horsefield, "Stop of the Exchequer," *Economic History Review*, 2d ser., 35 (1982): 526; Carruthers, *City of Capital*, 65, table 3.4.

[205] PCC, Berkeley 320, 1656.

[206] I. V. Hall, "Bristol's Second Sugar House," *Transactions of the Bristol and Gloucester Archaeological Society* 68 (1949): 126.

[207] Journal of Thomas Laxton, GLL, MS 17,146; M. Zell, "Credit in the Woollen Industry," *Economic History Review* 49 (1996): 675.

[208] G. D. Ramsay, ed., *John Isham Mercer*, vol. 21 (Northamptonshire Record Society, 1962), xxxix.

[209] KAO, MS U 1515/02; GLL, MS 23,953–4.   [210] GLL, MS 10,187, 10,188/1.

Although not easily quantified, it is evident from the abundant probate records and from judicial proceedings that a high proportion (probably 16–20 percent) of the assets of widows and spinsters consisted of loans to individuals.[211] Their portfolios combined mortgages with loans on bond and pawnbroking, primarily but not exclusively to kin.[212] Between 1711 and 1715 6.4 percent of creditors who sued bankrupts were women.[213] In provincial towns, like Worcester and Ipswich, women lent on a substantial scale.[214]

If they were not usurers, widows were major landladies, holding urban real estate that they usually managed themselves. Their husbands frequently left them either houses or an annuity tied to rents from a piece of real property: John Bindsey, for example, left his widow £60 p.a. for life from property in Bishopsgate.[215] In every town, from London to Rochester to Edinburgh, widows constituted a block of property owners living off rents.[216]

OBSTACLES TO PARTICIPATION

Why did so few independent businesswomen emerge? Prejudice may have been a deterrent.[217] There was certainly a sexual division of labor among artisans and the work undertaken by women was less specialized, less technical, and more intermittent. The contemporary advice literature emphasized the passive and subordinate role of a wife, even when she was a functional equal.[218] In a society where chaste women stayed close

---

[211] Brodsky, "Widows," 144.
[212] John Rylands Library, Manchester, Clarke Papers, 880–920; E. Kerridge, *Trade and Banking in Early Modern England* (Manchester, 1988), note 230; A. Eyre, *Diurnall*, ed. H. J. Moorehouse, vol. 65 (Surtees Society, 1878), 62, 66, 69; B. A. Holderness, "Widows in Pre-Industrial Society" in *Land, Kinship, and Life Cycle*, ed. R. M. Smith (Cambridge, 1984), 438–9; *idem.*, "Credit in Rural Society," *Agricultural History Review* 24 (1976): 106; *Yorkshire Diaries and Autobiographies of the Seventeenth Century*, vol. 77 (Surtees, Society, 1886), 14.
[213] Earle, *Making of the Middle Class*, 168.
[214] J. A. Johnston, "Worcester Probate Inventories," *Midland History* 4 (1978): table iv; M. Reed, "Economic Structure and Change" in P. Clark, *Country Towns in Pre-Industrial England* (New York, 1981), 117.
[215] PCC, Berkeley 434, 1656.
[216] A. J. F. Dulley, "People and Homes" in *Essays in Kentish History*, ed., M. Roake and J. Whyman (1977), 111; Sanderson, "Edinburgh Merchants," 187; E. R. C. Brinkworth and J. S. W. Gibson, *Banbury Wills and Inventories*, vol. 13 (Banbury Historical Society, 1985), 50.
[217] MacIntosh, *Community Transformed*, 295.
[218] Gouge, *Of Domestical Duties*, 255–6; S. D. Amussen, *An Ordered Society* (Oxford, 1988), 119–21; S. L. Thrupp, *Merchant Class of Medieval London* (Chicago, 1948), 173.

to home and the lustful widow was a literary stereotype, a widow who became head of a family firm could appear threatening to men and risked gossip about her reputation among those who identified economic with sexual independence.[219] It has been argued that the marketplace offended patriarchal sensibilities, that single women living alone or trading were bracketed with prostitutes.[220]

Businesswomen did have to face male hostility. Grocer Agnes Harrison and Widow Dolling both claimed that their trade had suffered from slander.[221] When the widow of Nehemiah Webb took over her late husband's share of a partnership, the other partners tried to exclude her, and she had to sue in chancery.[222] Elizabeth Dallison described to her brother the unreasonable men she had encountered: "it may be squire Brooks will write to thee of my being in the coffee house. It is true. I was and have been there several times. Need makes the old wife stroll. But know my deare brother President, I keep my grandeur for all the humiliation and will I warrant thee ever do so. Mr Papillon says my presence doth great advantage to the business."[223]

On the other hand, George Fox encouraged widows to trade.[224] Defoe denounced wives who were "above taking any notice of their husbands' affairs" and recommended that they be prepared to take over from their husbands; women "are not so helpless and shiftless creatures as some would make them appear."[225] Josiah Child wanted to train wives to be executrixes and thought that women could be "as knowing therein as the men."[226] In fact there was minimal discussion as to whether or

---

[219] K. M. Rogers, *The Troublesome Helpmate* (Seattle, 1966), 126–9; E. Ward, *London Spy*, ed. K. Fenwick (1955), 109; W. Fennor, *The Counters Commonwealth* (1617), 453; G. L. Gowing, "Gender and Insult," *History Workshop Journal* 35 (1993): 12, 18; M. C. Howell, *Women Production and Patriarchy* (Chicago, 1986), 183.

[220] J. G. Turner, "News from the New Exchange" in *The Consumption of Culture, 1600–1800*, ed. J. Brewer and A. Bermingham (1995), 419. This line of argument sometimes leads to bizarre speculation: L. Mendel, "Bawds and Merchants," *English Literary History* 59 (1992): 107, asserts on the basis of one tract by Mandeville (which the author admits is "unreadable") that women were identified with mercantile capitalism so that they could be blamed for its excesses, that profit maximization was both sexual in nature (either through violence or repression), and that the vagina was equated metaphorically with the home of a debt.

[221] Earle, *City Full of People*, 216; T. Meldrun, "A Womens' Court in London," *London Journal* 19 (1994): 12.

[222] Hall, "Whitson Court Sugar House," 46.

[223] Letters dated 13 and 24 March 1665 BL, Add. MS 40,700; letters dated 3 and 6 Apr. 1663, BL, Add. MS 40,711.

[224] A. Lloyd, *Quaker Social History* (1950), 9.

[225] D. Defoe, *The Compleat Tradesman*, vol. 2 (1727), 294, 302–3.

[226] J. Child, *A New Discourse about Trade* (1694), 5.

not women were inherently unsuited for business.[227] Arguing from negative evidence is always unsatisfactory, because the absence of comment
can mean either blanket acceptance or disapproval. It was, however,
generally assumed in the literature on the family and household
management that a wife would help her husband and participate in
the market.[228]

It is possible that women had been conditioned to have low expectations by a patriarchal society, but participation in business was more
a social than a gender issue. It was the separation of professional
from manual pursuits that penalized women, not their sex.[229] Women
were allocated specific functions in agriculture and manufacturing and
expected to work, as well as to run their households and rear their
children. But what was admissible for the wife of a tradesman was not
necessarily suitable for the widow of an alderman. Defoe and others
emphasized the increasing social pretensions of wives: "ladies scorn to
be seen in the compting house much less behind the counter."[230] No
status-conscious woman would have agreed with Chamberlayne that
"sitting in the shops" was "far more fit for women and their daughters"
than for gentlemen.[231] Husbands and wives could not unambiguously
reject a life of idleness because an independent income and voluntary
exclusion from production remained one test of gentility for both
sexes.[232]

Only the wealthiest could, however, afford to keep their wives
idle. Most depended on the help of their wives, and their daughters,
who must have acquired a familiarity with the routines of business in
the normal course of living.[233] Elizabeth Gurney kept the books and acted
as chief clerk.[234] Elizabeth Bury helped to cast accounts.[235] It is clear from
the few surviving accounts, like those of Joyce Jeffereys, Elizabeth Sneyd,
Anne Archer, Rachel Pengelly, Sarah Fell, and Anne Whitehead, that
women had some acquaintance with basic bookkeeping; the ledgers kept

[227] E. Tilney, *Brief and Pleasant Discourse of the Duties of Marriage* (1571), fo. L.4.
[228] H. Smith, *The Sermons* (1600), 35.   [229] Dingwall, *Edinburgh*, 203.
[230] Defoe, *Compleat English Tradesman*, vol. 2, 355.
[231] E. Chamberlayne, *Angliae Notitia* (1692 ed.), 259. The argument that women were
     devalued if they were not employed in the public sphere assumes incorrectly that Stuart
     England had embraced the work ethic of the nineteenth century.
[232] P. Earle, "The Middle Sort" in *The Middling Sort*, ed. J. Barry and C. Brooke
     (Basingstoke, 1994), 153.
[233] *Norwich City Records*, vol. 2, 308–9.
[234] V. B. Anderson, *Friends and Relations* (1980), 68.
[235] S. Bury, *Account of the Life and Death of Elizabeth Bury* (Bristol, 1721), 187–8.

by the six female trustees for the money, land, and bonds of the London Womens' Meeting were impeccable.[236]

Normally, however, women would have been handicapped by lack of training and experience. In order to survive in business, a woman needed not only basic technical skills but sufficient shrewdness and determination to control unruly apprentices, outwit manipulative efforts by relatives, and hold her own in the marketplace. Businesswomen often needed some male labor as well as support from husbands, fathers, and brothers, whereas men could often manage entirely without women.[237] Widows were more likely to take over a business that did not require employees outside the family. Many wives came from the landed or urban gentry and had no prior contact with business. Experience of running a household or even a shop was not necessarily enough to take over a complex business, and when a wife had experience, it was usually, as custom enjoined, in a trade different from that of her husband.[238]

Contemporaries were aware that widows often lacked the extensive knowledge necessary to wind up an estate.[239] The practical manuals for women did not include accounting, and William Scott advised men not to tell their wives about their business.[240] Defoe alleged that a widow was often forced to depend on and even marry her late husband's apprentice.[241] It does not seem to have been usual practice for propertied families to offer their daughters or wives a formal training in the appropriate skills for managing a business, though daughters were occasionally trained in bookkeeping and arithmetic so that they could

---

[236] BL, Cotton Vespasian I, xvi; BL, Add. MS 30,494; BL, Add. MS 32,456; BL, Egerton MS 3054; Griffiths, "Joyce Jeffries," 5; Lloyd, *Quaker Social History*, 114; Salt Library, Stafford MS HM/3736; S. Fell, *The Household Account Book*, ed. N. Penney (Cambridge, 1920). O. Hufton, *The Prospect before Her* (1996), 153, claims that sixteenth-century records speak of the casting of accounts by women, but no references are supplied.

[237] Hufton, "Women without Men," 365.

[238] *Marescoe-David Papers*, 6, 206; Ulrich, *Good Wives*, 48; Earle, "Female Labour Market," 339.

[239] Gouge, *Domesticall Duties*, 406; J. P. Cooper, ed., *Wentworth Papers*, 4th ser., vol. 12 (Camden Society, 1973), 20; J. Addy, *Death, Money, and the Vultures* (1992), 61–4, 84–5; A. Conyers, ed., *The Wiltshire Extents for Debts, Edw I–Eliz I*, vol. 28 (Wiltshire Record Society, 1973), 8; E. Roberts and K. Parker, eds., *Southampton Probate Inventories, 1447–1575*, vol. 1 (Southampton Record Society, 1992), 231. See also chapter 3.

[240] W. Scott, *Essay on Drapery* (1635), ed. S. L. Thrupp (Boston, 1953), 34; S. W. Hull, *Chaste, Select, and Obedient* (San Marino, 1982), 67–70.

[241] D. Defoe, *Works*, ed. W. Hazlitt, vol. 3 (1843), 42.

keep accounts for their father and husband.[242] Private business papers do not suggest that wives regularly assisted their husbands with their accounts.

An even greater disadvantage suffered by women was lack of capital, which made it almost impossible for a married woman or adult spinster to launch a major business. Some trades formerly in the hands of women, like brewing, may have passed to men simply because they became more heavily capitalized.[243] Female retailers suffered from the domination of the wholesale market by well-financed, large-scale traders. Although wives could have separate estates, as femes coverts, control of their personalty under common law was vested in their husbands (see chapter 2). If a daughter never married and still received a monetary portion at twenty-one, she could theoretically use this as venture capital. In Southampton a few single women received capital from their mothers and aunts and possibly from charitable loan funds.[244] Joyce Jeffereys was able to become a businesswoman because she had independent assets.[245] Usually, however, parents would provide either an annuity for an unmarried daughter or a portion, which on marriage would pass to the husband.

Widows had both the capital and the connections, and they could even roll over loans taken out by their late husbands.[246] But their main concern was economic security (see chapter 3). If they gambled on successful management of a business, they could easily fail, like Helen Hawks who overborrowed in the shop trade.[247] It was not surprising that widows consulted astrologers about the purchase of annuities and the setting up of shops.[248] When widows had children to raise, they would have been subject to increased pressure to find an investment

[242] L. Pollock, "The Making of Women," Continuity and Change 4 (1989): 237, 248; WAM, 9977, nos. 10, 139; Advice to the Women and Maidens of London (1678), 3, a tract written by a daughter who kept the household accounts; C. Mather, Ornaments for the Daughters of Zion (Boston, 1691), 82.

[243] J. M. Bennett, "Misogyny, Popular Culture," History Workshop Journal 31 (1991): 187; idem., Ale, Beer, and Brewsters (New York, 1996), 42, 54, 150.

[244] A. M. Froide, "Marital Status as a Category" in Singlewomen in the European Past, ed. J. M. Bennett and A. M. Froide (Philadelphia, 1999), 267; S. Mendelson and P. Crawford, Women in Early Modern England (Oxford, 1998), 169.

[245] BL, Egerton MS 3,054.

[246] Rappaport, Worlds within Worlds, 39–40.

[247] B. S. Snell, ed., Upperside. Minute Book of Friends, 1669–1690, vol. 1 (Buckinghamshire Architectural and Archaeological Society, 1937), 34.

[248] K. V. Thomas, Religion and the Decline of Magic (1971), 369.

vehicle that yielded a regular income without too much risk or commit-ment of time.[249] Many widows may have felt too old by the time that they inherited a business to take on more responsibility. It is also possible that they were less inclined to maximize their yield and more responsive to community needs.[250] Women often served as mediators in disputes over money, and Joyce Jeffereys may not have been the only woman to charge less than the maximum rate of interest.[251] Widow Pley might assert that business was her "sole delight in the world."[252] But most widows may not have been interested in self-advancement or in bearing the risks and labors of business. To those who could not afford to retire, remarriage might often have seemed preferable to running a business.[253] The greater the wealth of their husbands, the less likelihood that widows would stay in business.

SUMMARY

Apprenticeship brought women into the economy without changing the patriarchal character of society. Most women used their skills to assist their husbands, and marriage diluted a woman's occupational identity, which was always ill defined. Business was predominately a male pre-serve, linked to, but not dependent on, the household.

Women were discouraged rather than excluded from business. Busi-nesswomen were a visible minority found in most sectors of the economy but concentrated in the clothing, victualing, and retail trades. Most females were apprenticed as artisans, and most businesswomen learned their skills in the home and entered business through their husbands. Single women did operate in the lesser trades. A few married women traded both on their own and with their husbands. Widows in business

---

[249] B. J. Todd, "Freebench and Free Enterprise" in *English Rural Society, 1500–1800*, ed. J. Chartres and D. Hey (Cambridge, 1990), 199–200. The same attitude was adopted by Chancery, which limited the acceptable investments for trust capital after the Bubble; see M. R. Chesterman, "Family Settlement or Trust," *Law Economy and Society in England*, ed. G. R. Rubin and D. Sugarman (Abingdon, 1984), 159.
[250] Tittler, "Money Lending," 256.
[251] C. Muldew, "Culture of Reconciliation," 923. New York women, it has been argued, were the guardians of traditional communal values; see D. A. Rosen, *Courts and Commerce* (Columbus, Ohio, 1997), 140.
[252] *Calendar S. P. Domestic, 1665–6*, cited by A. Fraser, *The Weaker Vessel* (1984), 387.
[253] A. Vickery, "Historiographical Review," *Historical Journal* 36 (1993): 409.

were more common, but they were still in a clear minority, and they often traded in conjunction with male apprentices, children, partners, or kin. A few took over their husbands' businesses, but the majority turned the business assets into passive investments. There are several possible explanations for this retreat from the marketplace; the hostility of a patriarchal society, social ambition, lack of capital and experience, age, young children, the desire and the need for a secure, regular income, and indifference.

Spinsters and wives in Stuart England certainly faced greater obstacles in business than men. But the unwillingness of widows to assume managerial functions suggests that the small number of businesswomen cannot be explained just by discrimination or coercion. The actions of businessmen were constrained by the law of marginal utility and by the cost/benefit ratio. They did not hesitate to deal with clients of different faiths or cultures, with renegades or belligerents, papists, or pirates. No businessman worth his name was likely to reject a lucrative deal because the opposite party was a woman. The profit motive was a powerful antidote to any prejudice against women and took priority over traditional gender roles. Indeed, business always provided opportunities for those with talent who were excluded by religion, education, social background, or gender from the professions. The market was a neutral arena that treated all players alike; like death, it was a great leveler of persons.[254] Prosperous widows, like many gentlemen, may simply have preferred a life of leisure. They chose to be rentiers and not entrepreneurs.

---

[254] On the egalitarian characteristics of the market, see G. Simmel, *The Philosophy of Money* (1978).

9

Inheritance and Advancement

James Cole, in a treatise for which the merchant Dierick Host wrote a foreword, advised testators to "forecast all things that we may leave peace with them after our departure."[1] Some testators adopted a casual approach: Nicholas Lawson, a grocer, ignored his children in his will and then, as an afterthought, added "but upon some further consideration, I doe give my four children ten pounds a piece."[2] But one of the most important acts of a businessman was the drafting of his will, which, except in special situations such as undertaking a voyage, usually occurred close to death, sometimes because the testator was reluctant to anticipate his demise and sometimes because he did not wish the provisions of his will to become known and cause dissension. Wills often needed revision as circumstances changed; George Carew altered his will each time one of his daughters married, but unfortunately he died in his sleep in 1702 without signing it.

The transfer of property by bequest was the primary means by which a family was perpetuated, and the distribution of assets was a potential source of bitter conflict. Businessmen did not enjoy an absolute right of disposition; both law and custom privileged their widows and children. But the head of every family—whether male or female—still retained considerable power over the disposition of assets. A businessman was often in a position to choose his heir or heirs. He also had an additional obligation to advance his children in other ways: to place sons in promising careers and marriages and to find husbands and dowries for his daughters.

What laws governed the distribution of estates? To what extent

---

[1] J. Cole, *Of Death* (1629), 89.   [2] PCC, Berkeley 213, 1656.

did businessmen favor partible inheritance over primogeniture? Who was preferred in wills—the widow, the children, a particular child, or someone outside the nuclear family? Which careers did parents select for their sons, and what role did they play in the marriages of their sons and daughters? Did social advancement take priority over the interests of particular children? What received the higher priority—the business or the family?

INHERITANCE LAW

Property is a social construct that allocates rights to resources between individuals.[3] The transmission of property rights within a family, whether at maturity, marriage, or death, can be either lateral or lineal and can pass through either the male or female line. English law, where real property was concerned, always preferred direct descendants over collateral relatives and the lineal female over collateral male lines.[4] England did not adopt a lineage system in which property returns to kin if there is no direct heir.[5] Vertical inheritance reduced the number of potential heirs and discriminated against the extended family.[6]

After 1540 all freehold property could be devised freely by will, and transfer was governed by the rules of common law in case of intestacy. William Sutes, a goldsmith, emphasized several times in his will that the custom of London had no jurisdiction over his land, which he bequeathed to his sons whom he had apprenticed to trades.[7] In landed society sons were generally favored over daughters and eldest over younger sons. Widows were entitled to their dower; in both England and America the widow had a life interest, which continued even after remarriage.[8] Although partible inheritance survived in a few counties, primogeniture had become the norm by the seventeenth century because it was thought to safeguard the integrity of landed estates.

Although it could be justified by invoking the patriarchal model, primogeniture was often defended on implausible grounds: one advocate was reduced to an analogy with the birds and beasts, that they fed their

[3] J. Goody, *Death, Property, and the Ancestors* (Stanford, 1962), 287.
[4] J. Goody, *The Oriental, the Ancient, and the Primitive* (Cambridge, 1990), 5.
[5] E. P. Thompson, "Grid of Inheritance" in *Family and Inheritance*, ed. J. Goody, J. Thirsk and E. P. Thompson (Cambridge, 1976), 328–60.
[6] Goody, *Production and Reproduction*, 86–90.   [7] PCC, Clarke 187, 1625.
[8] Salmon, *Women and the Law of Property in Early America*, chapter 7.

eldest first, even though humans were usually differentiated absolutely from the creatures of the Earth.[9] The opponents, principally younger sons, had a stronger case in equity. John Locke recognized the power of fathers "to bestow their estates on those who please them best" even when the children were adults; but he rejected primogeniture and argued that "children have a title to part of it" because the family was a community of goods.[10] Some preachers, like William Gouge, recommended a double portion for the eldest for social reasons, but others urged that all children be treated equally, irrespective of birth order.[11]

The division of personalty was more egalitarian. Ecclesiastical law, which had jurisdiction over personalty, favored partible inheritance, as did the customary law of the towns. In London both sons and daughters of freemen inherited by custom equal shares of one-third of all personalty, and only one-third was at the discretion of the testator. Advancement of children, by prior gifts or in the form of apprenticeship fees and investment capital for sons or dowries for daughters, was taken into account when determining shares; legacies from relatives, however, and any bequests of freehold real estate were excluded. The custom safeguarded the interests of the bereaved, who were spared the abuses that dogged wardship in landed society; it received strong support until late in the seventeenth century and was thought to be a major attraction of the freedom.[12] When William Sole divided his estate unequally between his children, his decision became the subject of comment and was reported as significant news to Lionel Cranfield by his factor.[13]

Widows were especially favored. Unless a widow had waived her rights in return for a jointure in a prenuptial settlement, she was entitled by custom to either free bench or dower and to *legitim*.[14] In London free bench included one-third of the husband's real property for life or until remarriage as well as the principal domicile. Of even greater significance, a widow by custom in addition to her widow's chamber had absolute

[9] J. Page, *Jus Fratum* (1658), 106.
[10] Locke, *Two Treatises*, 315; J. Tully, *Discourse on Property* (Cambridge, 1980), 133–4.
[11] W. Vaughan, *The Golden Grove* (1600), chapter 2; Gouge, *Of Domesticall Duties*, 575–9; D. Rogers, *Matrimonial Honour* (1642), 91.
[12] H. Swinburn, *Brief Treatise of Testaments* (1590), 105–6; Londonophilus, *Proposals Moderately Offered for a Full Peopling the City* (1672).
[13] *HMC Sackville Cranfield Papers*, vol. 2, 153.
[14] M. Bateson, ed., *Borough Customs*, vol. 21 (Selden Society, 1906), 132–7; A. J. Kettle, "My Wife Shall have It" in *Marriage and Property*, ed. E. M. Craig (Aberdeen, 1984), 98; R. H. Helmholz, *Canon Law and the Law of England* (1987), 259.

enjoyment of one-third of her husband's personal estate (which included tangible and intangible assets) and half to two-thirds if there were no surviving children.[15] The custom in effect created community property.

Opposition to partible inheritance certainly gathered momentum during the seventeenth century. As early as 1638 a commission of London aldermen recommended accepting a will over the custom.[16] To a wealthy businessman the widow's one-third may have appeared overly generous.[17] A 1670 act did limit the widow to a one-third share in case of intestacy and reduce widows' rights when there were no surviving children; in 1725 the custom was abolished by statute.[18]

Until 1690 the aldermen of London, acting through the Court of Orphans, enforced the custom strictly against wills and prior bequests. Sir William Scawen was fearful that he would be penalized by the custom when he devised property to the children of his brother, who was a citizen. Among the cases collected by Sir John Moore as lord mayor was one that ruled on whether a daughter could inherit her one-third under custom if she had land settled on her at marriage; the court judged that all gifts must be included.[19] Before 1671 the ecclesiastical courts also regularly awarded widows more than their one-third (often two-thirds) in case of intestacy, and they usually allocated an additional one-third as alimony in cases of separation.[20] It was not until 1706 that chancery

[15] A. C. Carter, *Getting, Spending, and Investing* (Assen, 1975), 2, 6.

[16] C. Carlton, *The Court of Orphans* (Leicester, 1974), 61.

[17] S. Staves, *Married Womens Separate Property* (Cambridge, 1990), 35–6, and Erickson, *Women and Property*, 221, point out, disapprovingly, that women were accused of delaying inheritance of landed estates by males. It is, however, incorrect to assert that the custom was evaded by 1584; the *Briefe Discourse Approving the Maintenance of the Custom* (1584), 32–4, was in fact a vigorous defence. Nor were women in the business community just given enough to survive. Personalty, which included most business assets, was treated differently from real property and distributed without any gender preference.

[18] Erickson, *Women and Property*, 26. Kenny, *Law Marriage*, 69, states that the statute of distributions gave widows both their customary one-third and half of the testator's one-third if there were no children. L. Bonfield, "Testamentary Causes" in *Communities and Courts*, ed. C. W. Brooks and M. Lobban (Rio Grande, 1997), 135, note 20, corrects Erickson on the terms of the statute. C. Shammas, "English Inheritance Law" in *Inheritance in America*, ed. C. Shammas et al. (New Brunswick, 1987), 37, argues that acts (unspecified) in the 1680s prevented a mother from inheriting all her children's personalty. The widow of an orphaned freeman had no claim under custom, though chancery could overrule on equitable grounds: see Carlton, *The Court of Orphans*, 48, 62. On the situation in Wales, see K. W. Swett, "Widowhood, Custom, and Property," *Welsh History Review* 18 (1996): 189–227.

[19] GLL, MS 507.

[20] Erickson, *Women and Property*, 227; *idem.*, "An Introduction to Probate Accounts" in *The Records of the Nation*, ed. G. Martin and P. Spufford (1990), 281.

ruled that a widow could not claim both under a marriage settlement and a will.[21]

The same principle of division was applied in other towns and in the province of York. In the American colonies primogeniture was less common, and there were no strict settlements, though the eldest often received a double share.[22] Although common law principles eventually eroded partible inheritance in New York, the widow's one-third, which was called the "dower of personalty," survived longer in Virginia and Maryland than in England.[23] The New England colonies had multigeniture; in Connecticut widows were entitled to one-third of the personalty and the use of one-third of the real property.[24]

PARTIBLE INHERITANCE

A majority of London businessmen who left orphans distributed their personalty in their wills according to custom, though the proportion dropped from 74 percent in period I to 66 percent in period II, with the lowest proportion among the richest in bracket IV (35 percent). When testators who left no underage children are included, the proportion seeking equivalency between their widows and children was 70 percent in period I and 77 percent in period II, falling to 44 percent in bracket IV (see table 6.3). In the Commissary Court of London in the 1590s, 57 percent of freemen with orphans followed the custom in their wills.[25] Among the London elite, 56 percent followed the custom (1660–94), falling to 26 percent (1695–1725); partible inheritance was most char-

---

[21] *English Reports*, vol. 2, 959, Hern v. Hern; PRO, C 5/86/44 (1683); C 5/274/15 (1705). The widow of Sir Nathaniel Hern was alleged to have taken both her one-third and legacies that were conditional on waiving her customary rights. Under the statute of uses, provision of a jointure did not eliminate dower rights, though widows were not expected to enjoy both: see B. J. Harris, "Aristocratic Women" in *State Sovereign and Society*, ed. C. Carlton (New York, 1998), 13, 23.

[22] Some American colonies reduced the widow's one-third: see C. Shammas, "English Inheritance Law," *American Journal of Legal History* 31 (1987): 158; *idem.*, "English Inheritance Law," *Inheritance in America*, 39; G. L. Haskins, "Beginnings of Partible Inheritance" in *Essays in the History of Early American Law*, ed. D. H. Flaherty (Chapel Hill, 1969), 242; J. L. Alson and M. O. Schapiro, "Inheritance Laws," *Journal of Economic History* 44 (1984): table 1.

[23] R. B. Morris ed., *New York Select Cases Mayor's Court*, (Washington, 1935), 25; Salmon, *Women and Law Property*, 149–52; D. Merwick, *Possessing Albany* (New York, 1990), 150; D. E. Narrett, "Preparation for Death," *New York History*, 57 (1976): 419; J. D. Goodfriend, *Before the Melting Pot* (Princeton, 1992), 186.

[24] C. H. Dayton, *Women Before the Bar* (Chapel Hill, 1995), 41.

[25] Archer, *Pursuit of Stability*, 75.

acteristic of those active in business and those who were younger with more children; Sir Joseph Hern changed his mind between his first and second wills.[26]

Businessmen also practiced equal division in other towns such as Norwich, Exeter, Stockport, Chester, Manchester, King's Lynn, Retford, and Worcester.[27] In Shrewsbury 88 percent of testators divided equally, though sons, particularly the eldest, were still preferred by a minority; when real estate was bequeathed to sons, the daughters received money and goods of the same value.[28] The same was true in New England and New York; John Winthrop divided his estate equally, as did David Yale, to keep his family together.[29] In the Schuyler family of New York the children were so afraid of primogeniture after the English takeover, that special settlements were made.[30]

Many testators cited the custom of London as their model, though it was also taken for granted, and some divided equally with meticulous care. Lucas Jacobs divided his goods, including his pictures, furniture, and books, equally among his three daughters, drawing up an inventory and specifying each item including a "harpischord for his granddaughter to play upon with a wainscott frame."[31] As late as 1706 John Winn insisted that "of all his estate reall and personal his said wife should have $^{1}/_{3}$rd part and the other $^{2}/_{3}$rds should be equally divided amongst all his children share and share alike"; when Thomas Hansall, in 1711, bequeathed property in St. Helens to his eldest son, he provided that his widow and children should share the proceeds.[32] John Lemming, an ironmonger, willed that if his sons could not agree on how to divide his goods equally, then everything was to be sold and the money distributed.[33]

---

[26] H. Horwitz, "Testamentary Pratice," *Law and History Review* 2 (1984): 235–6.

[27] Levine, "Some Norwich Goldsmiths," 488; A. D. Dyer, *City of Worcester* (Leicester, 1972), 180; C. B. Phillips and J. H. Smith, eds., *Stockport Probate Records*, vol. 131 (Lancashire and Cheshire Record Society, 1993), 87; G. J. Piccope, ed., *Lancashire and Cheshire Wills from Chester*, vol. 54 (Chetham Society, 1861), 171–4; T. S. Willan, *Elizabethan Manchester*, 3d ser., vol. 27 (Chetham Society, 1980), 91–5; J. Youings, *Tuckers Hall Exeter* (Exeter, 1968), 69; S. M. Cooper, "Intergenerational Social Mobility," *Continuity and Change* 7 (1992): table 1; D. Marcombe, *English Small Town Life* (Nottingham, 1993), table 5.

[28] J. C. Hindson, "Family Structure, Inheritance, and Kinship" (Ph.D. diss., University of Wales, 1991), 145, table 3.6.

[29] *New York Abstract Wills, 1708–28*, vol. 26 (New York Historical Society, 1893), 9, 14, 19; R. S. Dunn, *Puritan and Yankee* (Princeton, 1962), 202; D. E. Narrett, *Inheritance and Family Life* (1993), 96; Bingham, *Elihu Yale*, 13.

[30] *New York Wills, 1708–28*, 69, 73, 88.   [31] PCC, Berkeley 258, 1656.

[32] CLRO, CSB 1693–1713.   [33] PCC, Cambell 95, 1642.

Table 9.1. *Holdings of Land and Urban Property: Division and Rank (Percentage of Known Cases)*

	Period I	Period II	Bracket I	Bracket II	Bracket III	Bracket IV	Cohort I	Cohort II	Cohort III	Cohort IV
Land Major	17.2	40.4	23.5	18.8	54.6	81.0	63.8	36.6	47.8	73.8
Land Minor	32.9	26.8	30.6	34.4	24.8	9.5	29.8	25.6	22.0	13.1
No Land	49.8	32.8	45.9	46.9	20.7	9.5	6.4	37.8	30.2	13.1
City Major	14.2	23.6	10.1	14.3	37.3	58.2	49.0	26.2	29.7	27.8
City Minor	29.8	33.6	30.4	39.1	29.9	13.4	38.8	35.2	27.1	27.8
City None	56.0	42.8	59.5	46.6	32.7	28.4	12.3	38.6	43.2	44.4
Equal Division	74.1	65.7	69.5	75.6	69.5	35.2	83.8	65.9	58.7	51.7
Unequal Division	25.9	34.3	30.5	24.4	30.5	64.8	16.3	34.1	41.3	48.3
Peer/Baronet	0.1	0.9	0.7	0.7	3.4	18.9	1.4	3.0	1.6	4.6
Knight	1.9	2.6	2.7	1.4	14.5	36.9	23.0	4.1	6.2	4.6

William Essington, a draper, spread his assets between his sons and daughters.[34] Anthony Cooper, a goldsmith, insisted that the money he had advanced to his elder married daughters be counted against their customary portion.[35]

When the eldest was given land, he was often excluded from a share of the personalty, as by Thomas Row and William Maddox, merchant tailors.[36] Edward Bellamy, a fishmonger, left one-third of his estate to the son whom he had not advanced.[37] Many testators interpreted the custom loosely as an obligation to be fair to all parties. In 1669 Henry Hunter gave his son, Nathaniel, a choice between his customary portion or a house plus £2,000. Salter John Salloway gave half of his estate to his widow and half to his children.[38] George Mitley, a Hamburg merchant, divided his estate into five parts: one-fifth to his wife and four-fifths to his children.[39] Thomas Hughes, a clothworker, who had advanced £1,300, or half his estate, to his eldest son over the previous eleven years, wanted to exclude him from his customary share and leave everything to his second son.[40] Edward Arbell, a goldsmith, gave land to his eldest son and daughter and wanted his personalty to be divided among his four youngest children.[41] John Thompson left most of his estate to his youngest son, who was appointed executor, because he had already advanced his two elder sons.[42] Dudley Lovell, a goldsmith, followed the custom, but he left land to trustees for his orphan son and married daughter, and he specified that more be purchased for his grandchildren.[43]

Some fathers wanted more choice than they were allowed by custom, so they established trusts, bought land, or gave their sons money surreptitiously during their lifetime to evade the custom. George Mellish, a merchant tailor, bequeathed everything to his eldest son; Henry Chitty and Thomas Tilsey specifically renounced the custom of London in their wills.[44] Richard Fox left specific legacies to each of his children, which his estate could not cover.[45] Several cases came before the Mayor's Court in which beneficiaries appealed to custom against their father's will.[46]

---

[34] PCC, Fairfax 18, 1649.   [35] PCC, Russell 96, 1633.
[36] PCC, Clarke 145, 1625; PCC, Swann 102, 1623, which lists in detail all his loans on mortgage.
[37] PCC, Berkeley 318, 1656.   [38] PCC, Evelyn 62, 1641.   [39] PCC, Alchin 295, 1659.
[40] PCC, Cambell 118, 1642.   [41] PCC, Fairfax 74, 1649.   [42] PCC, Ruthen 269, 1657.
[43] PCC, Hyde 26, 1665.   [44] PCC, Alchin 90, 1654; PCC, Fines 15, 1647.
[45] CLRO, CSB 1584–1614.   [46] Earle, *Making of the English Middle Class*, 392.

The overriding objective of most testators was equivalency rather than strict equality. Bequests of land were balanced by comparable bequests of moveables; children with legacies from grandparents and kin might receive less from their father.[47] The variations in division of property reflect different circumstances and different needs. Testators had to take into account many factors, including the distribution of their assets, the number, age, and sex of their children, and their marriage settlements. They usually tried to accommodate the different interests of their offspring, to satisfy their individual talents and give each child equal opportunity. There were always special cases. The residue of an estate might be distributed equally among the children, but often it passed to the more vulnerable children or those in greatest need.

GENDER AND BIRTH ORDER

Widows were frequently the first to inherit real estate; they were given an interest for life or during their widowhood or until their children came of age.[48] Anthony Bickerstaff left his land first to his wife, then his eldest son (who also had other land settled on him), then by elaborate descent to the children of his sons, and then to his male kin.[49] Richard Lane, who married the sister and heiress of Jonathan Blackwell, made his two brothers-in-law trustees for first his wife and then his daughters.[50] Robert Hayes, a merchant tailor, left his land first to his widow, then his son, and then his daughter.[51] John Harvey, a distiller, divided his personalty equally but left his land first to his widow and then to his son.[52] Walgrave Sidney, a merchant tailor, willed his extensive urban property to his widow for life and then to his son.[53] Joseph Pike, a vintner by company but a dyer by trade, left one-third of his land to his wife for life with reversion to his children; John Harris, a girdler, left his widow her dower of land and the residue to his eldest son, the younger sons being put apprentices.[54] Thomas Olcott, a dyer, left his Kentish land to his widow, then his eldest, and then his other sons in birth order.[55] Thomas Brown, a clothworker, bequeathed his house, "Cowfoot," to his widow (the rental income to be enjoyed by his mother-in-law) and then

[47] PCC, Twisse 169, 1646.
[48] J. Tuck, *Discourse on Property* (Cambridge, 1980), 134.
[49] PCC, Aylett 312, 1655.   [50] PRO, Prob 11/653/210–11, 1732.
[51] PCC, Meade 19, 1618.   [52] CLRO, CSB 1693–1713.   [53] PCC, Berkeley 318, 1656.
[54] PCC, Berkeley 316, 1656; PCC, Ruthen 271, 1657.   [55] PCC, Barrington 7, 1628.

to his eldest son.[56] Christopher Ile, an apothecary of Newcastle, left his real estate to his widow and then his daughters.[57]

A few testators sought to limit their widows' inheritance of land (see also chapter 2). Thomas Pitt purchased land in trust to bar his wife's claim to dower.[58] In 1709 Isaac Miller asked his widow to waive her dower rights over his real estate.[59] In 1590 Robert Lambert, a Colchester merchant, bequeathed his widow specific legacies in lieu of her dower.[60] Thomas Covell, a skinner, instructed that his land in Berkshire be sold to pay his debts and that his widow surrender her dower in return for one-third of his personalty.[61]

Some husbands also sought to limit the personalty inherited by their wives, who were entitled by custom to a larger share than any individual child. George Bourne of Newcastle, who had no children, left his wife £20 and the house if she did not claim her half under the custom; his main legatee was a gentleman, Mark Erington, who was appointed coexecutor with the widow.[62] William Sprott offered his widow 1,000 marks and his house in lieu of her mandatory half of the estate (their sole daughter being married) so long as she remained a widow.[63] Samuel Cartwright, a stationer, left his widow a house in London in lieu of her one-third.[64] William Parsons, a brewer, and Edmund Sheppard, a saddler, each gave £500 to their widows in lieu of custom.[65] Richard Wright offered his widow £4,000 if she did not claim under the custom, and he provided an elaborate descent for his land.[66] Valentine Bowles gave his widow £200 in lieu of her one-third and her dower rights to land in Essex, which was bequeathed to their daughters.[67] Andrew Impey, a vintner, gave his wife an annuity of £30 in lieu of her one-third and dower and left his lands to his three daughters.[68]

Prenuptial settlements were frequently invoked as a bar to customary rights.[69] The widow of Thomas Weeks, a clothworker, received what she had been promised on bond together with six months' board.[70] John

[56] PCC, Audley 93, 1632.
[57] *Durham Wills, 1604–49*, vol. 142 (Surtees Society, 1929), 87.
[58] H. M. C. *Fortescue*, vol. 2, xi.   [59] CLRO, CSB IV.
[60] F. G. Emmison, ed., *Wills of Essex Gentry and Yeomen* (Chelmsford, 1980), 293.
[61] PCC, Rivers 7, 1644.
[62] *Durham Wills, 1543–1607*, vol. 112 (Surtees Society, 1906), 154.
[63] PCC, Savile 104, 1622.   [64] PCC, Pembroke 89, 1650.
[65] PCC, Rivers 131, 1645; PCC, Cambell 22, 1642.
[66] PCC, Weldon 8, 1617.   [67] PCC, Goare 101, 1637.   [68] PCC, Aylett 190, 1655.
[69] Will of Sir Humphrey Handford, PCC, Clarke 142, 1625.
[70] PCC, Goare 79, 1637.

Parker sought to give his eldest son a double portion and ensure that his widow did not receive both the portion, which she had brought to the marriage, and her customary share.[71] Stephen Abberley, a grocer, regarded his marriage settlement as a substitute for the custom, though he still added £300 to the agreed £500 and asked his executors "to be loving and respctful to the widow."[72] Thomas Salter, in contrast, reversed normal practice by appealing to custom against his marriage settlement. He had agreed to bequeath his wife £180 at his death on penalty of £350, but he discovered that this would give her more than her entitlement under the custom of London. So he bequeathed her £6 for mourning, £20 in cash, his house in Middlesex, and all the clothing and silver plate, except for his virginals.[73]

When the custom was evaded, however, it was usually to favor the eldest son, not to exclude widows from their ancient entitlement, as happened on occasion in landed families.[74] Francis Child, an embroiderer, "bought noe land at all to the end I would not deprive her [his wife] of her full third."[75] When a portion was returned, the widow at least knew what she would receive, whereas a one-third share could be one-third of nothing.

In some cases, sons were preferred over daughters, who usually received money rather than land. Richard Scott, a draper of Shrewsbury, divided his urban property between his daughters and sons, but his eldest son received a farm and £200 more than the others.[76] Bigley Carleton, a grocer, left £1,000 from his testator's one-third to his eldest son but only £400 to his daughters.[77] Timothy Tirrell, whose wife was pregnant at the time he wrote his will, provided £1,500 if the child proved to be a son and £1,000 if she were a daughter.[78] Richard Pearson, a merchant tailor, provided £1,500 for his unborn child if a son, but £1,200 if a daughter.[79] William Hounsell, a merchant, allocated £4,000 if his wife had a daughter and half his estate if she had a son.[80] In Jamaica children were favored before wives and sons before daughters.[81] Widows usually received more than their daughters. In 1616 Robert Tempest, for example, left £1,000 to his widow and £500 to his daughter in a nun-cupative will.[82]

---

[71] CLRO, CSB 1693–1713.   [72] PCC, Rivers 41, 1645.   [73] PCC, Berkeley 126, 1656.
[74] E. Spring, "Law and the Theory of the Affective Family," *Albion* 16 (1984): 9.
[75] PCC, Evelyn 100, 1641.   [76] Shropshire RO, MS 49/601.   [77] PCC, Seager 78, 1634.
[78] PCC, Berkeley 314, 1656.   [79] PCC, Hale 90, 1626.   [80] PCC, Aylett 186, 1655.
[81] Burnard, "Family Continuity in Jamaica," 182, 188.
[82] *Durham Wills, 1604–49*, 107.

Daughters were, however, sometimes named principal beneficiaries, though it is difficult to know whether they were preferred above sons because there may have been no sons. George Boon left all his land and personalty to his daughters in trust, but he had no son and his wife had a jointure. Often a daughter received more personalty to compensate for the land bequeathed to the eldest son. Ralph Boutter, an armorer, left houses in Lewisham to his son provided that his daughter received a dowry of £150; otherwise they had to share.[83] Peter Mitton, a merchant tailor, left his son his house, but he had to pay his sister £15 a year.[84] The widowed Matthew Chapman of Newcastle did leave his son a larger share, but his daughters (one married) still received real estate.[85] Giles Crowche, a haberdasher, who had no sons, followed the custom for his three daughters, and, though he left his lands in Kent to his nephew and then by elaborate descent through his kin, he made his daughter, Anne, custodian of the deeds.[86]

In general, daughters seem to have been treated equally with younger sons; unmarried daughters often received special treatment. John Fowler followed the custom and then added £400 from his one-third to provide a portion for his daughter.[87] Michael Pope considered his surviving son unsatisfactory and made his daughter his heir.[88] Thomas Andrews, a draper, left his daughters portions of £300–400, whereas his younger son only received £80.[89] Philip Papillon left the Acrise estate to his eldest son, but he provided land and annuities for his younger sons and gave all his daughters equal portions of £3,000.[90]

Several businessmen imitated landowners and moved toward primogeniture. There are signs of increasing preference for eldest sons, even when the widow survived, between periods I and II, especially among the tycoons in bracket IV (see table 6.3). Sir Owen Buckingham, Sir Francis Child, Ambrose Crowley, Sir Peter Daniel, Sir Samuel Dashwood, and Sir Peter Delme all favored their eldest sons. Land was frequently settled on the eldest, even when the personalty was divided equally, as by William Hudson, a skinner.[91] Henry Reeve, a scrivener, left his land to his eldest son with reversion first to his younger sons and then to his

---

[83] PCC, Aylett 160, 1655.   [84] PCC, Nabbs 270, 1666.
[85] Durham Wills, 1604–49, 7.   [86] PROB, 11/94/150, 1599.
[87] P. W. Souers, The Matchless Orinda (Cambridge, 1931), 2.
[88] I. V. Hall, "Whitson Court Sugar House," Transactions of the Bristol and Gloucester Archaeological Society 65 (1944): 58.
[89] PCC, Clarke 123, 1625.   [90] KAO, MS U 1015 T 45/1.   [91] PCC, Twisse 57, 1646.

daughters.[92] Richard Crowche, a salter, who owned mainly urban property, gave his eldest his own house and then divided the other houses
between his younger son and daughter.[93] John Mabbe, Robert Wigge,
and Robert Hartop all left land to their eldest sons and urban property
to their younger sons.[94]

The eldest sometimes received a larger share of the personalty. Ralph
Harmon, a merchant tailor, preferred his eldest son with £2,400 to set
up, because he wanted to "strain myself to do him good."[95] Isaac Levy,
a New York merchant, left his eldest son £900, his second £800, and his
third and fourth £750.[96] Mathias Goodfellow, a girdler, gave his eldest
son £2,700, his second son £1,600, and two other sons £1,000 in lieu
of custom.[97] Samuel Bridges, a merchant tailor, had advanced all his children, so he left his whole estate to his eldest son.[98] Edmund Harrison,
who apprenticed his eldest son to a draper for £1,000, willed that his
children should each choose a piece of plate by order of age.[99]

In many cases younger sons received equal treatment and they often
inherited the estate because their eldest brother had died. Fathers took
ability into account as well as age. Sir James Houblon, in his will of
1700, left one-fifth of his estate to his son, James, "as more knowing in
my business though no unkindness" to his son, William, who was named
executor. Some eldest sons had antagonized their father: Robert Sanders
of New York left his eldest son 50 shillings "in full of ye pretence he
might have as being my eldest son and heir at law" and everything to
his wife.[100]

Even merchants who had turned landowners retained their preference
for partible inheritance and were generous to their younger sons.[101]
Sometimes all the children received some land, or the eldest was named
the legatee on condition that he pay annuities and portions to his mother
or siblings. Thomas Andrews, a draper, left land to his sons out of which
they had to pay an annuity to the widow.[102] Henry Bell gave his third
son his art collection.[103]

[92] PCC, Hele 43, 1626.   [93] PRO, PROB 11/98/173.
[94] T. F. Reddaway, "Elizabethan London," *Guildhall Miscellany*, 2 (1963): 187.
[95] PCC, Rudd 78, 1615.   [96] PRO, C 104/13–14.
[97] PCC, Cambell 12, 1642.   [98] PCC, Aylett 167, 1655.
[99] P. Wardle, "The King's Embroiderer," *Textile History* 35–36 (1994): 44.
[100] *New York Abstract Wills, 1665–1707*, vol. 25 (New York Historical Society, 1892),
368.
[101] H. J. Habakkuk, *Marriage, Debt, and the Estate Market* (Oxford, 1994), 100.
[102] PCC, Clarke 123, 1625.   [103] Cooper, "Intergenerational Social Mobility," 294.

The eldest was not necessarily the favorite or the most loved child, and parents frequently recognized that their younger children, who had still to establish themselves and marry, needed and deserved the most support. Thomas Blanchard, a draper, had apprenticed and set up his elder sons, and so he gave his youngest son his land in Shropshire.[104] William Dalby, a mercer, tried to favor his youngest son.[105] Remarriage raised additional problems; sometimes children from a first marriage were preferred to those from a second.[106] Edward Whorehouse defended himself successfully against charges that he had defrauded his widow and daughter by a second marriage in leaving land to his three children by his first wife.[107] In 1719 William Patterson had no wife or surviving children, so he left his money to the stepchildren of his two wives.

OTHER BENEFICIARIES

The primary beneficiaries of businessmen were always their widow and children. Rowland Wilson, Sr., told his son's widow that she would receive nothing from his estate.[108] But the unpredictability of mortality made it imperative that testators name several residual heirs. The wills of substantial merchants usually had contingency clauses rerouting bequests in case of death to make sure that property did not pass by default to the wrong person. Failure in the male line also prompted some testators to leave their land to male kin. Usually kin and friends received only token bequests, but in a few cases, they became principal legatees. They benefited more when the custom was followed, because a testator could distribute his one-third freely knowing that his widow and children already had their share.

The most common beneficiaries outside the nuclear family were grandchildren (see also chapter 5). When their children had already been set up, testators looked ahead to the third generation. A bequest to a married daughter was often in effect a gift to a grandchild. William Westrow, a clothworker, had already advanced his daughter, so he left the residue of his estate to his widow and then his grandchildren.[109] Richard Venner, a barber surgeon, had no sons, so he willed his land to

---

[104] PCC, Aylett 197, 1655.   [105] CLRO, CSB.
[106] W. Vaughan, *The Golden Grove* (1600), chapter 2; Gouge, *Of Domesticall Duties*, 578.
[107] CLRO, MC1/4B, 44. Eliz.
[108] R. Spalding, *Contemporaries of Bulstrode Whitelocke* (Oxford, 1990), 482.
[109] PCC, Alchin 51, 1654.

the children of his daughter.[110] Gowen Painter left £2,000 to his daughter and grandchildren to be invested in land.[111] David Knight wanted part of his daughter's customary one-third to pass to her newly born son. In 1616 Robert Clarkson left money to his grandson, Benjamin, "if obedient." In 1632 one clothworker in Sussex left his land to the daughter of his eldest son, not to his younger son who received stock.[112] William Cokayne scrupulously divided his estate between his sons, grandchildren, and kin and made his son, William, give bond for £10,000 to ensure performance.[113] Simon Wood, a merchant tailor, left his gold ring engraved with his arms and all his printed books to his grandson, his daughter having already been advanced.[114] Clement Underhill, a draper, had provided both his daughters with portions on marriage, so he left his estate to his grandchildren.[115] Richard Yearwood, a Southwark grocer, left his land in Surrey first to his son and then to his daughter's son.[116]

Some testators preferred their grandchildren to their children. In many cases, like that of William Sherrington and George Hough, it was because they were angry with their own children.[117] In 1720 tycoon Thomas Frederick left his main estate to his grandsons, because he considered that his sons and daughters had been disrepectful and had abandoned him in his old age; the eldest only received what he was entitled to by the marriage settlement, and his daughters and younger son only £1,000.[118]

Numerous kin could qualify as potential legatees. The childless Gilbert Casson, a fishmonger, left his urban property to his stepgrandson by his wife's first husband.[119] Sir Charles Peers was generous to his stepgrandchildren as well as his own grandchildren. But most bequests were confined to the spouses of a testator's children or to the children of their siblings. Land was often left to sons-in-law rather than daughters. Henry Jackson, a grocer, left his land to his daughter and her husband since he had no sons.[120] Sir Nathaniel Gould, in his will of 1726, left his land to his male kin and not his daughters. Richard Beal, a merchant, left his

---

[110] PCC, Berkeley 17, 1656.   [111] PCC, May 185, 1661.
[112] Erickson, *Women and Property*, 63.   [113] Cokayne, *Cokayne Memoranda*, 103.
[114] PCC, Fines 86, 1647.   [115] PCC, Brent 215, 1653.
[116] H. F. Waters, *Genealogical Gleanings in England*, vol. 1 (Salem, Mass., 1892), 123.
[117] PCC, Harvey 78, 1639.
[118] E. H. Fellowes, *Family of Frederick* (Windsor, 1988), 31.
[119] PCC, Pell 4, 1659.   [120] PCC, Pembroke 200, 1650.

land in Kent first to the son of his brother and then to other male kin.[121] Bachelors, like Sir Andrew King, usually favored their nephews.

A childless businessman, like Thomas Palmer, could provide for his widow but privilege his male kin. Palmer gave his widow his mansion in Mincing Lane with the vaults and tenements adjoining for life as well as a hoard of jewelery, paintings, coaches, and horses. A trust was set up to provide her with an annuity of £2,000, and she also received a lump sum of £1,000. But the major part of his fortune passed to a nephew, with £500 to each of his nephew's four daughters and £900 in trust for a niece.[122]

Kin in England also benefited from legacies of merchants living in America. George Heathcote of Pennsylvania bequeathed money to his sisters in England as well as to his cousin, Caleb, in New York.[123] In 1710 Giles Shelley of New York, a merchant and privateer, left a bequest to his aunt in England as well as to his adopted son, Edward Antill; in 1713 Nicholas Bowden of New York left one-third of his estate to the children of his deceased brother in Tiverton and to his sister in Cornwall.[124]

SONS IN BUSINESS

In period I 56 percent and in period II 60.8 percent of all sons became businessmen, though first sons in business slipped to 37 percent in bracket IV and to 38 and 40 percent in cohorts I and IV. Some 30 percent of all first sons became gentlemen, with a lower level in brackets I and II. The proportion of younger sons who became gentlemen fluctuated between 16 and 28 percent, with highs in bracket IV and cohorts I and IV. Younger sons who became professionals fluctuated considerably, with highs in brackets I and III and in cohort IV.[125]

In London rights of patrimony and the utility of the freedom ensured that sons would follow their fathers into the livery companies, even if they were not active in business. There were three generations of Haselfoots, for example, in the Haberdashers Company.[126] Certain

---

[121] PCC, Pile 93, 1636.   [122] PRO, Prob 11/564/131.
[123] *New York Abstract Wills, 1708–28*, 59.   [124] Ibid., 60, 108.
[125] A similar percentage (57.9 percent with a 10 percent margin of error) of sons followed their fathers into business in the modern period: see W. D. Rubinstein, *Capitalism, Culture, and Decline in Britain, 1750–1990* (1993), 120–1.
[126] Archer, *Haberdashers Company*, 49.

Table 9.2. *Occupations of Sons by Birth Order (Percentage of Known Cases)*

	Period I	Period II	Bracket I	Bracket II	Bracket III	Bracket IV	Cohort I	Cohort II	Cohort III	Cohort IV
First Son										
Businessman	55.61	55.77	51.52	68.33	48.45	36.84	37.93	54.25	55.11	40.00
Gentleman	29.82	31.05	21.21	22.50	43.22	56.14	53.45	34.91	32.12	54.00
Professional	14.57	13.18	27.27	9.17	8.33	7.02	8.62	10.85	12.77	6.00
Total	597	789	33	120	516	57	116	212	274	50
Second Son										
Businessman	55.74	66.97	54.55	84.78	61.81	44.44	50.00	67.35	71.55	47.62
Gentleman	23.36	15.46	18.18	8.70	21.65	38.89	32.89	17.35	14.63	28.57
Professional	20.90	17.58	27.27	6.52	16.54	16.67	17.11	15.31	13.82	23.81
Total	244	330	11	46	254	36	76	98	123	21
Third, Fourth, and Fifth Sons										
Businessmen	52.26	68.85	28.57	76.00	65.66	39.53	46.03	72.31	68.07	56.25
Gentlemen	27.74	15.57	57.14	16.00	19.19	48.84	38.10	15.39	20.17	12.50
Professional	20.00	15.57	14.29	8.00	15.15	11.63	15.87	12.31	11.77	31.25
Total	155	244	7	25	198	43	63	65	119	16

names evoked awe and deference in the business community, and there were patriarchal heads of tribes of merchants. Particular families in every period dominated the city and its trades, and their offspring were highly visible until the fourth generation. Richard Chamberlain, for example, put five of his six surviving sons in trade; the Gore family had seven sons in business at one time and were prominent for four generations. Sir William Garrard, the third in a line of Tudor mercantile oligarchs, had four surviving sons of which he intended the eldest for the landed gentry and the rest for business, though he gave them all land. Only one son, however, became a businessman; the second and fourth sons lived on annuities paid by their eldest brother, and the land that they inherited.[127]

Dynasties of elite families were to be found in all the major provincial towns. Newcastle had the Liddells, Blacketts, Riddels, Jenisons, Halls, Harleys, Sandersons, and Ellisons, some of them successfully reproducing for two centuries, though the Blacketts failed in the direct male line in the third generation.[128] Hull had the Listers, Ramsdens, Maisters, Crowleys, Moulds, and Barnards.[129] Exeter had the Elwells, Sanfords, Kings, Periams, and Woods; the Morris family of Exeter were carriers from the 1680s to the 1850s, but few families in fact lasted for more than two generations.[130] Bristol had the Knights, Earles, Gonings, Canns, Longs, Colstons, Carys, Browns, Wilkinsons, Aldsworths, Elbridges, Creswickes, Hookes, Jacksons, and Yates.[131] Liverpool had the Johnsons, Pembertons, Gildarts, Claytons, Cunliffes, Tarletons, Houghtons, Blundells, Norrises, and Warbricks.[132] On the other hand, although some families, like the Cuttings, Meadows, and Johnsons,

[127] Lang, "The Greater Merchants," appendixes.
[128] J. R. Boyle and D. W. Dendy, eds., *Newcastle Merchant Adventurers Records*, vol. 101 (Surtees Society, 1899), xxiii; J. Brand, *History of Newcastle upon Tyne*, vol. 1 (Newcastle, 1789), 113–14; H. Bourne, *History of Newcastle* (Newcastle, 1730), 66; R. Welford, *Men of Mark*, vol. 3 (1895), 37.
[129] J. Allison, ed., *V. C. H. Yorkshire East Riding*, vol. 1 (1969), 123; H. Calvert, *History of Kingston upon Hull* (1978), 180; G. Jackson, *Hull in the Eighteenth Century* (1972), 107.
[130] D. Gerhold, *Road Transport before the Railways* (Cambridge, 1993), figure 1; J. Youings, *Tuckers Hall Exeter* (Exeter, 1968), 80; W. G. Hoskins, "Elizabethan Merchants Exeter" in *Elizabethan Government and Society*, ed. S. T. Bindoff (1961), 172; W. T. MacCaffrey, *Exeter, 1540–1640* (Cambridge, Mass., 1958), 255–7.
[131] P. MacGrath, "Wills of Bristol Merchants," *Transactions of the Bristol and Gloucester Archaeological Society* 68 (1949): 93.
[132] H. Peet, ed., *Liverpool in the Reign of Queen Anne*, vol. 59 (Transactions of the Lancashire and Cheshire Historical Society, 1907), 6; P. G. E. Clements, "The Rise of Liverpool," *Economic History Review*, 2d ser., 29 (1976): 217.

lasted in Norwich for two to three generations, the majority dropped out one by one to move into the gentry and professions.[133] The same was true of lesser towns, like Shrewsbury.[134] King's Lynn had the Turners, Whartons, Percevals, Revetts, Baggs, Greens, and Allens; eldest sons were more likely to succeed their fathers than younger sons.[135] In Coventry sons followed their fathers, though there was little long-term continuity, and some moved to London, like in the Jesson family.[136] Chester had the Alderseys and Bavards.[137] York had the Robinsons, Dickinsons, Tophams, and Breareys.[138] Leeds had the Milners, Kitchinghams, Dixons, Wades, Stanhopes, Hodgsons, Lawsons, Rayners, and Lowthers.[139] Great Yarmouth had the Ingrams and Rivetts, Birmingham the Jenners, and Ipswich the Daundy, Sparrow, and Blois families.[140] In Petsworth rights of patrimony helped to sustain hereditary trades, and in Abingdon many sons followed their fathers (1540–1659), though numbers declined thereafter.[141] In contrast, in Rye, St. Ives, Oxford, and Swansea, although there were some artisanal lineages, successful business families came and went.[142]

Outside of England the situation was more mixed. Edinburgh had the Boyles, Dunlops, Corbetts, Mundreths, and Buchanans, and there was continuity between the seventeenth- and eighteenth-century business families; but this was less true of Aberdeen, Dundee, and Glasgow.[143]

---

[133] Pound, *Tudor and Stuart Norwich*, 82; J. T. Evans, "Decline of Oligarchy," *Journal of British Studies* 14 (1974): 8–52, 57; *idem.*, *Norwich* (Oxford, 1979), 24; C. Branford, "Powers of Association" (Ph.D. diss., University of East Anglia, 1993), 143.

[134] Hindson, "Family Structure," 204; T. C. Mendenhall, *Shrewsbury Drapers* (Oxford, 1953), 117.

[135] H. L. Bradfer-Lawrence, "The Merchants of Lynn" in *A Supplement to Blomefield's Norfolk*, ed. C. Ingelby (1929), 163; Cooper, "Intergenerational Social Mobility," 288.

[136] A. Hughes, *Politics, Society, and Civil War in Warwickshire* (Cambridge, 1987), 14; R. M. Berger, *Most Necessary Luxuries* (University Park, 1993), 244.

[137] D. M. Woodward, *The Trade of Elizabethan Chester* (Hull, 1970), 59.

[138] P. M. Tillcot, ed., *V. C. H. City of York* (1961), 181.

[139] R. G. Wilson, *Gentlemen Merchants* (Manchester, 1971), 15.

[140] P. Gauci, *Politics and Society in Great Yarmouth* (Oxford, 1996), appendixes 4–5.

[141] A. Everitt, "The Marketing of Agricultural Produce" in *The Agrarian History of England and Wales, 1500–1640*, ed. J. Thirsk, vol. 4 (Cambridge, 1967), 489.

[142] G. Mayhew, *Tudor Rye* (Falmer, 1989), 116; M. Griffiths, "Very Wealthy by Merchandise" in *Class, Community, and Culture in Tudor Wales*, ed. J. G. Jones (Cardiff, 1989), 212; C. I. Hammer, "Anatomy of an Oligarchy," *Journal of British Studies* 18 (1978): 25–6; M. Carter, "Town or Urban Society" in *Societies, Cultures, and Kinship*, ed. C. Phythian-Adams (Leicester, 1993), 118.

[143] Devine, *Tobacco Lords*, 3–6, 10, figure 1, appendix 1; *idem.*, "Merchant Class" in *Scottish Urban History*, ed. G. Gordon and B. Dicks (Aberdeen, 1983), 101; R. A. Houston, *Social Change* (Oxford, 1994), 82.

There was little continuity in Belfast, Philadelphia, Barbados, and the Chesapeake.[144] Many sons stuck to the same trades as their fathers. There were several generations of Bristows in the Virginia trade and Fryes in the sugar trade.[145] The Goulds, Heathcotes, Gores, and Lyells perpetuated their predominance in the Baltic.[146] The Levant trade was dominated by three-generation families such as the Bettons, Boddingtons, Des Bouveries, Salweys, Bosanquets, and Vernons; sixteen of the major players in the 1690s were sons of Levant merchants.[147] There were twelve generations of Durtnells in the building industry, eight generations of Earlys in the upholstery industry, and three generations of Petts in shipbuilding.[148] Six generations of Foleys were active in the Midland iron trade; the first Richard Foley (1588–1657) raised himself from nailer to ironmaster, and his son, Richard, and grandsons, Paul and Philip, continued the business.[149] In the Sheffield cutlery trade, the same surnames recur, and families, like the Hancocks and Steers, were multigenerational.[150] Several generations of Houltons were Trowbridge clothiers even though they bought land; the Odingsells of Sherburn had three sons and two grandsons in the drapery business.[151] The Luckes were mercers in Steyning for three generations, and there were dynasties of brewers in Rye.[152] Bookselling and banking were virtually hereditary trades with families such as the Clements, Childs, and Hoares.[153]

Other families spanned both time and space. The merchants who emi-

---

[144] G. B. Nash, "Philadelphia Merchants" in *The World of William Penn*, ed. R. S. and M. M. Dunn (Philadelphia, 1986), 337, 340, 344; Agnew, *Belfast Merchants*, 193.

[145] Virginia State Library, USL Acc 22,953; R. B. Sheridan, "The Sugar Trade" (Ph.D. diss., University of London, 1951), appendixes.

[146] Astrom, *From Cloth to Iron*, 162–3.

[147] Davis, *Aleppo and Devonshire Square*, 73.

[148] C. S. Durtnell, "Durtnell and Sons," *Business Archives* 40 (1974): 54; M. J. Power, "The East London Working Community" in *Work in Towns, 850–1850*, ed. P. J. Corfield and D. Keene (Leicester, 1990), 110; A. Plummer and R. E. Earl, *The Blanket Makers* (1969), introduction.

[149] M. B. Rowlands, *Masters and Men* (1975), 26–8.

[150] D. Hey, *Fiery Blades* (Leicester, 1991), 152, 198.

[151] J. B. Whitmore and A. W. H. Clarke, eds. *London Visitation Pedigrees, 1664*, vol. 92 (Harlean Society, 1940), 105; K. H. Rogers, "Trowbridge Clothiers" in *Textile History and Economic History*, ed. N. B. Harte and K. G. Ponting (Manchester, 1973), 142.

[152] J. Pennington and J. Sleight, "Steyning Town," *Sussex Archaeological Collections*, 130 (1992): 176; G. Mayhew, "Life Cycle Service," *Continuity and Change* 6 (1991): 213.

[153] G. Mandelbrote, "From the Warehouse" in *A Genius for Letters*, ed. R. Myers and M. Harris (Winchester, 1995), 51; T. Bennett, *Notebook*, ed. N. Hodgson and C. Blagden, vol. 6 (Oxford Bibliographical Society, 1956), 6; "Childs and Company," *Three Banks Review* 98 (1973): 43.

Table 9.3. *Generational Continuity in Business*

First Generation	Estimate per 100 families
Number who marry (89%)	89
Number of sons (77%)	69
Number of sons who enter business (58%)	40
Second Generation	
Number who marry (89%)	36
Number of sons (77%)	28
Number of sons who enter business (58%)	16
Third Generation	
Number who marry (89%)	14
Number of sons (77%)	11
Number of sons who enter business (58%)	6

grated to America from East Anglia had been in trade for three generations.[154] The Elwes, Cary, and Lever families surface in many different contexts.[155] Ten members of the Robinson family were merchants (1520–1660).[156] All three sons of Matthew Markland of Wigan went into his business.[157] Of the 173 merchant members of Parliament (1660–90), 50 percent were sons of merchants.[158]

All these examples are, however, deceptive, and they well illustrate how misleading individual cases can be. The truth can be determined by a simple mathematical calculation. Even though 58 percent of sons of businessmen entered business, when allowance is made for bachelors, infertility, and families with daughters but no sons, only fourteen out of every one hundred business families would have a son in business by the third generation, and six by the fourth generation. At any one time there would have been some 1,400 businessmen whose grandfather had been in business, more than sufficient to attract the notice of historians; but the great majority of families lasted in business for only one or two generations.

---

[154] Thompson, *Mobility and Migration*, 178.
[155] O. Barron, ed., *Northamptonshire Families* (1906), 63–6; A. Wallis, "Diary London Citizen," *Reliquary* 3 (1889): 92; J. M. Price, "Who was John Norton," *William and Mary Quarterly* 19 (1962): 401; F. Harrison, *The Devon Carys* (New York, 1920), 502.
[156] W. K. Jordan, *Men of Substance* (Chicago, 1942), 38.
[157] J. J. Bagley, "Matthew Markland," *Transactions of the Historical Society of Lancashire and Cheshire* 68 (1959): 45.
[158] B. D. Henning, ed., *House of Commons, 1660–1690* (1983), 10.

PARENTAL CHOICE

The advancement of sons was a universally acknowledged duty and often a long and anxious process (see chapter 5).[159] Parents had to take into account the temperament and skills of each son, based on their personal knowledge and his performance at school and vocational preferences. Rich businessmen frequently chose to set up their eldest sons as gentlemen living on rental income, but in most cases it was necessary to place sons in an occupation in which they could support themselves and assist their widowed mother and siblings. An incompetent, lazy, or dissolute son created serious problems, particularly if business was chosen as his occupation. In the family business a father might have to choose between merit and love, between bringing in talent from outside the family or accommodating an inadequate son.

Fathers frequently recommended apprenticeship for their sons in their wills. Richard Bolston, James Burkin, Sir Christian Desbouverie, Sir Joseph Woolf, and Sir Thomas Scawen all instructed that one of their sons be bred up as a merchant. Henry Lockey and Edwin Brown intended all their sons to be merchants.[160] Caleb Cockcroft, a skinner, allocated £120 of his one-third to apprentice his second son to a merchant adventurer.[161] Richard Baskerville wanted his only son to be a merchant.[162] In 1704 Sir Benjamin Bathurst planned to put all his sons into trade with £1,000 apiece.[163] Mothers also participated in the decision. Thomas Phipps told his son:

I take notice of what you write of your mother's contribution for your brother James. She never consulted me anything in it. It was her own sudden thoughts I presume which you know are not allways deep. I have no present intention to send him that way was he inclined to it but he is now fourteen years of age and I shall consult him whether he inclines to goe abroad or settle in England.[164]

Sons were sometimes set up in their father's trade. A mercer of Cirencester left his business to his younger son, who had run it, and nothing to his eldest, a parson.[165] John Foote, a grocer, left his shop and

---

[159] See also Grassby, The Business Community of Seventeenth-Century England, chapter 4.

[160] PCC, St. John 90, 1631.   [161] PCC, Rivers 55, 1645.

[162] J. H. Lea, ed., Prerogative Court Canterbury, Register Soame (Boston, 1904), 20.

[163] PCC, Ashe 87.

[164] Letter to James Phipps dated 20 Sept. 1710, PRO, C 113/280.

[165] I. Gandey, Round about the Little Steeple (Cirencester, 1989), 35.

warehouse to his sons, Thomas and Samuel.[166] David Hochstetter, who left £30 to apprentice his orphaned nephew, explained that he had lost "considerable sums of money" in recent years in the fishing trade; but he bequeathed one-fourth of his business interests to his brother, one-fourth to his sister, and half to his two sons and instructed that his account book should be preserved for his eldest son when he reached twenty-one; he also transferred his stock and freedom in the East India Company to his son, David.[167] George Orlaby wanted his son, Clement, to continue as a woollen draper.[168] Hans Cornelius Linckbeeck put two of his sons into the "tradesmans Traffick of merchandising" in company with three partners.[169] In 1730 Thomas Scawen wanted his son bred up as a merchant with his late partner; in 1719 Sir Richard Hoare wanted his son, Henry, to continue in partnership with his brother, Benjamin. Bartholomew Bulkeley left land and a portion of £3,000 to two sons, and his shop and £1,000 of stock to his second son, Thomas, to follow the trade.[170]

In richer business families, eldest sons and, to a certain extent, younger sons, were often set up as urban or landed gentlemen with an independent income from land, urban property, stocks, or annuities. Thomas Crompton, a mercer, left his eldest son £150 annually in lands and his younger son, who became a civil lawyer, £20 per year.[171] In 1726 Sir John Ward wanted his widow to raise £20,000 from the sale of stocks to buy land for his sons. Alderman Abdy, Abraham Elton, and Samuel Moyer, Sr., all entailed their land, and Vulture Hopkins attempted, but failed, to follow suit in 1727.[172] In 1718 Sir James Bateman adopted the strict settlement for his estates. Sir Nicholas Raynton, a haberdasher, bought the Enfield manor and erected Forty Hall.[173] The two sons of Sir William Blackett and the son of Joseph Brooksbank acquired major estates in Yorkshire.[174] Sir Abraham Elton of Bristol bought land for his second and third sons, as did the Hallets of Lyme Regis. Three sons of Sir Benjamin Bathurst had estates settled on them, and the eldest, Allen, was made a peer in 1712. The son and grandson of Richard Hanbury,

---

[166] PCC, Cope 127, 1616.   [167] PCC, Hyde 50, 1665.
[168] PCC, Cann 108, 1650.   [169] PCC, Aylett 378, 1655.
[170] D. W. Hasler, ed., *House of Commons, 1558–1603*, vol. 1 (1982), S. V. Bulkeley.
[171] B. P. Levack, *The Civil Lawyers* (Oxford, 1973), 15.
[172] J. Bramston, *Autobiography*, ed. L. Braybrook, vol. 40 (Camden Society, 1845), 107; M. Elton, *Annals of the Eltons* (Stroud, 1994), 44; PCC, Drax 372; D. Lysons, *Environs of London*, vol. 1 (1792–6), 534.
[173] *House of Commons, 1660–90*, 8, 55.   [174] Habbakuk, *Marriage Debt*, 424–7.

an ironmaster, became major landowners. Dorothy, relict and executrix of Moses Bathurst, sold her personal estate and bought the Cobham estate for her eldest son in 1705.[175] In 1707 Thomas Church instructed his trustees to buy land for his widow and children.[176] Thomas Petchell, a haberdasher, left money to his married daughter to be invested in land for his grandson.[177] John Lister of Hull gave land to four younger sons, and Edward Desbouverie bought estates for all his three sons who did, however, continue in business for another generation.[178] The eldest son of Sir William Gore stayed in business when he inherited land from his father in 1707, but he married the daughter of the Earl of Northampton, and his son became a gentleman.

Businessmen did of course consider other forms of employment for their children, and if they had several children, they were often distributed between several professions. This maximized the options available and minimized the risk of failure. Business families kept track of opportunities in the professions.[179] The whole Priestley family debated whether Jonathan should enter a university rather than a trade.[180] Edward Berry, John Stockham, William Clark, Richard Heywood, and Hugh Brown all directed in their wills that their sons should attend a university rather than be apprenticed.[181] William Feak, a goldsmith, directed his widow to put one son to a university until thirty and one son apprentice with £100.[182] Sarah Pitt left £100 for binding the sons of her brother "none of em be put to mean trades" and £100 to her nephew at twenty-one plus £25 per year for six years at a university "provided he be bred a scholar."[183] William Steer, a cutler, educated his eldest son for a career in the church and apprenticed his two younger sons to mercers.[184] Other sons were sent to the inns for a legal career, not always with success. The son of John Priestley, who inherited £50 per year and £1,500 in personal estate, went to Lincolns Inn instead of into his father's business, but he

[175] BL, Loan MS 57/73, fo. 127.
[176] CLRO, CSB 1693–1714.   [177] PCC, Lee 133, 1648.
[178] J. W. Clay, ed., *Yorkshire Abstract of Wills*, vol. 9 (Yorkshire Archaeological and Topographical Record Society, 1890), 165.
[179] Letter to William Sharpe dated 12 Oct. 1664, Shropshire RO, MS 1224.
[180] Priestley, *Memoirs*, 21.
[181] PCC, Clarke 143, 1625; PCC, Pell 247, 1659; MacGrath, *Merchants and Merchandize*, vol. 2, 19; A. P. Wadsworth and J. De L. Mann, *Cotton Trade* (Manchester, 1931), 33; J. H. Morison, ed., *Prerogative Court Canterbury Register Scroope* (1934), 156.
[182] PCC, Scott 34, 1595.
[183] BL, Egerton MS 1971, fo. 5.   [184] Hey, *Fiery Blades*, 229.

Table 9.4. *Impact of Father's Occupation on Behavior of Businessmen, 1580–1740 (Percentage of Known Cases)*

	Sons of businessmen	Sons of nonbusinessmen
Married daughter of businessman	70.27	62.47
Married other	29.73	37.53
Son in business	57.07	54.63
No son in business	42.93	45.37
Son married daughter of businessman	45.63	42.92
Son married other	54.38	57.08
Daughter married businessman	47.50	52.64
Daughter married other	52.50	47.36
Partible inheritance	60.59	67.57
Impartible inheritance	39.41	32.43
Major landholding	48.45	43.58
Minor landholding	22.91	23.28
No land	28.64	33.14
Active investments at death	55.97	49.12
Passive investments at death	44.03	50.88

kept bad company, spent extravagantly, and died young from heavy drinking.[185]

Many sons had no interest in business and refused to enter or left prematurely against the wishes of their parents. John Campbell's first son chose to become a soldier; it was his second son who became a partner in his business.[186] Hugh Hall was put into trade by his father against his wishes, although he had entered Harvard and wanted to enter the ministry; Samuel Sewall's son was intended for foreign trade, but he was allowed to become a bookseller.[187] Ambrose Crowley II's younger children were only interested in the money; the elder Crowley drew up a settlement to exclude them from the business, which led to much dispute. Wise parents realized that forcing their children to join the family business was self-defeating. Other children lacked the ability and personality to run a business and had to be removed and found sinecures. Caleb, son of Sir John Banks, proved to be sickly, idle, and incompetent, despite having John Locke as his tutor.[188] Benjamin Crowley could not cope, to the dismay of his father who wanted him to succeed.[189]

---

[185] Priestley, *Memoirs*, vol. 2, 21–4.
[186] E. Healey, *Coutts and Company* (1992), 22.   [187] Morgan, *Puritan Family*, 73–4.
[188] Coleman, *Sir John Banks*, 26–32.   [189] Flinn, *Men of Iron*, 18–20.

It is instructive to compare the performance and behavior of sons of businessmen with that of children from the rest of the population. Sons and grandsons of businessmen often married daughters of businessmen. Slightly more of them had at least one son in business, and more of their daughters married outside the business world. Sons of businessmen were more likely to reject partible inheritance and had slightly more assets actively invested when they died. In general, however, there was no fundamental difference.

MARRIAGE OF SONS

Since marriage was a passage to adulthood, it was usually the last issue that involved the exercise of parental authority.[190] Sons of course could veto any parental candidates, and they had more freedom than daughters. In their anxiety to prevent bad marriages, parents often found a suitable match and initiated negotiations, hoping that their sons would approve their choice. A son who had yet to receive his portion needed the concurrence of his parents, who could exercise economic as well as moral blackmail. If he detested their choice, he would refuse, but if he was just apathetic, given conventional deference and the widespread desire for parental approval, the marriage would probably take place.[191]

Parents had the most power over minors. Older and financially independent sons who were established in their careers could follow their own wishes. Many would have had no father alive by the time they married. A father would have to live into his fifties in order to witness the marriage of his first son at twenty-nine. Only about one-fourth of the children born later in the marriage would have been in that position; the evidence of marriage allegations suggests that children often married shortly after their father had died.[192] On the other hand, widows or guardians could substitute for the father, and in many cases one, if not both, parents lived long enough to see their children married.[193] In business families marriage was not conditional on inheriting the family

[190] The respective rights of parents and children with regard to marriage are discussed in chapter 1.
[191] M. Ingram, "The Reform of Popular Culture" in *Popular Culture in Seventeenth-Century England*, ed. B. Reay (1985), 135.
[192] Brodsky, *Single Women in the London Marriage Market*, 22.
[193] R. Wall, "Elderly Persons" in *Ageing in the Past*, ed. D. Kertzer and P. Laslett (Berkeley, 1995), 89.

estate, since most fathers could provide a sufficient portion in their lifetime.

Who did sons marry? There are no striking differences in the status of wives between eldest and younger sons, though more second sons married gentlewomen in brackets II and IV. Younger sons consistently, for no obvious reason, married more gentlewomen than daughters of businessmen in all four cohorts (with the reverse in bracket II), but the proportion of business wives never fell below 24 percent and ranged in both periods I and II from 41 to 48 percent. There are no indications that children married in birth order. The proportion of sons known to have never married did increase from 9 percent in cohort I to 14 to 17 percent in cohorts II to IV, but the marital history of too many sons is unknown to be sure that these cases are representative.

It is clear, however, that marriage was common between sons of London businessmen and daughters of minor gentry in search of income. It is also well documented in Chester, Exeter, Gloucester, Norwich, and Belfast.[194] In 1704 Richard Sykes of Hull married the daughter and coheir of Mark Kirby of Sledmore. Sir Job Harby's son married the daughter of Mildmay Fane, Earl of Westmoreland, and Henry Pranel also married the daughter of a peer. But a substantial proportion still married within the business community and usually within the same trades and companies; all the children of major players in the Muscovy Company, for example, intermarried.[195] By the time that new entrepreneurs had made sufficient money to marry into landed society, they had already married.[196]

Some parents were responsive to the wishes of their sons. Sir Gilbert Heathcote is said to have raised to £10,000 the portion of the woman with whom his eldest son, John, had fallen in love so that they could marry.[197] Samuel Heathcote poured his heart out to his uncle and guardian when he fell in love with Anne Woolf.[198] But many parents were dictatorial. Some tried to name or blackball spouses for their children in their wills; John Burchett would have disinherited his son, John,

---

[194] W. G. Hoskins, *Industry and People in Exeter, 1688–1800*, 2d ed. (Manchester, 1968), 168; P. Clark, "Civic Leaders Gloucester" in *The Transformation of English Provincial Towns*, ed. P. Clark (1984), 323–6; Woodward, *Trade of Elizabethan Chester*, 204; Evans, "Decline of Oligarchy," 57; Agnew, *Belfast Merchants*, 54.
[195] T. S. Willan, *The Muscovy Merchants of 1555* (Manchester, 1953), 14.
[196] Habakkuk, *Marriage Debt*, 201–7.
[197] Heathcote, *Families of Heathcote*, 85, 243.   [198] Ibid., 106.

Table 9.5. *Parental Status of Wives of Sons by Birth Order (Percentage of Known Cases)*

	Period I	Period II	Bracket I	Bracket II	Bracket III	Bracket IV	Cohort I	Cohort II	Cohort III	Cohort IV
First Son										
Businessman	42.27	46.67	33.33	54.35	45.64	30.00	43.59	42.98	42.75	37.04
Gentleman	51.89	45.28	53.33	39.13	47.65	52.50	50.00	48.25	46.38	55.56
Professional	5.84	8.06	13.33	6.52	6.71	17.50	6.41	8.77	10.87	7.41
Total	291	360	15	46	298	40	78	114	138	27
Second Son										
Businessman	44.76	48.21	16.67	60.00	50.48	28.57	40.00	36.11	55.00	25.00
Gentleman	49.52	42.86	50.00	30.00	45.71	66.67	56.00	55.56	32.50	62.50
Professional	5.71	8.93	33.33	10.00	3.81	4.76	4.00	8.33	12.50	12.50
Total	105	112	6	10	105	21	50	36	40	8
Third, Fourth, and Fifth Sons										
Businessmen	43.1	40.98	50.00	25.00	40.63	23.81	40.00	61.11	31.25	50.00
Gentlemen	53.9	45.90	50.00	75.00	54.69	71.42	56.67	27.78	62.50	50.00
Professional	3.1	13.11	–	–	4.69	4.76	3.33	11.11	6.25	–
Total	65	61	2	4	64	21	30	18	32	2

should he marry any daughter of Henry Wood of Kingston. Josiah Child drove a hard bargain for his son.[199] A correspondent of Sir Henry Johnson complained that his mother would not agree to his proposal: "she presently afterwards askt me if she should find out a neighbour's daughter with 8 or 10 thousand pounds whether or no I would tell your lordship that I was in love with her. I answered her that I could be in love with nothing but convenience. . . . I have now small comfort at home."[200]

Sons unsurprisingly rebelled against parental interference and usually paid a penalty. Caleb Banks married against his father's wishes.[201] William Lowther behaved likewise, and he consequently received a portion, but no land.[202] Hugh Lowther, while an apprentice in London, absconded and married without his father's consent.[203] Thomas Brown's son would have been disinherited if he had married "the gossip who was here before my maidservant which he denieth."[204] Sir Lionel Duckett, in a codicil to his will, explained that he was leaving all his testator's one-third to his widow, because his son had married without his consent.[205]

THE COURTSHIP OF PHILIP PAPILLON

The courtship of Philip Papillon is an excellent example of how hard a father would work to match his son and how difficult it was for mercantile wealth to penetrate landed society.[206] The lady Thomas Papillon and his son, Philip, had in mind was Dorothy Cartwright, an orphan with a £8,000 portion in the hands of the widow, Ursula Cartwright, who was both administrator and guardian. In a settlement that he drafted, Thomas proposed to settle on his son at marriage both the contents of the house and the estate at Acrise (which would provide both a jointure and provision for children), as well as land in Leicestershire, a

---

[199] Letter from Josiah Child to William Atwood dated 6 Aug. 1680, PRO, C 109/23/1.
[200] BL, Add. MS 22,186.   [201] Coleman, *Banks*, 134.
[202] D. R. Hainsworth, "Manor House to Counting House," in *European History and Its Historians*, ed. F. MacGregor and N. Wright (Adelaide, 1977), 73.
[203] D. R. Hainsworth, "The Lowther Younger Sons," *Transactions of the Cumberland and Westmoreland Archaeological and Antiquarian Society* 88 (1988): 156.
[204] PCC, Pye 342, 1673.
[205] PCC, Rutland 9, 1585 and 1587. His apprentice, who had abetted the marriage, also lost his legacy of £20.
[206] The following quotes are from letters of Thomas and Jane Papillon to and from Sir Joseph Ashe, Ursula Cartwright, William Carter, and Philip Boucher dated May 16 to July 18, 1684, with two letters from Philip Papillon, KAO, MS U 1015/C13/1–18.

brewhouse, other houses in Leadenhall and Fenchurch, and £8,000 in cash. He had to reckon, however, with the opposition of Lord Townshend.

In May 1684 Thomas and Jane Papillon met with Mrs. Wolstenholme, the aunt of Dorothy Cartwright, and an intermediary, Philip Boucher. Another intermediary, William Carter, made contact with the widow Cartwright who "put the question to me what steps I thought convenient to make towards my Ld Townshend (I telling her Ldpp that Mr Papillon were acquainted with Sir Joseph Ashe who is father in law to his Ldp). Her Ldpp replied that she thought of a shorter way by a Lady in London that was nearly related to my Lord Townshend but neither of the wayes was concluded till you meet again which is designed by her Ldpp Monday in the afternoone." Thomas met with Lady Cartwright and followed with a letter, which Philip Boucher agreed to

deliver with all secrecy and fidelity as soon as her Ldpp comes home which I doubt may be late, being as I heare gone to the park and if any answer be given I will take care to convey it. But I would deal by you as I would be dealt with, that is to let you know the plain truth so far as I can. She took occasion this afternoon to tell me you had been here and had some speech with her and that if you could use any means to induce my Lord to another mind touching the business. Otherwise she was not willing to proceed further.

In his letter Thomas proposed

to give 400 li per annum and a house with its furniture, and to take not one penny of the 8,000 li portion but to add 8,000 li more to it, to be imployed by my son in trade, the one half of the profit during mine and my wifes life to come to us and the whole to abide with my son after our decease with a prospect of 500 a yeare more after my decease. . . . I shall be willing to settle the greatest part of that 300 li a year to make it certain after mine and my wifes decease so it will be certain at 900 year and 16,000 li in mony besides the improvement of it. I am sure this will make you live more plentifully then any gentilmans estate of 2,000 li a year. My son is sober and free from all the evils of the present times and why a merchants son should not bee as well accounted of as a marchants daughter I understand not. . . . I must confess I and my wife have a great value for the young Lady as she hath had her education under you . . . but in case your Ladyship be not free to proceed and come to terms of agreement without delay, I must beg the favor that I may be at liberty and that nothing that hath hitherto passed may be reckoned any ingagement on my part. . . . Your Ladyship may advise with the earl of Claire or the lady Wolstenholme or such other relations as you shall think convenient but I desire to have a speedy result.

At the same time, Thomas wrote to Sir Joseph Ashe about Lord Townshend:

Though since my lst discourse with you upon my Ld Townshend's letter nothing hath been done in that affaire, yet I cannot satisfy my self without further application not that I think the portion any way Inviting, for I have had overtures of greater fortunes which I have not entertained and there are many now that with as large estates stick on hand and others that marry to less then what my sonn will be master of. But both I and my wife have good apprehensions of the young lady and of her sober and pious education. . . . I have ruminated with my self on what account it might be that my Lord seems at present to be averse. I have thought his Lordship might conceive I did not shew that respect I ought to his Lordship in not writing to him my self. If any thing of that nature be taken amisse you are obliged to make my excuse In regard I did forbear it on your advise. . . . Possibly his Lordship may have received misrepresentations of me as if I were a dissenter from or contrary to the Church of England To which I shall onely say That though generally I and my children do receive the sacrament at the french church in London yet it hath been our practise often at London and allways when in the country to attend on the publick worship of God and to receive the sacrament according to the liturgy and discipline of the Church of England. . . . As to my quality I hope that will not be objected against at this day when persons of the greatest figure count it noe dishonor to match into Merchants families and I may say by descent I am a Gentleman. My grandfather was a person of great repute in the court of France. . . . And as to estate I doe not find all circumstances considered but that my proposals are every way answerable to the ladys portion and dare say That if it please God that it be a match She will live and enjoy as much or more plenty and content then my estate of 2,500 li p. Annum is capable to afford. I might add that besides what I settle in marriage if God please to preserve me I intend a farther blessing to my son in mony having no other to bear my name but him and I must say of him that he hath been allwais a dutyfull child that he is sober and free from all the vices and debauchery of the age and of a very kind and loving nature so as to make a wife very happy and if this affair succeeds the Lady will be sure to have the virginity of his affections.

Ashe replied that the gentry had little esteem for merchants and wanted land, not money. Thomas took his advice and ended negotiations: "I suppose all persons have not the like opinion of merchants and that some will count it advantageous to have 2 strings to the bow, viz land and trade. I am sure (and you know) that the latter affords more plenty and content though the other be a good stake in the hedge." Meanwhile, Philip Boucher told Thomas Papillon that he had heard privately that Townshend had in mind as a suitor a nephew of Sir Joseph

Ashe: "If my intelligence be true you may for the time to come discern between true friends and friend only. I believe you to be a gentleman of better principles then to entertain any hard thoughts against Sir Joseph but will rather observe our Saviours rule to do good for evil."

The son tried a direct approach to the young lady in July 1684:

I cannot deny but I have been told that there is in your self a reciprocall affection, and I believe you know I have been acquainted therewith, but yet it is not the same thing to me as I had it under your own hand. Madam I am assured you know . . . how the whole matter stands and that it is not my affection will oblige your relations but your own will and that time lost may be of very ill consequences to us for I am perswaded that if you will manifest your respect to me nothing can prevent our being happie in and with each other. . . . [D]eere Madam doe not stand upon Nicety since with me you are sure of candour and trew honesty and I assure you a desire to make you happier further than my settlement for of the latter I could have prospects fair enough . . . it is the sweetness I believe you to be Mistriss of that does attract rather than a greater fortune.

It was, however, a lost cause. William Carter told Jane Papillon that Madam Cartwright wanted to match her daughter with a religious family. The prospective groom wrote another letter, but, on the advice of Philip Boucher, it was never sent:

Madame if you will give your self to me you shall sit regnant in my affection and my utmost indeavours shall be to improve what we have as may be to the greatest comfort. . . . Madam for your sake I have refused 1000 and a lady by birth and with others greater portion than yours. . . . I have been informed you have refused some for my sake. That gives me a little hope . . . so it is the strength of your love it must make your relations approve of any match and of me especially.

Thomas Papillon was not pleased with the actions of Madam Cartwright:

There is 2000 li charged on the real estate which will be saved if Miss Dorothy dies before marriage or the age of 21 yeers. There is 8000 li remaining in her hands for which while Miss Dorothy remains unmarried she allows not interest except only for such part of it as was put out on security. I will not saye but fear she is more a friend to her self than to Miss Dorothy and her insisting on a promise to my Lord not to dispose of the young lady without his consent seems to be used . . . as a pretence for her justification that she may alledge I proposed such a match and my Lord would not consent . . . she hath not proceeded with that candour and integrity as is suitable to persons of honor and affairs of that nature. The first motion was from her and she hath allways professed to us that it was what she desired, could my Lord Townsend be prevailed with to consent, and has told us she was sorry she had shewed soe much inclination to it for this she feared made my Lord soe much averse. . . . Wherein we have acted with all sincerity and clearness and used noe dubble or underhand dealing. That which Madam Cartwright wrote to his Lordship that we had made use of a mayde or wayting woman to induce the young ladys affections towards my son is a meere fiction for one of us never saw much less spake with her mayde or any wayting woman. . . . I reflect on this Madam Cartwright's comportment in this whole affair it seems as if she had no minde at all to marry Miss Dorothy and that this business was set on foote by her to prevent and put off other proposals and that she never intended it should take effect.

A note by Jane Papillon to her husband provides a sharp comment on the whole affair: "I would not croutch or at least have thee. I hope we are not guilty in order to that match, but if we bee, the Lord pardon it."

MARRIAGES OF DAUGHTERS

Parents had much more control over daughters than over their sons, because they could deny them financial assistance if they married undesirable spouses, and a daughter had little chance of surviving on her own without provision. At the very least parents could determine the age at which a daughter married and produce a short list of appropriate husbands as a basis for negotiation. Defiance was regarded as carnality. Some fathers kept their daughters single so that they could have nurses in their old age. But most dutifully did their best to settle their daughters for life.

In some respects the marriage of daughters was more important and stressful than that of sons because parents usually had to provide a substantial portion, which passed to another family. Fathers were anxious to find good husbands of equivalent or higher status for their daughters in order to protect and advance them. Often the mother was in charge of finding a spouse, since many daughters had lost their fathers by the time they married; 47 percent of London brides had no father by the time they reached twenty.[207]

Daughters had their own ambitions and often sought to upgrade their status, which women acquired by marriage rather than by birth or occupation. The daughters of aldermen were faulted for pride and overdressing and accused of ignoring their fathers and their "coarser kindred."[208] Defoe claimed that they were reluctant to marry trades-

---

[207] Brodsky, "Single Women," 22.   [208] F. Lenton, *Characterisimi* (1631), 37.

men.[209] "Citizens daughters," complained Francis Kirkman, "are better fed then taught," both surly and proud.[210] They certainly had an eye for a match. Thomas Papillon thanked Richard Oxenden for the diamonds he had sent to his wife and daughters: "I shall not forget you while we have those sparkling in our eyes" and his daughter "still remembers the person whom she looked to be the most a Gentleman that ever she saw."[211] Mary Cooling, daughter of a linen draper, contracted with a young man and then won over her father.[212] Merchants' daughters were often self-assured: when Joan, daughter of Sir Rowland Heyward, married John Thynne, she was cautiously assertive.[213]

Eldest daughters married businessmen more frequently than gentlemen, except in bracket IV and cohort IV, but the proportion who married gentlemen never dropped below 27 percent. The same was true of younger daughters, except for bracket IV and cohorts I and IV; indeed second daughters (and to a lesser extent their younger sisters) consistently married gentlemen more frequently than did their eldest sisters. The proportion of professional husbands fluctuated, but it was highest in bracket IV and cohort IV.

Marriage was certainly a channel of upward mobility for daughters who, particularly when their fathers were older, married younger sons of gentry families. In Elizabethan London daughters of tradesmen married upward, and in the early seventeenth century 11 percent of landed gentlemen married daughters of businessmen.[214] During the late seventeenth century, 60 percent of those daughters of London aldermen who married, married gentlemen.[215] The same was true of provincial towns, such as Norwich.[216]

Some daughters even married peers. Four of Sir William Cokayne's daughters married peers, and his widow remarried a peer.[217] But this was rare unless a daughter was an heiress; there were only six (1548–1617), nine (1618–30), and three (1631–60) of such marriages. Sir John Spencer

[209] Defoe, Compleat English Tradesmen, 313.
[210] F. Kirkman, The Unlucky Citizen (1673), 38.
[211] BL, Add. MS 40,700, fo. 67.   [212] Brodsky, "Mobility and Marriage," 303–4.
[213] A. Wall, "Elizabethan Precept and Feminine Practice," History 75 (1990): 27.
[214] Brodsky, "Mobility and Marriage," 348; L. and J. C. F. Stone, An Open Elite (Oxford, 1984), figure 7.8.
[215] N. Rogers, "Money, Land, and Lineage," Social History 4 (1979): 445; Defoe, Complete English Tradesman, chapter xxiv.
[216] Evans, Seventeenth-Century Norwich, 24.
[217] Stone, Crisis of the Aristocracy, 629–31.

Table 9.6. *Status of Husbands of Daughters by Birth Order (Percentage of Known Cases)*

	Period I	Period II	Bracket I	Bracket II	Bracket III	Bracket IV	Cohort I	Cohort II	Cohort III	Cohort IV
First Daughter										
Businessman	53.71	57.16	60.00	59.48	53.74	15.52	43.65	64.71	48.18	35.90
Gentleman	36.22	34.81	26.67	26.72	37.01	72.41	41.27	30.88	42.51	51.28
Professional	10.07	8.02	13.33	13.79	9.25	12.07	15.08	4.41	9.31	12.82
Total	566	698	30	116	562	58	126	204	247	39
Second Daughter										
Businessman	49.76	47.18	36.36	51.72	48.00	10.53	38.16	47.83	49.57	17.65
Gentleman	38.65	40.49	36.36	34.48	41.46	71.05	47.37	43.48	38.26	52.94
Professional	11.59	12.32	27.27	13.79	10.55	18.42	14.47	8.70	12.17	29.41
Total	207	284	11	29	275	38	76	92	115	17
Third, Fourth, and Fifth Daughters										
Businessmen	48.24	42.44	50.00	23.53	40.74	41.94	39.39	57.63	37.88	25.00
Gentlemen	38.82	46.51	50.00	70.59	45.37	48.39	45.45	35.59	53.03	12.50
Professional	12.94	11.05	–	5.88	13.89	9.68	15.15	6.78	9.09	62.50
Total	170	172	2	17	216	31	66	59	66	8

unsuccessfully opposed the marriage of his daughter and heiress, Elizabeth, to Lord Compton who used his influence at court to imprison Sir John and may have destroyed his father-in-law's will so that he and his wife could squander the vast estate.[218] Some were not even sanctioned by the parents. In 1672 the eldest son of the Second Earl of Scarsdale abducted the orphaned daughter and coheir of Sir John Lewis from her mother's London house.[219]

A substantial proportion of daughters still married within the business community and, like their brothers, often into the same trade, company, and financial bracket. George Clark's daughter, Rebecca, for example, married Richard Sherbrook, nephew of his partner. The daughter of Sir Peter Paravicino married George Torriano, allegedly a former butler.[220] The daughter of John Campbell married his partner after her father died.[221] In King's Lynn daughters married men in their father's trade.[222]

Parents were sometimes permissive. Of 181 wills in London, only fourteen imposed penalties if their daughters married without consent.[223] Joseph Collett did not want his daughter, Betty, to marry a bigot, whether Anglican or nonconformist, nor to marry without his consent. He conscientiously provided a large dowry and reflected that "it is said your sex need not be taught pride"; but he hoped that she would marry a husband of high station, and he assured his daughter, whom he addressed as "my tender love," that "I promise never to impose a husband on you. . . . I shall always have a great regard to your inclination."[224] George Boddington's daughter met Ebenezer Collier when boarding at Hackney and "was so set on having him" that George feared "she would pine away. . . . [S]he would rather go a begging with him"; so he reluctantly agreed to their marriage.[225] In 1700 the daughter of a London organ maker even had a suitor stay the night with her mother's permission.[226]

Usually, however, parents tried to control the marriages of their

---

[218] L. Stone, "The Peer and the Alderman's Daughter," *History Today* 10 (1961): 51.
[219] Habakkuk, *Marriage, Debt*, 193.
[220] Beinecke Library, Yale University, MS shipping records, 1669.
[221] Healey, *Coutts and Company*, 22.
[222] Cooper, "Intergenerational Social Mobility," 290.
[223] Earle, *Making of the Middle Class*, 187.
[224] Letters dated 16 Oct. 1713, 5 May 1714, and 10 Oct. 1715 in J. Collett, *Private Letterbook*, ed. H. H. Dodwell (1933). The same attitude was adopted by Thomas Crabb: see R. L. Greaves, *Dublin's Merchant Quaker* (Stanford, 1999), 18.
[225] GLL, MS 10,823.   [226] Stone, *Uncertain Unions*, 66.

daughters. Some fathers specified the type of husband: the widower Thomas Mann had a stepdaughter by his late wife's first husband who lived with him and whom he offered £50 in his will to marry his son.[227] William Tiffin, a clothworker, left his daughter, Alice, £1,000 from his Yorkshire lands, provided that she did not marry Thomas Newell of Shrewsbury.[228] In 1748 Samuel Shepherd had a natural daughter, but no heirs, and he gave her a portion of £36,000 plus a house in Cavendish Square, if she married Lord Montford, assuming that they liked each other, but he forbade her to marry any other peer, a Scotsman, or an Irishman. Elizabeth Walker was grateful to her father for refusing his consent to her marriage with an Ipswich merchant who later fell on hard times; instead she married a clergyman.[229]

Some businessmen arranged the entire match. Alderman Anthony Abdy married his daughter to Sir John Bramston through an intermediary, Dr. Spicer, a relative of the alderman.[230] Francis Dashwood offered his daughter to Sir Thomas Isham, claiming that she had an excellent temper and household skills.[231] John Crowley matched his three unmarried sisters.[232] Often the mother or widow played the most important role. Thomas Stanley did not think that his daughter and her swain "should in the first place see each other I doe not well approve of, especially here at my house, until all other matters are in some measure agreed. . . . [T]his matter I desire to be a while concealed from my wife who I know will oppose it . . . because she inclines to another."[233]

CONSENT

Since many fathers did not live to marry their daughters, they insisted in their wills that their daughters take advice from their widows or guardians, their siblings or kin, their executors or overseers, or their friends. In 1710 George Finch reduced his daughter's inheritance from £5,000 to £3,000 should she marry without consent. John Pynchon insisted that his daughters take advice from his widow and overseers.[234]

---

[227] PCC, Clarke 65, 1625.   [228] PCC, Goare 103, 1637.
[229] E. Walker, *The Holy Life*, ed. A. Walker (1690), 16.
[230] Bramston, *Autobiography*, 104.
[231] T. Isham, *Diary*, ed. G. Isham (Farnborough, 1971), 44.
[232] Flinn, *Men of Iron*, 70.
[233] Letter dated 18 Nov. 1649, KAO, MS U522/A3 Dalison MSS.
[234] C. Bridenbaugh and J. Tomlinson, eds., *Pynchon Papers*, vol. 1 (Colonial Society of Massachusetts, 1985), 48.

Joseph Jacques, a brewer, denied his daughter her inheritance should she marry without the consent of his overseers.[235] John Cary reduced his legacy to his daughter if she married without consent.[236] John Johnson advised that his daughters should not marry for money but "as God disposes and on the advice of their kin."[237] In 1706 Nicholas Cripps reduced his daughter's inheritance from £1,400 to £400, should she marry without her mother's consent. Other examples include Richard Downs, William Holgate, Charles Marescoe, Sir William Green, William Paggen, Sir Peter Paravicino, Sir Richard Levitt, Samuel Locke, and Sir Francis Dashwood.[238]

There were of course loopholes in the system. In 1623 heiress Elizabeth Barton was married to the son of the common crier, who was supposed to be protecting her against such an eventuality; the heiress Sarah Cox was simply abducted.[239] The orphaned granddaughter of Sir Thomas Campbell was enticed away and married without a license from the Court of Orphans.[240] In 1630 Anne Banks, the only daughter of a city merchant, eloped with the poet Edmund Waller. The daughter of a Chester goldsmith managed to correspond secretly, through a friend, and exchange tokens with George Ryder.[241]

Often daughters just ignored their fathers. Thomas Pilgrim had both a son who disobeyed him and a daughter who married without his consent.[242] Samuel Pepys noted that the daughter of Sir Richard Ford had married without the consent of friends.[243] The Pinney children ignored and constantly quarreled with their parents.[244] The cousin of James Fretwell married without consent, though the groom was taken into his father-in-law's tanning business.[245] William Hobson left only 40 shillings and apparel to his daughter, because she had married without his consent, and he had to take her back when her husband deserted her; he did, however, leave the residue of his estate in trust for her with the

[235] PCC, Pell 546, 1659.   [236] PCC, Dycer 58.
[237] B. Winchester, *Tudor Family Portrait* (1955), 62.
[238] Will of John Dawson, PCC, Seager 81, 1634; *Pynchon Papers*, vol. 2, 48.
[239] Carlton, *Court of Orphans*, 72.
[240] I. Pinchbeck and M. Hewitt, *Children in English Society*, vol. 1 (1973), 89.
[241] Stone, *Uncertain Unions*, 44.
[242] J. M. Sanders, ed., *Barbados Records, Wills and Administrations, 1700–1725*, vol. 3 (Houston, 1980), 268.
[243] Pepys, *Diary*, vol. 3, 264.
[244] R. Pares, *West India Fortune* (1950), 5.
[245] J. Fretwell, *Diary*, vol. 65 (Surtees Society, 1877), 201.

Vintner's Company.[246] Sir John Cutler's daughter married against her father's wishes, but two days before his death he forgave her.[247]

Other parents were not so forgiving. Richard Hull, a draper, left his daughter £150 but not her one-third, because she married against his advice.[248] John Robinson, a merchant of the Staple, described his daughter Elizabeth, who married without his consent, as "of a wilfull minde contrary as well to her duty as to the custome of London"; her legacy was reduced from £100 to £10.[249] Simon Bradstreet, a grocer, left his daughter just a cup and goods worth £500, because she had married a mercer "without my love, leave or consent"; his nephew inherited the estate.[250] Richard Norwood could not bring himself to accept his daughter's marriage to an Irish surgeon.[251] Francis Andrews, a merchant, cut off one daughter with £5 because she had married without his consent and threatened to disinherit his other daughter if she followed suit.[252]

DOWRIES

During the seventeenth century, it became more common for fathers to make their daughters' portions payable either at marriage or at a certain age, usually twenty-one, which gave them greater independence. The share of their father's personalty that they were entitled under the custom to receive at his death could also be treated as a dowry, and portions given at marriage were often increased in wills. There was no obligatory format for the dowry, which could include goods and furniture as well as money; daughters often received their mother's childbed linen, as in the will of Thomas Greenberg.[253] The dowry was nonetheless a major financial burden for a father, particularly if he had several daughters, and merchants usually paid portions in cash at the time of marriage.

The size of dowries was closely related to wealth. The median value of portions was higher in successive brackets, increasing in value over time. This is most obvious in bracket III, where an adequate number of cases demonstrates an increase in the median adjusted value of dowries from £1,000 (1580–1620) to £3,500 (1700–40) or by a factor of 3; there

---

[246] PCC, Cope 90, 1616.   [247] *D. N. B.*, vol. 5, 365.   [248] PCC, Fines 202, 1647.
[249] *North Country Wills, 1558–1604*, vol. 121 (Surtees Society, 1912), no. cxlvii.
[250] PCC, Barrington 14, 1628.
[251] R. Norwood, *Journal*, ed. W. B. Hayward and W. F. Craven (New York, 1945), 111.
[252] PCC, Hyde 11, 1665.   [253] PCC, Ruthen 166, 1657.

Table 9.7. *Dowries of Daughters (Median Value in £ Sterling Adjusted for Inflation)*

Period	Bracket I		Bracket II		Bracket III		Bracket IV	
	Median	Cases	Median	Cases	Median	Cases	Median	Cases
1580–1619	–	–	476	13	1,000	30	3,500	5
1620–1659	330	2	300	47	1,500	37	10,000	3
1660–1699	750	2	475	28	1,800	84	18,000	6
1700–1740	1,100	3	550	30	3,500	90	5,800	28

was, however, little change in bracket II.[254] There is a slight statistical correlation between portions, wealth, and the number of surviving children; the size of dowries increased proportionately to wealth and decreased proportionately to the number of children.[255]

In 1661 William Morrice claimed that merchants' daughters with portions of several thousand pounds were squeezing the daughters of the gentry out of the market.[256] In landed society portions do appear to have doubled during the century, probably because of a fall in the rate of interest; the portions of peers rose from £2,000 to £5,000.[257] Merchants who married their daughters to peers could expect to pay handsomely. Sir Stephen Fox, for example, gave his daughter £20,000 (with a jointure of £1,200) when she married the Fourth Earl of Northampton.[258] When the eldest son of the Earl of Kingston married the illegitimate daughter and heir of John Hall of Bradford, the portion was £23,000; the Second Lord Onslow married Elizabeth Knight, heiress to a Jamaican fortune.[259]

A few businessmen may have contributed to the inflation of portions. The turkey merchant, Richard Lane, for example, bequeathed £30,000 to each of his daughters as their marriage portion.[260] But only tycoons with no sons or extravagant social ambitions provided dowries at this

---

[254] The evidence on dowries is too random and incomplete to support solid conclusions, but there is a sufficient range of examples in brackets II and III to suggest the trend. In bracket IV the medians (1580–1699) are almost certainly exaggerated by a low N and the median of £5,800 (1700–40) is probably more representative.

[255] The Pearson R correlation between value of dowries and wealth at death = +0.339; the correlation between dowries and numbers of children = −0.119.

[256] M. Ashley, *The Stuarts in Love* (1963), 49.

[257] Stone, *Crisis of Aristocracy*, 638–40.

[258] C. G. Clay, *Public Finances* (Oxford, 1978), 295.

[259] Habakkuk, *Marriage Debt*, 195.   [260] PRO, Prob 11/653/210–11, 1732.

level; the large sums that some fortunate husbands received with their wives usually represented their whole inheritance rather than just their dowry. A Dutch merchant provided £4,700 plus some goods, and Joseph Collett found £5,000 for each of his daughters, representing half of his estate.[261] But the usual range for a businessmen with assets between £5,000 and £50,000 would have been £1,000 to £3,000. William Atwood gave £1,200 with his daughter to Edward Halford, plus £300 at a later date.[262] The Wealden ironmasters provided upward of £1,000.[263]

The information on portions is too spotty to be certain whether the conventional ratio of three times the annual income of the father applied to businessmen. The evidence from chancery cases suggests a range of £100 to £300 with a jointure of £40.[264] This is certainly consistent with the limited evidence for provincial towns, like Newcastle; Cuthbert Gray managed a portion of £200 for seven daughters, and other merchants offered £300.[265] The lesser London businessmen with assets of £500 to £5,000 would usually have provided around £500.

Some fathers imposed conditions. John Buck, a French Protestant merchant, said that his daughter would lose her inheritance of £2,300 if she married without the consent of her mother, and her husband must have a net worth of £1,500 and give bond to repay £800 should his daughter die without children.[266] Other fathers had to struggle to enforce the terms of their daughters' marriage settlement. When Thomas Boughey married his daughter to a son of Sir John Kempthorn, he was obliged to pay her portion in cash, although he would have preferred to provide shipping shares. Kempthorn gave bond to buy an inheritance of £2,000 within two years and settle it as a jointure on his daughter-in-law, but year after year passed without fulfillment of this provision, and, when Boughey protested, he was treated with disrespect.[267]

It appears that the marriage market in the business community was highly imperfect. In contrast to landed society, where a well-organized market set norms for portions, the price of dowries for daughters of

[261] V. Larminie, "Marriage and the Family," *Midland History* 9 (1984): 5–6; Collett, *Private Letter Book*, 146.
[262] PRO, C 109/21.   [263] A. Fletcher, *A County Community* (1975), 26.
[264] Erickson, *Married Women's Property*, 59.
[265] R. Welford, "Cuthbert Gray," *Archaeologia Aeliana* 11 (1885–6): 67, 160; will of Robert Shafto in *Durham Wills, 1604–49*.
[266] PCC, May 66, 1661.   [267] Letters dated 15 and 24 Aug. 1678, GLL, MS 18760/1.

businessmen seems to have been set case by case through negotiation with considerable fluctuations according to individual circumstances. The wealth of a father in relation to the number of his children usually determined how much he could offer, though some tycoons, such as Sir Gregory Page, gave paltry portions in relation to their wealth. Parents, however, could only give what they had; Defoe had delicate negotiations with Henry Baker over the dowry for his younger daughter.[268] As a rule, business families strained their resources to the limit to provide adequate dowries for both their daughters and granddaughters.

PEDIGREE

The prestige and importance of a family was determined by its ranking in a hierarchical society. An individual who distinguished himself in a profession or public office or who made a fortune in business and then married upward could transform the standing of his whole family. It was families that were elevated in society rather than individuals.[269] It was family connection rather than economic position that conferred genteel status. Pride in family consequently tempted businessmen to turn their backs on their occupation and to imitate the values, speech, manners, and lifestyle of the landed interest. Parents frequently tried to realize their social ambitions through their children. They set up their sons as professionals or gentlemen and married their daughters into the gentry. Usually the children were happy to comply, but in families with limited assets the desire for social advancement could conflict with the interests of individual children. A large dowry for a daughter often meant a reduced portion for a younger son. To elevate the eldest son, it might be necessary to raid the capital of the family business.

Some merchants had little interest in their ancestry. Sir Gilbert Heathcote, when visiting his father in Derbyshire, described how "several relations came to see me" with stories that he immediately forgot "it being more of man's business to look forward and retrieve than to look backward and repine."[270] The citizens of Shrewsbury displayed no awareness

---

[268] J. R. Moore, *Daniel Defoe* (1958), chapter 25; P. Backscheider, *Daniel Defoe* (Lexington, 1986), 500–2.
[269] J. A. Schumpeter, *The Economics and Sociology of Capitalism*, ed. R. Swedberg (Princeton, 1991), 248.
[270] Heathcote, *Families of Heathcote*, appendix vi.

of lineage.[271] But others were preoccupied with their family pedigree, which they did not hesitate to embellish or fake. Abraham Houblon left land to Isaac so that the "estate may continue in the family of Houblon and those descended from them."[272] Sir Richard Houblon, although a bachelor, was concerned about future generations of the family, so he left his fortune in trust for the purchase of estates to be entailed on his nephew, and the trustees purchased Hallingbury from Sir Edward Turner.[273] Thomas Lucas, a haberdasher, wanted his body moved to the parish church of Lindfield in Sussex "to be buried near kindred and ancestors."[274] Richard Leat, in a nuncupative will, left his house to his brother "because he said his Ancestors did dwell there and he and his brother had been born there."[275] Pride in family was displayed on funeral monuments and plaques. The Russell vault in St. Dunstans housed several generations—a father, two brothers, a father-in-law, two sons, two daughters, and seven grandchildren.[276] William Cloberry left money to Bradstone, Devonshire, "in remembrance of the love I have always had of the place from wherein myself and ancestors have antiently descended."[277]

Families also cultivated a collective memory by passing on physical artifacts and mementoes; movables were bequeathed with freehold property as heirlooms. Robert Goodwin, a salter, left his eldest son his bedroom furniture and his own portrait.[278] In 1726 Sir Samuel Ongley wanted the contents of his house to be preserved intact. Sir Peter Delme distributed the family pictures to his various children. Francis Saire, a mercer of Bernardcastle, included as heirlooms such items as buffet stools, books, silver, and armor.[279]

The principal reason why testators preferred their estate to pass by direct descent was that it preserved the family name. In 1721 Edward Colston rescinded his bequest of land to his nephew, when the nephew died leaving only a daughter, and settled it on a grandniece in trust for heirs male.[280] Businessmen, like the landed gentry, tried to transfer their surnames to preserve the illusion of continuity. Edward Colston wanted

---

[271] Hindson, "Family Structure," 48–57, 63–7, 243. Merchants represented 10 percent of this sample.
[272] Houblon, *The Houblon Family*, vol. 1, 4.
[273] Essex RO, Hallingbury MSS.   [274] PCC, Alchin 377, 1654.
[275] PCC, Sadler 69, 1635.   [276] Stow, *Survey of London*, vol. 2, 46.
[277] PCC, Coventry 4, 1640.   [278] PCC, Wingfield 91, 1610.
[279] *Durham Wills, 1604–49*, 12.   [280] PCC, Buckingham 236, 1721.

his heir to take his name, as did the bachelor, Sir John Lade, in 1740.[281] Sir Thomas Dunch left his estate to William Richards on the condition that he take the name Dunch.[282] In 1719 Sir Henry Johnson left a bequest to the second son of his daughter, who had married a peer, provided that he take the name Johnson. Michael Mitford, in his will of 1707, arranged that his nieces would inherit should they marry someone with the name Mitford.

The rich and successful also strove to fortify the status of their families by the acquisition of titles, particular those of peer and baronet, which were hereditary. Most had, however, to settle for individual knighthoods, a distinction still theoretically linked to land and military service, though an order of knightly bankers based on trade was proposed by one optimist.[283] Of all subjects in the database, 2 percent had a title in period I and 3.5 percent in period II; unsurprisingly they were heavily concentrated in brackets III and IV, in which 37 percent were knights and 19 percent baronets (see table 9.1). Only three merchants were, however, raised to the peerage before 1640 (together with the son of Sir William Craven), and only nine merchants and twenty-one sons of merchants became baronets (1611–49).[284]

SUMMARY

The character and future of capitalism in England was ultimately shaped by the attitude of parents toward the endowment, marriage, and advancement of their children. Lack of information on these critical questions is largely responsible for the long-standing but inconclusive debate over the emergence of the urban bourgeoisie. It can now be said that, despite a decline in the popularity of partible inheritance during the century, most fathers treated all their children equally, taking into account the circumstances, character, age, and needs of each child. They provided well for their widows and daughters and looked toward future generations. The will was a powerful weapon, but it was usually wielded responsibly. Each businessman had his own preferences and foibles and was driven by affection and guilt as well as by rational calculation. Fathers could be profligate or mean, meticulous or inept, clearheaded

[281] H. J. Wilkins, *Edward Colston* (Bristol, 1920), 128.
[282] R. Davies, *Chelsea Old Church* (1904), passim.
[283] BL, Cotton MS Titus BV, fos 250–1; see also BL, Add. MS 10,038.
[284] Stone, *Crisis of Aristocracy*, 190.

or confused, in their efforts to anticipate all contingencies, concentrate their assets, and perpetuate their families over time. There was no over-arching strategy of inheritance. Because they had no control over mortality, many estates were transferred through kin rather than by direct descent. Although priority was increasingly given to eldest sons, demographic failure ensured that property would be continuously distributed within the extended family.

All businessmen recognized an obligation to advance and protect their children and set them up for life. Many wanted at least one of their sons to follow in their occupation, and many sons did become businessmen, though not necessarily in their father's business. When their sons proved incompetent, fathers usually put love and loyalty before efficiency and enterprise. Many daughters also married into the business community. But the children were also distributed among different professions, and the richer merchants advanced the status of their families by putting their sons and daughters into the landed gentry. Parents sometimes acceded to the wishes of their children, but most still tried to control the marriages of their sons and especially of their daughters, because they had to sacrifice substantial capital to raise portions. Most businessmen sought to achieve immortality through their children. But the desire to elevate their families and perpetuate their line often threatened the integrity and cohesion of the family business.

Property was vested and consolidated in the family, not in the individual; a primary reason for the existence of the family as an institution was the need to hold property and transfer it between generations to legitimate heirs. The future of the whole family was supposed to take priority over the wishes of any individual member. But the growth of individual acquisitiveness and a clearer concept of property rights increasingly undermined family loyalty. Most parents, however, when it came to the crunch, put the interests of their children above those of the family and the interests of the family above their business.

Conclusion: Capitalism and the Life Cycle

The early modern family has often been represented as a theoretically based, passive institution manipulated by exogenous forces. In fact, it was an artifact, not a construct, and the product of human action rather than of design. The quantitative and qualitative data collected and presented here suggest that the business family had its own, often unpredictable, dynamic that functioned more like a traffic circle than a one-way street. Although in structure and process it conformed most closely to the developmental cycle model, the empirical evidence does not validate any current or past theory of the early modern family. Some specific patterns and norms of behavior have been identified statistically, but no fundamental change in form has been detected that might be construed as a transition to modernity.

It is important to assess at this point the relative impact of external and internal forces on the business family. Was its character changed by demographic, economic, or cultural factors in the faster-paced, credit-driven, expansionist market economy of Stuart England? Or was individual agency of equal or greater importance than environmental factors? Was the cohesion of the patriarchal family and its kinship networks undermined by possessive individualism? Or did the traditional structure survive intact? Is it defensible to retool Karl Marx's theory of alienation in the rarefied language of literary criticism and assert that all personal and social relationships were depersonalized in the late seventeenth century by the capitalist ethos, and that exchange transactions became anonymous and physical assets represented symbolically rather than valued for their utility? Or were relationships within the family never converted into alienable commodities?

Whereas an extensive literature has been devoted to the impact of

387

capitalism on the family, little attention has been paid to the autonomous impact of the family on capitalism. How did the family life cycle affect the economy, whose development over time is usually described in biological metaphors? Was the nuclear or extended family able to raise and employ capital efficiently and manage complex enterprises? How durable were family firms; did they perpetuate themselves and, if not, why not? What was the contribution of the family to economic growth?

MIXED MODELS

As the basic unit of society, the family was seen as immutable and immortal; representing it as "natural" rather than "artificial" gave it legitimacy. In fact it was a pliable institution that took many forms and was subject to continuous change, as was recognized by some perceptive contemporaries. In one sense the concept of traditional society is an illusion. The style and structure that contemporaries regarded as traditional had in fact been created in the not so distant past. In the seventeenth century the vocabulary of differentiation broadened, and behavior once tolerated or applauded was devalued and denounced.

There was no coherent, universally accepted ideology of the family, which was largely isolated from external role models. The identity of a family was defined by its distinctiveness, not by shared norms. Nor was there a set of attitudes or mode of reasoning governing family behavior that might be labeled a mentality.[1] The concept of mentality is too monolithic and makes no provision for interpenetration. Collective mentalities usually turn out to be a jumble of literary references mixed with some anthropology, not too different from the once-discredited concept of Zeitgeist. It is implausible that huge numbers of people would simultaneously recognize a system of shared meanings. There was too much conflict in English society, too many economic divisions, and too many autonomous subcultures, both religious and occupational. Nor is it plausible that an individual could simultaneously have several mentalities.

In the natural sciences the presence of uniform forces makes it possible to construct and test explanatory models. The human sciences, however, have to contend with the infinite variability of human nature.[2] The structure of society is not manifested in a unified or coherent manner

---

[1] G. E. R. Lloyd, *Demystifying Mentalities* (Cambridge, 1990), 4–5.
[2] E. Gellner, "Knowledge of Nature" in *Nature and Society*, ed. M. Teich et al. (Cambridge, 1997), 14.

and cannot be adequately captured even by complex models. No society is static; each reproduces itself in a variety of forms both vertically and spatially.[3] The principal effect of the "systems metaphor" has been to add more jargon: it is impossible to explain the nature of human society using abstract constructs like capitalism or patriarchy.[4] It is human agency that constructs identity and sets of relationships and the language in which those relationships are expressed. No satisfactory theory of social adjustment has even been devised, because all concepts are inevitably embedded in context, and arguing from one to the other is circular.[5]

Any model of the family is likely to be partially stereotypical. Families certainly shared expectations and faced recurring situations that had similar results. But, like the society in which they moved, they were not rational structures conforming to rules, but chaotic and infinitely diverse aggregations of individuals in motion. The experience of childhood became, in due course, parental behavior. To attempt to reduce them to categorical order might satisfy a psychological need or feed intellectual vanity, but it advances neither knowledge nor understanding. Indeed anyone who takes the trouble to study the actual sources, will soon appreciate the crucial role of opportunity and luck in the history of any family.

The family was not a rigid structure but a process. Every time that a new family was created, two other families each lost one member. There were as many family types as there were needs; the extended family itself was a phase rather than a type.[6] No paradigm can be devised for the business family, which was at the same time nuclear and extended, patriarchal and contractual. Heads of households transferred in and out of roles and made different choices under different circumstances. The family was both active and passive depending on the life cycle.[7] Despite some potential friction, family and kinship were not dichotomous.[8] Most kinship systems are flexible structures that provide social control in the absence of other instruments of government; they rely on goal congru-

---

[3] C. Phythian-Adams, ed., *Societies, Cultures, and Kinship* (Leicester, 1993), introduction, 4–5.

[4] H. Bradley, *Mens' Work, Womens' Work* (Minneapolis, 1989), 63; I. Kramnich, "Reflections on Revolution," *History and Theory* 11 (1972): 53.

[5] E. Gellner, *The Concept of Kinship* (Oxford, 1985), 21, 45, 51.

[6] C. Tilly, "Family History," *Journal of Family History* 12 (1987): 329.

[7] T. K. Haveren, "The Family Cycle" in *The Family Life Cycle*, ed. J. Cuisenier (The Hague, 1977), 347.

[8] J. Goody, *The East in the West* (Cambridge, 1996), 166.

ence, not on rationality.[9] No family form was completely stable, but each combined institutional, instrumental, and sentimental functions.

Change within the family and society was both slow and uneven; all cultures have a primary interest in self-perpetuation and need time to absorb and adjust to economic development.[10] What begins as reproduction can, however, end as transformation; there is a constant dialectic between the practice of structure and the structure of the practice.[11] Norms can be changed by cumulative interpretation while attempting to maintain the status quo; frequently social institutions are changed unintentionally because their functions are misunderstood. New norms usually took a generation to be unequivocally established, because a generation of children who had never been exposed to any alternative had to mature. The process of change was at the same time autonomous and imposed, random and deliberate, real and symbolic, and it developed from the bottom upward as well as from the top downward.[12] The business family was changed both by events and by the demands of its members.

The alleged "wholeness" of premodern society and the solidarity of the "traditional" family are both inventions. The principal flaw in modernization theory is that particular changes and improvements are generalized into a universal discontinuity and then explained in terms of abstract mental qualities such as rationality or egocentrism; it is assumed that one structure completely supersedes another, whereas, in fact, human progress is achieved by cumulative addition rather than by subtraction or division.[13] There was no fundamental break with the past—*natura non fecit saltum*. Modernization, when defined in terms of self-interest and rationality, is, like the market economy, a quantitative rather than a qualitative concept. Innovations within the family structure were largely changes of degree rather than of kind. The whole system did not change, but there were shifts in the relative frequency, importance, and distribution of behavior patterns and their relationship to each other.[14]

[9] W. G. Ouchi, "Markets, Bureaucracies, and Clans," *Administrative Science Quarterly* 25 (1980): 137.

[10] A. Janssens, *Family and Social Change* (Cambridge, 1993), 221.

[11] M. D. Sahlins, *Historical Metaphors and Mythical Realities* (Ann Arbor, 1981), 67, 72.

[12] C. Lloyd, *Explanation in Social History* (Oxford, 1986), 37, 163, 271.

[13] Goody, *The East in the West*, 81.

[14] R. Collins, *Weberian Sociological Theory* (Cambridge, 1987), 36.

It is tempting, but dangerous, to romanticize the past and to see history as either a linear march of progress or a decline from some ideal society. The family did not, however, evolve in one direction, like technology, which develops at different speeds but always toward greater efficiency.[15] Whereas change through differential reproductive success leads to stagnation and ultimately extinction and whereas technological change is irreversible, social institutions continously interact and adapt and can always be resurrected. Vestigial institutions and rituals survive even when they lose their functional utility. The family did not experience binary change from one model to another. Family forms are never totally eliminated; like Microsoft Windows software they are always present, if not immediately visible. A finite number of alternative modes are continuously recycled within the same framework. Like culture, the family changes by a syncretic process of successive compromises.[16]

The family was not a closed system but a flexible living organism in which new values and roles could appear without superseding the old ones.[17] The existing normative vocabulary was manipulated to legitimate new practices.[18] In England usable aspects of the old culture were selected and adapted; the nuclear family did not supersede but coexisted with the extended family, moving backward and forward, as also happened in medieval Italy.[19] Kinship ties would even survive the massive industrialization and urbanization of England in later centuries.

The traditional model, therefore, needs to be shelved. Stuart England did not move from gemeinschaft to gesellschaft but retained elements of both. Continuous bonding within the family served as a substitute for communitarian values in a civil society. Individual members could retain their personal identity without undermining the cohesion of the group. It was the extended family, not the nuclear family, that displaced the

---

[15] M. Segalen, *Historical Anthropology of the Family* (Cambridge, 1986), 44; J. Mokyr, *The Lever of Riches* (New York, 1990), 273.

[16] J. H. Bentley, *Old World Encounters* (New York, 1993), viii; L. Davidoff, "The Family in Britain" in *The Cambridge Social History of Britain*, ed. J. Thompson (Cambridge, 1990), 78–80.

[17] The older theory of the family as an equilibrium-seeking structure that changed permanently after transition periods is summarized by J. Cuisenier and M. Segalen, eds., *The Family Life Cycle in European Societies* (The Hague, 1977).

[18] Q. Skinner, "Social meaning" in *Meaning and Context*, ed. J. Tully (Princeton, 1988), 117.

[19] D. Herlihy, "Family Solidarity in Medieval Italian History" in *Economy, Society, and Government in Medieval Italy*, ed. D. Herlihy, R. S. Lopez, and V. Stessarer (Kent, Ohio, 1969), 175.

community; individualism flourished alongside kinship, which became more, not less, important. The business family in England was a hybrid structure in a hybrid society that sustained both a market and a moral economy. A dynamic equilibrium was created in which new values were superimposed and synthesized with old traditions. When the old family forms collided with the new market society, they mutated and were never completely destroyed.

RESPONSE AND INITIATIVE

The fate of any family was frequently determined by forces outside its members' control. Family formation and perpetuation were subject to demographic chance. Families could be extinguished by premature parental death, by infertility, or by infant mortality; they could also be destabilized by an excess or gender imbalance of children, by serial marriages, or by a succession of substitute parents. The fragility of the family must not, however, be exaggerated, nor the role of individuals dismissed. A majority of businessmen spent a full adult life with one spouse. Death was always in the hands of God, but the number of births could be regulated by the age at marriage, and this was determined by both social pressure and by the rational choice of individuals.[20] The arbitrariness of death was countered by elaborate contingency arrangements, and its impact was cushioned by the employment of subtle defence mechanisms.

The family was also subject to market forces. Marriage was a contract and a rearrangement of property; making a match was ultimately a question of supply and demand. Conflicts of economic interest at different stages of the life cycle created instability within both the nuclear and the extended family. An expanding economy raised expectations and encouraged individuals to pursue opportunities for advancement outside the family. The family could not insulate itself from a competitive world nor ignore the power of money and the smell of success. Wealth determined suitability in marriage, the future of widows, the occupations and independence of children, and the deference of kin.

But the widening of the market did not destroy the household as a means of production, divorce the nuclear family from its kin, nor convert

---

[20] R. J. Schofield, introduction to R. J. Schofield and J. Walter, eds., *Famine, Disease, and the Social Order* (Cambridge, 1989), 70.

it into a domestic retreat separate from the world, focused on reproduction and consumption. If the self-sufficient household ever existed, it
had been replaced by a market economy long before the seventeenth
century. Nor was there any distinct boundary between home and work.
Businessmen usually operated from or within close range of their homes;
only the corporate enterprises had offices. Kinship networks were not
replaced by a bourgeois family within a national society. They were not
only alive and well, but an integral and essential part of the business
family. The causal links between the family and the economy were
complex and reversible with variable shifts in the relative weight of different factors.[21] It is difficult to isolate the impact of economic change
on the family, because both were independently governed by numerous
other factors.

There is no doubt that the contract was increasingly adopted as an
organizing principle in seventeenth-century England. Indeed, the only
relationship within the family that was not contractual was that between
parent and child. Those Protestant divines who advocated religious
obedience within a patriarchal nuclear family facilitated the emergence
of possessive individualism, even though they rejected materialism.[22]
Economic individualism did discredit old familial ideals and values. In
order to satisfy new economic demands and needs, traditional practices
and customs were eroded by neglect or changed by political action.

It is surprising, however, that any historian should ever have envisaged early modern England as a society in which randomly associated,
possessive individuals competed in a disembodied marketplace. That is
the stuff of fiction, as in Defoe's novels where his characters have no
family.[23] Individualism and self-interest have a long history and were
always contained and diluted by the patriarchal structure of the family
and by the obligations of kinship. The basic social unit, as even Hobbes
conceded, was the family, not the individual.[24] Only the family could
train and socialize the next generation. Contract became an alternative
to, not a substitute for, status, descent, and connection. As children

[21] Goody, *Production and Reproduction*, 26.
[22] D. Ormrud, "Puritanism and Patriarchy" in *Studies in Modern Kentish History*, ed.
A. Detsicas and N. Yates (Maidstone, 1983), 125.
[23] I. P. Watt, *Rise of the Novel* (Berkeley, 1957), 65.
[24] G. J. Schochet, "Thomas Hobbes on the Family," *Political Science Quarterly* 82 (1967):
442. Hobbes regarded the family as a rational, artificial institution: see R. A. Chapman,
"Leviathan Writ Small," *American Political Science Review* 69 (1975): 78.

become more autonomous, however, they came to rely more for their education, advancement, and support on public institutions, whose growing professionalism and bureaucratic power constituted a greater threat to the integrity and authority of the family than the market.

The same was true of the patriarchal order, which survived because the theory was usually ignored in practice. Women were separated by gender at puberty and suffered from occupational discrimination; wives and daughters were expected to display obedience and deference to men in the household in return for protection and support. But familial roles were reciprocal as well as hierarchical. Wives had independent authority within the household and shared many functions with their husbands. Differential mortality and parental death undermined patriarchy, because so many wives survived their husbands and daughters survived their fathers to become executrixes and independent, full members of society. There was no strict division between the public and private spheres, both of which met in the family. The flood of advice on marriage and parenting, from both secular and clerical writers, was probably induced by a need to bolster cultural assumptions as women became more independent. The ideology of marriage was reactive, confused, and subject to continuous change, just like actual marriages that had inherent contradictions of interest and loyalty. The position of women in the business world differed from those in landed society, because they inherited liquid assets in their own right. To reconstruct their true status, it is necessary to follow the money. Nothing empowers like cold, hard cash.

The strength of romantic individualism is more difficult to calibrate. Love and affection surfaced frequently in both courtship and marriage, and it had existed long before the emergence of a sophisticated market economy; it was the nuclear family that allowed individualism to develop, and it was individualism that created both capitalism and love.[25] It is reasonable to suppose that the whole gamut of emotions was in play in all periods, although contemporary culture would always determine how they were expressed, and their display was contingent on the growth

---

[25] H. R. Lantz, "Romantic Love in the Premodern Period," *Journal of Social History* 15 (1982): 365; A. MacFarlane, *The Origins of English Individualism* (1978), 198; *idem.*, *Marriage and Love* (Oxford, 1985), 335. In Douai, love appears to have become more important in marriage after contract superseded custom: see M. C. Howell, *The Marriage Exchange* (Chicago, 1998), 237.

of private space in domestic interiors. There are signs of greater self-consciousness and intimacy with a parallel demand for greater privacy. It was not so much that individuals became more affectionate, but that the importance of affection was more widely acknowledged.[26] The quest for personal identity did not, however, destroy group cohesion. Common patterns of behavior coexisted with individual action.[27] Personal decisions were often family decisions.[28] The increasing demand for autonomy was quite compatible with bonding, fraternal values, and gentrification. Individuals could choose which of their kin to acknowledge and nurture, because kinship was personal, informal, and opportunistic, not prescriptive; kin complemented, but did not oust, friends. Family members had multiple roles, but those roles did not replace self. The family did not turn in on itself, and it was emotionally unified. The triumph of individualism was fundamentally a triumph of the individual household within a kinship structure.

The family, like all institutions, was both a product of and a participant in the prevailing culture, which defined needs and obligations. The actions of families were influenced by the world in which they functioned and in turn changed the nature of that world. The value system both shaped and was shaped by behavior.[29] What was given or normative was often taken as natural and self-evident; the rules were quietly accepted so long as they remained serviceable, because to change them required effort and risk and invited instability. Conformity was prudent and a consequence of inertia. Most individuals followed their instincts rather than ideas drawn from books or the prompting of an overarching mentality. Only the discontented and the ideologically committed were likely to complain. The majority, faced with inconvenient values, fell back on evasion, disregard, amnesia, hypocrisy, and the double standard. Principles of conduct were invented or the relevant rhetoric appropriated ex post facto to invest decisions made on other grounds with a spurious rationality and justification. Most families were governed by emotion and interest, not by ideology; they relied on practical compromise rather than representations of reality. They acted from habit as well as calculating their self-interest, while

---

[26] C. Taylor, *Sources of the Self* (Cambridge, Mass., 1989), 292.
[27] S. M. Greenfield and A. Strickson, "A New Paradigm for the Study of Entrepreneurship," *Economic Development and Cultural Change* 29 (1981): 487.
[28] Haveren, "The History of the Family," 107.
[29] J. E. Crowley, *This Sheba, Self* (Baltimore, 1974), 2.

simultaneously seeking to justify and confirm their actions by appeal to an external system of values.[30]

The history of the business family is a continuous struggle between individuals and their environment. They could only choose from the options available to them within a restricted time and space. Whatever their dreams, they were preoccupied with the mundane and the routine; they had to cope with life one day at a time. Their choice of marriage partners and their contact with kin was largely determined by geography. Many decisions, such as when to leave home or who to marry, were collective and based on external pressures, on needs rather than wants. But individuals still made choices, took action, and declined to become passive victims. Each age cohort had a unique historical experience.[31] It was up to each individual to make the final decision about when and who to marry, to make a marriage work through effort and sacrifice, and to raise children and build their characters. Conflicts of objectives and methods were resolved by compromise; a balance was struck between reciprocity and self-interest and between the public and private spheres.

CAPITAL

The accumulation of capital was largely a function of individual ability, luck, and length of life. But it was also promoted by late marriage and by family needs.[32] The structure of business families was closely related to their resources; they were forced to accumulate in order to start families, and it was largely the successful who procreated. The need to provide for children acted as a major incentive, despite the reluctance of sects like the Quakers to approve of accumulation even for children.[33] "The loss of my son," wrote Joseph Collett to his sister, "hath abated that desire of wealth which you justly observe was never very strong."[34] In Massachusetts merchants married first cousins in order to keep capital in the family.[35]

---

[30] C. Campbell, "Traditional and Modern Consumption" in *Consumption and the World of Goods*, ed. J. Brewer and R. Porter (1993), 41–5.
[31] N. Forer, "Age and Social Change" in *Age and Anthropological Theory*, ed. D. I. Kertzer (Ithaca, 1984), 206.
[32] A. Burgière, "De Malthus a Max Weber," *Annales* 7–10 (1972): 1138. The same argument can be applied to agriculture.
[33] Lloyd, *Quaker Social History*, 75.
[34] J. Collett, *Letter Book*, ed. H. H. Dodwell (1933), 134.
[35] P. H. Hall, "Family Structure" in *Family and Kin*, ed. T. K. Haveren (1977), 42.

Table 10.1. *Distribution of Wealth by Cohort, 1580–1740 (Percentage of Known Cases)*

	Bracket I	Bracket II	Bracket III	Bracket IV	Total
Cohort I	3.63	10.36	78.76	7.25	193
Cohort II	9.04	21.87	67.06	2.04	343
Cohort III	11.65	29.80	51.59	6.96	661
Cohort IV	8.82	30.00	50.00	11.18	170

Note: This table is based on that small proportion of subjects whose date of birth and whose wealth at death is known. The data is of interest but is not sufficient to calibrate changes in the distribution of wealth over time.

The assets of the business community grew continuously between 1580 and 1740, with a leap after 1700, though they were concentrated at the top. The proportion of subjects in bracket II increased over time from 10 to 30 percent between cohorts I and IV and the proportion in bracket IV from 7 to 11 percent; in bracket III, however, the proportion declined from 79 percent to 50 percent between cohorts I and IV.[36] There was a clear correlation between age at death and wealth; 79 percent of those in bracket IV and 71 percent in bracket III lived to sixty (see table 3.1).[37]

Wealth at death does not indicate the maximum levels that were reached.[38] The assets of children varied with the length of life of their parents. Because capital was distributed during a businessman's lifetime in portions to sons and daughters, the high point of his estate would have been the point after he had made his fortune and before his children matured. Edward Waterhouse thought that businessmen accumulated wealth between the ages of thirty and fifty, after which they began to distribute: "in 20 years, 10, 20, 30, 40, 60 or a 100 Thousand pounds clear Estate and more raised besides expences and losses."[39] When a busi-

---

[36] J. Alexander, "The City Revealed" in K. Schürer and T. Arkell, *Surveying the People* (Cambridge, 1992), table 3, found 3,000 households worth over £2,000, 3,500 worth £100–2,000, and 4,000 worth £50–500 in 1692.

[37] The Pearson R correlation between age at death and wealth = +0.105. See also P. Earle, "Age and Accumulation" in *Business, Life, and Public Policy*, ed. N. MacKendrick and R. B. Outhwaite (Cambridge, 1986), table 3.1; C. Shammas, "The Determinants of Personal Wealth," *Journal of Economic History* 37 (1977): 682.

[38] J. T. Main, "Standards of Living and the Life Cycle," *Journal of Economic History* 43 (1983): 159–60.

[39] E. Waterhouse, *The Gentleman's Monitor* (1665), 169, 208.

ness was closely held within a family, the capital assets were greater.[40] Some fortunes were quickly made after 1690 from quasimonopolistic profits by early entrants into government finance during the French wars; favoritism in contract allocation distributed unequally the massive gains from the world war.[41] Most fortunes were, however, accumulated over several generations through marriage and inheritance as well as by trade.

Family needs imposed limits on the supply and accumulation of capital. Primogeniture had both positive and negative effects on capital flows; partible inheritance, particularly if there were several children, usually diffused capital.[42] Early mortality could cause the rapid and unexpected transfer of assets. Capital was also absorbed by domestic expenditure, the cost of raising children (including orphans), and the transaction costs of transfer by inheritance without even counting losses in business. Working capital was regularly liquidated to pay for the portions of widows and children who never entered the business world. When Ralph Radcliffe inherited, he withdrew his share from the family business.[43] The great majority of businessmen accumulated little, and their assets were dispersed through their progeny.

Nonetheless, the hemorrhage of working capital must not be exaggerated. Not until a mean completed family size of 6.5 is reached in a population with a 50 percent chance of survival to the father's death does partibility become an issue in more than 50 percent of families; fertility and mortality interact to produce similar effects in high- and medium-pressure demographic regimes.[44] The transfer of assets to children was staggered over the life cycle. Property was vested mainly in the old and the long lived, and their children inherited their share of the whole estate (in contrast to their portions for setting up) late in life. Because parents hung on to their property to preserve their authority and keep their children in awe, capital was still concentrated in active hands. The education and apprenticeship of sons represented investment rather than expenditure of capital, as was pointed out by *The Complete Trades-*

---

[40] The Pearson R correlation coefficient between partners from immediate family and wealth at death = +0.227.

[41] Habakkuk, *Marriage, Debt, and the Estate Market*, 545.

[42] W. L. Miller, "Primogeniture Entails and Endowments," *History of Political Economy* 12 (1980): 568.

[43] Davis, *Aleppo and Devonshire Square*, 15–16.

[44] R. M. Smith, "Some Issues" in *Land, Kinship, and Life Cycle*, ed. R. M. Smith (Cambridge, 1984), 41, 43.

man.[45] Although the liquid portions of orphans were usually put out at interest, testators sometimes instructed that they be managed as active investments so that additional capital would accumulate during the minority. When sons entered business or daughters married businessmen, their inheritance remained in business; assets might be allocated to grandchildren, but distribution was long delayed.

The proportion of investment capital inherited by widows under the Custom is usually underestimated (see also chapter 2). Women whose second husbands were likely to outlive them were outnumbered by widowers who remarried younger women, thereby producing more widows (see also chapter 3). When there were no children, the widow was entitled to half the personalty, and frequently her husband left her all or most of his estate in these circumstances. Those widowed with underage children were not only entitled to one-third, but frequently managed the whole family estate as executrix until their children came of age. Widows might only act as temporary custodians of the property, but temporary could mean many years. Of all known cases, 16 percent of widows in period I and 6 percent in period II had no children; those responsible for raising orphans increased from 37 to 55 percent. Another sample of London wills shows that 40 percent of widows received a half share and 20 percent one-third.[46] A widow often received her share as a lump sum or in liquid assets rather than in the form of property or an annuity.

Older and childless widows with rich and trusting husbands were, therefore, disproportionately wealthy. There is abundant evidence, in wills, inventories, tax returns, and private business papers, of urban women, primarily widows, with more than £500 net worth.[47] In 1582 229 London women, or 4.2 percent of all denizens, were assessed for the subsidy, and widows of leading businessmen were clearly rich. Lady Holles was assessed at £1,900 and Lady Kitson at £1,333.[48] Between

---

[45] N. H., *The Complete Tradesman* (1684), 36.

[46] Earle, *Making of the Middle Class*, 315.

[47] D. G. Vaisey, ed., *Lichfield Probate Inventories*, 4th ser., vol. 5 (Coll. History Staffordshire, 1969), 12; E. and S. George, *Guide to the Probate Inventories of the Bristol Deanery* (Bristol Record Society, 1988), xxi; J. A. Johnston, "Probate Inventories," *Midland History* 1 (1971): table II; Pennington and Sleight, "Steyning Town," 176; Earle, "Female Labour Market," note 15.

[48] R. G. Lang, ed., *London. Two Tudor Subsidy Rolls*, vol. 29 (London Record Society, 1992), xxxv, lxxvi, table 1B; M. Reed, ed., *Ipswich Probate Inventories 1583–1631*, vol. 22 (Suffolk Record Society, 1981), 110; *idem.*, "Economic Structure in Ipswich" in *Country Towns*, ed. P. Clark (Leicester, 1981), 117.

Table 10.2. *Widows with Children, 1580–1740*
(Percentage of Known Cases)

	Period I	Period II
Widows with minor children	37.30	55.34
Widows with adult children	47.03	38.32
Widows with no children	15.68	6.34
Total number of cases	1,901	1,610

1480 and 1660 1,100 London women bequeathed £172,635 to charity, sixty-nine of whom left estates with a total value of £85,611; 260 women from the merchant community gave £68,304, and ninety-seven from the ranks of tradesmen gave £11,065.[49] The widows of the Muscovy merchants inherited sums of around £2,000, often more than their children.[50] In 1640 forty-one widows were listed among those with the resources to lend to the Crown and in 1689 twenty-three women lent between £25 and £500 to William of Orange; of the 1,665 families headed by females listed in the 1692 poll tax returns, twenty-one paid at the 10 shilling rate and sixty-six at the £1 rate.[51]

The same was true outside of London. Widows were major charitable benefactors in provincial towns, like Leeds, where they gave up to £2,000.[52] In 1607 Katherine, widow of alderman Thomas Grave of King's Lynn, left £5,000 to kin.[53] Even widows of small businessmen, like Abigail Watson and Katherine Sewell of Lincoln, left between £200 and £300.[54] Widow Goodeere of Ipswich left £675 plus £406 in debts owing to her, having been married to both a clothier and a merchant.[55]

Some of the assets that widows inherited must have found their way back into the hands of men, when sons and nephews inherited or

[49] W. K. Jordan, *Charities of London* (1960), 28–9.
[50] Willan, *Muscovy Merchants of 1555*, 55.
[51] W. J. Harvey, ed., *London List of the Principal Inhabitants, 1640* (Blackmansbury, 1969); D. V. Glass "Socio-Economic Status" in *Studies in London History*, ed. A. J. Hollaender and W. Kellaway (1969), tables 4 and 5; GLL, MS 5107; CLRO MS 40/35.
[52] Kirby, "Restoration Leeds," 171.
[53] Metters, "The Rulers and Merchants of King's Lynn," 58.
[54] J. A. Johnston, ed., *Lincoln Probate Inventories*, vol. 80 (Lincoln Record Society 1991), nos. 3, 27.
[55] *Ipswich Probate Inventories, 1583–1631*, 110.

Table 10.3. *Estimated Percentage of Business Assets Held By Widows*[a]

1. Assets inherited by widows:	
i. In families where at least one child had survived:	
A (0.89) × B (0.815) × H/C (0.23) × DE (0.29)	= 0.0484
ii. In families where no child had survived:	
A (0.89) × B (0.815) × H/C (0.23) × [F(1 − D)](0.11)	= 0.0184
Total owned outright by widows (i + ii)	= 0.0668
2. Assets controlled by widows:	
A (0.89) × B (0.815) × H/C (0.23)	
× D (0.89) × H/C (0.23) × [1 − E]) (0.67)	= 0.0229
Total (1 + 2)	= 0.09 (0.0897)

[a]Assumptions:

A. 0.89 of businessmen marry (91.23 percent married in period I and 88.93 percent in period II).

B. 0.815 of their wives survive them by a median of 12 years. The survival rate was 86 percent in period I and 77 percent in period II.

C. Twenty-six years constitutes the cycle of inheritance (husbands own the equity in their business on average for 20 years and their widows for 6 years, allowing for inheritance by children).

D. 0.89 of marriages, in which the widow survives, have at least one child who survives to inherit (84 percent in period I and 94 percent in period II).

E. 0.33 is inherited by a widow when there is a surviving child.

F. 0.50 is inherited by a widow when no children survive.

G. The entire estate is controlled by a widow so long as any child remains underage when she is appointed sole executrix.

H. Six years is the average period of time that a widow acts as executrix.

daughters' portions passed to their husbands. Wills frequently instructed that the widow should augment the children's portions in her will. The widow of Andrew Crook divided the estate she had inherited from her husband among her four daughters, three from previous marriages.[56] Nonetheless widows of successful businessmen were clearly women of property who picked up assets for a long time and had a major impact on consumption patterns.[57]

The capital involved was substantial. It can be projected that, at any one time, £9 out of every £100 of business assets in England was owned or controlled by widows.[58] Since businessmen in Stuart England were

[56] T. Hobbes, *Correspondence*, vol. 2, 823.
[57] M. Pointon, *Strategies for Showing* (Oxford, 1997), 36.
[58] W. K. Jordan, *Philanthropy in England* (1959), 354, also by coincidence suggests that women controlled nearly 9 percent of all wealth. Although he does not specify exactly how he arrived at this figure, it is probably derived from the £272,167 donated by all women between 1480–1660, which represented 8.77 of total charitable contributions.

worth collectively at least £25.3 million, the aggregate assets in the hands of widows probably amounted to over £2.28 million, more than the initial subscription for the Bank of England and more than sufficient to finance the entire Asian trade.[59]

The crucial difference between business and the landed interest, which is so often overlooked by historians, was that business assets consisted of personalty and were controlled absolutely by individuals, even though vested in the family. Trusts could be created to hold personalty, but it was generally difficult for businessmen to tie up their estates, and their capital was consequently mobile and liquid.[60] The business family acted as a holding company, distributing property between individual members and transmitting across generations; property was not pooled between family members or regarded by sons as a life interest.

The principal savers were men in business whose income depended on their ability to earn fees and profits and who had to accumulate sufficient reserves during their working life to provide a trouble-free income from rents or interest in their declining years. Since landowners were borrowers rather than lenders, it was business families that financed not just production and distribution, but government and war.[61]

Widows and children, however, took priority over the family business that few widows wished to continue. Transfers of assets between extended families within the kinship network were therefore necessary to finance family enterprises; few major businesses could have survived without outside capital from investors or lenders (see also chapter 7). One inherent weakness of the family firm was that its capital base was both narrow and unstable, whereas joint-stock companies could tap a national pool of capital.

INVESTMENT

The proportion of capital available for family businesses was also reduced by passive investment and a rentier strategy. Businessmen salted

---

[59] Grassby, *The Business Community of Seventeenth-Century England*, figure 8.1. This is a minimum estimate.

[60] Habakkuk, *Marriage Debt*, 5.

[61] One of the perplexing questions rarely asked is where the money came from to fund the ballooning government debt between 1690 and 1714. Some was clearly transferred from commercial investments, some came from abroad, and some was fictitious money from an anticipated future increase in the gross national product. But much of it must have represented savings accumulated out of earnings over the previous three generations, much of which passed through the hands of retirees, widows, and orphans.

away their profits in less risky investments, both as financial reserves against business reversals and to provide for their families and their own retirement. They had several choices for their portfolio: funds could be placed short term in private, corporate, and government loans, and mortgages, leases, and annuities, or long term in freehold land and urban property, company stocks, public offices, and long-term government debt. Trading in the primary and secondary capital markets for capital gains sometimes constituted an active business; professional brokers speculated in land, building, and stocks and became government financiers. But stocks and debt instruments were usually held for income.

Almost half of businessmen in period I and almost one-third in period II held no land, though that proportion fell to 21 percent in bracket III, 10 percent in bracket IV, and 13 percent in cohort IV; there was an increase in the number of major landholders in period II and a concentration in brackets III and IV and cohort IV; urban property was owned by around 50 percent, and those who had substantial holdings of one form of real estate usually had at least a foothold in the other (see table 9.1).

Other studies confirm this pattern. Half of the Jacobean aldermen possessed manors, though those who were large landowners were also well endowed with personalty.[62] London merchants were heavily involved in Crown and church lands during the interregnum.[63] One sample of citizens after 1660 shows that some two-fifths had land and one-fifth had urban property, with a higher concentration among the old and wealthy.[64] Approximately one-third of the property was in London and Middlesex and half in the southeastern counties. Insurance policies, like those of the Hand in Hand Insurance Company, also reveal that by the early eighteenth century many businessmen owned substantial homes, often combined with shops; numerous houses were insured by the same person and had presumably been acquired as rental properties.[65]

Outside of London, although the data is uneven, land was routinely acquired by businessmen in Gloucester, Norwich, Manchester, Bristol,

---

[62] Lang, "Greater Merchants of London," appendixes.
[63] H. J. Habbakuk, "The Land Settlement," *Transactions of the Royal Historical Society*, 5th ser., 28 (1978): 205.
[64] Earle, *Making of the Middle Class*, 153–5, tables 5.6 and 5.7; Boulton, *Neighbourhood and Society*, 87.
[65] GLL, MS 8674/2, fos. 185, 333.

and Leeds, although it was less common in Belfast.[66] Hull merchants owned both urban property and land near the town.[67] In Lincolnshire nine families purchased estates, and in Northamptonshire, Northumberland, and Hertfordshire 6 percent of new owners and one-third of all purchasers were businessmen.[68] Wealthy clothiers, like those in the Weald, usually owned land.[69] The same was true of Scotland.[70] One-fourth of merchant members of Parliament acquired country estates through inheritance, marriage, or purchase, mostly before their election.[71]

The majority of businessmen did not, however, have landed estates. Even the successful businessman first invested on a small scale, and families gradually built up an estate over more than one generation. Few had the financial resources to acquire large properties and leave trades altogether; they had to settle for suburban property and a villa. Around 30 percent of those whose assets are known had only small parcels in both periods I and II, brackets I and II, and cohorts I to II (see table 9.1). Two typical examples are Emmanuel Stallin, a haberdasher, who had twenty acres in Essex, and Thomas Andrews, a dyer, who had thirty acres in Springfield and a few acres in Lancashire.[72] In Scotland merchants usually had around fifty acres.[73]

One criterion for investing in land was the comparative yield of different securities. The decline in interest rates on mortgages seems to have driven capital from land into business after 1660.[74] In 1665 Edward Waterhouse argued that gains from trade had discouraged investment in land in the 1630s.[75] To many businessmen, like Thomas Pengelly who bought land for his uncle, investment in real property was simply a busi-

[66] N. Herbert, ed., *V. C. H. Gloucester IV. City of Gloucester* (1988), 81; Evans, *Seventeenth-Century Norwich*, 24; Wilson, *Gentlemen Merchants*, 17; J. F. Pound, *Tudor and Stuart Norwich* (Chicester, 1988), 81; Agnew, *Belfast Merchants*, 46; P. MacGrath, "Wills Bristol Merchants," *Transactions of the Bristol and Gloucester Archaeological Society* 68 (1949): 95.
[67] K. J. Allison, ed., *V. C. H. Yorkshire East Riding*, vol. 1 (1969), 122.
[68] A. R. Maddison, ed., *Lincolnshire Wills, 1600–1711* (1891), xxv; L. and J. C. F. Stone, *An Open Elite* (Oxford, 1984), 403.
[69] M. Zell, *Industry in the Countryside* (Cambridge, 1994), 224.
[70] N. T. Phillipson, "The Faculty of Advocates" in *Law Making and Law Makers in British History*, ed. A. Harding (1980), 146–56.
[71] B. D. Henning, ed., *The House of Commons, 1660–90* (1983), 8, 55.
[72] PCC, Coventry 27, 1640; PCC, Evelyn 72, 1641.
[73] Devine, "Merchant Class," 102.
[74] I. Blanchard, A. Goodman, and J. Newman, eds., *Industry and Finance in Early Modern History* (Stuttgart, 1992), 22.
[75] Waterhouse, *The Gentleman's Monitor*, 169, 208.

ness with the prospect of capital appreciation: "Be sure to get it as cheap as possible and make sure that the title is good and free from decimation and mortgages."[76] George Treadway ran an urban estate in Hammersmith in partnership with his father-in-law.[77] Bankers needed the visibility of landownership in order to reassure the landowners who constituted their principal clients, and they could often pick up bargains. Sir Francis Child and his son, Robert, acquired Osterley by purchasing from the mortgagees.

The great attraction of land was its security. Subject to the law of entropy, land is permanent, and the demand for its main product, food, remains constant unless the population suffers a demographic collapse. That was why it was popular with those who had made their fortunes quickly in risky enterprises and was so frequently chosen by businessmen to settle dowries and jointures and provide for widows and children. John Paige's father-in-law and partner asked him to put the money he owed him into land for his daughter.[78] Thomas Mun instructed, in his will, that £3,000 be invested in land by his overseers for his widow and children.[79]

The main reason for buying a landed estate, versus parcels of land or urban property, was to join or put a son into the landed gentry. When the move from town to country occurred, it was usually in the second or third generation, and it was an option only open to the rich; it was more common for sons to enter the urban gentry and the professions than landed society. Land not only conferred status, but it perpetuated the family name. Those without sons were less likely to buy, though some businessmen bought in anticipation, like John Randolph, a merchant tailor, who had only a daughter.[80] William Dwight, a clothworker, had three daughters but no male heir for his land.[81] In these circumstances testators usually endowed the sons of their married daughters.[82]

Sometimes land was not acquired as a deliberate choice or was treated as a temporary investment, not as a patrimony. It could be inherited from ancestors, siblings, or kin. In Shrewsbury merchants did acquire real property outside the town, but it was often divided and sold rather than

---

[76] Letter to his brother dated 13 Nov. 1656, Bod, Add. MS C 267.
[77] CLRO, CSB.
[78] J. Paige, *Letters, 1648–58*, ed. G. F. Steckley, vol. 21 (London Record Society, 1984), xxxiv.
[79] PCC, Evelyn 92, 1641.   [80] PCC, Barrington 25, 1628.
[81] PCC, Goare 79, 1637.   [82] Habakkuk, *Marriage Debt*, 558, 567.

kept intact within the family.[83] Thomas Lane, a salter, instructed that his
land be sold to increase his personal estate and pay his legacies.[84] Edward
Rennick had no children, so he ordered his trustees to sell his land and
distribute the proceeds to his wife and kin.[85] Sometimes businessmen
became landholders by default: Philip Ford, the London business
manager for William Penn, found himself the owner of most of
Pennsylvania.[86]

The acquisition of landed estates by businessmen was not determined
just by demand and wealth; the frequency, timing, and scale of purchase
also depended on the supply of land in the market and the availability
of their capital.[87] Businessmen were frequently trapped in illiquid investments at the critical time when an opportunity materialized. Most maintained a balance between their commercial and landed investments.
William Cotesworth moved gradually from trade into land, but retained
his colliery interests.[88] Families, like the Myddletons, or businessmen,
like Josiah Child, were "amphibious" landowners, bridging land and
trade.[89]

By the end of the seventeenth century preferences had changed. Land
lost ground as a rentier investment to company stocks and government
debt. There were now many moderately wealthy businessmen who
lacked the resources to buy estates but who still sought a safe and liquid
outlet for their surplus capital.[90] The funded debt after 1690 benefited
from the public confidence generated by parliamentary government
and served the same purpose as venal office in continental countries.
Company shares (and so the government debt which the companies
carried) were assignable, alienable, and relatively liquid, though management of rentier holdings was never that simple or easy. It was a sign
of changing times when the merchant, Jeremy Sambrooke, in November
1702, bought twenty-three annuities of £14 for six members of his family
for £4,830.[91]

Family needs and the life cycle therefore determined the allocation of
capital between active and passive investments. It is sometimes argued

[83] J. C. Hindson, "Family Structure" (Ph.D. diss., University of Wales, 1991), 159–61.
[84] PCC, Alchin 471, 1654.   [85] PCC, Rivers 135, 1645.
[86] R. S. Dunn, "Penny Wise" in *The World of William Penn*, ed. R. S. and M. M. Dunn
(Philadelphia, 1986), 51.
[87] Habakkuk, *Marriage Debt*, 549.   [88] Ellis, *William Cotesworth*, 8.
[89] D. Stephenson, "The Myddletons," *Essex Archaeology and History* 8 (1977): 286.
[90] Habakkuk, *Marriage Debt*, 617.   [91] Ibid., 504.

that the husband's control of a wife's property was the "keystone of family capitalism."[92] Exogamy did indeed result in the circulation of women and therefore of capital.[93] But age was the dominant factor. Disinvestment from trade accelerated from the age of fifty onwards; the elderly were more likely to be cautious rentiers and more interested in regularity than in scale of return.[94]

Widowhood had a positive effect—a fact underestimated by historians—because they recycled the capital they inherited to other active businessmen. The proceeds from liquidated businesses re-emerged as passive investments in the stock, annuity, and loan markets. The individual amounts invested were often modest, but when all the small loans are aggregated, they assume real importance.[95] Widows financed young apprentices, sons, nephews, and cousins throughout the country and abroad.[96] Advances were often made informally to those who could not offer collateral and at much more modest rates of interest than loans by professional scriveners and usurers, who had always charged more than the legal maximum rate to small business borrowers.[97]

The inability of the centralized capital markets to meet the needs of small or unsecured individual borrowers created a paradoxical situation: the stock market was awash with money, while, at the same time, aspiring merchants and craftsmen, especially in the provinces, suffered from a shortage of capital. What was needed was trade credit rather than funding for fixed assets.[98] Even though corporations and some landowners could borrow at low rates, the cost of money for new entrepreneurs often exceeded the profit that they could reasonably expect to attain.

[92] C. Shammas, M. Salmon, and M. Dahlin, eds., *Inheritance in America* (New Brunswick, 1987), 48, 212; families are described as "firms."
[93] D. Herlihy, *Medieval Households* (Cambridge, Mass., 1985), 136; P. D. Hall, "Family Structure and Economic Organization" in *Family and Kin*, ed. T. K. Haveren (1977), 42.
[94] Earle, *Making of the Middle Class*, tables 5.1 and 5.2.
[95] *Ipswich Probate Inventories*, 89.
[96] Ellis, *William Cotesworth*, 5; C. H. Dayton, *Women before the Bar* (Chapel Hill, 1995), 94.
[97] N. Jones, *God and the Moneylenders* (Oxford, 1989), 68; M. K. McIntosh, "Money Lending," *Albion* 20 (1988): 570; B. A. Holderness, "Elizabeth Parkin," *Transactions of the Hunter Archaeology Society* 10 (1972): 85; J. Webb, "Joyce Jeffries," *Archaeologia* 37 (1857): 201; R. G. Griffiths, "Joyce Jeffries," *Transactions of the Worcester Archaeological Society* 10–11 (1933–5): 13; E. Roberts and K. Parker, ed., *Southampton Probate Inventories*, vol. 34–5 (Southampton Record Society, 1992), 154.
[98] B. L. Anderson, "Money and the Structure of Credit," *Business History* 12 (1970): 100; J. Ellis, "Risk Capital" in *From Family Firm to Corporate Capitalism*, ed. P. K. O'Brien (Oxford, 1998), 84.

Widows reduced this prominent gap in the credit system. Throughout the country and the century, the capital set aside by businessmen for retirement was inherited by widows who then provided continuous and productive, short-term finance for farmers, merchants, tradesmen, factors, craftsmen, and consumers. In their search for passive income widows recirculated capital and greased the wheels of enterprise. By increasing the supply of loan funds, they helped to bring down the interest rate, and they provided flexible credit and liquidity where it was most needed at the grassroots of the domestic economy.

MANAGEMENT

A family firm was limited by the number and ability of its members. It could, and did, draw on the whole extended family for manpower, but nepotism often took precedence over merit. Children and kin did not always measure up to expectations; in Coventry outsiders performed better than the second generation of businessmen.[99] Human capital is different from other assets because the return on investment depends on ability and declines as more is invested.[100] A business could be debilitated by inbreeding and needed regular infusions of new blood. But families often succumbed instead to the lure of oligarchy and shut out new men.[101]

Another major problem in a family business, which usually escapes notice, was physical deterioration through ill health or aging. Without any effective medical care many businessmen were likely to suffer from intermittent or persistent difficulties with their sight, hearing, teeth, backs, and limbs, and their mental faculties could be expected to decline with age. Given the personal nature of business, this must have affected the quality of management. William Phillips, when asked to invest on behalf of his son in Turkey, recognized that he was past his best: "I am now too old to commence merchant."[102] Michael Mitford bowed to his infirmities in a series of letters to his correspondents:

It is but little I do at present. . . . I have not been 3 times in London this 6 weeks having been much indisposed with an asthma or shortness of breath . . . living in the country, I am resolved to wind up any bottom as soon as possible being now

---

[99] R. M. Berger, *Necessary Luxuries* (University Park, 1993), 278.
[100] G. S. Becker, *A Treatise on the Family* (Cambridge, Mass., 1981), 5.
[101] C. Brooks, "Apprenticeship" in *The Middling Sort*, ed. J. Barry and C. Brooke (1994), 54.
[102] Letter dated 28 April 1726, Folger Library, MS UB 818.

in the 50th year of my age. . . . I doe assure you that for these 6 months past I have found a very great decay of nature in myself for it is not one day in three but I am troubled with a sore vomiting and oppression upon my stomack which has also occasioned such a dimness in my eyes that I can scarce see to write so that I think to withdraw from all business and leave my wife and relations as little involved in business as possible I can . . . not having my health it is a trouble and a burden to me. . . . I have given over my lodgings at London and am wholly retired to Clapham going and coming 2 or 3 times a week as my occasions may require to hear how matters are going upon the Exchange and at Skinner's Hall with the East India Company.[103]

Aging must also have influenced the judgment of businessmen, since their response to events would have been determined by habits and values acquired some forty years earlier, during their formative years between eighteen and twenty-five. Major events, such as the 1620 depression or the civil wars, would have resonated with individuals long after they had ceased to be relevant. The old clung to their offices, which usually passed by seniority, and often resented the young and dismissed their views.[104] Only in a few cases did generations work together. Indeed English society might be better described as a gerontocracy than as a patriarchy.

The effectiveness of the family as a unit of production is always a function of time and place.[105] Time is a scarce resource, and the number of hours supplied to the market is positively related to the price of time over the life cycle.[106] Family firms sometimes had too much emotional investment; family pride tended to create obstacles to mergers with other partners and firms. The wants and whims of children and kin often took priority over the needs of the business. Sons fought for more power and responsibility; relatives pressed for burdensome loans and sureties.

Motivation could also be smothered within the embrace of the family. The best entrepreneurs emerge from obscurity. Alfred Marshall once argued that children brought up by servants would lack the drive of their parents and undermine family businesses.[107] It has been argued that the

---

[103] Letters to Mallabar and Lowther dated 15 Sept., 7 Oct., 1704, and 6 March 1705 GLL, MS 11,892; letter to Booth and Barnardiston, 3 Jan. 1705/6, GLL, MS 11,892A.

[104] Thomas, *Age and Authority*, 71.

[105] G. Jones and M. B. Rose, "Family Capitalism," *Business History* 35 (1993), 4.

[106] G. Ghez and G. S. Becker, *The Allocation of Time and Goods over the Life Cycle* (New York, 1978), xv.

[107] A. Marshall, *Principles of Economics*, 8th ed., 299–300; W. Lazonick, *Business Organization and the Myth of the Market Economy* (Cambridge, 1992), 340.

breakup of family firms develops a more dynamic ideology of enterprise; a distinction has been made between personal, entrepreneurial, and managerial enterprise.[108] Patriarchal direction could fossilize firms and slow the response to economic opportunities; fraternal obligations and kinship ties could undermine competition and efficiency.[109] The whole kinship network both rose and fell together.[110]

For some purposes the family firm had to be supplemented or replaced by more objective institutions. As the market continously expanded, the credit system became increasingly complex and vulnerable and could not be regulated just by family ties or informal arbitration. Institutions therefore emerged that promoted sociability rather than kinship and redefined trust as an abstract and calculable social good, backed by legal enforcement.[111] It can be argued that only institutions can prevent individual actions from having collective irrational results.[112] It became increasingly difficult for small firms to compete either economically or politically with the huge, well-capitalized, monopolistic joint-stock companies. Max Weber, it should be recalled, argued that capitalism developed through bureaucratization, not through the family.

Family firms, in contrast to landed estates, were also discontinuous. Only five goldsmith bankers created permanent firms—the Hoares, Martins, Childs, Hankeys, and Coutts.[113] In Bristol the sugar trade founded some dynasties, but not the tobacco trade.[114] There were no family businesses in the sense that successive generations controlled and managed the same business. Businesses were never sold as a unitary asset. Few were even transferred intact. One exception is the shipping firm of Sir John Frederick and John Haines of Dartmouth, which was taken over by Joseph Herne.[115] Only a minority of sons followed their fathers into

---

[108] D. Bell, *The End of Ideology* (Cambridge, Mass., 1988), 44; A. D. Chandler, "Structure and Investment" in *The Rise of Managerial Capitalism*, ed. H. Daems and H. Van der Wee (The Hague, 1974), 36; P. O'Brien, "Political Pre-Conditions" in *The Industrial Revolution and British Society*, ed. P. O'Brien and R. Quinault (Cambridge, 1993), 134; S. Pollard, *Genesis of Modern Management* (Cambridge, Mass., 1965), 16–36; G. Cookson, "Family Firms and Business Networks," *Business History* 39 (1997): 1–20.

[109] B. Benedict, "Family Firms and Economic Development," *Southwestern Journal of Anthropology* 1 (1968): 18; R. Pares, *West India Fortune* (1950), 212.

[110] Price, *Perry of London*, viii.

[111] Muldrew, "The Culture of Reconciliation," 920; *idem.*, "Interpreting the Market," 183.

[112] M. Granovetter and R. Swedberg, eds., *The Sociology of Economic Life* (Oxford, 1992), 1–26.

[113] F. T. Melton, *Sir Robert Clayton* (Cambridge, 1986), 235.

[114] Morgan, "Bristol West India Merchants," 202.

[115] *House of Commons, 1660–90*, vol. 2, 517.

the same business and few took over lock, stock, and barrel (see chapter 9). They might begin in partnership with their father, operate in the same area of trade, use the same contacts, and sometimes assume the lease of the business premises, but each business was independently founded, and sons usually had higher ambitions than their fathers.

Historians have neglected to observe that, even when there was continuity of trade, there was no continuity of the firm. Many businesses were liquidated before the children matured, and few kinship groups were identified exclusively with one business. In Quaker families continuity was sustained by partible inheritance and by exclusion from the professions, but many of them still moved from high-risk to low-risk trades or into banking.[116] The majority of working businesses could expect to last no more than two generations. Every household firm was destined for oblivion; businessmen had power over money, but not over time.

Clusters of hereditary families were relatively common in the guilds and municipal offices. Although towns differed in the rate of turnover of their officeholders, the frequency of municipal dynasties did increase in the late seventeenth century.[117] But these groups were bound by wealth and politics and frequently had little contact with active business.[118] Gideon Sjoberg was probably correct in his view that urban elites were founded not on business but on religious and political connections bolstered by administrative and ceremonial functions.

A major explanation for discontinuity was a lack of competent male heirs. William Pepperill wanted to return to England and leave his sons to run the business, but one died.[119] Robert Aldworth died without any heirs, so he left his sugar house to his business manager.[120] It was extremely difficult to perpetuate a business in direct male descent (see also chapter 4). The probability of a son succeeding his father was only one in three, and there was a high probability that an heiress would not produce a male heir.[121]

---

[116] Price, "The Great Quaker Business Families," 372, 382.
[117] A. Everitt, "Landscape and Community" in *The Tudor and Stuart Town*, ed. J. Barry (1990), 303.
[118] F. F. Foster, *Politics of Stability* (1977), 102.
[119] B. Fairchild, *William Pepperell* (Ithaca, 1954), 48.
[120] I. V. Hall, "Bristol's Second Sugar House," *Transactions of the Bristol and Gloucester Archaeological Society* 68 (1949): 114.
[121] J. Goody, "Strategies of Heirship," *Comparative Studies in Society History* 15 (1973): 16.

Nor were widows or children necessarily able or willing to pick up the reins. Many family firms were dissolved because the widow could not or would not take over when there was no adult male heir or kinsman to assume this function. Businessmen often anticipated this eventuality and wound up their affairs to protect their dependents and to make their estates easier to administer and harder to despoil. Business also had to compete with other occupations and professions; opportunities for mobility undermined family solidarity.

Since it was property that gave a family continuity, the form in which the assets were held was crucial. In contrast to a landed estate, a business could be liquidated with relative ease but transferred only with difficulty. Landed families failed in the male line as often as businessmen, but their estates passed on intact for centuries because they were administrative units that did not require personal management by their owners, and farming, the ultimate source of their income, was less vulnerable to changes in technology, product, and markets than business. The enterprises of shipowners, ironmasters, and bankers survived longer because their fixed assets could not easily be realized, as was the case with Scottish partnerships. Those businesses closely linked to real property or physical plant had a much greater chance of survival. It is often forgotten, however, that every business is built on sand; the conditions that initially make it profitable do not last, and its fixed assets eventually depreciate to zero.

The objectives of merchants are often misconstrued. Some wanted their businesses to continue through their sons or kin and even made the transfer during their lifetime.[122] Edward Colston's business was taken over by one of his brothers. John Bradshaw, a brewer, instructed that his brewery be run by his executors with the help of his brother-in-law.[123] Robert Abbot, on the other hand, intended his widow to dissolve his business; it passed, however, to Clayton and Morris, and when Abbot's sons failed to contest the takeover, they were excluded from the firm. Clayton ironically left no heirs.[124]

Most businessmen, in fact, never intended their businesses to be permanent. They lacked the ethos of the landowner who regarded himself as steward of property lent to his family by God and as a link between the past and the future. The urban businessman, in sharp contrast, had

[122] Coster, "Kinship and Inheritance," 10.
[123] PCC, Hudleston 25, 1606.   [124] Melton, *Clayton*, 70.

a less-rarified attitude about property. He did not behave as a temporary custodian of his wealth, usually made by his own efforts, but as the absolute owner of his movable assets. As George Simmel observed, economic individualism began where inheritance ended.[125] There was a psychological dimension to the fundamental legal distinction between realty and personalty.

FAMILIAL CAPITALISM

The weaknesses of the family business were more than offset by great strengths. Families never lacked adequate manpower because they did not hesitate to recruit talent as needed from outside the family. New recruits were, moreover, frequently subsumed within the family structure; outsiders were either treated as family members or literally absorbed by intermarriage. Each new generation was trained within a family; the desire to marry and have children stimulated the drive for achievement and provided an incentive to defer gratification.[126] Obligations to children and kin served as a justification for rejecting the prescriptions of the moral economy.

The family business was organized around kin who acted as agents and partners. Different branches of a family cooperated without suppressing healthy competition. Blood ties and family patronage were as important as rationality and cost accounting. Families helped to shape and expand the channels and flows of the market, through breeding, migration, and dispersion.[127] Although mutual exchange and credit facilitated bonding, individual autonomy was not created by the market, but the opposite: kinship networks created a market culture.[128] Family networks could corner markets more effectively than simple partnerships or syndicates of individuals. Business risks were shouldered by the whole extended family, which provided an essential safety net in a society in which private assets were not separated from public liabilities. Businesses that dealt informally with kin benefited from lower

---

[125] G. Simmel, *The Philosophy of Money*, trans. T. Bottomore and D. Frisby, 2d ed. (1990), 354. L. Dumont, *Essays on Individualism* (Chicago, 1986), 107, argues that movable wealth is more highly regarded in the modern world.

[126] The nuclear family is traditionally associated with guilt, and the extended family with shame: see W. Eberhard, *Guilt and Sin in Traditional China* (1962).

[127] B. Bailyn, "Communications and Trade," *Journal of Economic History* 13 (1953): 382.

[128] D. Rollison, *The Local Origins of Modern Society* (1993), 11.

transaction costs that follow any reduction in uncertainty. Even modern firms prefer mergers to the hazards of contract.[129] Fewer resources, for example, had to be allocated to monitor behavior.[130] Trust can be grounded on religious belief or on interest, but it is most effectively secured by a common value system such as that shared by gentlemen or kin; it is usually undermined by the division of labor and by reduced solidarity.[131] Individual businessmen, in their dealings with the outside world, could also draw on the reputation their extended family had acquired over time.

The family business was more than a household unit. It was usually a partnership or series of partnerships with both outsiders and kin. Joint associations of this kind had been the norm in large-scale enterprise, at least since the innovations of medieval Italy. All business was based on personal relationships; even the impersonal functions of companies rested on personalized relations. Every business had a familial structure—even the joint-stock companies. Skill, experience, loyalty, and commitment compensated for shortages of capital. Small unincorporated firms functioned well within a workshop economy, even in the eighteenth century, and the extended family was both compatible with and an active factor in industrialization.[132] In Japan, it has been said, the firm behaved like a family and families functioned like firms.[133]

[129] O. E. Williamson, *Markets and Hierarchies* (New York, 1975), 107; *idem., The Economic Institutions of Capitalism* (New York, 1985), 45; R. A. Pollard, "A Transaction Cost Approach" in *The Economics of the Family*, ed. N. Folbre (Cheltenham, 1996), 596.

[130] M. Casson, *The Economics of Business Culture* (Oxford, 1991), passim.

[131] P. Dasgupta, "Trust as a Commodity," and J. Dunn, "Trust and Political Agency" in *Trust*, ed. D. Gambetta (Oxford, 1988), 53, 81; A. Pagne, "The Destruction of Trust," *Trust*, ed. D. Gambetta, 126–41, argues, however, that kinship networks delay the development of trust by dividing society into outgroups and ingroups.

[132] Haveren and Plakans, eds., *Family History at the Crossroads*, xi; E. A. Wrigley, "Reflections on the History of Family," *Daedalus* 106 (1977): 81; S. N. Eisenstadt, *Tradition, Change, and Modernity* (New York, 1983), 108; M. Berg, "Small Producer Capitalism," *Business History* 35 (1993): 36; B. Supple, "Aspects of Private Investment" in *Rise of Managerial Capitalism*, ed. H. Daems and H. Van der Wee (The Hague, 1974), 85. H. Medick, "The Proto-Industrial Family Economy," *Social History* 3 (1976): 300, argues that there was a symbiotic relationship between family economies and merchant capital. As late as the 1880s most manufacturing firms were unincorporated family businesses, and the predominant business unit was the partnership: see P. Payne, *British Entrepreneurship in the Nineteenth Century*, 2d ed. (1988), 14–16.

[133] Japan provides a sharp contrast because it adopted primogeniture (unlike China) but rejected the nuclear family in favor of group orientation. See T. C. Smith, *The Agrarian Origins of Modern Japan* (Stanford, 1959), 89; W. M. Fruin, "The Family as a Firm," *Journal of Family History* 5 (1980): 432; C. Usui, "Can Japanese Society Promote Individualism," in *Age Structuring in Comparative Perspective*, ed. D. I.

If businesses rarely descended through the male line, they frequently descended through kin, often by a devious route (see also chapter 9). Two generations of Carlills were goldsmiths in Hull, for example, and then Robert Robinson married a Carlill and took on a nephew, James Birkley, who died and left the premises to his wife or Birkley's son.[134] The Monmouthshire ironworks of the Hanbury family were transferred through kin.[135] The son of James Cole of Gateshead diversified his father's business, and his nephew in turn inherited and moved into coal mining, followed by his two sons.[136] Thomas Fowle, who was one of four brothers who were all apprenticed as goldsmiths, was followed by his nephew, Robert.[137] Two Chethams were succeeded by nephews, and two of their grandchildren in turn became merchants.[138] Many London dynasties were perpetuated through the female line.[139]

Even though every business ultimately disappeared and even though kinship networks lacked generational depth, the business family was still serially important. Two generations, it should be emphasized, is not exactly the blink of an eye; few modern corporations survive intact for sixty years.[140] The English economy benefited from both continuity and discontinuity. Richard Steele thought that the "next end and last end" of building an estate was to do good and that the old successful traders should retire to give the young their chance.[141] All firms are vulnerable to the law of retardation, because they are too heavily invested in their past glory and are unable to adapt when diminishing returns set in. There was sufficient continuity to transfer skills between generations and sufficient discontinuity to escape the trap of oligarchy and foster merit and entrepreneurship.

In the early modern economy it was inevitable that most business activity would be in the hands of small family firms. There were rela-

Kertzer and K. W. Schaie (Hillsdale, N.J. 1989), 140; H. Morikawa, *Zaibatsu* (1992), xvii.

[134] A. Bennett, "The Goldsmiths in Church Lane," *Yorkshire Archaeological Journal* 60 (1988): 117.

[135] A. A. Locke, *The Hanbury Family*, vol. 1 (1916), 119–51.

[136] F. W. D. Manders, *History of Gateshead* (1973), 55.

[137] D. M. Mitchell, "Mr Fowle," *Business and Economic History* 23 (1994): 27–9.

[138] Wadsworth and Mann, *Cotton Trade*, 33.

[139] A. R. Wagner, *English Genealogy*, 2d ed. (Oxford, 1972), 160.

[140] According to Cardwell's law, no society can retain its lead in technological innovation for more than two to three generations. The preponderance of nation-states or empires also seems to be governed by the same cycle.

[141] R. Steele, *Tradesmans Calling*, 2d ed. (1698), 204, 235.

tively few sectors where large-scale organizations were either needed or viable. The combined resources of kinship networks with their acceptance of collective responsibility gave family businesses the strength to compete in the marketplace with larger entities. Above all, they were spared the costs and rigidities of bureaucracy. Public firms set up hierarchies to allocate resources and make decisions and consequently have longer time lags and higher transaction costs.[142] Family businesses, in contrast, were flexible and could adjust more quickly to changing circumstances. Family firms might lack staying power, but when weak and uncompetitive they simply fell by the wayside, whereas corporations continued under their own momentum despite diminishing returns to management. The business family had to be efficient or it did not survive.

It has been noted that the family, by determining the age of marriage, was an active factor in demographic change.[143] What has never been fully understood until now is that the family made a positive contribution to economic growth, that it was an independent and not simply a dependent variable. It was an instrument of change, not a refuge from change. Indeed the main thrust of development had to come from small business. The business family created its own economic identity. It occupied the middle ground between the bureaucratic management of the joint-stock companies and the rootless entrepreneurship of economic individualism. Familial capitalism combined the self-reliance of the nuclear family with the dutifulness of the extended family. The business family provided a socially acceptable framework within which individual talent and energy could be encouraged and harnessed. The English economy would ultimately be industrialized by small, entrepreneurial family firms without separating ownership from management.

The business family was in several respects the individual writ large. It differed from the landed family in that its head expected to liquidate his firm and share his assets among his children. Each generation had to start afresh and found new businesses. Landed estates could be transferred intact to the eldest son and run by professional managers. Business, however, could not be governed by the hereditary principle, because it required personal direction and because talent did not necessarily run

---

[142] R. H. Coase, "The Nature of the Firm" in *The Nature of the Firm*, ed. O. E. Williamson and S. G. Winter (Oxford, 1991), 3.
[143] E. A. Wrigley, *People, Cities, and Wealth* (Oxford, 1987), 13.

in families. On the other hand, individuals were mortal. Although it was individual entrepreneurship that generated fortunes, it was the family that consolidated, accumulated, and redistributed property over time through marriage and inheritance. In a perilous and unforgiving world, any individual, however aggressive and independent, needed all the help he could muster, and his first line of defense was his kin. The family provided both a secure base, a deterrent against irresponsibility, and a reason to succeed. The introduction of financial markets did not depersonalize business, which, on the contrary, operated in a face-to-face society.

The family firm played a paradoxical role in the economy. It operated at a disadvantage in those sectors of the economy dominated by highly capitalized, centralized, large-scale institutions. Undue preference for kin as partners and associates reduced the pool of talent. The interests and objectives of the family did not necessarily coincide with those of the family business; the values and attitudes appropriate to one could become a liability to the other. The desire to perpetuate the family name could only be achieved by leaving active business and investing in land or institutionalized assets or a perpetual charity. On the other hand, the great strength of the family was its infinite flexibility and its hybrid structure. Families were able to compartmentalize their behavior to meet conflicting demands. In the early modern period the economy would have grown at a slower pace without corporations and lone adventurers, but it would not have functioned at all without family networks.

Because the family was the dominant social institution, it was inevitable that it would change as the economy changed. A credit-driven economy created new opportunities and needs and forced families to adjust. The self-correcting mechanism of the market eliminated the inefficient. Greater wealth enabled greater individual choice, more privacy, and a gendered division of labor, though it was aspirations to gentility rather than capitalism or patriarchy that imposed a life of idleness on the wives of prosperous businessmen. But the family was also a dynamic force in the economy. Without the capital and applied skills of family firms, there would have been no economic growth. All families were subject to the same external forces, but their response was not uniform, and some seized opportunities when others stagnated. In the early modern period kinship and capitalism complemented and reinforced each other; their relationship was not antagonistic but symbiotic.

Appendix A

Sources for the Database

Archival records, supplemented by both primary and secondary literary sources, constitute the bedrock of the database for this book. It has been assembled both from contemporary quantitative data and by accumulating thousands of references from a cross section of sources. Some classes of records have been systematically exploited and others sampled; some data have been compiled from the original documents, some from indexes and abstracts, and some from later compilations.[1] Certain fields, which do not bear directly on the main questions posed in this book, have been accorded a low priority. Information about common councilmen, for example, has been entered in passing, but the records have not been systematically searched to identify all those in the database who held that office. In most cases biographical information in printed genealogical sources and dictionaries has been assumed to be correct. Before listing the sources individually, it may be helpful to summarize the principal categories of evidence and indicate those sources that have not been used.

STATE RECORDS

- Petitions of individuals and groups on political and economic issues[2]
- Official correspondence

---

[1] Much basic data can be gathered from the card indexes in the GLL and CLRO of names of common councilors, liverymen, taxpayers, lenders, and oath takers. Perceval Boyd's massive index of London citizens now in the Society of Genealogists has not been used because of inaccessibility. Boyd summarizes on alphabetically ordered cards the genealogical and guild information available from printed sources, but not the actual occupations of citizens.

[2] Periods of political instability, like the 1640s, generated multiple lists of petitioners, but

- Lists of aliens, denizens, naturalized citizens, foreign Protestants
- Lists of nonconformists and oath takers
- Lists of patentees, grantees, charter members, and office holders
- Proceedings and reports of parliamentary committees and commissions of enquiry
- Immigration records (during the interregnum)
- Tax assessments, including the poll and marriage taxes and the subsidies[3]
- Port books for London for 1618–9, 1639–40, 1672–3 (systematic); 1587–8, 1629–30, 1633–4, 1660, 1663, 1665, 1685, 1695 (partial)
- Bills of entry
- Lists of businessmen able to pay taxes or lend money to the Crown
- Subscribers to lotteries and tontines[4]
- Exclusions: hearth and window tax records; muster rolls; apprenticeship returns in PRO IR/1

CHURCH

- Marriage allegations and bonds for licenses (mainly those in print)
- Parochial registers (those in print or available on microfiches in the IGG)
- PCC wills and inventories and administration records, including the wills of English merchants resident overseas and resident aliens
- Jewish congregations (printed)
- French Protestant and other nonconformist churches (printed)
- Quaker genealogies (printed)
- Boyd's index of marriages
- Exclusions: records of the High Court of Delegates, the Commissary and Consistory Courts, and the Court of Arches (matrimonial and testamentary cases); Huguenot collection at University College; Easter books, churchwardens' presentments, and vestry books; Original records in Friends House, Baptist Union Library, congregational library, Bevis Marks, French and Dutch Reformed Churches, and Presbyterian congregations

only those that specify occupations are suitable for analysis. See, for example, L. W. L. Edwards, "The Protestation Returns of 1641–2," *Genealogical Magazine* 19 (1977).

[3] The poll and hearth taxes are fully described by T. Arkell, "Poll Taxes" in *Surveying the People*, ed. K. Schurer and T. Arkel (Oxford, 1992), 142–80; J. S. W. Gibson, *Hearth Tax, Other Later Stuart Tax Lists* (1990).

[4] The original lists are in PRO C 114/9–23; E 401/2599–2600; E 401/1992–1993; E 401/2018. See also F. Leeson, *A Guide to the Records of the British State Tontines* (Isle of Wight, 1968).

JUDICIAL (ALL SELECTIVE)

- Court of Requests
- Court of Chancery
- Bankruptcy Docquets
- Court of Exchequer
- High Court of Admiralty

CITY OF LONDON

- Court of Orphans: common serjeants books, inventories and administration accounts, journals and ledgers, recognizances
- Poll books
- Lists of brokers, jobbers, victualers, licensees, oath takers, freemen, liverymen, common councilmen
- Subscription lists of lenders to the Chamber of London
- Lord Mayor's Court
- Tax assessments
- Exclusions: letter books, journals, and repertories, insolvent debtors schedules, city properties, committee books, wardmote books, certificates of sacrament, and declarations

PRIVATE INSTITUTIONS

- Livery companies: apprenticeship and freedom registers (partial)
- Visitation records (printed)
- School registers (printed)
- Charitable endowments and trusts
- Genealogical records and pedigrees
- Joint-stock companies (commercial, industrial, and financial): lists of adventurers and subscribers, stockholders and directors from company minutes and printed registers
- Regulated chartered companies: lists of members and officeholders from charters and company records
- Exclusions: original visitation records, pedigrees and funeral certificates in the College of Arms; Bank of England subscription books and ledgers

LITERARY SOURCES

- Directories and topographical dictionaries
- Transcripts of monumental inscriptions
- Genealogies, pedigrees, lists of titled and armorial families

- Family histories
- Newsletters, newpapers, ballads, and almanacs
- Pamphlets, tracts, sermons, travelogues, and advice books
- Funeral orations and elegies
- Dramatic works and novels
- Contemporary biographies of business families and editions of letters
- Contemporary histories of towns and counties near London
- Exclusions: the commissioners declarations of bankruptcy in the *London Gazette* and *Gentleman's Magazine*

PRIVATE SOURCES

- Family correspondence, including marriage negotiations
- Diaries, sea journals, day books, commonplace and memorandum books, books of remembrance, memoirs, autobiographies
- Business papers—ledgers, journals, and correspondence
- Legal papers (partnership indentures, deeds, bonds, assignations, settlements, conveyances, contracts for debt)
- Household accounts, invoices, retailers' bills
- Physical artifacts, portraits, monumental inscriptions, trade tokens, merchants' marks
- Exclusions: medical records, like Mayerne's casebook in BL, Sloane 2075, and astrological records, like those of William Lilly

SECONDARY

- Family histories and genealogies[5] (the printed visitations by the Heralds are often embellished with pedigrees provided by the editor)[6]
- Biographical dictionaries, obituaries, and lists of investors, adventurers, indentured servants, trades (booksellers, goldsmiths), citizens, officeholders, aliens, MPs, lawyers, physicians, clergy, soldiers, and sailors (many dictionaries include details of children, relatives, or parents who were businessmen)[7]
- Biographies of businessmen and business families

[5] The reservoir of information buried in genealogical works is scarcely ever used by historians because of their antipathy to genealogy. It is not altogether clear why historians should treat genealogists and antiquarians with contempt, but it probably can be traced back to the point at which the writing of history was professionalized, and it was felt that true historians had to be fundamentally distinguished from "amateur" and "nonscientific" practioners.

[6] G. D. Squibb, *Visitation Pedigrees* (Canterbury, 1964), 11.

[7] The *Dictionary of National Biography* is of little value because so few businessmen are included: see E. S. De Beer, "The DNB," *Genealogical Magazine* 8 (1938): 126–7.

- Admission registers to schools, inns, and universities
- Studies of specific religious denominations
- Guild and urban histories, including topographical works and studies of urban groups
- Histories of parish churches and schools
- Histories of companies, industries, and trades that provide biographical information

PRINCIPAL SOURCES OF THE DATABASE[8]

Manuscripts

British Library

Additional

5,489: Petition of merchants
8,225: Royal Exchange Assurance Company
22,185: List of stockholders in the East India Company
34,015: Register of travelers entering England 1655–7
36,448: Aston papers

Cotton

Nero B 8: List of members of the Turkey Company

Harlean

167: List of merchants
1,238: Petition of the grocers, circa 1685
7,497: List of subscribers to the South Sea Company investing more than £3,000 (1711)

Lansdowne

41: List of Spanish importers (1584)
81: List of merchants
683: List of eminent merchants (1580)

[8] This is a selective list of the principal sources that provided *quantitative* information for the database, many of which are not cited in the footnotes to the main text. It does not include sources for individual subjects or the ledgers and correspondence of merchants, which are listed in the bibliography of manuscripts.

India Office

L/AG/14/3: Register of transfers
A/1/54: Subscribers to the New East India Company
List of stockholders (1709)
Subscriptions of 1657 and 1669
Stock transfers (1681–8)
H/1/1: Alphabetical Index Third joint stock 1631–42
H/1/2: List of adventurers 1675, 1691, 1693
H/1/3: Additional stock paid (1693)
H/2: List of adventurers (1694–6), (1699)
H/3: List of adventurers (1701–3), (1707)
H/40/51: New general stock
Parchment records 54A–B: Original subscribers (1698)

Corporation of London Record Office

Common Serjeants Books (1586–1614), (1662–1713)
Orphans Inventories
Chamber orphanage accounts; monies paid (1643–6), (1661–78);
  finding book (1656–77); monies received (1627–93); recognizances
  (1590 onward)
40/31: Loans on the poll tax (1678)
40/35–71: Loans to the Crown (1689–97)
40/57 Loan on the 4 shilling aid (1693–4)
Alchin MS B/33/5: List of petitioners (1679)
BR/B: Brokers bonds (1697–1720)
BR/C: List of brokers (1697)
Misc. MSS 344.2: Aliens admitted as brokers (1697)
Petitions from brokers (1708)
BR/P: Register of brokers (1697–1708)
Victualers licenses
Oath books

Guildhall London Library

2,879: Transcriptions of the monumental inscriptions in the Guildhall
  chapel
2,942–2,942A–B: Subsidy assessments (1572–1662)
3,119: Monumental inscriptions, church of St. Lawrence

3,283–4: Assessments collected (1673–4)
3,342: Commanders of the trained bands
3,359: Genealogical notes on lord mayors
6,848: Inhabitants of St. Helen's, Bishopsgate
8,674: Hand in Hand Insurance Company
10,091/1–7: Marriage allegations
11,316: Land tax assessments
11,741: Russia Company minutes
11,758: Eastland Company minutes
11,892–3: Eastland Company treasurer's book
11,936: Sun Fire Office registers

House of Lords Record Office

South Sea Company papers

Public Record Office

B 4/1–2: Bankruptcy docquet books
E 190 13, 21–22, 36, 43–44, 50, 55–56, 123: Port books, London
PROB 2: Prerogative Court of Canterbury inventories
PROB 4: Engrossed copies of wills and administration accounts
PROB 5: Paper inventories
PROB 6: Act books of administrations
PROB 8: Act books of probate
PROB 11: Registered copies of wills
PROB 31–32: Exhibits and inventories
SP 105/157–168: Levant Company's ledger and entry books
SP 12/160/10: Venice Company patentees
SP 16/492/76: Lenders to Crown (1641)
SP 28/162: List of leading merchants
SP 28/217: Inventories of delinquents
SP 28/350/2: Voucher book of subscribers to the loan of 1647
SP 29/387, 418, 435: Lists of common councilors
T 52/19: National Land Bank subscriptions
T 70/189, 191: Royal Africa Company stock ledger

Westminster Abbey Muniments

54,982: List of merchants and tradesmen (1696)

Center Kentish Studies

U 1015, Papillon archives: lists of adventurers in East India Company (1683–4) and list of the livery of the Mercers Company

Center for Metropolitan Studies, University of London

Database of assessments for the poll tax of 1692

Bodleian Library, Oxford

Rawlinson D. 1312: Societies for Reformation (1696)
Smith Newsbooks c. 10: List of subscribers toward a present for the King in Cheapside ward (1661)

Printed Primary Sources

Admiralty Depositions, 1637–8, ed. D. O. Shilton and R. Holworth (1932)
Akerman, J. Y., *Tradesmen's Tokens Current in London, 1648 and 1672* (1849; reprint New York, 1969)
Aliens: Returns of Strangers in the Metropolis, ed. I. Scouloudi, vol. 57 (Huguenot Society of London Publications, 1985)
Aliens: The Marriage, Baptismal, and Burial Register, 1571–1874, of the Dutch Reformed Church, Austin Friars, ed. J. C. Moens (Lymington, 1884)
Aliens: Register of the French Church at Threadneedle Street, vol. 16 (Huguenot Society of London Publications, 1906)
Aliens: Letters of Denization and Acts of Naturalization, 1603–1800, ed. W. A. Shaw, vols. 18 and 27 (Huguenot Society of London Publications, 1911)
Aliens: Returns of Aliens, vols. 8, 10, and 25 (Huguenot Society of London Publications, 1899–1931)
Aliens: French Protestant Refugees Relieved, 1681–7, ed. A. P. Hands and I. Scouloudi, vol. 49 (Huguenot Society of London Publications, 1971)
Aliens: List of Foreign Protestants and Aliens, 1618–1688, ed. W. D. Cooper (Camden Society, 1862)
Aliens: Register of the Church of La Patent, Spittlefields, 1681–1785, ed. W. Minet and W. C. Waller, vol. 11 (Huguenot Society of London Publications, 1898)
Aliens: Registers of the Churches of Chapel Royal St. James and Swallow Street, ed. W. and S. Minet, vol. 28 (Huguenot Society of London Publications, 1924)
Alley, H., *Caveatt*, ed. I. Archer and others, vol. 137 (London Topographical Society Publications, 1988)
American Wills Proved in London, 1611–1775, ed. P. W. Coldham (Baltimore, 1992)

American Wills in the Prerogative Court of Canterbury, 1660–1857, ed. P. W. Coldham (1989)

Archdeacons Court of London. Index to Testamentary Records, ed. C. Thurby and M. Fitch, vols. 88–89, 98 (British Record Society, Index Library, 1976, 1979, 1985)

Court of Arches. Index of Cases, 1660–1913, ed. J. Houston, vol. 85 (British Record Society Index Library, 1972)

Arnold, A. P., "A List of Jews and Their Households in London," *Transactions of the Jewish Historical Society in England* 6 (1962)

Bank of England: A List of the Names of All the Subscribers (1694)

Bank of England: A List of the Names of All the Proprietors (1701)

Barbados Baptisms, 1637–1800, ed. J. M. Sanders (Baltimore, 1984)

Barbados Marriages, 1643–1800, ed. J. M. Sanders (Houston, 1987)

Barbados Records, Wills, and Administrations, 1639–1725, ed. J. M. Sanders, 3 vols. (Baltimore, 1979–82)

Bevis Marks Records, ed. L. D. Barnett, 2 vols. (Oxford, 1940, 1949)

Bunhill Fields. Inscriptions upon the Tombs of Dissenters (1717)

Burn, J. H., *A Descriptive Catalogue of the London Traders Tavern and Coffee House Tokens* (1853)

Carpenters Company. Apprentices Entry Book, 1654–94, ed. B. Marsh (1913)

Carr, C. T., ed., *Select Charters of Trading Companies, 1530–1707*, vol. 28 (Selden Society, 1913)

Chancery Decree Rolls. Calendar, ed. M. W. Beresford, 3 vols.

Charterhouse Chapel. Register of Monumental Inscriptions (1892)

Christ's Hospital Admissions, 1554–99 (1937)

Clay, J. W., *Familiae Minorum Gentium*, vol. 40 (Harlean Society, 1896)

Commissary Court of London. Index to Testamentary Records, ed. M. Fitch, vols. 97 and 102 (British Record Society, Index Library, 1985, 1992)

Cotton, J. J., *List of Inscriptions on the Tombs in Madras* (Madras, 1905)

Currer-Briggs, N., *Virginia Settlers and English Adventurers*, 3 vols. (Baltimore, 1969–71)

Currer-Briggs, N., *English Wills of Colonial Families*

Dickinson, M., *Seventeenth-Century Tokens of the British Isles* (1986)

Dugdale, Sir William, *Staffordshire Pedigrees*, ed. Sir G. J. Armytage and H. Rylands (1912)

Durham Wills and Inventories from the Registry at Durham, 1543–1649, vols. 112 and 142 (Surtees Society, 1906, 1929)

East Anglian Pedigrees, ed. A. Campling, vols. 91 and 97 (Harlean Society, 1939, 1945)

East India Company. Register of Letters, 1600–19, ed. Sir George M. Birdwood and W. Foster (1893)

East India Company. Petition of Merchants Trading to the East Indies (1641)

East India Company. Calender of the Court Minutes, 1635–1679, ed. E. B. Sainsbury, 11 vols. (Oxford, 1907–38)

East India Company. The Names of the Governor, Deputy, and 24 Committees (1680, 1685)

East India Company. List of Adventurers (1684, 1685, 1700)

Eastland Company. Acts and Ordinances, ed. M. Sellers, 3d ser., vol. 11 (Camden Society, 1906)

Elmhirst, E. M., *English Merchant Marks*, ed. L. Dow, vol. 108 (Harlean Society, 1956)

English Adventurers and Emigrants, 1609–1773, ed. P. W. Coldham, 2 vols. (Baltimore, 1984–5)

Fisher, M. P. and G. B. Morgan, *Catalogue of the Tombs in the Churches of London, 1666* (1668; reprint 1885)

Gent, T., *History of Hull* (1735; reprint Hull, 1869)

Girling, F. A., *English Merchants Marks* (Oxford, 1964)

R. Hakluyt, *Principal Navigations*, vol. 39 (1589; reprint Hakluyt Society, 1965)

Hatton, E., *A New View of London*, 2 vols. (1708)

Hudsons Bay Company. List of Adventurers (1696)

Hudsons Bay Company Minutes 1671–84, ed. E. E. Rich, vols. 8–9 (Hudsons Bay Company Record Series, 1942–6)

Hughes, C. A. W., ed., *Monumental Inscriptions in the Church of St. Mary's, Wimbledon* (1934)

Hughes, W. E., *Monumental Inscriptions and Extracts from the Registers at St. Anne's Church, Soho* (1905)

Jaggard, W., *A View of All the Lord Mayors of London* (1661)

Kent's Directory for the Year 1745 (1745)

Kirby, H., ed., *The Monumental Inscriptions in the Church of St. Mary, Lewisham* (1889)

Lancashire and Cheshire Wills and Inventories from the Ecclesiastical Court of Chester, ed. G. J. Piccope, J. P. Earwalker, and J. P. Rylands, vols. (o.s.) 51 and 54 (n.s.), 3, 28, and 37 (Chetham Society, 1860, 1861, 1884, 1893, 1897)

Land Bank. A List of Names of Subscribers (1695)

Lawrence-Archer, J. H., *Monumental Inscriptions of the British West Indies* (1875)

Leroy, J. H., *Memorials of the Discovery and Early Settlement of the Bermudas, 1515–1685*, 2 vols. (1932, 1981)

LeNeve, P., *Monumenta Anglicana*, 5 vols. (1715–19)

LeNeve, P., *Pedigrees of the Knights*, ed. G. W. Marshall, vol. 8 (Harlean Society, 1873)

LeNeve, P., *Lives and Characters Who Died, 1712* (1714)

Levant Company. List of English Factors at Constantinople, 1704 (Bod, folio h 665)

Levant Company. List of Factors at Smyrna, January 1704 (Bod, folio h 665)

Levant Company. List of Members, 1701 (Bod, folio h 665)

London. Visitation Pedigrees, 1664, ed. J. B. Whitmore and A. W. H. Clarke, vol. 92 (Harlean Society, 1940)

London. Inhabitants within the Walls, 1695, ed. D. V. Glass, vol. 2 (London Record Society, 1966)

London. The Port and Trade of Early Elizabethan London, ed. B. Dietz, vol. 8 (London Record Society, 1972)

London. Marriage Licenses, 1521–1869, ed. J. Foster (1887)

London. Two Tudor Subsidy Assessment Rolls for London, ed. R. G. Lang, vol. 29 (London Record Society, 1992)

London. Citizens in 1651, ed. J. C. and W. Whitebrook (1910)

"London. Characters of the Lord Mayors and the Court of Aldermen Presented to Charles II," *Gentleman's Magazine* 39 (1769)

London. The Inhabitants of London in 1638, ed. T. C. Dale, 2 vols. (Society of Genealogists, 1931)

London. Marriages at St. James, Duke's Place, ed. W. P. W. Phillimore and G. E. Cokayne, 4 vols. (1900–2)

London. Calendar of Wills Proved in the Court of Hustings, 1258–1688, ed. R. R. Sharpe (1890)

London. Parish Registers, vols. 1–89 (Harlean Society Publications Registers, 1877 onward)

London. The List of Inhabitants Liable for the 1641 Poll Tax, transcribed by T. C. Dale (Society of Genealogists, 1934–9)

London. The Inhabitants of Westminster, 1636–42, transcribed by T. C. Dale

London. Lord Mayor's Court. Depositions Relating to America, 1641–1736, ed. P. W. Coldham (Washington, 1980)

London. List of the Principal Inhabitants, 1640, ed. W. J. Harvey *Miscellenea Genealogica* 2 (1886; reprint Blackmansbury, 1969)

London. Allegations for Marriage Licenses Issued by the Bishop of London, 1520–1828, ed. J. L. Chester and G. J. Armytage, vols. 25–26 (Harlean Society, 1887)

London. A Calendar of Marriage License Allegations in the Registry of the Bishop of London, 1597–1700, ed. R. M. Glencross, vols. 62 and 66 (British Record Society, Index Library, 1937, 1940)

London. Allegations for Marriage Licenses Issued by the Faculty Office of the Archbishop of Canterbury, 1632–1702, ed. J. L. Chester and G. J. Armytage, vol. 24 (Harlean Society, 1886)

London. Allegations for Marriage Licenses Issued by the Vicar General of the Archbishop of Canterbury, 1660–94, ed. G. J. Armytage, vols. 30–31, 33–34 (Harlean Society, 1890–92)

London. Calendar of Marriage Licenses Issued by the Faculty Office, 1632–1714, ed. G. E. Cokayne and E. A. Fry, vol. 33 (British Record Society, Index Library, 1905)

London. Allegations for Marriage Licenses Issued by the Dean and Chapter of Westminster, 1558–1699, vol. 23 (Harlean Society, 1885)

London. Monumental Inscriptions in the Church of St. Olave, Jewry, ed. F. A. Crisp (1887)

London. A Collection of the Merchants Living in and about London (1677)

London. Register Book of the Fourth Classis, 1646–59, ed. C. E. Surman, vols. 82–83 (Harlean Society, 1953)

London. Royal Commission on Historical Monuments (England). An Inventory of the Historical Monuments of London IV. The City (1929)

London. Pollbooks, 1713, ed. W. A. Speck and W. A. Gray, vol. 17 (London Record Society, 1981)

Lysons, D., *The Environs of London*, 4 vols. (1792–6)

Mackerell, B., *The History of King's Lynn* (1736)

Merchant Taylor's School Register, 1561–1934, ed. E. P. Hart, 2 vols. (1936)

Middlesex Pedigrees Collected by Richard Mundy, ed. Sir G. J. Armytage, vol. 65 (Harlean Society, 1914)

Million Bank. List of Subscribers (1693–4)

Milner-Gibson-Cullum, G., and F. C. Macauley, *The Inscriptions in the Old British Cemetery of Leghorn* (Leghorn, 1906)

Morant, P., *The History and Antiquities of Colchester* (1748)

Morant, P., *The History of the County of Essex*, 2 vols. (1763–8)

New York. Select Cases of the Mayor's Court of New York 1674–1785, ed. R. B. Morris (Washington, 1935)

New York. Abstract of Wills Surrogates Office, 1665–1728, vols. 25–26 (New York Historical Society Collection, 1892–3)

North Country Wills, 1558–1604, vol. 121 (Surtees Society, 1912)

Oliver, V. L., *The Monumental Inscriptions of the British West Indies* (Dorchester, 1927)

Oliver, V. L., *The Monumental Inscriptions of Barbados* (Glendale, 1989)

Parliamentary Papers. Reports of the Charity Commissioners, vols. 39, 49, and 71 (1884, 1903–4)

Playhouse Wills, 1558–1642, ed. E. A. J. Honigman and S. Brock (Manchester, 1993)

Prerogative Court of Canterbury. Abstracts of Probates and Sentences, 1620–55, ed. J. and G. F. Matthews, 6 vols. (1902–11)

Prerogative Court of Canterbury. Genealogical Abstracts of Wills, Register of Wootton, 1658, ed. W. Brigg, 7 vols. (Leeds, 1894–1914)

Prerogative Court of Canterbury. Index to Wills, 1580–1635, 1654–1700, 12 vols. (British Record Society, Index Library)

Prerogative Court of Canterbury. Wills, Sentences, and Probate Acts, 1660–70, ed. J. H. Morrison (1935)

Prerogative Court of Canterbury. Register Scroope, 1630, ed. J. H. Morrison (1934)

Prerogative Court of Canterbury Abstracts of Will in Register of Soame, 1620, ed. J. H. Lea (Boston, Mass., 1904)

Prerogative Court of Canterbury. Indexes to Administrations 1581–1660, ed. R. M. Glencross and M. Fitch, vols. 66, 68, 72, 74, 75, 81, 83, and 100 (British Record Society, Index Library, 1912–86) and ed. J. H. Morrison (1935)

Prerogative Court of Canterbury. Paper Inventories, 1661–1725, vol. 149 (British Record Society, Index Library, 1978)

Prerogative Court of Canterbury. Parchment Inventories, vol. 221 (British Record Society, Index Library, 1988)

St. Paul's School Register, 1509–1748, ed. Sir M. F. J. MacDonnell (1977)

Scriveners Company Papers, ed. F. W. Steer, vol. 4 (London Record Society Publications, 1968)

The Second Centurie (1648)

Skinners Company of London Records, ed. J. J. Lambert (1934)

Skinner Company Apprentices, ed. G. E. Cokayne (*Miscellanea Genealogica et Heraldica,* 3d ser., 1, 1896)

Smythe, R., *The Obituary of Richard Smythe, 1627–1674,* ed. Sir Henry Ellis, vol. 44 (Camden Society, 1849)

South Sea Company. List of the Names Mentioned in the Report of the Committee of Secrecy (1722)

South Sea Company. Account of the Estates of the Directors (1722)

The Spanish Company, ed. P. Croft, vol. 9 (London Record Society, 1973)

Staffordshire Pedigrees, ed. Sir G. Armytage and W. H. Rylands, vol. 63 (Harlean Society, 1912)

State Papers. Calendar State Papers America and West Indies, 1661–1738, ed. W. N. Sainsbury et al. (1860–1953, vol. 18, 1699–1700)

Stationers Company Apprentices, 1605–1640, ed. D. F. MacKenzie (Bibliographical Society, University of Virginia, Charlottesville, 1961)

Stationers Company Apprentices, 1641–1700 (Oxford Bibliographical Society, 1974)

Stationers: Abstracts from the Wills of English Printers and Stationers, 1492–1630, ed. H. R. Plomer (1903)

Stationers: Loan Book of the Stationers Company, ed. F. W. Craig, vol. 4 (Bibliographical Society Occasional Papers, 1989)

Stow, J., *A Survey of London,* ed. C. L. Kingsford, 2 vols. (Oxford, 1971)

Stow, J., *Survey of London,* ed. J. Strype, 2 vols. (1720)

Tontine. List of Nominees of the State Tontine of 1693 (1693)

Two Millions. A List of the Subscribers to a Loan of Two Millions (1698)

Virginia Company Records, ed. S. M. Kingsbury, 4 vols. (Washington, 1906–35)

Visitation of Bedfordshire, 1634, ed. F. A. Blaydes, vol. 19 (Harlean Society, 1884)

Visitation of Berkshire, 1623, 1663–5, ed. W. H. Rylands, vol. 56 (Harlean Society, 1907)

Visitation of Buckinghamshire, 1634, ed. W. H. Rylands, vol. 58 (Harlean Society, 1909)

Visitation of Derbyshire, 1662 and 1664, ed. G. D. Squibb, n.s., vol. 8 (Harlean Society, 1989)

Visitation of Dorset, 1677, ed. G. D. Squibb, vol. 117 (Harlean Society, 1977)

Visitation of Essex, 1612, 1634, ed. W. C. Metcalfe, vols. 13–14 (Harlean Society, 1878–9)

Visitation of Hampshire, 1686, ed. G. D. Squibb, n.s., vol. 10 (Harlean Society, 1991)

Visitations of Hertfordshire in 1572 and 1634, ed. W. C. Metcalf, vol. 22 (Harlean Society, 1886)

Visitation of Huntingdon 1684, ed. J. Bedells, n.s., vol. 13 (Harlean Society, 1994)

Visitations of Kent, 1619, 1663, and 1668, ed. R. Hoveden and Sir G. J. Armytage, vols. 42 and 54 (Harlean Society, 1898, 1906)

Visitation of County Palatine of Lancaster, ed. F. R. Raines, vols. 82, 84, 85, and 88 (Chetham Society, 1871–3)

Visitation of London, 1568, ed. J. J. Howard and G. J. Armytage, vol. 1, ed. H. S. London and S. W. Rawlins, vol. 109 (Harlean Society, 1869, 1963)

Visitation of London Anno Domini, 1633, 1634, and 1635, ed. J. J. Howard and J. L. Chester, vols. 15 and 17 (Harlean Society, 1880, 1883)

Visitation of London Pedigrees, 1664, ed. J. B. Whitmore and A. W. H. Clarke, vol. 92 (Harlean Society, 1940)

Visitation of Norfolk, 1664, ed. A. W. H. Clarke and A. Camplin, vols. 85–86 (Harlean Society, 1933–4)

Visitation of Northamptonshire, 1681, ed. H. Longden, vol. 87 (Harlean Society, 1935)

Visitation of Nottinghamshire and Derbyshire, ed. G. D. Squibb, n.s., vols. 5–6, and 8 (Harlean Society, 1986–7, 1989)

Visitation of Nottinghamshire, 1662–4, vol. 13 (Thoroton Society, 1949)

Visitation of Oxfordshire, 1634, 1669, and 1675, ed. G. D. Squibb, vols. 5 and 12 (Harlean Society, 1871, 1993)

Visitation of Shropshire, 1623, ed. G. Grazebrook and J. P. Rylands, vols. 28–29 (Harlean Society, 1889)

Visitation of Somerset and Bristol, 1672, ed. G. D. Squibb, n.s., vol. 11 (Harlean Society, 1992)

Visitation of Staffordshire, 1614, 1663–4, ed. H. S. Grasebrook, vol. 5 (Collection of History of Staffordshire, 1885)

Visitation of Suffolk, 1664–1668, by Sir Edward Bysshe, vol. 61 (Harlean Society, 1910)

Visitation of Surrey, 1623, 1662, 1668, ed. W. B. Bannerman and Sir G. J. Armytage, vols. 43 and 60 (Harlean Society, 1899, 1910)

Visitation of Sussex, 1662, ed. A. W. H. Clarke, vol. 89 (Harlean Society, 1937)

Visitation of Warwick, 1682–3, ed. W. H. Rylands, vol. 62 (Harlean Society, 1911)

Visitation of Wiltshire, 1623, ed. G. D. Squibb, vols. 105–6 (Harlean Society, 1953–4)

Visitation of Worcestershire, 1634, ed. A. T. Butler, vol. 90 (Harlean Society, 1938)

Visitation of the County of York, 1665–6 (Sir William Dugdale) vol. 36 (Surtees Society, 1872)

Warburton, J., *London and Middlesex Illustrated* (1749)

Weeven, J., *Ancient Funeral Monuments* (1631)

Williams, N. J., "The English Tobacco Trade," *Virginia Magazine History and Biography* 65 (1957): 403–49

Wootton, T., *The English Baronetage* (1741)

Wright, P., *Monumental Inscriptions of Jamaica* (Society of Genealogists, 1966)

Yorkshire Pedigrees, ed. J. W. Walker, vols. 95–96 (Harlean Society, 1943–4)

SECONDARY SOURCES

Abraham, D., "Jew Brokers of London," *Jewish Historical Society of England Miscellany* 3 (1937): 80–94

Acres, W. M., *The Bank of England from Within* (1931)

Acres, W. M., "Directors of the Bank of England," *Notes & Queries* 179 (1940)

Acres, W. M., "Huguenot Directors of the Bank," *Proceedings of the Huguenot Society of London*, 15 (1934–7)

Agnew, J., *Belfast Merchant Families in the Seventeenth Century* (Dublin, 1996)

Ambrose, G. L., "The Levant Company Mainly from 1640 to 1753" (B. Litt. Thesis, University of Oxford, 1933)

Anderson, S., *An English Consul in Turkey* (Oxford, 1989)

Anderson, V. D., *New England's Generation* (Cambridge, 1991)

Andrews, K. R., *Elizabethan Privateering during the Spanish War* (Cambridge, 1964)

Andrews, K. R., *Ships, Money, and Politics* (Cambridge, 1991)

Archer, I. W., *The Pursuit of Stability* (Cambridge, 1991)

Arnold, A. P., *Anglo Jewish Notabilities* (Jewish Historical Society of England, 1949)

Ashton, R., *The City and the Court, 1603–43* (Cambridge, 1979)

Ashton, R., *The Crown and the Money Market, 1603–40* (Oxford, 1960)

Astrom, S. E., *From Cloth to Iron* (Helsingfors, 1963–5)

Baddeley, J. J., *The Aldermen of Cripplegate Ward, 1276–1900* (1900)

Bailyn, B. and L., *Massachusetts Shipping, 1697–1714* (Cambridge, Mass., 1959)

Bailyn, B., *The New England Merchants* (1955; reprint New York, 1964)

Banks, C. E., *Planters of the Commonwealth, 1620–40* (Boston, 1930)

Baumann, W. R., *The Merchant Adventurers and the Continental Cloth Trade* (Berlin, 1990)

Beaven, A., *The Aldermen of the City of London*, 2 vols. (1908–13)

Benbow, R. M., "Index of Londoners Involved in City Government, 1558–1603" (typescript in Institute of Historical Research, London)

Berry, G., *Seventeenth-Century England's Traders and Their Tokens* (1988)

Berry, W., *County Genealogies. Pedigrees of the Families of Berkshire, Essex, Hampshire, Kent, Hertfordshire, Staffordshire, Sussex* (1830–1844)

Blackmore, H. L., *A Dictionary of London Gunmakers, 1350–1850* (Oxford, 1986)

Boddington, R. S., *Pedigree of the Gould Family* (1880)

Bosher, J. F., "Huguenot Merchants and the Protestant International," *William and Mary Quarterly*, 3d ser., 52 (1995): 77–102

Bottigheimer, K. S., *English Money and Irish Land* (Oxford, 1971)

Boulton, J., *Neighbourhood and Society. A London Suburb in the Seventeenth Century* (Cambridge, 1987)

Bowen, G. C., and H. W. Harwood, "Pedigree of Offley," *Genealogist*, n.s., 19–20 (1903–4)

Boyd, P., *Roll of the Draper's Company of London* (Croydon, 1934)

Brenner, R., *Merchants and Revolution* (Princeton, 1993)

Brigg, W., *Genealogical Abstracts of Wills*, 7 vols. (Leeds, 1894)

Buisseret, D., and M. Pawson, *Port Royal Jamaica* (Oxford, 1975)

Burgess, F., *English Churchyard Memorials* (1979)

Carr, L. G., and D. W. Jordan, *Maryland's Revolution in Government* (Ithaca, 1974)

Carswell, J., *The South Sea Bubble* (1960)

Cell, G. T., "The Newfoundland Company," *William and Mary Quarterly*, 3d ser., 22 (1965): 611–25

Chandler, M. J., "Emigrants from Britain to the Colonies," *Journal of the Barbados Museum and Historical Society* 36 (1979)

Cherry, G. L., *The Convention Parliament of 1689* (New York, 1960)

Clark, D. C., "A Restoration Banking House" in *Essays in Honour of W. C. Abbott* (Cambridge, Mass., 1941)

Clay, C. G. A., "Henry Hoare" in F. M. L. Thompson, ed., *Landowners Capitalists and Entrepreneurs* (Oxford, 1994), 113–38

Clode, C. M., *The Early History of the Merchant Taylors of London*, 2 vols. (1888)

Clutterbuck, R., *History of Hertford*, 4 vols. (1815–27)

Coghill, J. H., *Family of Coghill, 1377–1879* (privately printed, 1879)

Cokayne, G. E., *Complete Baronetage*, 6 vols. (1900–09)

Cokayne, G. E., *Complete Peerage* (1910–50)

Cokayne, G. E., *Some Account of the Lord Mayors and Sheriffs of London, 1601–25* (1897)

Cokayne, G. E., *Cokayne Memoranda* (privately printed, 1873)

Cox, W., *Annals of St. Helen's Bishopsgate* (1897)

Cusans, J. E., *History of Hertfordshire*, 4 vols. (1879–81)

Davies, R., *Chelsea Old Church* (1904)

Davies, K. G., *The Royal Africa Company* (1957)

DeKrey, G. S., *A Fractured Society* (Oxford, 1985)

DeKrey, G. S., "Trade, Religion, and Politics in London in the Reign of William III" (Ph.D. thesis, Princeton, 1978). The biographical appendixes have been removed in the loanable copy.

DeMarly, D., "Fashionable Suppliers," *The Antiquaries Journal* 58 (1979)

Diamond, A. S., "The Community of the Resettlement," *Transactions of the Jewish Historical Sociey of England* 24 (1974): 134–50

Dickson, P. G. M., *The Financial Revolution in England* (1967)

Donald, M. B., *Elizabethan Copper* (1965)

Donald, M. B., *Elizabethan Monopolies. The History of the Company of Mineral and Battery Works from 1565 to 1604* (Edinburgh, 1861)

Earle, P., *A City Full of People* (1994)

Earle, P., *The Making of the Middle Class* (1989)

East Anglian Pedigrees, ed. A. Campling, vol. 13 (Norfolk Record Society, 1940)

Edmond, M., "Limners and Picture Makers," *Walpole Society* 47 (1978–80): 60–242

Edwards, A. C., "Sir John Petrie," *London Topographical Record* 23 (1972)

Ehrenburg, R., *Hamburg und England* (Jena, 1896)

Elliot, D. C., "Elections to the Common Council, 1659," *Guildhall Studies in London History* 4 (1981)

Ellis, L. B., "The Lethieullier Family," *Proceedings of the Huguenot Society of London* 19 (1953–9): 60–7

Farnell, J. E., "The Navigation Act of 1651," *Economic History Review*, 2d ser., 16 (1964): 439–54

Faulkner, T., *History of Chelsea* (1810)

Faulkner, T., *History of Kensington* (1820)

Fedorowicz, J. K., *England's Baltic Trade in the Early Seventeenth Century* (Cambridge, 1980)

Fellowes, E. H., *The Family of Frederick* (Windsor, 1988)

Fitzhugh, T., "East India Company Families," *Family History* 12 (1982): 279–86

Forbes, T. R., "Weavers and Cordwainers," *Guildhall Studies in London History* 4 (1980): 119–32

Forse, J. H., *Art Imitates Business* (Bowling Green, Ohio, 1993)

Foster, F. F., *Politics of Stability* (1977)

Friis, A., *Alderman Cockayne's Project and the Cloth Trade* (1927)

Glanville, P., and J. Goldsborough, *Women Silversmiths, 1685–1845* (1990)

Godfrey, E. S., *The Development of English Glassmaking, 1560–1640* (Chapel Hill, 1975)

Godfrey, W. H., *The Church of St. Bride, Fleet Street* (1944)

Goss, C. W. F., *Crosby Hall* (1908)

Gough, B. M., "The Adventurers of England Trading into Hudsons Bay," *Albion* 2 (1970): 35–47

Gough, J. W., *Sir Hugh Middleton* (Oxford, 1964)

Gray, I. E., "Merchants at Alexandretta," *Genealogist Magazine* 9 (1945): 469–71

Grimwade, A. G., *London Goldsmiths, 1697–1837*, 2d ed. (1982)

Guiseppi, J. A., "Families of Long Service in the Bank of England," *Genealogical Magazine* 10 (1947–50)

Guiseppi, J. A., "Sephardic Jews and the Early Years of the Bank of England," *Transactions of the Jewish Historical Society of England* 19 (1960): 53–64

Gwynn, R. D., *Huguenot Heritage* (1985)

Habakkuk, H. J., *Marriage, Debt, and the Estate System. English Landownership, 1650–1950* (Oxford, 1994)

Hadley, G., *Citizens and Founders* (1976)

Harrison, F., *The Devon Carys*, 2 vols. (New York, 1920)

Heal, A., *The London Goldsmiths, 1200–1800* (Cambridge, 1935)

Heal, A., *London Tradesmen's Cards of the Seventeenth Century* (1924)

Heal, A., *The Signboards of Old London Shops* (1947)

Heathcote, E. D., *An Account of the Families of Heathcote* (Derby, 1899)

Hinton, R. W. K., *The Eastland Trade and the Common Weal* (Cambridge, 1959)

Hoare, E., *Some Account of the Families of Hore and Hoare* (1883)

Hoare, H. P. R., *Hoares Bank. A Record* (1932)

Hobhouse, H., *The Ward of Cheap* (privately printed, n.d.)

Houblon, A. A., *The Houblon Family* (1907)

Hyamson, A. M., *History of the Jews in England* (1928)

Hyamson, A. M., *The Sephardim of England* (1951)

Jackson, Sir C. J., *The English Goldsmiths*, 2d ed. (1921; reprint 1964)

Johnson, A. H. R., *History of the Company of Drapers*, 4 vols. (Oxford, 1914–22)

Jones, D. W., *War and Economy in the Age of William III* (Oxford, 1988)

Jones, J. R., *London's Import Trade with France during the Reign of Elizabeth* (Philadelphia, 1944)

Jordan, W. K., *The Charities of London, 1480–1660* (New York, 1960)

Keeler, M., *The Long Parliament* (Philadelphia, 1954)

Kellaway, W., *The New England Company, 1649–1776* (1961)

Kerridge, E., *Trade and Banking in Early Modern England* (Manchester, 1988)

Kirby, D. A., "The Radicals of St. Stephen's, Coleman Street, 1624–42," *Guildhall Miscellany* 3 (1970): 98–110

Knights, M., "London Petitions in 1679," *Parliamentary History* 1 (1993): 19–46

Lacey, D. R., *Dissent and Parliamentary Politics in England, 1661–89* (New Brunswick, 1969)

Lang, R. G., "The Greater Merchants of London in the Early Seventeenth Century" (D.Phil, University of Oxford, 1963)

Levison-Gower, G. W., *Genealogy of the Family of Gresham* (1883)

Lincolnshire Pedigrees, ed. A. R. Maddison, vols. 50–52, 54 (Harlean Society, 1902–4, 1906)

Lipcombe, G., *The History of the County of Buckingham*, 4 vols. (1847)

Liu, T., *Puritan London* (Newark, 1986)

Love, H. D., *Vestiges of Old Madras, 1640–1800*, 4 vols. (1913)

MacCusker, J. J., and C. Gravesteijn, *The Beginnings of Commercial and Financial Journalism* (Amsterdam, 1991)

MacKerrow, R. B., *A Dictionary of Printers and Booksellers, 1555–1640* (1910; reprint 1968)

Manchée, M., "Some Huguenot Smugglers," *Proceedings of the Huguenot Society of London* 15 (1936–70)

Mandelbrote, G., "From the Warehouse to the Counting House" in R. Myers and M. Harris, eds., *A Genius for Letters* (Winchester, 1995)

Manning, B. W., *History and Antiquities of Surrey* (1808–14; reprint 1974)

Martin, J. B., *The Grasshopper in Lombard Street* (1892)

Master, G. S., *Some Notices of the Family of Master* (privately printed, 1874)

Meekings, C. A. F., "The City Loans on the Hearth Tax" in A. E. J. Hollaender and W. Kellaway, eds., *Studies in London History* (1969), 333–63

Meroney, G., "The London Entrepot Merchants," *William and Mary Quarterly* 25 (1968): 230–44

Meyer, V. M., and J. F. Dorman, *Adventurers of Purse and Person. Virginia, 1607–1624* (Richmond, 1987)

Milbourne, T., *The History of the Church of St. Mildred the Virgin* (1872)

Milbourne, T., *The Vintners Company* (1888)

Milner-Gibson-Cullum, G. G., *The Corsellis Family* (1914)

Milner-Gibson-Cullum, G. G., *Pedigree of Middleton* (1897)

Milner-Gibson-Cullum, G. G., *Pedigree of Wittewrong* (1905)

Minet, W., *Some Account of the Family of Minet* (1892)

Miscellanea Genealogica et Heraldica, 1st ser., I–IV (1874–84), 2d ser., I–IV (1886–92), 3d ser., IV (1902), 5th ser., II–IV (1915–22)

Mitchell, D., ed., *Goldsmiths, Silversmiths, and Bankers* (1995)

Moore, N., *The Church of St. Bartholomew the Great* (1915)

Morgan, P., "Warwickshire Apprentices to the Stationers Company," *Dugdale Society Occasional Papers* 25 (1978)

Musgrave, W., *Obituary Prior to 1800*, ed. Sir G. J. Armytage, vols. 44–49 (Harlean Society Publications, 1899–1901)

Nicholl, J., *History of the Ironmongers Company* (1851)

Noble, T. C., *A Brief History of the Company of Ironmongers of London* (1889)

Northamptonshire Families, ed. O. Barron (1906)

Olson, A. G., "The Virginia Merchants of London," *William and Mary Quarterly*, 3d ser., 40 (1983)

Orridge, B. B., *Some Account of the Citizens of London, 1060–1867* (1867)

Pagano de Divitiis, G., *English Merchants in Seventeenth-Century Italy*, trans. S. Parkin (Cambridge, 1990)

Parliament: The House of Commons, 1558–1603, ed. P. W. Hasler, 3 vols. (1982)

Parliament: The House of Commons, 1509–58, ed. S. T. Bindoff (1982)

Parliament: The House of Commons, 1660–1690, ed. B. D. Henning (1983)

Parliament: The House of Commons, 1715–54, ed. R. Sedgwick (1970)

Pearl, V., *London and the Outbreak of the Puritan Revolution* (Oxford, 1961)

Plomer, H. R., *Dictionary of Printers and Booksellers in England* (1910)

Povah, A., *Annals of St. Olaves, Hart Street* (1894)

Price, F. G. H., *Handbook of London Bankers*, 2d ed. (1890–1)

Price, J. M., *Perry and Company* (Cambridge, Mass., 1992)

Price, J. M., "The Great Quaker Families" in R. S. and M. M. Dunn, eds., *The World of William Penn* (Philadelphia, 1986), 363–99

Price, W. H., *The English Patents of Monopoly* (Boston, 1906)

Puckrein, G. A., *Little England: Plantation Society and Anglo-Barbadian Politics, 1627–1700* (New York, 1984)

Quinn, S., "Balances and Goldsmith Bankers" in D. Mitchell, ed., *Goldsmiths, Silversmiths, and Bankers* (1995)

Rabb, T. K., *Enterprise and Empire* (Cambridge, Mass., 1967)

Reddaway, T. F., "Elizabethan London," *Guildhall Miscellany* 2 (1963), 181–206

Richards, R. D., *The Early History of Banking in England* (1929; reprint New York, 1965)

Robbins, W. G., "The Massachusetts Bay Company," *The Historian* 32 (1969), 83–98

Robinson, W., *The History of the Parish of Hackney* (1842)

Rose-Troup, F., *The Massachusetts Bay Company and Its Predecessors* (New York, 1930)

Roseveare, H., "Wiggins Key Revisited," *Journal of Transport History*, 3d ser., 16 (1995)

Rushen, P. C., *The Churchyard Inscriptions of London* (1910)

Samuel, E. R., "Portuguese Jews in Jacobean London," *Transactions of the Jewish Historical Society of England* 18 (1958)

Samuel, W. S., *A Review of the Jewish Colonists in Barbados* (1936)

Savage, J., *A Genealogical Dictionary of the First Settlers of New England*, 4 vols. (1965)

Scammell, G. V., *Ships, Oceans, and Empires* (1995)

Shaw, W. A., *The Knights of England*, 2 vols. (1906)

Sherwood, G., *The Pedigree Register*, 4 vols. (1913–16)

Sherwood, G. F., *American Colonists in English Records*, 2 vols. (1932–3)

Simon, A. L., *History of the Wine Trade in England*, 3 vols. (1909)

Simpson, R., ed., *Memorials of St. Johns at Hackney* (1882)

Simpson, R., *Some Account of the Monuments in Hackney Church* (1884)

Sisson, C. J., "A Colony of Jews in Shakespearian London," *Essays and Studies* 23 (1938): 38–51

Spalding, R., *Contemporaries of Bulstrode Whitelocke, 1605–1675* (Oxford, 1990)

Stephenson, M., *A Revised List of Monumental Brasses in the British Isles* (1977)

Taylor, G. A., "A List of London Merchants Trading with New England," *Genealogical Magazine* 8 (1938)

Thornton, A. P., *West India Policy under the Restoration* (Oxford, 1956)

Tyack, N. C. P., "English Exports to New England, 1632–40," *New England Historical and Genealogical Register* 135 (1981): 213–38

Upton, W. H., *Upton Family Records* (1893)

Victoria History of the Counties of England (Berkshire, Buckinghamshire, Essex, Gloucestershire, Hertfordshire, Middlesex, Staffordshire, Warwickshire, Yorkshire)

Vulliamy, C. E., *The Onslow Family* (1953)

Vyner, C. J., *Vyner: A Family History* (1885)

Walcott, R., *English Politics in the Early Eighteenth Century* (Oxford, 1956)

Wall, R. E., *Massachusetts Bay, 1640–50* (New Haven, 1972)

Warren, T., *History and Genealogy of the Warren Family* (1902; reprint Baltimore, 1989)

Waters, H. F., *Genealogical Gleanings in England*, 2 vols. (Salem, Mass., 1892)

Watlington, H. T., *Family Narratives* (1980)

Welch, C., *History of the Cutlers Company of London* (1916–23)

West, S. G., "Members of the Lisbon Factory in the Late Seventeenth Century," *12th Annual Report of the Historical Association, Lisbon Branch* (1954)

Whitmore, W. H., *Whitmore Tract* (Boston, 1875)

Wilkinson, H. C., *The Adventurers of Bermuda*, 2d ed. (1958)

Willan, T. S., *The Muscovy Merchants of 1555* (Manchester, 1953)

Willan, T. S., *Studies in Elizabethan Foreign Trade* (Manchester, 1959)

Williams, D. A., "Puritanism in City Government, 1610–40," *Guildhall Miscellany* 1 (1955): 3–14

Williamson, G. C., *Trade Tokens of the Seventeenth Century* (1889)

Woodhead, J. R., *The Rulers of London, 1660–89* (London and Middlesex Archaeological Society, 1965)

Woolf, M., "Foreign Trade of London Jews," *Transactions of the Jewish Historical Society of England* 24 (1974): 38–58

Worden, B., *The Rump Parliament* (Cambridge, 1974)

Young, S., *Annals of the Barber Surgeons of London* (1890)

Zahedieh, N., "London and the Colonial Consumer," *Economic History Review* 47 (1994): 239–61

Zins, H., *England and the Baltic in the Elizabethan Era* (Manchester, 1973)

Appendix B

Criteria for Coding Inputs

It is not feasible to detail every coding decision behind the thousands of entries. Some fields, such as marriage to daughters or widows of masters, require no explanation. But the principal criteria employed to categorize the evidence should be made explicit. A systematic approach has been adopted to ensure consistency; all data has been entered in a standard format to facilitate comparison and correlation. But the guiding principles have been simplicity and flexibility.

In some fields, as with types of executor, the number of alternative categories was reduced when they proved unwieldy. Several fields were jettisoned because of insufficient data or because the number of cases was too small. These include the number of orphaned apprentices (which required a death date for the father), the occupations of unmarried daughters, disinheritance of sons, restrictions on remarriage by widows, and cases of estrangement between parents and children. Some potentially useful fields occurred to the author too late for inclusion in the main database. A few of these (including numbers of grandchildren, marriage settlements, and deaths overseas) were added in memo fields, but data in this form could not be manipulated as effectively as in regular fields.

The documentary evidence has necessarily been simplified and some discretion exercised in ambiguous and borderline cases. There is no satisfactory solution to the problem of unknown values. Nor can unconscious bias be eliminated; it is difficult, for example, to avoid privileging subjects who have left fuller records or who have familiar names. Nonetheless, every effort has been made to obtain equal numbers for comparison over equal intervals of time and to specify whether there is full, partial, or no data. The database has been cleaned by random

441

Table B.1. *Number of Known Values in All Fields of the Database*

Field	Period I (1580–1659)	Period II (1660–1740)
Surnames	14,060	14,156
Females	75	85
Place of birth	2,699	2,667
Birth date	862	3,253
Estimated date of death	6,943	6,684
Known date of death	7,117	7,472
Age at death	470	1,909
Citizenship	8,389	6,859
Resident abroad	1,267	1,613
Titles	274	4,98
Religion	695	1,277
Status of father	2,098	2,378
Type of training	1,192	1,598
Type of trade	9,835	11,120
Same business as father	63	284
Office	1,006	1,530
Marital status	5,666	6,684
First marriage:		
Age groom	258	1,820
Marital status of bride	2,180	2,936
Maiden name of bride	2,198	3,265
Age of marriage of first bride	194	1,390
Social status of bride	1,257	1,548
Location of first bride	1,639	2,496
Married daughter/widow of master	19	44
Marriage settlement	50	158
Surviving sons	3,356	3,234
Sons marry	369	426
Surviving daughters	3,022	3,032
Daughters marry	839	864
Second marriage:		
Marital status of bride	261	610
Maiden name of bride	277	696
Age of bride	29	299
Social status of bride	154	269
Location of bride	192	484
Surviving sons	149	193
Sons married	29	45
Surviving daughters	134	165
Daughters married	30	64
Third marriage:		
Marital status of bride	29	51
Maiden name of bride	32	65
Age of bride	1	15
Social status of bride	16	27
Location of bride	20	42
Surviving sons	17	15
Sons married	2	3
Surviving daughters	16	14
Daughters married	1	4
Dowries	172	299

Table B.1. *(cont.)*

Field	Period I (1580–1659)	Period II (1660–1740)
Families with surviving child	3,578	3,763
First son occupation	597	789
First son training	154	214
First son status of bride	291	360
Second son occupation	244	330
Second son training	54	85
Second son status of bride	105	112
Third son occupation	96	145
Third son training	25	55
Third son status of bride	41	41
Fourth son occupation	43	71
Fourth son training	10	22
Fourth son status of bride	16	13
Fifth son occupation	16	28
Fifth son training	2	8
Fifth son status of bride	8	7
First daughter status of husband	566	698
Second daughter status of husband	207	284
Third daughter status of husband	102	110
Fourth daughter status of husband	49	52
Fifth daughter status of husband	22	10
Widow survives	3,062	2,428
Length of widowhood	169	350
Length of marriage	45	242
Widow runs business	25	22
Widow remarries	226	216
Orphans	864	1,059
Personal wealth	1,882	3,973
City property	1,774	1,413
Land	2,070	1,698
Primary assets at death	96	341
Wills	6,523	6,290
Inventories	79	1,406
Executors	3,612	2,041
Overseers	832	244
Partible inheritance	1,570	1,397
Charity	2,235	1,047
Primary beneficiary	1,946	1,442
Kin mentioned in will	1,710	911
Friends mentioned in will	1,652	805
Partners in immediate family	246	582
Partners from kin	59	133
Partners unrelated	314	663
Primary capital	22	96
Additional capital	32	122
Grandchildren	204	122
Personal papers	18	38
Business papers	34	118
Apprentices in immediate family	6	13
Apprentices from kin	46	43
Apprentices unrelated	399	333

Note: Known values include negative information (e.g. giving nothing to charity) but exclude all unknown values (e.g. when there is no information on charitable bequests).

reliability tests and checked for logical inconsistencies and duplication. Entries have been continuously updated and sometimes deleted in light of later evidence.

RECORDS

Each record consists of an individual subject identified by surname and first name.[1] Common names and multiple spellings of names have of course created problems; to encounter yet another Thomas Smith was not a welcome prospect. All spellings have been standardized (e.g. *y* to *i*, *ough* to *off*, *ochs* to *ox*; the *e* dropped, as in Thorp(e); *de* converted to a prefix as in Delaun or Decosta). Occasionally two sons proved to have the same first name, but interestingly only Dutch residents had more than one first name. Male businessmen, whose first names could not be ascertained, have been excluded, but an exception to this rule has been allowed for widows. Foreign names have presented great difficulties. Jews did not use surnames, and French, German, Italian, and Dutch names were anglicized and misspelled, often in bizarre forms.[2]

Only businessmen aged at least twenty-five from the metropolitan area of London have been included. After 1556 twenty-four was the minimum age for a freeman of London, and twenty-five was the age at which most set up as independent businessmen. Businessmen have been defined principally by their equity, usually but not exclusively at death; a minimum of £500 (1660–1740, adjusted downward for inflation 1580–1660). In many cases, subjects have been presumed to qualify even though their exact wealth is unknown: for example, surtax payers, Liverymen of major companies, and bankrupts in the docket books.

Businessmen have also been defined by their level of activity rather than by the raw materials they handled or by their function (i.e. distribution versus production). Those who were purely passive investors have been excluded, but not those who lent money, managed property, or invested in stocks as a full-time business. Members of some companies, like the pewterers, have usually been assumed to practice their formal

---

[1] I. Winchester, "Record Linkage" and R. Schofield, "Automatic Family Reconstitution," *Historical Methods* 25 (1992): 75–9, 151–2; E. A. Wrigley, *Identifying People in the Past* (1973), 99–103.
[2] R. D. Gwynn, *Huguenot Heritage* (1985), 178–80, has a useful glossary of corruption of French names.

trade, but no such assumption has been made in companies such as the drapers and clothworkers. Many types of evidence have been employed to determine occupation, including wills, orphanage records, business papers, tax records, legal cases, and company lists. Undoubtedly, mistakes have been made in allocation; some businessmen may have been wrongly omitted from the database and some entered when they do not qualify.

All those whose business activities centered on London have been included, even if they lived outside the city or abroad. The period divisions have been determined by date of death, with a few exceptions for long-lived merchants who died close to 1740. Spinsters and widows active in business have been included, but not wives or daughters helping their husbands or fathers.

PARTICULAR FIELDS

Birth date. When only the year of birth is known, it has been entered as January 1. The accuracy of birth dates varies with the source. Those taken from parish registers, family genealogies, and monumental inscriptions are more reliable than those taken from legal depositions and marriage allegations, which are often notional. Some have been calculated from apprenticeship enrollments (assuming eighteen was the age of registration), but none have been based on dates of entry into the freedom or livery. No distinction has been made between date of birth and date of baptism, except when the baptism occurred within the first seven days of a new year.

Death date. When the exact date of death is unknown, an approximate date has been substituted. For example, the date of probate or (in the case of the Court of Orphans) the first date that an inventory was exhibited has been taken as the date of death. If probate was granted in the first month of a calendar year, it has been assumed that the subject died in the previous year. When the month of death is unknown, the date has been entered as January 1. Burial dates have been taken as dates of death unless they occurred within the first four days of a new year. All estimated dates of death refer to the last date that the subject was known to be alive. Residence at death has not been recorded in the database, nor the birth or death dates of wives. Date of death has not been estimated from a birth date.

Age at death. The year in which a subject died has been counted as a full year; someone who was born in 1600 and died in 1650 in his fiftieth year has been regarded as aged fifty not forty-nine. When the calendar in use is unspecified, it has been assumed to be Old Style in primary sources and New Style in secondary sources. Age at death has not been calculated when the actual date of death is unknown.

Place of birth. This has been equated with normal residence of the father. Four categories have been used: London (the whole metropolitan area, including Southwark and Westminster, outlying towns such as Hackney or Wapping and the county of Middlesex), local region (counties adjacent to London and Middlesex), distant region (all other English counties), and abroad (including Scotland and Ireland). Addresses have not been recorded in the database.

Status of father. Six categories have been employed with an emphasis on occupational rather than purely social status. Business is defined by the same criteria as in other fields. Gentlemen include peers, baronets, knights, esquires, and gentlemen, but excludes working businessmen or professionals who had titles or gentle status. Professionals include army officers, clergy, lawyers, shipmasters (unless also merchants), and office holders in the law, household, and royal government (but not municipal officers). Artisans and tradesmen include all small craftsmen and laborers operating in manufacturing and distribution below the level of businessmen. Farmers include yeomen and husbandmen. Aliens include all those born abroad, even when they were denizens or naturalized. The birth order of subjects in the family has not been recorded. Status has been determined from many different types of evidence and is necessarily approximate in many cases, with many overlaps between the broad categories. Whereas descriptions in the visitations and apprenticeship registers have been taken at face value, businessmen who declared themselves gentlemen in wills or depositions have been disallowed. The same definitions have been used in all fields.

Citizenship. This field has been divided into three categories: freeman of London, nonfreeman, and alien.

Titles. These include titles (peer, baronet, knight) acquired or inherited by a subject.

Religion. Five categories have been employed: Catholic, Dissenter, Quaker, foreign Protestant, and Jew. Dissenters include those opposition groups within the established church before 1640 usually labeled as Puritans (Presbyterians and sectaries) and all nonconformist groups as defined by the Clarendon Code after the Restoration, except for Quakers who have been recorded separately. Foreign Protestants include German, French (Huguenot), and Dutch immigrants and refugees. Nonconformity has been determined less by evidence of personal belief, than by church membership, political activity, refusal of the sacrament or office, bequests in wills, place of burial, and links with Protestants abroad. Sons of Huguenots, for example, have been counted as Huguenots, except when they are known to have embraced Anglicanism. It has proved hard to detect Catholics, and no attempt has been made to identify positively Anglicans who usually practiced quietly. Businessmen have been taken to be orthodox unless there is evidence to the contrary.

Training. Six categories have been employed: apprenticed within the immediate family (father or grandfather), to kin (including siblings) or outside the family, entry by patrimony or redemption, and a professional education at a university, Inn of Court, or abroad. Some categories do overlap: apprenticeship was sometimes combined with entry by patrimony or a legal education. When a subject had more than one master, the first has been entered; in some cases whoever freed a subject has been assumed to be his master. Undoubtedly some kin acting as masters have been missed because they had a different surname.

Type of business. The many complex and overlapping sectors of business have been reduced to six categories: foreign trade, domestic trade, retailing, manufacturing, finance, and a combination of several types. The *Apologie of the City*, printed in Stow's *Survey of London*, distinguished between navigation (merchants), invection (importing and supplying the nation), and negotiation (shopkeeping), all activities distinct from handicrafts (labor plus cunning), and laboring.[3] Foreign trade includes shipowners and some shipmasters as well as trade with Scotland and Ireland. Active directors of companies have been treated as merchants unless they were primarily stockbrokers. Domestic trade includes woolmen, clothiers, woodmongers, warehousemen, drysalters, iron-

---

[3] J. Stow, *A Survey of London*, ed. C. L. Kingsford (Oxford, 1971), 207.

mongers, factors, vintners (though some were wine merchants), trans-portation, and wholesale distribution of food, raw materials, and fuel. Retailing includes shopkeepers, like jewelers and booksellers, tallow-chandlers, haberdashers, chapmen, victualers, embroiderers, tavern keepers, and providers of services such as scriveners, apothecaries, and barber surgeons. Among the surtax payers in the 1692 poll tax were members of several minor companies and trades, including one distiller, ten tobacconists, and fifty-seven tradesmen.[4]

Manufacturing includes brewers, working goldsmiths (but not bankers), dyers, cutlers, soap boilers, processors, builders, textile pro-ducers, girdlers, armorers, and braziers. Businessmen were more common in distribution than in production, though both functions could be combined; many drapers, mercers, skinners, furriers, leathersellers, and saddlers qualify, but few tailors, milliners, weavers, fullers, cur-riers, cordwainers, hosiers, carpenters, glaziers, masons, sawyers, plas-terers, locksmiths, plumbers, smiths, pouchmakers, tawyers, or tanners. Finance includes banking, stock jobbing, and large-scale lending to the government, cities, and individuals.

These divisions are of course oversimplified; foreign trade, for example, was often combined with the domestic trade and supplied goods for the internal market. The precise business of a subject can only be determined from business papers and inventories. It can be assumed, however, that the great majority of subjects whose trade is unknown would have been in one of the domestic trades, since overseas merchants are highly visible in the sources.

Office. Although holders of minor offices in London (from common councilmen downward) have been recorded in passing, only two cate-gories have been used: subjects who served as aldermen, sheriffs, or gov-ernors of city institutions; and those who held national office as members of Parliament or the royal administration.

Residence abroad. This field counts all businessmen who either traveled or lived abroad, including aliens and immigrants from the colonies.

Same business as father. Subjects placed in this field did not necessarily take over their father's firm.

[4] D. V. Glass, "Socio-Economic Status" in A. E. J. Hollaender and W. Kellaway, eds., *Studies in London History* (1969), table 7.

Marital status of subject. Four categories have been employed: never married, married once, married twice, and married three or more times. Only subjects whose marital status is known have been entered.

Age at first marriage (subject and wife). It has been assumed that a marriage took place within seven days of a license being granted or within six months of the signing of a marriage contract. Unless both the birth date and marriage date are known, this data consists of declared ages.

Marital status of first wife. Either single or widowed.

First marriage, maiden name of wife. When a widow, both maiden and married names are recorded.

First marriage, occupation of father of wife. This field has been reduced to four categories: business, gentleman, professional, and other. In the case of widows, the occupation of the father and not the husband has been recorded.

First marriage, location of wife. Four categories have been employed: London (as defined above), other urban (all other provincial towns), country, and abroad (including Scotland and Ireland).

First marriage, surviving sons. All births have been recorded, but only the data on those surviving have been used. Many children have undoubtedly been overlooked. Frequently a source identifies one son, but there is no additional evidence on other children in the family. Pedigrees and wills usually omit those who died in infancy, and it has proved impossible to check all parish registers for births and burials. Sometimes the number, but not the sex, of children is given, and in these cases the total has been equally divided between sons and daughters. Children have been treated as surviving when they predeceased their father, if they had lived long enough to be apprenticed or married. The names and birth and death dates of children have only been recorded if they enter the database as practicing businessmen. Stepchildren have not been recorded.

First marriage, sons who marry. The data cannot be regarded as complete because some sources used (a visitation, pedigree, or will) are time specific and a marriage may have occurred at a later date. When a son is definitely known never to have married this has been recorded, but the data is too limited to use.

Identical fields have been used for up to five sons and five daughters.

Identical fields have been introduced for second and third marriages, except age at marriage of husband is omitted.

First son, occupation. Three categories have been employed: business, gentleman, or professional. When a son had no obvious occupation and lived on rents or interest from land, urban property, or stocks, he has been classified as a gentleman. No attempt has been made to compare his status with that of his father to measure upward or downward mobility.

First son, occupation of wife. The same categories have been used as with wives of subjects in the database.

Identical fields have been employed for second, third, fourth, and fifth sons.

First daughter, status of husband. Three categories have been employed: business, gentleman, and professional, as defined above.

Identical fields have been introduced for second, third, fourth, and fifth daughters.

Dowries of daughters. The data has been entered in pounds sterling and averaged if there were several daughters per family. It has not always been possible to distinguish a dowry from normal inheritance in wills.

Duration of marriages and duration of widowhood. Length of marriage has been calculated from date of marriage to date of death of either husband or wife. Widows who remarried have been excluded.

Remarriage of widows. The name, status, and age of second husbands have not been recorded.

Orphans surviving at death of father. Orphans are here defined as any child under twenty-one and unmarried.

Personal wealth at death. All data have been entered in pounds sterling.

Usually only personalty has been counted, but in some cases it has proved impossible to differentiate movables from real estate. In other cases, relying just on personalty would place a subject in the wrong bracket: John Batkin, merchant tailor, for example had only £308 in personalty, but extensive lands in Middlesex. Some estates have been estimated, but not on the basis of contemporary rumor. Among the methods used are multiplying from tax assessments, the declarations in the port books and the bonds furnished by administrators. Property qualifications for office have also been taken as the minimum estate.[5] Surtax payers in the assessments of the 1690s have, however, only been included when their occupation is given or when they are known from other sources to have been businessmen.

A major source has been the net estates in the common serjeant's books, all of which have been entered.[6] Those with net assets under £500 (even nil) have been included when it is clear from their liabilities that they were trading in the £500 range. Most of those sued for bankruptcy had more than £500, and frequently a businessman appears first as a petitioner and then as a bankrupt.

All these methods carry risk—even scale of trading: "If it be known what a merchant trades for, it doth not appeare thereby what he is worth."[7] Inventories at death are not representative of the living population. But the net worth of many subjects has been accurately ascertained, and the principal objective in this field has been to place subjects in a particular financial bracket.

Primary assets. This field is divided into just two categories: active (invested in a working business, including lending money as a business) and passive (invested in rent-producing assets, such as land, houses, or stocks, with no active buying and selling).

---

[5] Liverymen had to be worth £1,000, after 1697 and £500 in artisan companies. After 1580, although the minimum was never clearly specified, an alderman could be discharged if worth less than £4,000; in 1622 the level was 10,000 marks, in 1672 £10,000, and in 1710 £15,000. Peter Blayney kindly extracted this information from the repertories.

[6] Debts owing to the testator have been excluded and consquently the data differ from that supplied by J. R. Woodhead, G. S. De Krey, and P. Earle, who cite gross figures. See also N. J. Cox, "Probate Inventories," *Local Historian* 16 (1984): 133–45, 217–27, 467–77.

[7] *The Balance of Trade* (1622), reprinted in F. G. M. Price, *Handbook London Bankers* (1876), 147.

Probate. The following categories have been employed: will, intestate (admon), and probate through the Court of Orphans.

Executors. Over twenty initial categories have been reduced to ten: parents/siblings, kin, kin combined with outside executors, outside executors, widow as sole executor, widow combined with son, widow combined with outside executor, sons, daughters, and all the children.[8]

Kin and friends mentioned in wills. It has not always been possible to differentiate friends from relatives, since relatives were often referred to as friends and vice versa. Often the phrasing of a will suggests whether an individual (including ministers of religion, clients, and business partners) were friends rather than associates, but considerable ambiguity still remains. Godchildren have been classified as friends unless they are specifically identified as kin; grandchildren were on occasion called godsons, as by James Williams, a merchant tailor, in 1621. The term "mother" can refer to either a biological mother (often remarried with a new surname) or to a mother-in-law; stepfathers were sometimes called fathers-in-law. No attempt has been made to grade legacies (which were often given no monetary value) by financial scale. The principal aim of this field has been to determine which individuals were remembered rather than rewarded by a testator.

Overseers. Six categories have been employed: widow, children, parents/siblings, kin, kin plus outsiders, and others.

Primary beneficiaries. Sixteen categories have been employed in various combinations: eldest son, daughters, all children, grandchildren, children plus grandchildren, kin, others, widow, widow plus children, widow plus kin, widow plus others, siblings, siblings plus others, father/mother, and equal (an equitable distribution between widow and children not in strict accordance with the custom of London).

Charity. Only three categories have been employed: major, minor, and no benefactions. Gifts have been rated by percentage of an estate, not

---

[8] There are numerous ways of categorizing legatees; for two different approaches see P. Earle, *Making of the Middle Class* (1989), table 11.4, and J. A. Johnston, "Family, Kin, and Community," *Rural History* 6 (1995): 179.

by absolute value; a benefaction of £100 by a subject worth £50,000 has been treated as minor, whereas a benefaction of £50 by a subject worth £500 has been treated as major.

Inheritance by custom. This field records whether or not a testator followed or intentionally evaded the custom of London.

Land and urban real estate. Three broad categories have been employed: major, minor, and no holdings. It was difficult to estimate acreage from wills when the rental income is not given, but usually the approximate scale can be inferred from descriptions.[9] Land and urban property held on long-term leases has also been included, particularly when managed as rental property.

Partners. Three categories have been employed: immediate family (grandfather, father, siblings, children, or grandchildren), kin (all other relatives), and unrelated.

Apprentices. Three categories have been employed: immediate family, kin, and unrelated.

Principal source of initial capital. Five categories have been employed: immediate family, kin, marriage, master, and others.

Principal source of additional capital. Three categories have been employed: immediate family, kin, and others.

Memo fields (2). One records additional information about a subject and one lists the principal sources of information.

SUBSETS

Periods I and II. By date of death (estimated or known):

- I: 1580–1659
- II: 1660–1740

---

[9] Earle, *Making of the Middle Class,* table 5.9, uses five gradations of landholding.

Financial brackets I–IV. By net worth at death adjusted for inflation (taking 1660 as the baseline, all monetary figures have been adjusted using the Phelps-Brown and Hopkins Index):

* I: £0–500 (only businessmen who are known to have managed businesses with a net equity of over £500 at some point in their lives)
* II: £501–5000
* III: £5,001–50,000
* IV: over £50,000

It should be noted that the financial bracket in which a subject died may have been quite different from the bracket he was in when he married.

Birth cohorts I–IV: by birth date

* I: 1540–1579
* II: 1580–1619
* III: 1620–1659
* IV: 1660–1700

Subjects whose date of birth is known but not their actual date of death have been excluded. Cohort IV is not a completed cohort because many born in the 1690s would have lived beyond 1740, the terminal date of the database. All cohorts are necessarily restricted to those who lived to at least twenty-five and whose birth date is known (6 percent of all subjects in period I and 23 percent in period II).[10] For analytical purposes, a generation has been taken as forty years, even though it is often regarded as thirty-three years or measured by the mean age of maternity.[11]

---

[10] In comparison, T. Hollingsworth, *Demography of the Peerage* (1969), 92, found birth and death dates for 11.3 percent of his secondary universe, and R. Houston, "Mortality in Early Modern Scotland," *Continuity and Change* 7 (1992): 49, for 43.6 percent of his advocates.

[11] R. A. Houston, *The Population History of Britain* (Cambridge, 1995), 22, puts the mean length at forty years; Hollingsworth, *Demography of the Peerage*, 62, at thirty-five years. See also F. F. Mendel, "Age of Maternity," *Journal of Family History*, 3 (1978): 237; D. B. Rutman, "People in Process" in *Family and Kin*, ed. T. K. Haveren (New York, 1977), 32.

Sources

BRITISH LIBRARY[1]

Additional MSS

- 4,224: Memoirs of Sir Patience Ward
- 5,488–9: Hill papers
- 5,540: Papers of John Cary of Bristol
- 11,409–11: Papers of Thomas Povey
- 12,423: Journal of Colonel Edward d'Oyles
- 21,133: Lustring Company
- 22,183–7: Papers of Sir Henry Johnson
- 22,842–56: Papers of Thomas Pitt
- 22,006–7: Oxenden papers
- 22,910
- 23,199: Correspondence of Sir John Shaw
- 24,107: Letter book of Sir Charles Hedges
- 27,622: Accounts of Anne Crouch
- 28,714: Inventory of Thomas Bulman
- 29,873: Memorandum book of Sir Daniel Tyas
- 30,494: Household accounts of Anne Archer
- 32,456: Household accounts of Rachel Pengelly
- 33,085: Letters of Thomas Pelham
- 34,273: Correspondence of Hale family
- 40,696–713: Oxenden papers
- 42,122–3: Scattergood papers

---

[1] Private business papers which were not included in the list provided in R. Grassby, *The Business Community of Seventeenth-Century England* (Cambridge, 1996), 427–38, are marked with an asterisk. Manuscripts listed in appendix A have been excluded here.

- 43,730–3: Scattergood papers
- 54,332: Oxenden papers
- 61,935: Account book of a Seville merchant
- 70,145: Harley papers
- 70,160–5: Harley papers
- 70,223: Harley papers
- 72,481–620: Trumbull papers

Cotton

- Otho E viii: Papers of Michael Lock
- Titus BV: Miscellaneous tracts
- Vespasian F. xvi: Household accounts of a merchant's wife
- Vespasian F. xvii: Merchant's account book

Egerton

- 1,971: Pitt papers
- 2,224: Accounts of John Walbank
- 2,395: Povey papers
- 3,054: Diary of Joyce Jeffries

Harlean

- 1,231: Inventory of Sir John Rudstone
- 2,104
- 2,243
- 6,821: Correspondence of Gregory King

Lansdowne

- 88: Papers of Sir Michael Hicks
- 162
- 241: Sanderson papers
- 1,156: Daybook of Lord Delaware

Sloane

- 320: A tradesman's account book
- 857: Letter of John Green

- 2,902: Papers of Abraham Hill
- 3,515: Courteen papers
- 4,454: Diary of Katherine Austen

Stowe

- 759: Letter book of Philip Williams

Loan

- 57: Bathurst papers

Oriental and India Office Collections

- European MS E 387/A–C: Letter book of Isaac Lawrence
- G 19/36: Diary of Richard Mohun
- H/36/6: Estate of Nathaniel Wych
- H/40/5: Letter book of John Massingberd
- H/40/26: Correspondence of Humphrey Holcomb
- H/40/54: Letter book of John Manifold
- H/40/114: Letter book of Mrs. Uvedale
- H/40/120: Correspondence of Sir Josiah Child

CORPORATION OF LONDON RECORD OFFICE

- MCD 1/1–123: Mayors Court
- MC 1/: Mayors Court

GREATER LONDON RECORD OFFICE

- New River Company Papers
- E/&D/30: Will of William Boulter

GUILDHALL LONDON LIBRARY

- 204: Diary of Nehemiah Wallington
- 233: Daybook of Edward Strong
- 404–5: Papers of Sir John Chapman
- 507–507A: Papers of Sir John Moore

- 1,525: Correspondence of Sir John Gayer
- 2,708: Memorandum book of Richard Farrington
- 2,951: Account book of Robert Abbott
- 3,041/1–4: Papers of Thomas Bowrey
- 3,181–4: Probate documents of Thomas Reeve
- 3,324: Notes on Lord Mayors
- 3,504: Papers of Sir John Moore
- 3,547: Papers of Edmund Sherman
- 3,723: Papers of Thomas Palmer
- 5,101–A: Papers of Sir William Turner
- 5,301–A: Business papers of Charles Payne
- 5,626: Business papers of Joseph Bosworth*
- 5,677: Inventory of Giles Crouch
- 6,372: Papers of Frederick Herne
- 6,666: Inventory of William Gilby
- 7,388: Account book of a Dutch merchant*
- 8,489–92A: Papers of Sir William Rawstorn
- 9,563: Papers of Thomas d'Aeth senior and junior
- 10,187–8: Journal of Sir Charles Peers
- 10,770: Papers of Sir William Turner
- 10,823: Papers of Boddington family
- 10,857: Papers of Skilbeck family
- 11,096: Papers of John Pope*
- 11,892–2A: Papers of Michael Mitford
- 11,896: Papers of John Mead
- 12,017: Autobiography of John Fryer
- 13,248B: Will of Thomas Fisher
- 14,289: Papers of a tobacco and sugar merchant*
- 16,283: Partnership agreement
- 17,145–6: Business papers of Thomas Laxton and Timothy Betton*
- 18,472: Papers of William Brooke*
- 18,760/1: Papers of Thomas Boughey and Nathaniel Cole
- 19,017: Papers of John Richards and John Rooke
- 20,347: Partnership agreement of John Timbrell and Abel Wilkinson*
- 20,756: Partnership agreement of Henry Hovener and James Brown*
- 22,317–21: Correspondence of Corsini family
- 22,825: Partnership deed of William Baldwyn and John Tynte*
- 22,945: Papers of Thomas Fisher
- 23,493: Accounts of servant of Sir John Gore*
- 23,902: Accounts of a cutler*
- 23,953–5: Papers of Richard Archdale
- 24,201: Papers of Thomas Fisher

- 24,553–4: Papers of John Wyse*
- 25,681: Ledger of Cadiz merchant*

NATIONAL MARITIME MUSEUM

- AMS/1: Account book of Thomas Pye
- LBK/3: Correspondence of Sir Anthony Deane

PUBLIC RECORD OFFICE

- 30/26/52: Correspondence of Daniel Chardin
- C 5: 35/13; 86/44; 87/57; 90/17; 274/15; 460/31; 501/110
- C 6: 252/49; 260/113; 301/18
- C 7: 61/37; 292/54; 334/9; 363/34; 373/40
- C 8: 352/248; 356/30; 384/8; 484/6; 522/45; 672/12
- C 9: 84/24; 489/20
- C 10: 161/16; 304/59; 381/47; 514/90
- C 24: 765
- C 66: 1158/1–6
- C 78: 61/15; 90/9; 100/10; 155/5; 161/4; 167/16; 173/1–2; 181/4–10; 185/9; 191/11, 14; 193/5, 11; 195/7; 263/12
- C 103: 40, 158, 160–1, 186*, 194*, 198*
- C 104: 3*, 11–16, 44–5, 77–80*, 107–8, 123–31, 141–5*, 156*
- C 105: 5*, 12, 15, 27*, 29
- C 107: 12, 17–18, 20, 70–2, 112–13*, 158*, 161, 172*, 180*
- C 108: 30, 34, 44*, 82*, 132, 203*, 280*, 284*, 414*
- C 109: 19–24, 248*
- C 110: 15*, 19–20*, 25*, 42–3, 81, 87, 140, 151–2, 158*, 167*, 179*, 181, 185*
- C 111: 50, 95–6*, 127, 135*
- C 112: 4*, 24*, 176*, 181*, 189*, 205*
- C 113: 11–14, 31–2, 34–7, 175*, 261–95*
- C 114: 9*, 16*, 55–60, 164–5, 179–80, 182*
- C 214: 9
- E 101: 521/7, 10, 13–17; 634/4; 635/39–41
- E 154: 3/35–4/40, inventories
- E 178: Special commissions, inventories, and inquisitions
- HCA 2: 560
- HCA 30: 635–54*, 636
- Req 2: 296, 307, 389
- SP 9: 96, 106

- SP 23: 183*
- SP 46: 83–8
- SP 105: 110–341
- SP 110: 10–59

UNIVERSITY OF LONDON

- 71: Inventory of Thomas Church
- 186: Inventory of Sir Godfrey Copley
- 265: Journal of William Hoskins
- 448: Household accounts
- 473: Accounts of Madam Tayler
- 553–4: Papers of Clutterbuck and Tyndale
- 628: Letter book of William Chalmers
- 655: Accounts of Richard Davis

WESTMINSTER ABBEY MUNIMENTS

- 9,977: Indentures
- 12,911: Clothing bills
- 10,367–11,586: Papers of Sir Andrew King
- 54,114: Invoice book
- 58,137: Account book

VICTORIA LIBRARY, WESTMINSTER ARCHIVE DEPARTMENT

- 985: Account book of Joseph Ashley*

DR. WILLIAMS LIBRARY

- Henry MS 4: Letter book of Sarah Savage
- 284: Diary of Elias Pledge

BERKSHIRE RECORD OFFICE

- D/EBbu: Burdett papers
- D/ED B: Merchant's ledger
- D/EE: Commercial ledger

- D/EN F 6: Business correspondence
- D/EZ5 and H/R: Papers of Henry Hunter

CAMBRIDGE UNIVERSITY LIBRARY

- Add. 91: Correspondence of Michael Blackett
- Add. 3303: Daybook Cambridge Draper
- Add. 8793: Hill papers
- Dd.vii.26: Blackett correspondence

DERBYSHIRE RECORD OFFICE

- D. 258: Gell papers*
- D. 2086: Papers of William Hogkinson

EXETER CITY LIBRARY

- 61/6/1/: Jeffries ledger

ESSEX RECORD OFFICE

- D/DBF: Hallingbury Place archives
- D/DDC: Du Cane papers
- D/DEL: Accounts of Edwin Rawstorn
- D/DU: Business correspondence of Nicholas Corsellis
- D/D Bin Z: Notebook of Joseph Buxton*

GLOUCESTER RECORD OFFICE

- D 1086–7: Business papers of John Whalley and John Nelmer
- D 1799: Dyrham papers

BRISTOL CITY ARCHIVES

- 10521: Papers of Shershaw Cary
- Ashton Court papers
- Papers of John King

BRISTOL REFERENCE LIBRARY

• Jefferies MSS

BRISTOL UNIVERSITY LIBRARY

• Pinney papers
• Society of Merchant Venturers

HAMPSHIRE RECORD OFFICE

• Heathcote of Hursley papers

HEREFORD AND WORCESTER RECORD OFFICE

• BA 4328/9899: Letters of Anne North
• BA/8541: Account book Thomas Yardley
• F/iv/c: Business papers of John Foley

HERTFORDSHIRE RECORD OFFICE

• Radcliffe papers
• Pashanger archive: Papers of Robert Booth and William Cowper

CENTER KENTISH STUDIES

• U. 22: Denne papers
• U. 47: Dodwell papers
• U. 119: Masters MSS
• U. 133: Dering MSS
• U. 145: Faunce Delaune MSS*
• U. 234: Aylesford papers
• U. 289: Business accounts
• U. 312: Accounts of a wine merchant
• U. 350: Dering papers
• U 352: Indentures
• U. 386: Indentures
• U. 480: Best MSS
• U. 522: Dalison MSS
• U. 593: Tylden MSS

- U. 1015: Papillon MSS
- U. 1515: Papers of John Hill
- Ch2/12: Accounts of a Hamburg merchant

LANCASHIRE RECORD OFFICE

- DDB: Barcroft papers
- DDC: Cavendish of Holker MSS
- DDH: Hopwood MSS
- DDW: Willis of Halnead MSS
- Accounts of Salford hosier

CHETHAM LIBRARY, MANCHESTER

- Raines MSS

PRESTON RECORD OFFICE

- Accounts of Thomas Rawlinson

LIVERPOOL UNIVERSITY LIBRARY

- Moore MSS

LEICESTER MUSEUM ARCHIVES DEPARTMENT

- D 57: Braye of Stanford and papers of John Schoppens

LEICESTERSHIRE RECORD OFFICE

- Correspondence of Sir John Moore

LINCOLNSHIRE ARCHIVES OFFICE

- 1B: Whichcote MSS
- 2PG: Pearson Gregory MSS
- 4/: Nelthorpe MSS
- 7/7: Monson MSS
- 9/D: Ancaster MSS
- 21/: Massingberd of Gunby MSS

- 28 B/5: Eyre Papers
- Trollope Bellew MSS
- Broadley MSS
- Holywell MSS
- Diocesan Archives inventories

NORTHAMPTONSHIRE RECORD OFFICE

- Cokayne MSS
- Accounts of Newnham candle vendor

NORFOLK RECORD OFFICE

- 21/12/92: Accounts of Thomas Andrews*

UNIVERSITY OF NOTTINGHAM

- ME: Mellish of Hodsock MSS

BODLEIAN LIBRARY

- Add. A 49: Diary of Timothy Marriott
- Add. C. 267: Letters of Thomas Pengelly
- Ashmole 1809: Accounts of William Smythe
- Ashurst DD c. 1: Correspondence of Henry Ashurst
- Ch London and Midd. 50: Inventories
- Dashwood MSS*
- Dep. C. 23: Papers of Henry Sanford
- Eng. hist. C. 44: Correspondence of Sir John Shaw
- Eng. hist. C. 63: Letters of Nicholas Buckeridge
- Eng. hist. D. 156–63: Scattergood papers
- Eng. lett. C. 192: Business correspondence of John Aylward
- Eng. misc. C. 14: Armorial collection of Ralph Starkey
- Eng. misc. C. 260: Letter book of a merchant
- Eng. misc. C. 292: Inventory of George Hadley
- Eng. misc. C. 563: Letter book of Matthew Ashton
- Eng. misc. C. 602: Letter book of Matthew Ashton
- Eng. misc. F. 78: Diary of John Cogge
- Malone 2: Account book of Richard Newall, 1623
- Rawlinson A. 21: Accounts of an insurance underwriter
- Rawlinson A. 414: Inventory of Richard Wyche

- Rawlinson C. 66: Letter book of merchant*
- Rawlinson C. 395 (and 7476): Letter books of Nicholas Buckeridge
- Rawlinson C. 745–7: Factors letters of the Royal Africa Company
- Rawlinson C. 861: Diary of a wigmaker
- Rawlinson D. 72: Letters of John Dunton
- Rawlinson D. 114: Business diary of Samuel Marriott*
- Rawlinson D. 1483: Ledger of a factor at Aleppo
- Rawlinson letters 66: Letter book of a merchant
- Rylands E. 17: Heraldic collections

SHROPSHIRE RECORD OFFICE

- 49: Scott MSS
- 112: Attingham MSS
- 567: Plymley correspondence
- 1224: Brooke (Forester) MSS
- 4572: Papers of Robert Moore

SOMERSET RECORD OFFICE

- Hylton MSS: Ledger of John Morley and memorandum book of James Twyford
- Dd/GB/148: Gibb MSS and papers of William Gore*

WILLIAM SALT LIBRARY, STAFFORD

- HM 37/36: Papers of Elizabeth Sneyd
- Papers of Gregory King

EAST SUFFOLK RECORD OFFICE

- AP/S1: Ashe papers
- GB 1: Mills papers
- HA 170/246: Marnock papers
- HA 53: Barne papers
- HE 30: Blois papers

EAST SUSSEX RECORD OFFICE

- FRE 4870 (145/11): Ledger and correspondence of Samuel Jeake

WEST SUSSEX RECORD OFFICE

- Accounts of Newdigate Owsley

WARWICKSHIRE RECORD OFFICE

- CR 314/114: Business papers Nathaniel Alsopp

YORKSHIRE NORTH RIDING RECORD OFFICE

- Cholmeley MSS

LEEDS CENTRAL LIBRARY

- DB/36: Denison papers
- NH: Newby Hall MSS
- TN/OA/D13: Correspondence of a clothier
- Stansfield MSS

BROTHERTON LIBRARY, UNIVERSITY OF LEEDS

- Diary of John Bufton
- Autobiography of G. Aptall
- Ltq 1: Commonplace book of John Tempest
- Volume of merchants accounts (1675–92)
- Dep c. 231: Accounts of a Spanish merchant

SHEFFIELD CENTRAL LIBRARY

- Business correspondence of Ferdinando Wingfield
- Autobiography of William Statham
- Pye MSS
- Bright papers
- Spencer-Stanhope archive: Business papers of Benjamin and William Spencer
- Tibbitts collection: Dawson papers

COMPANY OF MERCHANT ADVENTURERS OF YORK

- Correspondence of James Hutchins*

NATIONAL LIBRARY OF WALES

- Myddleton MSS (Chirk castle)
- Wynn MSS
- Bodewnd MSS
- 9685 B: Commonplace book of William Thomas

BEINECKE LIBRARY, YALE UNIVERSITY

- Chardin MSS
- Shipping records, 1669

BERMUDA ARCHIVES

- Colonial records, 1618–80
- Government records
- Book of wills

CLARK LIBRARY, LOS ANGELES

- 531: Account book of Rebecca Steel

FOLGER LIBRARY, WASHINGTON, D.C.

- UB 18: Letter book of William Phillips*
- V/a/459: Commonplace book

HUNTINGTON LIBRARY, SAN MARINO

- 1264: Papers of Nehemiah Grew

KRESS LIBRARY, COLUMBIA UNIVERSITY

- 148: Account of Humphrey Hill
- 787: Ledger of John Warner

NEW YORK PUBLIC LIBRARY

- Letter book of Hugh Hall
- Smythe of Nibley papers

UNIVERSITY OF VIRGINIA

• Letter book of Robert Anderson

VIRGINIA STATE LIBRARY, RICHMOND

• USL Acc 22,953: Letter book of Robert Bristow

Index

Abberley, Elizabeth, 194
Abberley, Stephen, 226, 351
Abbot, Robert, 80, 94, 412
abduction, 378
Abdy, Sir Anthony, 305–6, 363, 377
Abell, William, 178
Aberdeen, 359
Abingdon, 47, 102, 127, 137, 142, 278, 329, 331, 359
absence of husband. *See* travel
accidents, 173, 176, 185
accounting, 193–4, 324, 336–8, 413
achievement. *See* motivation
Acrise, 205, 352, 369
Acton, Richard, 58
Addison, Gulston, 246
adolescence, 31, 155, 158, 178–9, 183–7, 244
adoption, 234, 356
adultery. *See* infidelity
adult mortality. *See* life expectancy
adulthood, 187, 189, 204, 366
advice books, 89, 116, 170–1, 179–82, 184, 208, 334, 336–7, 394–5
affection. *See* love
affinity. *See* friends
Africa, 190
Africa Company, 332
age, at death, 118–21, 167, 224, 260, 397, 446; difference of, 40, 70, 93, 102, 137–9, 151; of majority, 379. *See also* minors

agency, individual, 387, 389, 392–6, 410. *See also* individualism
agents, business, 289–90, 292–7, 303, 317, 321, 323–4, 413
agents outside the family, 296–7
Akehurst, Ralph, 148
Albin, Ferdinand, 324
Alchorn, William, 244
Aldenham, Hertfordshire, 137
Aldworth, Robert, 411
ale houses. *See* taverns
Aleppo, 192, 229, 280, 283, 296, 306
Alexander, James, 21
Algiers, 211
aliens, 54–6, 161, 252, 255, 271, 273, 307–8, 324, 446, 448
alimony, 344
Allen, Edward, 109, 286
Allen, Hannah, 328
Allestree, Richard, 180
Alley, Richard, 178
Alleyn, Edward, 290
almanacs, 91, 171
alms. *See* charity
America, 192, 308, 318, 323, 342, 345, 356, 361
Ames, Edward, 100
Amsterdam, 54, 106, 285, 292–3, 308
Amthil, 324
Amy, John, 219
anachronism, 15
ancestry. *See* lineage

469

Andover, 163, 257
Andrews, Edmund, 141
Andrews, Francis, 379
Andrews, Thomas, 352–3, 404
Anglesey, George, 247
annuities, 72–3, 105–6, 131, 142,
  148–9, 200, 204, 241, 244, 331,
  333–4, 338, 349–50, 352–3, 363,
  399, 403, 406–7. *See also* debt
annulment, 107–8
Antill, Edward, 356
Antrobus, Thomas, 245, 327
apothecary, 120, 133, 178, 196, 199,
  237, 247, 286, 295, 315, 327,
  350, 448
Apothecary's Company, 315
Appleton, Elizabeth, 333
appraisers, 246, 250. *See also*
  inventories
apprentices, 41, 45, 53, 65, 95, 97,
  99, 106, 113, 134, 142, 145, 160,
  168, 179–80, 183–4, 187,
  189–90, 210, 213, 224–5,
  229–30, 235–7, 240, 242, 244,
  248–9, 252, 269, 271–83, 287,
  293, 295, 299, 302, 310, 312–13,
  315–16, 322–6, 330–1, 337,
  339–40, 342–3, 349, 353–4,
  362–4, 369, 398, 407, 446–7,
  453; bound outside the family,
  279–82; bound to fathers, 277–8;
  bound to kin, 278–81; bound to
  siblings, 278; geographical origins
  of, 274–5; litigation over, 168,
  182; marriage of, 38, 43, 50, 64,
  69, 337; parental occupations of,
  273–4, 446; trading with widow
  of master, 134, 287, 326, 330,
  337; with widows as masters,
  325–7; women, 314–16
apprenticeship. *See* apprentices
Arbell, Edward, 348
arbitration, 202, 249, 251, 253, 259,
  301, 339, 410
Archangel, 212, 289
Archdale, Martin, 131
Archdale, Richard, 202, 297, 333
Archer, Anne, 336
Archer, Richard, 21
Aries, Philippe, 10

armourer, 205, 352, 448
Arnaud, Jean, 322
Arnold, Richard, 223
Arnold, Thomas, 106
d'Arvieux, Chevalier, 40
Ashe, Abraham, 74, 124, 195
Ashe, Edward, 296
Ashe, James, 284–5, 296–7
Ashe, John, 296
Ashe, Jonathan, 296
Ashe, Sir Joseph, 371–2
Ashe, Margaret, 86, 195
Ashe, Robert, 284, 296, 328
Ashton, Henry, 227, 301
Ashton, Lawrence, 195
Ashton, Matthew, 67, 104, 113, 297,
  301, 303
Ashurst, Sir William, 201
Ashwell, William, 173
Asia, 402
assets. *See* capital
Astell, Mary, 193
Astell, Richard, 233
astrology, 17, 148, 338
Asty, Francis, 57
Atherall, Thomas, 326
Atkin, William, 290
Atkinson, Robert, 53
Atlantic, 256, 269, 294–5, 310, 317,
  327
attorneys. *See* lawyers
Atwood, Mary, 88, 104, 185–7, 208
Atwood, Richard, 185
Atwood, Robert, 170
Atwood, Thomas, 290
Atwood, Walter, 290
Atwood, William, Sr. and Jr., 146,
  165, 175, 180, 185–6, 195, 228,
  231, 245, 282, 294, 296, 301,
  381
Aubrey, John, 117, 244
Audley, Sir Henry, 207, 308
aunts, 57, 103, 179, 217, 219, 232,
  234, 236, 240, 285, 325, 338,
  356, 370
Austen, John, 74
Austen, Katherine, 149–50
autobiographies, 27, 176
Avery, Samuel, 293
Awdesley, Richard, 147

Aylmer, Tobell, 135
Aylward, John, 295, 303

babies. *See* infancy
Babington, John, 164
bachelordom. *See* bachelors,
    marriage, avoidance of, *and* never
    married
bachelors, 64, 77–81, 89, 227, 233,
    240, 243, 249, 260, 244, 247,
    269, 356, 361, 383–4
Bacon, Francis, 16
Badger, George, 157
Bagnall, Richard, 286, 290
Bailey, John, 45
Baker, Henry, 382
Baker, John, 294
bakers, 316, 329, 331
Balam, Anthony, 57
Baldwin, Dereham, 157
Baldwin, Thomas, 285
Ball, Bryan, 245
Ball, Charles, 299
Ball, George, 293
Ball, Robert, 293, 299
Ball, Thomas, 293
Ball, William, 176, 294
Balle. *See* Ball
ballads, 38, 47, 89
Ballard, Thomas, 207
Baltic, 54, 307, 360
Bamforth, George, 147
Banbury, 296
Banford, Patrick, 202
Bangs, Benjamin, 282
Bank of England, 50, 332, 402
banker, 281, 297, 301, 305, 307,
    329, 332–3, 360, 384, 405,
    410–12, 448. *See also* goldsmith
Bankes, James, 196
banking. *See* banker
bankruptcy. *See* bankrupts
bankrupts, 106, 195, 299, 301, 313,
    334, 444, 451
Banks, Anne, 378
Banks, Caleb, 365, 369
Banks, John, 221, 243
Banks, Sir John, 75, 290, 365
Banks, Richard, 194
Banks, Thomas, 199

Bantam, 248
baptism. *See* birth
Baptist. *See* sects
Barbados, 109, 187, 191, 226, 284,
    293–4, 300, 307–9, 360
Barbary, 269
barber surgeon, 106, 234, 318, 354,
    370, 448
Barber Surgeons Company, 178, 326
Barcroft, Charles, 293
Barefoot, Thomas, 194
Barker, Catherine, 76
Barker, John, 141
Barlow, Thomas, 157
Barnaby, Alexander, 93
Barnaby, Catherine, 103
Barnardiston, Arthur, 47
Barnardiston, Sir Pelatia, 230
Barnardiston, Sir Samuel, 88, 230
Barnes, Ambrose, 80, 139, 181, 193,
    230, 318
Barnstable, 121, 170, 294
Baron, Anthony, 244
Baron, Benjamin, 172, 233
baronets. *See* peerage
barristers. *See* lawyers
Barrow, Thomas, 67
Barton, Elizabeth, 378
Barton, William, 142
Baskerville, Richard, 362
bastards, 45, 66, 81, 99, 168–9, 377,
    380
Bateson, Matthew, 207
Bath, city of, 100, 110
Bathurst, Allen, 363
Bathurst, Sir Benjamin, 113, 134,
    280, 362–3
Bathurst, Dorothy, 364
Bathurst, Henry, 199
Bathurst, John, 199
Bathurst, Moses, 364
Batkin, John, 451
Battie, John, 112
Baxter, Richard, 43
Bayman, Richard, 204, 234
Bayning, Andrew, 293
Bayning, Paul, 108, 287, 293
Beal, Richard, 355
Beare, John, 100
beauty, 39–41, 46, 69, 83, 107

Beazley, Thomas, 234
Beeston, Christopher, 130
behavior, 11, 27–9, 31, 90, 115, 175,
    366, 382, 387, 388–90, 395, 409,
    414, 417
Belfast, 130, 137, 224, 235, 260,
    305, 330, 360, 367, 404
Bell, Henry, 353
Bell, Joseph, 195
Bell, Richard, 195
Bell, Robert, 243
Bell, Sarah, 108
Bellamy, Edward, 283, 348
benchers. *See* lawyers
beneficiaries, primary, 452
Bennett, John, 87
bequests, 66, 132, 203, 212, 219–20,
    231–2, 236–43, 247, 249–50,
    259, 262, 282, 341, 343–4,
    348–50, 354, 356, 379, 384;
    restrictive, 141–5, 148; timing of,
    398
bereavement. *See* loss
Berkshire, 350
Bermuda, 294
Bernardcastle, 383
Berry, Edward, 144, 248, 364
Berwick, 190
Betts, Nicholas, 72
Bewick, Edward, 212
bias, 441
Bickerstaff, Anthony, 349
Bickerstaff, Arthur, 208, 228
bigamy, 135
bigotry, 376
Bilbao, 292
Billings, John, 240
Billingsley, Elizabeth, 315
bills of mortality, 163
binding, 277–81, 325–6. *See also*
    apprentices
Bindsey, John, 334
Birkley, Jane, 415
Birmingham, 289, 359
birth, 31, 37, 113, 194; control,
    169–70; date of, 24, 445, 454;
    birthdays, 193, 213, 228; defects,
    170; order, 163, 208, 342–3,
    345–6, 353–4, 367, 446; place of,
    54, 224, 261, 275, 446; rituals,

228, 232, 257. *See also* childbirth,
    primogeniture
Bisby, Alexander, 289
Bishop, Thomas, 144
Bishopsgate, 334
Blackburn, John, 85
Blackett, Edward, 227
Blackett, Michael, 298
Blackett, Sir William, 363
Blackfan, John, 330
Blackmore, Sir Richard, 97
Blackwell, Jonathan, 349
Blackwell Hall, 293, 328
Blanchard, Thomas, 354
Bland, John, 230
Blencoe, William, 204
Blois, William, 294
Blomefield, Poel, 50
blood kin. *See* kin, consanguineous
Bludworth, Sir Thomas, 306
Blundell, Nicholas, 211, 289
Blundell, Richard, 66, 289
Blunt, Charles, 213, 233, 236, 297,
    304
Blunt, John, 139, 173, 233, 297
Blunt, Samuel, 192, 304
boarding school. *See* children,
    education of
Boddington, Benjamin, 278
Boddington, George, 45, 57, 146,
    164, 169–70, 178, 196, 236, 278,
    283, 376
Boddington, John, 196
Boddington, Sarah, 106–7
Boddington, Thomas, 145
Bodley, Thomas, 70
Boldero, Henry, 87
Bolston, Richard, 362
Bolton, Lancashire, 292
Bolton, William, 176, 289
bonds, 71, 73, 85, 132, 143–4,
    229–30, 298, 321, 331, 333–4,
    337, 350, 355, 381, 451
Bonfoy, Sebastian, 308
books, 346, 355, 383
bookseller, 100, 295, 324, 331, 360,
    365, 448
Boone, George, 209, 353
Booth, Robert, 227
Bordeaux, 324

Borough, Jane, 332
Boroughside, 248
Boston, Massachusetts, 226, 235, 290, 294, 306
Botheby, Thomas, 223
Bott, John, 200
Boucher, Benjamin, 192
Boucher, Louis, 290
Boucher, Paul, 290
Boucher, Philip, 370–2
Boudaen, Martin, 133
Boughey, Thomas, 230, 381
Boulter, William, 232
Boulton, Ambrose, 279
Boulton, William, 279
bourgeois, 3, 5–7, 9, 13–14, 384, 393
Bourne, George, 350
Bourne, Nehemiah, 166
Boutflower, William, 57
Boutter, Ralph, 352
Bowater, Edward, 241
Bowcock, George, 145
Bowden, Nicholas, 356
Bowes, Sir Martin, 199
Bowles, Valentine, 192, 350
Bowmer, Richard, 244
Bowrey, Mary, 110, 324
Bowrey, Thomas, 57, 110, 225, 295, 324
Bowyer, Robert, 112, 241
Bowyer, William, 71, 212, 248
Boyd, Perceval, 21
Boyer, Ralph, 112
Bradford, 380
Bradley, Samuel, 285
Bradley, William, 299
Bradshaw, John, 412
Bradshaw, Peter, 58
Bradstone, 383
Bradstreet, Simon, 379
Bramston, Edward, 50, 284
Bramston, Sir John, 377
Brand, William, 74, 86
Brazil, 293
breast feeding, 170–2. *See also* nursing
Brent, Anne, 328
Brent, Edward, 327
Brerewood, Francis, 132

Breta, Jacob Mendez de, 198
Breton, George, 130, 253
Breton, Nicholas, 26, 46
brewer, 100, 145, 240, 248–9, 285, 295, 307, 315, 318, 320, 324, 326, 330–1, 338, 350, 360, 378, 412, 448
brewing industry. *See* brewer
Brewster, Anne, 318
Bridewell, 78, 255
Bridges, Delitia, 41
Bridges, Samuel, 166, 353
Briggins, Peter, 86, 192
Briggs, David, 321
Bright, Edward, 305
Bright, Heigham, 211, 245, 279
Bright, Thomas, 233
Bristol, England, 47–8, 51, 75, 78, 93, 137, 148, 161, 166, 168, 177, 193, 199, 237, 255, 261, 274, 277, 284, 292, 305, 315, 317, 324–5, 328, 331, 358, 363, 403, 410
Bristol, colonial, 63, 163
Bristow, Robert, 71, 178, 203
Britaine, William de, 38
Brocas, Mary, 332
Brockett, Thomas, 130
Brodnax, William, 229
Brodsky, Vivien, 21
broker. *See* brokerage
brokerage, 93, 241, 296, 324, 403
Bromley, Joseph, 325
Brook, John, 172
Brooksbank, Joseph, 363
brothels, 45, 102, 318
brother-in-law. *See* in-laws
Brown, Abraham, 107
Brown, Edwin, 306–7, 362
Brown, Elizabeth, 306
Brown, Hugh, 364
Brown, Humphrey, 157, 248
Brown, John, 306
Brown, Joshua, 325
Brown, Mun, 306
Brown, Thomas, 349, 369
Brown, Tom, 68, 81, 99
Brown, William, 290
Browne, John, 291
Browne, Joshua, 50

Browne, Sir Thomas, 117, 179
Brudenell, Anne, 134
Brudenell, William, 230
Brussels, 289
Buck, John, 381
Buckeridge, Nicholas, 213
Buckeridge, Richard, 145
Buckingham, Sir Owen, 135, 352
Buckinghamshire, 286
Buckland, John, 197
Buckland, Robert, 197
Buckle, Sir Cuthbert, 114
Buckworth, Elizabeth, 306
Buckworth, Sir John, 306
Buckworth, Mary, 307
Bufford, Samuel, 138, 181
building industry, 360, 448
Bulkeley, Bartholomew, 363
Bulkeley, Thomas, 363
Bull, Edmund, 142
Bull, John, 307
Bullock, Augustin, 225
Bullwart, William, 281
Bunby, Richard, 313
Bunyan, John, 69, 214
Burchett, John, 367
bureaucracy, 5, 262, 269, 271, 394,
    410, 416
Burgess, Francis, 328
Burgess, Humphrey, 249
Burgess Court of Westminster, 326
Burgis, John, 29
burial. *See* funeral
burial, place of, 114–15, 197, 207–8,
    383
Burkin, James, 189, 362
Burkin, John, 189
Burlamachi, Philip, 308
Burnell, Francis, 131
Burnell, John, 206, 290
Burnell, Mary, 124
Burrell, John, 54
Burton, Simon, 207
Bury, Elizabeth, 336
Bury, Humphrey, 112
Bush, John, 326
business, enterprise, 302, 309–10,
    312, 340, 367, 407, 409–10,
    415–17; family, 415–16;
    institutions, *see* companies; losses,

398, 403; businessman, definition
    of, 444, *see also* merchant,
    overseas, *and* domestic;
    management, 246, 271, 296, 298,
    310–11, 324, 330–2, 337–8, 340,
    406, 408–13, 416; morality,
    249–51, 300, 308–9, 319, 410,
    414, *see also* dishonesty;
    organization, scale of, 415–17, *see
    also* firm; papers, 29–31, 72, 288,
    296, 320, 324–5, 328, 336, 338,
    363, 399, 444; parental choice of,
    362–3, 412–13, *see also* sons in
    business; sectors, 275–6, 444–5,
    447, *see also* trade;
    businesswoman, *see* women
Butler, Sir Nicholas, 219
Buttermore, John, 200
button maker, 320
Byrd, William, 279, 300

Caius College, Cambridge, 122
Calcott, Arthur, 247
calendar, Old and New Style, 445–
    6
Calthorp, Margaret, 77
Calthorp, Martin, 280
Calverley, Thomas, 280
Calvert, Elizabeth, 318
Calvinists. *See* Nonconformists
Cambridge, 124, 161, 180, 244, 305,
    329
Cambridge University, 240–1
Campbell, Agnes, 330
Campbell, Sir James, 240, 289, 305
Campbell, John, 365, 376
Campbell, Sir Thomas, 305, 378
Canary Islands, 68, 229, 299
Canham, Henry, 287
Cann, Elizabeth, 81
Canterbury, diocese of, 63, 136
Capell, Hugh, 201
capital, 32, 47, 72–3, 80, 134, 146,
    148, 151, 241, 271, 334, 348,
    381–2, 385, 388, 394, 396–402,
    406, 416; accumulation, *see*
    wealth; appreciation, *see* wealth;
    affinal, 284–8, 305; allocation of,
    see investment; consanguineous,
    282–4; external, 288, 402; fixed,

282, 412; human, 408; sources of, 453; starting, 282–5, 343; working, 282, 398
capitalism, 1–2, 4–8, 10, 16, 33, 310–11, 384, 387–90, 394, 410, 417
Carcas, James, 112
Carew, George, 341
Carleton, Bigley, 351
Carleton, Matthew, 301
Carleton, Thomas, 58
Carpenter, John, 237
Carpenters Company, 315
carrier, 318, 358
Carswell, James, 308
cartels. *See* monopolies
Carter, James, 295
Carter, Susan, 249
Carter, Thomas, 249
Cartwright, Dorothy, 369–73
Cartwright, Jarvis, 167
Cartwright, Samuel, 350
Cartwright, Ursula, 369–73
Cary, John, 189, 378
Cary, William, 137
cash, 176, 185–6, 236, 351, 356, 370–1, 379, 381, 383, 394, 399, 411. *See also* capital, liquidity
Cassel, Philip van, 322
Casson, Elizabeth, 329
Casson, Gilbert, 355
Castelyn, Elizabeth, 115
Caswell, William, 236
caterers. *See* food trades
Catholics, 257, 308, 447
causation, 15, 393, 416. *See also* probability
Cavendish Square, 377
Chadwell, William, 134
Chaffer, Joseph, 106
Chamberlain, Richard, 247, 358
Chamberlain, Thomas, 199, 209
Chamberlayne, Edward, 336
Chancery, 66, 68, 86, 109, 133, 151, 203, 209, 335, 344, 381
change, 390, 391, 394, 416
chapbooks, 38–39
chapmen, chapwomen, 299, 324, 332, 448
Chapman, Adam, 132, 134

Chapman, Jasper, 114, 221
Chapman, John, 199
Chapman, Matthew, 352
character. *See* personality
Chard, Edward, 195, 250
charitable societies, 261
charity, 77, 130, 199, 230, 240–1, 244, 250, 253, 260–2, 400, 452–3
Charleston, 205
chastity, 38, 44, 90, 97, 334
Chauncey, Elizabeth, 320
Chelsea, 176
Cheney, Edward, 326
Chesapeake, 92, 122, 235, 360
Cheshire, 240
Cheslin, William, 58
Chester, 161, 184, 289, 323, 325, 328, 346, 359, 367, 378
Chester, Elizabeth, 67, 74
Chetham, George, 328
Chetham, Humphrey, 77, 248, 282, 291
Chetham, James, 51
childbirth, 94, 124, 145, 170
Child, Sir Francis, 132, 351–2, 405
Child, Sir Josiah, 133, 143, 146, 194, 335, 369, 406
Child, Robert, 405
Child, Stephen, 140
Childey, Katherine, 317
childless couples, 9, 106, 109, 145, 155–7, 160, 162–3, 187, 225, 235, 249, 260, 344, 350, 352, 354–6, 399, 406
children, attitude to parents, 31–2, 177, 197–200, 204–8, 215–16; attitude to stepparents, 178–9; attitude to widowed mother, 113, 117, 150, 200–204; behavior of, 31, 181, 195–6; conflict between, 146; cost of, 215; custody of, 130, 234; discipline of, 176, 182–4; disinheritance of, 199, 355, 377–9; education of, 88, 104, 143–4, 171, 175–6, 180, 183–4, 186, 190, 193–4; employment of, 196; experience of childhood, 31, 174–6, 187, 242, 389; games of, 175–6, 182, 186, 249; independence of, 179, 183–4, 189,

children (*cont.*)
197, 216; loss of, 196–7; marriage of, 194; moral instruction of, 174, 181–2; mortality of, 157–8; number of surviving, 31, 125, 131, 157–9, 187, 224, 242, 281, 380, 449; obedience of, 180–2, 197, 199, 202, 237; provision for, 32, 65–6, 73, 130, 143, 180, 182, 215, 343, 369, 385, 396, 398; rearing of, 172–3, 178, 187, 195, 233–5, 336, 338; rights of, 180; sending away, 183, 189, 234, 281–2; sex ratios of, 31, 155, 163–4, 187, 392; spoiling of, 175, 182–3, 195, 367, 376; weaning, 172. *See also* sons, daughters, guardians, toys
Chilton, Thomas, 220
Chilvers Cotton, Warwickshire, 161
Chipping Camden, 199
Chipping Sodbury, 205
Chiswick House, 93
Chitty, Henry, 348
Chiverton, Elizabeth, 203
Chiverton, Sir Richard, 203
Cholmeley, Mary, 74
Cholmeley, Nathaniel, 57
Christian, John, 143, 209
Christ's Hospital, 168, 255
Church of England, 257–60, 364, 371, 447
Church, Thomas, 269, 364
Churchhouse, George, 106
Cirencester, 362
civic elite, 47, 54, 63, 83, 102, 121, 137, 161, 163, 243, 251–5, 257, 273, 305, 345, 358, 411
civic consciousness. *See* community, civic
civil society, 2, 6, 251, 256–7, 264, 391
Civil Law, 66, 343–4
Civil Wars, 177, 207, 409
civility. *See* behavior
Civill, Peter, 209
Clare, Earl of, 280
Clark, Alice, 8
Clark, Sir Edward, 87
Clark, George, 376

Clark, Rebecca, 376
Clark, Robert, 228, 327
Clark, Thomas, 147
Clark, Tristam, 233
Clark, William, 201, 283, 364
Clarke, Deborah, 299
Clarke, Matthew, 133
Clarke, William, 288
Clarkson, Robert, 355
Clavering, Anne, 326
Claypoole, James, 243
Clayton, Sir Robert, 80, 92
Clayton, William, 72
Cleaver, Robert, 39, 46, 90
Cleev, Henry, 283
clergy. *See* professions
clerical writers, 39, 42–3, 56, 58, 89–91, 171, 173–4, 181, 185, 260, 343, 393–4
clientage. *See* patronage
clients, 296–7, 302, 322, 328, 333, 340, 405
Clifford, George, 281
Clitherow, Sir Christopher, 305–6
Cloberry, William, 50, 132, 209, 383
clothier, 145, 157, 245, 275, 281, 287, 295–6, 360, 400, 404, 447
clothing, 94–6, 104–5, 180, 185, 194, 212–13, 236, 245–6, 248, 261
clothworker, 106, 112, 114, 120, 132, 157, 220, 221, 233, 236–7, 240, 247, 279, 348–50, 354–5, 377, 405, 444
Clurgeon, John, 247
coach and horses, 112, 356
coal trade, 318, 328, 406, 415
Cobham estate, 364
Cockcroft, Caleb, 241, 362
coding, criteria for, 441–54
coffee houses, 318
Cogge, John, 74, 185, 236, 279
cohorts, 11, 19, 22, 198, 396
Coish, Richard, 241
coitus interruptus, 170. *See also* birth control
Cokayne, Sir Thomas, 283
Cokayne, Sir William, 355, 374
Coke, Thomas, 247
Colchester, 56, 243, 350
Coldham, John, 87

Cole, James, 93, 341, 415
Cole, Ralph, 168
Coleman, William, 247
Coles, Benjamin, 203
Collett, Betty, 376
Collett, Joseph, 56, 138, 177, 193, 196, 206, 213, 235, 376, 381, 396
Collett, Nicholas, 235
Collier, Ebenezer, 376
Collins, John, 290
Collins, Richard, 131
Colston, Edward, 77, 81, 240, 383, 412
Colston, William Jr. 292
Colston, William Sr. 292
Colthurst, Henry, 306
Colyton, 102
commemoration. *See* monuments
commission trade. *See* agents, business
Common Serjeant. *See* London, Court of Orphans
common law, 66, 338, 342, 345
community, 2, 250–2, 264, 339, 392; civic, 252–57; expatriate, 294
companies, holding, 270, 398, 402; joint stock, 270–1, 310, 332–3, 402, 410, 414, 416, 447; regulated, 270, 317. *See also* London, livery companies
companionship, 80, 92, 116, 145, 263
competition, 410, 413
Complete Tradesman, 47, 398
compromise, 395–6
Compton, Lord, 376
Connecticut, 122, 330, 345
connection, 302–5, 393, 414, 417. *See also* kin networks
Constantinople, 45, 244, 247, 262, 306
consumption, 5, 9, 85, 92, 95, 104, 196, 277, 365, 393, 398, 401, 408
continuity of families. *See* dynasties, generations
contract, 1, 5, 8, 66, 75–6, 85, 91, 179, 184, 277, 300–301, 309, 389, 392–3, 414

contraception. *See* birth control
Cony, Thomas, 157
Cook, Samuel, 130
Cook, Thomas, 87
cooking. *See* food
Cooling, Mary, 374
cooper, 137, 145, 167, 194, 247, 278, 315, 323, 325, 330, 339
Cooper, Anne, 314
Cooper, Anthony, 358
Cooper, Daniel, 245
Coopers Company, 319
Cope, James, 282
Cope, Susan, 232
Cope, Thomas, 151
Copley, Sir Godfrey, 112
Corbin, Henry, 294
cordwainers, 282, 316, 330, 448
coresidence, 80, 189, 205, 224–6, 289
Cork, 309
Cornwall, 356
Coronell, Isaac, 70
corporations, 252–3, 271, 407, 415–16
correlation coefficients, 18, 23
correspondence, 26, 28–31, 66, 69, 95, 109, 175, 185, 190, 206, 210, 216, 226–8, 242, 249, 320, 333
cost/benefit ratio, 340
Cotesworth, William, 81, 158, 287, 406
Cotton, Sampson, 326–7
Cotton, William, 207
Cotymore, Catherine, 205
Coulson, Thomas, 169
Courn, Thomas, 100
Court of Requests, 86
Court of Aldermen. *See* London, Court of Aldermen
Court of Arches, 109
Courteen, Margaret, 133
Courteen, Sir William, 133, 146
courtesy literature, 89. *See also* advice books
courtship, 37, 40, 50, 65–70, 82, 374, 394; failure of, 76–7, 83; manuals, 39; of Philip Papillon, 369–73; strategy of matchmaking, 82, 96, 392

cousins, 57, 218–19, 225, 226–7, 233–6, 240–1, 247, 279–81, 285, 290, 292, 294–5, 297–9, 301, 304, 306, 309, 356, 378, 396, 407
Coutts, James, 293
Coutts, Hercule, 293
Coutts, Thomas, 293
couverture, 85–6, 142, 148, 313, 407
Covel, Francis, 100
Covell, Thomas, 350
Coventry, 161, 255, 260, 274, 287, 313, 325, 315, 359, 408
Cox, Nicholas, 200
Cox, Sarah, 378
Coxere, Edward, 323
Cranfield, Lionel, 1st Earl of Middlesex, 50, 68, 103, 198, 230, 245, 289, 343
Cranfield, Mary, 322
Craven, Sir William, 384
credit, 93–4, 104, 106, 134, 195, 230, 235, 250, 270, 282, 284–5, 288, 298–9, 309–10, 321–2, 331, 334, 338, 403, 407–10, 417
Cresswell, Elizabeth, 99, 319
Cressy, David, 21
crime, 319
Crispe, Ellis, 219
Crispe, Nicholas, 112, 141, 321, 378
Crispe, Samuel, 321
Crommelin, Catherine, 146
Crompton, Thomas, 363
Crooke, Andrew, 278, 401
Crooke, William, 278, 331
Cropland, Luke, 247
Crowche, Anne, 194, 352
Crowche, Giles, 352
Crowche, Richard, 219, 353
Crowley, Ambrose, 158, 270, 352, 365
Crowley, Benjamin, 365
Crowley, John, 330, 377
Crowley, Judith, 206
Crowther, John, 73, 130
Cruttenden, Joseph, 226
cuckoldry. See infidelity
Cuffe, Henry, 171, 155, 184
Cullen, Abraham, 322
Cullum, Mary, 100
Cullum, Sir Thomas, 284

Culmer, Philip, 237
Culpepper, William, 168
culture, 1, 4, 6, 9, 13, 15, 32, 37, 82, 89, 187, 198, 217, 255, 264, 340, 387, 390–1, 394–5, 413
Cumberland, 304
Currer, Henry, 240
Currer, John, 112
Cust, Samuel, 295
Custom of London. See London, Custom of
customers. See clients
cutler, 112, 134, 173, 182, 295, 318, 360, 364, 448
Cutler, George, 200
Cutler, John, 304
Cutler, Sir John, 221, 379
Cutts, Nicholas, 328

D'Aeth, Thomas, 45, 298
Dalby, William, 354
Dalison, Elizabeth, 211, 322, 335
dancing, 193–4, 198
Daniel, John, 227
Daniel, Sir Peter, 352
Daniel, Serle, 176
Dansell, Sir William, 169
Dant, Joan, 332
Dantzig, 292–3
Darnell, Daniel, 199
Darnell, Richard, 199
Dartmouth, 410
Darwin, Charles, 15
Dashwood, Abraham, 291
Dashwood, Sir Francis, 377–8
Dashwood, Madam, 245
Dashwood, Sir Samuel, 298, 352
data. See sources
database, 19–23, 28, 32, 273, 260, 277, 384; checks and balances, 441–2; chronological parameters, 445, 453; cohort divisions, 454; fields of, 441, 445–53; financial brackets, 444, 454; geographical parameters, 445; sources for, 423–40; structure of, 444–5
Daton, Robert, 203
daughter-in-law. See in-laws
daughters, adult, 192–5; disinheritance of, 200; as executrices, 195, 202, 352;

education of, 374, 376; marriages of, 32, 54, 341, 373–7, 450; rights of patrimony, 312; unmarried, 206; younger, 47, 144. *See also* children, provision for
Davenant, Jane, 324
Davenant, John, 50, 157
David, Jacob, 145, 330
Davis, John, 323
Davis, Thomas, 294
Davies, Sir Thomas, 278
Dawbeney, Arthur, 306
Dawson, William, 290, 306
Dean, Sir Richard, 112
Deane, Thomas, 205
death, premature, 173, 392, 398; dates of, 21–2, 445, 454; deathbed, 93, 111, 115, 183, 192, 206, 251
DeBritto, Joseph, 200
debtors. *See* debts
debts, 73, 85–6, 93, 130, 132–5, 141, 177, 189, 195, 203, 209, 223, 230, 233, 235–6, 246, 261, 285–8, 299–300, 310, 328, 350, 403, 406
Decosta, Catherine, 77
Decosta, Jacob, 77
Decosta, Joseph, 77
Decosta Philip, 77
Dedham, 64, 163, 281
defamation. *See* slander
deference, 197, 204, 394
Defoe, Daniel, 29, 58, 104, 150, 299, 320, 329, 335–7, 373, 382, 393
Dekker, Thomas, 47
Delamotte, Judith, 328
Delaun, Gideon, 166
Delaval, Sir John, 235
Delawood, William, 81
Deleat, John, 212
Delilliers, Jacob, 114
Dellbridge, John, 294
Delme, Sir Peter, 352, 383
Denew, James, 164, 277
Denew, Joas, 237
Denmark, 110
Denner, Oliver, 112
Dennis, Elizabeth, 306
Deptford, 243
Derbyshire, 382

Dering, Sir Edward, 147
Derrack, William, 201
Des Carriere, John, 139, 175
Desbouverie, Sir Christian, 362
Desbouverie, Edward, 364
descent, lineal and lateral, 219, 221, 226, 342, 352, 383, 393, 411
Dethick, Charles, 290
Deuxville, John de, 240
developmental cycle, 11, 387
Devon, 328
devotion. *See* love
diaries, 26–30, 45, 98, 111, 147, 185
Dickinson, Henry, 196
Dickinson, Jonathan, 279
Dickinson, William, 72
dinners. *See* food
directorships, 270–1, 296, 447
discrimination. *See* gender prejudice
disease. *See* sickness
dishonesty, 196, 230, 298, 300, 310
disinheritance. *See* children, disinheritance of
Disney, Gervaise, 68, 111, 279
Dissent. *See* Nonconformists
dissolute. *See* libertinism
distiller, 159, 205, 349, 448
Distillers Company, 255
division of labor, 1, 91–2, 94, 271, 302, 334, 414, 417
divorce, 38, 98, 108,
Dobbins, William, 177
Dod, John, 39, 46, 90
Dodderidge, Richard, 294
Dodson, Ellen, 330
Dodson, James, 330
Dodson, Mary, 325
Doncaster, 234
Dore, John, 198
Dornell, Robert, 199
Dorrington, Francis, 199
double portion, 343, 345, 351
double standard, 99
Dowcett, Francis, 147
dower. *See* inheritance, rights of
Downs, Richard, 378
dowry. *See* portion
Drake, John, 57
Drake, Roger, 57
dramatists. *See* theater

draper, 61, 109, 133–4, 142, 157, 194, 202, 225, 234, 240, 279, 281, 286–7, 289, 315, 324, 326, 348, 351, 352–5, 360, 379, 444, 448
Drapers Company, 205, 273, 287
dreams, 113, 214–15
dress. *See* clothing
drinking, 96, 106–7, 170, 190, 196, 228, 241, 244, 249, 365
Druce, Abell, 321
Duboc, Judith, 87, 322
Dubois, John, 110
DuCane, Peter, 76, 110, 131
Duckett, Sir Lionel, 369
Dunch, John, 325
Dunch, Sir Thomas, 384
Duncomb, Charles, 81
Dundee, 359
Dunster, John, 132
Dunton, Iris, 324
Dunton, John, 69, 111, 179, 198, 324
Dutch, 54–6, 310, 381, 444, 447
Dutch church, 56, 106
Dutton, Sarah, 315
Dutton, Thomas, 315
Dutton, Sir Thomas, 179
Dwight, William, 405
dyer, 87, 151, 178, 228, 283, 291, 326, 328–9, 349, 404, 448
Dyer, Richard, 113
dynasties, business, 358–61, 410–13, 415. *See also* civic elite, heirs, lack of

Earle, John, 174, 209, 243
Earle, Peter, 20
Earle, Sir Thomas, 292
Earls Colne, 63
East Anglia, 224, 361
East India Company, 54, 56, 180, 199, 229, 280, 301, 304, 307, 313, 322, 332–3, 363, 409
Eastland Company, 304, 332
economic development, 388, 390, 392–3, 416–7. *See also* capitalism
economic individualism. *See* individualism
Edinburgh, 162, 251, 255, 293, 305, 321, 330, 332, 334, 359

Edinburgh Merchants Company, 321
Edsaw, Anne, 329
Edwards, Jonathan, 40
Edwards, William, 323
efficiency. *See* business management
Egerton, John, 244
ego. *See* personality
Elbing, 10, 168
Elbridge, Giles, 148
Elder, Daniel, 81, 208
elderly. *See* old age
Elias, Norbert, 30
Elliott, Daniel, 221
Ellison, John, 234
Elton, Abraham, 100, 278, 363
Elton, Sir Abraham, 363
Elwes, Geoffrey, 140
Elwes, Jeremiah, 245
embroiderer, 351, 448
embroidery. *See* needlework
Emms, Samuel, 327
emotions, 27–8, 39–41, 43–4, 47, 95, 102, 106, 148, 171, 175–6, 181, 183, 185, 187, 197, 210–11, 216, 394–5, 409. *See also* love
empiricism, 13, 16, 32
employees, 296, 337. *See also* servants
Enfield manor, 363
Engels, Friedrich, 7
Ent, Peter, 290
entail, 383. *See also* strict settlement
entertainment, public, 96, 249–50, 253, 255
entertainment, private, 244
equal division of property. *See* London, Custom of
equality of sexes, 90–1, 94. *See also* family, obedience within, gender differentiation
equilibrium, 2
Erikson, Erik, 184
Erington, Mark, 350
Essex, 73, 166, 350, 404
Essington, William, 166, 348
Ethersey, Alexander, 286
Evans, John, 307
Everenden, John, 283
evidence. *See* sources
evolution, 391

Ewen, Mark, 113
exchangewoman, 317
executors, 230, 233–4, 348, 377
executorship, 132–5, 150–1, 452. *See also* widows
Exeter, 70, 162, 224, 226, 286, 305, 346, 358, 367
Eyon, John, 199
Eyon, William, 199

factors, 65, 180, 190, 230, 243, 286, 293–6, 306–7, 328, 408, 448
family, boundaries, 263, 393; business, value of, 309–11; business, women in, 322–5; capitalism, 413–17; extended, 4, 10, 32, 66, 217, 224, 228, 235, 257, 259, 263–4, 269, 286, 288, 309, 385, 388–9, 391, 402, 408, 413, 416; firm, 32, 269–70, 309, 321, 330, 335, 385, 388, 398, 408, 409–10, 412–17; formation, 187–8, 387, 389–90; ideology of, 388; models of, 9–13, 387–92; networks, 417; nuclear, 2, 10, 32, 189, 233, 249, 263, 269, 309, 342, 354, 388–9, 391–4, 416; obedience within, 43, 90–3, 96, 103, 111; perpetuation of, *see* lineage; size of, 31, 155–9; stem, 189; structure and process of, 387, 389–90; theories of, 2–4, 7, 9–13, 31–2, 82, 85, 88–9, 92, 387
Fane, Mildmay, 367
farming, 405, 412
Farnaby, John, 53
Farquahar, George, 46
Farrar, Nicholas, 120, 177
Farrington, Richard, 75, 110–11, 158–9, 166, 170, 172, 205, 225, 233, 248, 255, 259, 292
Farrington, William, 304
father-in-law. *See* in-laws
Faucus, Roger, 203
favoritism, 201, 208, 210. *See also* patronage
Feak, William, 364
Fell, Sarah, 329, 336
Fellows, William, 105
femes soles, 320–2

feminism. *See* gender theory
Fenn, Mary, 147
Fern, Joseph, 232
Ferrar, Mary, 150
Ferrers, John, 197
fertility, 157–9, 169, 361, 392
feudalism, 5, 7
fiction, 25, 44, 393
fictive kin. *See* friends
fidelity. *See* infidelity
Field, Edward, 195
Filmer, Sir Robert, 262
finance, 277, 398, 403, 407–8, 447
financial services. *See* finance
financial brackets. *See* database, wealth
Finch, George, 377
Finch, Heneage, 147
Finch, Joseph, 232
firm, 283, 303, 305, 319, 333, 411–12, 414–16
Firmin, Thomas, 113
Fishborn, Richard, 253, 291
fishing, 186
fishing industry, 186, 363
fishmonger, 175, 182, 315, 329, 348, 355
flagellation, 100
Fleet prison, 133
Fleet, John, 304, 307, 319
Fleetwood, William, 46, 193, 197
Fletcher, Henry, 200
Fletcher, Prudence, 20
Fludd, Roger, 54
Foley, Paul, 270
Foley, Philip, 270
Foley, Thomas, 270
food, 91, 94, 102, 105, 171–2, 190, 212, 225, 244, 250, 253, 255, 261, 280, 302, 405, 448
food trades, 318–19, 321, 323–4, 329, 339
Foot, Samuel, 250
Foote, John, 201, 281, 362
Foote, Samuel, 363
Foote, Thomas, 363
Forbes, Francis, 213
Forbes, William, 213
Ford, Philip, 406
Ford, Sir Richard, 232, 378

foreign trade. *See* trade, foreign
Forman, Simon, 41
Forty Hall, 363
Foster, Edmund, 99
fostering. *See* children, sending away
Founders Company, 253, 315
Founes, Warwick, 250
Fountain, Mary, 231
Fountain, Peter, 231, 308
Fowle, Robert, 269, 415
Fowle, Sir Thomas, 75, 232, 415
Fowler, John, 352
Fox, George, 335
Fox, Jane, 193
Fox, Richard, 348
Fox, Sir Stephen, 93–4, 137, 177, 193–4, 235–6, 380
Fox, Thomas, 221
France, 229, 444
Franci, Vallentine, 110
Franklin, Edward, 67
Franklin, Richard, 248
fraternalism, 253, 255, 395, 410
Frederick, Sir John, 231, 410
Frederick, Thomas, 108, 199, 355
free bench, 343
freedom, municipal and guild, 47, 53, 64, 314, 343, 356, 411. *See also* London, citizens of
freedom, transfer of, 53, 313
freehold land, 343, 383, 403
Freeman, Blanche, 324
Freeman, John, 295
Freeman, William, 290, 324
French church, 66, 259. *See also* Huguenots
French Protestant. *See* Huguenots
French wars, 398, 402
Frere, George, 225
Freshford, 296
Fretwell, James, 183, 279, 378
Frewen, Stephen, 78
Frewin, Richard, 99
friends, 132–3, 234, 240–7, 263, 281, 296, 303, 309–10, 377–8, 395, 452; advice of, 171; as advisors, 66; as beneficiaries, 106, 243, 354; as companions, 95; as guardians, 145; as intermediaries, 245–6; loyalty of, 245; number of, 242

Fryer, Sir John, 75, 135, 181, 285
fulling, 329
funerals, 132, 202, 214, 219, 226, 228, 236, 250, 253
Furnese, Sir Henry, 57
Furnese, Robert, 57
furniture, 104, 114, 187, 200, 209, 246, 248, 346, 379, 383

Gainsford, Thomas, 39, 91, 96
Galpin, Nathaniel, 281
Gardiner, John, 250
Gardiner, Mary, 57
Garland, Robert, 285
Garrard, Sir William, 358
Garway, Sir Henry, 286
Gaseley, Thomas, 130
Gataker, Thomas, 39
Gateshead, 415
Gatley, John, 240
Gay, Anthony, 330
Gay, Martha, 330
Gell, John, 284, 299
Gell, Sir John, 227
Gell, Philip, 227
gemeinschaft, 1, 12–13, 310, 390–1. *See also* community
gender differentiation, 173–4, 181, 189, 192–3, 215–16, 243, 336, 339, 349–52, 394, 417
gender prejudice, 131, 334, 340, 342. *See also* women
gender theory, 7–9, 89–93, 96, 320, 334
genealogy, 20, 28, 218, 221, 419, 422, 445
generations, 19, 22, 31–2, 155, 164, 187, 198, 215, 218, 221, 354, 356–61, 383, 390, 405, 408–11, 413, 415–16, 454. *See also* dynasties, business
Genoa, 282, 292–3
Gent, Thomas, 40, 65, 70, 280, 330
gentility. *See* social differentiation
gentleman. *See* landed gentry
Gentlewoman's Companion, 76, 185
gentrification. *See* social ambition
Geraldine, Nicholas, 303
German Protestant, 259

Germany, 54, 241, 245, 292, 297, 444
gesellschaft, 1, 310, 391
Gethen, Maurice, 286
Gibbon, Edward, 58
Gibbs, Sarah, 133
gifts, 70, 87, 111, 176, 185, 192–3, 204, 212–13, 226, 228, 235–6, 244, 261, 378
Gilborn, Thomas, 247
girdler, 73, 142, 157, 219–20, 248, 327, 349, 353, 448
Glasgow, 121–2, 270, 274, 287, 295, 359
glassmaker, 285, 289, 328
Gloucester, 121, 136, 224, 257, 332, 367, 403
glover, 197, 320
Glover, Francis, 151
Glover, Henry, 270
Glover, Richard, 281
Glover, Thomas, 281
godchildren, 218, 225, 242–4, 250, 281, 452; number of, 243–4
Godfrey, Michael, 229
Godfrey, Peter, 323
Godfrey, Richard, 50
godliness, 56, 69, 80, 181, 190, 192, 259
godparents, 57, 235, 243–4
Godschall, James, 74, 285
Godschall, John, 164
Godschall, Samuel, 285
Goff, James, 71
goldsmith, 50, 81, 96, 106, 130, 143, 163, 167, 192, 200, 204, 221, 223–4, 249, 269, 279, 317, 320, 324, 328, 333, 342, 348, 364, 378, 415, 448
Goldsmiths Company, 328
Gonsales, Abraham, 196
Good, Priscilla, 314
Goodfellow, Matthew, 353
Goodwin, Robert, 383
Goodyear, Moses, 307
Gordon, James, 169
Gordon, Jane, 169
Gore, Gerard, 164, 306
Gore, Sir John, 305
Gore, Nicholas, 134
Gore, Thomas, 247

Gore, Sir William, 219, 364
gossip, 103, 213, 243, 249, 251–2, 335, 369
gossips, 95, 170
Gouge, Thomas, 58
Gouge, William, 42, 90–1, 96, 172, 197, 218, 343
Gough, George, 355
Gough, Sir Richard, 74
Gould, John, 290
Gould, Sir Nathaniel, 355
government, 252–3, 255, 262, 446
grandchildren, 162, 165–6, 199–200, 203, 205–6, 218, 220, 236, 247, 250, 325, 348, 354–5, 360, 363–4, 366, 399, 415, 452
grandparents, 177–8, 204, 233, 284, 289, 349
Grange, Hugh, 145
Graunt, John, 163
Grave, Katherine, 40
Grave, Thomas, 290, 400
Gravener, John, 247
Gray, Cuthbert, 381
Gray, Robert, 111, 323
Great Yarmouth, 127, 225, 359
Green, Lawrence, 262
Green, Roger, 93
Green, Thomas, 206
Green, Sir Thomas, 111
Green, William, 247
Green, Sir William, 378
Greenberg, Thomas, 379
Greenwich, 228
Gregory, Edward, 243
Gresham, John, 210
Gresham, Judith, 320
Gresham, Mary, 210, 320
Gresham, Sir Thomas, 150, 158
Gressley, Lady Francis, 139
Grew, Nehemiah, 194
Grey, Thomas, 143
Griffin, Francis, 225, 291
Grimeston, Elizabeth, 43
grocer, 65, 106, 112, 145, 147, 168, 172, 196, 201, 204–6, 221, 226, 230, 233–4, 237, 240–1, 243, 247, 278, 281, 285, 314–15, 318, 320, 328, 341, 351, 355, 362, 379
guardians, 66, 131, 143–5, 201, 234, 247, 366, 369, 377

guilds. *See* London, livery companies, freedom
Guinea, 294
gunmakers, 318
Gurney, Elizabeth, 336
Guston, Henry, 324
Guy, Alice, 40
Guyot, John, 72
Gwin, Thomas, 90

haberdasher, 45, 112, 120, 200–1, 205, 219, 234, 237, 240, 261, 279, 295, 315, 324, 352, 363–4, 383, 404, 448
Haberdashers Company, 118, 253, 356
Habermas, Jurgen, 6
habit. *See* behavior
Hackney, 376, 446
Haines, John, 410
Haines, William, 221, 327
Hale, Edmund, 114, 221
Halford, Edward, 381
Halford, William, 294
Hall, Ezekiell, 299
Hall, Hugh, 365
Hall, John, 234
Hall, John of Bradford, 380
Hall, Joseph, 192
Hall, Judith, 99
Hall, Thomas, 26
Halley, Edmund, 117
Hallingbury, 383
Hallwood, Thomas, 240
Hamburg, 241, 243, 283, 292–3, 326, 348
Hammersley, Sir Hugh, 111–12
Hammersmith, 405
Hampton, Walter, 290
Hanbury, Richard, 363
Hancorn, Michael, 249
Hand in Hand insurance company, 403
Hanger, Ann, 333
Hanger, George, 291
Hannay, Patrick, 46
Hansall, Thomas, 346
Harby, Clement, 290
Harby, Sir Job, 367
Hardebroeck, Margaret, 330

Hardwin, Grace, 314
Hardwin, John, 285
Harley, Nathaniel, 69, 184, 210, 212–13, 229, 282, 285
Harmon, Ralph, 353
Harrington, James, 38
Harris, Edward, 285
Harris, Innocentius, 240
Harris, John, 349
Harris, Mary, 286
Harris, Nicholas, 145
Harrison, Agnes, 335
Harrison, Edmund, 72, 353
Harrison, John, 50
Hartopp, Robert, 353
Hartopp, Thomas, 306
Harvard, 365
Harvey, Abigail, 210
Harvey, Charles, 326
Harvey, Daniel, 77, 306
Harvey, Dorothy, 134
Harvey, Edward, 50
Harvey, Eliab, 306
Harvey, Sir Eliab, 73, 112, 306
Harvey, Elinor, 139
Harvey, Sir James, 209, 247
Harvey, John, 111, 112, 134, 240
Harvey, John, distiller, 349
Harvey, Samuel, 280
Harwich, 180
Haselden, William, 193
Hassall, Hugh, 300
Hatton, Edmund, 160
Hatton, Roger, 148
Havel, Susanne, 325
Hawke, William, 327
Hawkins, Humphrey, 178
Hawkins, Thomas, 313
Hawks, Helen, 338
Hayes, Robert, 349
Haynes, John, 70, 94
Hayward, John, 205
Hayward, Robert, 237
Heath, William, 220
Heathcote, Caleb, 77, 292, 356
Heathcote, George, 292, 356
Heathcote, Gilbert Jr., 292
Heathcote, Sir Gilbert, 292, 304, 308, 367
Heathcote, John, 292, 367

Heathcote, Josiah, 292
Heathcote, Samuel, 77, 281, 290, 292, 306, 367, 382
Heathcote, William, 292
Hebblethwaite, Henry, 240
Hedges, Robert, 203
Hedges, William, 203, 307
heiresses, 47, 367, 373–4, 376, 378, 380, 411
heirlooms, 383
heirs, lack of, 73, 142, 157, 162–3, 192, 231, 309, 321, 354, 377, 383, 405, 411–12
heirs, residual. *See* residual legacies
Hellinas, Elizabeth, 328
Helyar, Cary, 281
Hemming, Bartholomew, 144
Henley, Susan, 70
Henshawe, Charles, 233
Henslow, Philip, 146, 201, 290
heraldic visitations, 275, 296, 446
Herd, Isaac, 296
hereditary trades. *See* generations, sons in business, lineage
Herlan, John, 133
Hern, Frederick, 203
Hern, Sir Joseph, 87, 346, 410
Hern, Nathaniel, 304
Herrick, Mary, 166
Herrick, Robert, 141
Hertau, John, 250
Hertfordshire, 169, 404
Hewitt, John, 81
Hewitt, Judith, 135
Heyward, Joan, 374
Heyward, Sir Rowland, 374
Heywood, Oliver, 46
Heywood, Richard, 364
Hicks, Baptist, 70, 212, 291, 304
Hicks, Elizabeth, 279
Hicks, Michael, 304
Higgens, Edward, 243
Higginbottom, Henry, 237
Hill, Hilary, 299
Hill, John, 297, 333
Hill, Richard, 210, 281, 296
Hill, Samuel, 293
Hill, Thomas, 92, 281, 293
Hill, Valentine, 294
Hill, William, 134, 146

Hilson, Robert, 54
Himner, Catherine, 76
Hind, John, 151
Hingham, 163
Hoare, Benjamin, 363
Hoare, Henry, 363
Hoare, James, 190, 292
Hoare, John, 292
Hoare, Sir Richard, 72, 190, 196, 228, 288, 292, 305, 363
Hoare, Thomas, 196
Hobbes, Thomas, 5, 179, 393
Hobson, Ursula, 318
Hobson, William, 378
Hochstetter, David Jr., 363
Hochstetter, David Sr., 363
Hodges, John, 167
Hodges, Sir Joseph, 196
Hodgson, Giles, 53
Hodgson, Samuel, 202
Holgate, William, 51, 378
holidays, 105, 244
Holland, Hester, 228
Holland, Joshua, 296
Holles, Lady, 399
Hollis, Thomas, 164, 295
Holmes, Henry, 201
home, 252, 264, 393, 403
homosexuality, 78
honor, 44, 58, 88, 99, 335, 414
Hooke, Humphrey, 166, 177
Hope, John, 167
Hopegood, Edmund, 291
Hopkins, Henry, 204
Horner, John, 144
Horwitz, Henry, 20
Hosea, Alexander, 285
Host, Derrick, 73, 341
Houblon, Abraham, 383
Houblon, Isaac, 383
Houblon, James Jr., 353
Houblon, Sir James, 166, 353
Houblon, Mary, 173
Houblon, Sir Richard, 383
Houblon, William, 353
Hough, William, 157
Hounsell, William, 351
household, 2, 5, 10, 17, 76, 81, 89–90, 92, 124, 150, 179, 183, 187, 189, 192–3, 196, 205–6,

household (*cont.*)
225, 243, 248, 251–2, 262–4,
269, 314, 339, 389, 392–5, 414;
accounts, 27, 94, 103, 193–4;
entertainment, 91, 94, 229;
extended, 225; management, 31,
91, 93–6, 193, 316, 336–7, 377;
separate, 198; size, 92, 160–3
householder. *See* household
housekeepers, 53, 81, 138, 146, 187,
236
houses, 98, 102–3. *See also* home
housewifery. *See* household
management
housework. *See* household
management
How, Sir John, 285
Howatt, Elizabeth, 321
Howell, James, 287
Howell, Thomas, 287
Howes, John, 132
Howland, Elizabeth, 332
Hudleston, Wilfrid, 298
Hudson, James, 284, 286
Hudson, John, 206, 212, 300
Hudson, William, 352
Hudson Bay Company, 332
Hughes, Thomas, 348
Huguenots, 56, 87, 171, 194, 259,
308, 322, 381, 447
Hull, 85, 146, 157, 269, 293, 317,
324, 329, 358, 364, 367, 404, 415
Hull, John, 173, 294
Hull, Richard, 379
Hulse, Hugh, 201
Humber, 329
Humphries, Sir William, 143
Hunt, William, 201
Hunter, Henry, 348
Hunter, John, 214
Hunter, Nathaniel, 282, 348
husband abuse, 103, 107
husbandmen, 274
husbands, generosity of, 112–13
Hussey, Sir William, 306–7
Hutchinson, Richard, 294
Hynde, Sarah, 232

ideal types, 4
ideology, 6, 8, 16–17, 30, 255, 388,
390–3, 395–6, 410, 414

idleness, 92, 99, 103, 184, 336, 362,
365, 417
Ile, Christopher, 350
immigration. *See* migrants
immortality, 385
Impey, Andrew, 350
in-laws, 41, 50, 57–8, 67, 87–8, 131,
134, 218–19, 225–6, 228, 230,
232–7, 279, 281, 283, 285,
290–1, 293–9, 301, 305–6, 309,
327, 330, 349, 354–5, 376, 378,
405, 412, 452; income, 339–40,
362–3, 367, 381, 404, 415, 450,
453. *See also* profits, passive
investment
indenture. *See* binding
India, 40, 54, 67, 76, 135, 139, 145,
147, 169, 177, 184, 192, 206,
211–13, 229, 235, 286, 293,
321–2, 324
individualism, 2, 5, 16, 33, 183, 255,
385, 392–3, 394, 413–14, 416–17
industrialization, 1–2, 391, 414, 416
infancy, 31, 171–2
infant mortality, 118, 157–60, 163,
171–2, 174, 187, 392, 449
infatuation. *See* love
infidelity, 31, 43, 45, 97–100, 108.
See also chastity, libertinism
inflation, 380, 444, 454
Ingram, Ralph, 221
inheritance, of house, 72–4, 87, 105–
6, 112, 114, 132, 141, 169, 200,
202, 205, 207, 213, 321, 325–7,
334, 343–4, 348–52, 356, 383; of
land, 66, 112, 148, 205, 218, 237,
342, 349–50, 352–5, 358, 363,
383; partible, 32, 73, 99, 106,
324–5, 342, 353, 366, 384, 398,
411; rights or law of, 71–3, 86,
96, 200, 341–5, 349–51; strategy
of, 385. *See also* London, Custom
of, bequests, primogeniture
innholder, innkeeper. *See* food trades
Inns of Court, 364, 447
inns. *See* taverns
insolvency. *See* bankrupt
insurance, 286, 299
interest rates. *See* usury
intergenesic interval, 169
intermarriage, 9, 20, 32, 47, 54,

56–7, 257, 271, 290, 295, 310, 367, 371, 374, 413
international networks, 308. *See also* kin networks
intestacy, 127, 133, 342, 344. *See also* nuncupative wills
intimacy. *See* emotions
inventories, 21, 24, 29, 95, 97, 132, 151, 187, 233, 318, 331, 346, 399, 445, 451
investment manager. *See* business management
investment, 91, 283–4, 398–9, 402–8, 417. *See also* passive investment
Ipswich, 212, 233, 304, 334, 359, 377, 400
Ireland, 194, 198, 292, 304, 308, 446–7, 449
Ireland, John, 100
Irish, 377, 379
Irish Adventurers, 291
Irish, Richard, 249
iron industry, 270, 288–9, 304, 307, 328–9, 360, 415
ironmaster, 364, 381, 412
ironmonger, 130, 199, 221, 240, 249, 295, 298, 317–18, 323, 346, 448
Isham, John, 228, 333
Isham, Sir Thomas, 377
Isle of Thanet, 223
Italian, 444
Italy, 45, 293, 391, 414. *See also* Leghorn, Venice

Jackson, Henry, 355
Jackson, John, 179
Jackson, Sir Philip, 3–6
Jackson, Robert, 300
Jacob, Alexander, 199
Jacobs, Lucas, 346
Jacobson, Rimbold, 145
Jacques, Joseph, 378
Jamaica, 63, 102, 163, 235, 281, 293, 330, 351, 380
James, Thomas, 293
Janus, George, 237
Japan, 414
Jeaffreson, Christopher, 76, 226
Jeake, Samuel Jr., 75, 77, 98, 172, 176–7, 225, 234, 260, 295

Jeake, Samuel Sr., 77
jealousy. *See* emotions
Jeffereys, John, 137, 241
Jeffereys, Joyce, 321, 336, 338–9
Jeffereys, Thomas, 286
Jennens, Ambrose, 289
Jennens, John, 130, 289
Jennings, William, 285
Jermyn, Stephen, 108
Jerusalem, Alley, 326
Jesson, Jacob, 226
jewelry, 104–6, 111, 135, 150–1, 178, 193, 247–8, 250, 253, 351, 353, 355–6, 374, 383
Jews, 54, 56, 118, 133, 163, 198, 200, 255, 257, 308, 324, 444, 447
Johnson, Sir Henry, 75, 111, 194, 207, 230, 307, 369, 384
Johnson, John, 109, 378
Johnson, Nicholas, 115
Johnson, Robert, 130
joint stocks, 288, 290, 326, 331. *See also* companies, joint stock
jointures, 71–2, 74, 77, 106, 112, 143, 145, 343, 352, 369, 380–1, 405
Jones, John, 142
Jones, Thomas, 133
Jones, William, 78, 261
Josselin, Ralph, 26
Jourdain, Elizabeth, 330
Joyce, Robert, 144
Joyce, William, 225
judicial proceedings, 25, 29, 86, 249, 251, 300, 325, 334
judicial records, 445
Jupe, Thomas, 327
Juxon, Arthur, 150
Juxon, John, 253, 327
Juxon, Thomas, 213

Kaley, Christopher, 113
Kaley, Robert, 212
Keayne, Robert, 235
Kellett, Henry, 145
Kempster, John, 285
Kempthorne, Sir John, 194–5, 381
Kendale, William, 199
Kendall, Grace, 235
Kendall, Jack, 235

Kendall, James, 235
Kendall, John, 288
Kendrick, John, 230, 281
Kent, 47, 63, 125, 228, 269, 287, 329, 349, 352, 356
Kent, James, 234
Kent, Robert, 234
Kent, Thomas, 322
Kent, Walter, 81
Kersteman, Anne, 151
Key, Thomas, 333
kin, as administrators, 230; as advisors, 66, 170–1, 235, 263; affinal and consanguineous, 10, 32, 57, 217, 219, 242; as beneficiaries, 106, 143, 236–7, 354–6; conflicts with, 229–32, 409; definition of, 217–18, 220, 263, 389, 395; as executors, 130–1, 144, 230, 233; frequency of contact, 226–9, 263; as guardians, 131, 144, 179, 225, 230, 234; litigation between, 230, 232; location of, 219, 223, 237, 396; loss of, 228; loyalty of, 263; as masters, 106, 230; networks, 2, 12, 32–3, 225–6, 233, 252, 262, 265, 295–6, 301–2, 305, 309, 311, 387, 393, 402, 410–11, 413, 415–16; numbers of, 217, 220–4, 226, 263; as overseers, 234; paternal, 263; recognition as, 218–20, 395, 452; risks of, 229–32, 298–9; as servants, 53, 81, 248; as source of capital, 235, 282, 285–6; as source of credit, 93, 334; support of, 232–6; as suretors, 235–6, 286; value to business, 297–301, 410, 413, 417; as witnesses, 235
King, Sir Andrew, 81, 315, 328, 356
King, Gregory, 25, 58, 134, 160
King, Raymond, 180
Kingsmill, Andrew, 58
Kingston, 369
Kingston, Earl of, 380
Kingston upon Thames, 325
King's Lynn, 40, 121, 133, 161, 224, 274, 277, 290, 305, 321, 346, 359, 376

kinship. *See* kin
Kirby, Jefferey, 287
Kirby, Mark, 157, 367
Kirkman, Francis, 184, 278, 374
Kitch, Reginald, 212
Kitson, Lady, 399
Kneller, Sir Godfrey, 112
Knight, David, 355
Knight, Elizabeth, 380
Knight, John, 333
Knight, Robert, 242
knighthoods, 384
Knipe, Randolph, 284
Knipe, Richard, 248
Knowles, Thomas, 115

Labon, Robert, 248
Ladds, William, 287
Lade, Sir John, 384
Lait, Thomas, 166
Lambert, Anthony, 157
Lambert, Charles, 226
Lambert, Robert, 350
Lancashire, 206, 229, 241, 404
Lancashire, Robert, 143
Lancaster, Isabel, 329
land law. *See* real property, inheritance, rights of
land, purchase of, 47, 87, 234, 348, 350–1, 353, 355, 360, 363–4, 383, 403, 405–6
land, sale of, 405–6
land, scale of holdings, 403–4, 406
landed estates. *See* landed gentry
landed gentry, 47, 50, 78, 137, 162, 274, 279, 315, 322, 325, 336–7, 340, 342, 350–1, 356, 358–9, 363–4, 367, 374, 380–2, 385, 402, 405, 410, 412, 414, 416, 446, 449, 450. *See also* peerage
landladies, 150, 324, 334
Lane, Elizabeth, 197
Lane, George, 292
Lane, Richard, 74, 112, 197, 210, 349, 380
Lane, Thomas, 113, 327, 406
Lane, William, 140
Langford, William, 167
Langham, Elizabeth, 306
Langham, Sir John, 157, 306

Langham, Samuel, 306
Langham, Sir Stephen, 306
Langhorn, William, 243
Langley, Christopher, 141, 243
Langley, John, 304
Langley, Richard, 304
languages, 180, 194, 225
Lannoy, Ann, 51
Lant, Robert, 86
Larrett, Jane, 314
Laughton, Lucy, 200
laundry, 20, 94, 180, 213
law of retardation, 415
Lawrence, Adam, 322
Lawrence, Isaac, 80, 211–12, 245
Lawrence, William, 76, 80, 82, 211,
    214, 241
Lawson, Nicholas, 341
lawyers, 122, 332, 363
Lea, Philip, 328
lead industry, 318
Lead, John, 233
Leat, Richard, 383
leatherseller, 71, 165, 240, 327, 448
lecherous. *See* libertinism
ledgers. *See* business papers
Lee, Arthur, 73
Lee, Henry, 71
Lee, Sir Henry, 292
Lee, Joshua, 327
Lee, Lawrence, 200
Lee, Rowland, 286
Lee, Susanna, 328
Leeds, 48, 54, 63, 102, 118, 121,
    161, 305, 329, 359, 400, 404
legacies. *See* bequests, residual
    legacies
Legatt, George, 297
Leghorn (Livorno), 210, 293, 289,
    299
legitim, 343
Leicester, 317, 329
Leicestershire, 369
Leigh, Dorothy, 44
Leigh, John, 133
Lemming, John, 105, 346
Le Noble, David, 148
Lenton, Francis, 98
Leppington, Lemuel, 290
Lethieullier, John, 40, 42

Lethieullier, Thomas, 283
letters of renunciation. *See*
    executorship
Levant. *See* Turkey
Levant trade, 306, 360
Levant Company, 270, 275, 304, 306
Levett, James, 229
Levi-Strauss, Claude, 12
Levins, Humphrey, 197
Levitt, Sir Richard, 87, 378
Levy, Isaac, 295, 353
Levy, Joseph, 295
Levy, Moses, 295
Levy, Nathan, 295, 308
Levy, Oliver, 295
Levy, Samuel, 241, 295
Lewis, Edmund, 202
Lewis, Sir John, 376
Lewis, Richard, 233
Lewisham, 352
liabilities. *See* risks, debts
libertinism, 43, 45, 81, 97–8, 165,
    362
Lichfield, 124, 328
Liddell, Elizabeth, 100
Liddell, Francis, 234
Liddell, Henry, 326
Liddell, Thomas, 115
life cycle, 19, 33, 117, 155, 184, 187,
    198, 264, 320, 388–9, 392, 398,
    406, 409
life expectancy, 31, 80, 117–23, 151,
    235, 354, 366, 373, 396–7
life interest. *See* annuities
Linckbeeck, Hans Cornelius, 363
Lincoln, 400
Lincolns Inn. *See* Inns of Court
Lincolnshire, 63, 102, 404
lineage, 143, 342, 352, 382–4, 385,
    405, 411, 417
linen draper, 321–3, 374
liquidation, 132–4, 331, 407, 411–12
liquidity, 398–9, 402, 406, 408
Lisbon, 292
Lister, John, 295, 364
literacy, 193
literary criticism, 3n, 6, 43n, 51,
    387
literary sources, 115, 335, 419. *See
    also* advice books

litigation. *See* judicial proceedings
Liverpool, 72, 289, 319, 332, 358
living in sin. *See* libertinism
Livingstone, Robert, 323
Lloyd, John, 300
loan charities, 240, 253, 287, 338
loans. *See* credit
Locke, John, 5, 14, 25, 91, 182, 208, 343, 365
Locke, Samuel, 378
Lockey, Henry, 362
Lodge, Thomas, 163
lodgers, 92, 160, 187, 225, 243, 318, 331
logwood, 292
London, aldermen of, 20, 118–20, 123, 135, 146, 160, 175, 253, 275, 305, 344, 373–4, 403, 448, *see also* civic elite; citizens of, 20, 120, 168, 242–3, 252–3, 255, 271–3, 275, 312, 314, 316, 343–5, 403, 446, *see also* freedom; city of, 252, 298; Commissary Court of, 345; common councilors, 20, 255; Consistory Court of, 86, 108, 120, 160, 317; Court of Aldermen, 66; Court of Orphans, 24, 143, 331, 344, 378, 445, 451–2; Custom of, 71, 87, 113, 116, 124, 196, 312, 342–6, 348, 351–2, 379, 399, 452, *see also* primogeniture; evasion of the Custom, 342–5, 348, 350–1, 453; livery companies, 47, 51, 149, 240, 242, 252–3, 255–6, 261, 280, 314–16, 356, *see also* under names of individual companies; Lord Mayor's Court, 168, 348; marriages in, 61
London Cuckold, 97
London Libertine, 97
London Womens' Meeting, 337
looms, 313
Lore, Sir Peter van, 146
love, 4, 7–9, 10, 27, 37–42, 46–7, 58, 74, 80, 82–3, 87, 90, 109–10, 111–12, 147–8, 173, 175, 177, 180, 182, 190, 192, 206, 209, 354, 362, 367, 369, 394–5
Lovell, Dudley, 348

Low, Francis, 333
Low, Sir Thomas, 113
Lowe, Roger, 41, 207, 277
Lowther, Anthony, 213
Lowther, Christopher, 292
Lowther, Hugh, 369
Lowther, Richard, 292
Lowther, Robert, 292
Lowther, William, 279, 369
Lucas, Thomas, 383
Lucke, Martha, 321, 329
Lucke, Samuel, 329
lust. *See* sexuality
Lustring company, 313
Lyle, Anne, 244
Lyme, Regis, 363
Lyon, Thomas, 164
Lysons, Daniel, 118

Mabbe, John, 353
Machell, Nicholas, 112
Maddison, Elizabeth, 100
Maddison, Henry, 100
Maddox, William, 348
Madeira, 176
madness, 107, 151, 170
Maidstone, 307
Main, Robert, 288
Maister, Henry, 157
Maitland, Frederick William, 15
Mallett, William, 57
Mallory, Edward, 240
Malynes, Gerard, 262
Manchester, 147, 168, 260, 295, 299, 305, 329, 346, 403
Mancio, Abraham, 248
Mandeville, Bernard de, 38
Manifold, John, 290
Mann, Daniel, 304
Mann, John, 303
Mann, Nathaniel, 207
Mann, Robert, 143, 237
Mann, Thomas, 377
manners. *See* behavior
manpower. *See* recruitment
manuals. *See* advice books
manufacturing, 328–9, 275–7, 317, 336, 446–7
Manwaring, Charles, 234
mapselling, 328
Marblehead, 257

March, Francis, 72
Marcus, Moses, 198
Marescoe, Charles, 179, 330, 378
Marescoe, Leonora, 145, 150, 330
marginal utility, law of, 340
market economy, 264, 335, 336–7,
   340, 387, 390, 392–4, 410,
   416–17. *See also* capitalism
marketplace. *See* market economy
Markland, Matthew, 361
marriage, age of, 24, 44, 58–65, 83,
   125, 138, 158, 164, 396, 416,
   449; allegations, 24, 61, 366, 445;
   arranged, 31, 37, 46, 83;
   avoidance of, 64, 78, 80, *see also*
   bachelors; by banns, 24, 75;
   bonds, 24, 68; brokers, 68;
   clandestine, 65; conflicts within,
   102–8; with consent, 65–6, 75,
   237, 366, 377–9; with consent of
   kin, 377–8; with consent of
   siblings, 377; with consent of
   widow, 377–8; without consent,
   41, 43, 209, 231–2, 369, 378–9,
   376, 378–9, 381; conventions, 37,
   76, 88–92; denominational, 56–7,
   259; duration of, 31, 100–2, 392,
   450; exogenous, 9, 83, 407;
   expectations, 83–4; with kin,
   57–8; law of, 37, 65–6, 85–8,
   107; by license, 24, 63, 75;
   litigation, 77, 98, 108–9, 253;
   market, 46, 66, 82–3, 380–2; with
   master's daughter or widow, 50–1;
   for money, 46–8, 69, 82, 146–7;
   postnuptial agreements, 72, 88;
   postponement of, 80; process of,
   31, 85, 92–7, 115–16;
   prohibitions, 57–8, 65–6; quality
   of, 108–10; risks of, 83; rituals,
   228, 232; settlements, 32, 66,
   70–6, 86, 109, 112–13, 148, 151,
   203, 230, 343–5, 349–51,
   369–70, 381; for status, 48–50,
   83; theories of, 115–16, 394;
   timing of, 37, 58–65, 75; value to
   business, 281, 286, 305–8. *See
   also* spouse
Marriott, Samuel, 298
Marsden, Thomas, 292
Marseille, 292, 294

Marshall, Alfred, 409
Marshall, Joshua, 144
Marshall, William, 278
Marten, Malachy, 248
Martin, Roger, 115
Marx, Karl, 4–7, 387
Marxism. *See* Marx, Karl
Maryland, 314, 345
mason, 313, 448
Massachusetts, 396
Massinger, Philip, 46, 97
Master, Streynsham, 40, 76, 146
masters of apprentices, 38, 50–1,
   178, 184–5, 213, 242, 277, 303,
   306; as source of capital, 283,
   286–7
Masters, Anne, 211
Masters, Richard, 284
Masters, Robert, 211
Masterton, Francis, 46
maternal mortality, 124
maternity, age of, 169
matriarchs, 150
Maurois, Jeanne, 76
Maxwell, James, 176
May, Richard, 133
Mayer, Ralph, 78
Mayor, Jereman, 166
meals. *See* food
mediation. *See* arbitration
Mediterranean, 293
Meese, Henry, 112
Melling, Thomas, 205
Mellish, Edward, 280
Mellish, George, 348
Mellish, Robert, 280
mementoes, 178, 213, 383
memo fields, 441, 453
mentalities, 2, 6, 175, 185, 388,
   395
mercer, 61, 120, 170, 199, 221, 240,
   247–8, 250, 274, 279, 281, 283,
   291, 296, 315, 318, 321–2, 329,
   354, 360, 362–4, 379, 383, 448
Mercers Company, 150
Merchant Adventurers, 45, 121, 168,
   237, 275, 278, 280–1, 315, 362
merchant, domestic, 23, 61, 161,
   253, 289, 315, 318, 320–1, 350,
   377, 400, 404–5, 407–8, 415,
   447

merchant, overseas, 23, 112, 162, 167, 169, 178, 180, 200, 204, 207–8, 212, 220, 226–7, 240–1, 243, 248, 250, 262, 281, 285, 289, 293–4, 296, 300, 304, 306–8, 317, 321–2, 328, 341, 346, 348, 351, 353–4, 355–6, 360–2, 364, 379–81, 404, 447
merchant tailor, 53, 112, 132, 142–3, 164, 178, 194–5, 205, 209, 219, 221, 223, 225, 233, 244–5, 247–50, 253, 274–5, 283, 290–1, 314, 321, 326, 348–9, 351–3, 355, 405, 451–2
Merchant tailors company, 315
Merchants Map of Commerce, 243
Merttins, Sir George, 87
Meux, Samuel, 289
Meux, Thomas, 289
middle age, 155, 204
Middlesex, 275, 403, 446, 451
Middleton, Sir Hugh, 57, 137, 212
Middleton, Sir Thomas, 57, 212, 306
Midlands, 307
midwives, 170, 319, 321
migrants, 47, 56, 61, 66, 118, 225, 227, 243, 251–2, 259, 275, 294, 296, 307, 314, 413. *See also* aliens
Mildmay, Sir Humphrey, 243
Miller, Isaac, 350
milliner, 320–1, 448
Millington, Edward, 134
Millington, Roger, 50
Mills, John, 106
Millward, William, 242
Milner, Benjamin, 279
Milner, Joseph, 279
Minehead, 157
Mingay, William, 71
minors, 65–6, 112, 155, 366
misbehavior. *See* behavior
miscarriage, 170
misogyny, 78
Mitchell, Hester, 71
Mitchell, John, 99
Mitchell, Thomas, 71
Mitford, Michael, 73, 151, 213, 226, 235–6, 243–4, 246, 302–3, 384, 408–9

Mitley, George, 348
Mitton, Peter, 227, 286, 352
modernization, 1–4, 6, 8, 10, 32, 390
Molyneux, John, 72
Mompesson, Drew, 103, 285
Mompesson, Thomas, 231
Monmouthshire, 415
monopolies, 270, 302, 304, 410
Montford, Lord, 377
Montgomery, Adam, 290
monuments, 111, 114–15, 197, 199, 207–8, 211, 247, 383, 445
Moore, Cicely, 53
Moore, Francis, 144
Moore, John, 248
Moore, Sir John, 139, 223, 80, 301, 344
Moore, Susanna, 318
moral economy, 6, 264, 392, 413
Morea joint stock, 290
Morgan, Joshua, 72
Morgan, Lewis, 7
Morrice, Humphrey, 75
Morrice, William, 197, 380
Morris, Jane, 81
Morris, John, 80
Morse, Henry, 298
mortgages, 334, 403–5
Mosley, Nicholas, 289
Mosley, Rowland, 289
mother-in-law. *See* in-laws
motherhood, 171, 173, 179, 181, 192
motivation, 409–10, 412–13
mourning, 114, 142, 218–19, 228, 250, 261
Mowse, Richard, 41, 87
Moyer, Jacob, 204
Moyer, Sir Samuel, 248, 286, 298, 363
Mun, John, 280
Mun, Thomas, 87, 280, 405
Muschamp, Thomas, 285
Muscovy. *See* Russia
music, 96, 180, 194, 346, 351
mutuality, 90, 116
Myers, Walter, 218
myths, 16

names, first, 22, 170–1, 242–3; last, 9, 22, 48, 85, 90, 196, 273, 279,

360, 383, 447; maiden, 449; transcription of, 444
Napier, Richard, 42
Narva, 289
Nash, Thomas, 98
national debt, 333, 406
Needham, Francis, 247
needlework, 95, 112, 193–4, 315, 317
neighbors, 246, 249–52, 263–4, 329; as overseers, 250; as source of credit, 250
Nelson, John, 306
Nelthorp, Richard, 287
nephews, 225, 230, 231–2, 235–7, 240, 279–81, 285, 291, 293, 294–5, 301, 304, 307, 328, 352, 356, 363–4, 376, 379, 383, 400, 407, 415
nepotism, 5, 262, 271, 408
net worth. *See* wealth
Netherlands, 56, 207, 236, 292
never married, 78, 217, 235, 247, 322, 367, 449–50. *See also* bachelors
new economic history, 17, 19
New England, 63, 122, 163, 223, 226, 235, 255, 278, 293–4, 308–9, 314, 345–6
New Jersey, 309
New York City, 54, 64, 130, 163, 212, 226, 241, 292–5, 305, 308–9, 313, 321, 323, 330, 345–6, 353, 356
Newcastle, 45, 48, 99, 115, 121, 131, 168, 193, 225, 234, 252, 278, 280–1, 293, 315, 325–6, 350, 352, 358, 381
Newcombe, Henry, 103, 178
Newell, Thomas, 377
Newfoundland, 227
Newfoundland Company, 294
Newton, Richard, 72
Newton, Samuel, 244
Niccholes, Alexander, 43, 141
Nicholls, William, 247
Nichols, Abraham, 229
Nicholson, Clement, 300
Nicholson, John, 303
nicknames, 174

Nicks, Catherine, 321
Nicks, John, 321
nieces, 57, 87, 135, 225, 227, 231, 235–7, 240, 249, 307, 315, 384
Nodes, George, 51
Noell, Martin, 293
Noell, Thomas, 293
Nonconformists, 56, 255, 257, 259, 308, 376, 447. *See also* Quakers
Norfolk, 105
Norman, Alexander, 137
norms. *See* ideology
Norris, Henry, 303
Norris, James, 67, 227
Norris, Thomas, 286
North, Sir Dudley, 131, 172, 206
North, Montague, 80
Northampton, Earl of, 364, 380
Northamptonshire, 47, 125, 329, 404
Northumberland, 404
Northwest Company, 332
Norway, 293
Norwich, 57, 64, 100, 121, 134, 161, 224, 255, 273–4, 277, 279, 295, 304–5, 308, 314–15, 326, 328–9, 346, 359, 367, 374, 403
Norwood, Richard, 379
Nottingham, 313, 331
nuncupative wills, 111, 201, 242, 351, 383
nursing, 111, 138, 153, 159, 172–3, 179, 373

Oakley, Edward, 194
obligations. *See* business morality
occupations. *See* careers
office holders. *See* public office
Offley, Henry, 172
Offley, John, 157
Olcott, Thomas, 349
old age, 80, 117–18, 134, 137–8, 193, 198, 204, 206, 301, 339, 398, 407–9
oligarchy. *See* civic elite
Ongley, Sir Samuel, 231, 323, 383
Onslow, 2nd Lord, 380
Oporto, 212, 246
Oram, Nicholas, 175
Ord, Tryphena, 76
Orlaby, Clement, 363

Orlaby, George, 363
orphans, 20, 53, 65–6, 74, 112, 120,
    143, 146–7, 155, 166–8, 187,
    197, 203, 213, 225, 230, 232–3,
    259, 287, 315, 345, 348, 363,
    369, 376, 378, 398–9; number of,
    31, 450
Orton, Abraham, 247
Osborn, Edward, 50
Osterley, 405
Otgar, David, 58
Otton, Mathias, 308
overseers, 127, 145, 202, 233–4,
    242, 246, 250, 377–8, 452
Overton, Robert, 204
Owen, Charles, 326
Owen, Thomas, 245
ownership. *See* shareholders, capital
Oxenden, Sir George, 69, 229, 235
Oxenden, Henry, 76
Oxenden, Richard, 211, 226, 229,
    280, 374
Oxford, 50, 102, 175, 277, 317, 321,
    325–6, 329, 359

Page, Sir Gregory, 382
Page, John, 250
Paggen, Peter, 170
Paggen, Sarah, 170
Paggen, William, 378
Paice, Joseph, 40
Paige, John, 298, 405
Pain, Robert, 53
Painter, Gowen, 355
paintings, 112, 172–3, 193, 211,
    319, 346, 353, 356, 383
Paiva, Jacques da, 81
Palavicino, Sir Horatio, 133
Palmer, Thomas, 244, 247, 356
Palmer, William, 201
Papillon, David, 67, 176, 308
Papillon, Elizabeth, 192, 207
Papillon, George, 67
Papillon, Jane, 96, 103, 109, 177,
    179, 233, 259, 370, 373
Papillon, Philip, 177, 233, 285, 308,
    352, 369–73
Papillon, Samuel, 233
Papillon, Sarah, 177, 207
Papillon, Thomas, 50, 57, 74, 93,
    103, 109, 172, 175, 177, 205,

    229–31, 235–6, 244, 260, 292,
    335, 369–74
Paravicini, Sir Peter, 308, 376, 378
parents, 25, 31–2, 53, 91, 94, 172–4;
    attitude to children, 196–7;
    authority, 179–80, 187, 196–7,
    366–7, 385; death, 394;
    disappointment, 195–6, 215, 365,
    408; occupation, 274–5;
    responsibilities of, 173, 176,
    180–1, 196, 215, 341–2, 362,
    384–5, 413; rights of, 179–81;
    substitute, 155, 172, 176–9, 187,
    392; worries, 194, 215
Pargiter, Giles, 282
Pargiter, Richard, 230
Paris, 296
parishes, 61, 123–4, 160, 224, 250,
    261, 326, 383, 445, 449
Parker, Christopher, 308
Parker, John, 71, 351
Parker, Robert, 221
Parker, Thomas, 248, 293
Parker, Timothy, 325
Parkin, Elizabeth, 321
Parliament, houses of, 47, 50, 78,
    108, 122, 136, 255, 262, 328,
    332, 361, 404, 406, 448
Parsons, Hannah, 214
Parsons, Humphrey, 232
Parsons, John, 245, 291
Parsons, William, 350
partnerships, 231, 283–4, 290, 294;
    business, 32, 134, 140, 243,
    247–8, 269–71, 278, 281, 302,
    305–6, 308–9, 310, 322, 325,
    327, 330, 335, 363, 365, 376,
    405, 409, 412–14, 453; colliery,
    270; father and sons, 288–9, 411;
    husband and wife, 91–2, 94, 97,
    325; with kin, 290–1, 414; outside
    the family, 291–2, 414; siblings,
    289, 363; widow and children,
    327, 330, 340; widow and kin,
    327, 340; widow and second
    husband, 330
Partridge, Richard, 232
Parvis, Henry, 227
passion. *See* emotion
passive investment, 32, 150, 271,
    282, 288, 309, 312, 322, 331–4,

340, 366, 402, 406–7, 444, 451.
    See also investments
paternity, age of, 169
patriarchy, 7–9, 33, 91–2, 116, 179,
    208, 216, 248, 264, 312, 335–6,
    339–40, 342, 358, 387, 389,
    393–4, 409–10, 417
patrimony, 271–2, 312, 315, 356,
    359, 405, 412–13, 447
patronage, 96, 229, 235, 243, 262,
    280, 302, 304, 309, 413
Patterson, William, 354
pawnbrokers, 319, 321, 334. *See also*
    credit
Payne, Charles, 67, 211, 227
Peacham, Henry, 99
Peak, Edward, 246
Peak, Sir Robert, 81, 88
Pearson, Nicholas, 284
Pearson, Richard, 142, 351
peer group. *See* adolescence
peerage, 50, 63, 80, 102, 122,
    124–5, 137, 140, 146, 162, 164,
    168, 367, 374, 377, 380, 384,
    446
Peers, Sir Charles, 233, 297, 333,
    355
Pelham, Lucy, 42, 211
Pelham, Peregrine, 146
Pelham, Thomas, 300
Pengelly, Rachel, 96, 150, 225, 336
Pengelly, Thomas, 294, 404
Penn, William, 406
Penning, Nicholas, 141
Pennoyer, Samuel, 219
Pennsylvania, 309, 313, 356, 406
Pepperill, William, 411
Pepys, Charles, 106
Pepys, Mary, 106
Pepys, Samuel, 40, 92, 98, 100, 378
Pereira, Rebecca, 70
Perrin, Edith, 135
Perry, Robert, 111
personal identity. *See* personality
personal relationship. *See* connection
personality, 65, 83, 88–9, 96, 102–3,
    115, 171, 173–4, 181, 187, 195,
    197, 208, 216, 263, 362, 365, 377,
    385, 391, 395
personalty, 85–6, 112, 203, 338,
    343–6, 348–50, 352–3, 379, 383,

399, 402–3, 406, 413, 451. *See*
    also property
Pescod, Nicholas, 68
Petchell, Thomas, 141, 364
Peterson, Peter, 327
Petrie, Lady Katherine, 315
Petsworth, 329, 359
Pett, Peter, 68
Pett, Phineas, 40, 68
Pettiwood, Roger, 87, 282
Petty, Sir William, 117
pewterer, 96, 106, 444
Pewterer's Company, 53, 315
Philadelphia, 163, 360
Phill, Henry, 296, 333
Phillips, Charles, 283
Phillips, John, 250
Phillips, Robert, 73
Phillips, William, 77, 207, 211, 244,
    283, 297, 302, 408
Phipps, James, 190, 232, 289
Phipps, Thomas, 362
piety. *See* godliness
Pike, Joseph, 309, 349
Pilgrim, Thomas, 378
Pillstone, James, 295
pinmaking, 329
Pinney, Azariah, 145, 206
Piton, James, 178
Pitt, John, 231, 246
Pitt, Phineas, 213
Pitt, Robert, 41, 103, 180, 199,
    240
Pitt, Sarah, 145, 246, 364
Pitt, Thomas, 56, 67, 100, 103–4,
    199, 231, 234, 240, 323, 350
placement. *See* patronage
Plaisterer, Henry, 144
Plampin, Thomas, 202
plate. *See* jewelry
Platt, Richard, 240
play. *See* children, games of
plumber, 327, 448
Plymouth, 202
poll tax, 400, 448. *See also* tax
    records
Pool, Francis, 42
Poole, 161
poor, 214, 240–1, 251, 256, 260–1,
    331
Pope, Michael, 352

population, general, 63, 124, 138, 163–4, 166, 168–9, 224, 366
port books, 23, 317, 327, 451
Port Royal, Jamaica, 321
Porter, Anne, 320
portions, 41, 43, 46–7, 58, 65, 68, 70–1, 87, 130, 139, 146–7, 194, 212, 240, 247, 284, 286, 338, 341, 342, 351–2, 355, 367, 369–73, 376–7, 379–82, 385, 397–8, 401, 405, 450; method of payment, 379; portion-jointure ratio, *see* jointures; size of, 73–5; as source of capital, 286; value of, 379–81
portraits. *See* paintings
Portugal, 281, 292
Portuguese, 54–6
possessive individualism. *See* individualism
Potts, Nathan, 200–1
Poulton, Silvester, 145
Povey, Richard, 293
Povey, Thomas, 210, 231
Povey, William, 210, 293
Powell, Rowland, 220
Power, Katherine, 329
Pranel, Henry, 367
pregnancy, 44–5, 53, 93, 109, 143–4, 167–8, 170, 194, 351
premature death, 178
premium. *See* binding
Presbyterians. *See* Nonconformists
prescriptive literature. *See* family, theories of
pride. *See* social ambition
Priestley, John, 75, 285, 293, 364
Priestley, Jonathan, 40, 47, 286, 364
Priestley, Thomas, 199
primary assets, 451. *See also* investment
primogeniture, 32, 86, 210, 342, 345–6, 352, 398
principals, 288–92
printing. *See* publishing
privacy, 187, 251–2, 264, 395, 417
private and public sphere, 6–7, 92–3, 96, 251–2, 260, 394, 396
probability, 17, 20, 162, 166, 168, 398, 401, 411

probate administration, 25, 28, 127, 132, 246, 452. *See also* wills, inventories, executors
probate litigation, 132–3, 143, 151, 197, 202–3, 209. *See also* judicial proceedings
Proctor, Edward, 143
Proctor, Thomas, 234
production, 92, 277, 282, 392, 402, 409, 448
professions, 48, 257, 273–4, 315, 336, 340, 356, 359, 362, 364, 374, 377, 382, 394, 405, 411–12, 446–7, 449–50
profit, 340, 398, 402–3, 407. *See also* income
property, movable, *see* personalty; rights, 4–8, 25, 37, 46, 67, 76, 82, 149, 174, 180, 204–5, 341–2, 412, 417; rights of women, *see* couverture, inheritance, rights of; separate, 73, 86–7, 103, 106, 134, 321–2, 388; transfer of, 32, 204, 209, 220, 282, 341–2, 385, 398, 402, 417. *See also* inheritance
Prowde, Richard, 214, 285
puberty, 38, 184–5, 189
public office, 224, 253, 255, 262, 273, 314, 382, 406, 409, 411, 446, 448
publishing, 318, 328, 330, 332
Pullis, Sir Thomas, 205
Purcell, Thomas, 278
Pye, Thomas, 282
Pynchon, John, 289, 377
Pynchon, William, 289

Quakers, 41–2, 56, 64, 66, 102, 107, 122, 137, 162, 181, 259, 270, 279, 308–9, 329, 396, 411, 447
Quaker's Wife, 97
Quarles, John, 281
Quarles, William, 201
Quince, John, 114

Rabb, Theodore, 20
Radcliffe, Jane, 169
Radcliffe, Ralph, 398
Radcliffe, Walter, 71
ragione. *See* firm

Raikes, William, 280
Rainton, Sir Nicholas, 221
Raleigh, Sir Walter, 290
Ramesey, William, 89
Ramsey, John, 232
Ramsey, Sir Thomas, 242
Randall, Alice, 41
Randall, John, 281
Randall, Vincent, 289
Randolph, John, 405
rape, 182
Rappaport, Steve, 20
rationality, 11, 14, 44, 182, 384, 389–90, 395, 410, 413
Ravenscroft, George, 289
Rawdon, Marmaduke, 41, 68, 80, 176, 184, 206–7, 229, 242, 279
Rawdon, Sir Marmaduke, 47
Rawston, Samuel, 236
Rawstorn, Sir William, 306
Raynold, Jonas, 200
Raynton, Sir Nicholas, 363
real property, 66, 72–3, 86, 142, 203, 209, 212, 331, 343, 345–6, 350, 352, 403–5, 412–13, 453. *See also* urban property, inheritance of land
reasonable part. *See* inheritance, rights of
recommendations. *See* references
recruitment, 32, 71–7, 309, 408, 413
redemption, 271–3, 447
Reeve, Henry, 144, 352
references, 280–1
refugees, 56, 308, 328. *See also* aliens
religion, conversion, 198, 200; denominations of, 447; value to business, 308–9
remarriage, attitude of children, 145, 151; attitude of husbands, 141–5, 151; benefits of, 149–51; choice of partner, 139–40; decision to remarry, 135, 138–9, 145–9, 151, 339; frequency of, 31, 50, 125, 135–7, 151; general view of, 44, 137, 140–5, 151; location of spouse, 140; timing of, 137–9, 151
Renew, Daniel, 294
Renew, Peter, 294

rentier. *See* passive investment
representation, 16, 25, 89, 395
reputation. *See* honor
residence abroad, 93, 176, 184, 206, 212, 224, 248, 253, 289, 448
residential segregation, 251
residual estate. *See* residual legacies
residual legacies, 106, 112, 158, 201, 205, 237, 241, 249, 349, 354
retailers, 94, 161, 253, 261, 277, 315, 317, 318–20, 321–3, 324–5, 328–9, 336, 338–9, 447–8
Retford, 346
retirement income, 205, 339, 402–3, 408
returns. *See* income
reversion. *See* descent
Reynardson, Sir Abraham, 141, 288
Reynolds, Anthony, 297
Reynolds, Elizabeth, 327
rhetoric. *See* representation
Rich, Sir Charles, 209
Rich, Elizabeth, 209
Rich, Leonard, 244
Richards, Richard, 247
Richards, William, 384
Richardson, Christopher, 280
Richardson, Peter, 85
Rickert, Heinrich, 4
Riddell, Henry, 100
Riles, Susanna, 328
risk, 286, 299, 338, 403, 405, 411, 413–14, 417
Rivers, Samuel, 143
Roberts, Barne, 111
Roberts, Lewis, 243
Robinson, Elizabeth, 379
Robinson, John, 379
Robinson, Sir John, 141
Robinson, Robert, 179, 182, 415
Robinson, Sarah, 104
Robinson, Thomas, 157
Robsart, Arthur, 237
Rochester, 334
Rodway, William, 219
Rogers, Francis, 40, 46, 90–1
Rogers, John, 157
Rogers, Philip, 241
Rogers, Richard, 143
Rogerson, John, 294

roles, 265, 389, 395
Rolles, Gertrude, 320
romances, 38, 70
Rombouts, Helen, 330
Rome, 211
Romford, 161
Rotterdam, 293
Row, Thomas, 348
Rowse, John, 182
Roxana, 320
Royal Africa Company, 236
Royal Exchange, 318, 320
runaways, 197–8
Russell, Francis, 76
Russell, Thomas, 219
Russia, 86, 290, 293
Russia Company, 332–3, 367
Russian trade, 278, 400
Rutter, William, 326
Rycaut, James, 299
Rycaut, Paul, 299
Ryder, George, 378
Rye, Sussex, 168, 330, 359–60
Ryton, 225

sabbath, 192
saddler, 248, 328, 350, 448
Saddlers company, 253
Sadler, John, 168
Saire, Francis, 106, 279, 383
Salem, 313
Salisbury, 166, 321
Salloway, John, 348
salter, 87, 144, 150, 164, 195, 201, 219, 282, 289–90, 292, 321, 348, 353, 383, 406
Salter, Thomas, 351
Saltonstall, Wye, 38, 141
Sambrook, Sir Jeremy, 151, 406
San Lucar, 293
Sanders, Robert, 353
Sanderson, John, 45, 77, 93, 192, 209, 211–12, 225, 240, 280
Sanderson, Lucy, 315
Sanderson, William, 105, 290
Savage, Sarah, 114, 183
Saville, Robert, 282
saving, 402
Sawbridge, George, 50
Sawbridge, Hannah, 328

Scarsdale, Earl of, 376
Scattergood, Betty, 192
Scattergood, John, 103, 192, 210, 232
Scattergood, Roger, 103
Scawen, Sir Thomas, 362–3
Scawen, Sir William, 344
schoolmaster, 178, 180, 183, 185–6
scolds, 90–1, 103, 198
Scotland, 122, 270, 274, 404, 412, 446–7, 449
Scots, 56, 377
Scott, Elizabeth, 73
Scott, John, 185
Scott, Jonathan, 296
Scott, Richard, 351
Scott, William, 337
scrivener, 146, 243, 352, 407, 448
Scrivener's Company, 315
Scudamore, John, 283
seamstress. *See* needlework
secrecy, 249, 302, 337
sects, 308, 323, 447
security. *See* bond
Segalen, Martine, 12
self consciousness, 84, 395
Self, 100
self–help, 302, 392–3, 416. *See also* individualism, agency
self–interest. *See* individualism
Sell, John, 133
Selly, Simon, 327
Selwood, Bartholomew, 144
sensuality. *See* emotions
sentiment. *See* emotions
separate residence, 198, 206. *See also* coresidence
separation, legal, 98, 107–8, 344
Seracole, George, 283
Seracole, Ralph, 283
Serra, Antonio Gomes, 150
servants, 45, 53, 69, 73, 81, 92, 94–5, 98, 103, 106–7, 113, 137, 179, 184, 187, 224–5, 242, 248–9, 376, 409
Sevenoaks, 329
Sewall, Samuel, 365
Sewell, Katherine, 40
sexuality, 8–9, 37–9, 42–5, 76, 90, 97–9, 137, 141, 147–8, 170, 335,

373; abstinence, 45, 170; diseases, 43, 56, 97; disorders, 98, 181; premarital, 43–5, 65
Shadwell, Thomas, 97
Shaker, Margery, 178
Shallett, Arthur, 308
shareholders, 313, 332, 406
Sharpe, William, 109, 191, 226
Shaw, Hester, 319
Shaw, Ralph, 328
Sheaffe, Edmund, 157
Sheffield, 360
Shelley, Giles, 356
Shepherd, Samuel, 377
Sheppard, Edmund, 350
Sheppard, Richard, 68, 196
Sheppard, Thomas, 230
Sherbrook, John, 100
Sherbrook, Richard, 376
Sherburn, 360
Sheriff, Richard, 106
Sherman, Edmund, 73, 281
Sherman, Richard, 145, 283
Sherman, Rowland, 282
Sherrington, William, 355
Shershaw, Henry, 105,
shipping industry, 203, 288, 290, 295, 307, 323, 325, 327, 332, 360, 381, 410, 412, 447
shoemaker. *See* cordwainer
shopkeeper. *See* retailer
Showell, Richard, 296
Shrewsbury, 63, 130, 161, 171, 225, 242, 260, 289, 346, 351, 359, 377, 382, 405
Shropshire, 72, 227, 296, 354
siblings, as advisors, 66; as agents, 293–6; harmony, 32, 210–15; loss of, 211–12; rivalry, 199, 208–10, 354; as source of capital, 214, 284
sickness, 93–4, 100, 105, 113, 120, 150, 159–60, 180, 185, 190, 205–7, 212, 232, 245, 319, 323, 365, 408–9
Sidney, Walgrave, 349
silkman, 279, 291
silk weavers, 313, 315
Silverlock, James, 135
silversmith, 318, 322

Silvester, Elizabeth, 81
Simmel, George, 413
Simmons, Samuel, 197
Simpson, George, 113
Simpson, Nathan, 213
Simson, Duffy, 330
Simson, Nathan, 69
single parenting, 166, 177–8
singlewomen, 32, 145, 212, 312, 319, 329. *See also* women, femes soles
sister-in-law. *See* in-laws
Sitwell, Francis, 329
Sitwell, George, 283, 292
Sjoberg, Gideon, 411
skinner, 200, 207–8, 218, 228, 240–1, 243, 248, 293, 314, 317, 321, 350, 352, 362, 448
Skinner, Matthew, 212
Skinner, Thomasine, 87
Skinners Company, 53, 253, 409
slander, 44, 86, 103, 335. *See also* judicial proceedings
Sledmore, 367
small world theory, 310
Smallbridge, Anne, 328
smallpox. *See* sickness
Smallwood, Humphrey, 213
Smirna, 176, 243, 294, 302
smith, 313, 448
Smith, Adam, 38 n11
Smith, Agnes, 326
Smith, Henry, 91, 95, 172, 241
Smith, James, 87
Smith, John, 168
Smith, Robert, 205
Smith, Simon, 166
Smith, Thomas, 248
Smith, Wolfran, 241
Smythe, Customer, 111, 141, 157
Smythe, Helena, 333
Smythe, James, 292
Smythe, Richard, 103, 114
Sneyd, Elizabeth, 336
social ambition, 96–7, 336, 340, 342, 373–4, 376, 380, 383, 417
social differentiation, 37, 184, 251–2, 263, 382, 388, 395, 446. *See also* status
sodomy, 44. *See also* homosexuality

Sole, William, 343
Solomon, Francis, 247
Somersetshire, 325
Sondes, Sir George, 230
son-in-law. *See* in-laws
sons, adult, 189–92; in business, 273,
    356–62, 385, 416; careers of, 32,
    197, 341, 362–5, 450; choice of
    career, 362–6; education of, 362;
    eldest, 199, 234, 345–6, 348,
    350–1, 353, 355–6, 359, 362–4,
    367, 382–3, 385, 416, *see also*
    birth order; as executors, 200,
    353; financial provision for,
    282–4, *see also* children, provision
    for; marriages of, 32, 366–9, 449,
    450; marriage without consent,
    369; rejection of business, 365;
    sector of trade, 273, 283, 288,
    356, 360–1, 410–11, 448; talents
    of, 362; younger, 47, 78, 80, 198,
    209–10, 213, 237, 279, 283, 287,
    289, 292, 294, 348–9, 352–6,
    359, 363, 365, 367, 374, *see also*
    birth order
sources, 3, 9, 17, 19, 21–30, 275,
    277, 287, 319–20, 334, 387,
    419–23
South Sea Company, 332
Southampton, 93, 161, 225, 277,
    329, 338
Southwark, 54, 160, 224–5, 253,
    314, 318, 355, 446
Sowers, Robert, 237
space, 187
Spain, 54, 95, 133, 289, 292–3, 297,
    299
Spateman, Rebecca, 68
Spencer, Elizabeth, 376
Spencer, Sir John, 374, 376
Spencer, Nicholas, 286
spinster. *See* never married,
    singlewomen
spousals, 65–6, 75,
spouse, choice of, 20, 31, 37, 46–7,
    56–7, 64, 81–4, 396; equality of,
    111, 116, 334; location of 37,
    53–6, 83, 449; loss of, 113–15,
    151; marital status, 51, 60–3, 449;
    religion of, 56–7, 83; social status

of, 37, 367, 449
Springfield, 404
Sprott, William, 350
Spurstow, Henry, 41
St. Botolph within Aldgate, 160
St. Dunstans, 383
St. Giles within Cripplegate, 320
St. Helens, 346
St. Ives, 224, 359
St James, Duke's Place, 51, 61, 138–9
St. John's College, Oxford, 151
St. Leonards, Eastcheap, 160
St. Loe, Mary, 81
Stafford, Lord, 194
Stallin, Emmanuel, 404
Stanford, Hugh, 134
Stanier, James, 207
Stanley, Thomas, 377
Staple, merchant of, 379
Starkey, Thomas, 298
Starling, Sir Samuel, 108
state, 262
stationer, 87, 133, 200–1, 242, 278,
    328, 350
Stationers company, 279, 325
statistical correlation, 242, 380, 397
statistics, use of, 3 n5, 17–20
status, 1, 5, 46–8, 89, 92, 181, 336,
    373, 376, 382, 384, 393, 405,
    446
Statute of Artificers, 312
Staverd, John, 234
Stead, Edmund, 206
Stead, James, 46
Stead, Thomas, 219
Stebbing, Benjamin, 186
Steeg, William, 247
Steel, Michael, 248
Steele, Benjamin, 114
Steele, Richard, 184, 415
Steer, William, 364
Stegg, Thomas, 279
stepchildren, 146, 157, 160, 182,
    203, 218, 307, 354–5, 377, 449
stepfather, 203, 280
Stephens, Edward, 184
stepmother, 203, 212
Stepney, 138
stepparents, 178–9
stepsiblings, 212–13

Stevens, John, 279
Stevens, Thomas, 248
Steyning, 321, 329, 360
Stile, Joseph Haskins, 144
Stile, Sir Oliver, 306
Stiles, Robert, 114
stock market, 255
Stockham, John, 364
Stockholm, 290, 293
Stockport, 346
stocks, 321, 331, 355, 363, 403, 406–7
Stone, Dorcas, 328
Stone, Richard, 69
Stone, Thomas, 146
Story, Anne, 315
Stout, Elin, 81
Stout, William, 58, 77, 81, 179, 182, 205, 284
Stow, John, 209, 260, 447
Strange, Jacob, 301
strangers, 242, 296, 281, 299, 309, 408. *See also* aliens, freedom
Stratford, 63, 65, 121, 157, 161, 168
Stratford, John, 289
Stratford, Ralph, 289
strict settlement, 345, 363
structuralism, 6, 14, 30, 390
Strype, John, 260
Stuart, Alexander, 221
Stubbs, Robert, 281
submission. *See* obedience
subordination. *See* spouses, equality of
succession. *See* inheritance of land
Suffolk, 63, 68, 275
sugar trade, 291, 309, 317, 327, 333, 360, 410–11
suicide, 107, 198, 306
Summers, Francis, 133
Sun Fire office, 319
sureties. *See* bonds
surnames. *See* names, last
Surrey, 355
Sussex, 355, 383
Sutes, William, 342
Suttleworth, Henry, 285
Sutton, Thomas, 94, 168
swaddling, 172
Swansea, 359

Swetnam, Joseph, 46, 58, 141
Sykes, Richard, 367
syndicates, 271, 288, 302, 413
syphilis. *See* sexual diseases
systems metaphor, 389

Tailer, William, 306
tailor, 279, 331, 448
Talbot, Titus, 234
talent, 365, 385, 396, 408, 413–14, 416–17
tallow chandler, 71, 144, 193, 213, 248, 250, 321, 448
Tandin, James, 151
tanner, 313, 378, 448
Tanner, John, 296
Tanner, Nathaniel, 70
Tanturier, Daniel, 282
Taunton, 322
taverns, 96, 179, 318, 320, 324, 329–30, 448
tax records, 24, 317, 399, 444, 451
Taylor, Christopher, 64
Taylor, David, 193
Taylor, Edward, 53
Taylor, Elizabeth, 330
Taylor, Randall, 87
teething, 172
Telford, 328
Tellen, Andrew, 321
temperament. *See* personality
Tempest, Robert, 351
Temple, John, 81, 96
Tench, George, 219
Tench, Nathaniel, 57
Tennant, Neville, 240
testator. *See* wills
textile trades, 317, 319, 321–3, 328, 339, 448
Thacker, Richard, 195
theater, 25–6, 29, 46, 64, 89, 97–8, 103, 141, 194, 198, 290, 320
theoretical approach, 13–17, 30
thirds. *See* inheritance, rights of
Thompson, John, 348
Thompson, Maurice, 295
Thomson, Francis, 87
Thoresby, Ralph, 74, 118, 158, 175, 207, 279
Thornburn, Samuel, 167

Thorowgood, Richard, 301
Thrale, Ralph, 285
thrift, 91, 111, 181, 195
Throwbridge, Thomas, 41
Thurston, Malachy, 199
Thynn, John, 374
Thynn, Thomas, 248
Tiberkin, Daniel, 291
Tichborn, Elizabeth, 107
Tichborn, Robert, 178, 240
Tiffin, Alice, 377
Tiffin, Isobel, 329
Tiffin, William, 377
Tileman, Germain, 307
Tilly, Sir James, 203
Tilney, Edmund, 89
Tilsey, Thomas, 348
time, 185, 409, 411
Tindal, Dru, 326
Tirrell, Timothy, 351
Tirrey, William, 164
Tite, Thomas, 230
titles, 384, 446
Tiverton, 356
tobacco trade, 269, 295, 300, 317, 327, 410, 448
tobacconist, 200
Toennies, Ferdinand, 2
toilet training, 172
tokens. *See* gifts
Tomlinson, Christopher, 150
tontine, 122, 333
Torriano, Elizabeth, 70, 190
Torriano, George, 180, 376
Torriano, Nathaniel Jr., 180, 190, 213, 333
Torriano, Nathaniel Sr., 294
Torriano, Peter, 180, 190–1
Tower of London, 248
Towlin, Samuel, 240
Townshend, Lord, 370–2
toys, 172, 175
trade, domestic, 275, 277, 290–1, 295–6, 307, 317, 328–9, 408, 447
trade, overseas, 275, 302, 317, 321, 324, 327, 365, 447
tradesmen, 61, 138, 142, 149, 160, 162, 168, 175, 194, 273, 336–7, 373–4, 400, 408, 446, 448
tradesmen's tokens, 318
trading networks, 279. *See also*

kinship networks
tradition, 1, 33, 388, 390, 392
training, 32, 189–90, 235, 277–82, 337, 339–40, 447
transaction costs, 398, 414, 416
translation. *See* binding
travel, 92–3, 110, 111, 132, 176–7, 192, 323
Treadway, George, 51, 405
Trelawney, Robert, 202
Trenchfield, Caleb, 76, 90–1, 182–3
Trenchfield, John, 289
Trenchfield, Thomas, 210, 289
Trinity House, 218
Trollopp, Mary, 75
Trosse, George, 45, 107, 281
Trowbridge, 360
trust, 73, 86, 148, 203, 230, 240, 246, 279, 285, 337, 348, 352, 356, 364, 378, 383, 402, 406, 410. *See also* morality
trustee. *See* trust
Tryon, Thomas, 170–1, 312
Tucker, Hannah, 170
Tucker, Walter, 170
Tudman, Benjamin, 140
Turkey, 45, 66, 190, 247, 283, 285, 292–3, 296, 303, 380, 408
Turner, Charles, 235
Turner, Sir Edward, 383
Turner, Jacob, 158, 176
Turner, Rachel, 151
Turner, Sir William, 78, 81, 182, 207, 211, 235–6, 285
Turner's Company, 253, 273
Turton, Anne, 278, 329
Twisden, Heneage, 306
Twisden, Margaret, 306
Tyrell, Thomas, 133

uncertainty. *See* risk
uncles, 57, 179, 217, 219, 228, 232, 234, 236, 240, 246, 279, 285, 281, 289, 292, 294–5, 297–8
Underwood, Clement, 355
Underwood, Edmond, 141
university, 364, 447
unknown values, 441
upholstery industry, 360
Upton, Arthur, 51
Upton, John, 71, 204

urban gentry, 363, 405. *See also* professions
urban property, 112, 143, 295, 334, 349, 351–2, 353, 355, 363, 370, 403–5, 453
usury, 150, 246, 285–7, 321, 331–4, 339, 380, 399, 402, 404, 407. *See also* credit

values. *See* ideology, culture
Vanderput, Margaret, 194
Vanderput, Sir Peter, 306
Van de Veldes, William, 112
Vanlore, Peter, 203
Vansittart, Robert, 194
variable. *See* causation
Vassall, John, 106
Vassall, Samuel, 120
Vaughan, Hugh, 81
Vaughan, James, 57
Vaughan, William, 102
venereal disease. *See* sexual diseases
Venice, 147, 289, 294
Venner, Richard, 354
Verney, John, 39–40, 109, 178, 286
victualler, 161, 448
victualling. *See* food trades
Villiers, Harriet, 41
Vincent, Sir William, 306
vintner, 107, 147, 167, 192, 204, 207, 219, 237, 240, 281, 315, 322, 329, 349–50, 448. *See also* taverns, food trades, drinking
Vintner's Company, 379
Virginia, 112, 199–200, 226, 279, 289, 293–4, 299, 309, 313, 330, 345, 360
virgins, 44, 146, 315. *See also* chastity
visiting, 229, 382
voluntary associations, 255
Vyner, Sir Robert, 114, 301, 333

Wakeman, George, 178
Wakeman, Robert, 107
Walbank, John, 235
Walbrook ward, 243
Walcott, Sarah, 73
Walden, Thomas, 330
Wales, 245
Walker, Elizabeth, 377
Walker, John, 65
Walker, Robert, 237
Walker, Thomas, 113, 144
Wall, Jane, 73
Waller, Edmund, 378
Waller, Henry, 250
Waller, William, 202
Walley, John, 226
Wallingford, 329
Wallington, Nehemiah, 98, 118, 228
Wallis, Henry, 87
Wallis, Samuel, 270
Wallis, Thomas, 281
Walter, Richard, 220
Walters, Thomas, 291, 330
Wansey, Hester, 317
Wapping, 446
Ward, Benjamin, 146
Ward, Sir John, 363
Ward, Ned, 76, 90, 99, 108, 141, 175, 193, 204
Wardle, Thomas, 112
wardship, 343
Ware, Christopher, 212
Warner, George, 67, 69–70, 74, 212, 236, 245, 247, 280, 286, 297
Warner, Janet, 211–12
Warner, Nicholas, 130
Warner, Richard, 200
Warwick, 329
Warwickshire, 307
Waterhouse, Edward, 397, 404
Watson, Abigail, 400
Watson, Thomas, 249
Watts, John, 306
waxchandler, 285, 314
Waythman, John, 326
Weald, 381, 404
wealth, 22, 31–2, 46–8, 60–1, 78, 91, 104, 127, 130, 136, 141, 146–7, 149, 151, 155, 159, 187, 194, 204, 220, 225–6, 252, 231, 233, 237, 242, 255, 261–3, 275, 305, 319, 329, 336, 339, 344–5, 362–3, 369, 374, 376, 379–80, 382, 384, 392, 396–402, 405–6, 411, 417, 450
weaning. *See* children
Weatherill, Lorna, 21
weaver, 93, 144, 250, 316, 448
Weavers Company, 167, 313, 326

Webb, Nehemiah, 335
Weber, Max, 3–5, 150, 410
Webster, Jacob, 287
Webster, William, 71
wedding rituals, 76
weddings, cost of, 75–6
Weedon, Robert, 147
Weeks, Thomas, 350
Welby, Richard, 165
Wells, Joseph, 144
West, John, 205
West, Sarah, 321
West, Thomas, 329
West Indies, 226, 277, 290, 292, 294, 308–9. *See also* Jamaica, Barbados
West country, 275
Westcomb, Edward, 281
Westcombe, 296
Westminster, 446
Weston, William, 114, 135, 250
Westrow, William, 354
Wetherall, Thomas, 132
Wetwood, Katherine, 315
Whateley, William, 56, 90, 182, 204
Wheake, Philip, 279
Wheatley, Samuel, 144
Wheeler, John, 296
Wheeler, Nicholas, 228
Whitcombe, Simon, 130
White, John, 303
White, Richard, 205
White, Thomas, 201
White, Sir Thomas, 151
Whitehaven, 327
Whitehead, Anne, 336
Whitelocke, Richard, 148
Whitmore, George, 305
Whitson, John, 45, 48, 50, 120, 135, 232, 244
wholesalers. *See* merchants, domestic
whore, 99, 319, 335. *See also* brothels
Whorehouse, Edward, 354
whoring. *See* libertinism
Wich, Richard, 157
Wick, Thomas, 290
widowers, number of, 31, 47; remarriage of, 166, 169, 450
widowhood, length of, 31, 125, 151, 450

widows, in business, 148, 150, 324, 327–31, 340, 412; chamber, 343, *see also* inheritance of house; competence of, 150, *see also* women; economic importance of, 407–8; as executrix, 394, 399; as executrix, joint, 31, 125–32, 151, 202, 350; as executrix, sole, 31, 125–32, 151, 399; hostility to, 141, 335; independence of, 141, 147, 150–1, 225, 335; leisure activities, 149; number of, 31, 399; ratio to widowers, 123–5, 151; remarriage of, 46–7, 67, 70; wealth of, 399–402
wives, abuse of, 90–1, 106–7, 148; aggression of, 95, 322–3; beating of, *see* wife abuse; in business, 312, 317, 320–2, 339; independence of, 92–6, 107, 322, 374, 394; loyalty of, 109, 112; marginalization of, 92; obedience of, 394; treatment of, 97, 194; type of trade, 312, 337; wifehood, 7–9, 32, 89, 91. *See also* marriage, spouses, husbands, generosity of
Wigan, 361
Wigfall, Daniel, 227
Wigfall, Dorothy, 88
Wigge, Robert, 353
Wightwick, John, 134
Wildboar, Sarah, 88
Wildgoose, John, 134
Wilding, John, 167
Wilkins, John, 285
wills, 24–9, 28–9, 32, 66, 71–2, 81, 85, 95, 105, 107, 112–13, 127, 130, 141, 147, 151, 168, 195–6, 199, 203–7, 212, 215, 234, 237, 242–3, 246, 248, 250, 260, 277, 314, 341–2, 344–5, 348, 351, 353–5, 362, 367, 369, 376, 379, 384, 399, 401, 405, 446, 449, 452–3. *See also* nuncupative wills
Willaum, Anne, 322
Willcox, John, 76
Willetts, Samuel, 329
William III, 400
Williams, Dr. Daniel, 185
Williams, Humphrey, 214

Williams, James, 225, 452
Williams, John, 237
Williams, Philip, 41
Williams, Robert, 133
Williams, William, 177
Wilson, Jane, 304
Wilson, Robert, 225, 279
Wilson, Rowland, 166, 279, 354
Wiltshire, 307
Winchcomb, Sir Henry, 66
Windus, James, 315
wine trade, 289, 292, 296, 308, 327, 448
Wingrave, Robert, 293
Wingrave, Thomas, 293
Winn, John, 346
Winthrop, John, 346
Wirral, 295
Withnall, Thurston, 292
witnesses, 131–2, 246, 249
Wittwrong, Jacob, 307
women, 2, 7–8, 32, 40, 51, 82–3, 255, 264, 330, 335, 337–8, 340, 394; competence of, 130, 323–5, 332, 335–7; education of, 193–4, 312; exclusion from business, 312–14, 339; lack of capital, 338, 340; never married, 333–5, 338–40; obstacles in business, 312, 334–9, 340; ratio to men, 124–5; training of, 140; type of trade, 312, 316–20
Wood, Henry, 369
Wood, Samuel, 141
Wood, Simon, 248, 355
Woodcock, Ralph, 157
Woodhead, J. R., 20
woodmonger, 240, 447

Woodrow, Thomas, 205
Woodward, John, 178
wool merchant, 328
Woolf, Anne, 367
Woolf, Sir Joseph, 362
woollen draper, 144, 363
Woolley, Hannah, 96
Woolley, John, 250
Worcester, 161, 334, 346
work, 5, 10, 336–7, 393. *See also* idleness
Worral, John, 201
Wotton, Thomas, 269
Wright, Gilbert, 107
Wright, Leonard, 91
Wright, Richard, 200, 350
Wright, Thomas, 89
Wriothesley, Thomas, 240
Wycherley, William, 46
Wyett, Sir Nicholas, 135
Wynn, Maurice, 198, 245
Wynn, Thomas, 145

Yale, David, 346
Yale, Elihu, 68, 76, 81, 169, 203, 287
Yardley, Ralph, 178, 286
Yearwood, Richard, 196, 355
Yeats, William, 199
yeomen, 273–5, 446
yield. *See* income
Yonge, James, 100, 114
York, 48, 121, 137, 161, 234, 273, 303, 313, 316, 325, 329, 359
York, province of, 345
Yorkshire, 236, 249, 295, 307, 317, 322, 328, 363, 377
Young, Arthur, 106
youth. *See* adolescence

Other books in the series (*continued from page iii*)

Blair A. Ruble, *Money Sings: The Changing Politics of Urban Space in Post-Soviet Yaroslavl*

Deborah S. Davis, Richard Kraus, Barry Naughton, and Elizabeth J. Perry, editors, *Urban Spaces in Contemporary China: The Potential for Autonomy and Community in Post-Mao China*

William M. Shea and Peter A. Huff, editors, *Knowledge and Belief in America: Enlightenment Traditions and Modern Religious Thought*

W. Elliot Brownlee, editor, *Funding the Modern American State, 1941–1995: The Rise and Fall of the Era of Easy Finance*

W. Elliot Brownlee, *Federal Taxation in America: A Short History*

R. H. Taylor, editor, *The Politics of Elections in Southeast Asia*

Šumit Ganguly, *The Crisis in Kashmir: Portents of War, Hopes of Peace*

James W. Muller, editor, *Churchill as Peacemaker*

Donald R. Kelley and David Harris Sacks, editors, *The Historical Imagination in Early Modern Britain: History, Rhetoric, and Fiction, 1500–1800*

Richard Wightman Fox and Robert B. Westbrook, editors, *In Face of the Facts: Moral Inquiry in American Scholarship*

Selig S. Harrison, Paul H. Kreisberg, and Dennis Kux, editors, *India and Pakistan: The First Fifty Years*

Morton Keller and R. Shep Melnick, editors, *Taking Stock: American Government in the Twentieth Century*

Martha Derthick, editor, *Dilemmas of Scale in America's Federal Democracy*